The Summer Atlas
of
North American Birds

Jeff Price, Sam Droege, and Amy Price

We proudly dedicate this book to Chan Robbins and to the thousands of volunteers, past, present, and future, who rise before dawn to participate in collecting the data for the Breeding Bird Survey.

The Summer Atlas of North American Birds

Jeff Price, Sam Droege, and Amy Price

Illustrated by David D. Beadle

ACADEMIC PRESS
Harcourt Brace & Company, Publishers
LONDON SAN DIEGO NEW YORK
BOSTON SYDNEY TOKYO TORONTO

ACADEMIC PRESS LIMITED
24–28 Oval Road
LONDON NW1 7DX

U.S. Edition Published by
ACADEMIC PRESS INC.
San Diego, CA 92101

This book is printed on acid free paper

Copyright © 1995 ACADEMIC PRESS LIMITED
Illustrations © 1995 David D. Beadle

All rights reserved
No part of this book may be reproduced or transmitted in any form or by any means,
electronic or mechanical including photocopying, recording, or any information storage
and retrieval system without permission in writing from the publisher

A catalogue record for this book is available from the British Library

ISBN 0-12-5646607

Typeset by Wyvern Typesetting Ltd, Bristol.
Printed in Great Britain by Butler and Tanner, Frome, Somerset.

Contents

Acknowledgements		*vi*
Foreword		*vii*
Preface		*ix*
Chapter 1.	*Overview of the Breeding Bird Survey*	*1*
Chapter 2.	*Analysis of the Breeding Bird Survey data – creating the maps*	*7*
Chapter 3.	*Relative abundance maps*	*15*
Chapter 4.	*Annotated list of species, habitats, and areas with high relative abundance values*	*253*
Chapter 5.	*Conservation issues and population trends*	*317*
Appendix A.	*Common and scientific names*	*337*
Appendix B.	*Selected bird-finding guides, breeding bird atlases, and other references*	*343*
Appendix C.	*Cited references and suggested readings*	*349*
Appendix D.	*Birding ethics*	*353*
Index		*355*

Acknowledgements

A book based on Breeding Bird Survey (BBS) data could not have been written without the existence of the survey, the cooperation of its staff, and its dedicated cadre of volunteers. We would like to start by acknowledging Chan Robbins for his foresight and dedication in establishing the BBS; Bruce Peterjohn for providing data and trends; the past and present BBS coordinators: Danny Bystrak, Connie Downes, Sam Droege, Anthony Erskine, Ellen Hayakawa, Lucie Metras, Bruce Peterjohn, and Ted Van Velzen; and Paul Geissler, John Sauer, and the rest of the statisticians who developed the route regression analysis for detecting population trends. For keeping the BBS going we credit all of the state and provincial BBS coordinators who have found the volunteers to go out into the field and collect the data. And, most importantly, the volunteers, without whom the data would not be collected.

Early and continuing support for this project came from Terry Root, who showed that the techniques existed for using computers to develop relative abundance maps; and William S. Moore, who provided the initial equipment and support to develop the techniques used in creating early versions of these maps. It was Andrew Richford, our editor at Academic Press, who believed in this project when it was first presented to him in 1990, and had the patience to see it through to completion. Pat Madison, Tom Bresnahan, and the staff of Golden Software, Inc. provided technical support and an advance copy of their new software, SURFER® for Windows, without which there would be no filled contours.

Some of these maps originally appeared, in a slightly different form, in *The Birds of North America* series, a joint project of the American Ornithologists' Union and the Academy of Natural Sciences of Philadelphia. We thank Alan Poole, Frank Gill, and Christine Bush for seeing the benefit behind including relative abundance maps in the series, and for the many comments which helped to improve the maps.

John B. Dunning, Pete Blancher, Greg Butcher, Danny Bystrak, Tony Erskine, Kenn Kaufman, Bruce Peterjohn, Chan Robbins, and John Sauer all reviewed at least parts of the book and their suggestions greatly improved the final copy. In addition to these reviewers, many others have commented on the relative abundance maps. This has enabled us to improve the look of the maps before publication.

Finally, we want to acknowledge our families, who have now seen the difficulties of writing a book, and who continued to support us nevertheless.

Foreword

People who are interested in birds often have a special fascination with maps. We daydream over maps of places we want to go birding; we puzzle over road maps after we go there and get lost; and we often study maps of bird species distribution.

If looking at range maps is a favorite activity, then criticizing them must be a close second. However, the critics miss a basic point: compiling perfect range maps is not just difficult, it's literally impossible.

Most bird cartography takes what might be called a "broad brush" approach. Every known locality is plotted, the outermost points are connected, and then the whole enclosed area is painted in with one solid color. Such a map is comforting because it looks so absolute. But it is also, invariably, misleading.

Real bird distribution does not work that way, filling in an area solidly, cutting off at an abrupt line. Normally the edge of a bird's range comes gradually, with gaps and outlying populations. Even within the range, there are major variations in abundance. For example, Indigo Buntings seem to sing from every bush in Kentucky, while in Arizona they are scarce and local: but the "standard" map will fill in both areas with the same broad brush – or leave out the Arizona birds entirely. Either way is misleading. Many of us have wished for range maps that would show relative abundance, but gathering the necessary data has seemed an impossible task.

The Breeding Bird Survey (BBS), brainchild of the great Chan Robbins, was designed to track changes in bird numbers over time; but Jeff Price suggested that it could show relative numbers on a geographic scale as well. Of course, BBS data are not perfect. Rare and inconspicuous birds are often missed. Other problems are thoroughly explained in this book's introductory chapters. So the resulting maps are not perfect either, but they give us a remarkable new perspective.

For anyone interested in birds, this *Summer Atlas* will be an essential reference, a gold mine of information and ideas. It is appropriate that the book includes chapters on population trends and conservation. The maps will help to foster the understanding needed for bird conservation: seeing the distribution of each species not as a swath of solid color on the map, but as a mosaic of rarity and abundance, of sensitive response to habitat and climate, revealing each bird as part of the living landscape.

Kenn Kaufman
Tucson, Arizona
April 1995

Preface

An atlas can be described as a bound collection of maps, sometimes with supporting figures and tables. This book is truly an avian atlas. It contains maps, figures, and tables pertaining to birds found in summer in North America (south of approximately 51° N latitude and north of Mexico). More specifically, it contains relative abundance maps of 450 species and identifiable forms. A relative abundance map differs from the typical map in a field guide in that it shows not only the distribution of a species, but also portrays an index of how abundant a species is in the different parts of its range.

These maps are based on data collected by the North American Breeding Bird Survey (BBS). For the most part, the maps are based on data collected during the period 1985–1991. This is a summer atlas because the BBS does not monitor the *breeding* status of a species, but its *relative abundance* in a given area during the early summer (late May to early July depending upon latitude). This atlas also contains an annotated list that provides information on the routes that have detected the highest abundance of each of 531 species and identifiable forms. Whereas the maps are limited to areas in the United States and southern Canada, the annotated list contains information from routes in Alaska and northern Canada as well. Finally, there is a chapter outlining some of the conservation concerns facing different groups of North American birds, and the population trends for these species. Each of the chapters have been designed, as much as possible, to stand alone. This was done so that you could use the chapter that interests you and read the others at a later time.

As a beginning birder, I quickly learned that the distribution maps in field guides were only rough approximations of the actual distribution of each species. Typical maps do not differentiate that a species is uncommon in some parts of its range and common in other parts; all levels of abundance are depicted the same way. I wondered whether there was any way to indicate not only where a species was found, but also provide an index of how abundant the species was in a given area.

Over time my interest in birds grew until I chose to make a career out of studying them. In those intervening years I learned about bird distributions the way most birders do, by reading the regional bird guides that were then available. As a graduate student I was fortunate enough to see the galley proofs of the *Atlas of Wintering North American Birds* (Root 1988). For the first time I saw that the types of maps I wanted to produce were possible, but a source of data and improved technology still needed to be found. About that same time I saw the maps in the *Breeding Bird Survey: Its first fifteen years* (Robbins *et al.* 1986) and I knew that I had found the data to use to create a summer atlas.

Over the next few years I gained access to a fast (for its time) microcomputer and learned the techniques necessary to produce computer-generated relative abundance maps. During this time I became acquainted with Sam Droege, then Coordinator of the BBS. Sam provided a great deal of insight into the BBS and also into relative abundance mapping. I asked Sam if he would like to join me in producing a book of relative abundance maps. When it came down to actually generating and fine-tuning all of the maps in this book I asked my wife, Amy, to help with the multitude of tasks that had to be done to transfer the ideas, data, and words into the finished product.

I certainly hope that this book at least meets its original goal of helping birders find birds. The maps provide some indication of areas where birding from the roadside may yield a species of interest, or point out new areas worthy of exploration. The annotated list should help pinpoint areas for some of the more sought after birds (which seems to be a different species for every birder). Taken together with the list of bird-finding guides in Appendix B, this book should make it easier for birders to plan trips and enjoy the birds and their habitats.

While this book originally started as a book for birders, I hope that its use will go far beyond that. These maps can provide guidance to land managers and conservation organizations about where certain groups of species are found and where they are the most abundant. The annotated list helps pinpoint areas that may be of special concern within a state or province. An overview of some of the difficulties many species are facing can be found in chapter 5. I hope that the information from the conservation chapter, along with the maps showing centers of abundance as detected by the BBS, will help land-use planners and managers identify specific areas that might merit more conservation attention.

As an avian biogeographer, the patterns in these maps continue to fascinate me. Why are some species absent from an area while other species are more abundant? What are the factors associated with some species' disjunct ranges? The possible questions go on and on. For ornithologists, perhaps these maps will provide additional insight into a species' relative abundance pattern and stimulate further research into North America's summer birds.

Jeff Price

Overview of the Breeding Bird Survey

1

Publication of the book *Silent Spring* (Carson 1962), and subsequent media coverage, galvanized public attention. Citizens became alarmed when they learned that the United States' national symbol, the Bald Eagle, and common birds such as robins, terns, and gulls were being harmed by the toxicity of pesticides. In the early 1960s considerable publicity focused on large die-offs of American Robins following the application of DDT on college campuses in Michigan and other states. A concerned citizen wrote Chandler Robbins, then Chief of the Section of Migratory Non-Game Studies at the Bureau of Sport Fisheries and Wildlife's Patuxent Wildlife Research Center, to inquire whether such seemingly widespread losses of robins from DDT were sufficiently serious to cause overall declines in the national population. Robbins realized that neither he, nor any other ornithologist, could answer that question. The answer would require the development of bird surveys that estimated population changes at the state, national, and international levels.

This simple query compelled Robbins to design, develop, and implement a continental early warning system for bird population changes.

Robbins was convinced that it was important for bird conservation to create a new, more rigorous, monitoring program and that the technology was there to manage and analyse the large amounts of resulting data. That program ultimately became the North American Breeding Bird Survey (BBS).

At the time, the importance of quantifying bird population changes using standardized techniques and statistical analyses was gaining widespread recognition. Amateur ornithologists had been conducting Christmas Bird Counts since the turn of the century, but the results had not been computerized nor used for estimating population changes. Coordinated efforts to collect estimates of bird densities from plot-based mapping of bird territories (Breeding Bird Censuses and Winter Bird Population Studies) had started in 1937. Unfortunately, the small number of plots and their limited distribution precluded anything but summaries of local population trends. It would have been misleading to combine such scattered surveys into state or regional estimates.

Robbins realized that he could use a different survey technique, the point count, combined with new statistical analyses and large numbers of volunteers to answer the questions asked about national population trends. Point counts had been widely used to survey game birds in the early 1930s and, unlike plot-based censusing, were designed to sample bird populations rather than completely enumerate all birds present.

Point counts are literally counts made from a single point. Observers go to predesignated places (in the case of the BBS a stop along a secondary road) and count everything they see or hear from that point for a predesignated period of time (three minutes for the BBS). In that period of time only a fraction of the birds actually present at the point will be recorded. During the first few minutes of a point count the number of new birds detected increases quickly, then rapidly tapers off. Consequently, the greatest number of birds can be recorded by spending relatively little time at any one point, counting at many points, and moving quickly between points. As the number of stops accumulates, a relatively representative picture develops of the bird population in that landscape. By using the statistical properties of randomness, coupled with probability theory, a system of representative point counts could be devised to estimate relative abundance and population trends over large geographic areas.

Robbins spent 1964 testing point count techniques both in Maryland and New Hampshire. With the cooperation of Maryland and Delaware bird watchers, the effects of time-of-day, length of point count, spacing of points, and observer skills were examined. These investigations resulted in the methods still used today by the BBS to survey North American birds.

The survey structure decided upon involves a series of point counts, spaced evenly 0.5 miles (0.8 km) apart, largely along secondary roads. The observer drives from point to point, stopping at each for three minutes to count every bird seen or heard. Early studies had shown that the period of time when bird activity was highest lasted for about five hours after sunrise (Robbins 1981). Since an average observer could reasonably do 50, 3-minute point counts during this time, the survey route was chosen to be 24.5 miles (40 km) long. To assure relatively even coverage in each state, and to meet the statistical need for randomness, each of these sets of point counts (routes), are randomly located within blocks of one degree of latitude and longitude.

Following the development of a sampling framework and methodology for the BBS, there remained the question of whether enough volunteers could be found. In 1965, a pilot program, with 50 BBS routes in

Maryland and 10 in Delaware, was designed. The pilot was successful owing to the efforts of the volunteers who ran every route. During the fall and winter of 1965/66, United States and Canadian coordinators for the BBS were located for all of the eastern states and every eastern province except Ontario. These coordinators were asked to help Robbins lay out survey routes within their regions and to recruit observers to run those routes. In 1967, the central states and provinces were added, and in 1968 the western states and provinces completed the system. The number of routes located in each degree-block of latitude/longitude is determined by the number of volunteers available to run survey routes. Even today, some of the western states have only one survey route per block, while some of the eastern states have as many as 16.

In 1968, the Canadian Wildlife Service asked Anthony Erskine to help coordinate the BBS in Canada. Although Chan Robbins had contacted Canadian bird clubs early in the development of the BBS, it took several years before the federal Canadian Wildlife Service took an active role. Erskine greatly expanded the number of routes run in Canada, including the addition of routes in remote areas. Even in the absence of formal agreements between the two countries, the BBS has always been run as a cooperative international program. The Canadian and United States coordinators have ensured that consistent methodologies are applied on both sides of the border. Recently, a series of routes have been started in Mexico. It is to be hoped that this pilot program will be successful and the number of routes expanded so that the BBS will be truly North American in coverage.

The BBS owes its existence to Robbins' fortitude. Within the administration of the Bureau of Sport Fisheries and Wildlife few thought it possible to develop such a comprehensive program without large numbers of personnel. Existing waterfowl population and harvest surveys required, then and now, the maintenance of a large permanent staff of biologists, pilots, administrators, and technicians. In contrast, for little more than the cost of a coordinator, technician, and computer support, the BBS collects information on over 500 bird species. The importance of volunteers to the BBS cannot be overemphasized. The annual value of the volunteer contribution to the BBS program has been conservatively placed at nearly $300,000. In acknowledgement of his efforts, Robbins received an official reprimand from the Director of the U.S. Fish and Wildlife Service for not following official procedures.

In 1989, a paper was published that used BBS data to document what many had suspected; northeastern populations of neotropical migrants had declined precipitously (Robbins et al. 1989). Inspired by that report and the subsequent publicity, the National Fish and Wildlife Foundation and a coalition of federal, state, and non-government organizations created Partners in Flight. The goal of this program is to reverse the declines of neotropical migrants and foster the scientific study of the causes of declines in these migrants. Chapter 5 details some of these population changes and the conservation problems confronting neotropical migrants and other birds.

Conservation activities, such as those leading to the formation of Partners in Flight, have been the primary focus of both the Canadian Wildlife Service and Fish and Wildlife Service's analyses of the BBS data. However, other researchers have used BBS data to explore biogeographical, energetic, and community issues that only a survey program that is continental in scope can address.

While the design of the BBS is adequate for estimating trends of many species, it also has a number of characteristics that add noise and bias to those estimates. Coverage is inadequate in the interior West, the boreal zone, and portions of the Great Plains. Observers vary in how they estimate numbers, and roadside habitats and changes along them often differ from the surrounding region. For further details on BBS biases and their statistical corrections see Sauer and Droege (1990a).

Another of the difficulties researchers face in using BBS data are problems with differential detectability among species, and the roadside bias of the sample. The relative detectability of birds varies with species. Some, such as Northern Bobwhite, Red-eyed Vireo, or hawks of the open countryside, are conspicuous in their calls, songs, or visibility. Others, such as rails or owls, call so infrequently during the time that data on BBS routes are being collected that they are greatly under-represented on BBS routes.

The time of day and time of year of the survey can both have an influence on the detectability of certain species. Many raptors would probably be better surveyed if the routes were run later in the day; owls if the routes were run earlier in the morning. Even though the BBS is run early in the summer (late May in the southern states up until early July for the more northern routes), the singing activity of some species has already begun to taper off. In Louisiana, the rate of singing of many species is reduced by early May. By the time the BBS routes are run in North Dakota, Black-capped Chickadees are already incubating eggs and much less vocal than earlier in the season. A possible solution to this problem would be to run routes earlier in the season. This would create additional problems owing to the detection of birds migrating through the area which, in turn, would cause problems in the calculation of population trends. For all of these reasons, the relative abundance of birds on BBS routes is not necessarily an accurate reflection of the true abundance of birds in the community. For the calculation of species-specific population trends, this does not present a problem unless the detectability of an individual species on a route changes greatly over time. However, these differences in detectability, especially *among* species, means that comparisons of relative abundance maps of different species should only be done with a full understanding of the problems and limitations.

The placement of BBS stops along the sides of roads enhances the ability of an observer to quickly and efficiently survey a large transect of the landscape. Unfortunately, habitats along roads are often different from those of the landscape as a whole. Edge habitats predominate and wetland habitats are often avoided. For the calculation of trends, it may not matter that habitats are differentially represented along roads, so long as changes in habitats reflect changes to the landscape as a whole. Because of the difference in roaded vs. unroaded habitats it must be kept in mind that the relative abundance of birds on BBS routes represents the relative abundance of birds in North America along roads.

In 1993, the BBS was transferred to the newly created National Biological Survey. This new agency now houses most of the major monitoring and research functions of the Department of the Interior and plans are underway to develop more surveys similar to the BBS. While the BBS is coordinated by the United States and Canadian governments, most of the data collection and observer recruitment is done by volunteers. BBS observers are among the best amateur and professional ornithologists in North America. To be assigned a route, each observer must not only know how to identify all of the breeding birds in the area by sight, but also know all of the local songs and call notes. The point count technique is simple in methodology, but demanding in observer capabilities. Most birds on BBS routes (well over 90%) are detected by call or song (Faanes and Bystrak 1981). The three minutes allotted at each stop leaves no time for an observer to investigate unfamiliar sounds. Consequently, only the most experienced observers are recruited to run BBS routes. In regions of high density and diversity of bird communities, even experienced birders find running BBS routes to be an intense experience, calling on all their faculties to record accurately what they see and hear.

While some BBS observers are employees of federal, state, and provincial governments, many of them do their routes on their own time. The majority of observers are amateur ornithologists, many of whom have been running their routes from the earliest days of the BBS. These observers often run more than one route and go to great personal effort and expense to run their surveys.

Volunteers are always needed to run more routes. If you are interested in taking on the responsibility of running a BBS route, and possess the necessary birding skills, you can contact the Breeding Bird Survey at:

Breeding Bird Survey National Biological Service Patuxent Environmental Science Center Laurel, MD 20708

or

Breeding Bird Survey Canadian Wildlife Service 100 Gamelin Boulevard Hull, Quebec K1A 0H3

The BBS Coordinator will either put you in direct contact with the local coordinator, or will send you a map of the routes currently available.

It is difficult to define what motivates observers to take on the responsibility of running a BBS route. There is no pay, you have to get up outrageously early, and collecting the data can be exhaustingly intense. In part, it must be the experience of quiet dawns full of the fresh scents of early summer; the time spent alone with the world and its birds before civilization awakens; watching and tracking the ornithological landscape as it changes yearly along the route; and finally, the knowledge that the data collected become a permanent record of changes of the local bird community.

Analysis of the Breeding Bird Survey data – creating the maps

2

What follows is a detailed description of how the data were processed to create the maps. This information is provided for those who want to learn more about the mapping process. Brief overviews of these topics can be found at the beginning of chapters 3 (maps) and 4 (annotated list) for those who just want to begin using the maps and annotated list.

Once the data were received from the U.S. Fish and Wildlife Service, the first task was error checking. This involved two separate processes: one to check the data, and one to check the coordinates supplied for each route. The data were used to generate lists of species detected on Breeding Bird Survey (BBS) routes for each state and province. These lists were then compared with those in the *Distributional Checklist of North American Birds* (DeSante and Pyle 1986), and regional bird guides. In some cases, errors were obvious (Cactus Wren in West Virginia, White-tailed Hawk in British Columbia). These were checked against the original data and found to represent improperly entered data that were then corrected (Carolina Wren for

Cactus Wren, Red-tailed Hawk for White-tailed Hawk). It is important to remember that the BBS does not detect breeding birds *per se*, but most of the species detected on a route were probably breeding in the area at the time. Other species detected may be lingering migrants, vagrant individuals, or birds which may be spending the summer in the area – even though it may be some distance from their breeding grounds. In cases where it was clear that the species were either lingering migrants, vagrant individuals, or potential misidentifications, the data for those species were eliminated. Data for those species that occasionally linger in an area throughout the survey period, or which may represent true range expansions (as confirmed by regional bird guides), were retained. For this reason it is best to consider the information in this atlas as summer data *not* breeding data.

The database was then checked for errors in route coordinates. The BBS provided the latitude and longitude for the start point of each of the routes. These coordinates were then checked to see that they lay within the boundaries of the appropriate state or province. Errors were checked against the original route maps and corrections were made. A sub-sample of routes was further checked to see if the coordinates of the start point lay on a road. Finally, the starting coordinates of each route were checked against a geographic place names database to determine the closest town or crossroads for each of the routes. Since the name of the BBS route is often the name of a nearby town, crossroads, or geographic feature, this provided an additional check on the accuracy of the starting coordinates of the route.

Data from the BBS go back to 1966 so a decision had to be made on the number of years to include in the maps and annotated list. In the last decade or so, many bird species have undergone significant declines (see chapter 5). Some of these declines are probably due to habitat alteration on their breeding grounds. A long-term average could mask these changes, showing a species as being present in an area that is now unsuitable. To minimize these effects, almost all of the data used in this book were from BBS routes run between 1985 and 1991. To be included in this group, a route had to be run at least three times during this seven-year period. Sometimes a larger than normal number of individuals of a single species will be detected on a route. This may be a real occurrence, or it may be a result of bias on the part of the observer. By averaging the data over all of the years the route was run during this period, and including only those routes run a minimum of three years, the influence of this bias should have been minimized.

Unfortunately, not every BBS route is run every year. The number of BBS routes run in any one year is a function of the availability of volunteers. In some areas, the geographic coverage of the BBS is thorough owing to the number of qualified volunteers available. In other areas, especially much of the West, there are few volunteers to cover all of the available routes. For that reason, some routes might have been run annually prior to 1985, only to have the observer move out of the area with no one willing to replace them. With recent concerns over the population declines in numerous bird species, many routes have been added in the last few years. This is due, in part, to the development of Partners in Flight, and the subsequent formation of regional and state chapters, many of which have been actively recruiting people to run BBS routes.

Although most of the routes used in this book were run during the period 1985–1991, this did not provide adequate coverage for some portions of the included area. The better the geographic coverage of routes, the better the final maps would be. For that reason, some routes that had been run

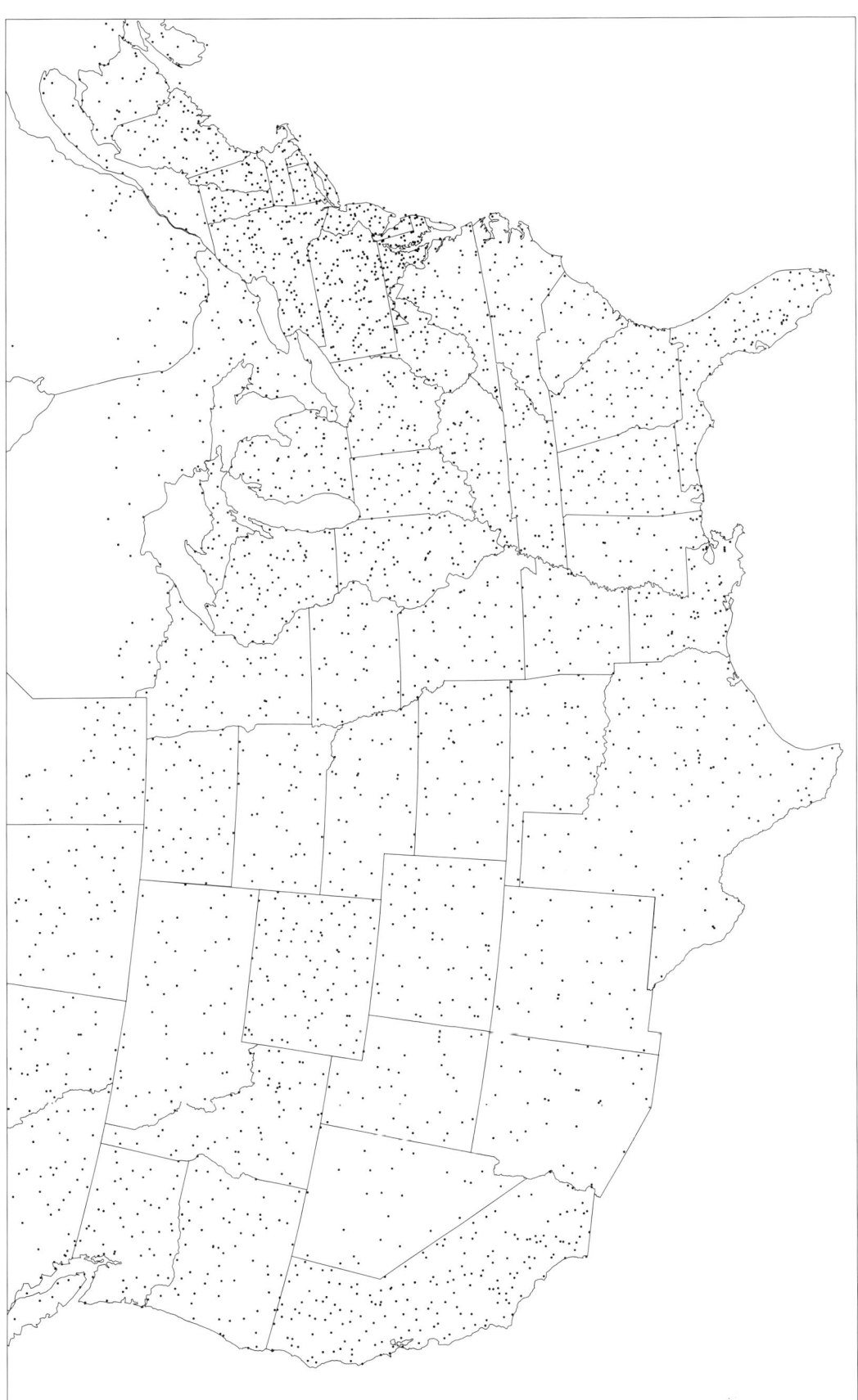

Figure 1. Breeding Bird Survey (BBS) routes used in the creation of the maps. Each symbol represents the starting coordinates of a BBS route.

prior to 1985 and some routes that have only been run in the 1990s have been included in order to improve the geographic coverage. Some of the routes that began in 1990 were established in U.S. National Parks or Monuments. These routes often represent habitats that have been protected or are different from the surrounding landscape and thus were important to include in the data used in this book. While most of the routes included were run in both 1990 and 1991, a few were included that were only run in 1991. For those routes to be included that pre-dated 1985, a similar set of rules were applied as for those run during the period 1985–1991. For these routes, the seven-year window was shifted back one year (e.g., 1984–1990, 1983–1989) until at least three years could be included. A map (fig. 1) has been provided showing the locations of all of the routes used in creating the relative abundance maps.

The BBS is a sample of bird populations in North America. While it is not a 'true' random sample (being restricted solely to areas with roads), it does represent a reasonable sample of the populations of many species. Most routes are more similar to routes close by than to routes farther away. This is largely owing to local similarities in habitat, topography, soils, climate, and land-use practices. This spatial correlation among routes makes it possible to create spatially interpolated maps based on these sample points.

There are many ways of creating maps from irregularly spaced sample data. The easiest, and least satisfactory, is simply to connect all of the points with similar values together. This provides a very crude map. Another way is to take advantage of the autocorrelated nature of the data and spatially interpolate it onto a grid of regularly spaced points. One of the best techniques for creating a regularly spaced grid out of irregularly spaced data, and the technique used in creating all of these maps, is kriging. Kriging is a geostatistical technique developed to predict the average grade of gold ore in a mining block based on data from nearby mining blocks (Cressie 1990). It is one of the better techniques in that it is both an unbiased estimator (or predictor) of the point and because it minimizes the error variance (Isaaks and Srivastava 1989, Cressie 1989). Kriging provides a weighted linear average for each point to be estimated based on both the spatial relationship and the covariation of the surrounding data.

A spatially interpolated map starts as a map of irregularly spaced sample points (fig. 2a). A decision is then made as to the proper grid spacing to use. This grid is composed of the regularly spaced points to be estimated by kriging. The choice of grid size is very important. If the grid is too coarse, much information will be lost and the value of the maps will be diminished. If the grid is too fine, the value of the maps is questionable because they are presenting more information than the data can support. For these maps the grid spacing was chosen to be 31 miles (50 km), or slightly longer than the length of a BBS route. Even though the irregularly spaced data are shown

---

Figure 2. Creating relative abundance maps. Maps often start as irregularly spaced data (fig. 2a). A decision is made as to the spacing of the nodes in a regularly spaced grid (the + symbols in fig. 2b). Kriging is then used to estimate the value at each regularly spaced grid node (+) based on the irregularly spaced data (▲). The arrow in the rectangular box in figure 2b points to the location being estimated (+). Lines connect the point being estimated with the five (in this example) closest data points (▲). The data provide a weighted estimate of the value at the grid node. Figure 2c shows the completed map based on the estimated values. See text for more complete details and references.

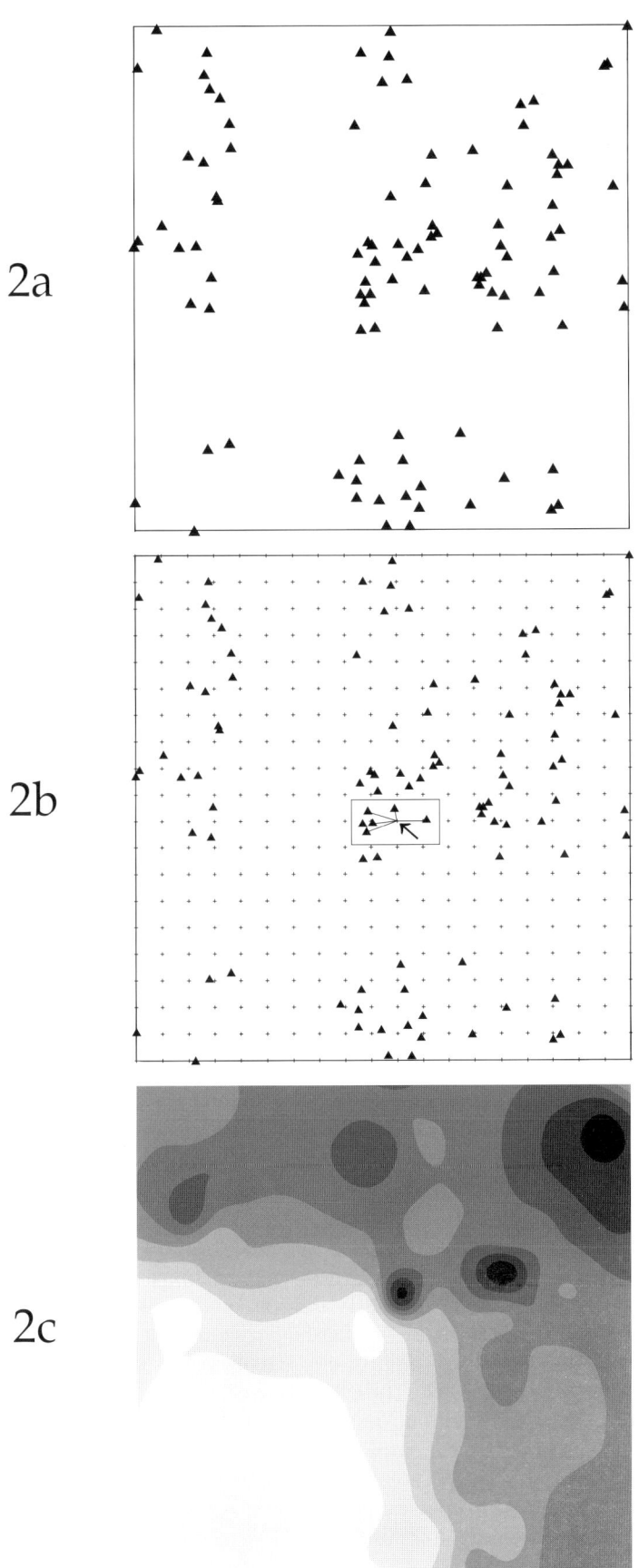

as points, those points actually represent all of the data collected over the entire 24.5-mile (40 km) length of the BBS routes. The points thus represent a mixture, or generalized representation, of all of the habitat types found along the length of the route. The grid to be estimated is shown in figure 2b.

Kriging is then used to estimate the value at each of these grid nodes. The ten closest BBS routes are used in the estimation of the value for each node. Each of these ten routes is weighted so that those that are closer and have a similar covariance provide more weight than those farther away. The more actual data near the point to be estimated, the better the overall estimation will be. Thus, the estimated data underlying the maps are better in areas with many BBS routes (much of the East and California), and somewhat less accurate in areas with few nearby data points (many parts of the West, and northern Ontario and Quebec). The reason for this is that in data-sparse regions the search distance will be greater to find the closest data. If the habitats remain similar over this greater distance then the estimates are likely to be similar. However, if the habitats are dissimilar then the estimates are likely to be less reflective of the actual bird population at that point.

It is important to remember that the scale of these maps is relatively coarse. Since each grid node is 31 miles (50 km) from its nearest neighbor, the maps are estimated values for blocks 31 miles by 31 miles (50 km by 50 km). Interpret this as meaning that the bird is likely to be found, along a road, in the proper habitat, somewhere within this block. Therefore, any 'point' on the relative abundance maps should actually be considered to have a spatial resolution of a 50 km by 50 km block.

The next step is to turn the regularly spaced grid into a map. There are two decisions that must be made in placing contours on a map. The first has to do with the contour interval. On a topographic map, the contour interval is regularly spaced (e.g., every 20 feet (6 m)). The abundance of biological organisms is usually not regularly distributed. Most sites will have relatively few individuals while a few sites may have many individuals. For that reason a regularly spaced scale is not appropriate when dealing with biological data. The scale used in these maps has the following levels: <5; 5–20; 20–50; and >50 individuals per route, per year.

The second decision has to do with the edge of a species' distribution. It is difficult to determine the actual edge of any species' distribution. From day to day, and especially from year to year, the edge of the distribution will differ. While zero might be a logical choice, this would potentially lead to the inclusion of areas where the species has been seen only once in seven years. Many regional bird guides would consider this to be an accidental occurrence. For most of the species represented in the maps in this book, the edge of the distribution was chosen to be 0.5 birds per route per year. That is, approximately one individual of that species seen on that route every other year. For some species, especially those which might be present in reasonably high numbers but not as easily detectable, the edge of the distribution was chosen to be 0.25 or even 0.1 birds per route per year. Similar species tended to cluster together (e.g., most warblers have their range edge at 0.25). This makes sense as the detectability of these species tends to be similar. The mapped distribution of each species was examined using each of the three edge values (0.5, 0.25, and 0.1). These distributions were then compared with that from other sources to determine the best value to use in defining the edge of the species' distribution. Once the distributional limit was chosen, a contouring algorithm created contours based on the underlying estimated values (fig. 2c).

Even though the original data had been checked for potential errors, the maps were also checked for outliers and for errors that might have been introduced in the mapping process. There were two aspects to this: examining the positive data (the actual distribution and abundance patterns on the maps), and the negative data (areas where the species was not detected). For positive data, distribution boundaries and potential outliers were checked against existing distribution maps and regional guides and atlases. For some species, the edge of the distribution had been 'over-interpolated' and the map showed the edge of the species' range as occurring in areas where the species has never been found. In these cases, the distribution was shifted to better match the known distributions. In other cases the data checking process revealed that many of the small areas that appeared to be outliers (e.g., Bronzed Cowbird and Common Tern in Louisiana) were actually small isolated colonies of those species. Other outliers were often found to represent individuals that are often seen in those areas, at least during the early summer period when the BBS is run (e.g., many species of waterfowl and gulls). In some cases the outliers were found to represent errors introduced in the mapping process, or errors not identified in the initial data screening. Those outliers were eliminated.

Careful attention was also paid to negative data. Negative data are from routes that were run but that did not detect the species during the period of time used in these maps. These data are represented both as much of the unshaded areas on the map, and as small unshaded areas within the shaded portions of the map. Birds often have a relatively patchy distribution owing to the distribution of their habitat within the surrounding landscape. For example, a given BBS route rarely runs through 24.5 miles of a continuous habitat type; the route may start in a deciduous woodland, run through areas with cultivated fields, and end in a suburban area. Since the routes are selected at random from the roads in a given area, it is possible that some species found in the general area are missed on the survey. It is not only possible, but probable that many wetland species (e.g., herons, rails) are missed because roads tend not to run through wetlands. For those reasons it is possible to have small areas with negative data (no individuals detected) within large areas where the species is likely to be found.

Future directions in bird mapping

There were no maps in the earliest field guides. The distributions of birds were described in the text. Current field guides have maps showing a coarse depiction of the distributions of most species; some even showing the interesting discontinuities in the distributions of many species. Relative abundance maps represent the newest generation of bird maps.

Every year of breeding bird atlas data collected improves the knowledge of the breeding distributions of North American bird species (see appendix B for a list of some of the breeding bird atlases available). Each atlas that has been published has changed what was known about the distributions of most species, either by showing actual range expansions or contractions, or in providing a finer scale understanding of where range boundaries lay. Range boundaries are also being studied in terms of the factors, particularly climate and habitat, that might be limiting the distributions of the species. These studies have led, and are continuing to lead, to the development of models that predict, often quite successfully, where a species distributional limit lays.

While the Breeding Bird Survey is still the only truly continent-wide survey of birds during the summer, there are many states and provinces running mini-BBS routes as part of their atlas programs. Some states and provinces have also established other point count transects, at least in some areas. Data collected from these surveys all help to refine the knowledge of the relative abundance pattern of many bird species.

These new types of data represent a challenge for avian biogeographers and cartographers. The next generation of maps is likely to represent a combination of data collected at many different scales from many different sources. These maps are likely to include, at a minimum, a combination of existing breeding bird atlas data with relative abundance maps based on data collected by the BBS. Advances in the understanding of the factors associated with the distribution and abundance patterns of birds will also lead to improved relative abundance maps. While the maps in this book only examine the relationships of routes with each other, future maps will be based on interpolations that take into account surrounding habitat and climate types.

Technical Details

All work on the data and much of the work for the annotated list was done using dBASE IV® (Borland International). The maps were created in SURFER® for Windows (Golden Software). Final editing and map layout was done in CorelDRAW® 3.0 (Corel Corporation) with the final maps being sent in digital form to the printers. The text and annotated list were written in WordPerfect® (Novell) and submitted in digital form to the publisher.

Relative abundance maps 3

Bird distributions are very dynamic. They can vary markedly among years, and during times of migration or dispersal the changes are continual. Some species undergo dramatic fluctuations in population size, or in distribution, from year to year. For example, Lark Buntings will often be absent from an area for several years only to reappear in high numbers. This is thought primarily to be a result of fluctuations in the timing and amount of precipitation. Invading species may also show dramatic changes in their distribution over a very short period of time.

Maps, however, are very static. A map of the relative abundance of a species is a snapshot, either of a single time period or an average over multiple time periods. While it is possible to portray temporal changes on a map, it requires a very different type of map than the standard distribution map found in most field guides, or the relative abundance maps presented here. These maps represent an *average* of the species' relative abundance pattern for the years 1985–1991 (with some exceptions, see chapter 2 for complete details). It is important to emphasize that these maps are based on a very selected sample of the bird populations (those along roads). The biases associated with the BBS affect how well the maps represent the true average population.

When examining these maps it is important to understand the difference between positive and negative data. Positive data represents known information about the presence of a species – a BBS route was run in the area and a species was detected. Negative data represents known information about the absence of a species – a BBS route was run and no individuals of that species were detected. If a map shows a species as being absent from an area it could be due to two reasons. Either it is an area where a route was run and no individuals of that species were detected (negative data), or there could be no routes in that area and thus no data have been collected (*terra incognita*, 'Here there be dragons').

Areas showing a species as being absent must be treated with a great deal of caution. Even if a route has been run in the general area, differences in habitat between the route and the surrounding area could cause a species to be missed. Even relatively common species could be missed due to difficulty in detecting the species (e.g., raptors, rails, owls, nightjars, and skulking species).

These maps should be considered primarily for the information portrayed by the positive data. In order for an area on the map to be shaded a route had to be run in the general area and the species had to be detected. The overall distribution of many species is more extensive than that shown on these maps. There can be many reasons for this. The simplest reason is that no BBS route has been run in that area (see chapter 1 for information on how to volunteer to run a BBS route). Figure 1 in chapter 2 shows the locations of the BBS routes used in creating these maps. If a species is shown as being absent in an area, and there were no routes near that general area, then the species may or may not be present in that area. Under these circumstances other sources should be consulted to verify whether the species is found in that area or not.

This chapter contains relative abundance maps of 450 species and identifiable forms. These are not maps of the breeding distribution, rather they represent the distribution and abundance pattern of the species during early summer (late May to early July depending upon latitude). For the most part the maps represent the breeding distribution and abundance pattern of the species. However, some maps also show areas outside the breeding range where the species are regularly found during early summer (especially some of the waterfowl and gulls).

Not all of the maps of the species can be thought of as being representative of that species' range. Rather the species was included because it was detected, in portions of its range, at a high enough rate to be meaningful. These species are potentially much more widespread in their proper habitat. These maps make no attempt to portray all of a species' distribution but are based *entirely* on data collected by the BBS. For some species the relative abundance map and maps in other sources agree closely. For other species, maps in other sources may show a more widespread distribution. Many of these differences will be owing to habitat differences, and whether the road on which a route is run bisects the typical habitats in the area. Finally, keep in mind that many published maps of bird distributions are very broad, coarse approximations. The maps in this book portray a finer level of resolution (50 km by 50 km blocks) of the distributions of many species. As such, areas near the edge of a species' distribution often resemble a patchwork of the species being present or absent. This may be more indicative of the true patchy distribution of the species and its habitat. Breeding bird atlases, completed for a number of states and provinces, provide an even finer level of resolution (often 10 km by 10 km blocks), especially near the edge of a species' distribution. A list of many of these atlases, and other bird and bird-finding guides, can be found in appendix B.

The technique used to create these maps works best in areas where many routes were run (much of the East and California). The fewer the routes, the greater the potential error in the interpolation. For that reason, species' distributions in much of northern Ontario and northern Quebec must be treated as being very uncertain. While the interpolated distributions were compared against those from other sources, the scarcity of routes in those areas (largely due to lack of roads) means that the species' distributions should be considered as coarse approximations.

Each map contains up to four different levels of abundance, represented as successively darker shades of color. The levels are: <5; 5–20; 20–50; and >50 birds detected per route per year. The lowest level does not extend to zero as the actual position of a species' distributional boundary varies from year to year. A decision was made to fix the minimum mapped value in such a way that the map was representative of the range but excluded accidental detections (1 in 7 years) and spurious values (errors created by the interpolation). The minimum mapped value for most species was 0.5 birds per route per year. This would represent one individual of a species being detected on a BBS route every other year. Chapter 2 provides more information on how the species' range edge was determined.

There are a few things to keep in mind while examining the maps. The first is that there is a relationship between relative abundance and detectability. Species with high abundance values tend to be more easily detectable than species with low abundance values. It is possible for a species to be relatively common in an area but be difficult to detect and thus have a low relative abundance value. The second is that a BBS observer only spends three minutes at each stop, or 150 minutes (2.5 hours) of active observation along the 24.5-mile length of the route. For most routes, three minutes is not enough time to detect all of the individuals of all of the species at that stop. If more time was spent at the stop more individuals and species would be detected. Finally, the relative abundance in a given area on these maps represents an average over an area of 50 km by 50 km (approximately 31 miles by 31 miles). Taken together, all of these factors mean that no one *spot* will likely have a given species at the relative abundance shown on the map. Instead, the relative abundance value is indicative of the numbers of individuals that might be detected, providing that enough time is spent along roads in the proper habitat within a given area.

REFERENCES: Cadman *et al.* 1987; Campbell *et al.* 1990; DeSante and Pyle 1986; Godfrey 1986; Holt 1989, 1992; Janssen 1987; Martin and Lester 1990; Monson and Phillips 1981; National Geographic Society 1983; Oullet 1993; Peterson and Peterson 1980, 1990; Rappole and Blacklock 1994; Robbins *et al.* 1983; Stephens and Sturts 1991; Toops and Dilley 1986; Unitt 1984.

Relative abundance maps based on Breeding Bird Survey data.

☐ < 5
☐ 5 - 20
☐ 20 - 50
☐ > 50

Scale represents the average number of individuals detected per route per year.

Common Loon

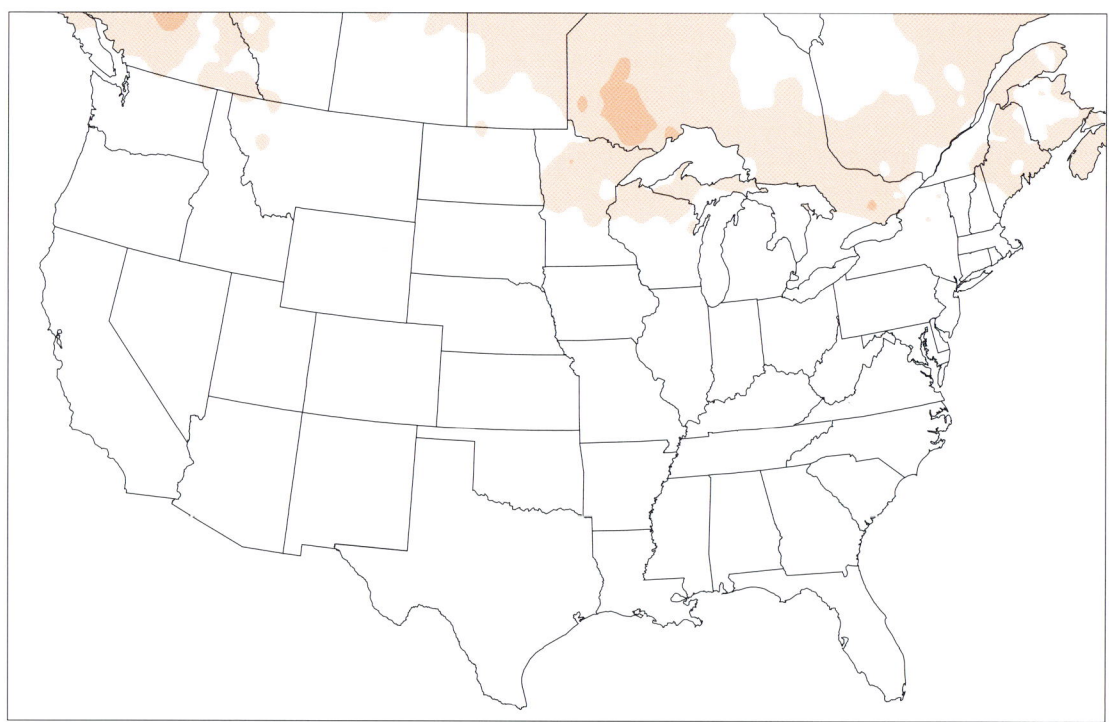

Pied-billed Grebe

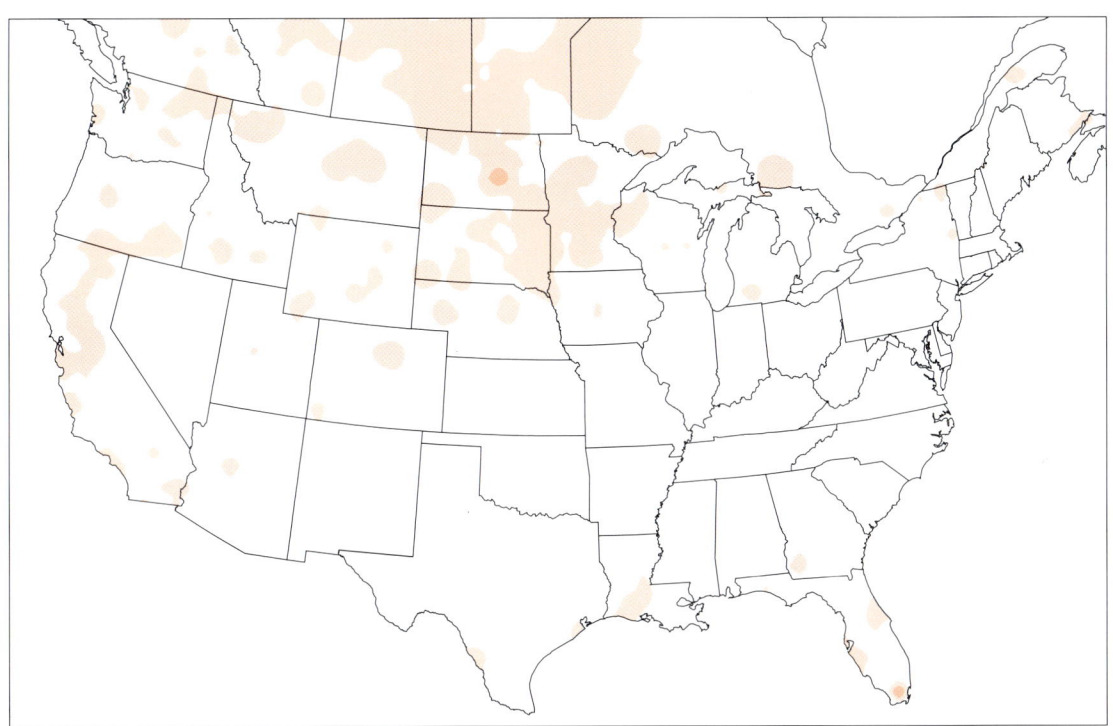

Horned Grebe

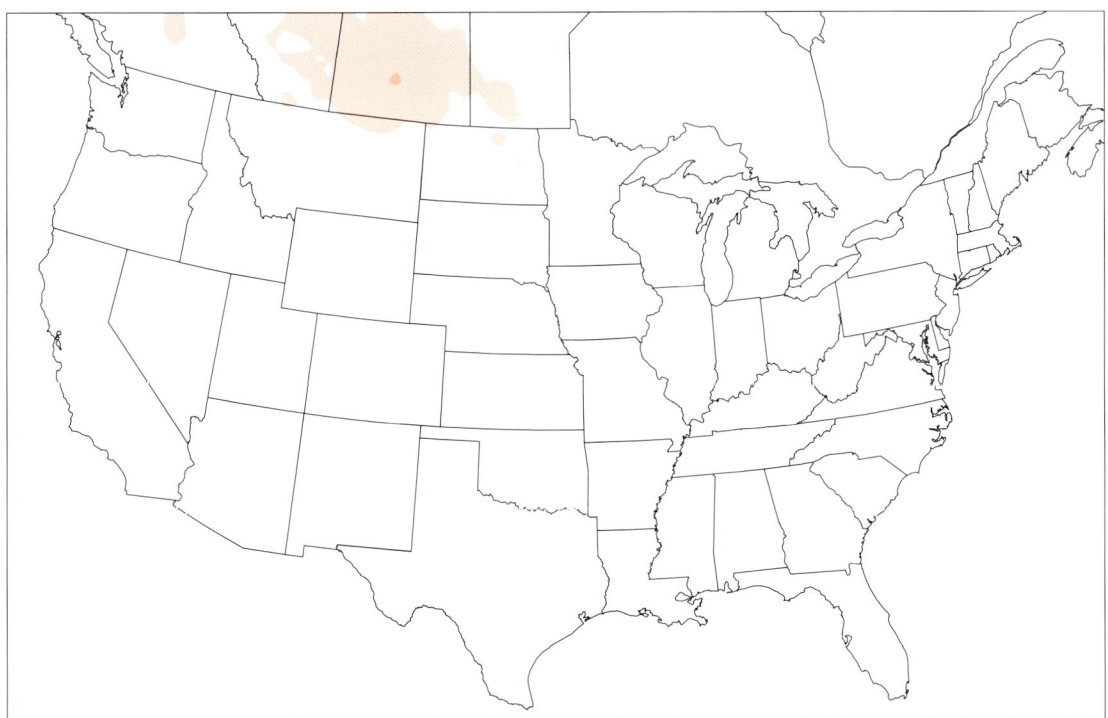

Eared Grebe

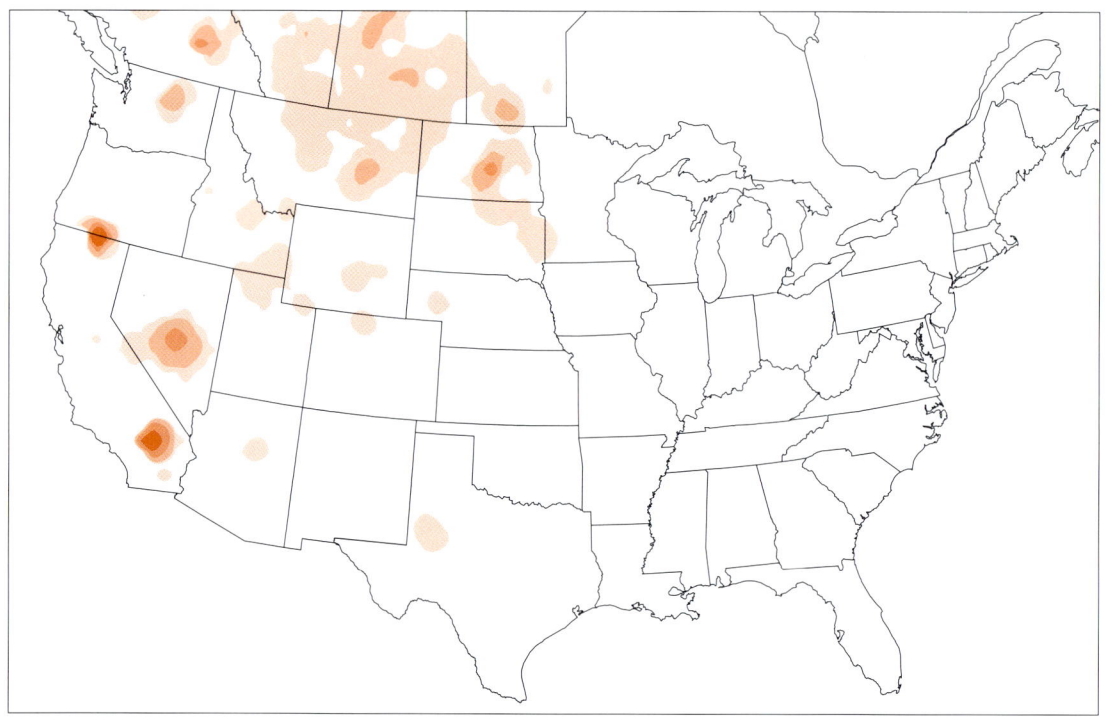

Western Grebe

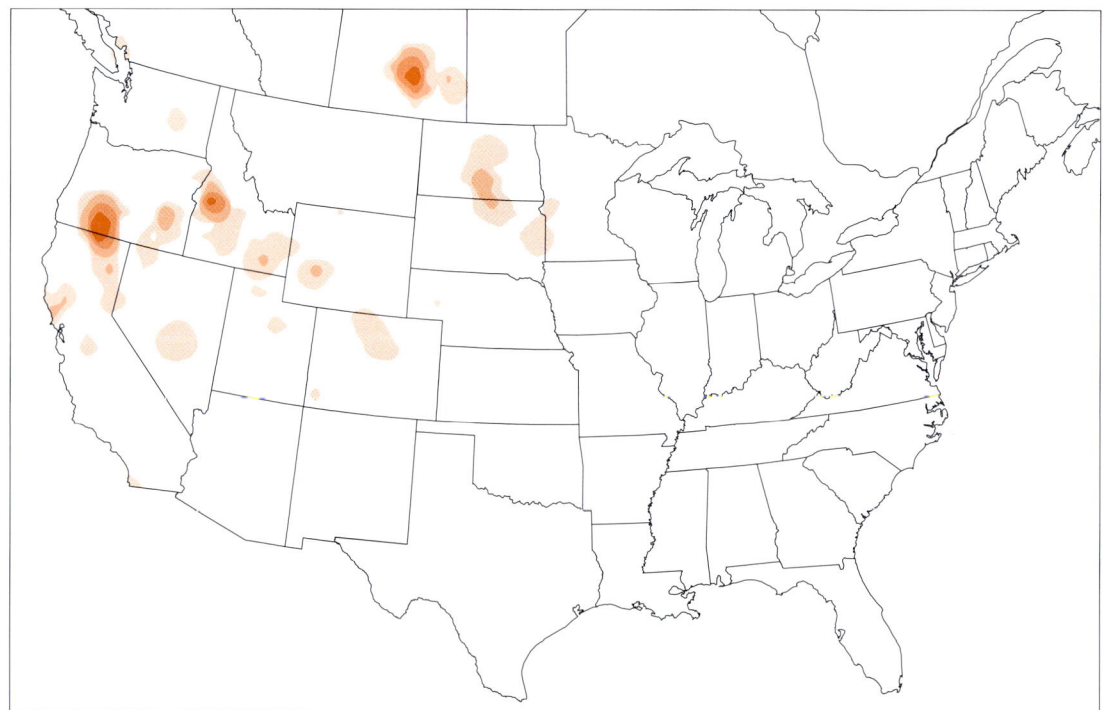

American White Pelican

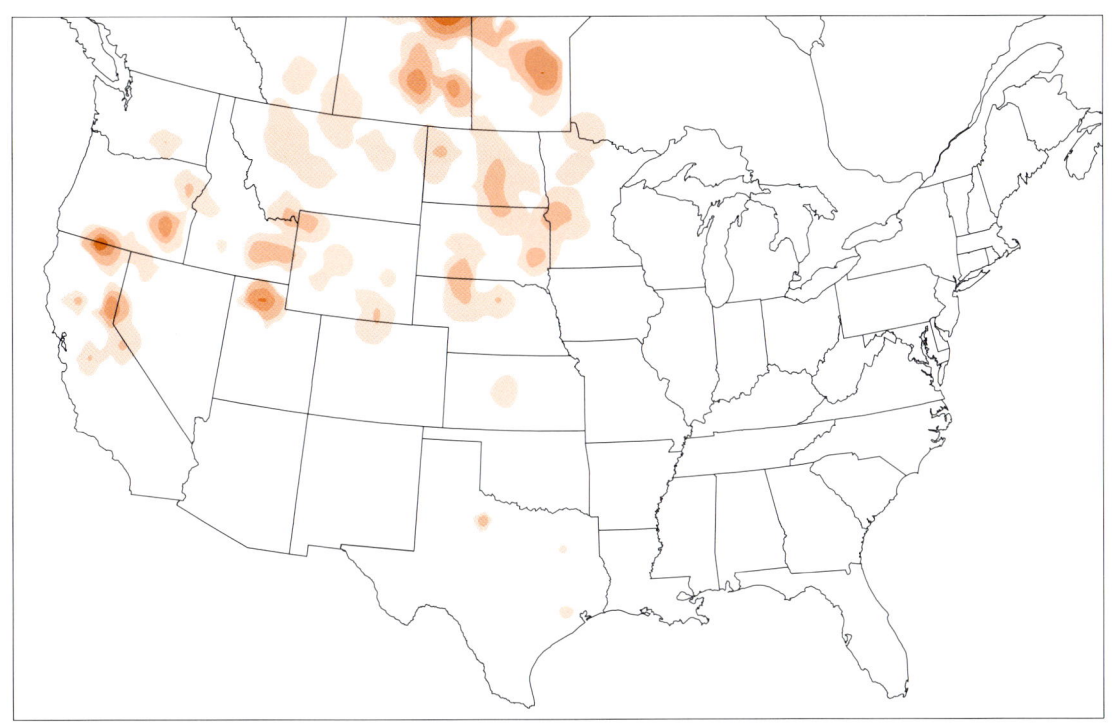

Brown Pelican

Double-crested Cormorant

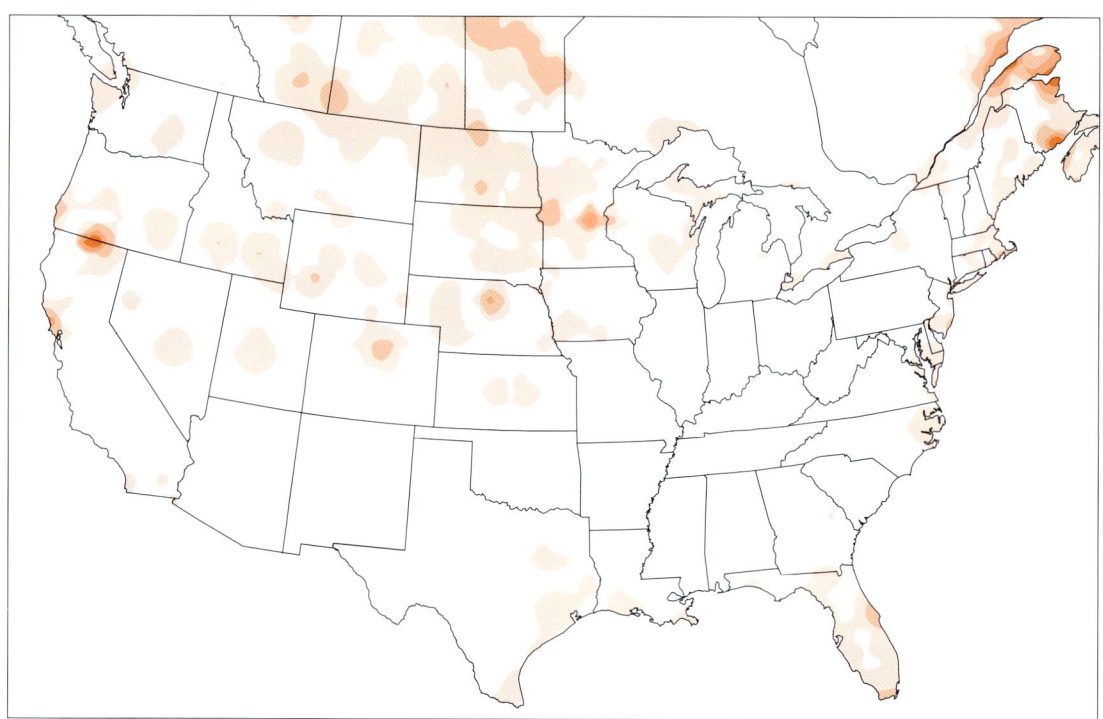

Neotropic Cormorant

Anhinga

Magnificent Frigatebird

American Bittern

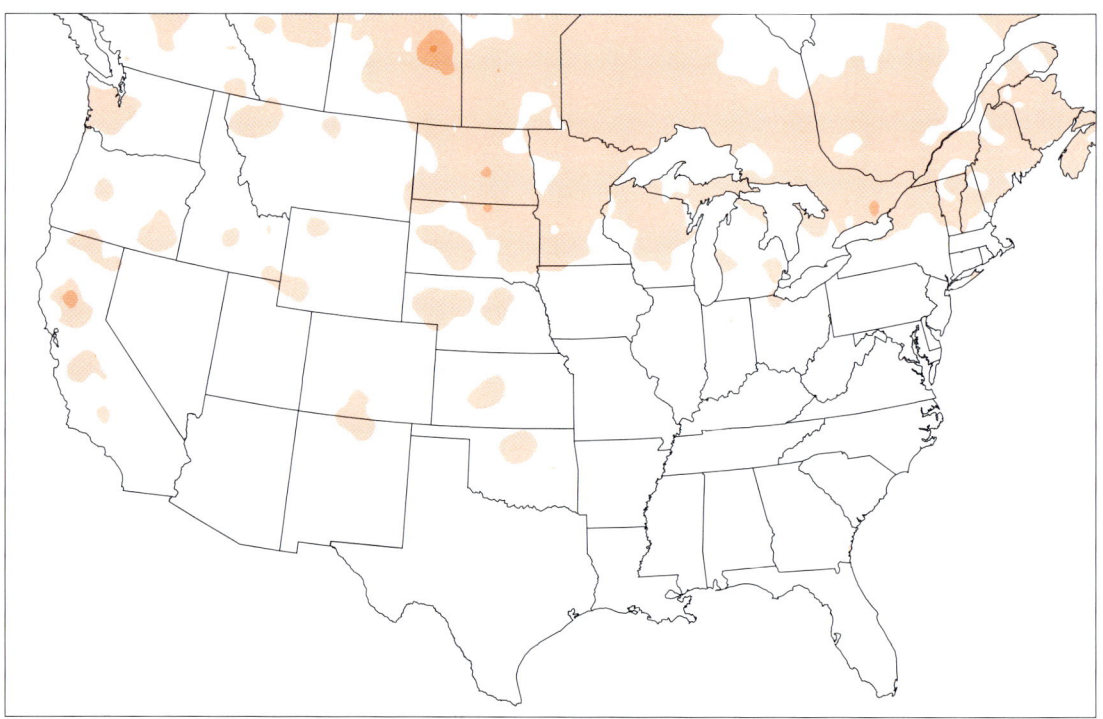

Great Blue Heron

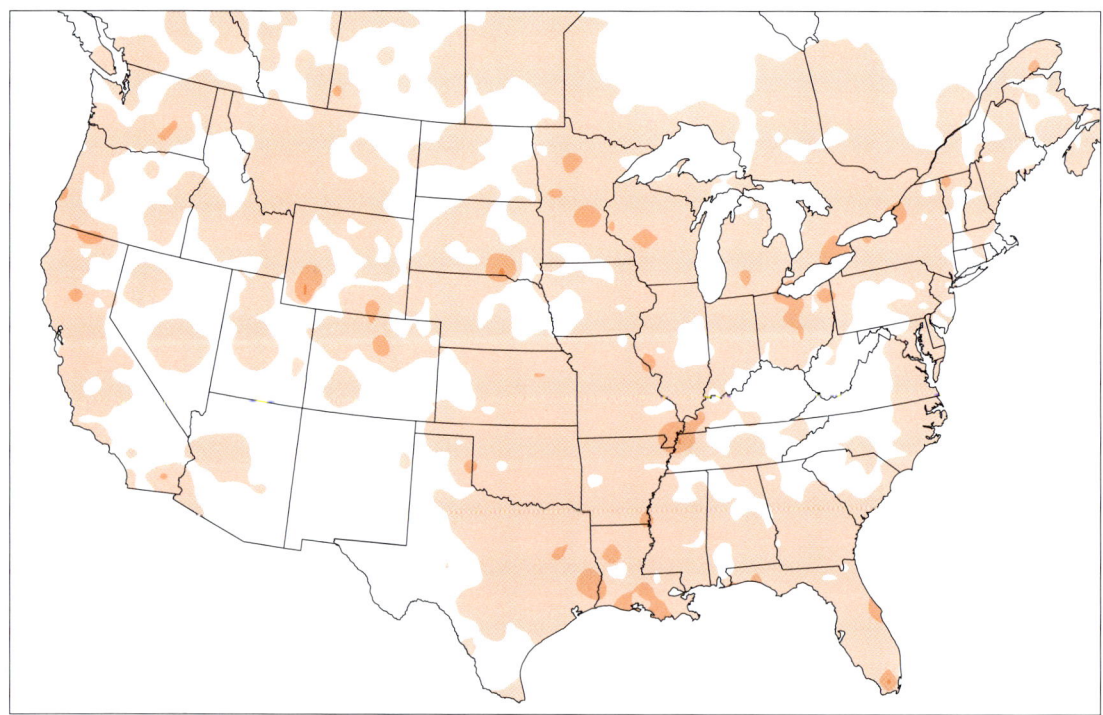

Great Egret

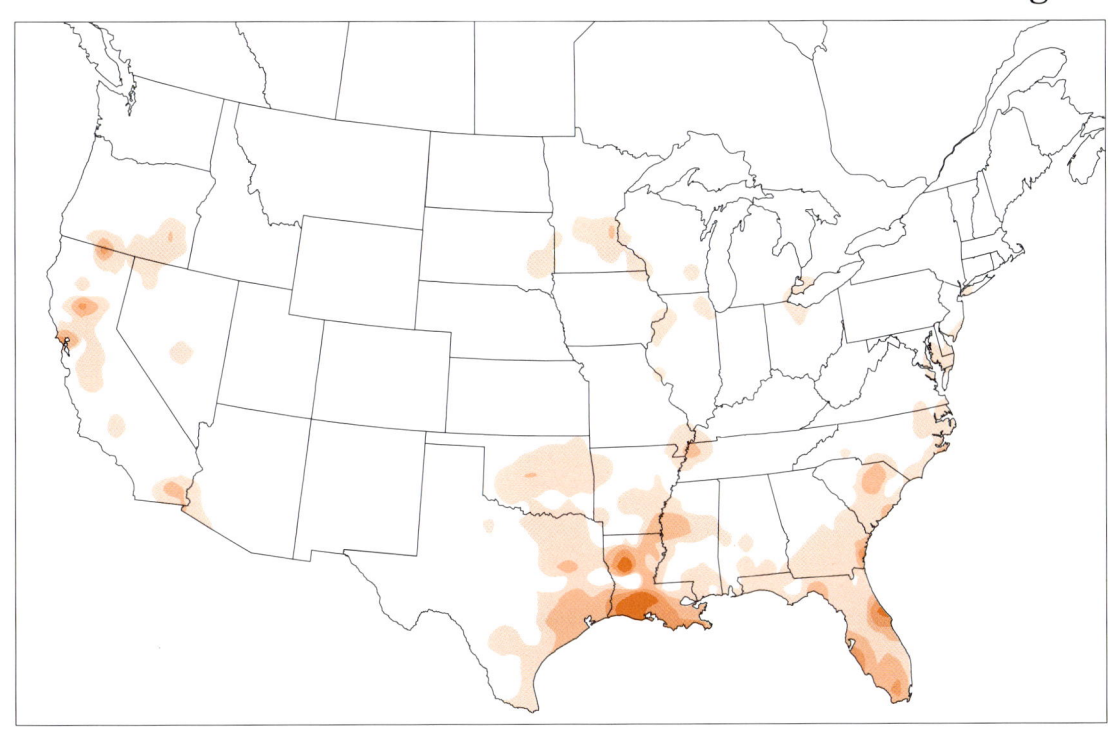

Snowy Egret

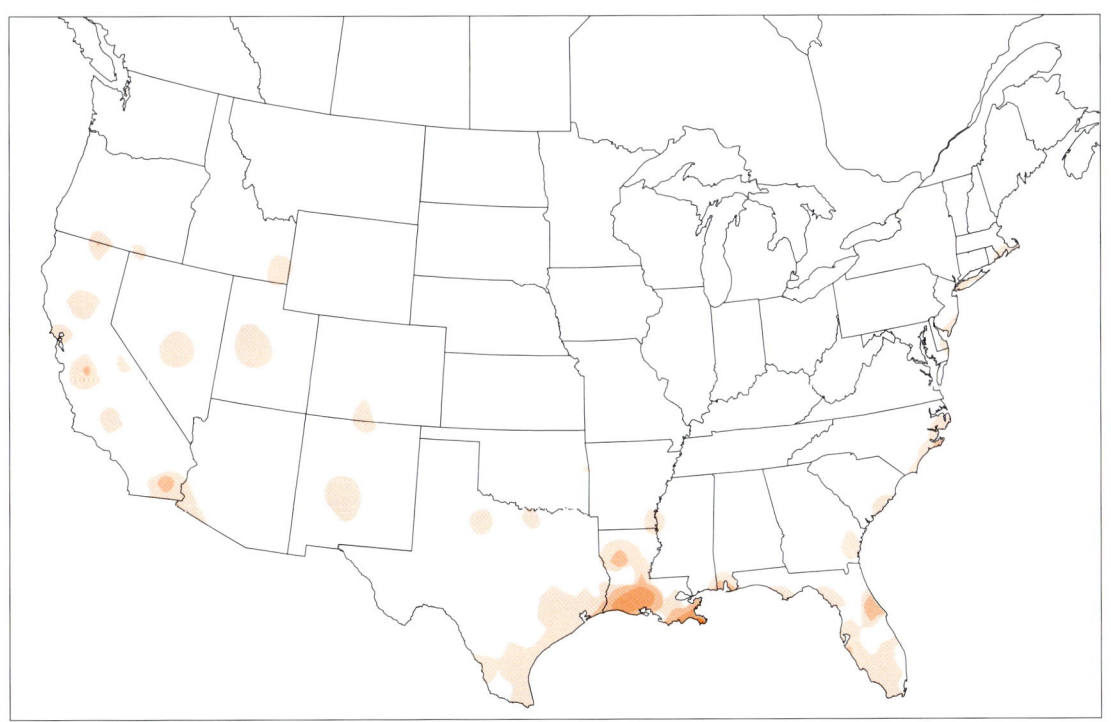

Little Blue Heron

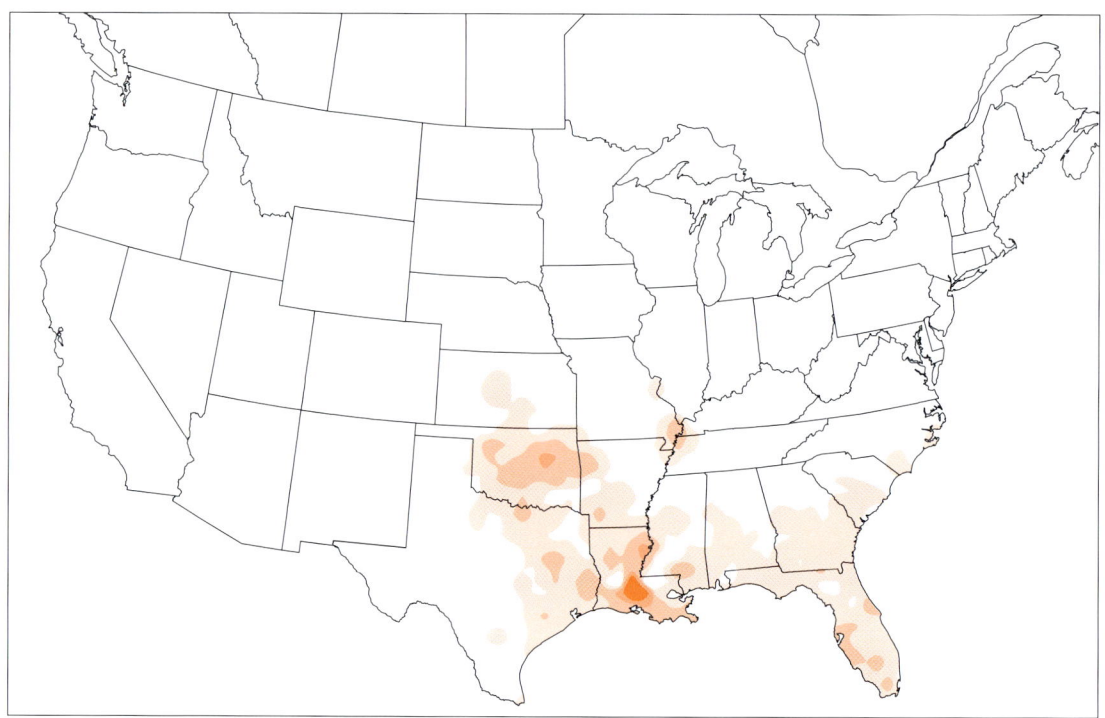

Tricolored Heron

Reddish Egret

Cattle Egret

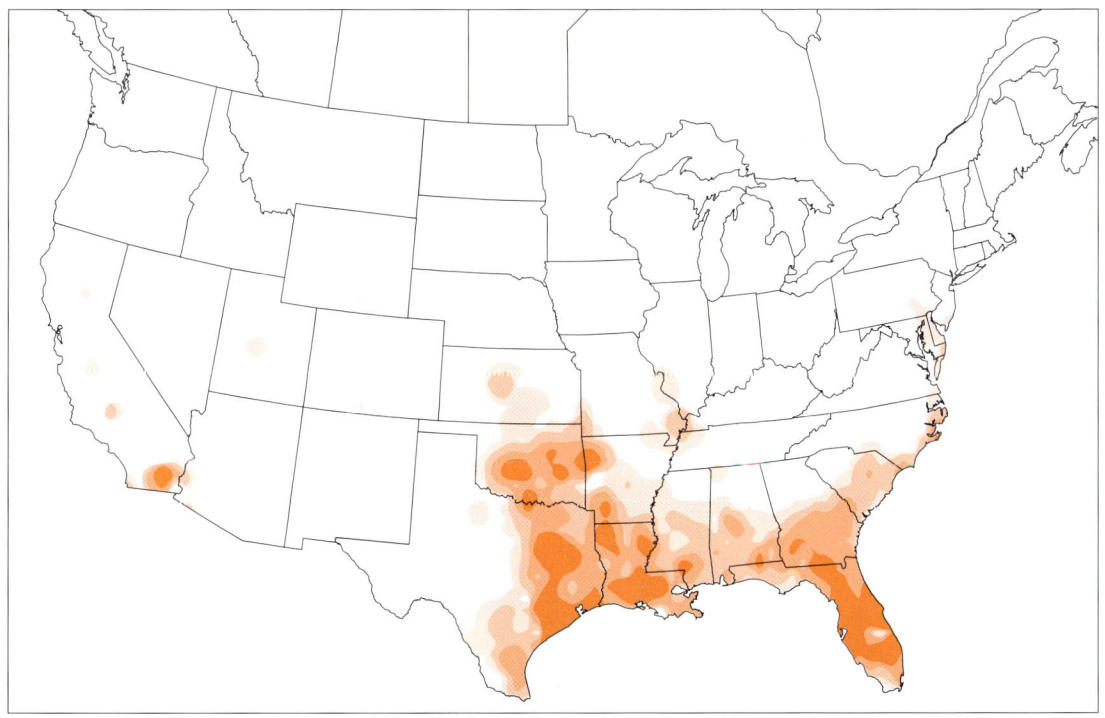

Green Heron

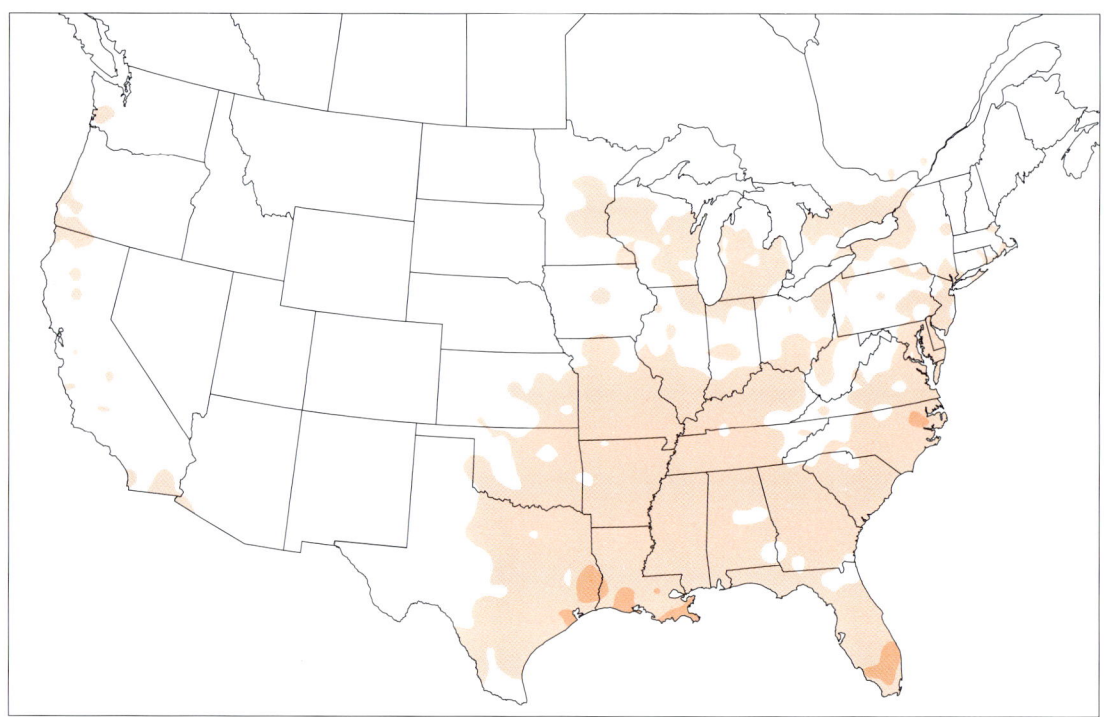

Yellow-crowned Night-Heron

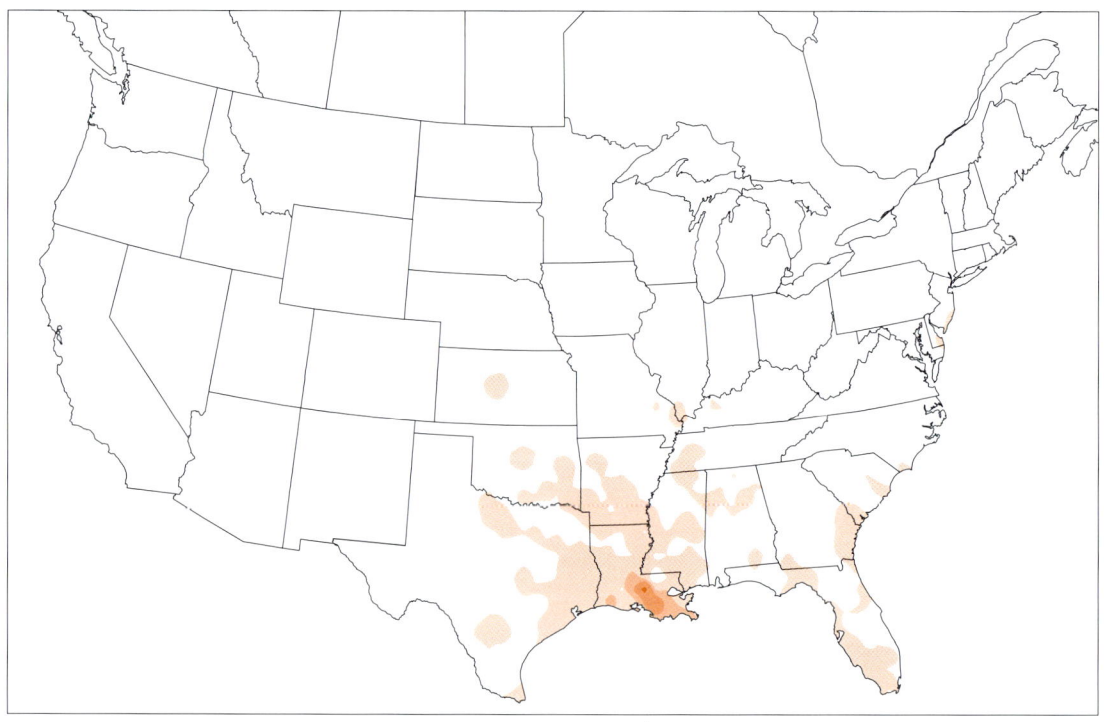

White Ibis

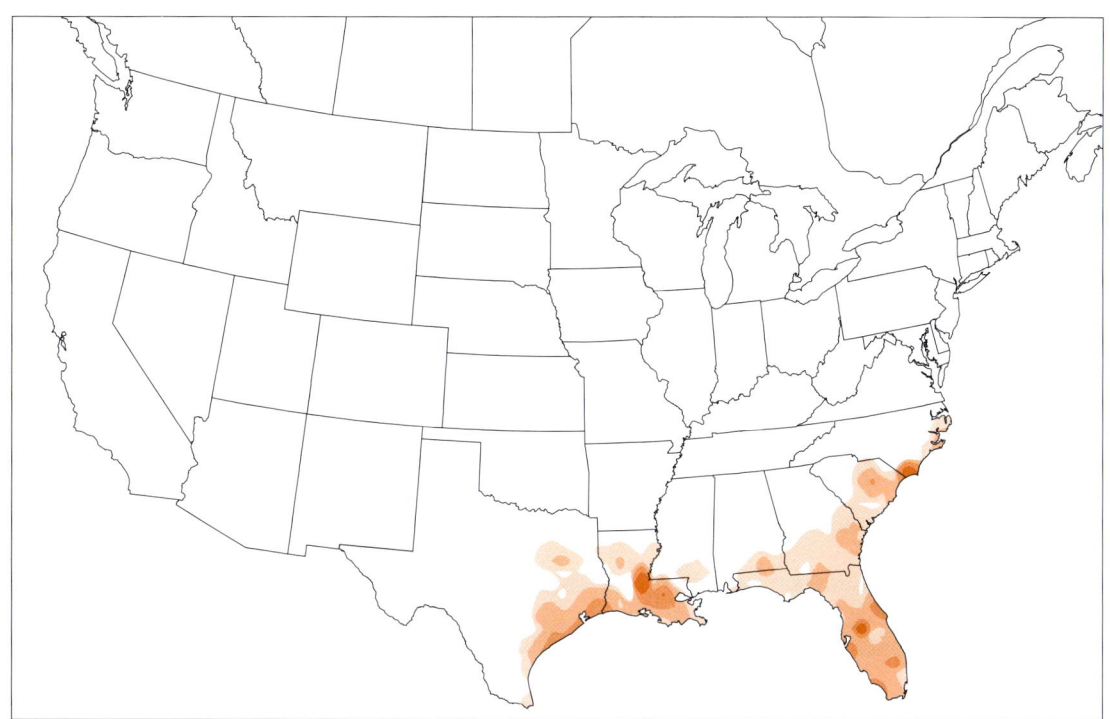

Glossy Ibis

White-faced Ibis

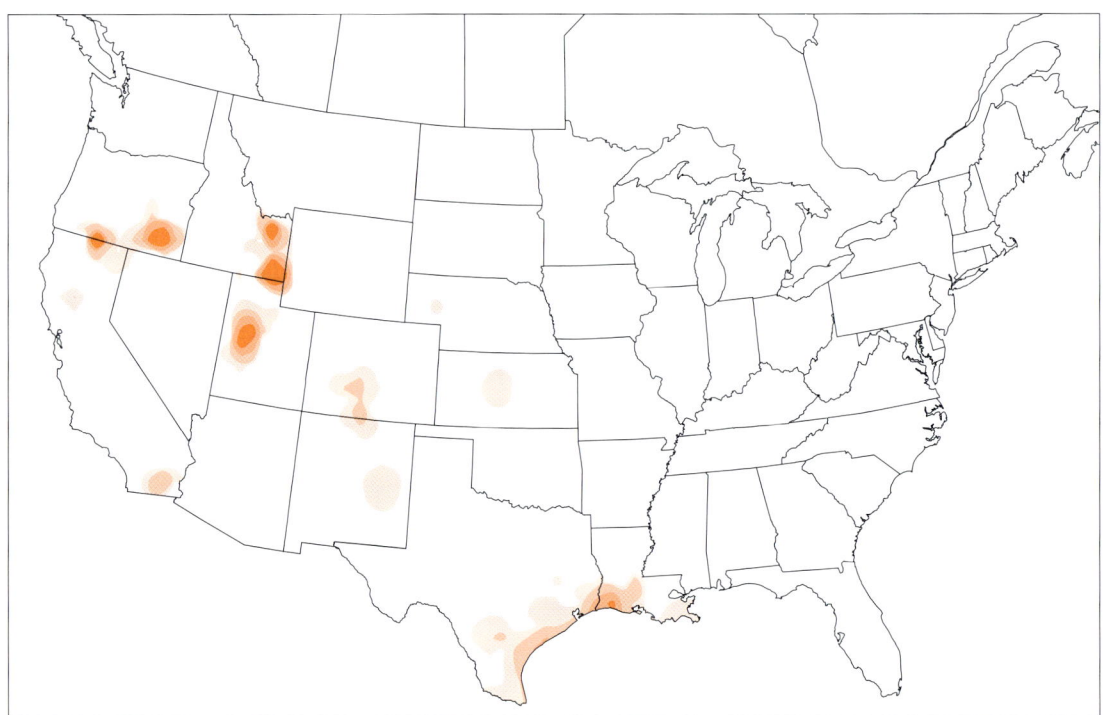

Roseate Spoonbill

Wood Stork

Fulvous Whistling-Duck

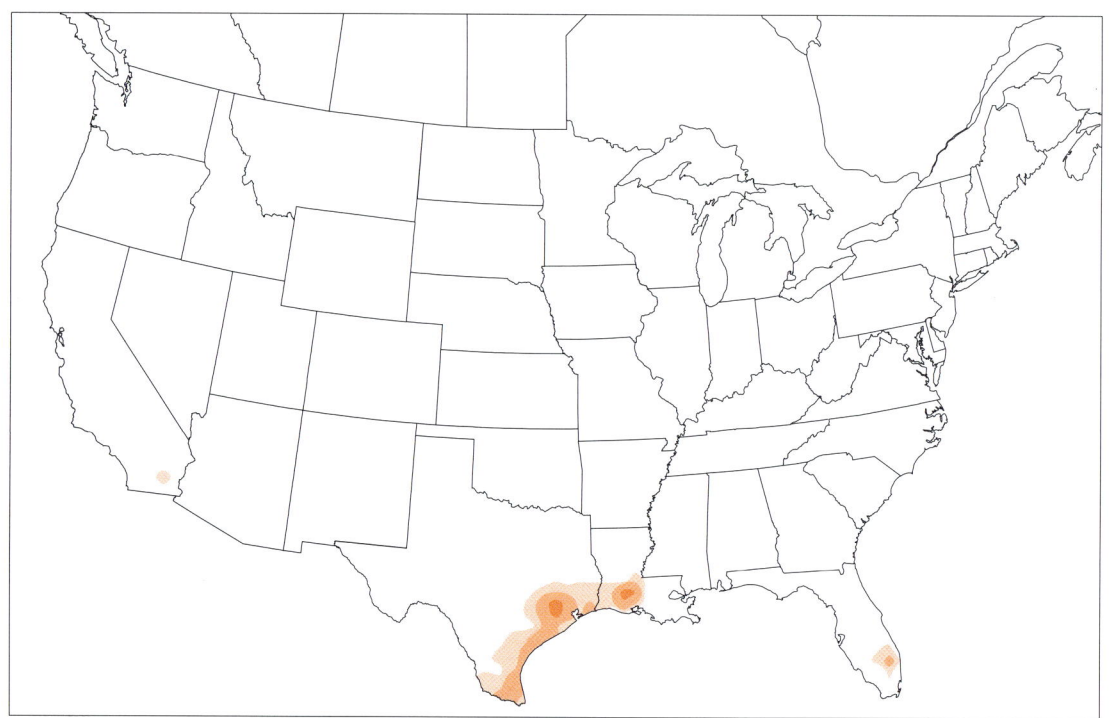

Black-bellied Whistling-Duck

Trumpeter Swan

Mute Swan

Canada Goose

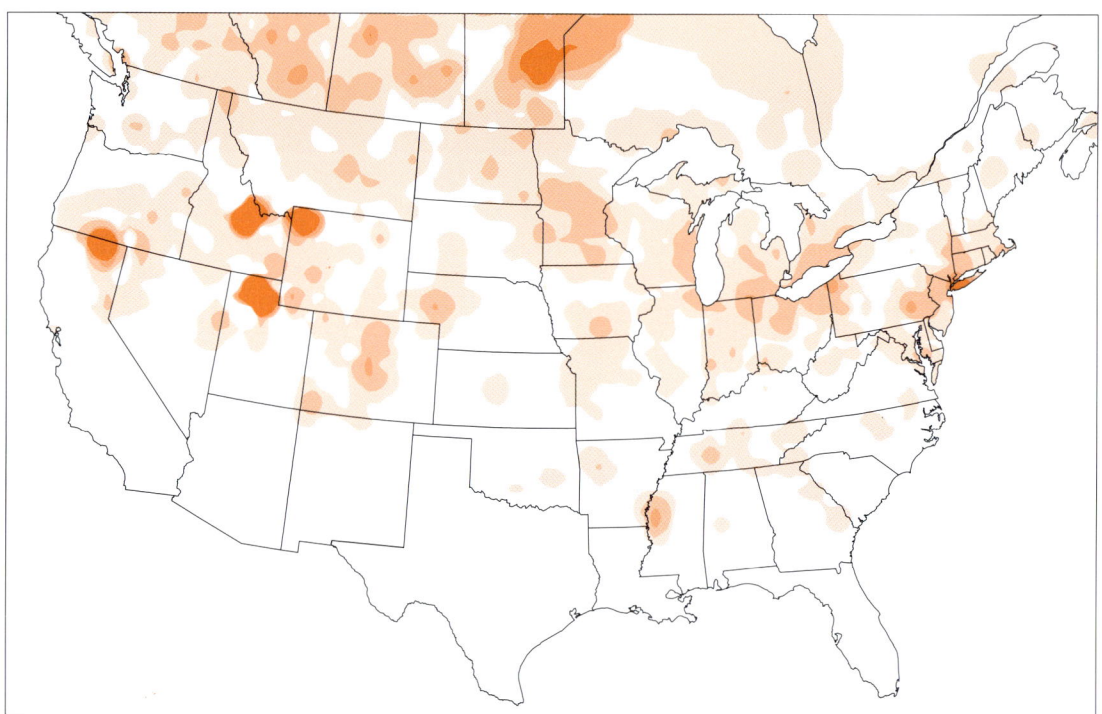

Wood Duck

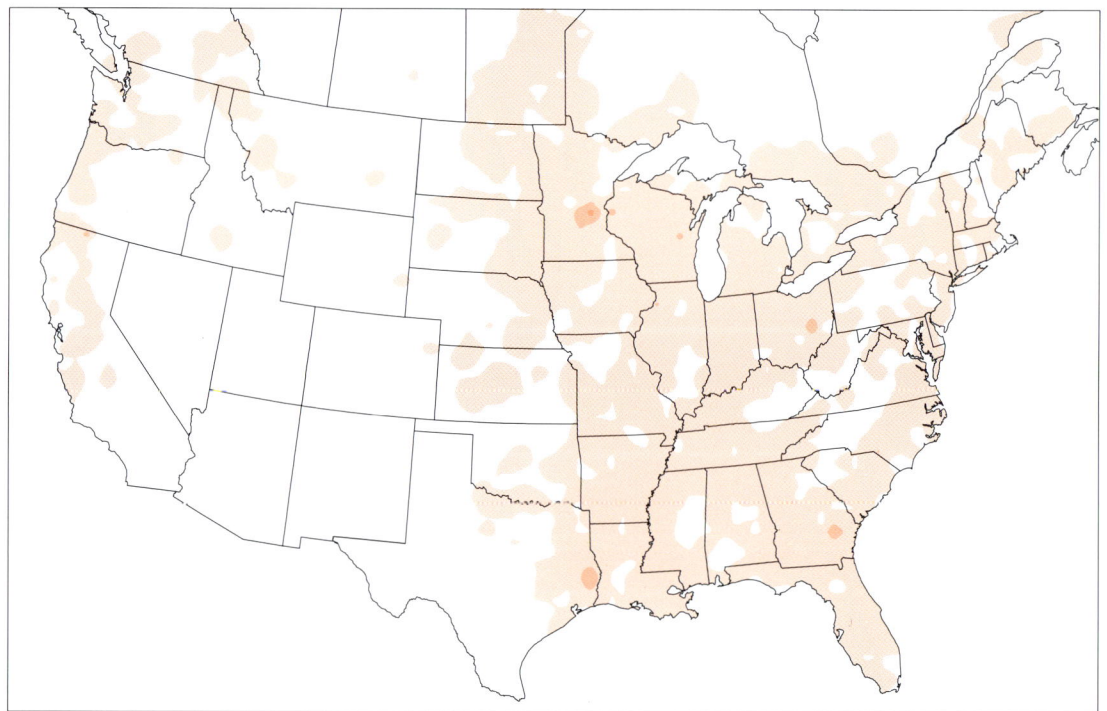

Green-winged Teal

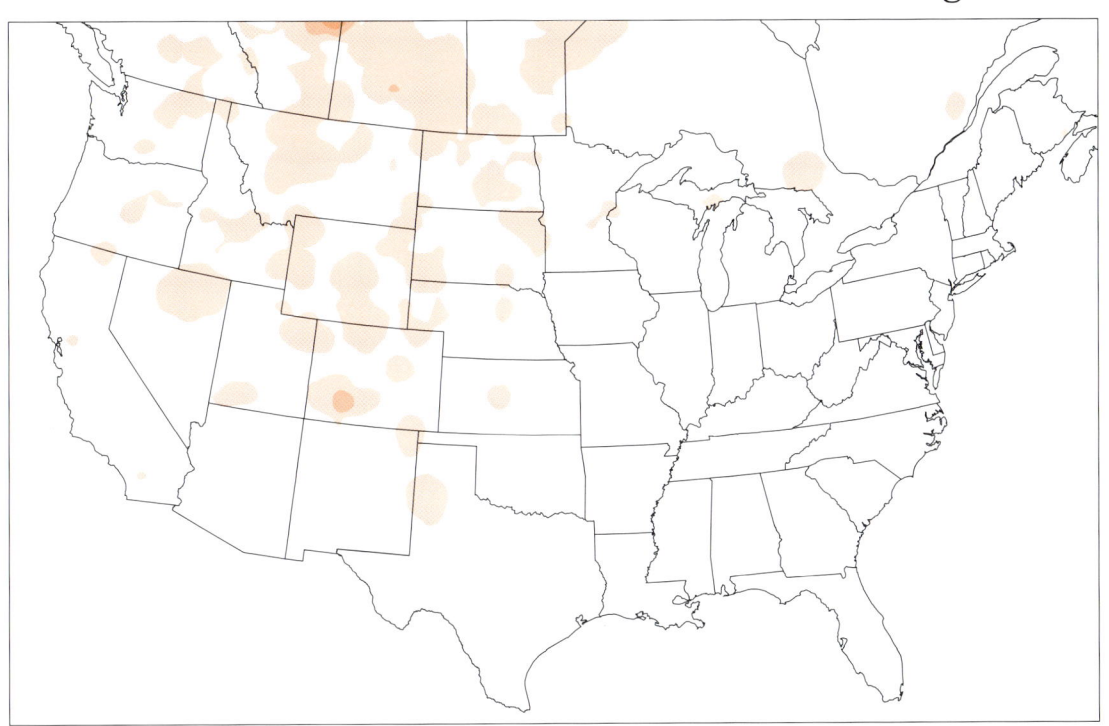

American Black Duck

Mottled Duck

Mallard

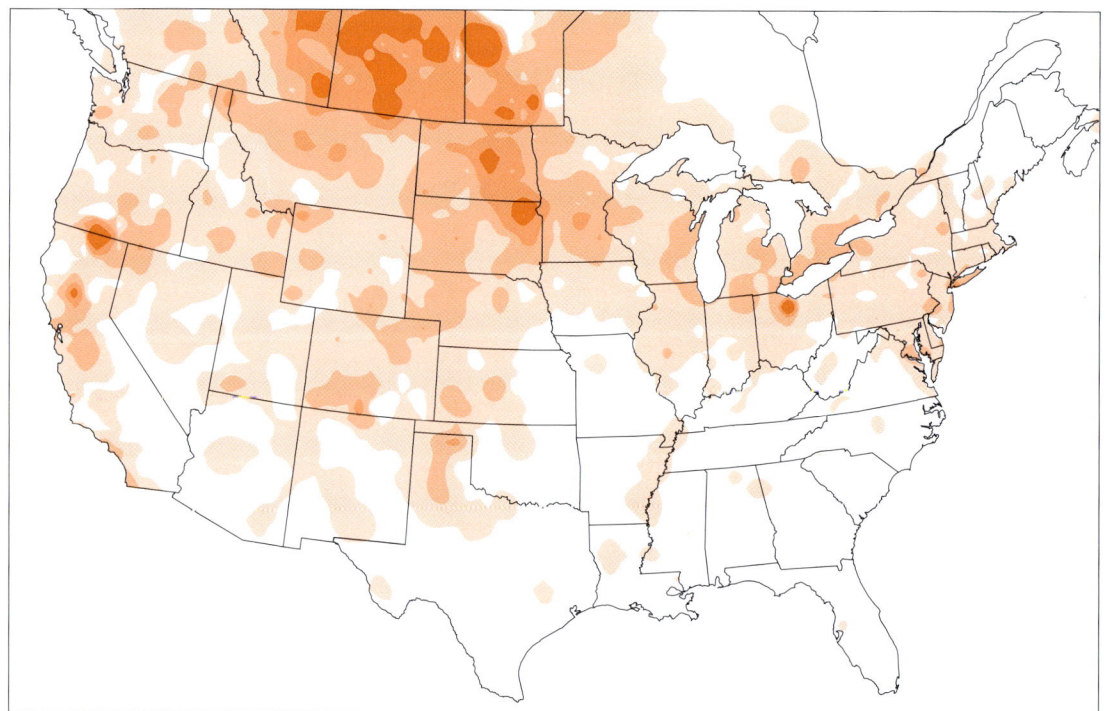

Northern Pintail

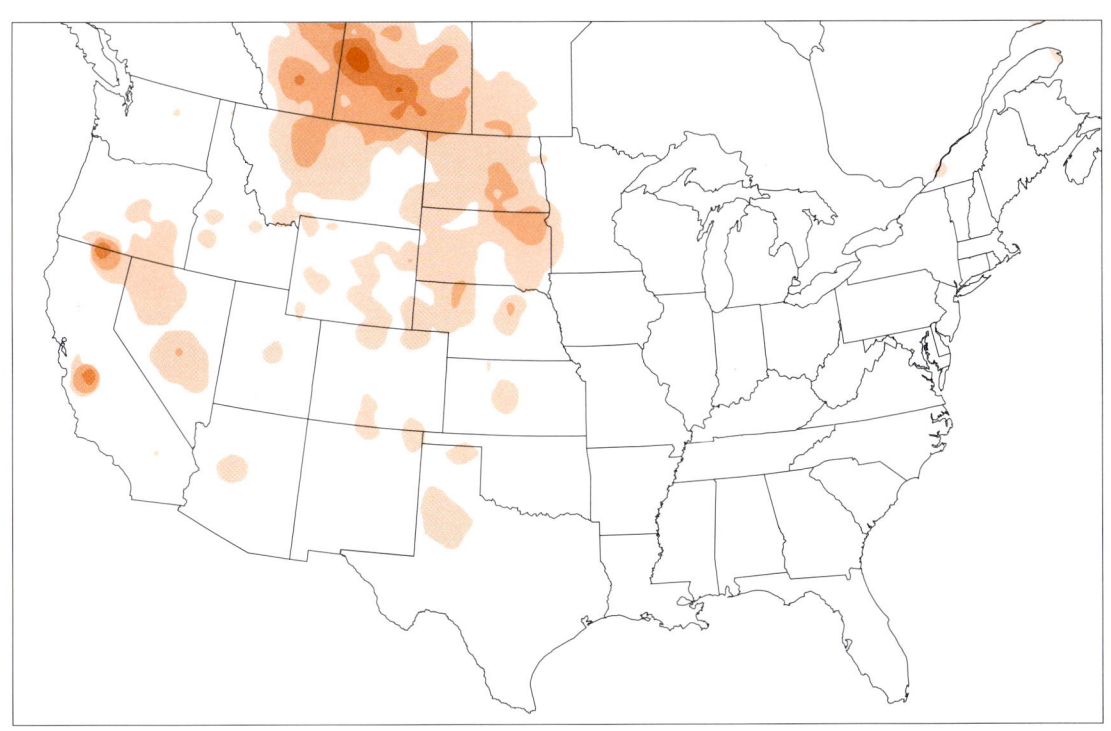

Blue-winged Teal

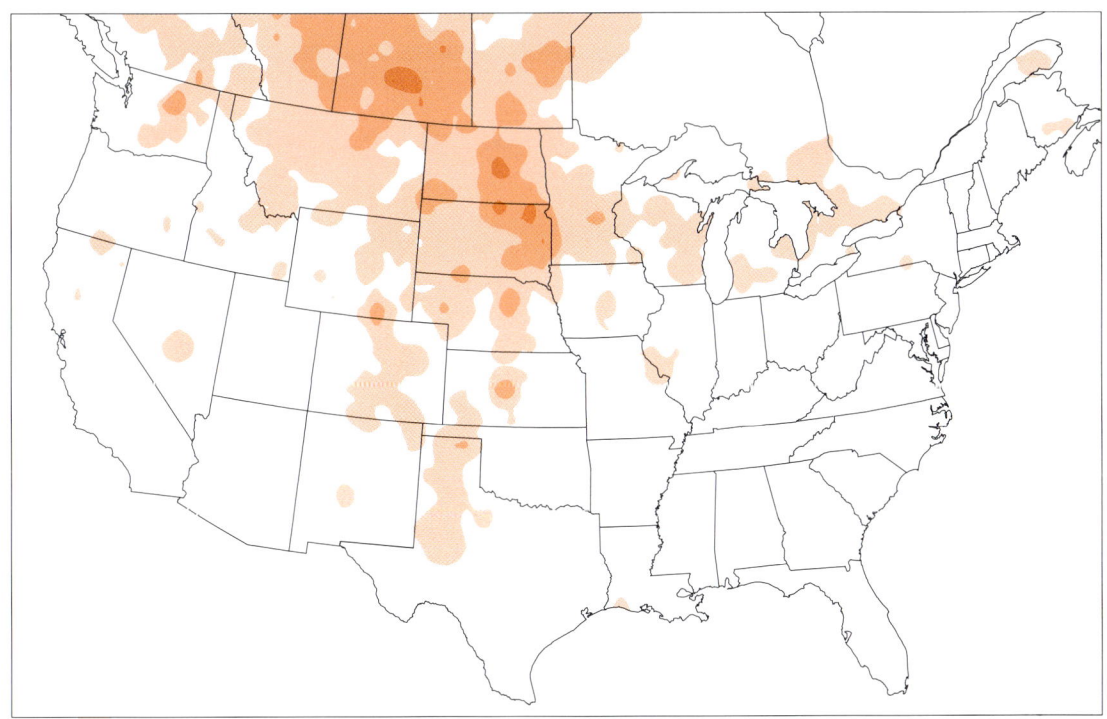

Cinnamon Teal

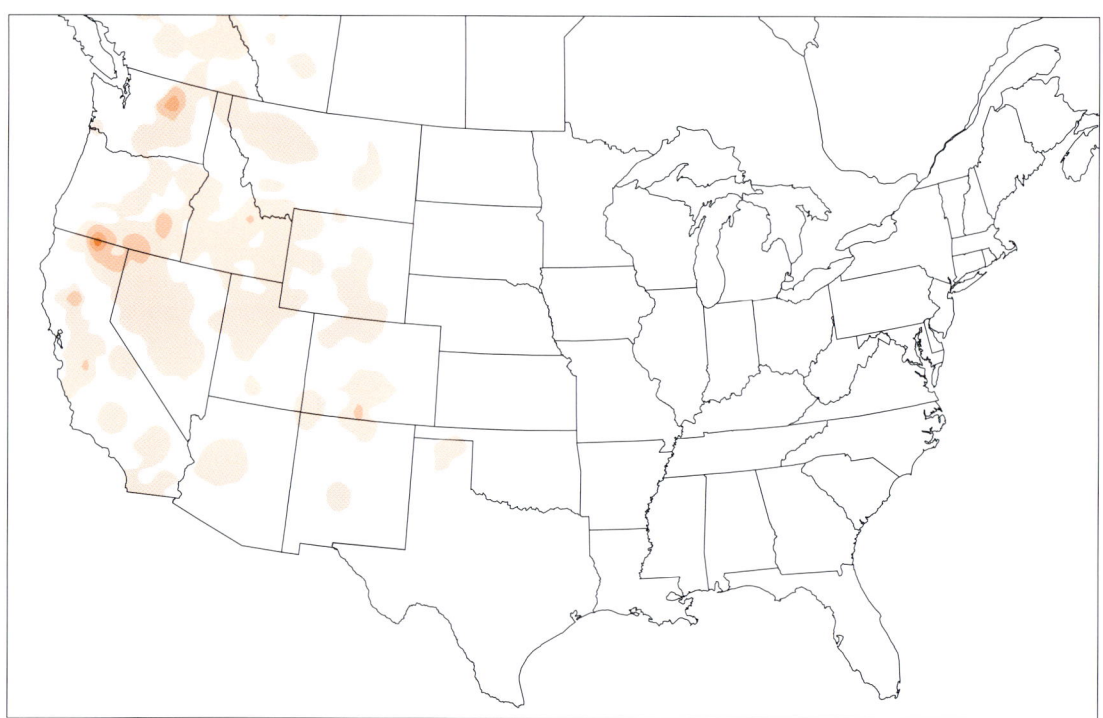

Northern Shoveler

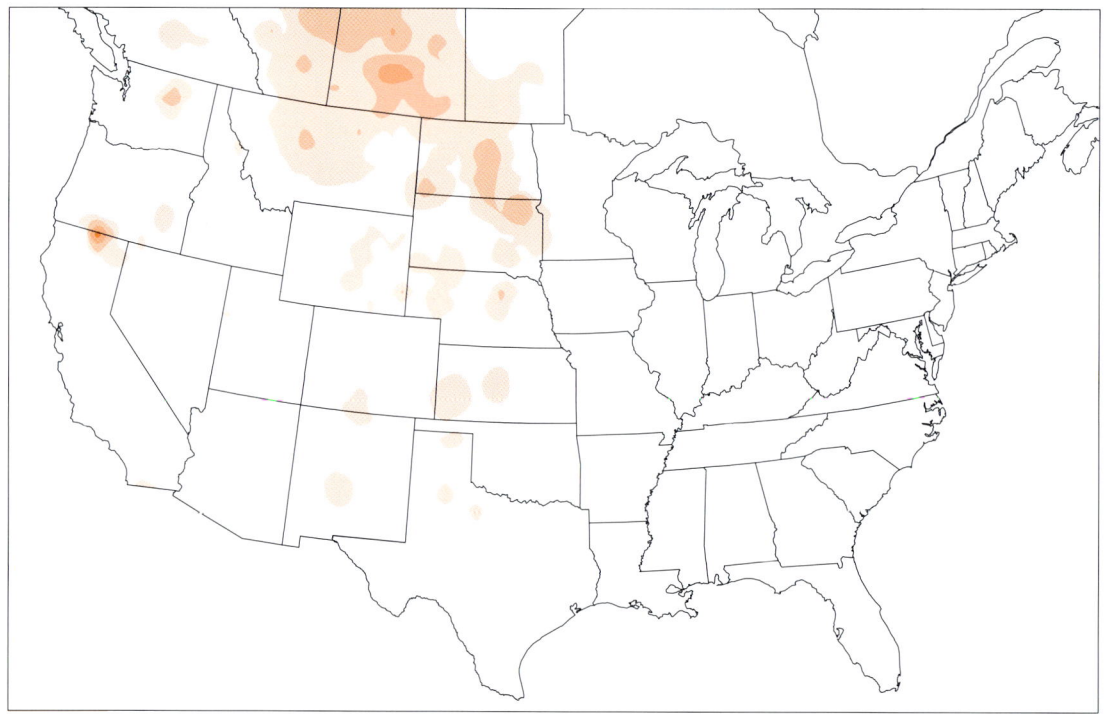

Gadwall

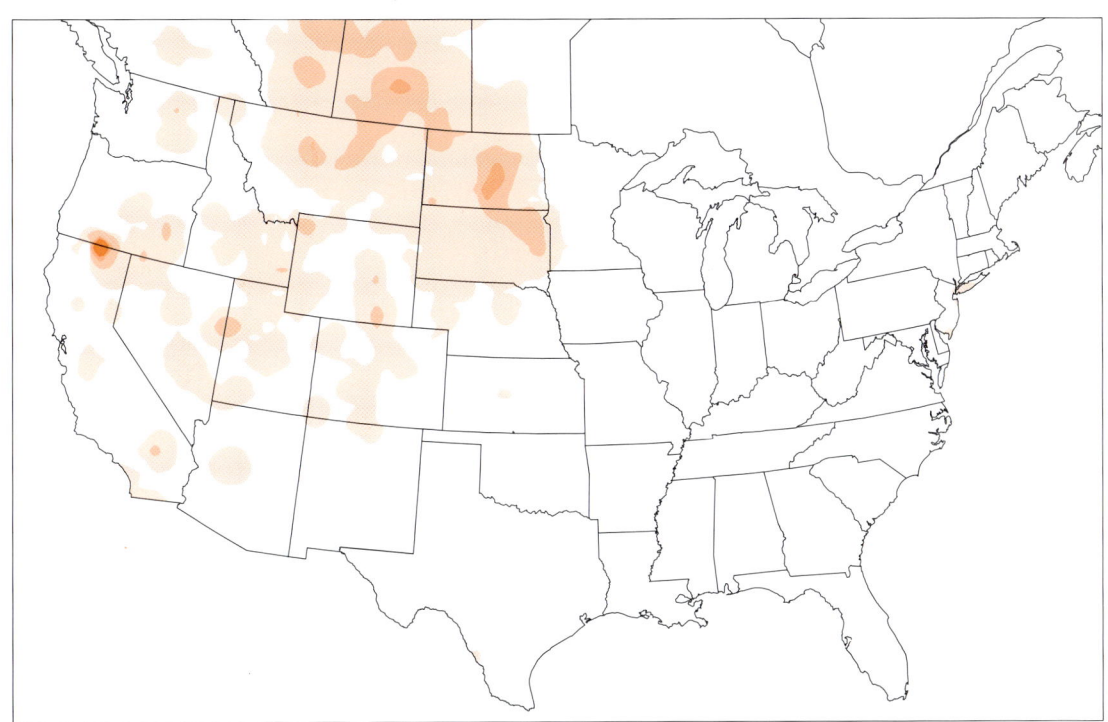

American Wigeon

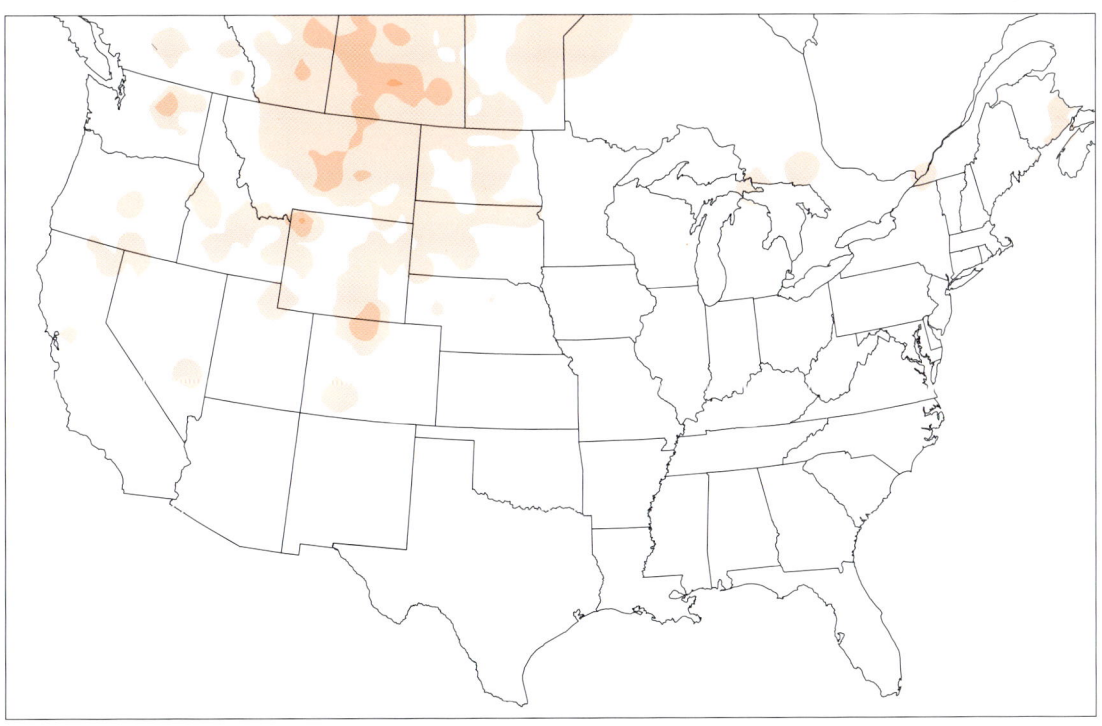

Canvasback

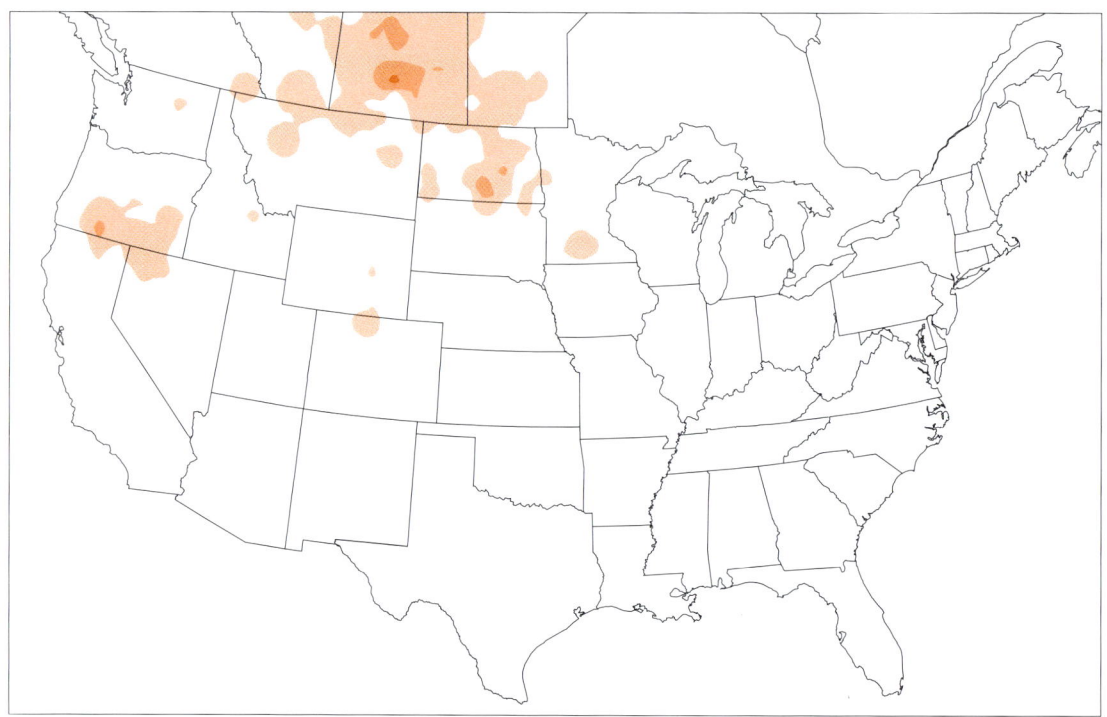

Redhead

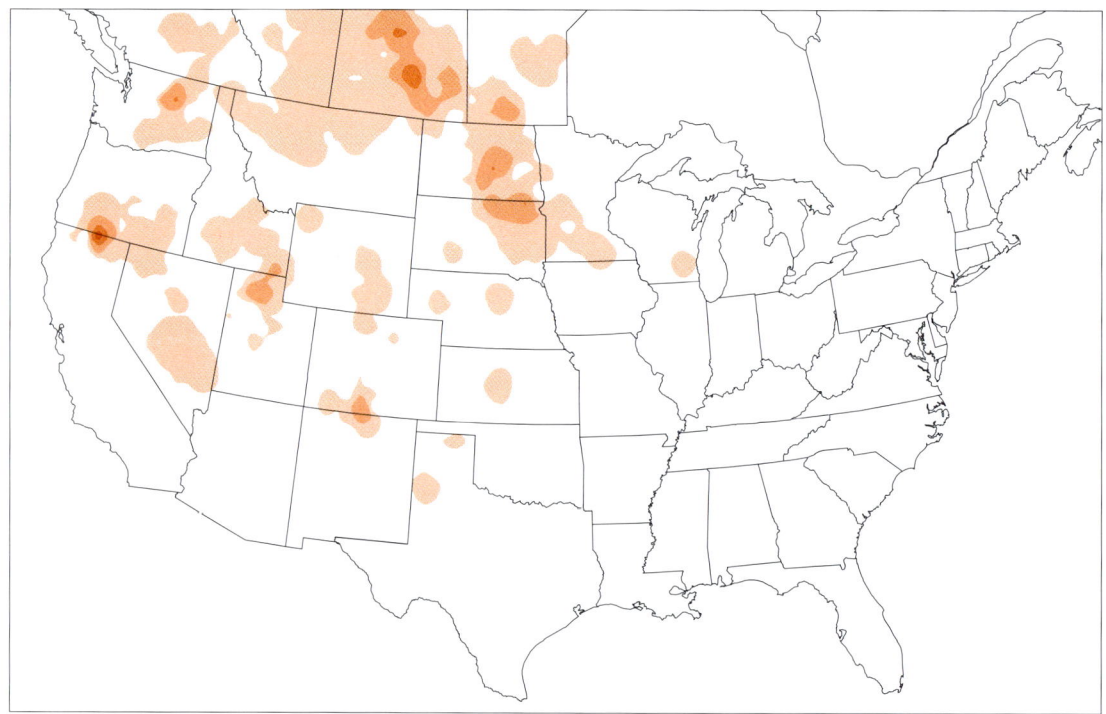

Ring-necked Duck

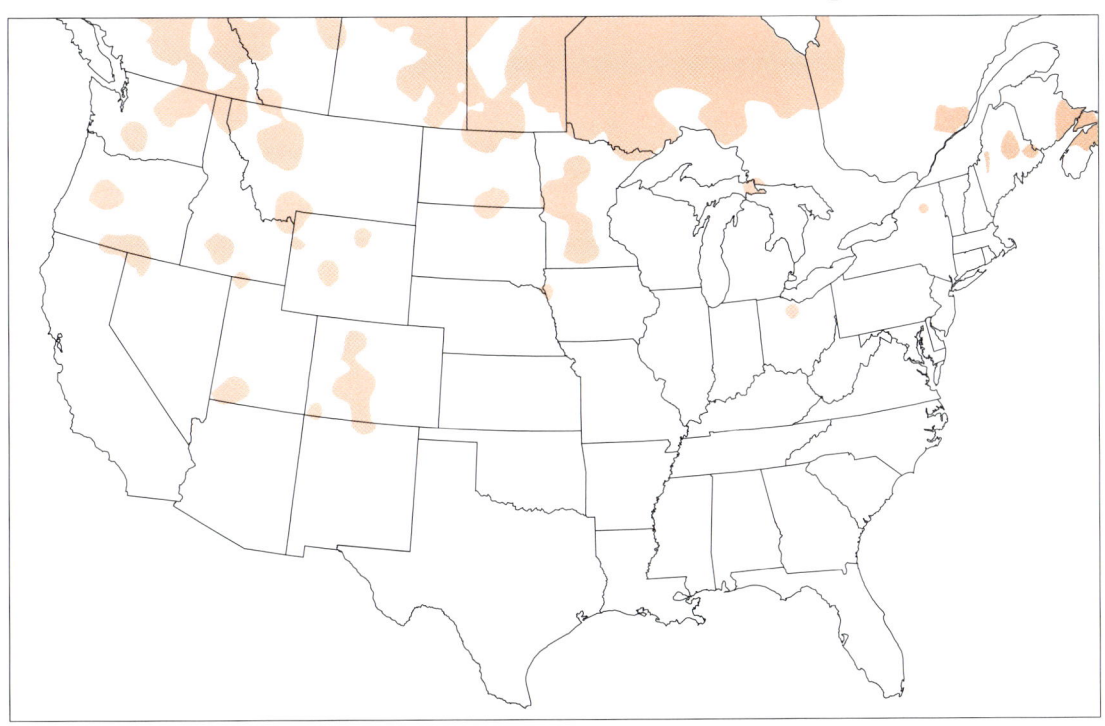

Lesser Scaup

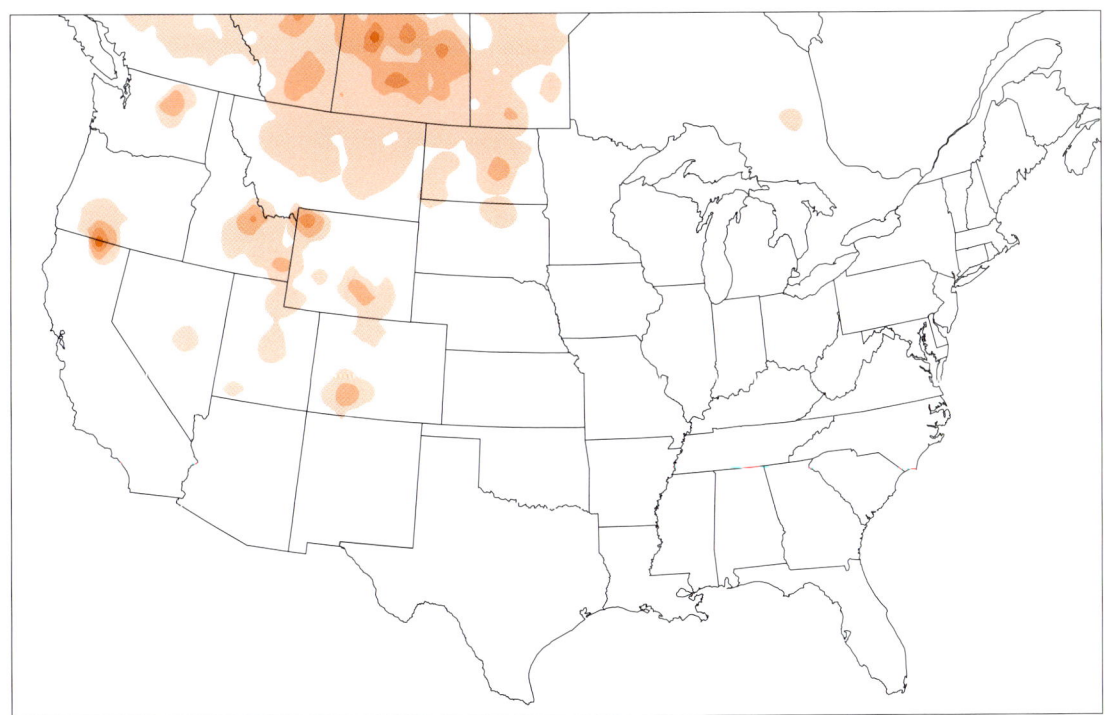

Common Eider

Common Goldeneye

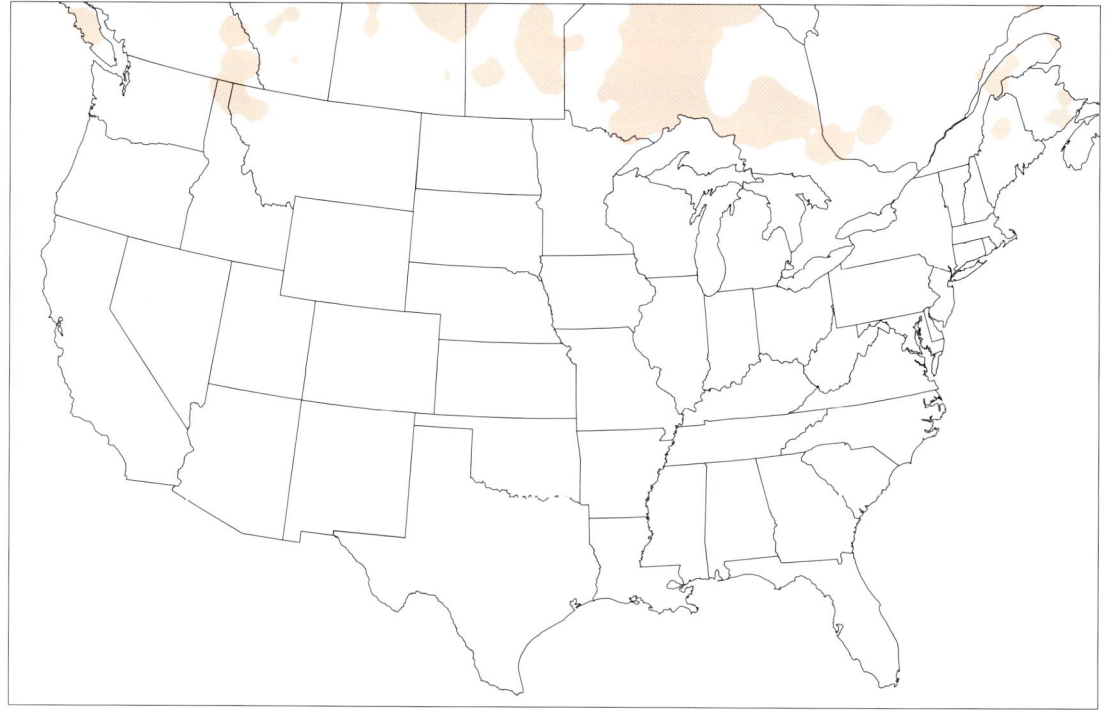

Barrow's Goldeneye

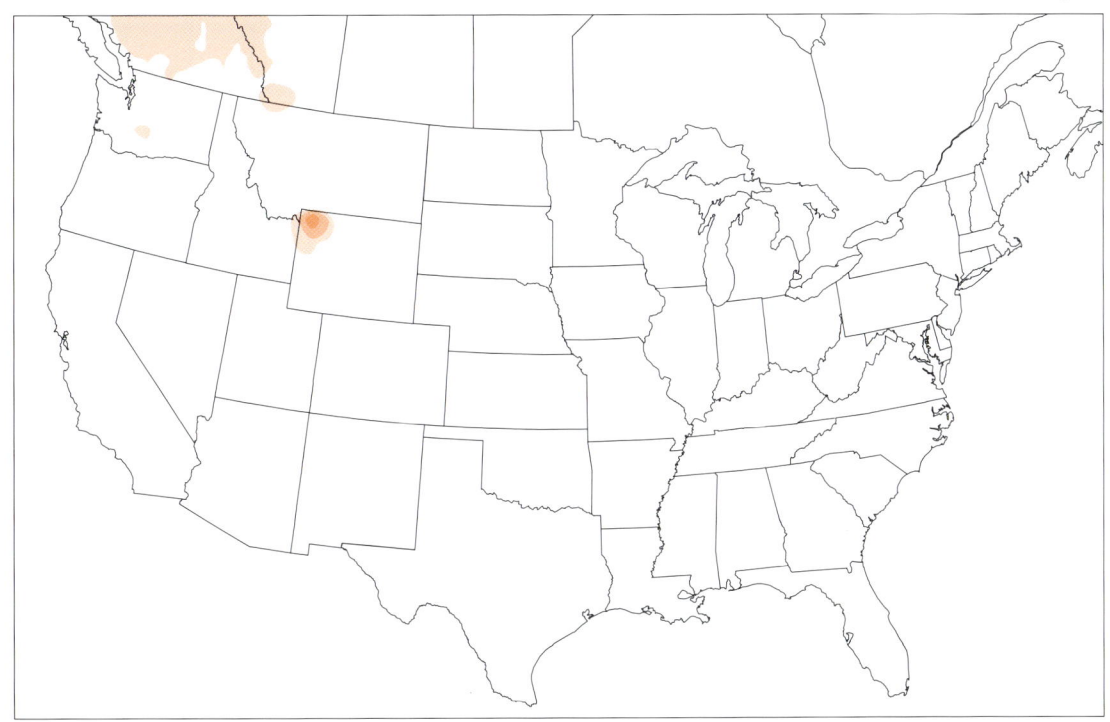

Common Merganser

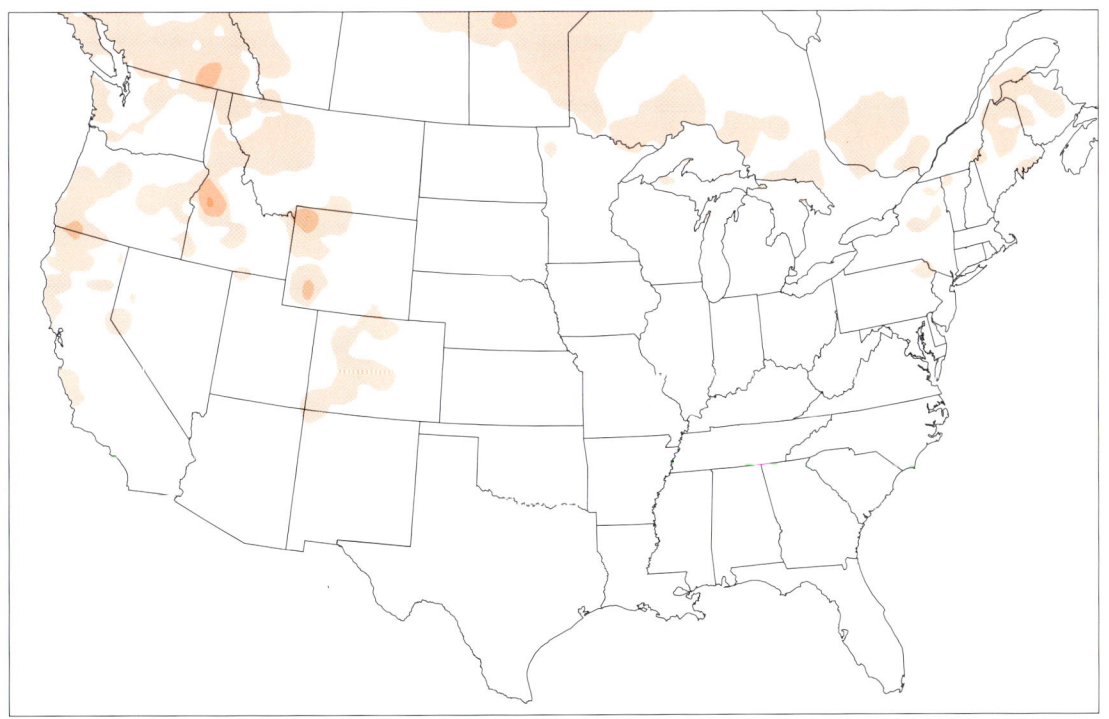

Red-breasted Merganser

Ruddy Duck

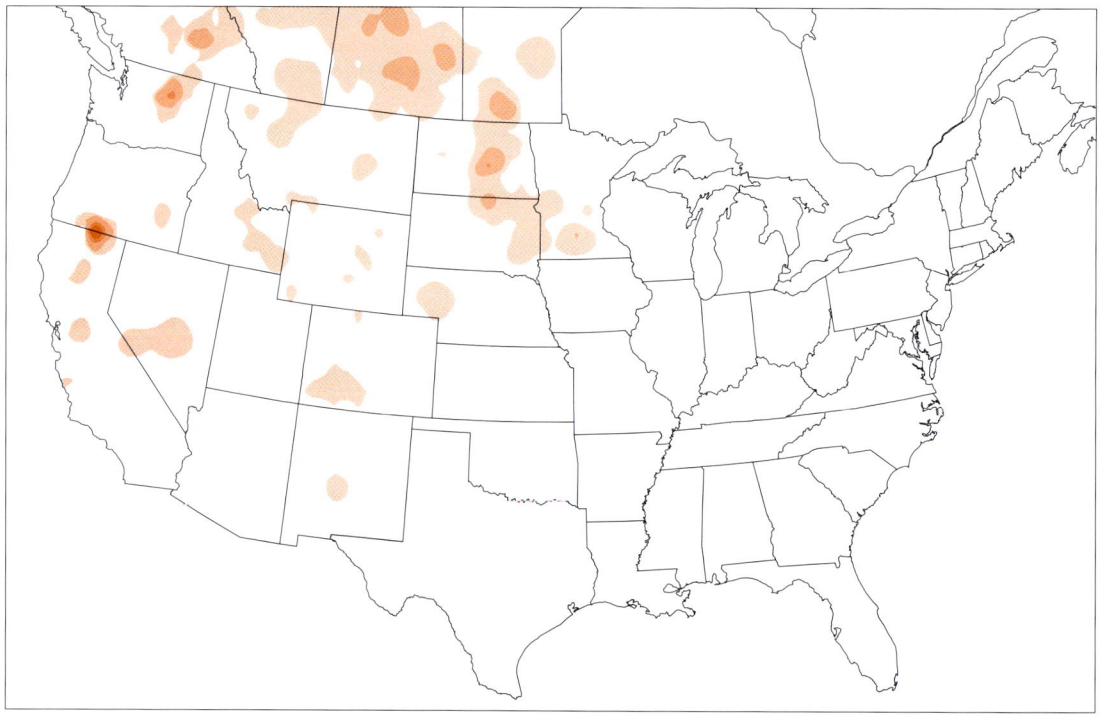

Black Vulture

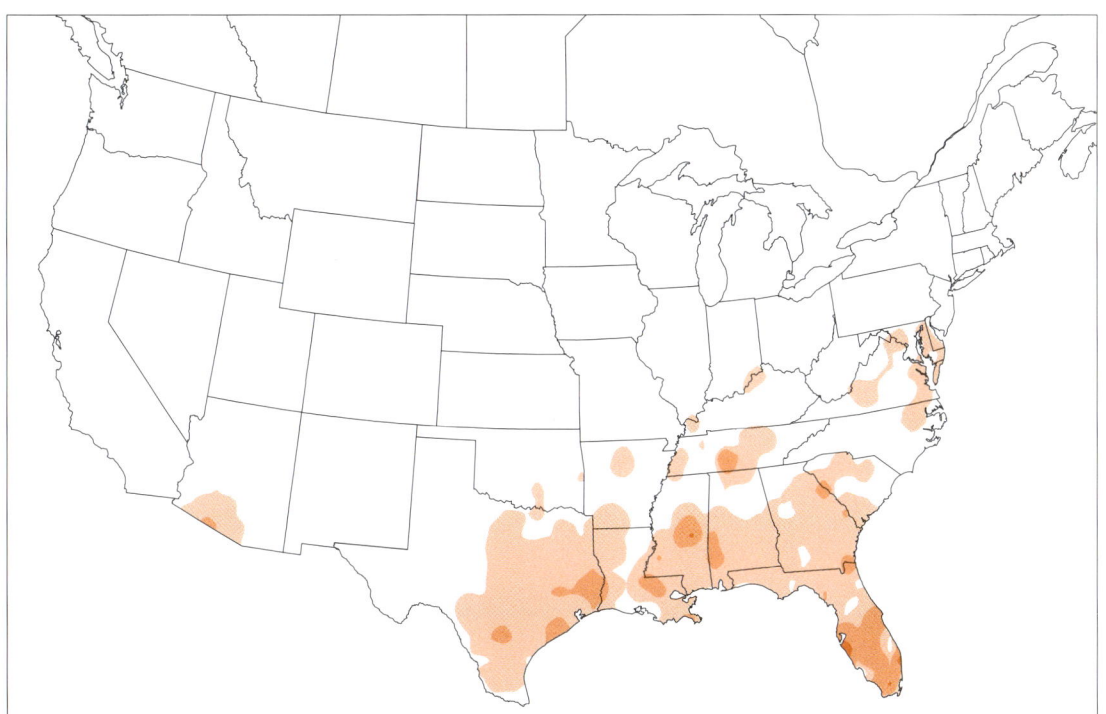

Turkey Vulture

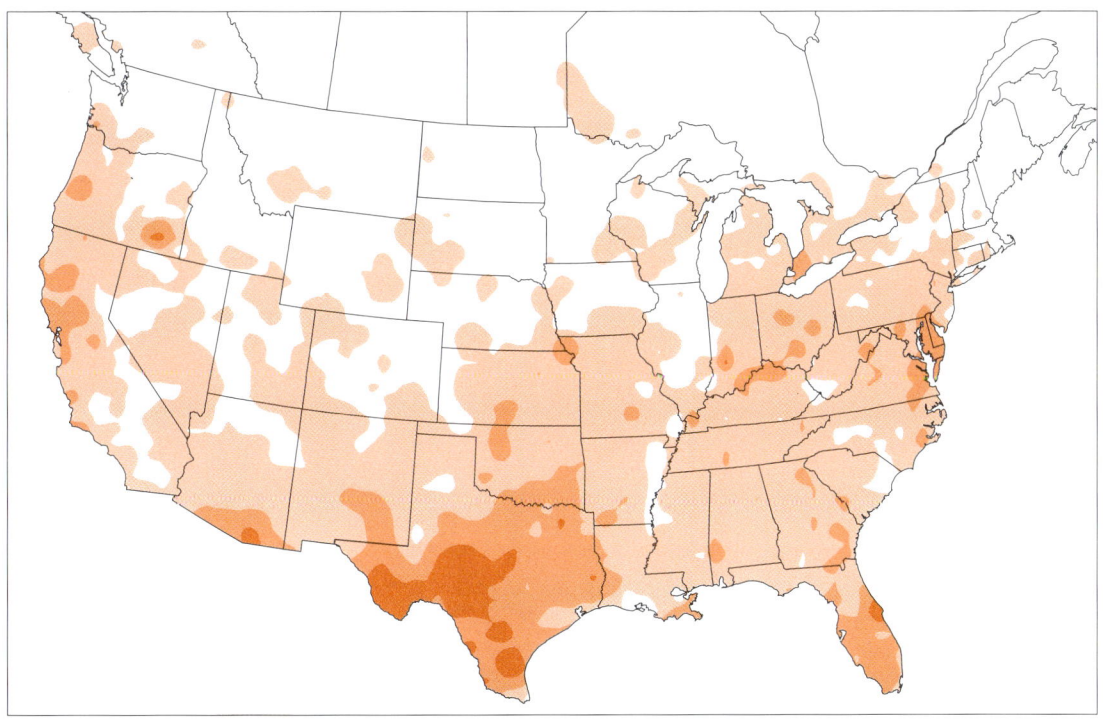

Osprey

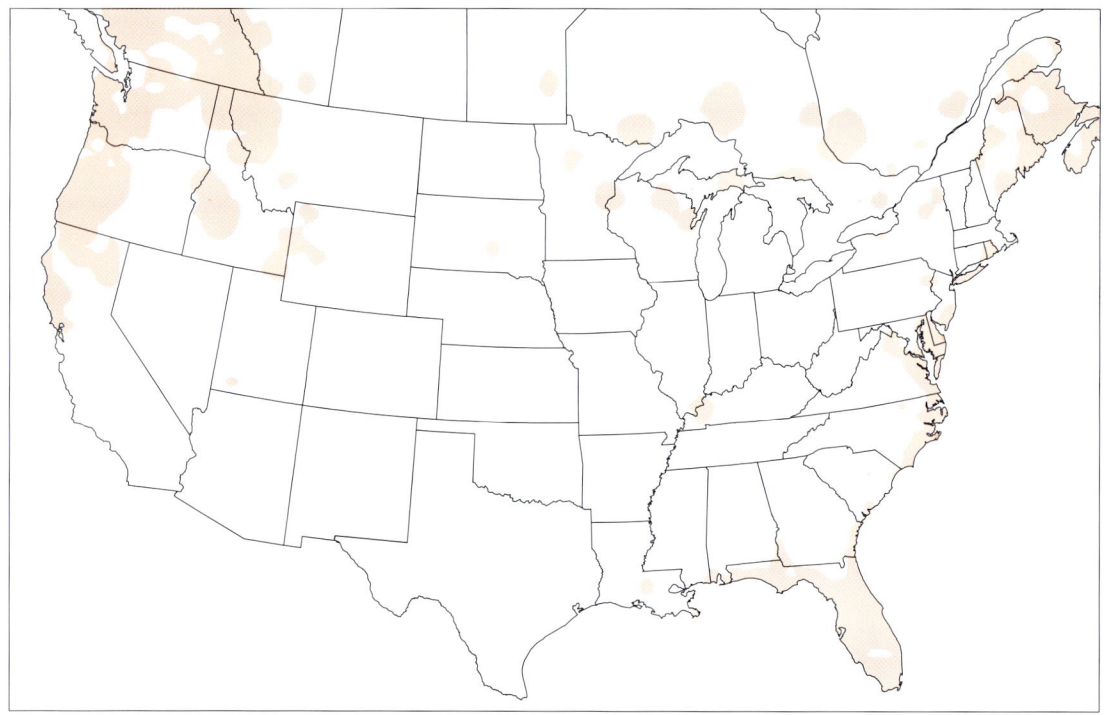

American Swallow-tailed Kite

White-tailed Kite

Snail Kite

Mississippi Kite

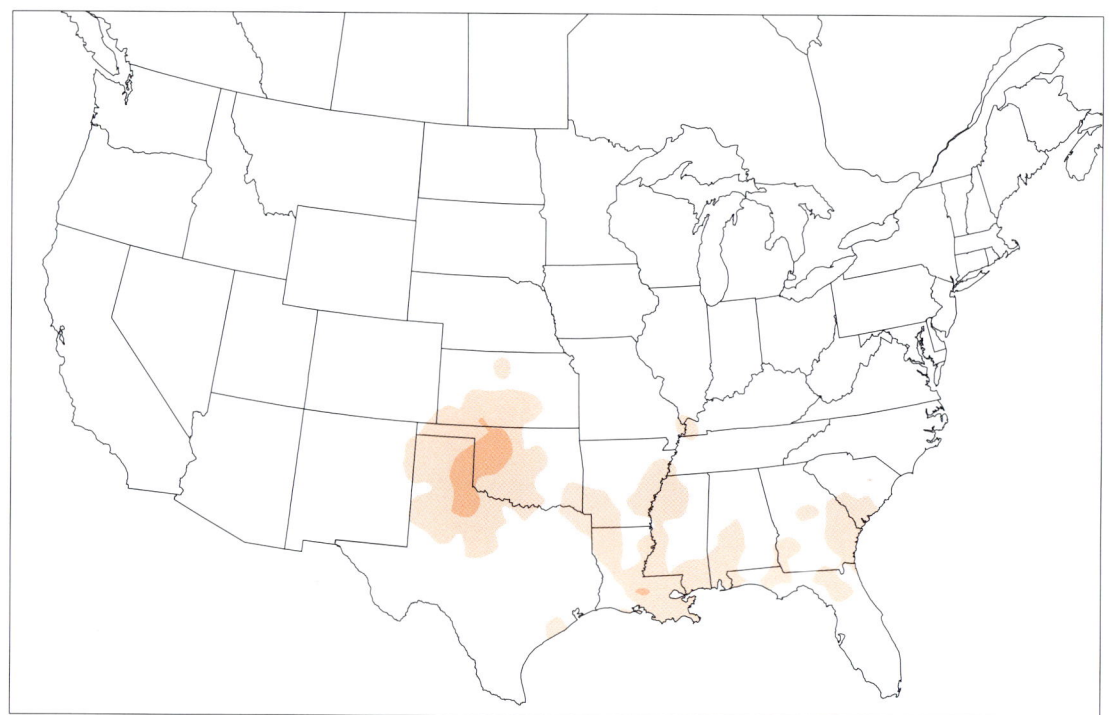

Bald Eagle

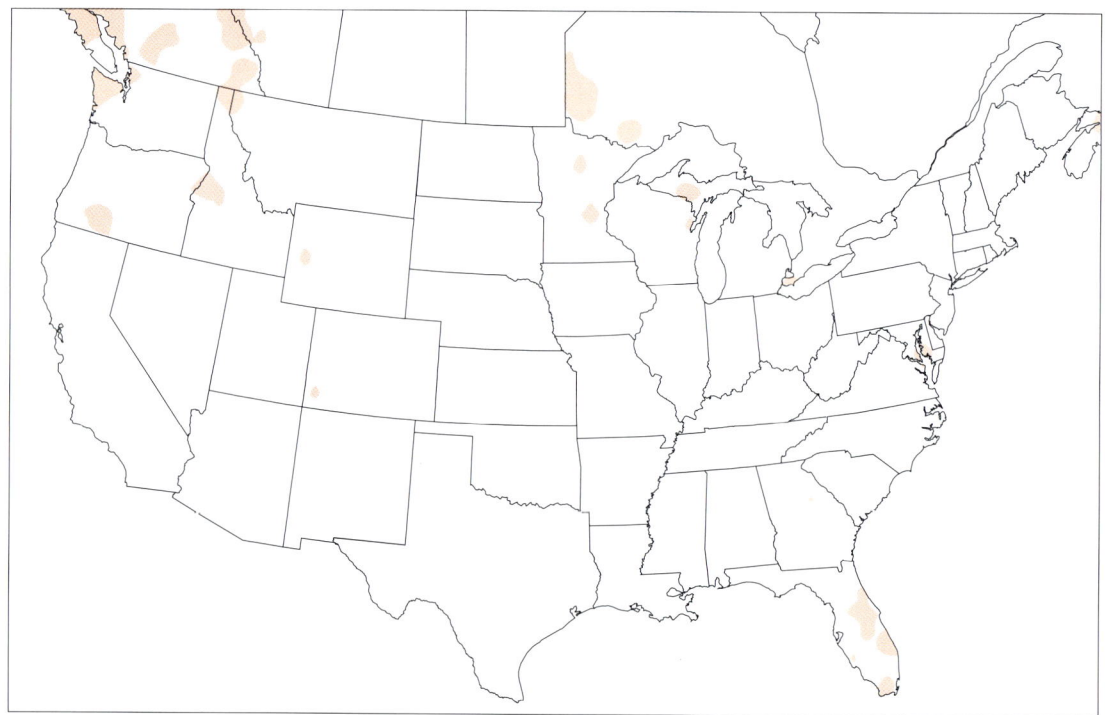

Northern Harrier

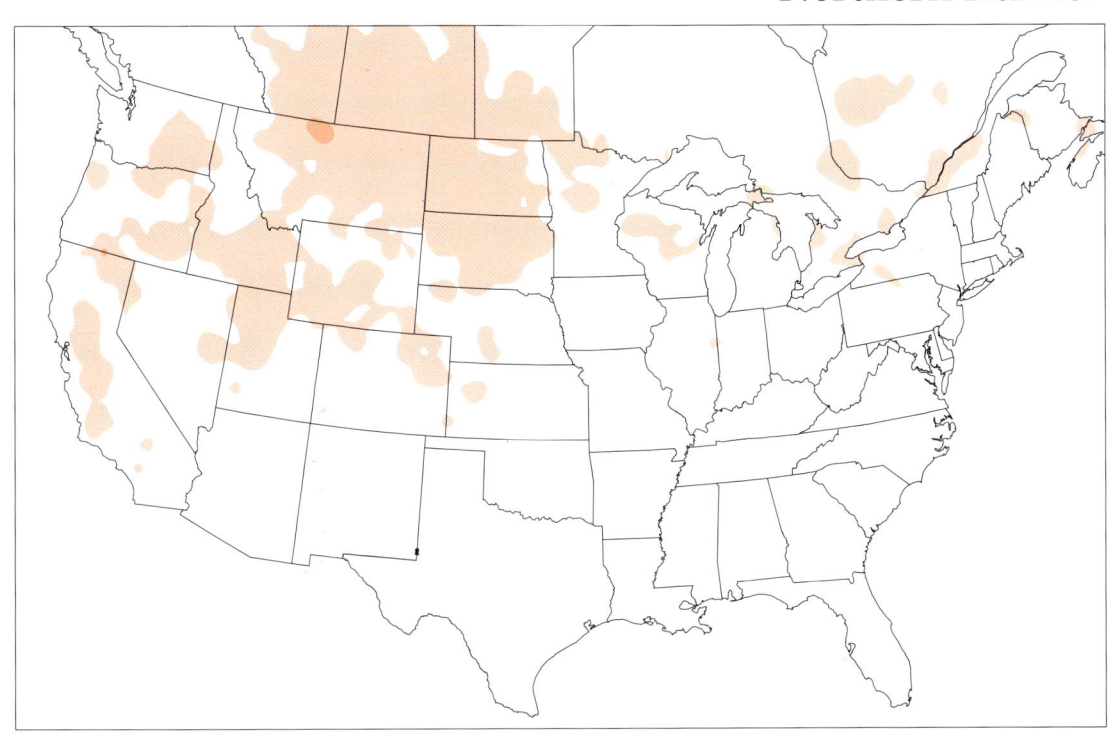

Harris' Hawk

Gray Hawk

Red-shouldered Hawk

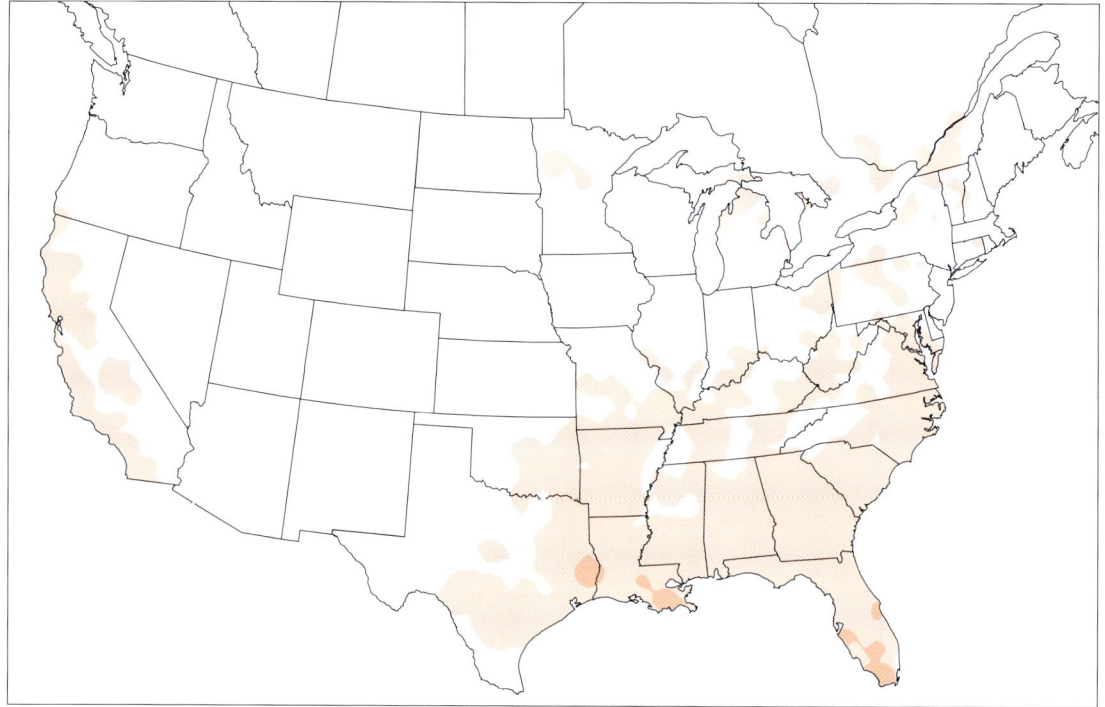

Broad-winged Hawk

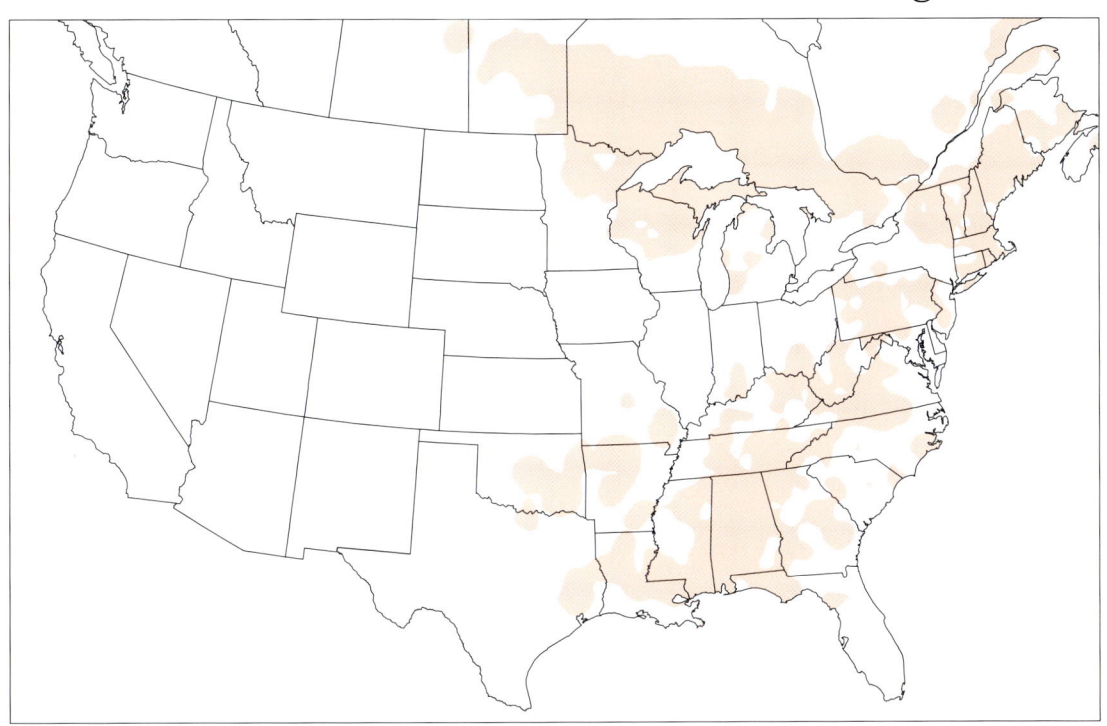

Swainson's Hawk

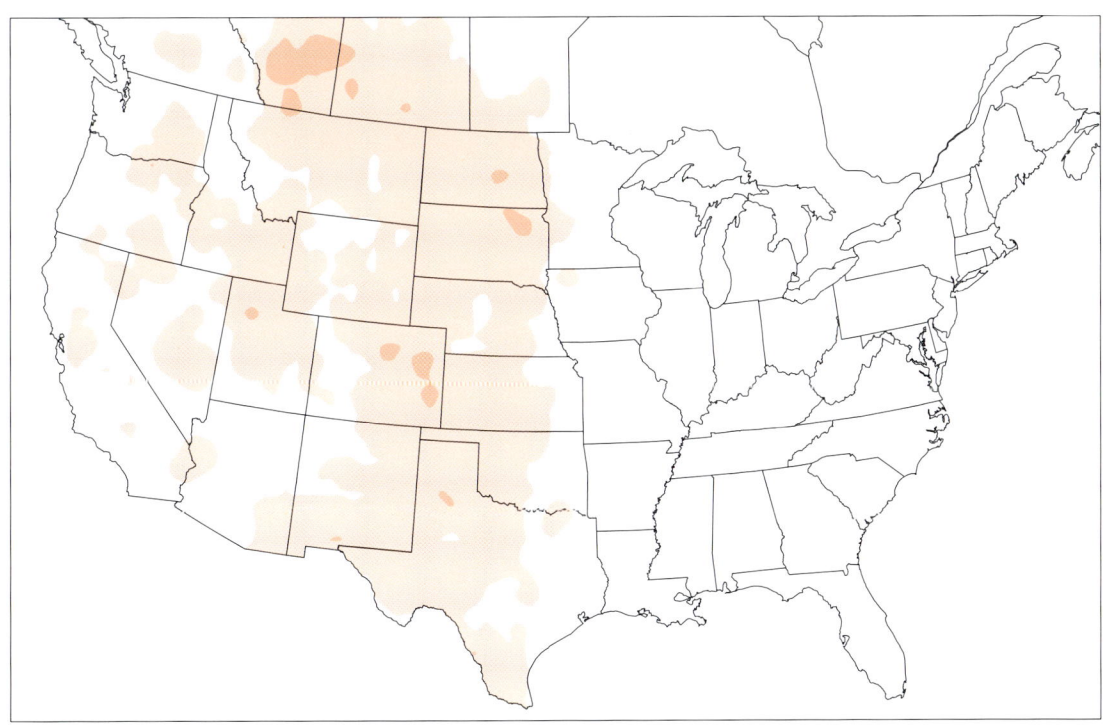

White-tailed Hawk

Red-tailed Hawk

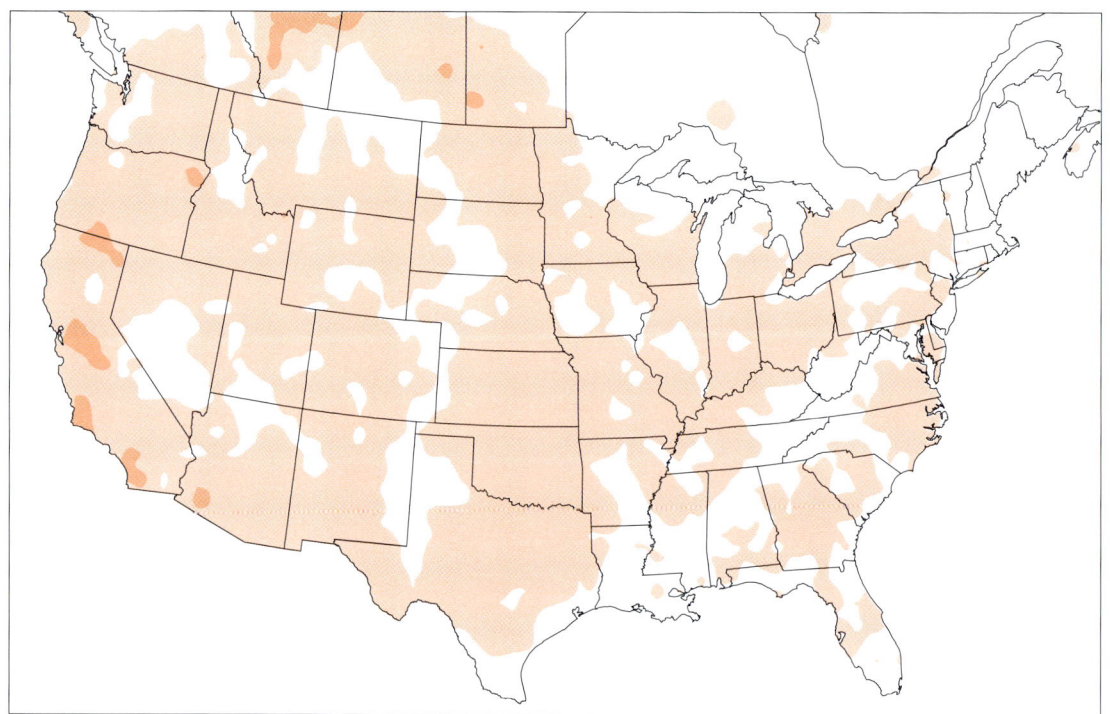

Ferruginous Hawk

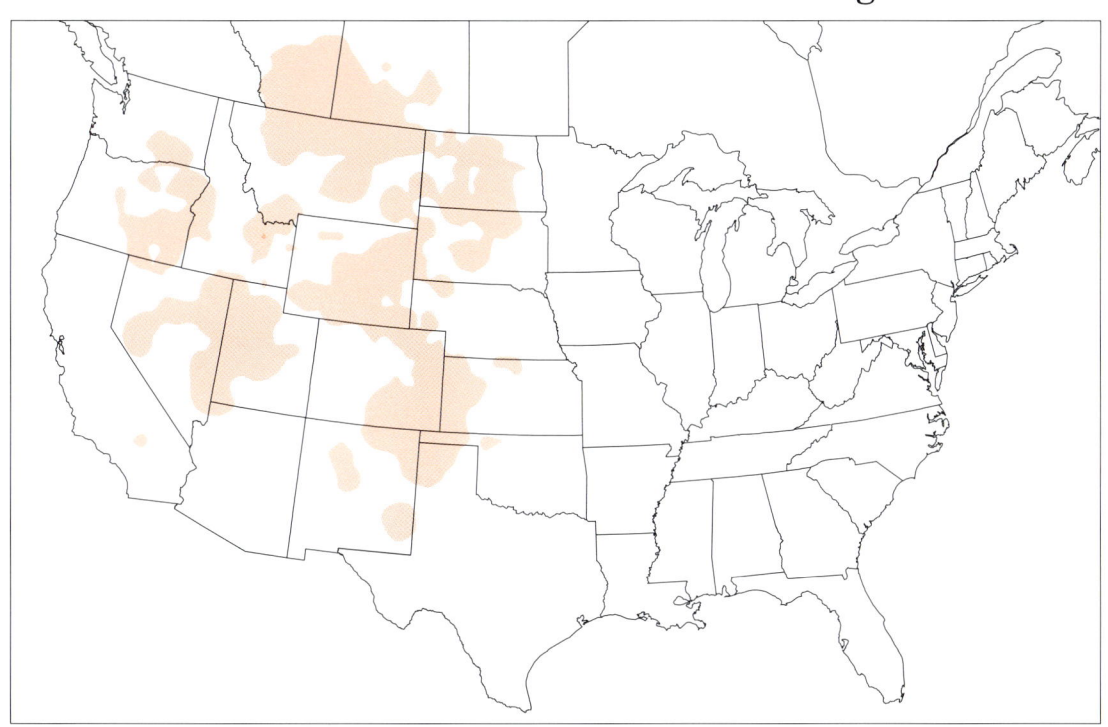

Golden Eagle

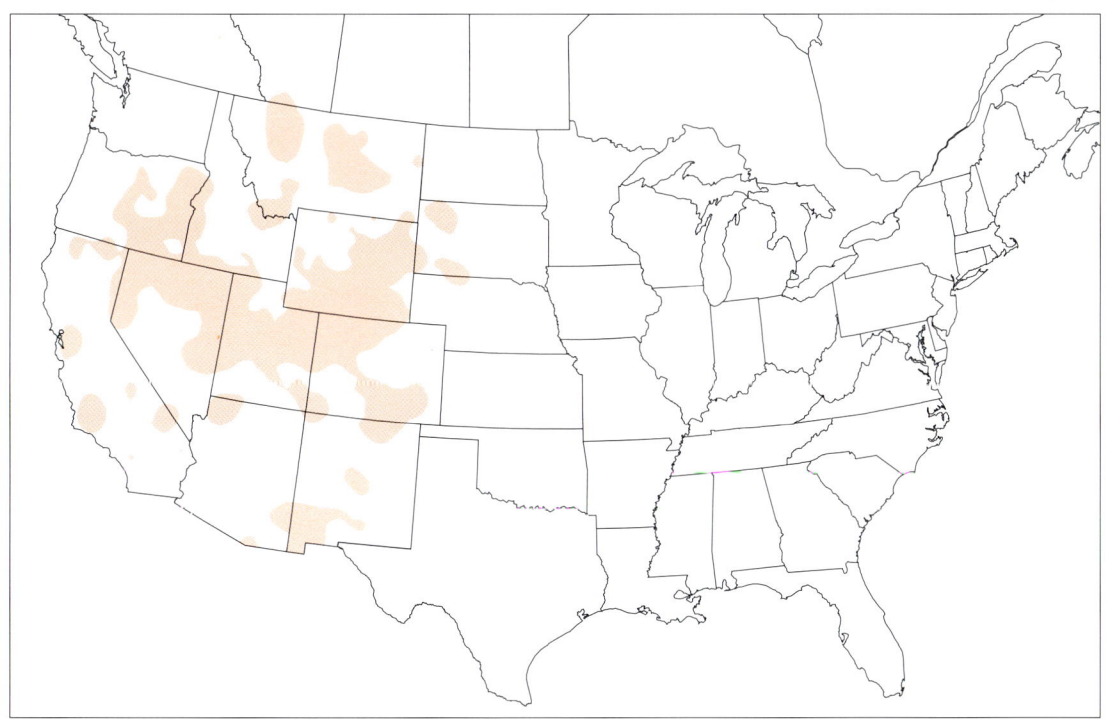

Crested Caracara

American Kestrel

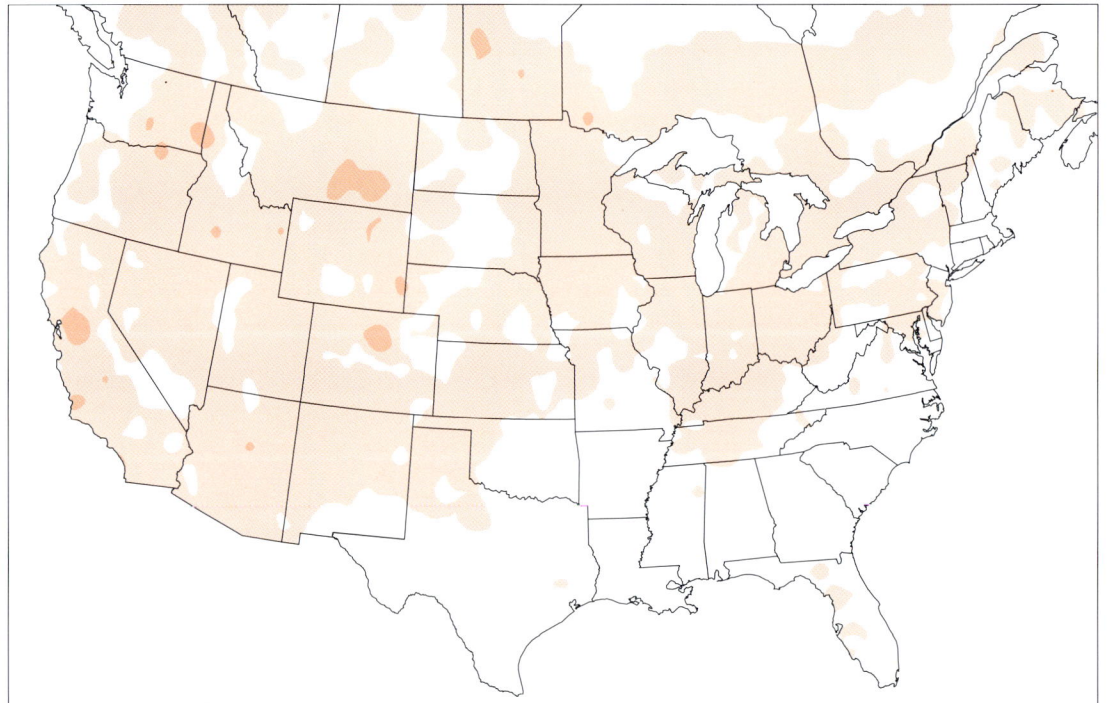

Merlin

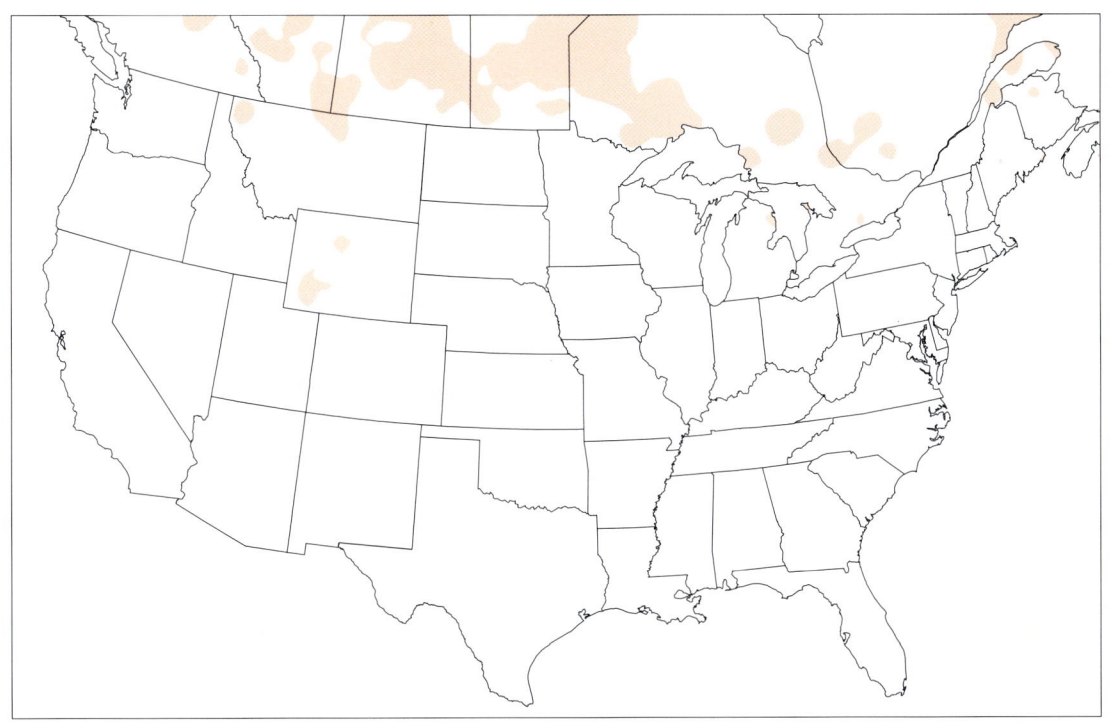

Peregrine Falcon

Prairie Falcon

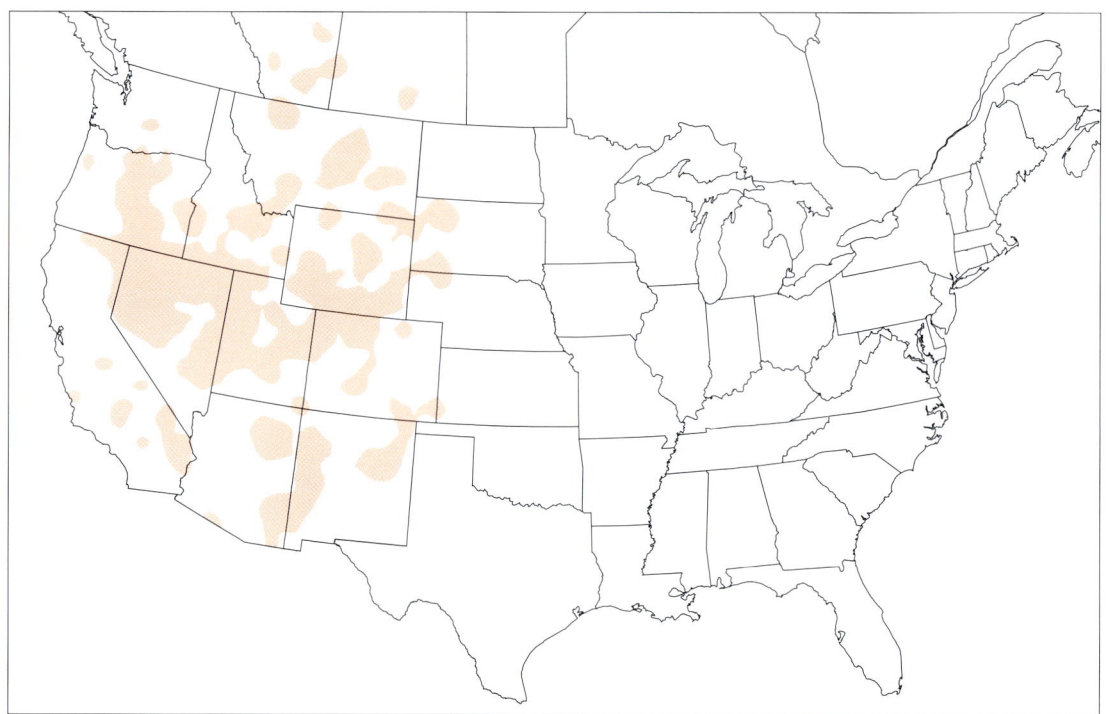

Plain Chachalaca

Gray Partridge

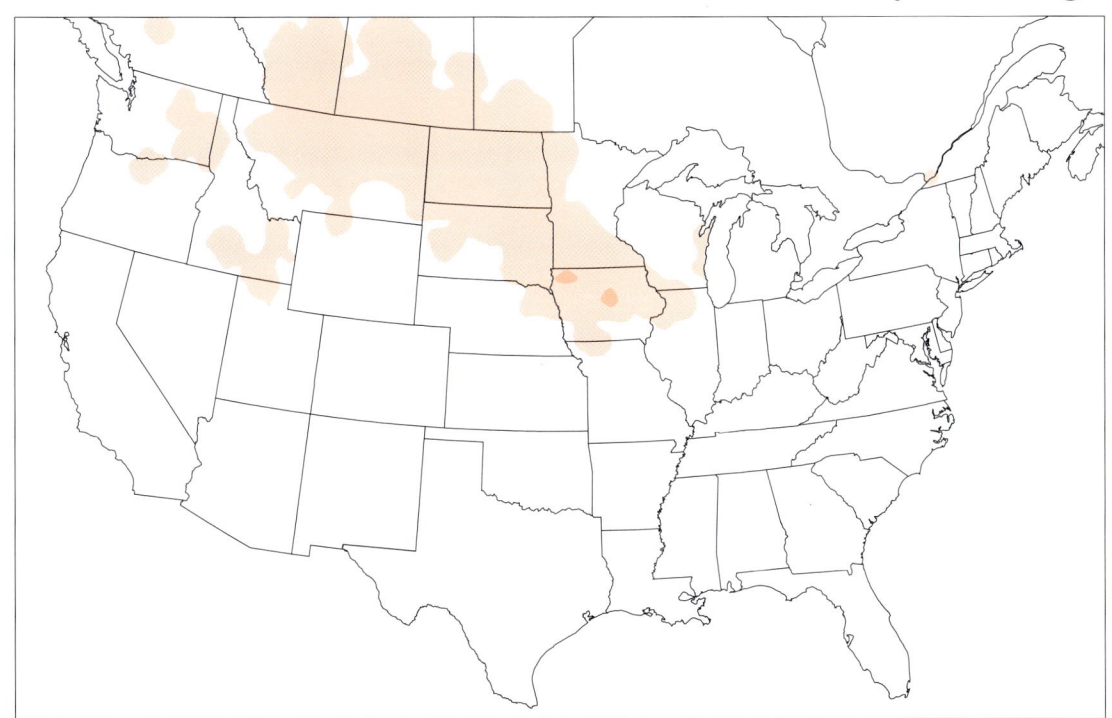

Chukar

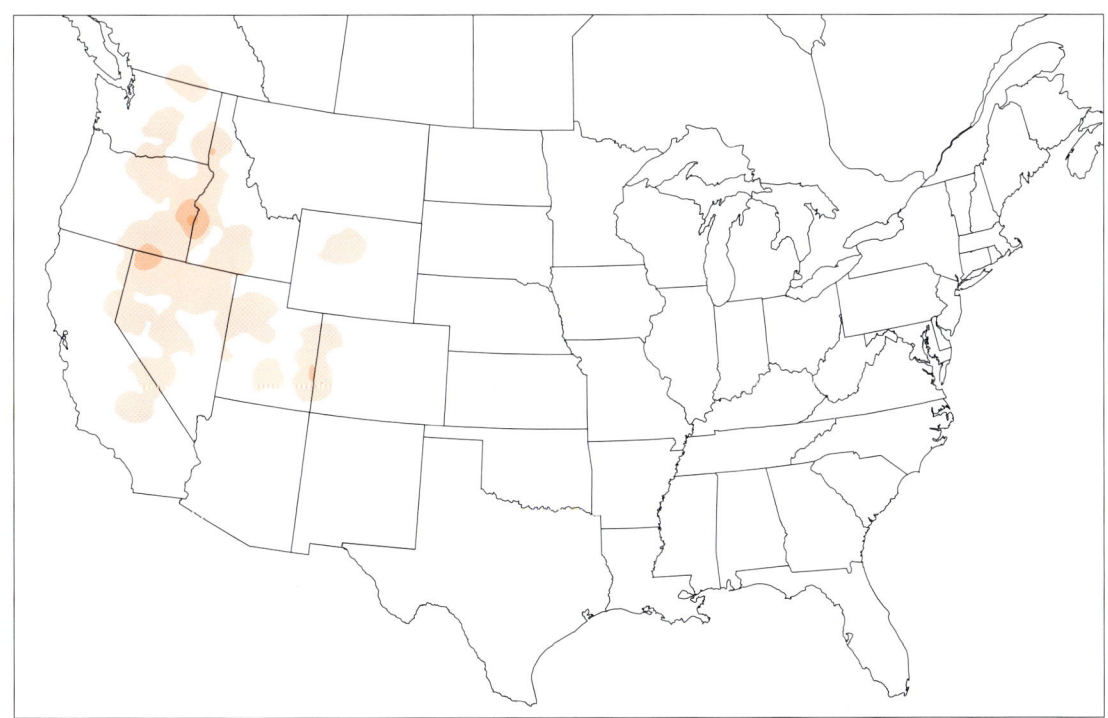

Ring-necked Pheasant

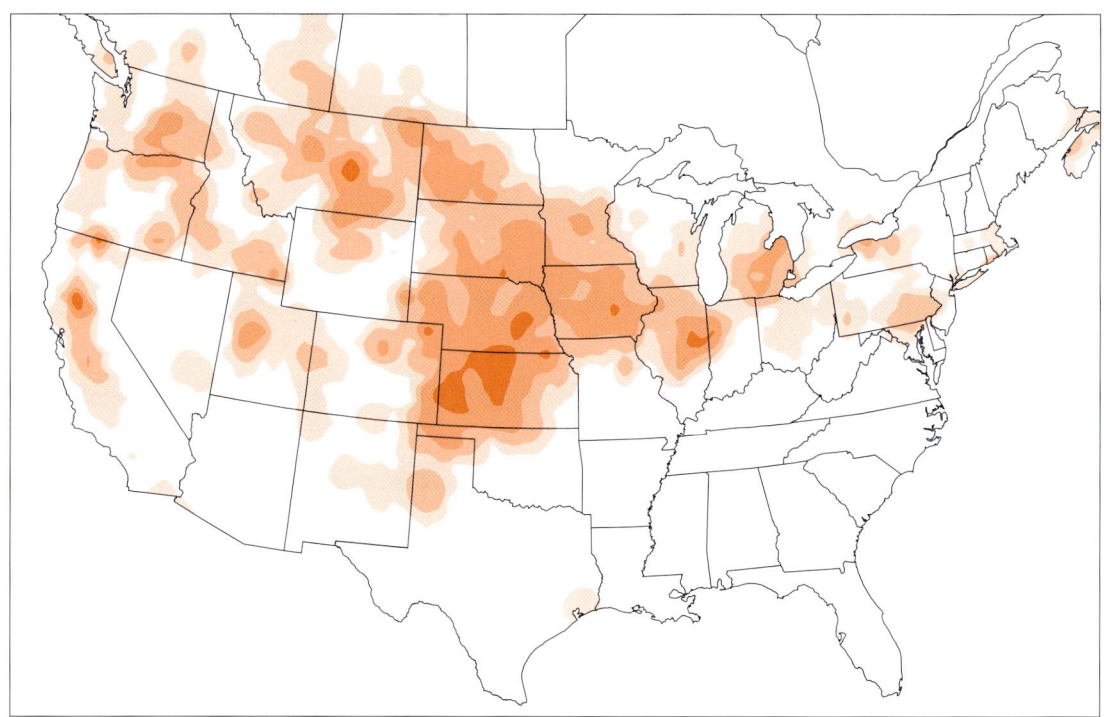

Blue Grouse

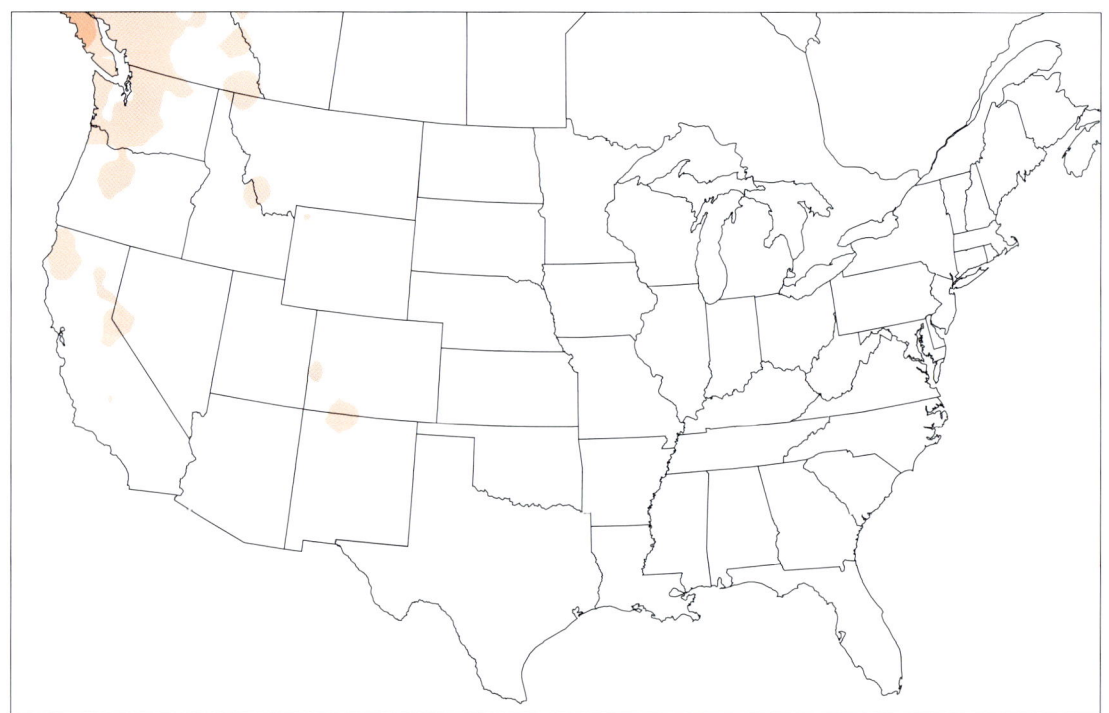

Ruffed Grouse

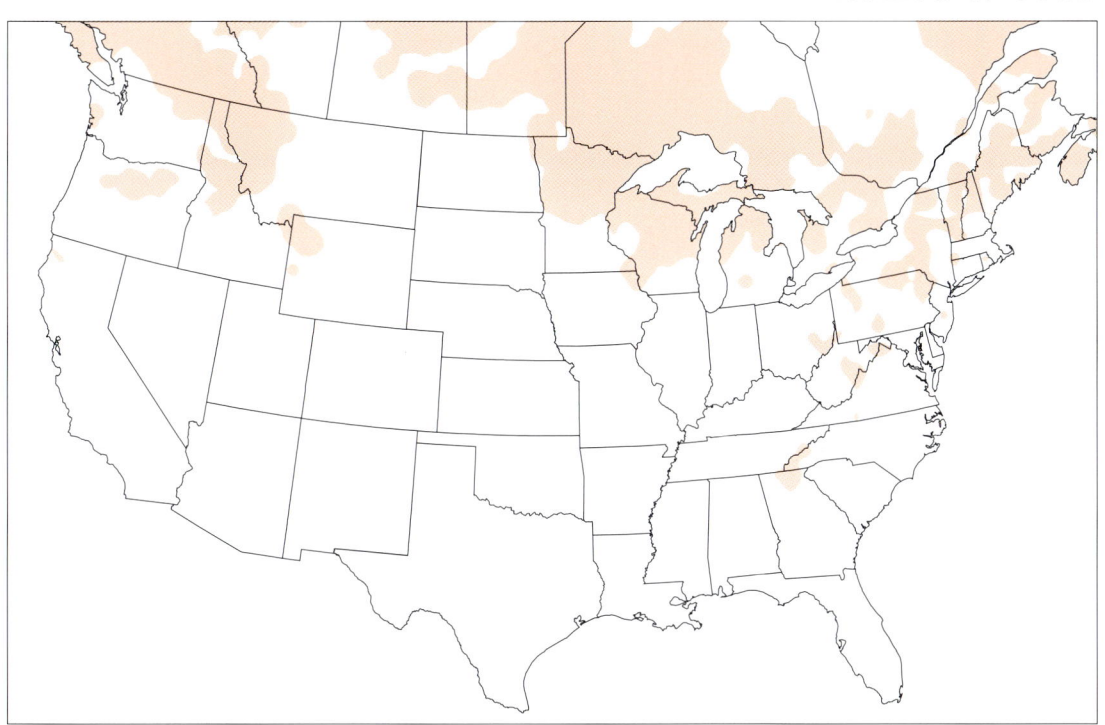

Sage Grouse

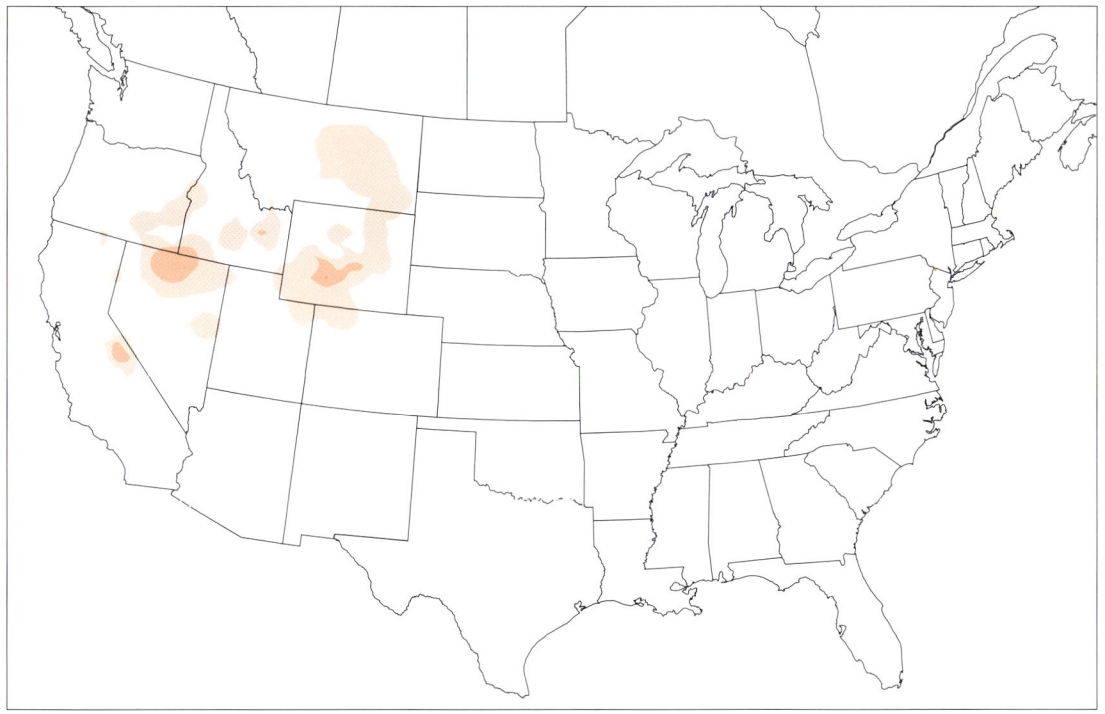

Greater Prairie-Chicken

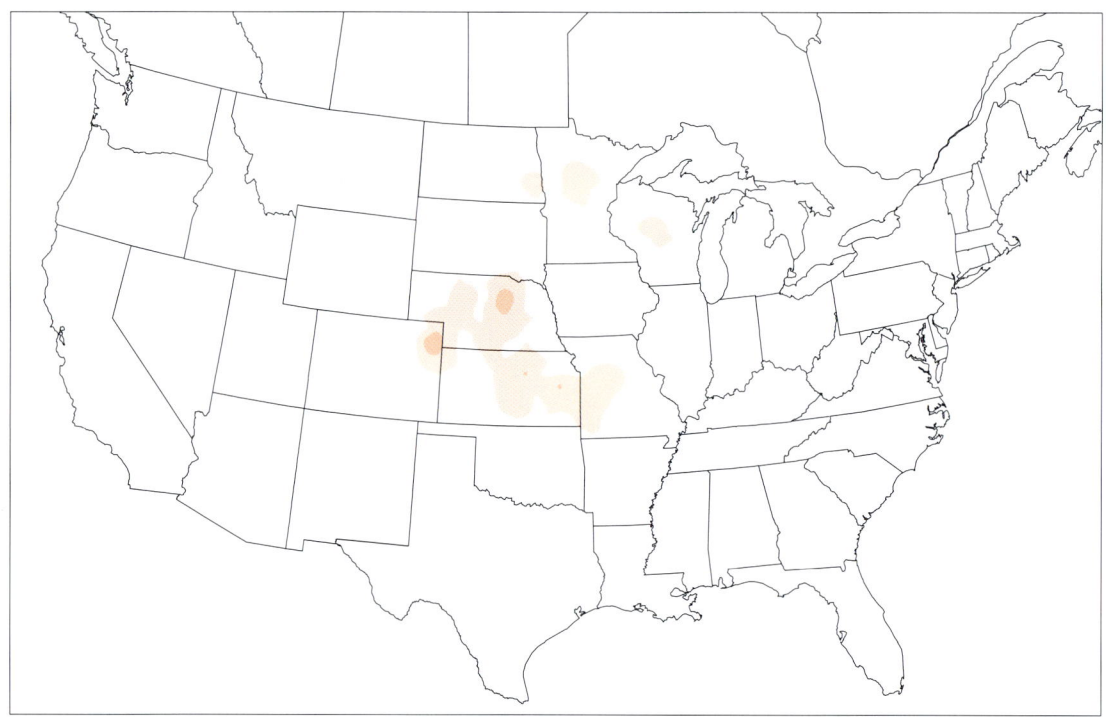

Lesser Prairie-Chicken

Sharp-tailed Grouse

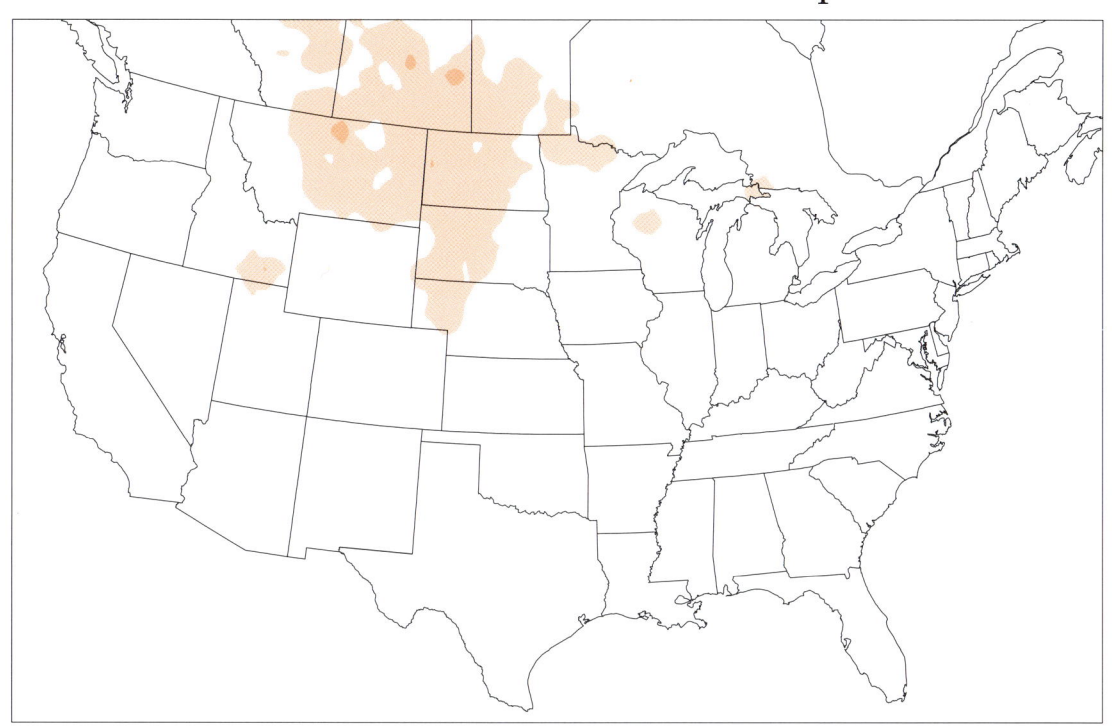

Wild Turkey

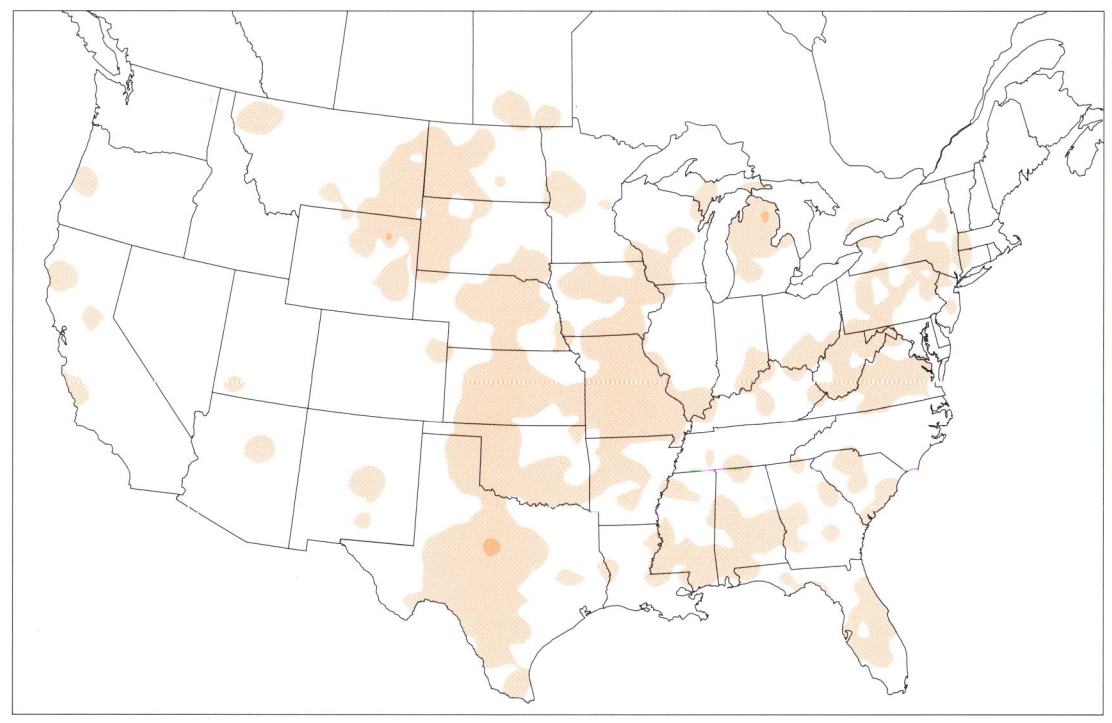

Montezuma Quail

Northern Bobwhite

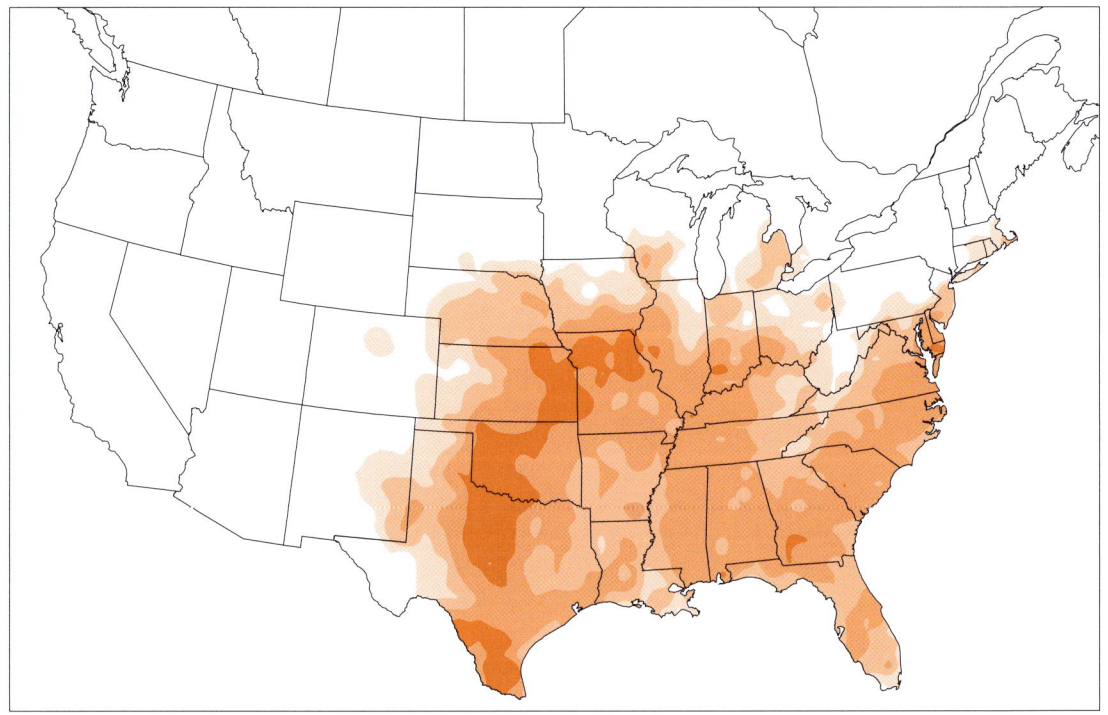

Scaled Quail

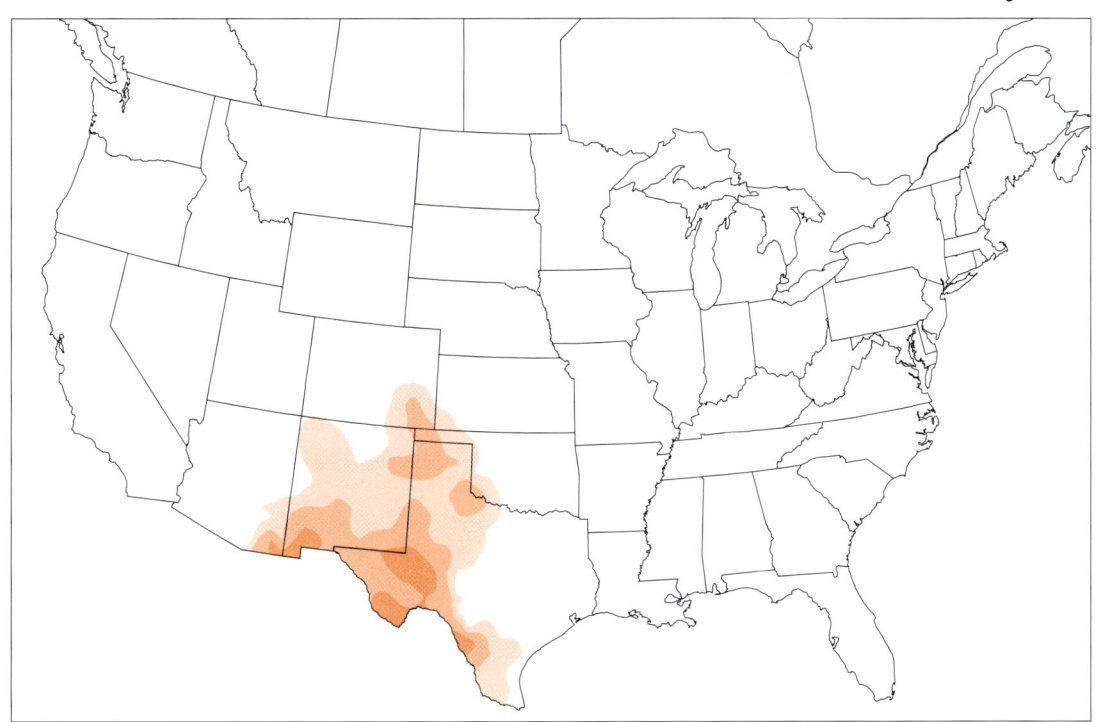

Gambel's Quail

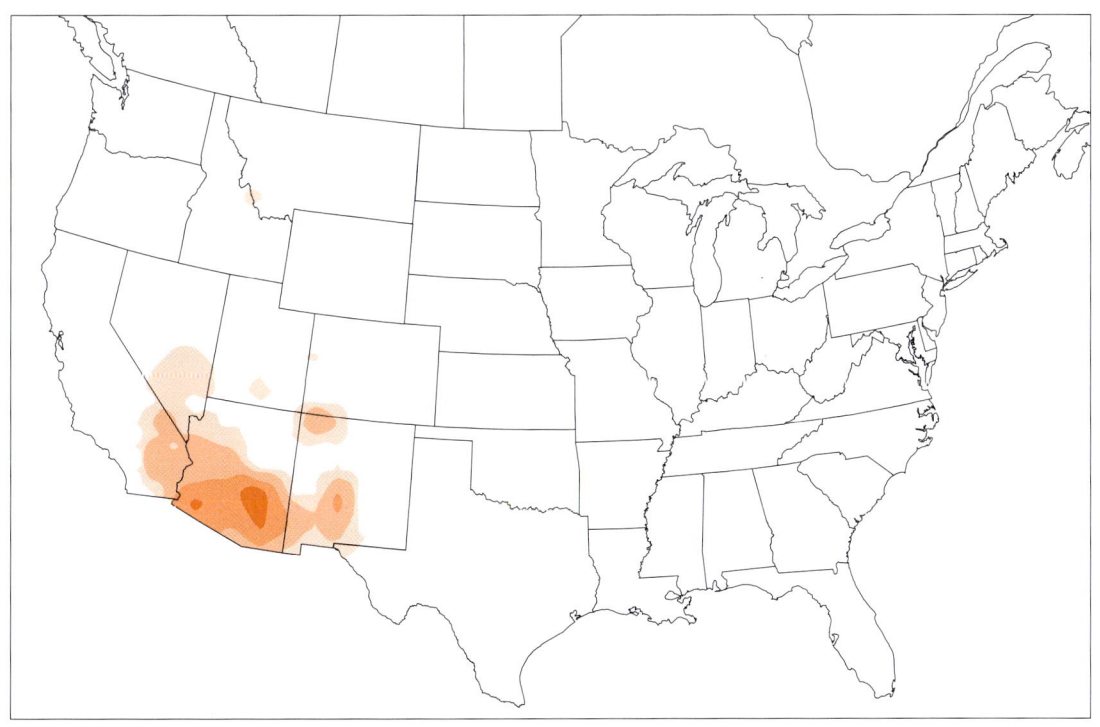

California Quail

Mountain Quail

Clapper Rail

Sora

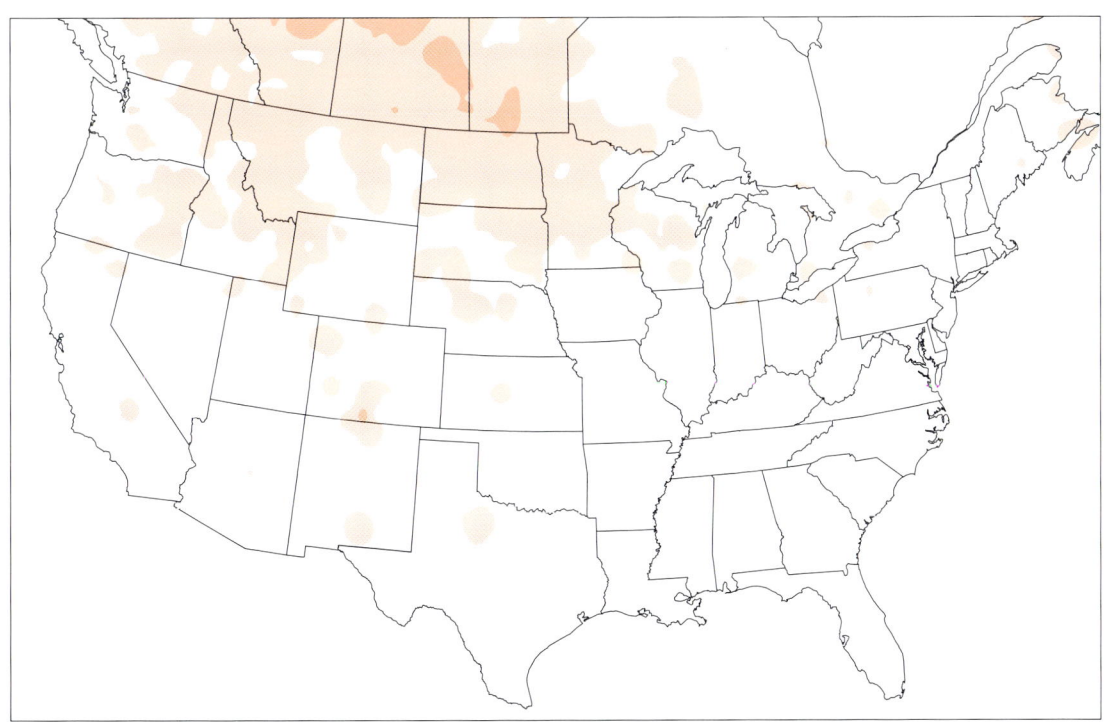

Purple Gallinule

American Coot

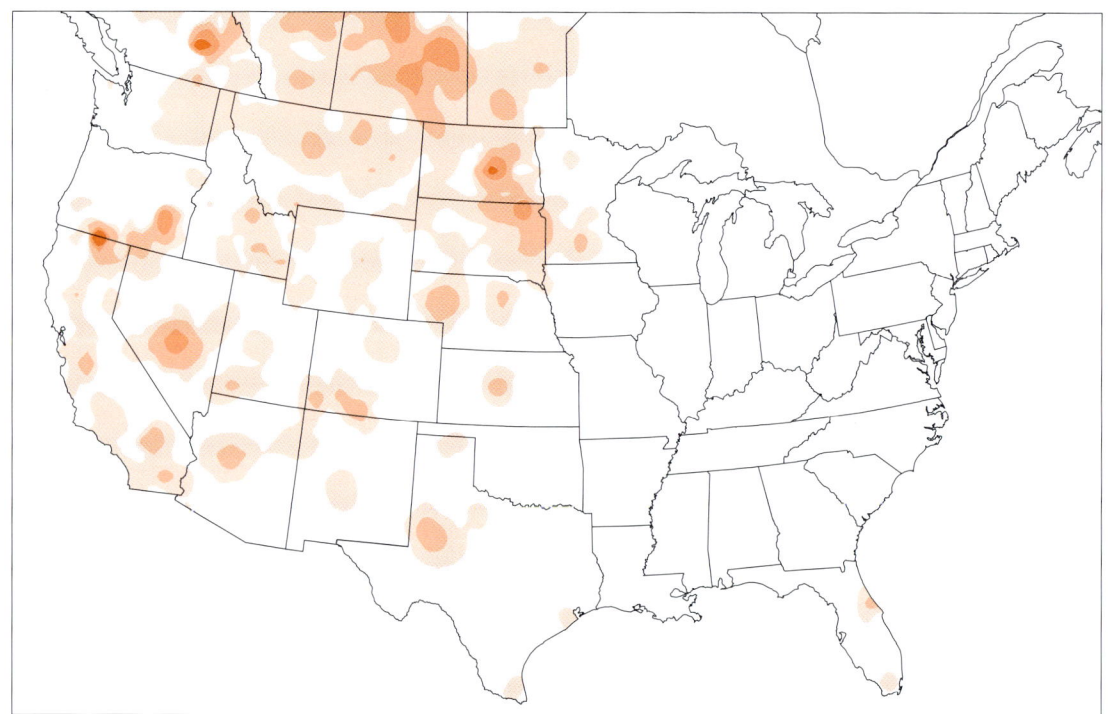

Limpkin

Sandhill Crane

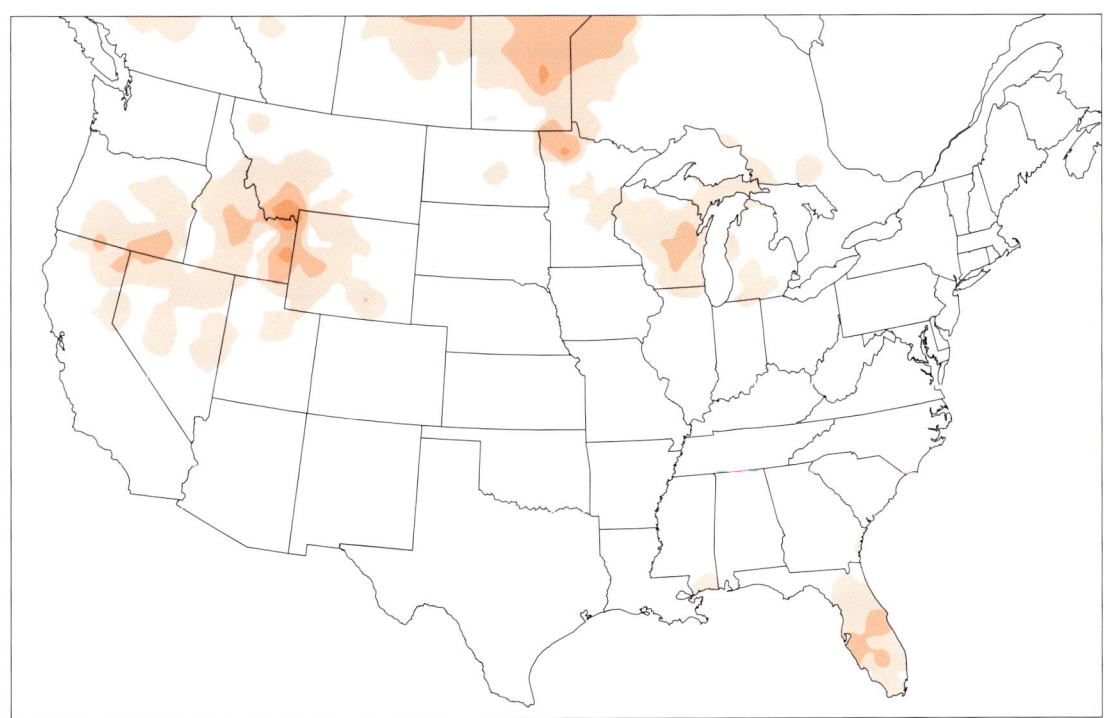

Killdeer

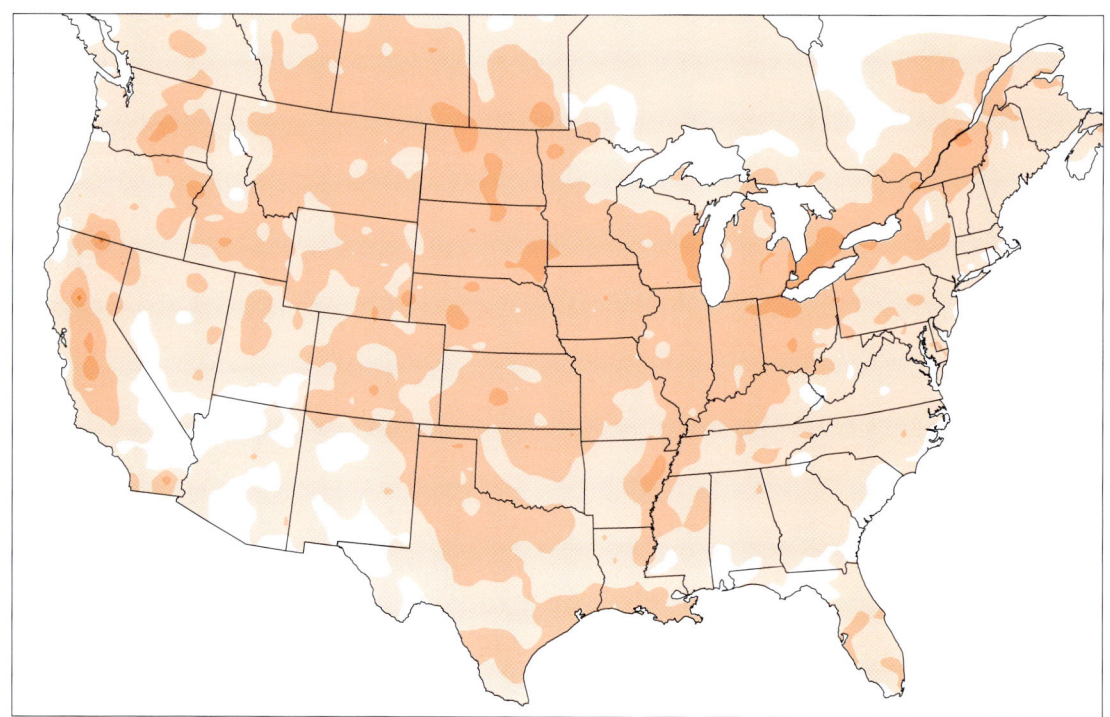

Mountain Plover

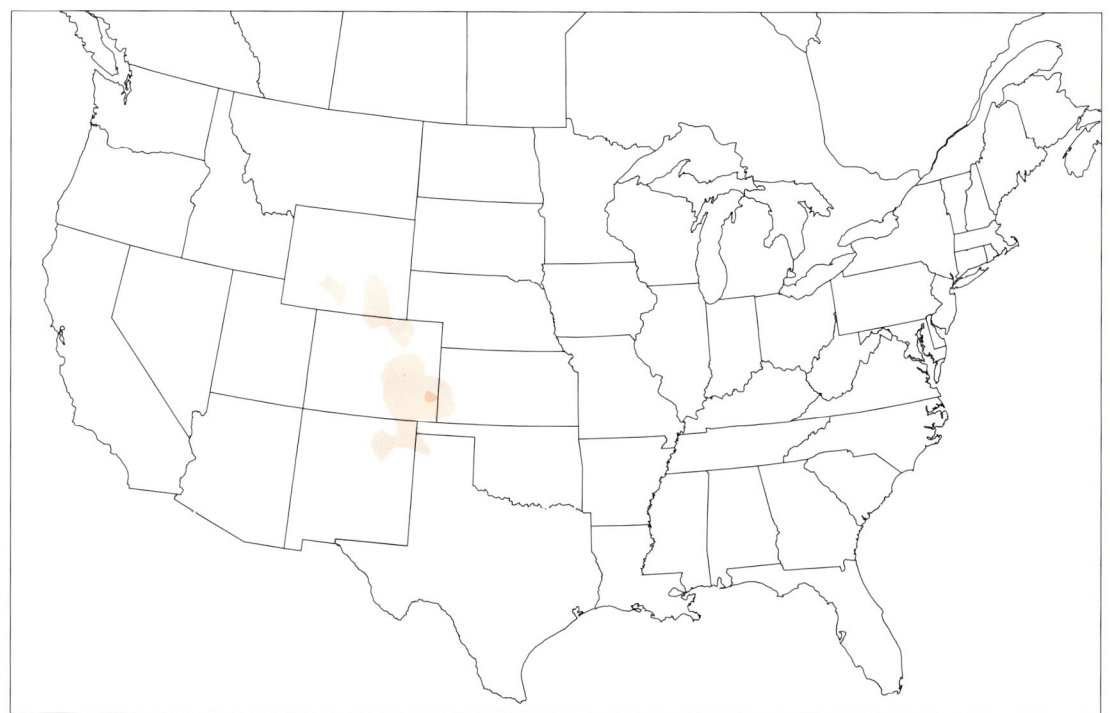

American Oystercatcher

Black Oystercatcher

Black-necked Stilt

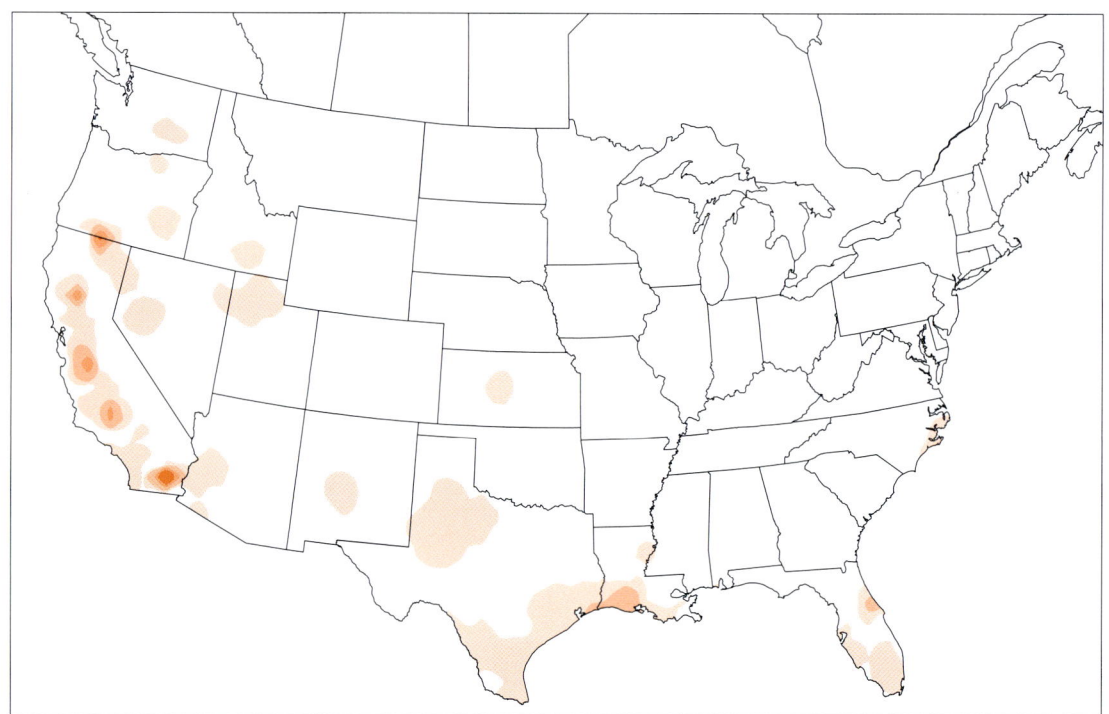

American Avocet

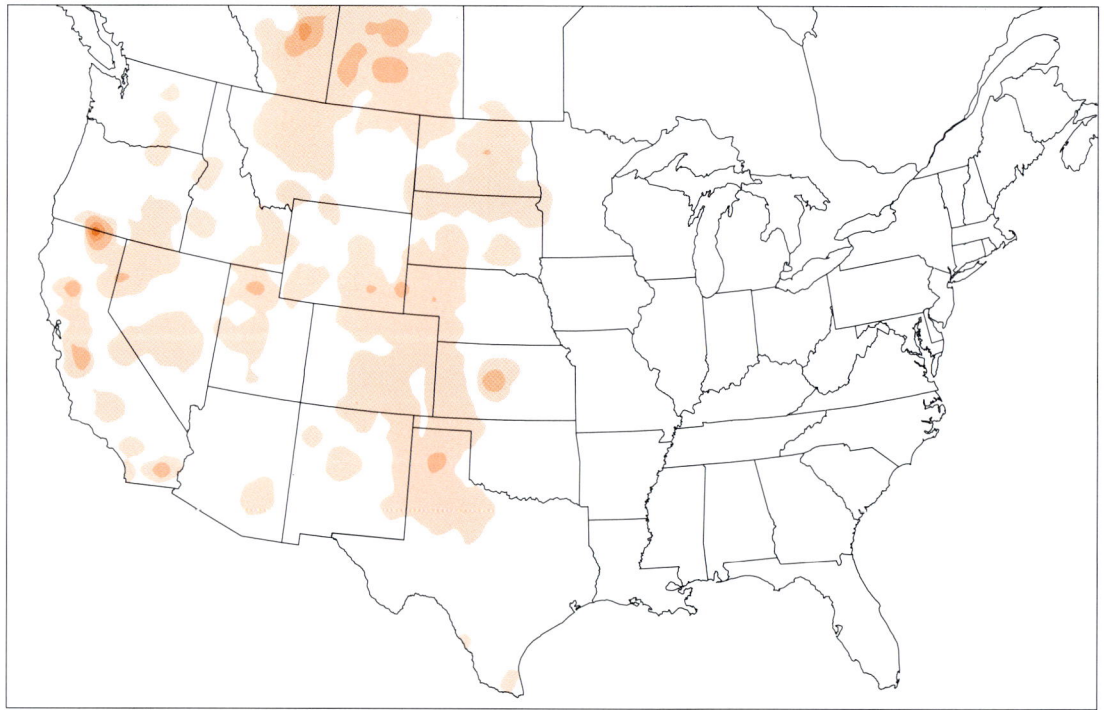

Willet

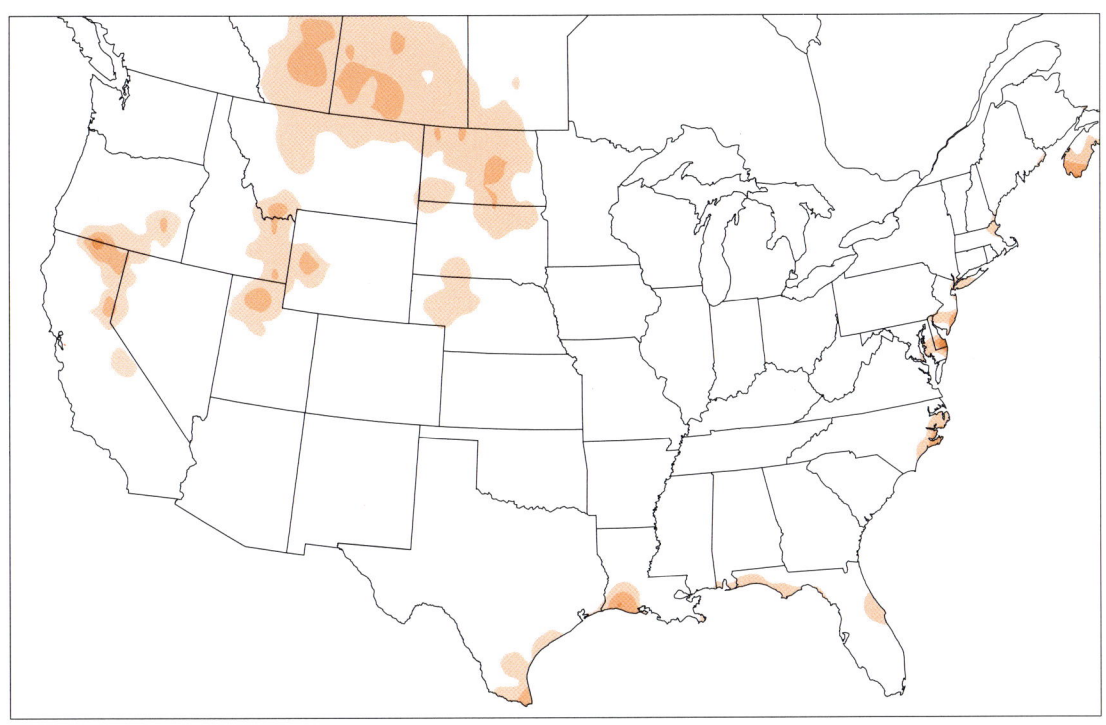

Spotted Sandpiper

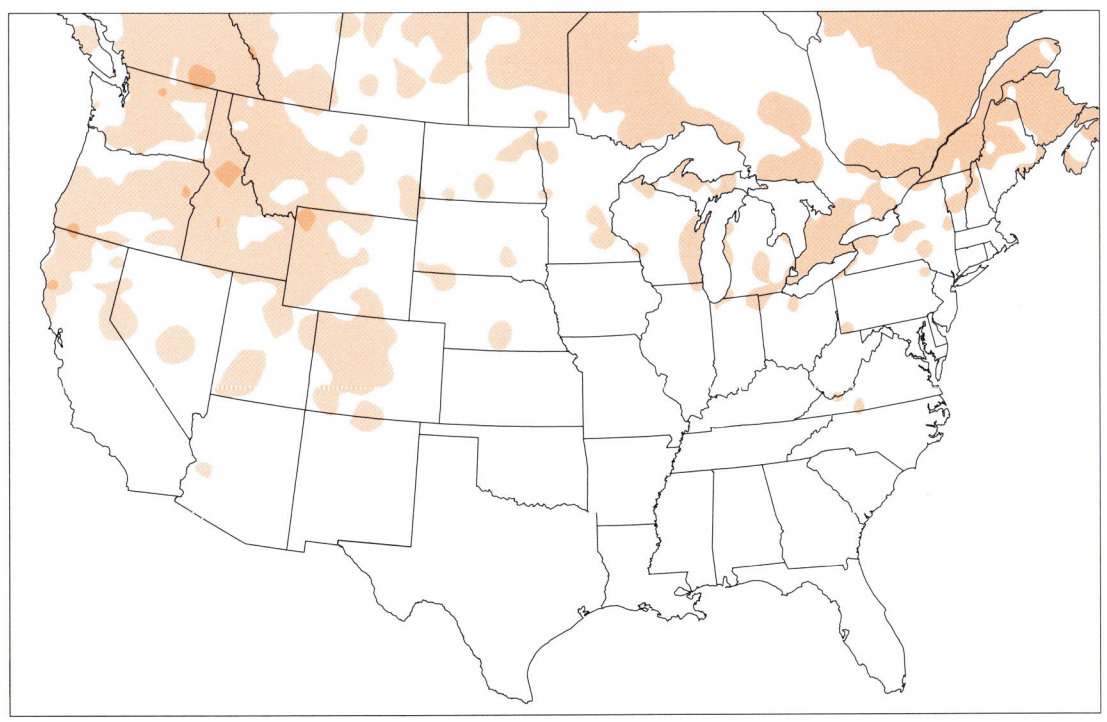

Upland Sandpiper

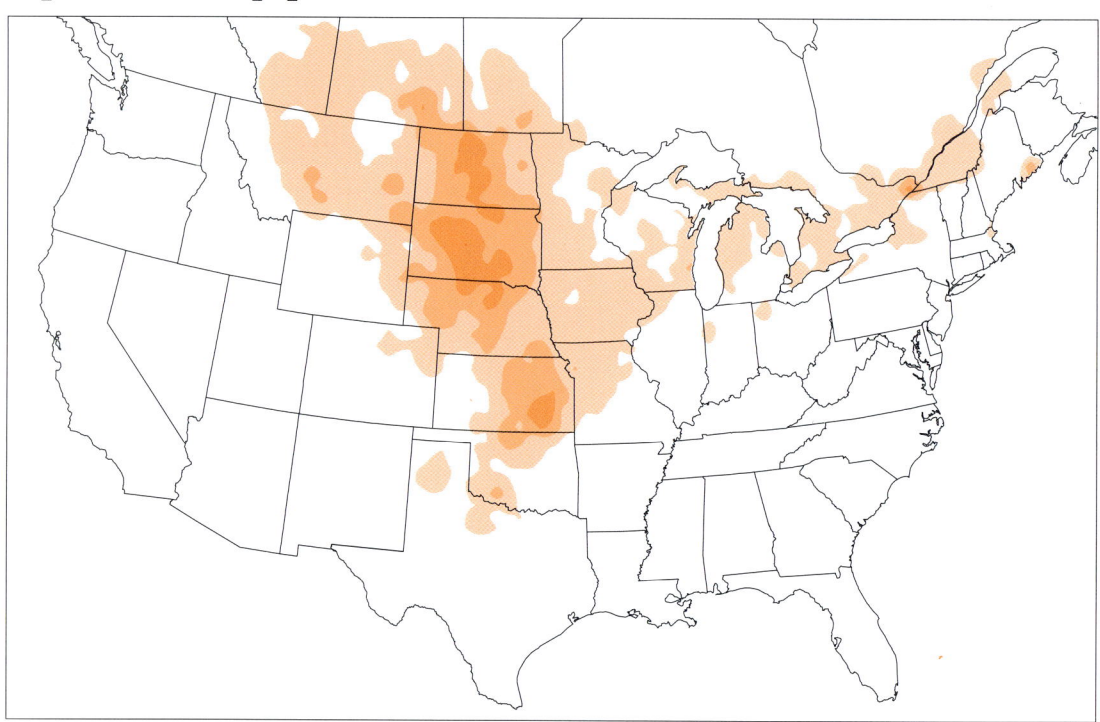

Long-billed Curlew

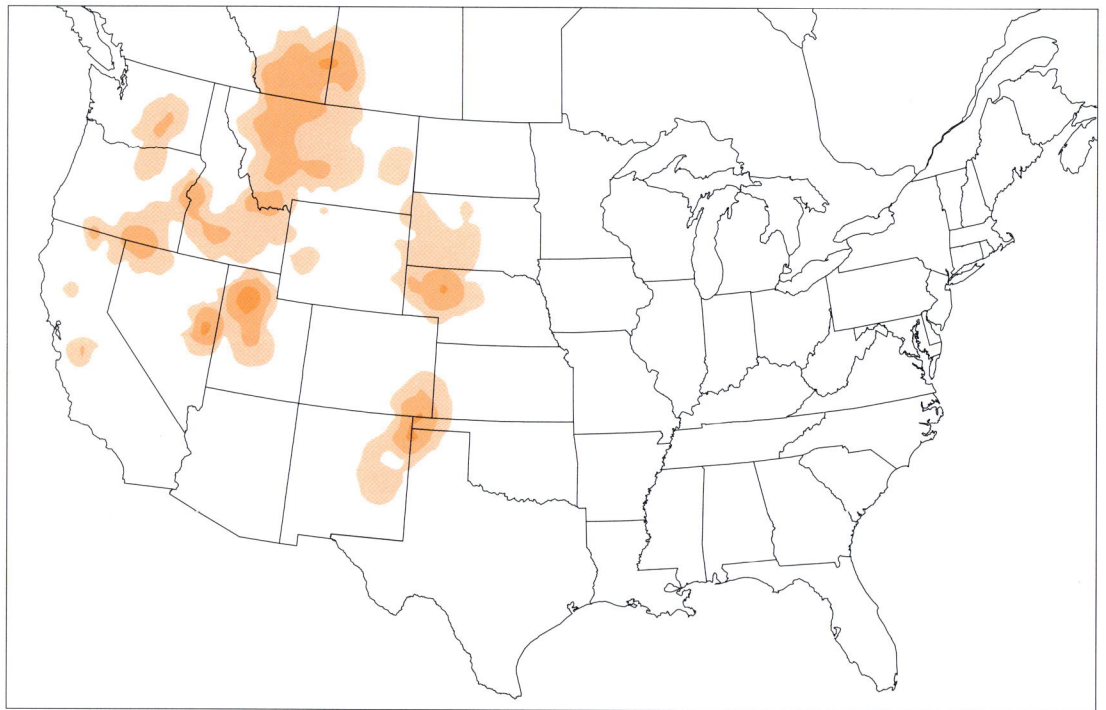

Marbled Godwit

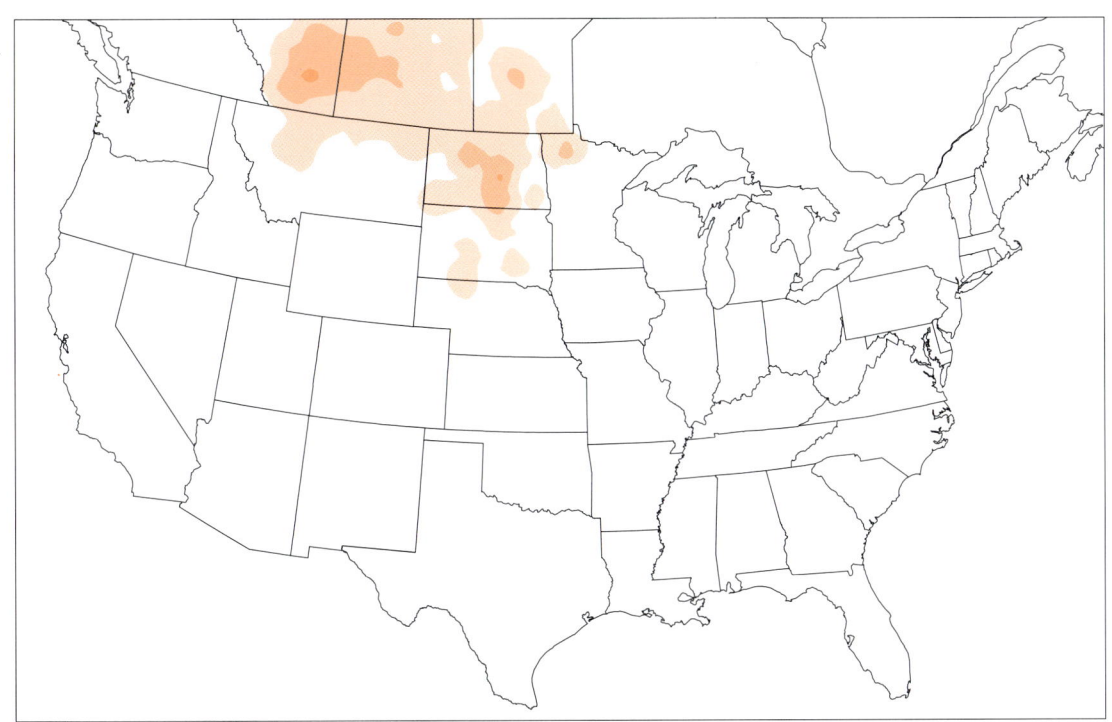

Common Snipe

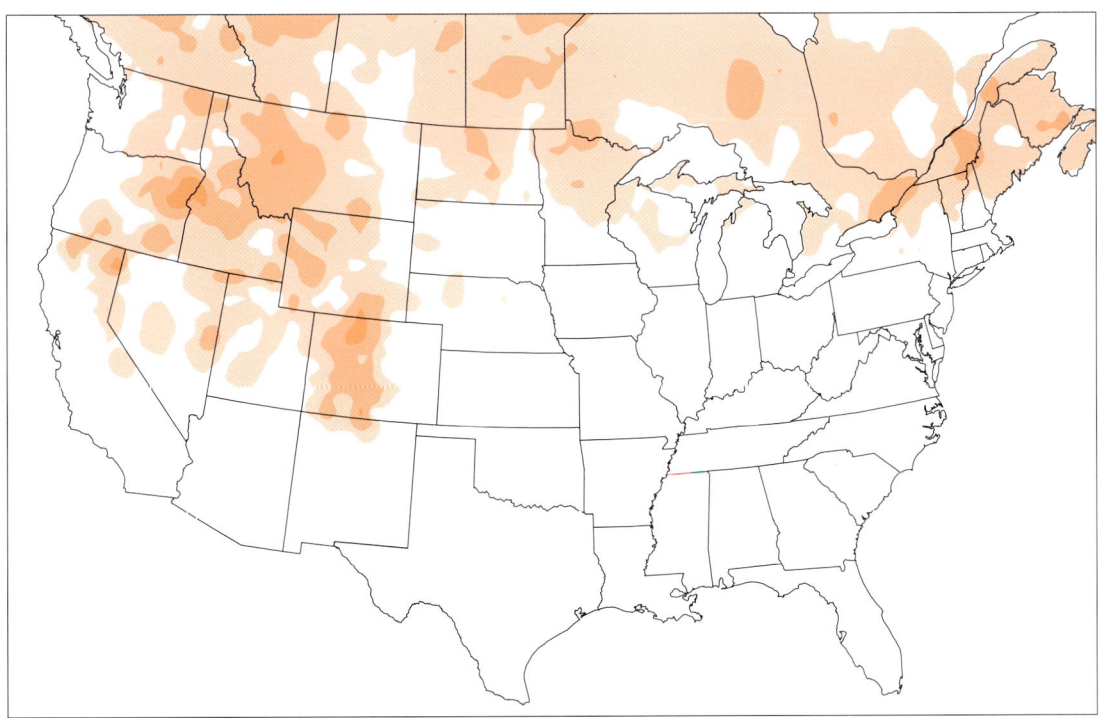

Wilson's Phalarope

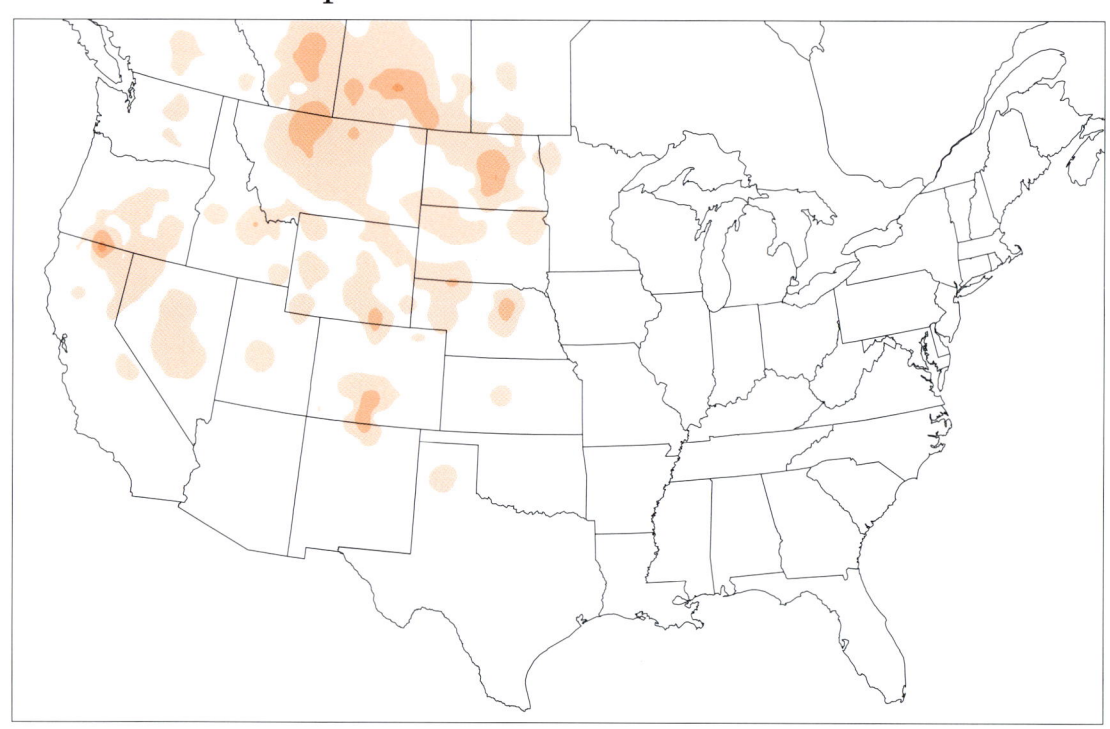

Laughing Gull

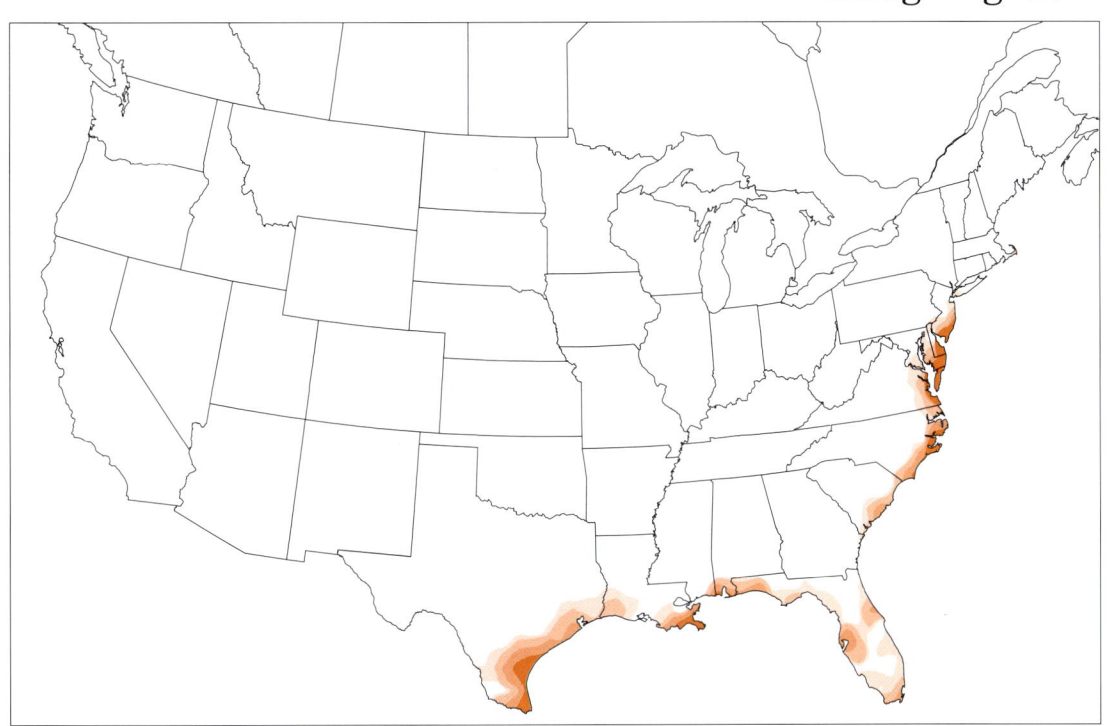

Franklin's Gull

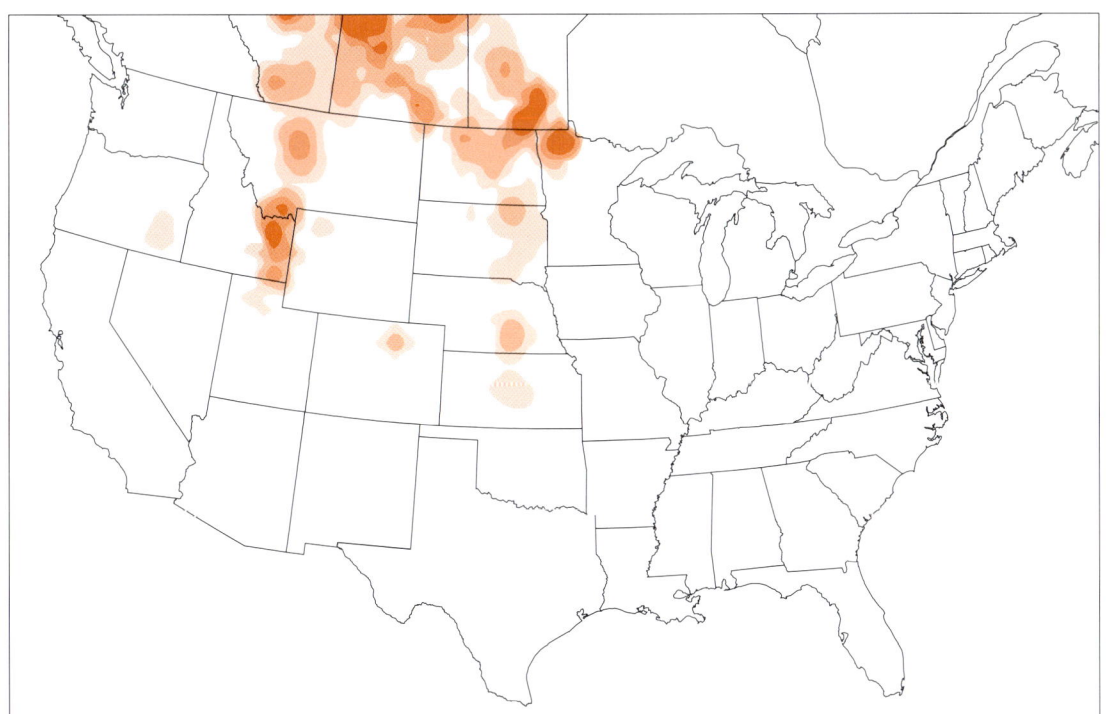

Heerman's Gull

Ring-billed Gull

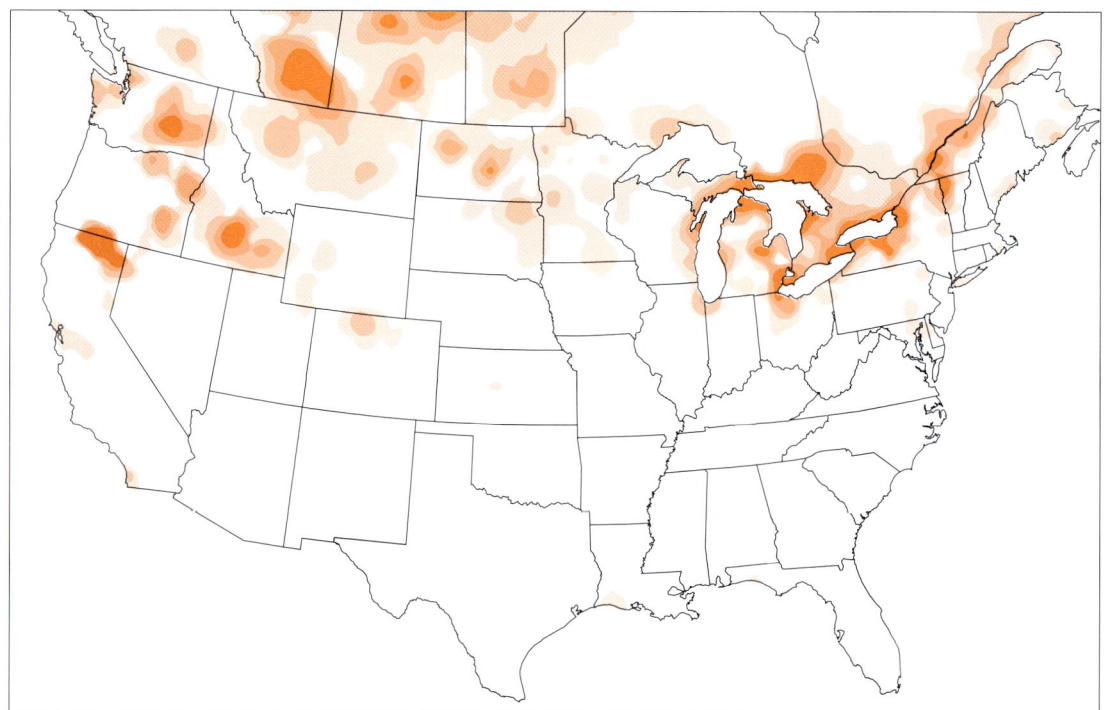

California Gull

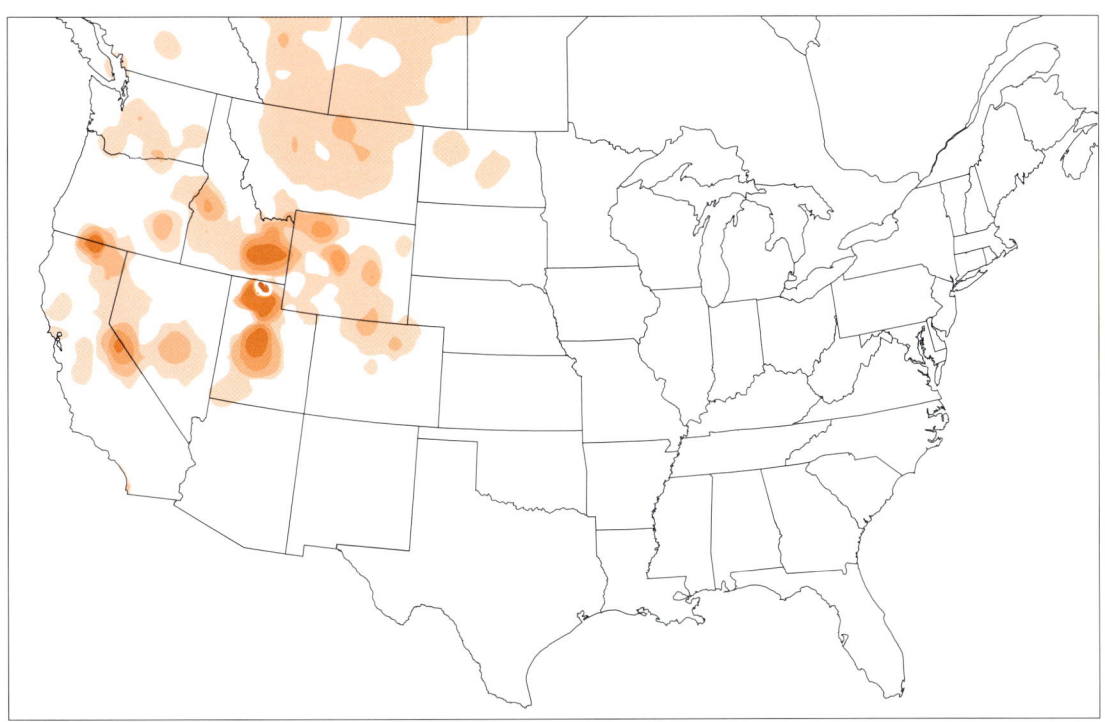

Herring Gull

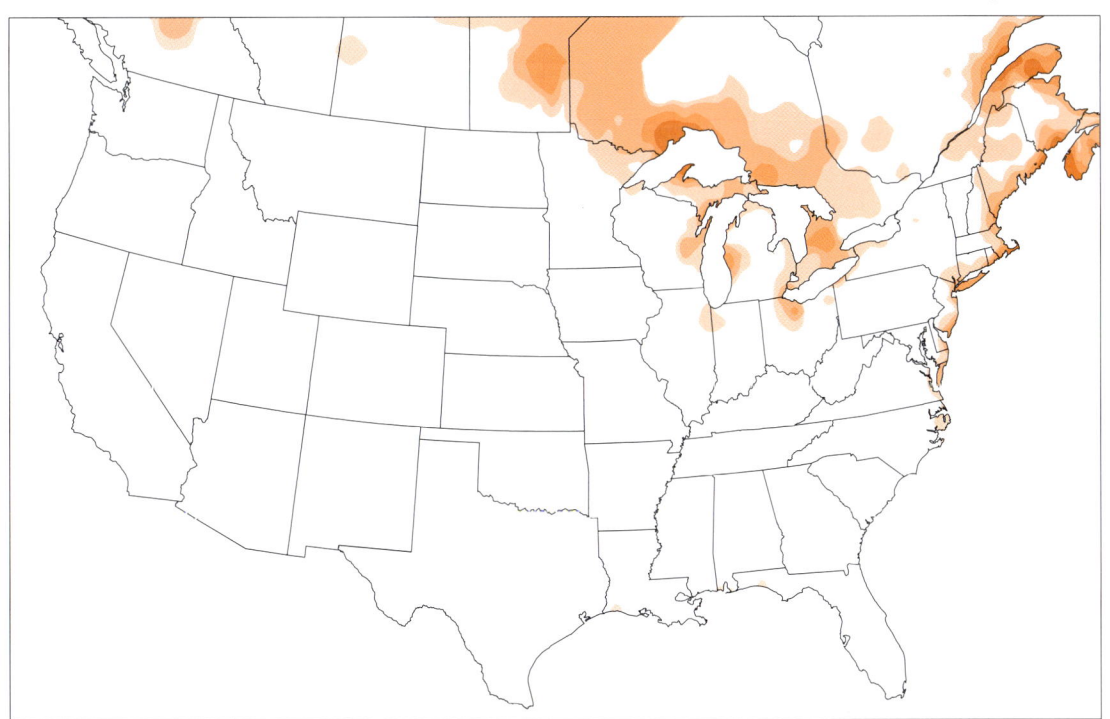

Western Gull

Glaucous-winged Gull

Great Black-backed Gull

Gull-billed Tern

Caspian Tern

Royal Tern

Common Tern

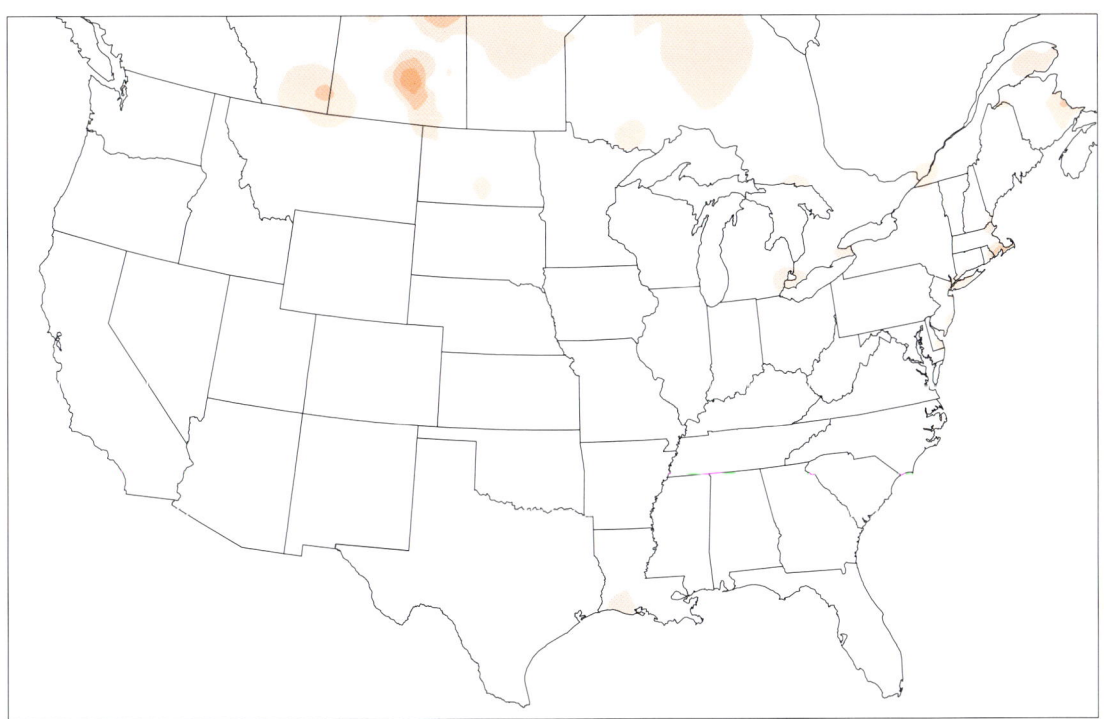

Forster's Tern

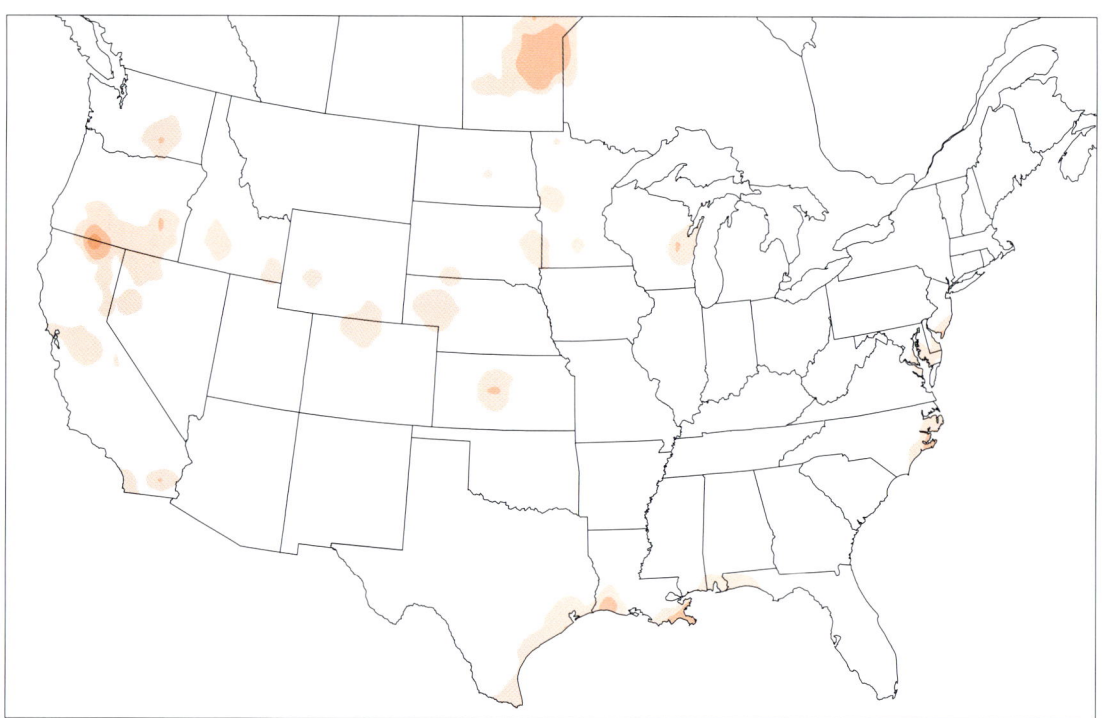

Least Tern

Black Tern

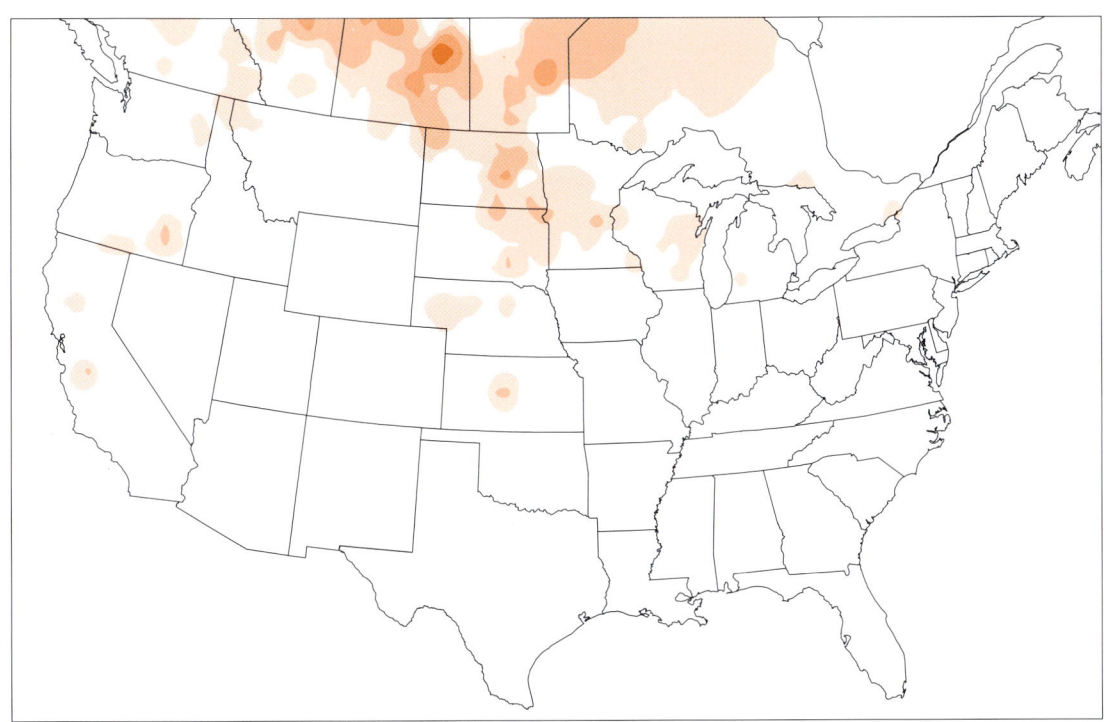

Black Skimmer

Rock Dove

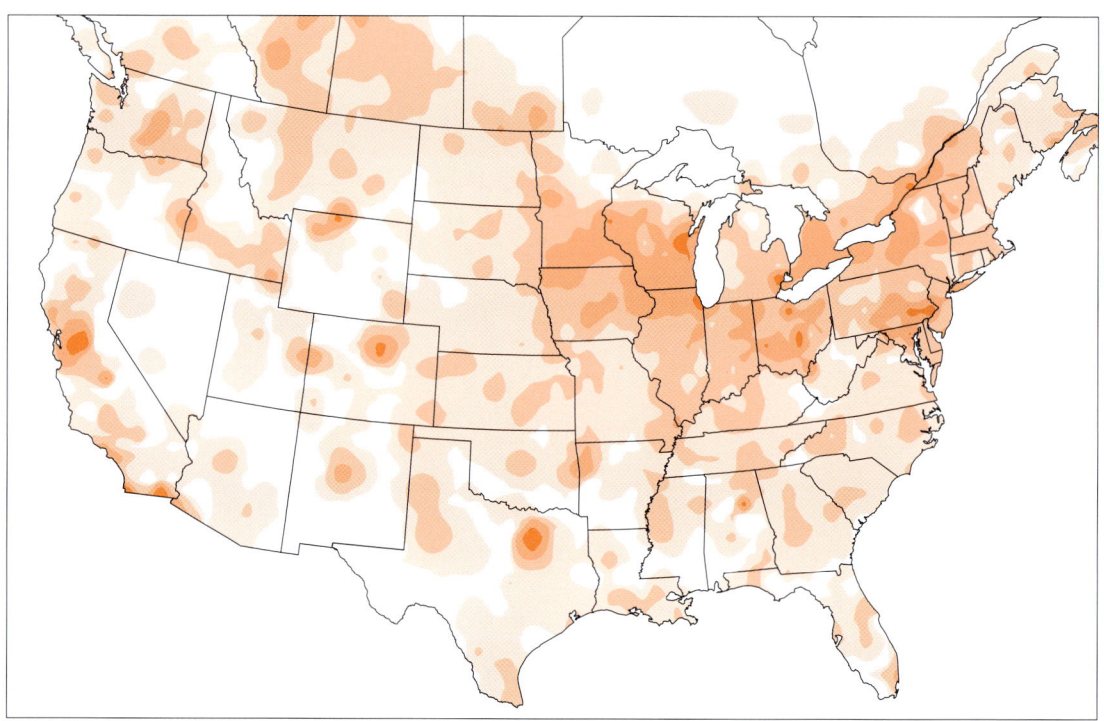

White-crowned Pigeon

Band-tailed Pigeon

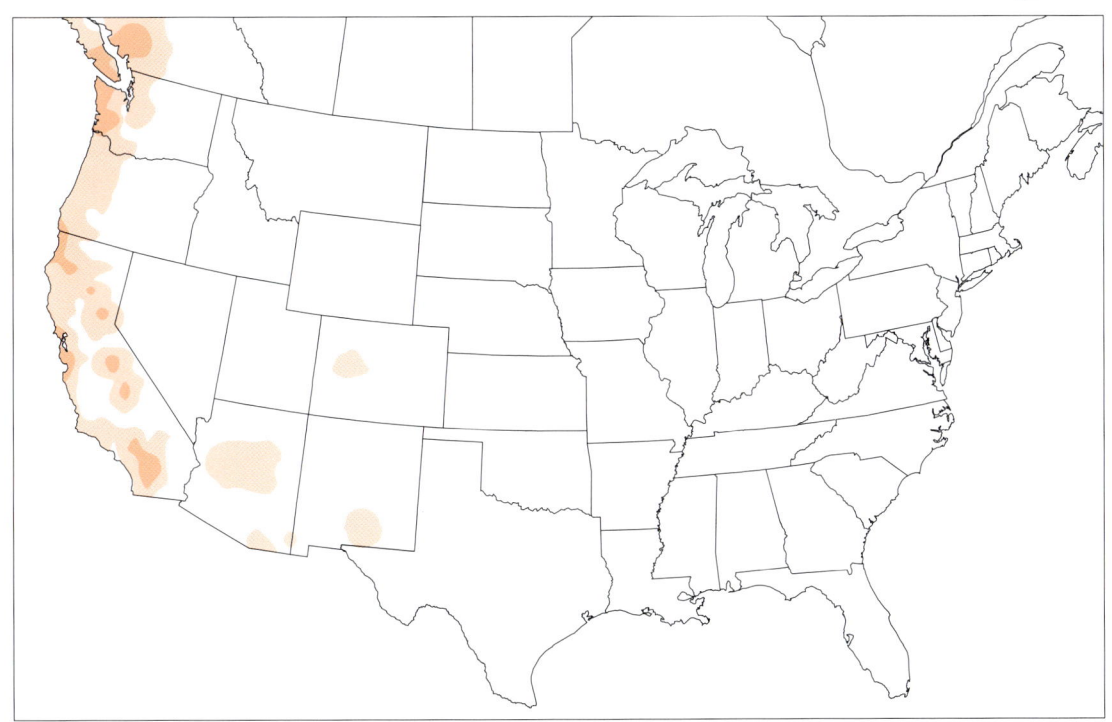

Spotted Dove

White-winged Dove

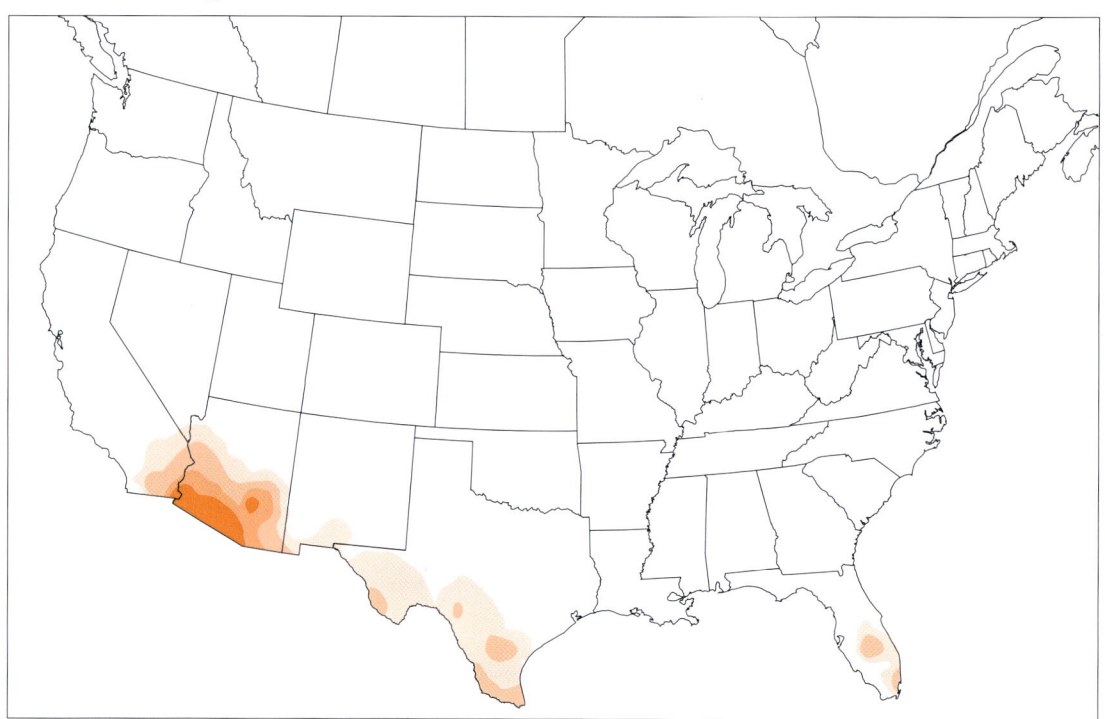

Mourning Dove

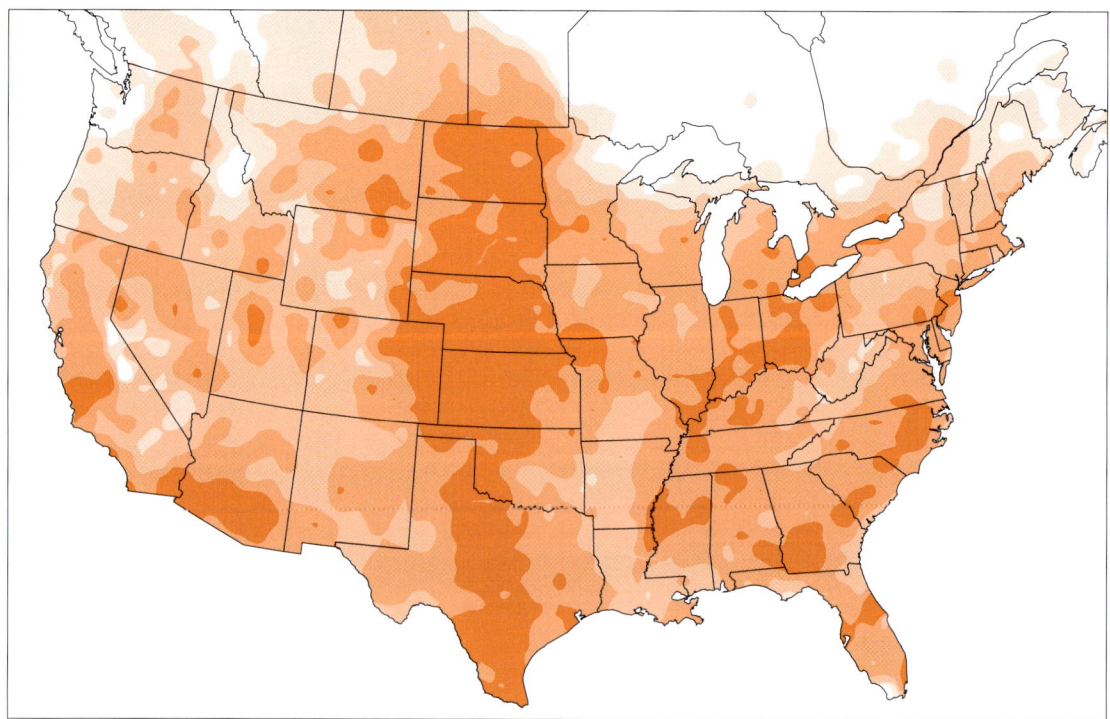

Inca Dove

Common Ground-Dove

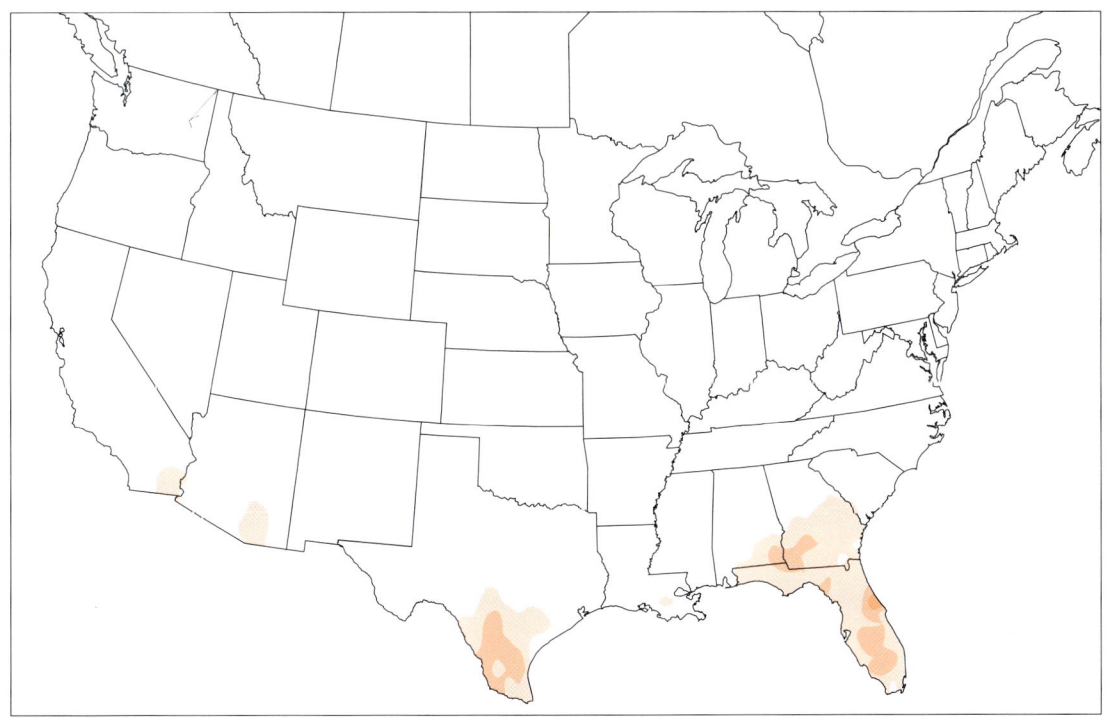

White-tipped Dove

Black-billed Cuckoo

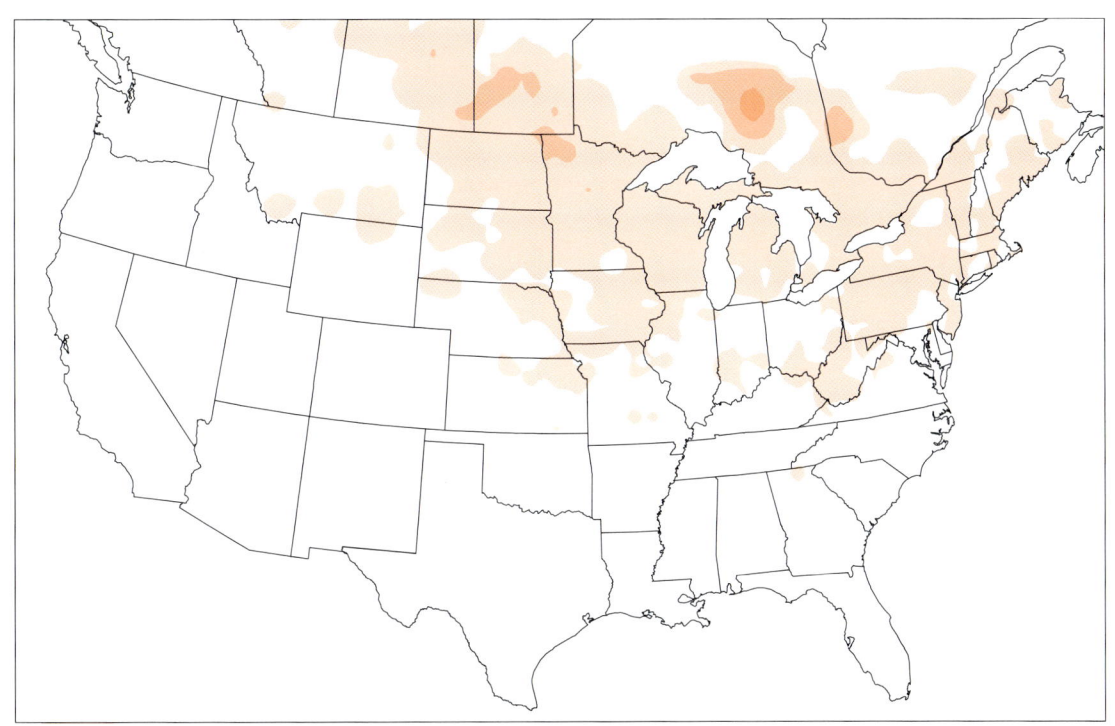

Yellow-billed Cuckoo

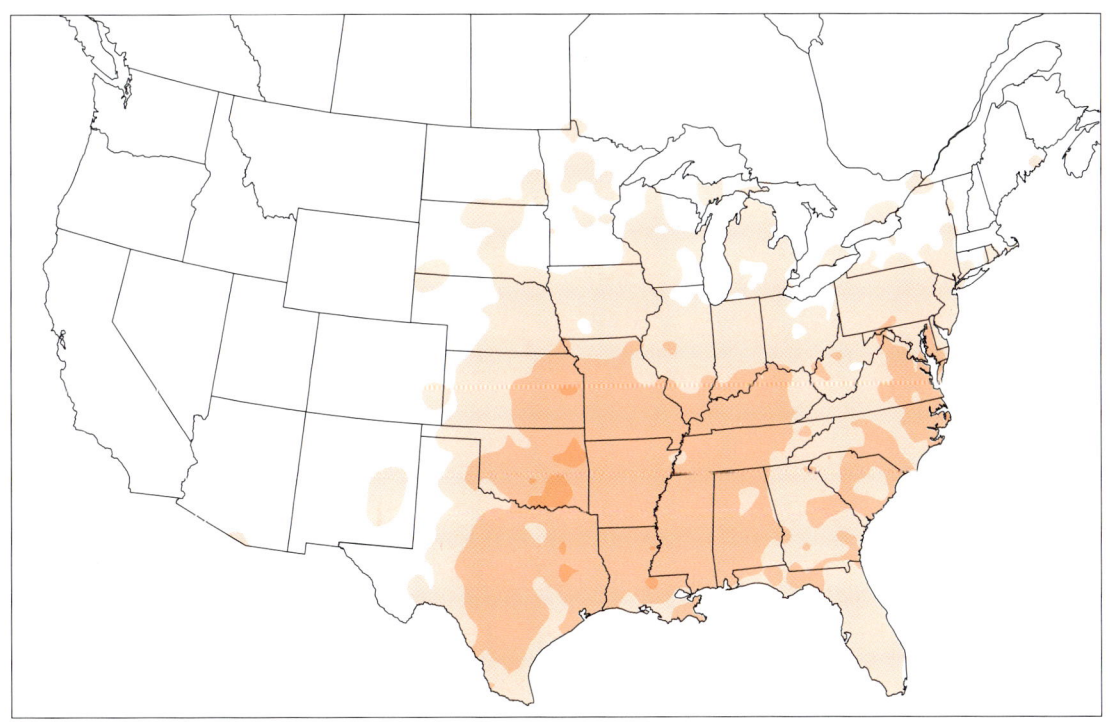

Mangrove Cuckoo

Greater Roadrunner

Smooth-billed Ani

Groove-billed Ani

Great Horned Owl

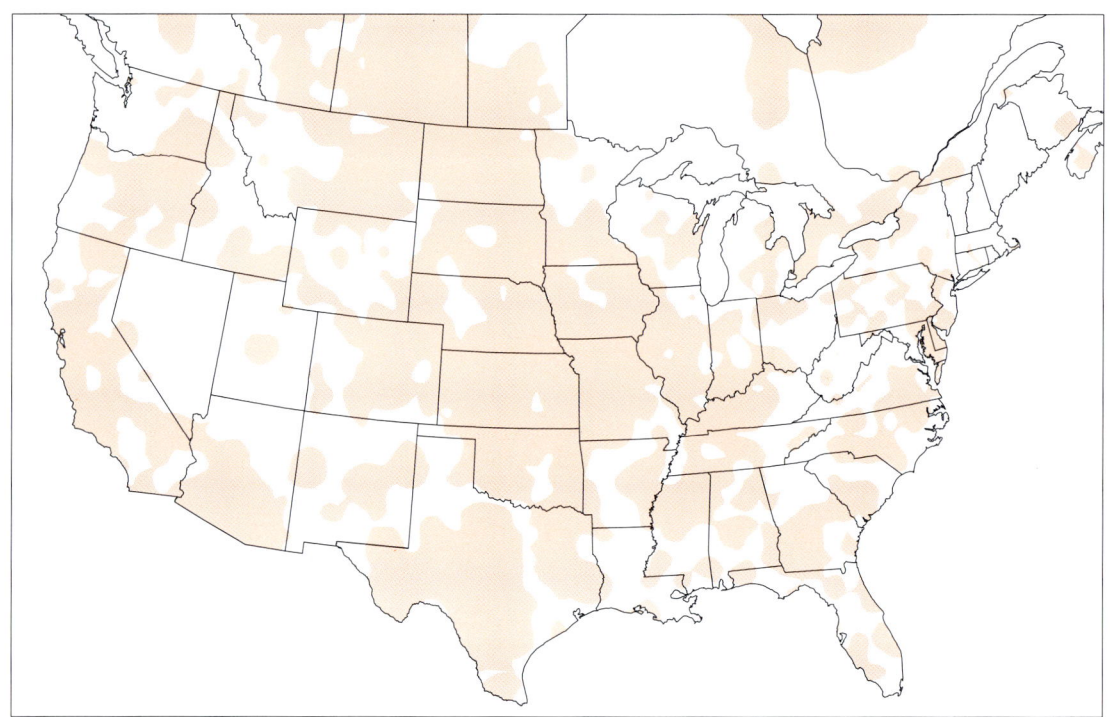

Burrowing Owl

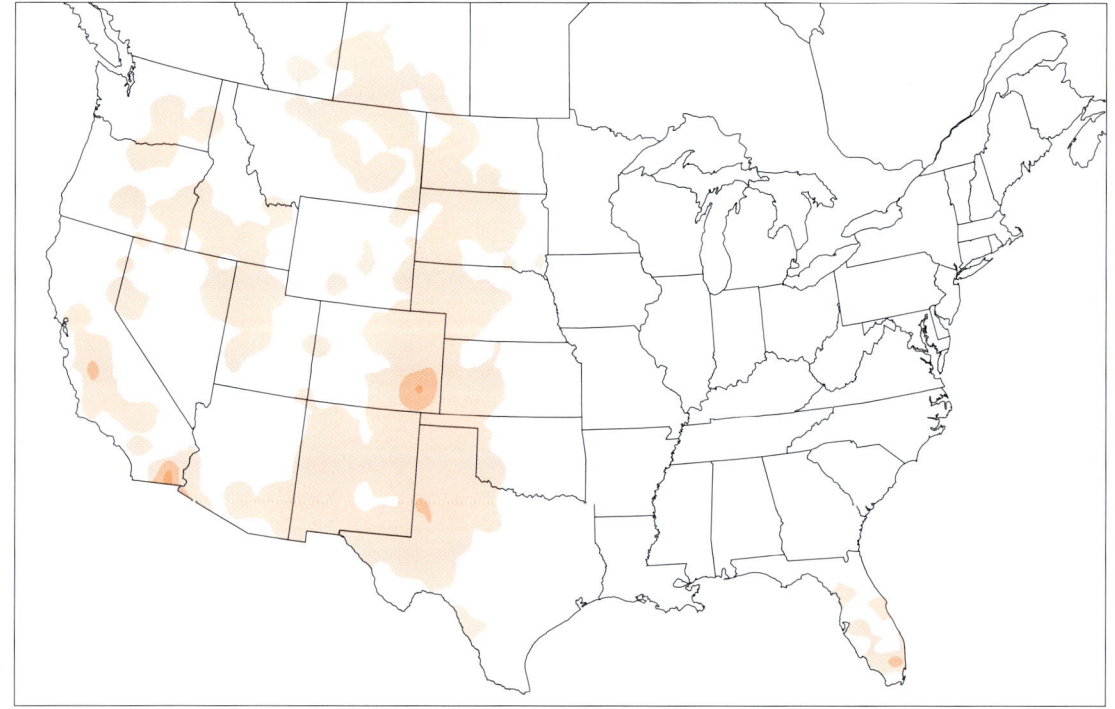

Barred Owl

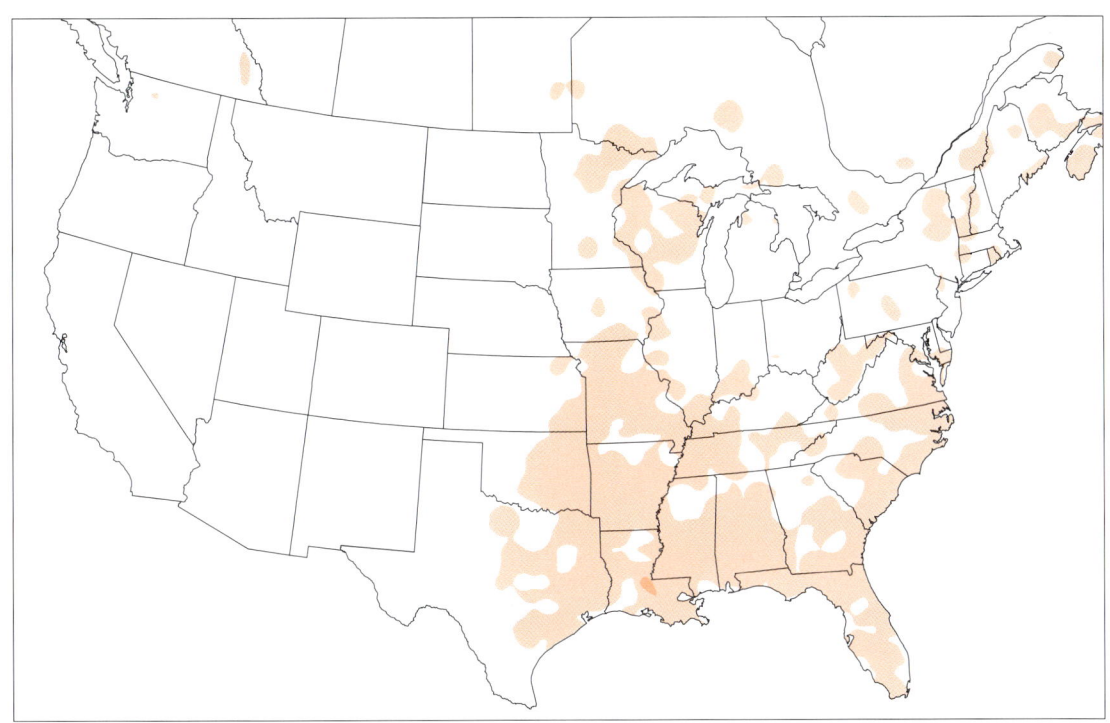

Lesser Nighthawk

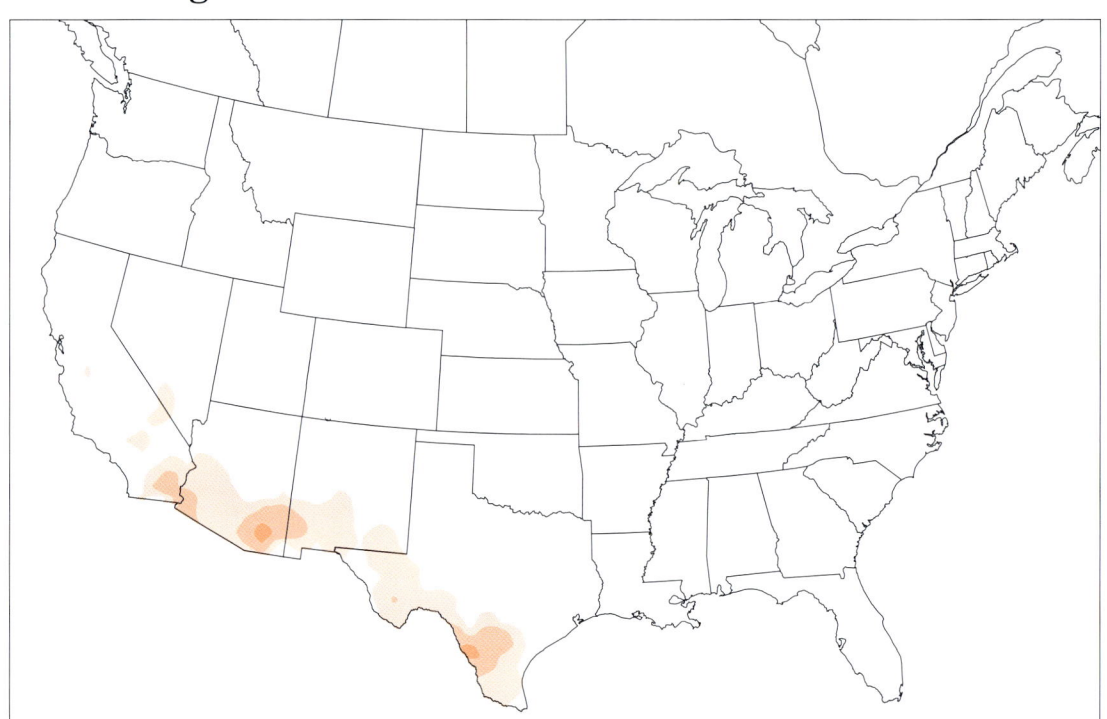

Common Nighthawk

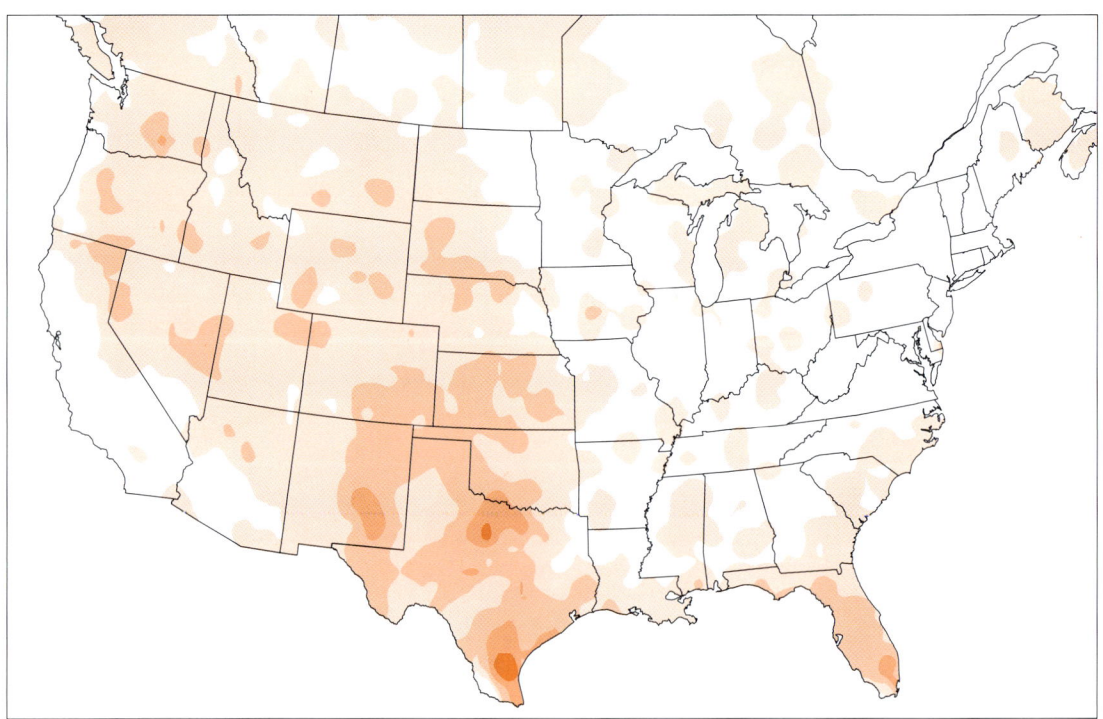

Pauraque

Common Poorwill

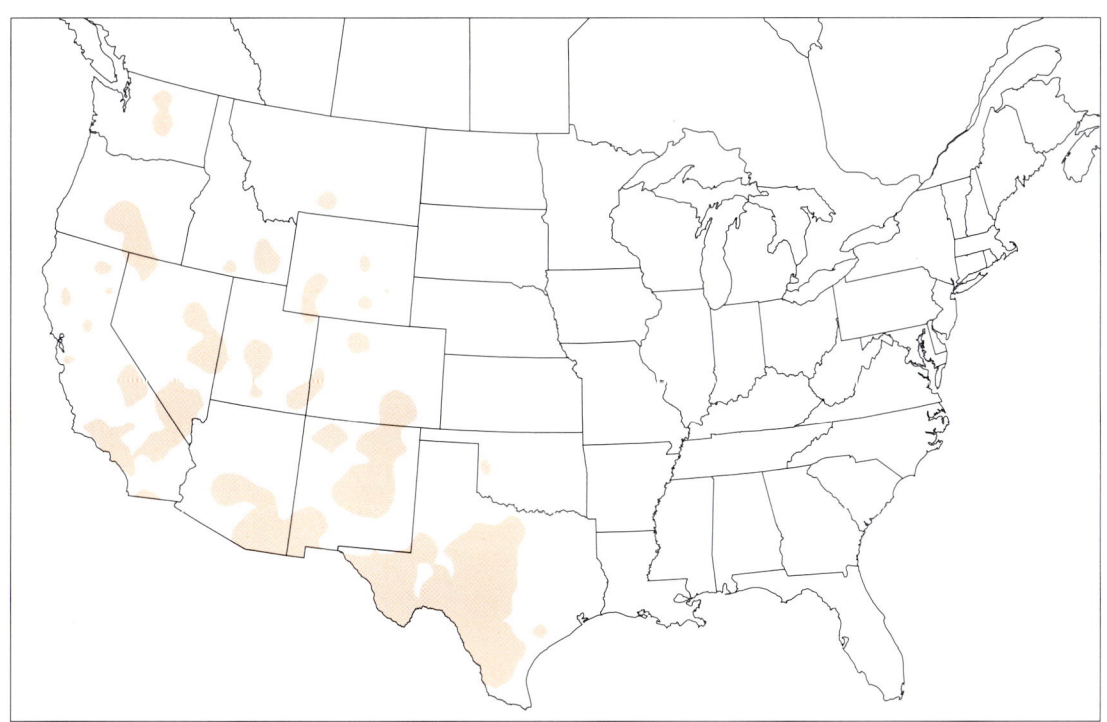

Chuck-will's-widow

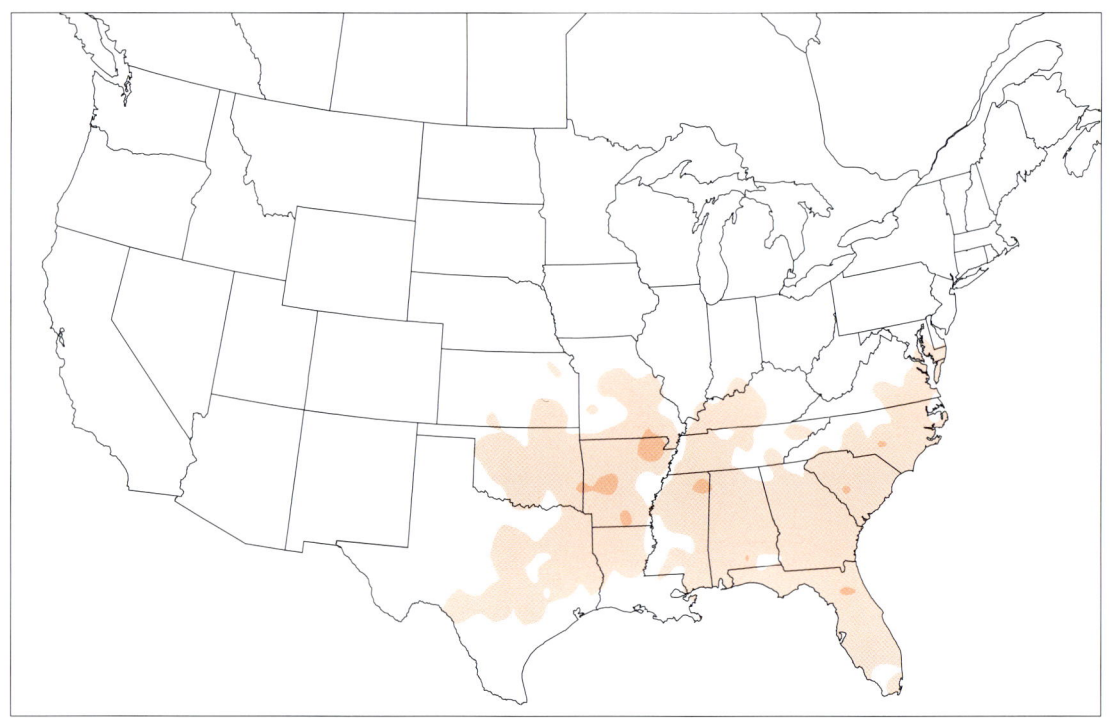

Whip-poor-will

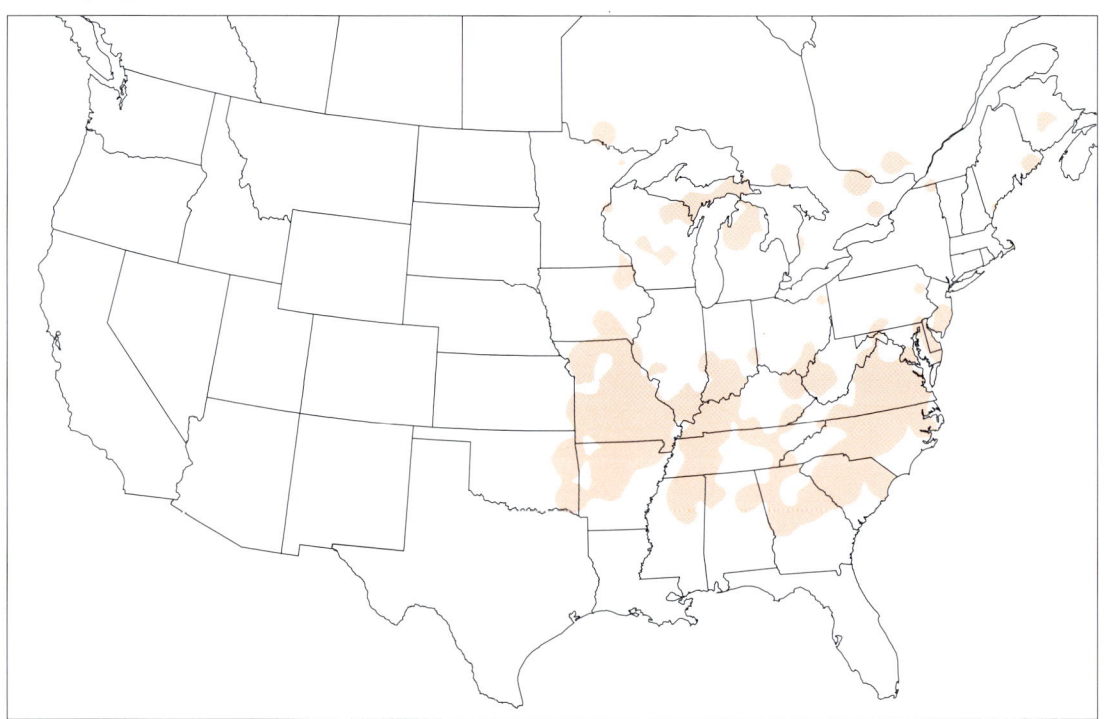

Black Swift

Chimney Swift

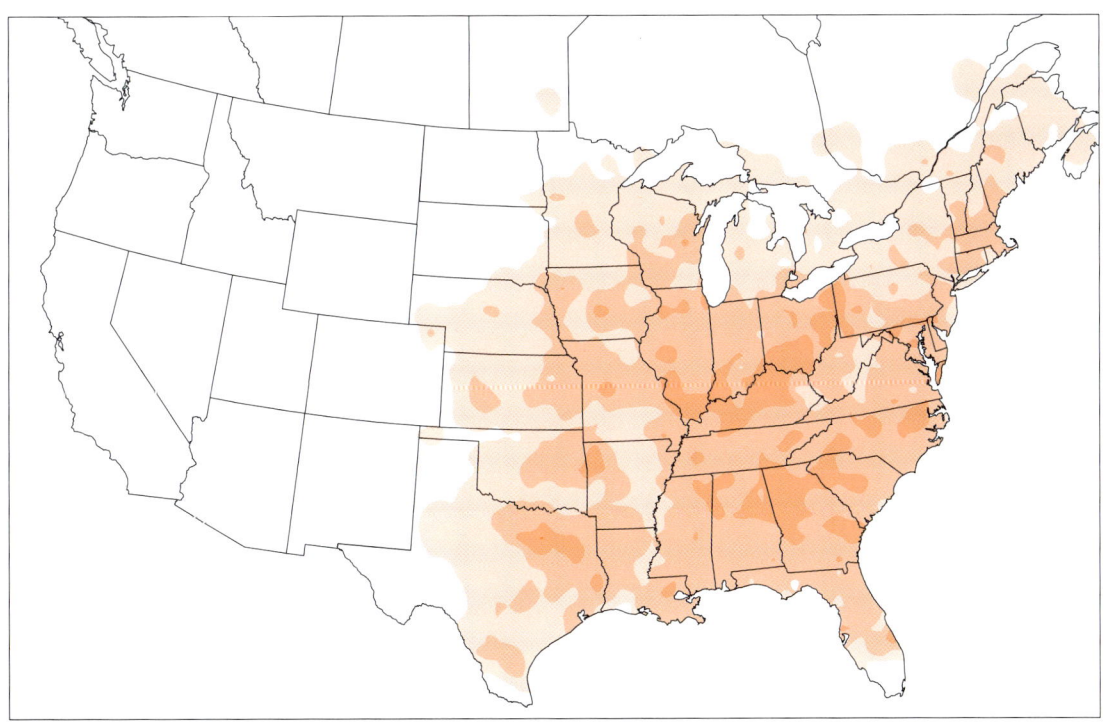

Vaux's Swift

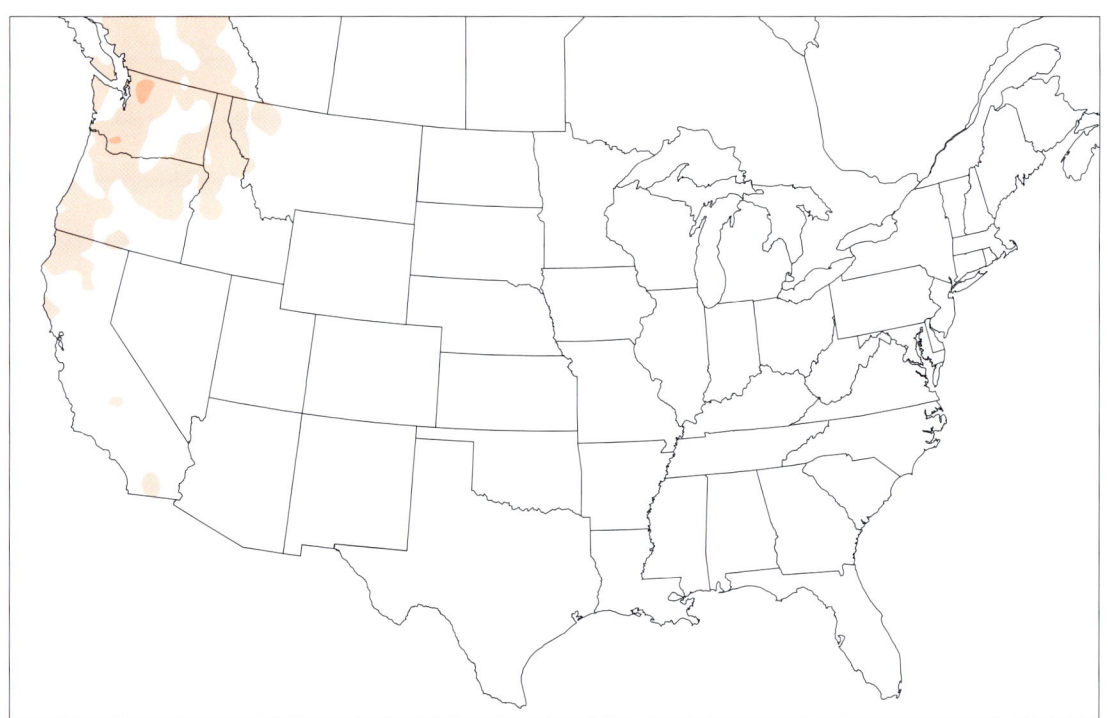

White-throated Swift

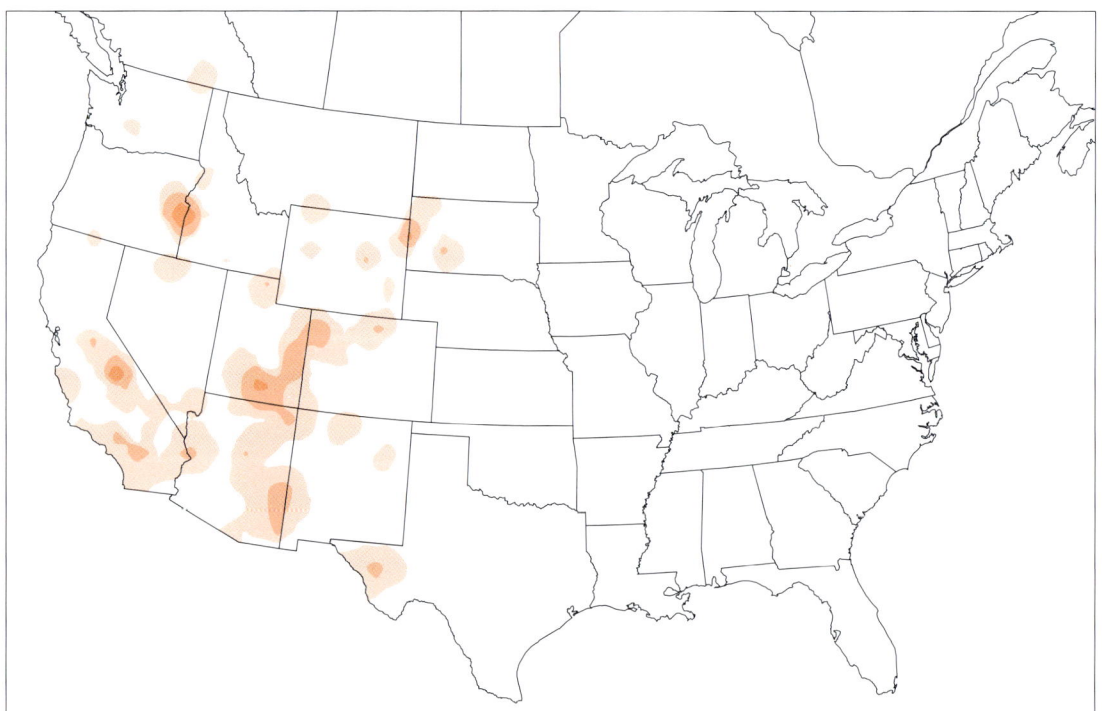

Broad-billed Hummingbird

Blue-throated Hummingbird

Ruby-throated Hummingbird

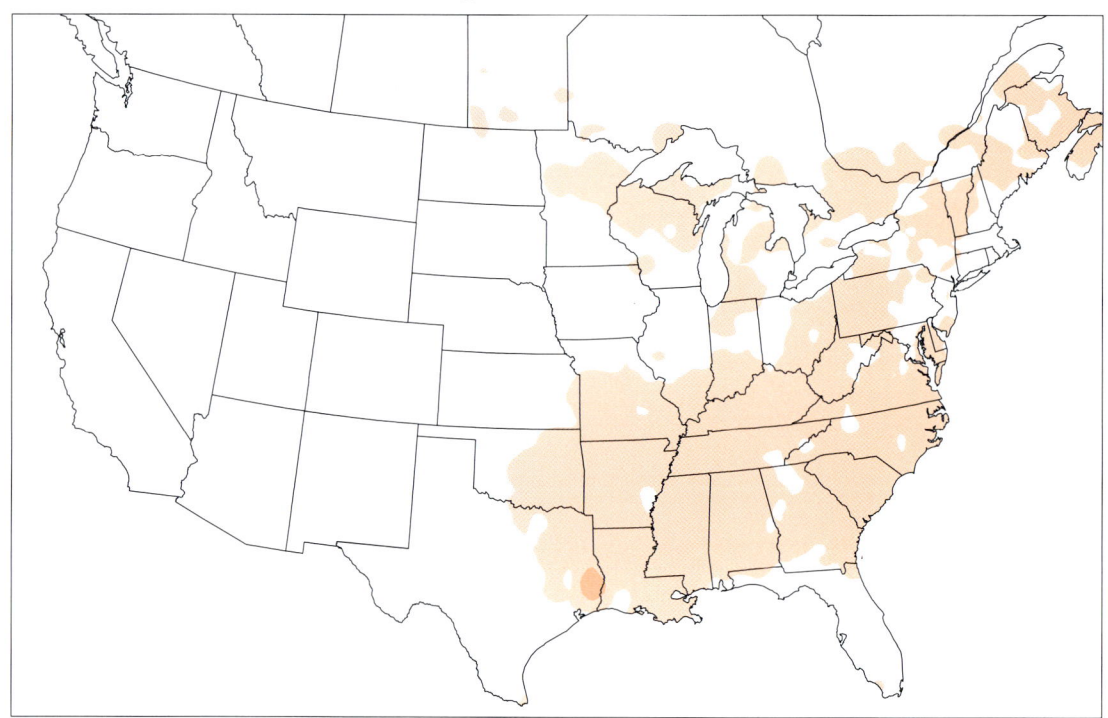

Black-chinned Hummingbird

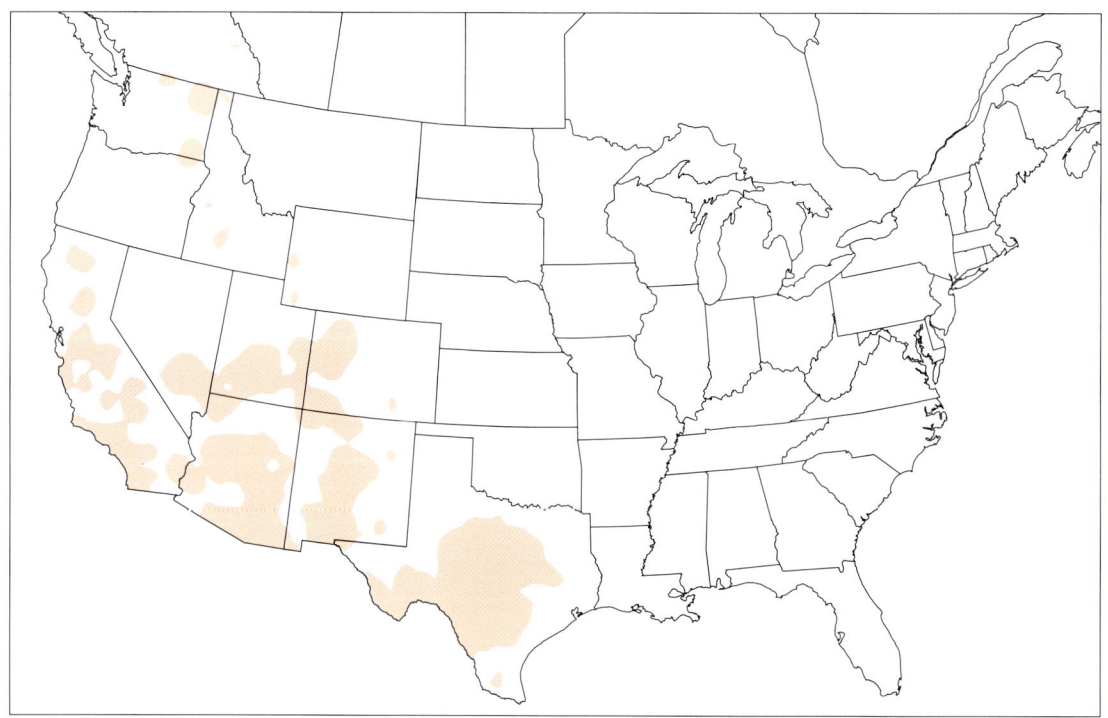

Anna's Hummingbird

Costa's Hummingbird

Calliope Hummingbird

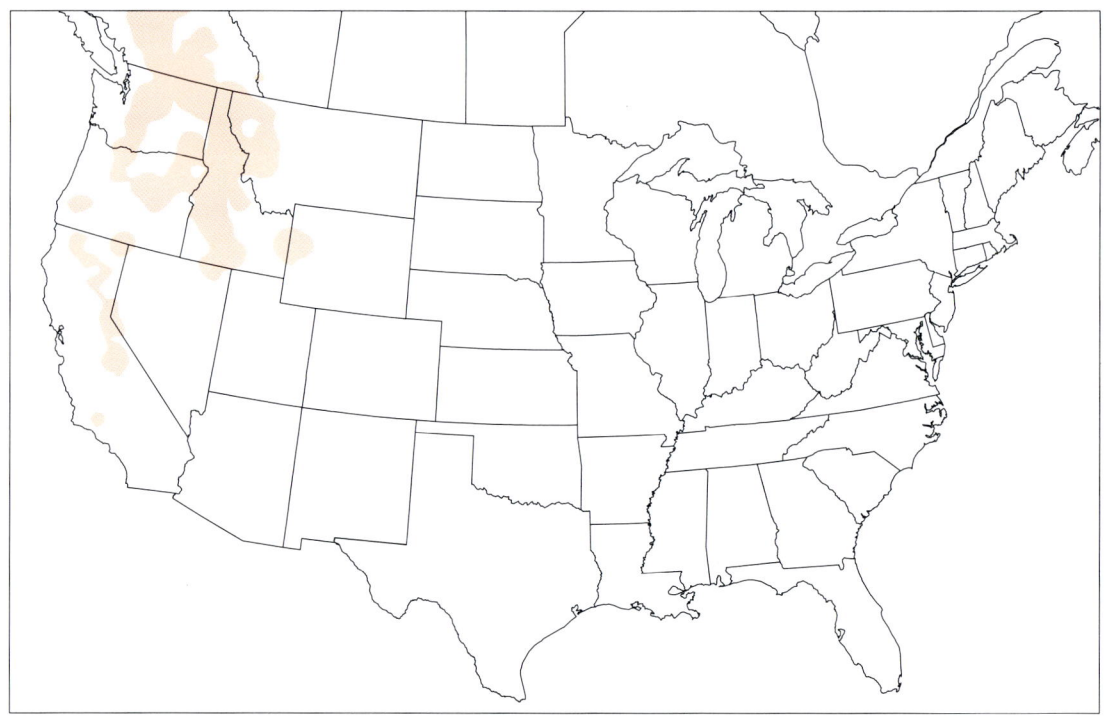

Broad-tailed Hummingbird

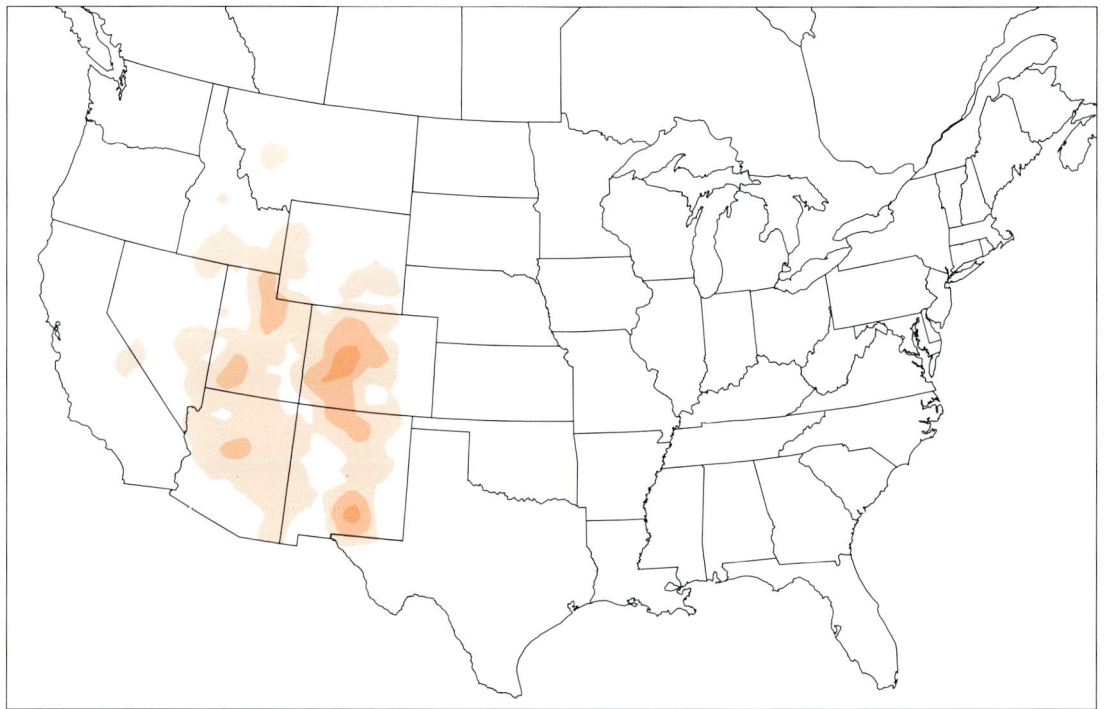

Rufous Hummingbird

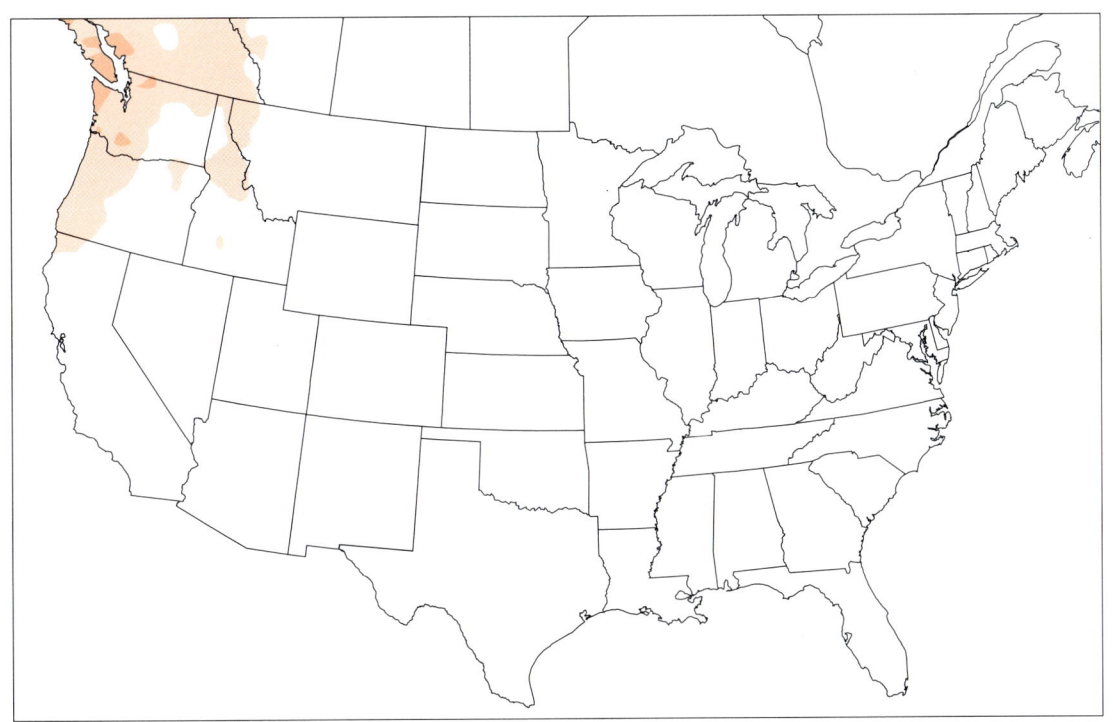

Allen's Hummingbird

Elegant Trogon

Belted Kingfisher

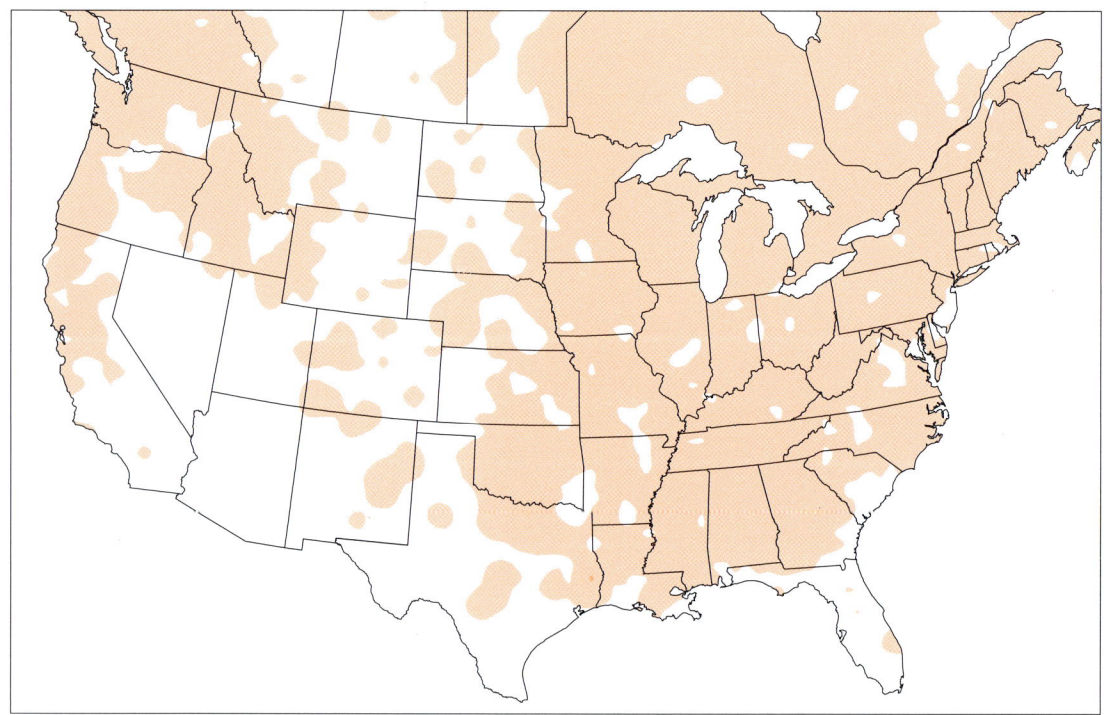

Red-headed Woodpecker

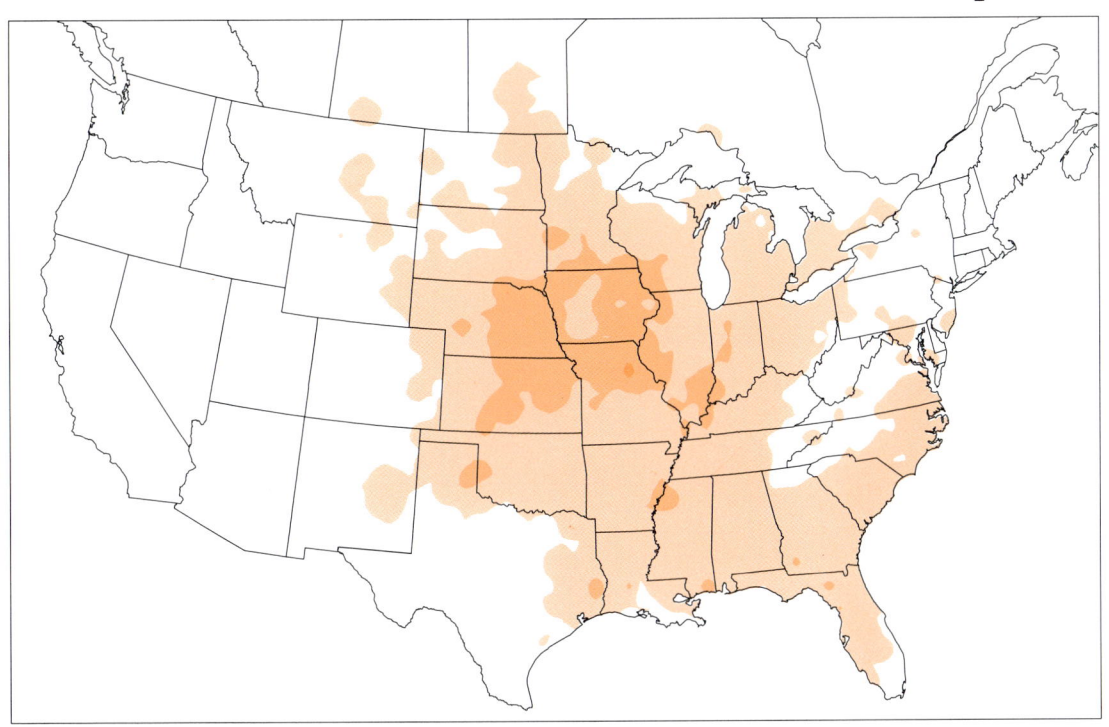

Acorn Woodpecker

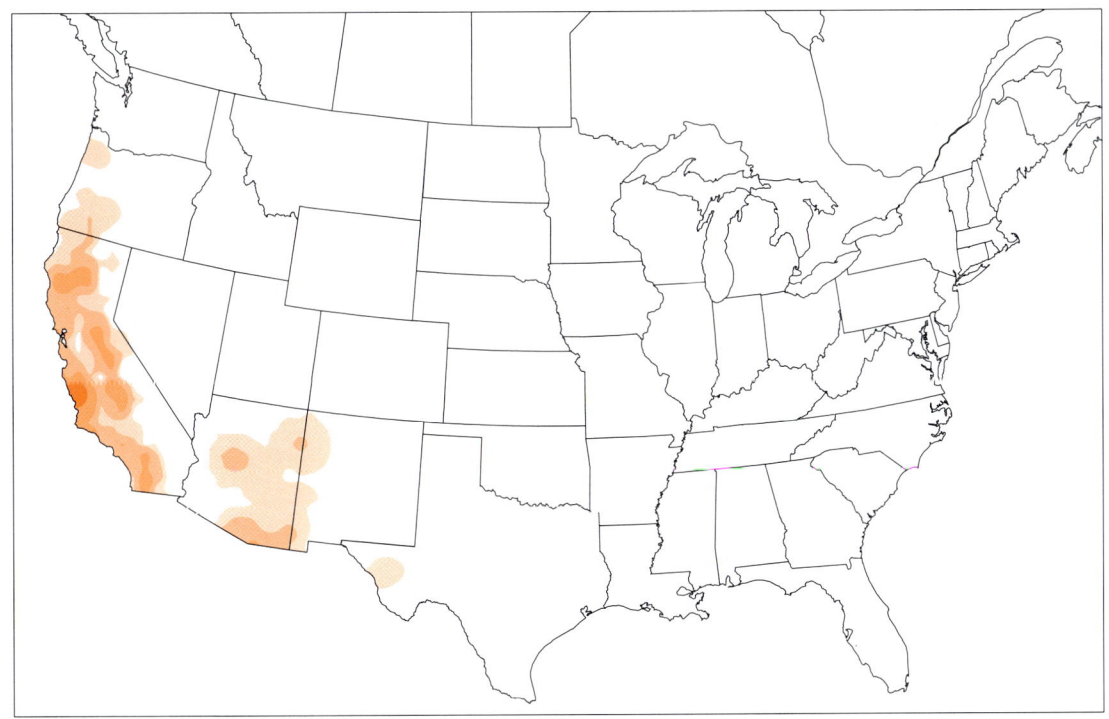

Gila Woodpecker

Golden-fronted Woodpecker

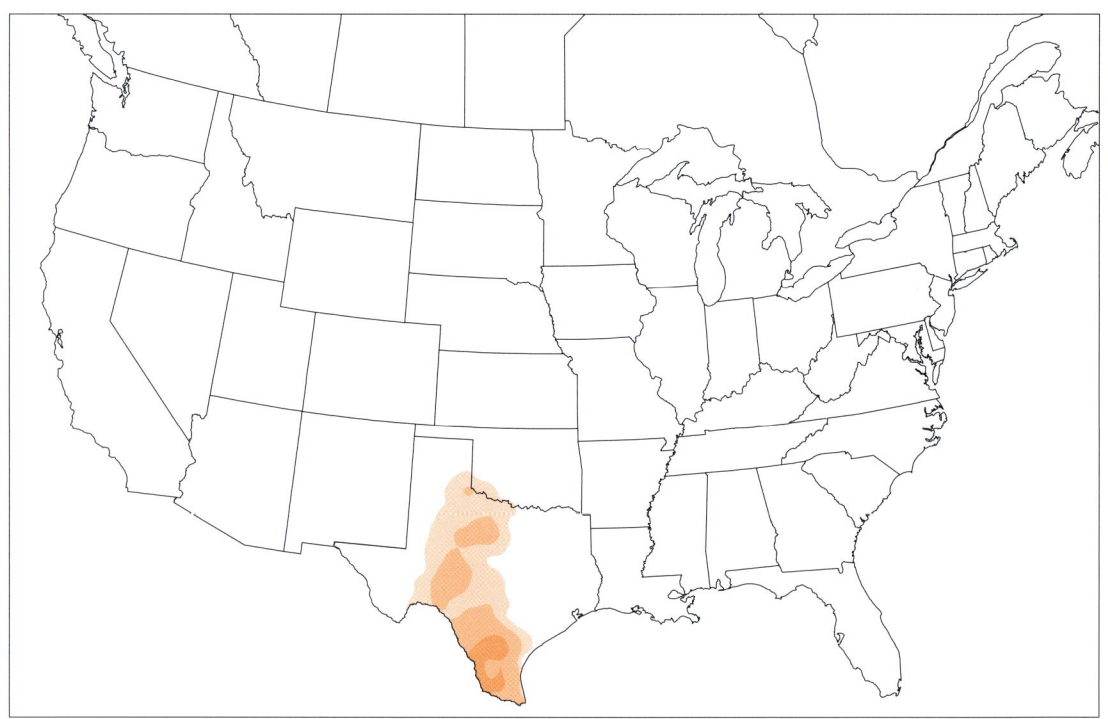

Red-bellied Woodpecker

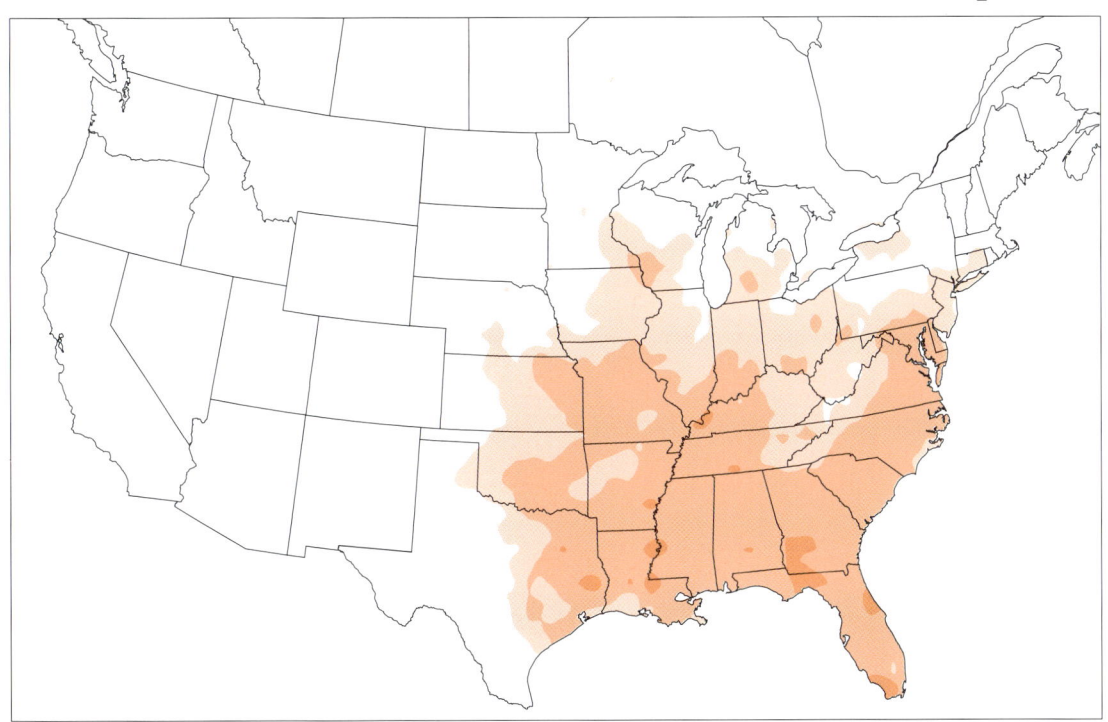

Yellow-bellied Sapsucker

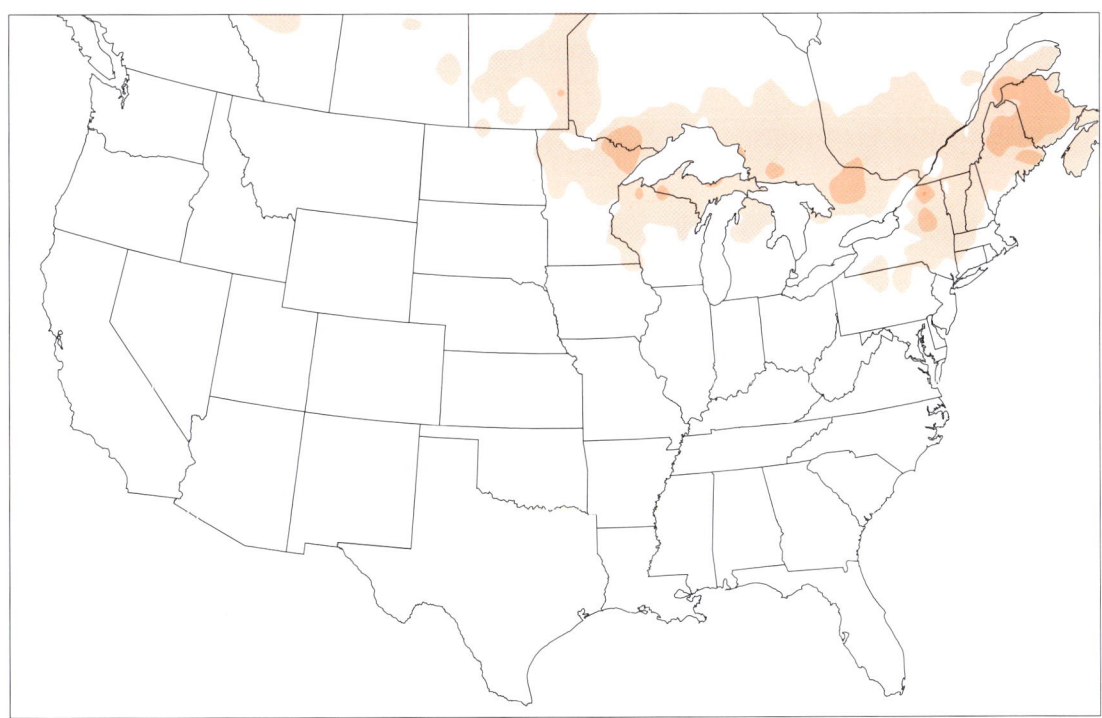

Red-naped Sapsucker

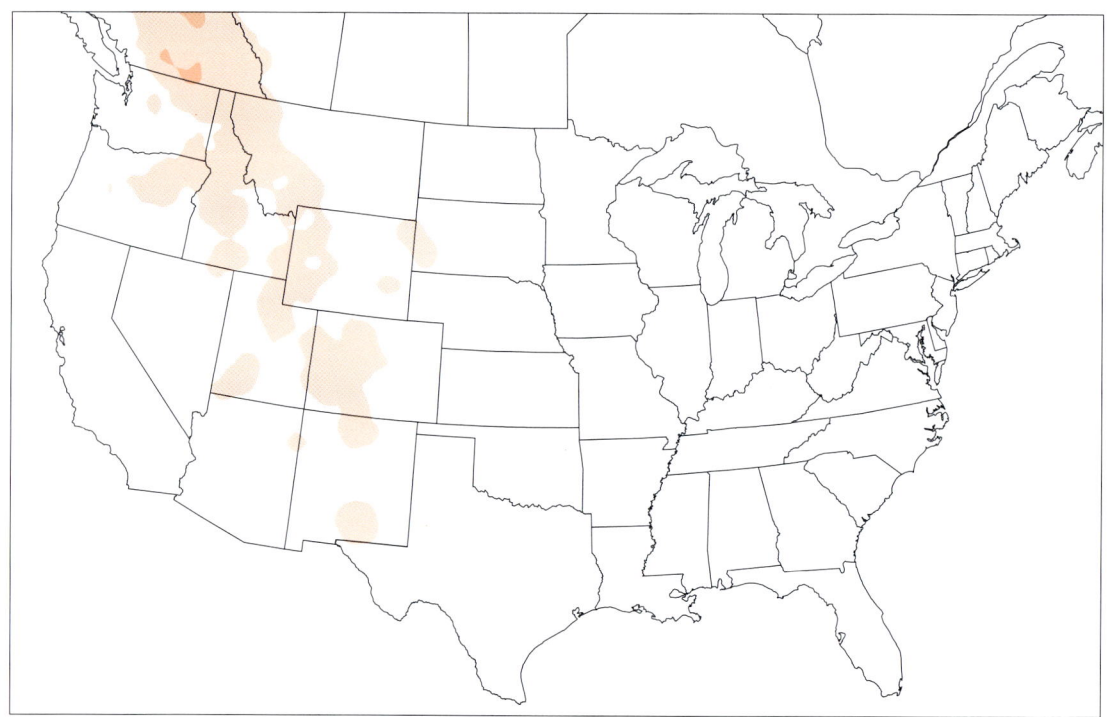

Red-breasted Sapsucker

Williamson's Sapsucker

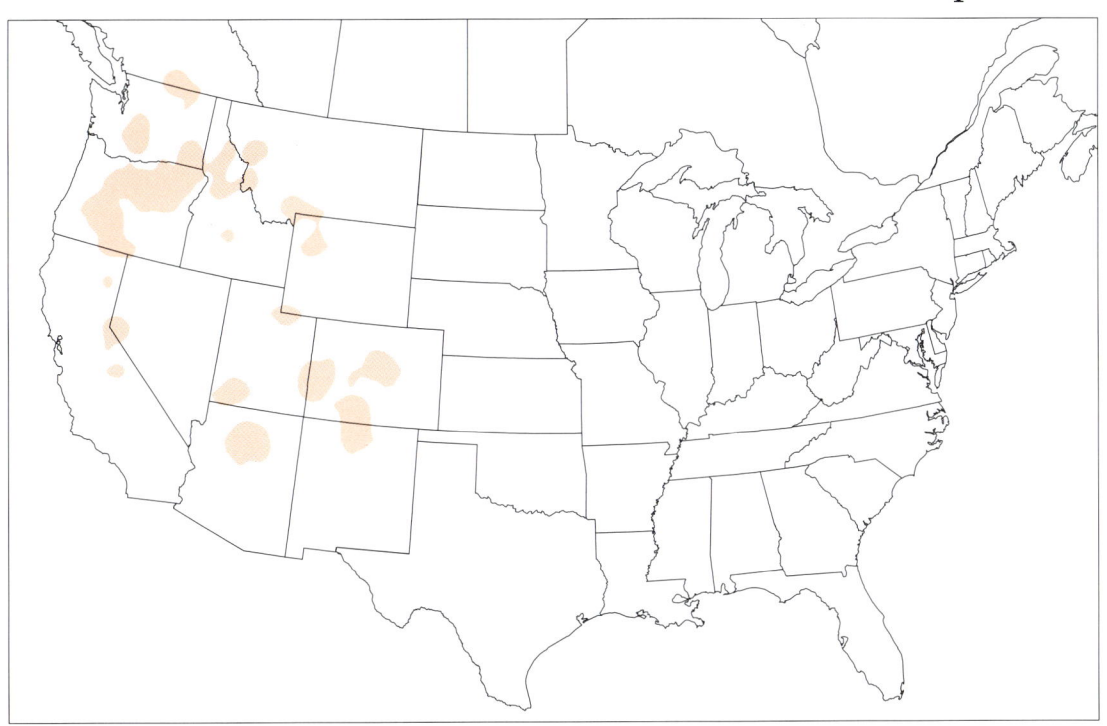

Ladder-backed Woodpecker

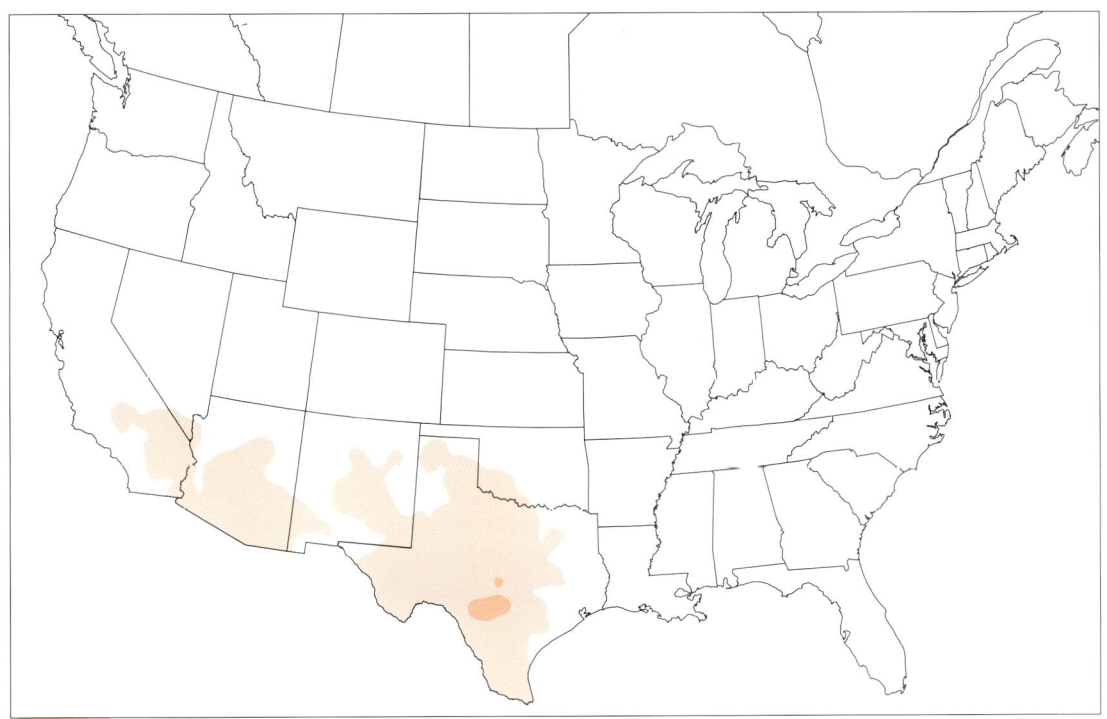

Nuttall's Woodpecker

Downy Woodpecker

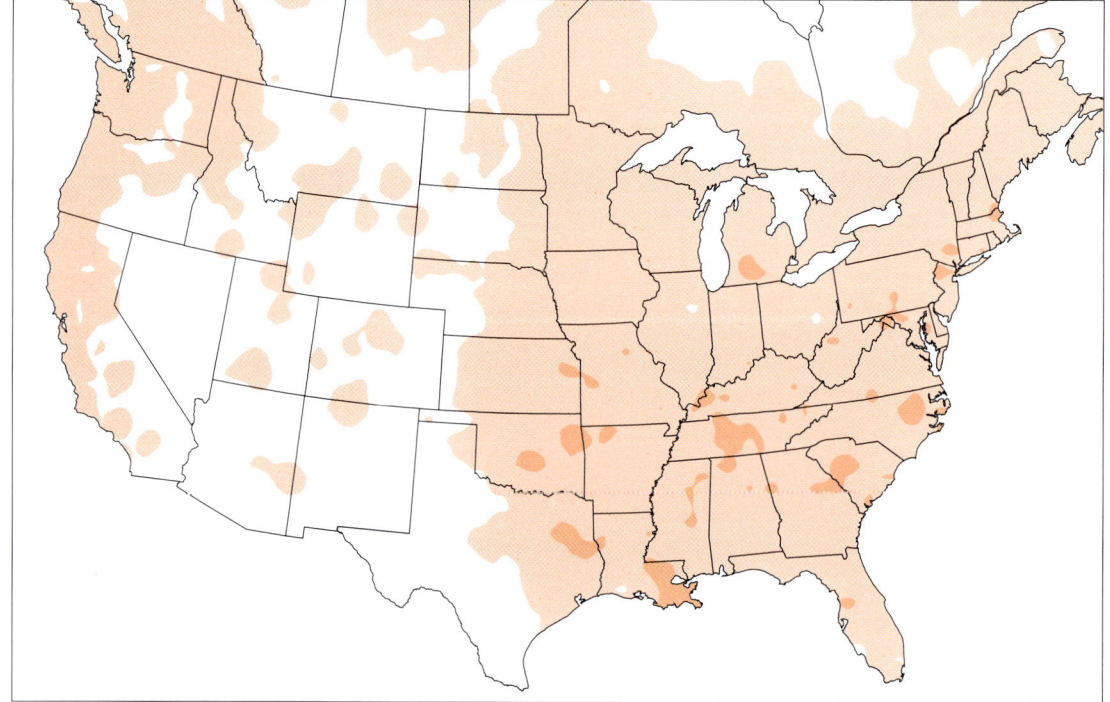

Hairy Woodpecker

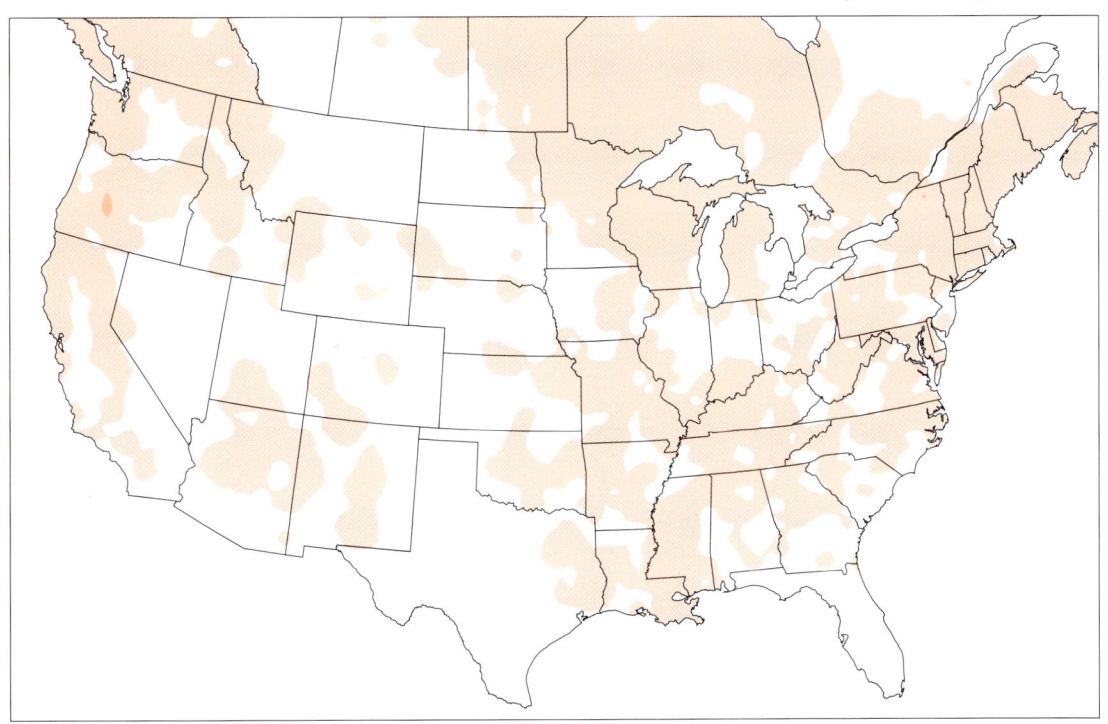

Strickland's Woodpecker

White-headed Woodpecker

Northern Flicker

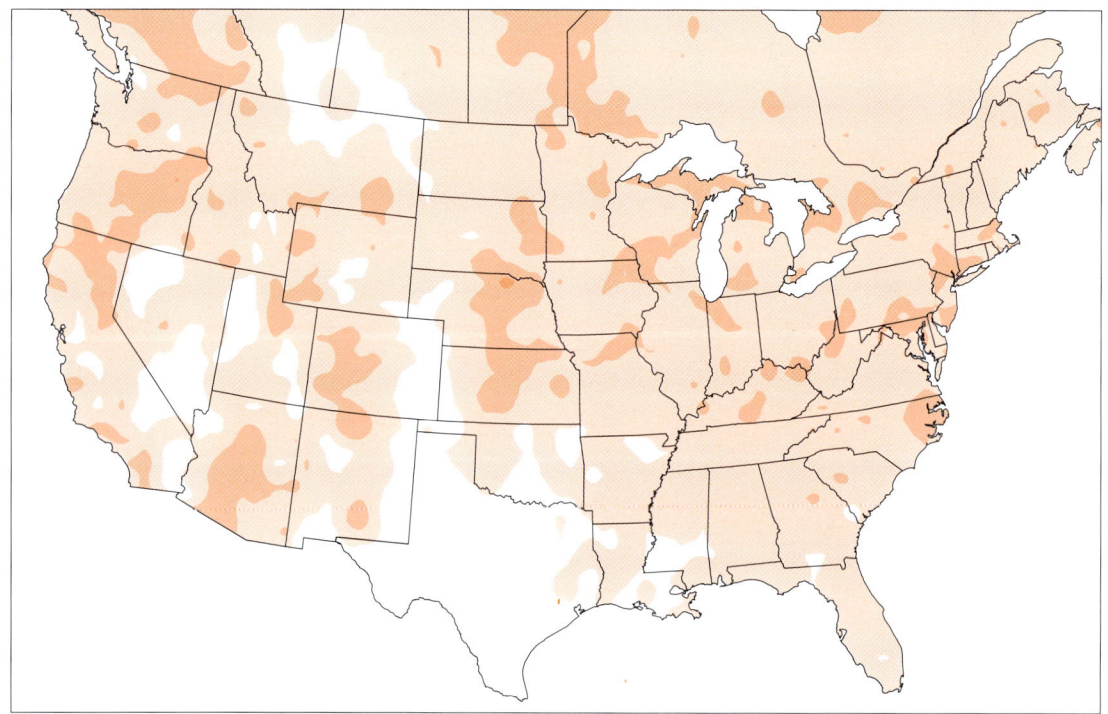

Northern Flicker (Yellow-shafted)

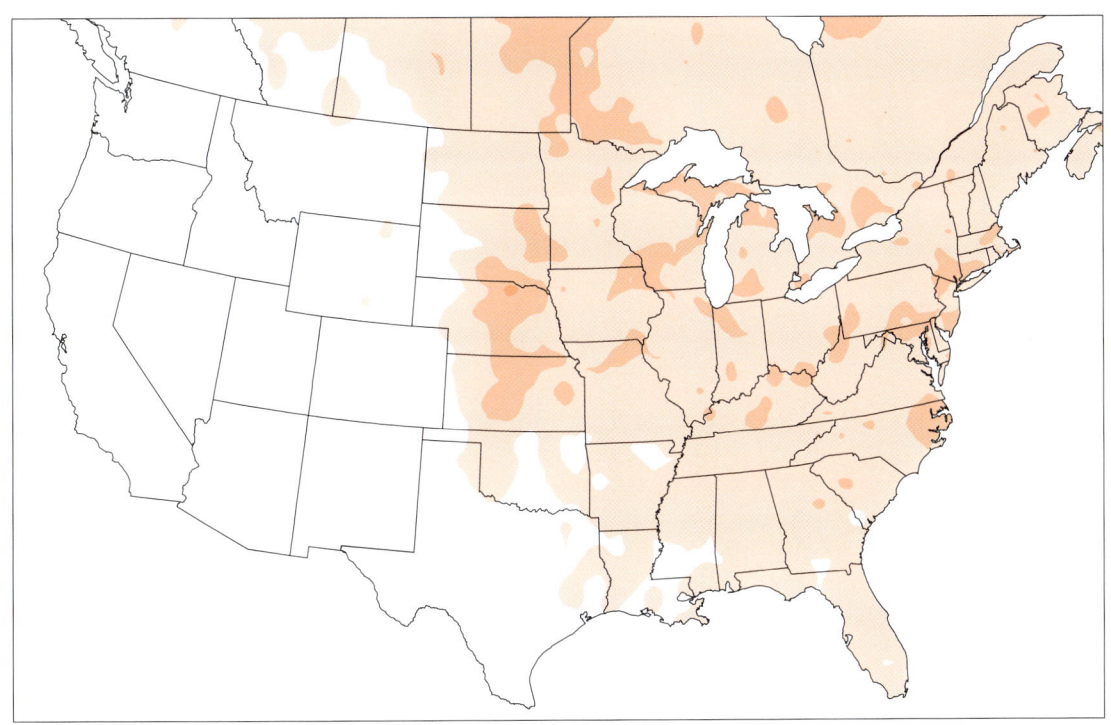

Northern Flicker (Red-shafted)

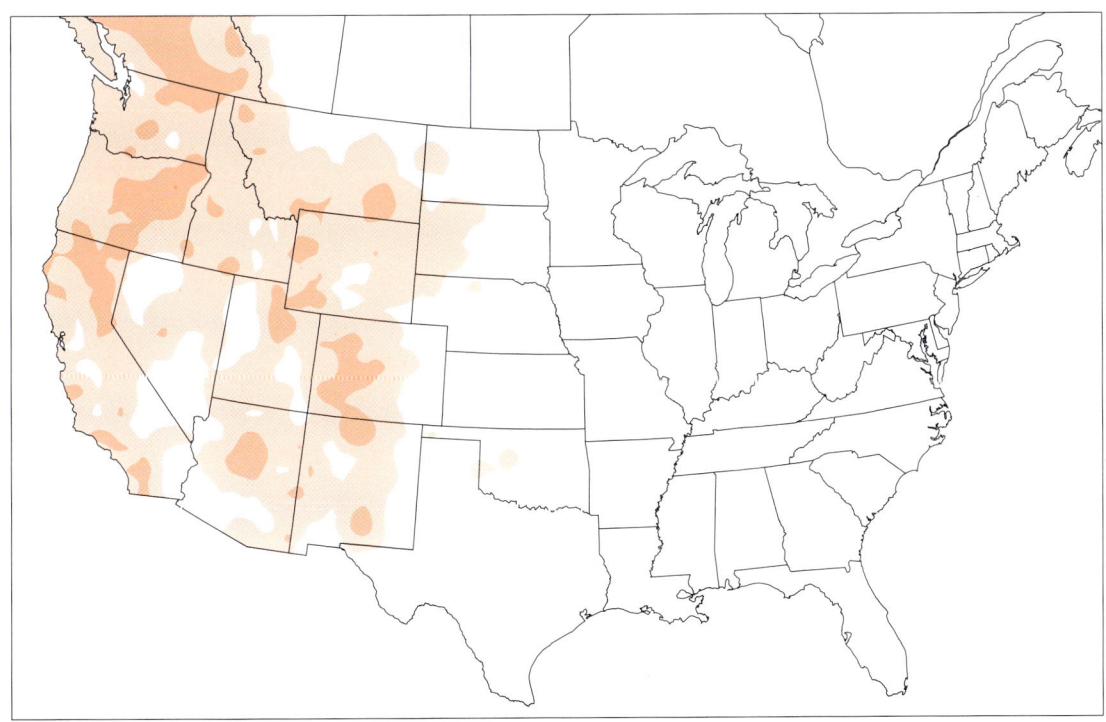

Northern Flicker (Gilded)

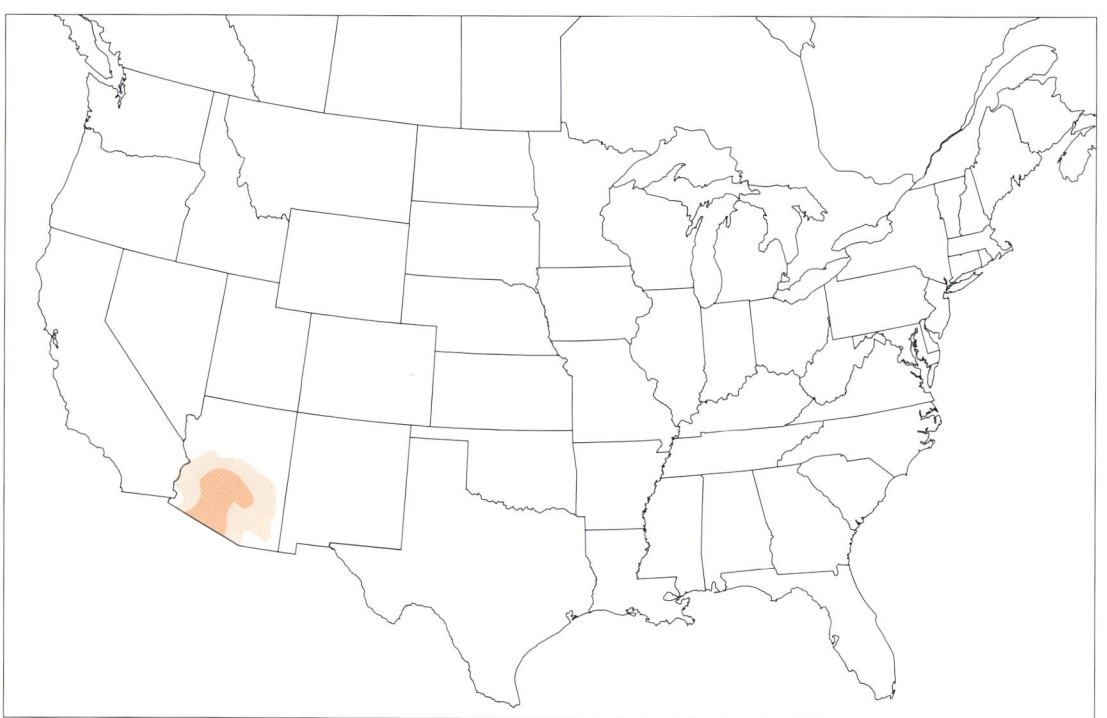

Pileated Woodpecker

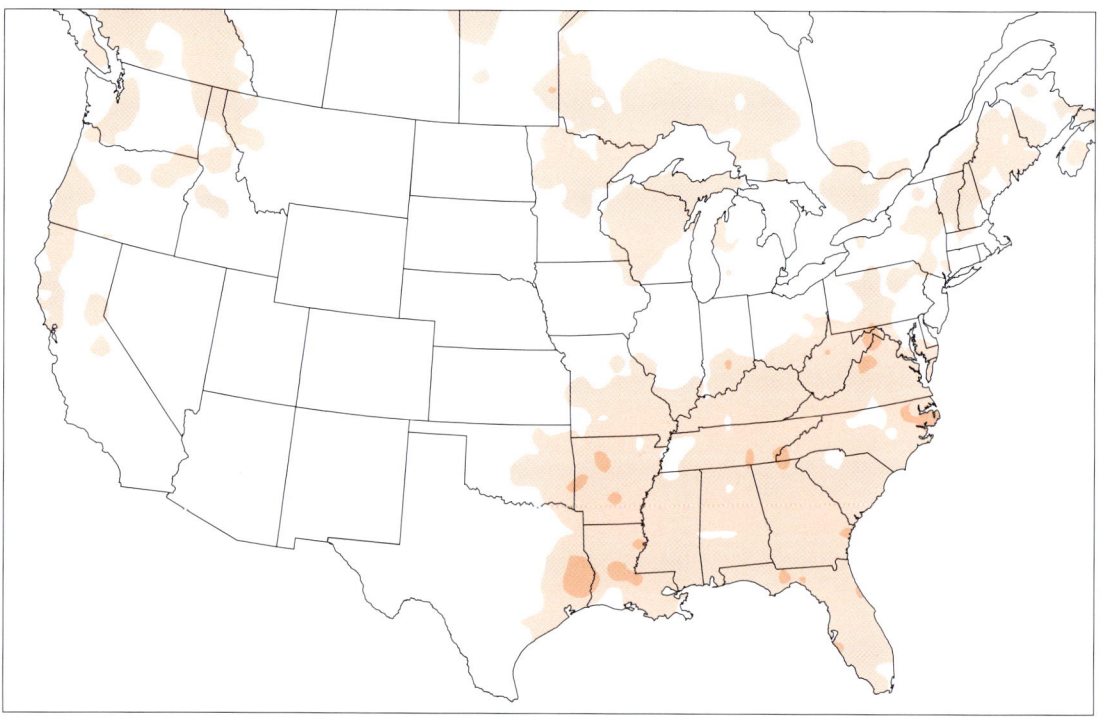

Northern Beardless-Tyrannulet

Olive-sided Flycatcher

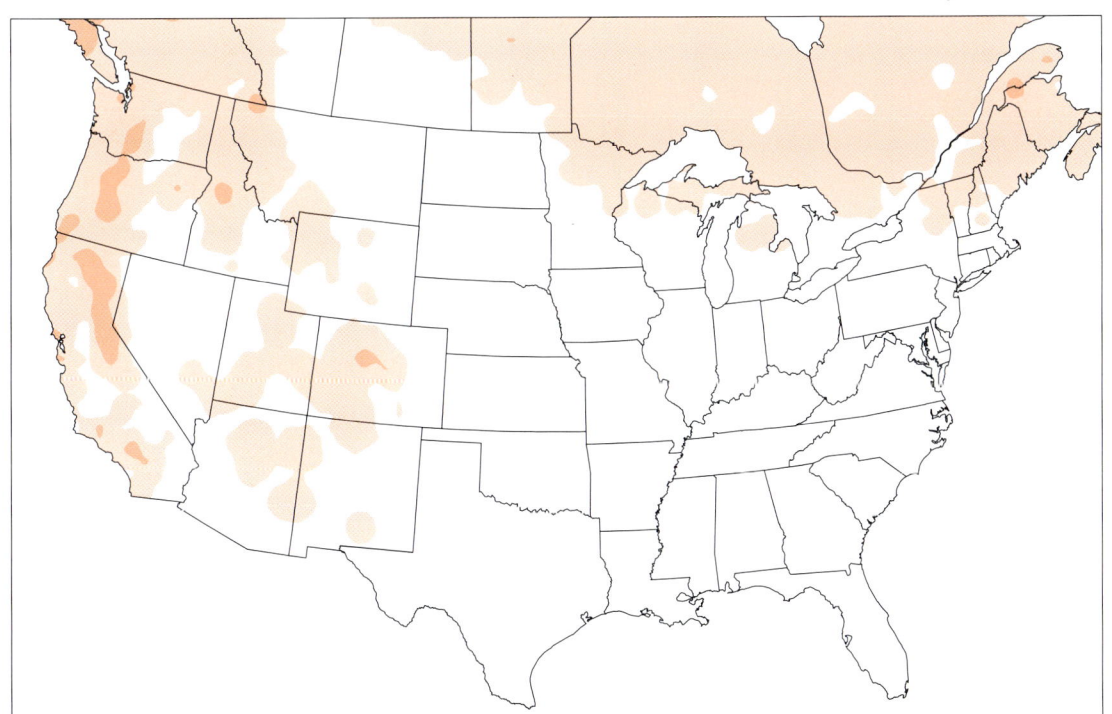

Greater Pewee

Western Wood-Pewee

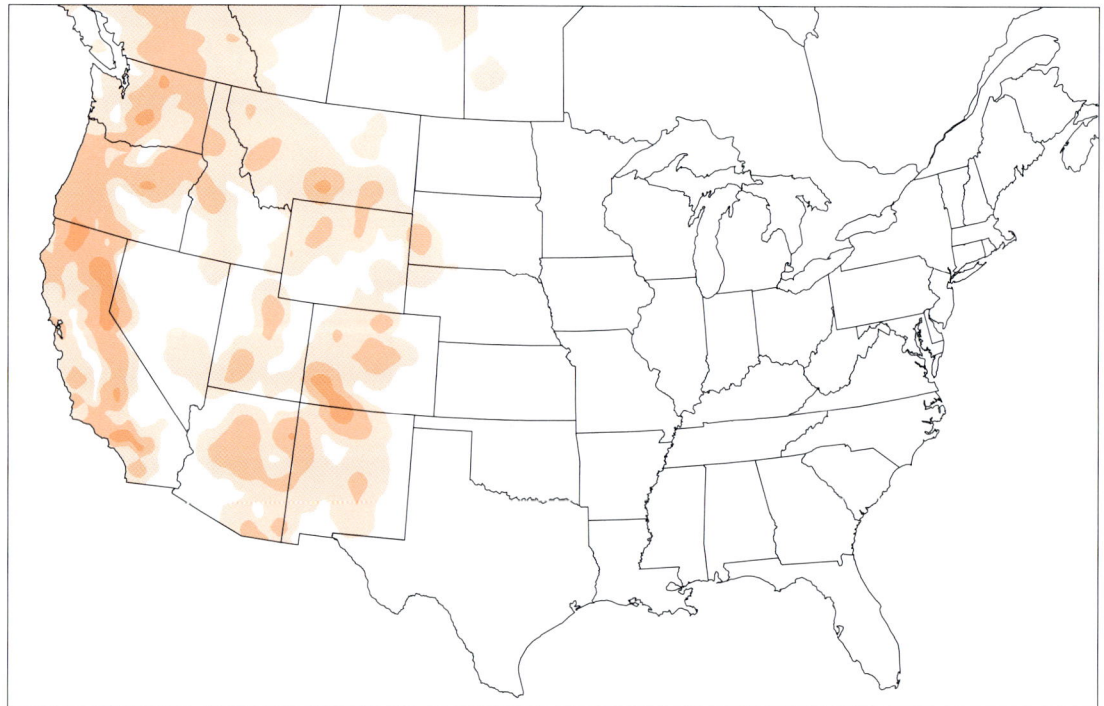

Eastern Wood-Pewee

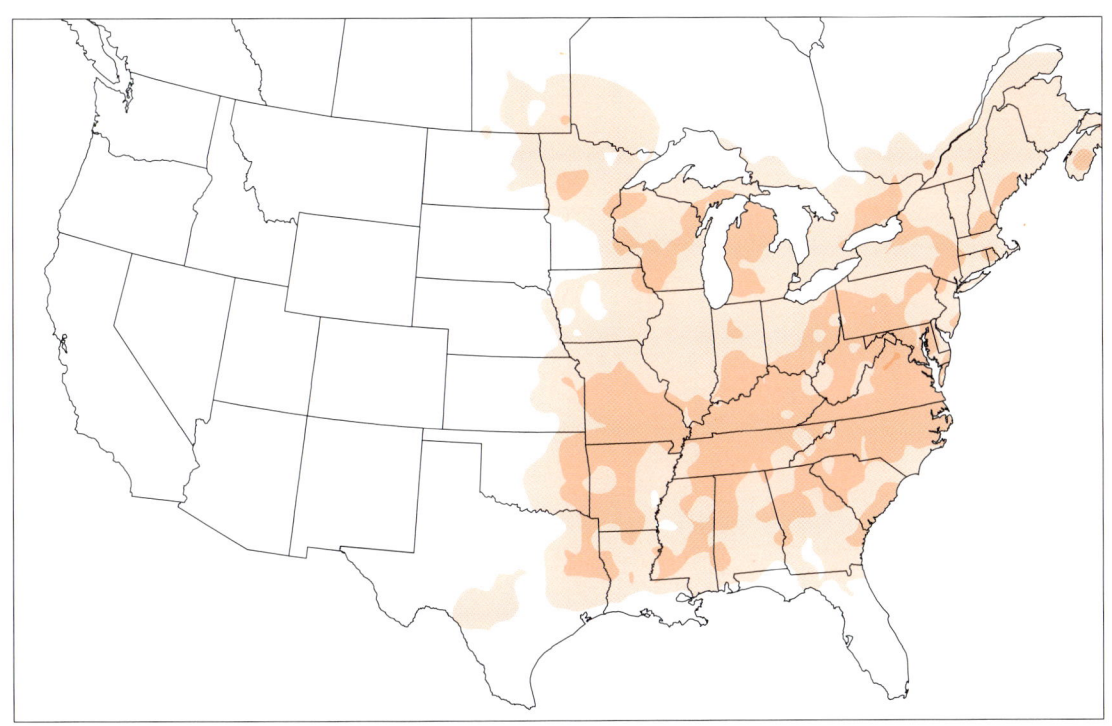

Yellow-bellied Flycatcher

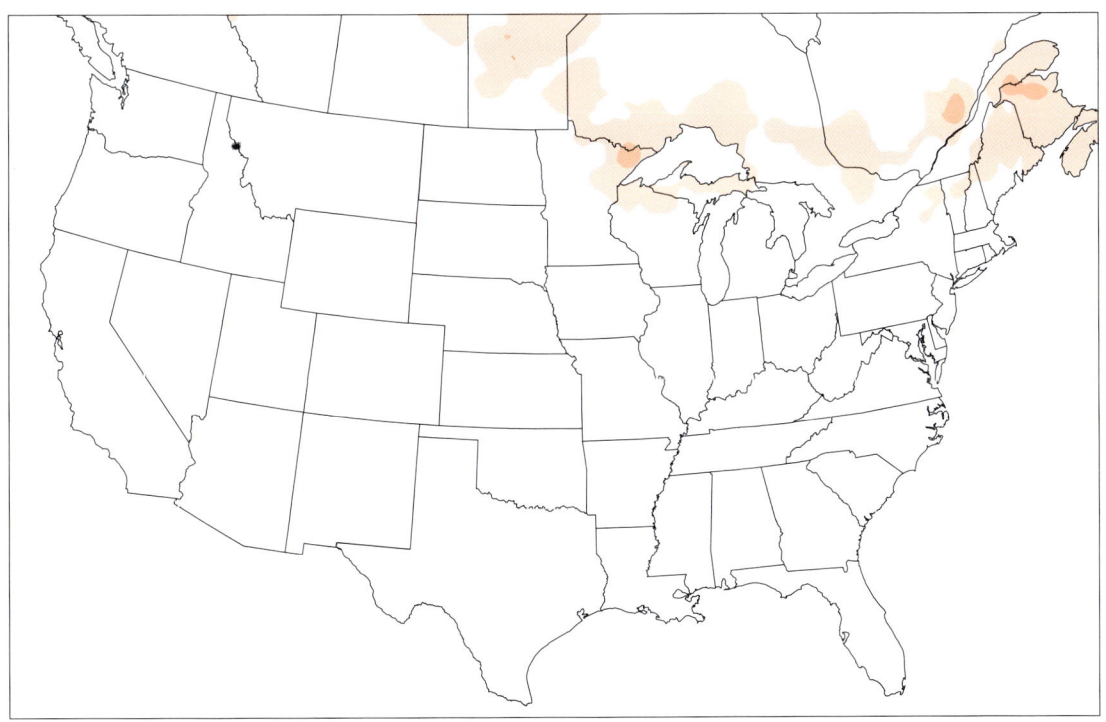

Acadian Flycatcher

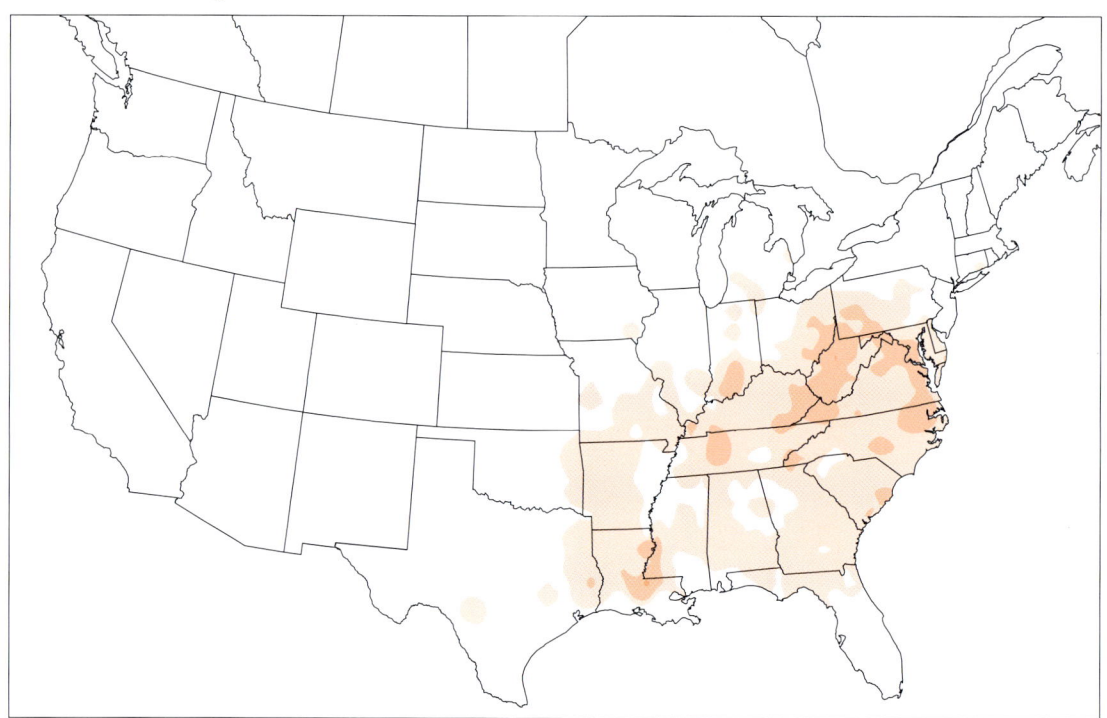

Alder Flycatcher

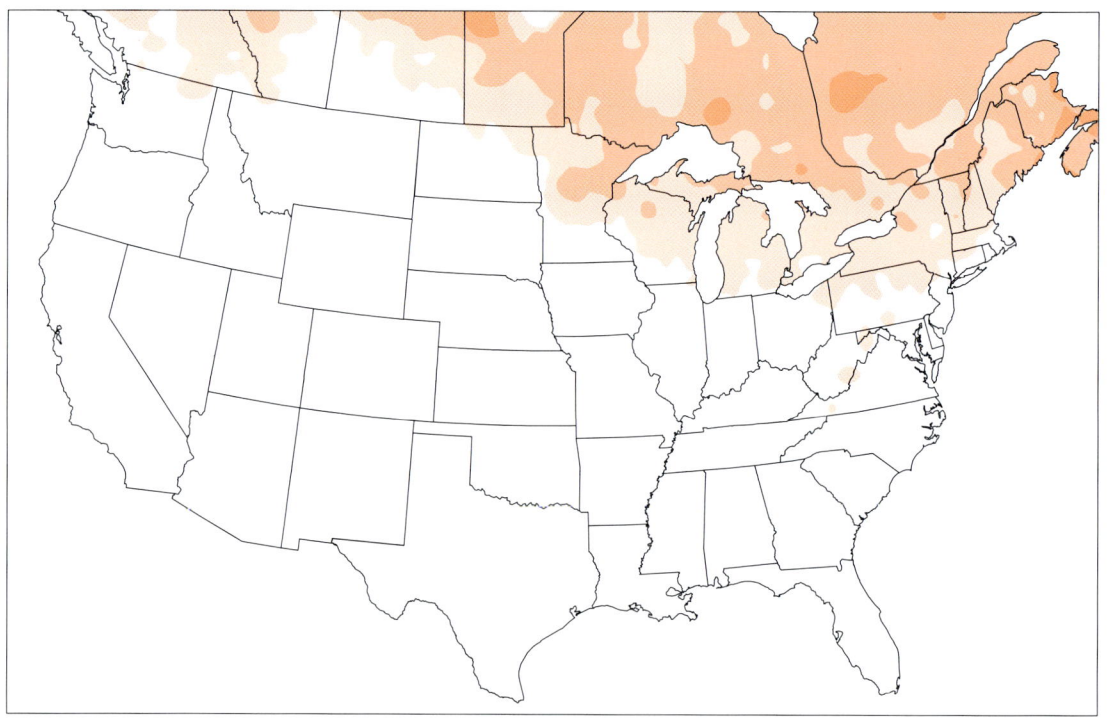

Willow Flycatcher

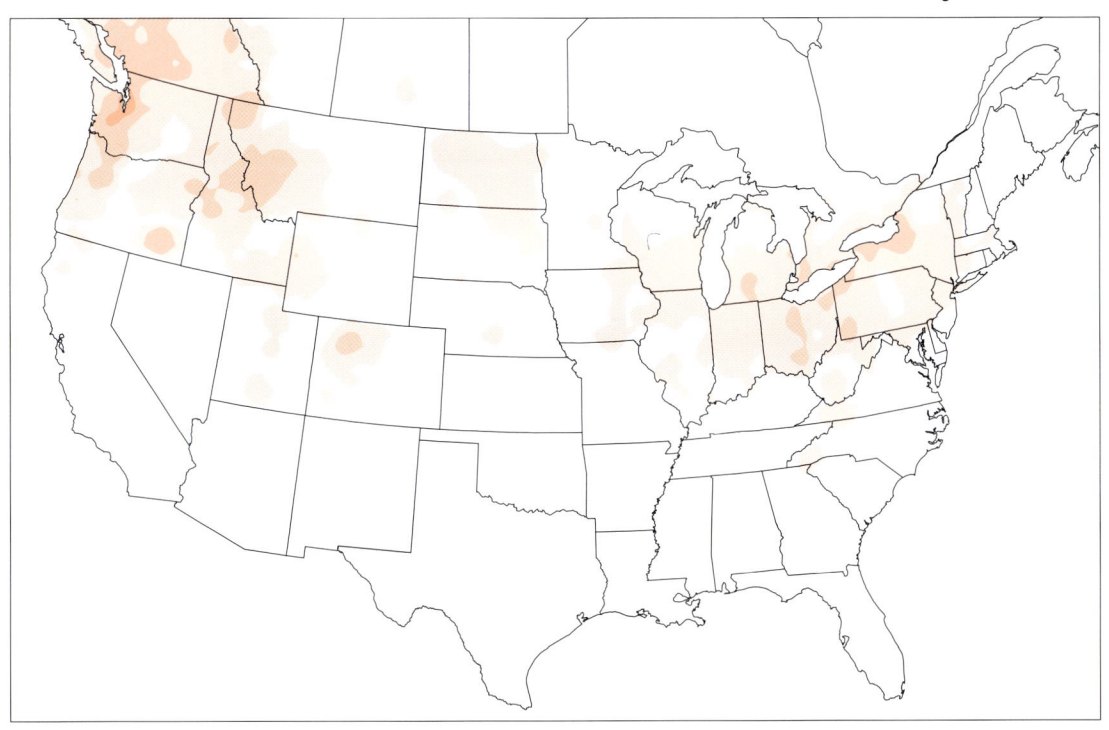

Least Flycatcher

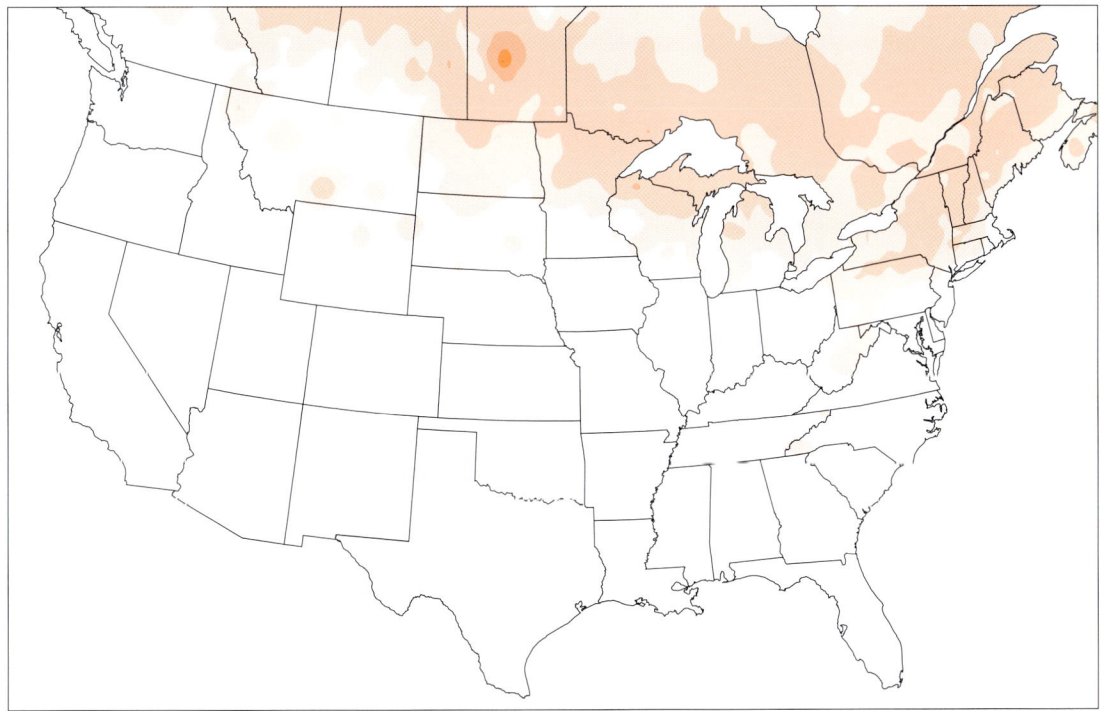

Hammond's Flycatcher

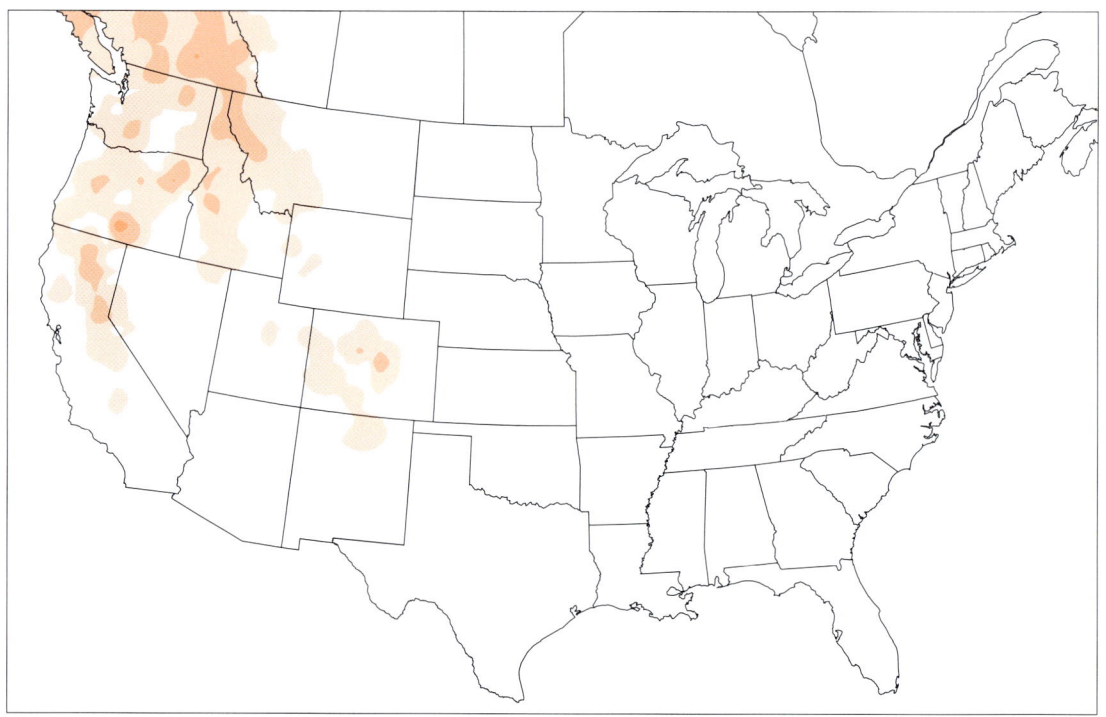

Dusky Flycatcher

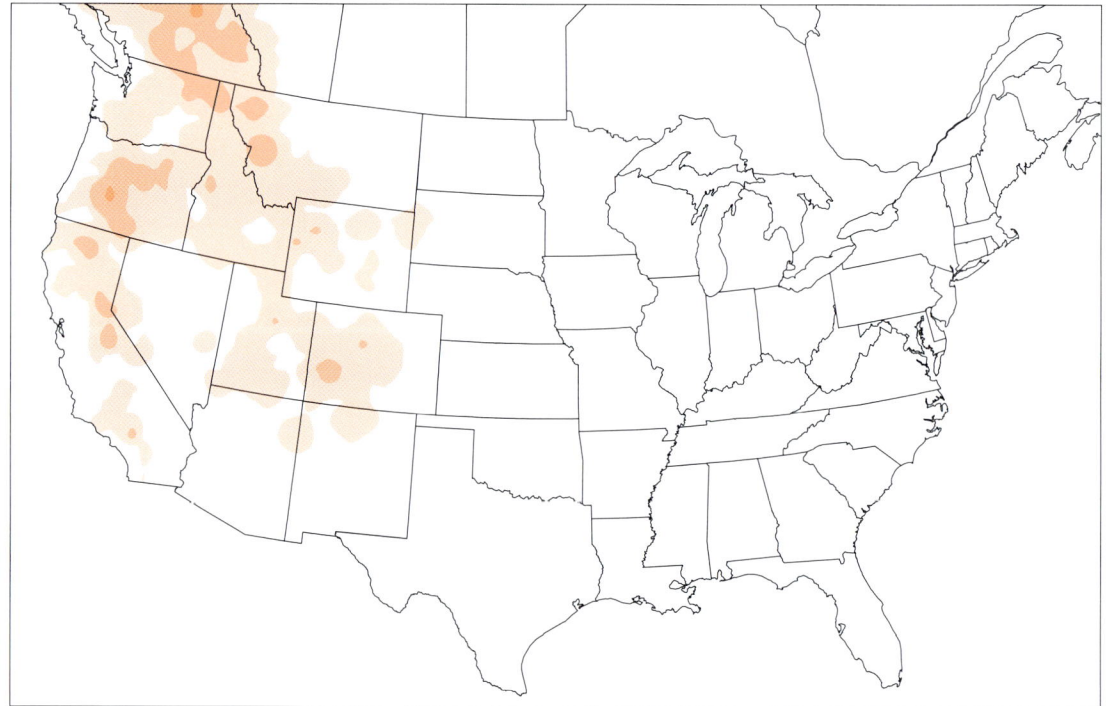

Gray Flycatcher

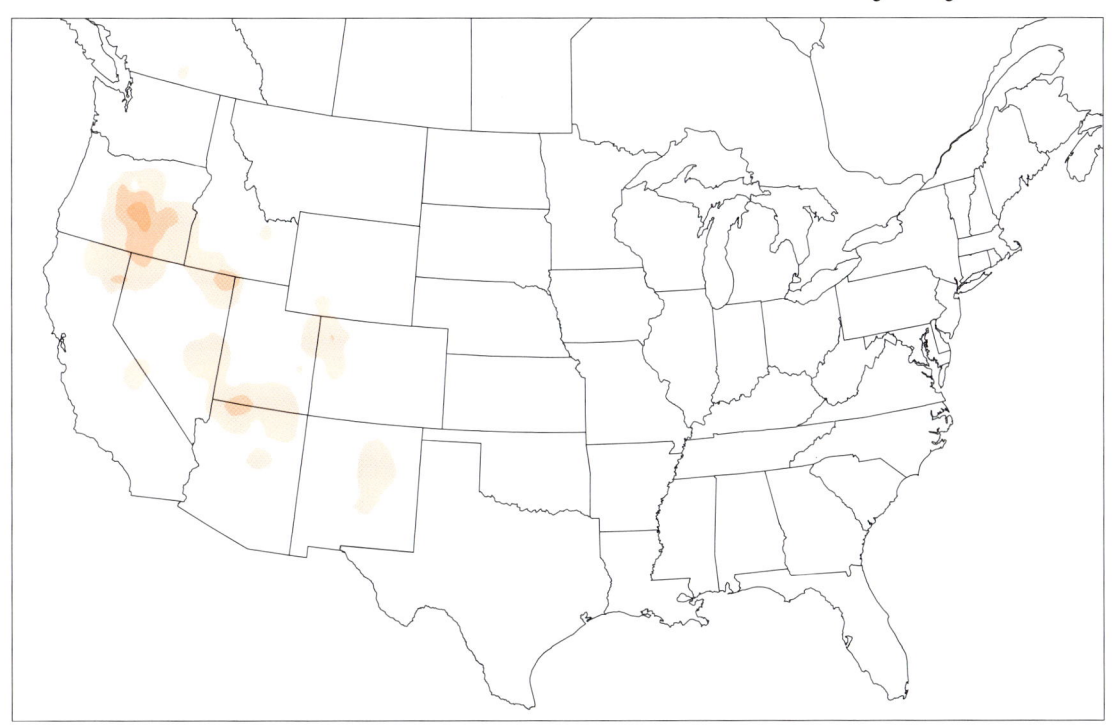

Pacific-slope Flycatcher

Cordilleran Flycatcher

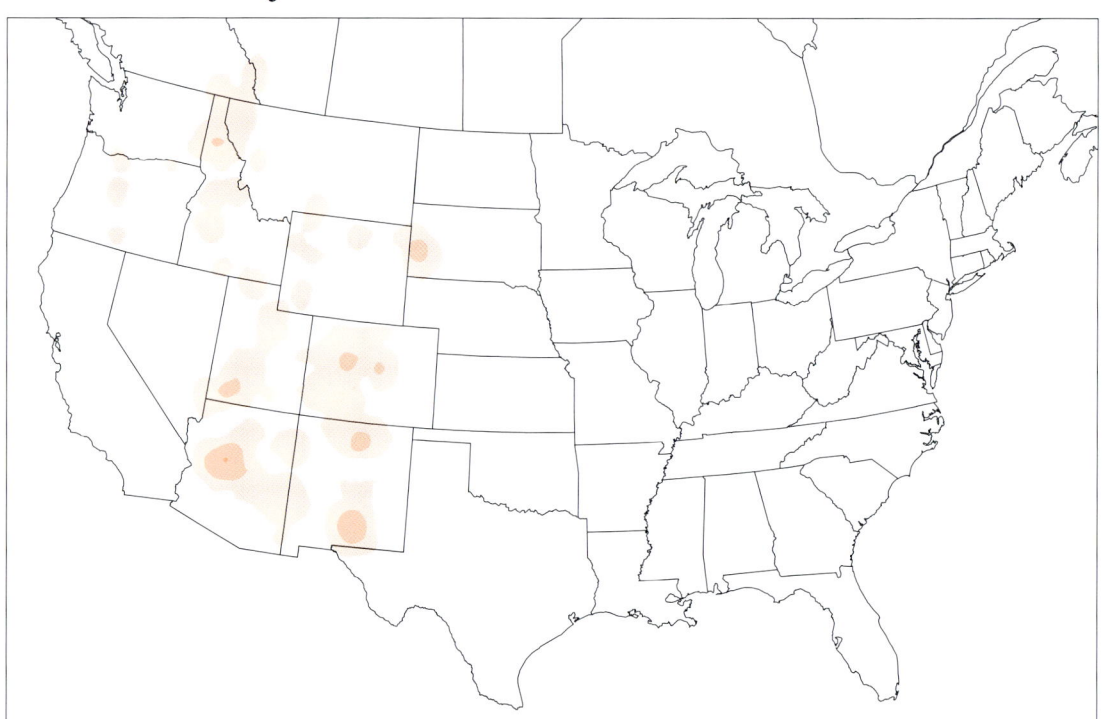

Black Phoebe

Eastern Phoebe

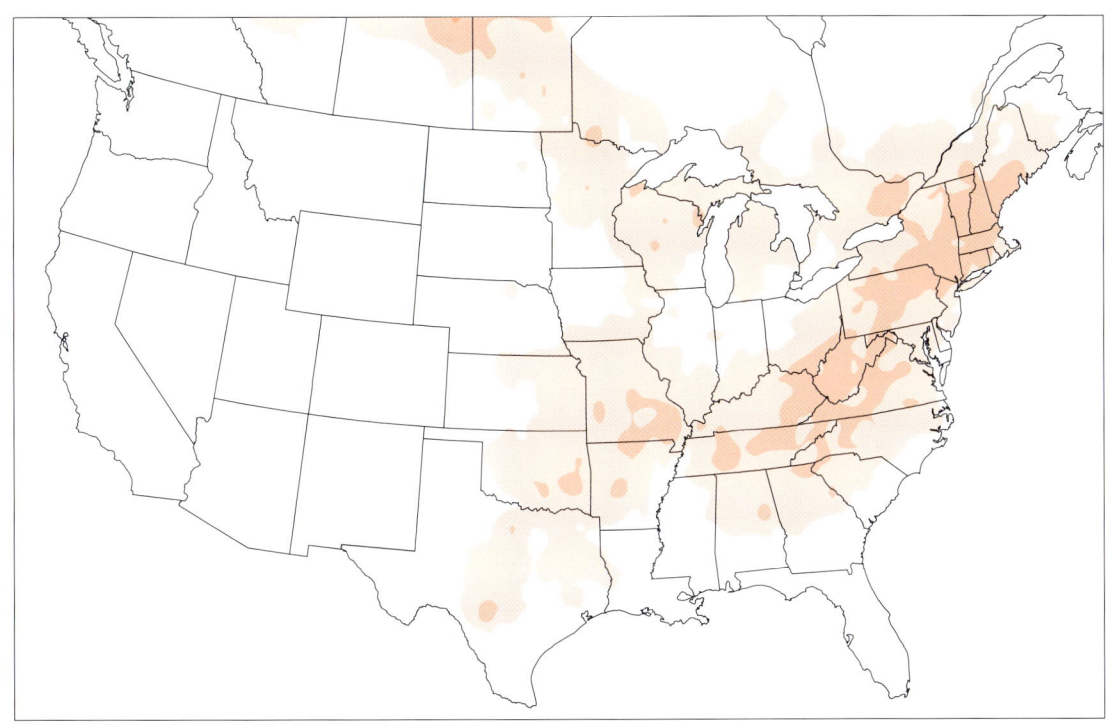

Say's Phoebe

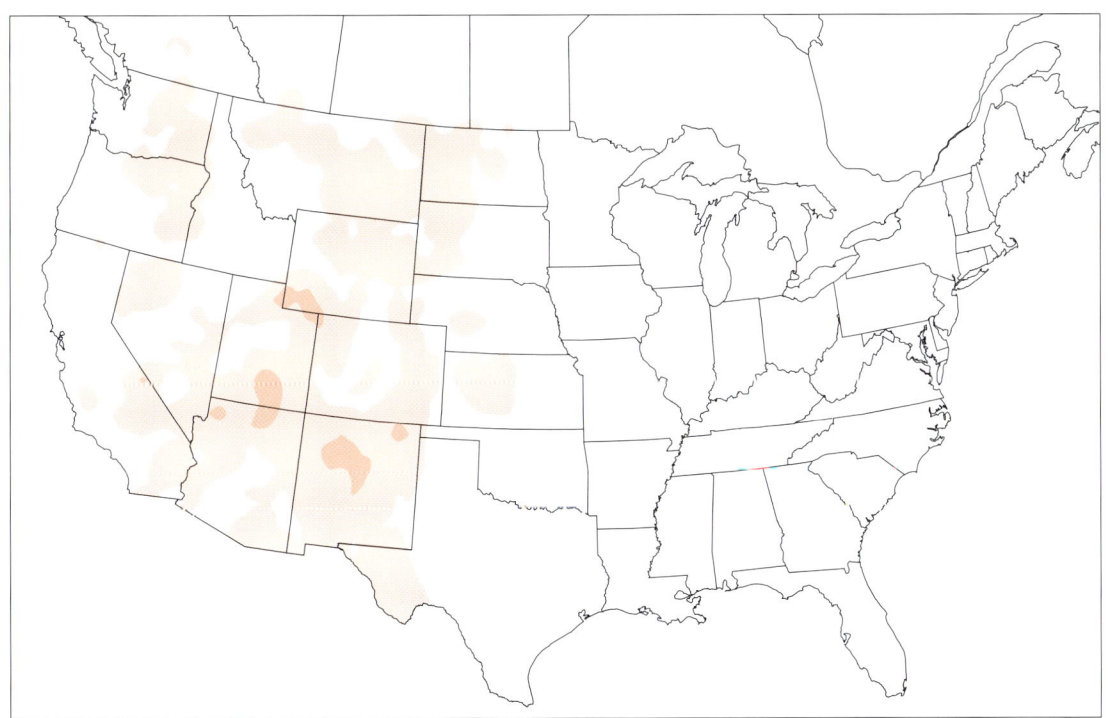

Vermilion Flycatcher

Dusky-capped Flycatcher

Ash-throated Flycatcher

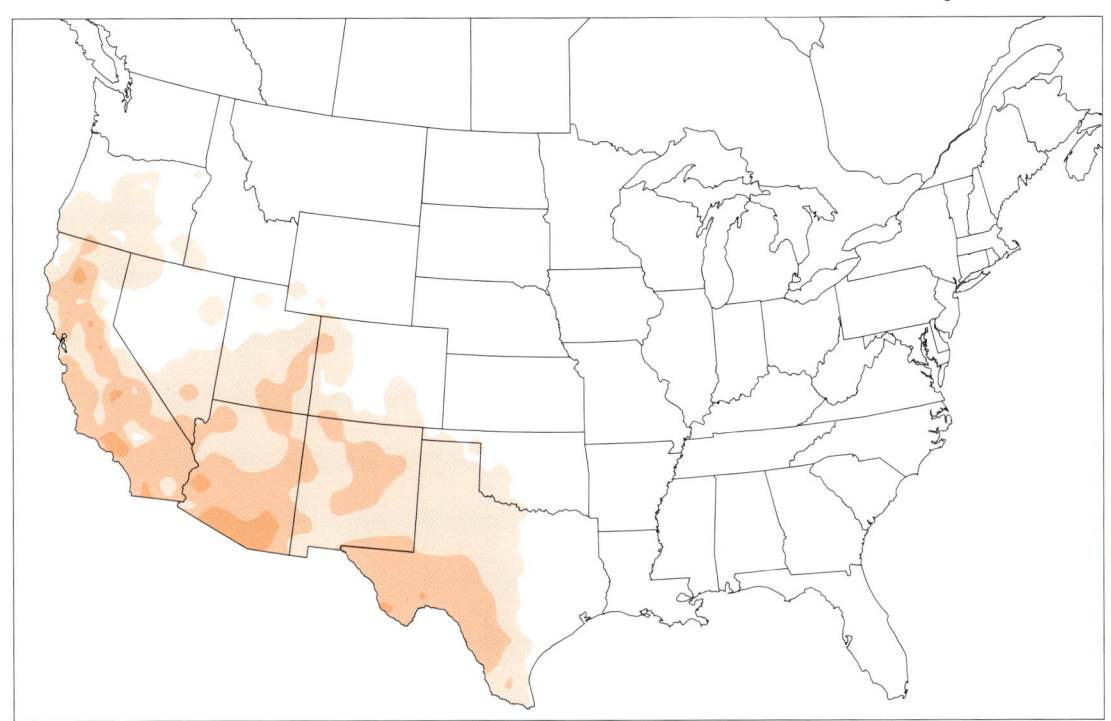

Great Crested Flycatcher

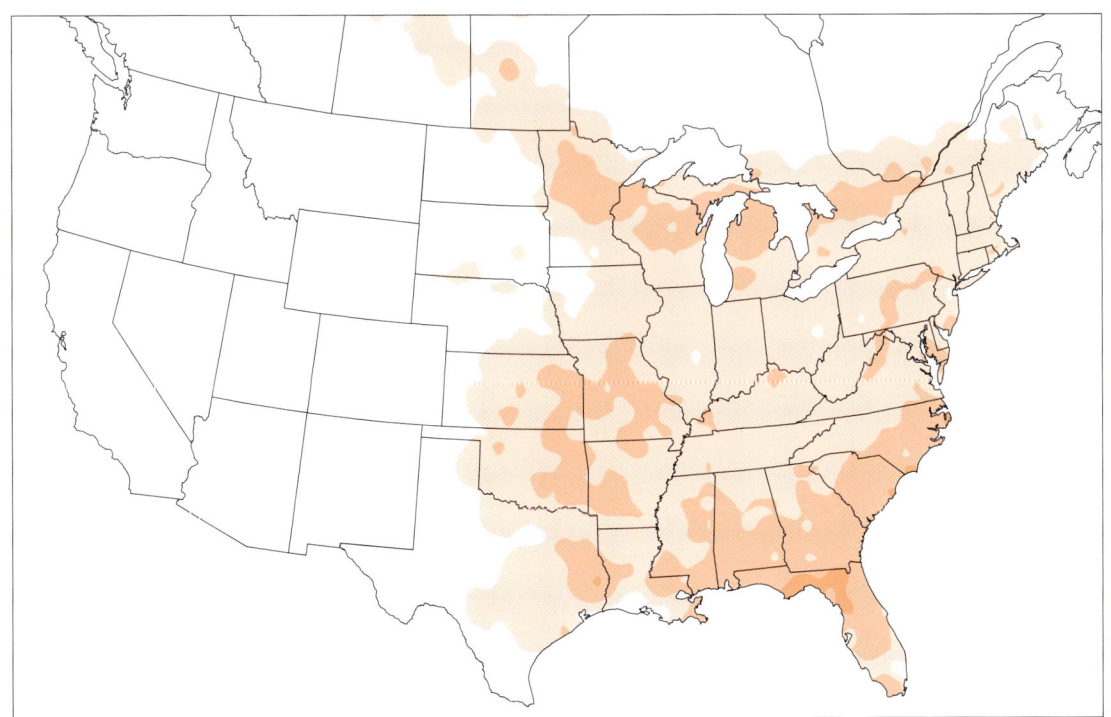

Brown-crested Flycatcher

Great Kiskadee

Sulphur-bellied Flycatcher

Couch's Kingbird

Cassin's Kingbird

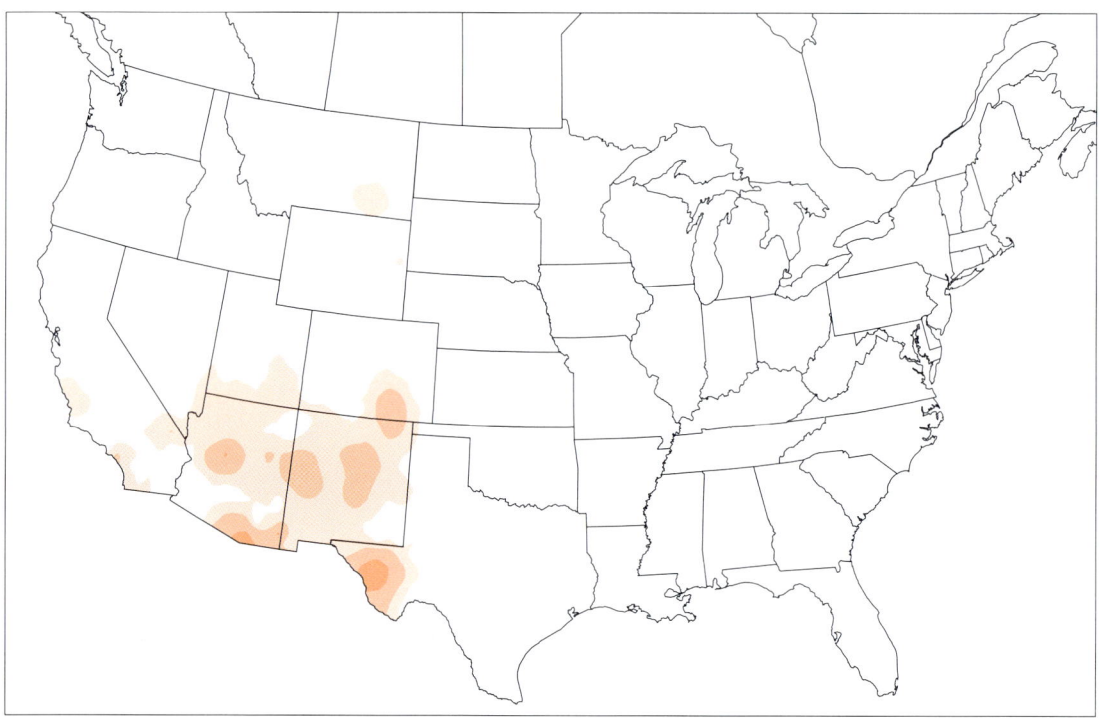

Thick-billed Kingbird

Western Kingbird

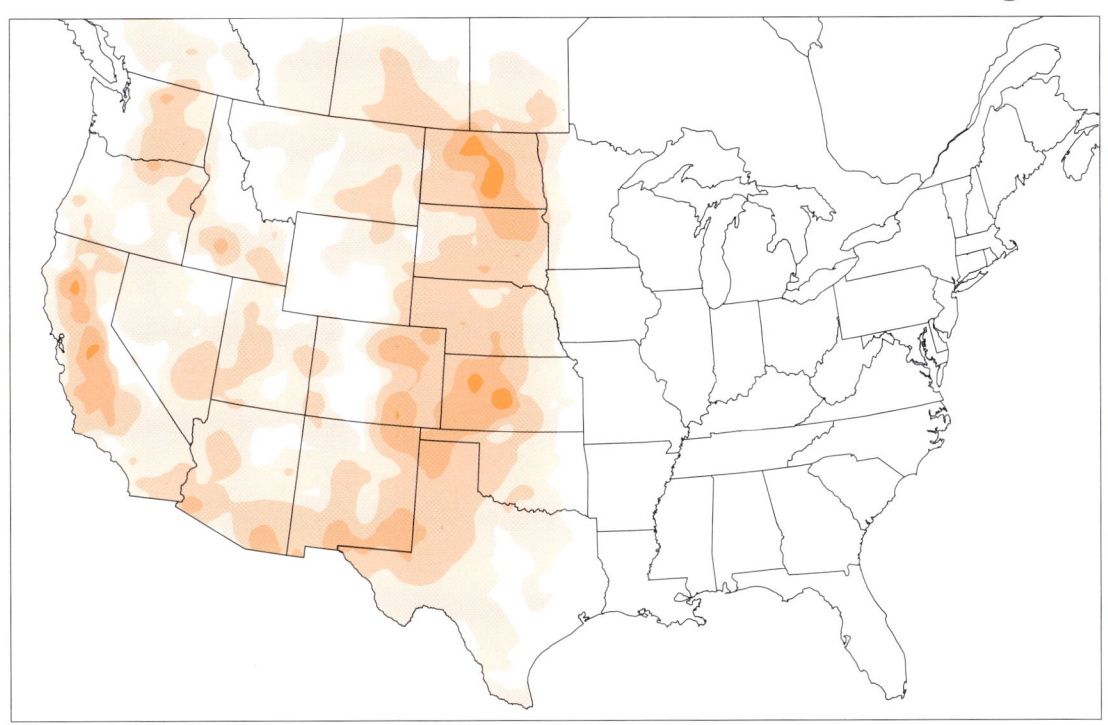

Eastern Kingbird

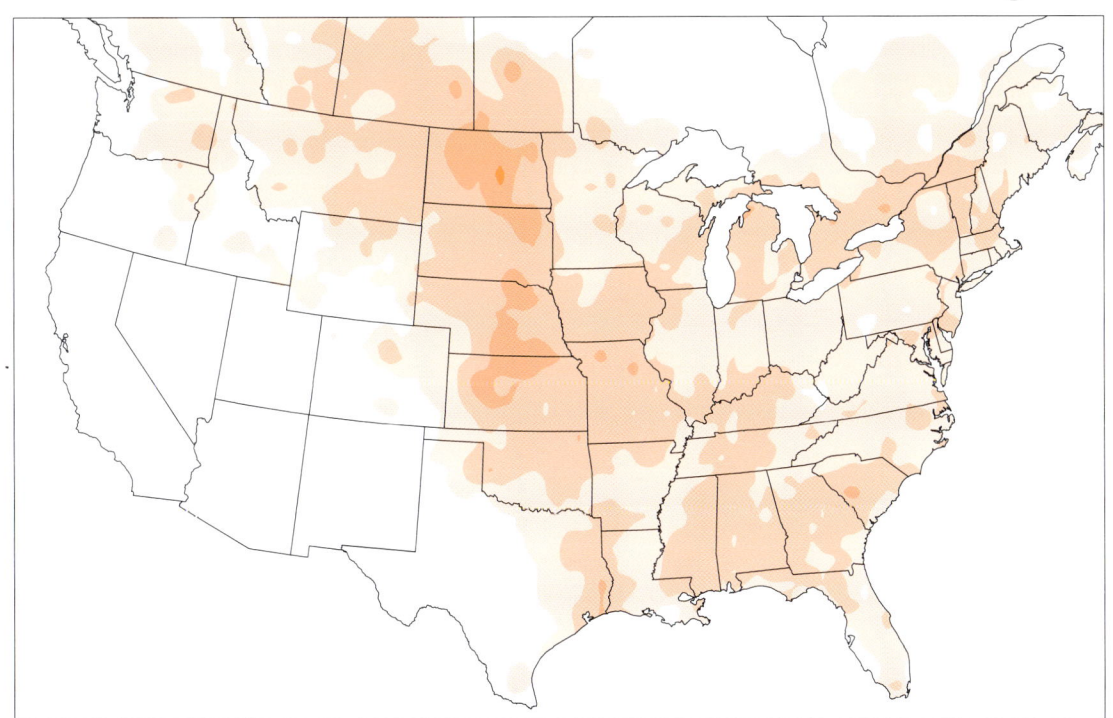

Gray Kingbird

Scissor-tailed Flycatcher

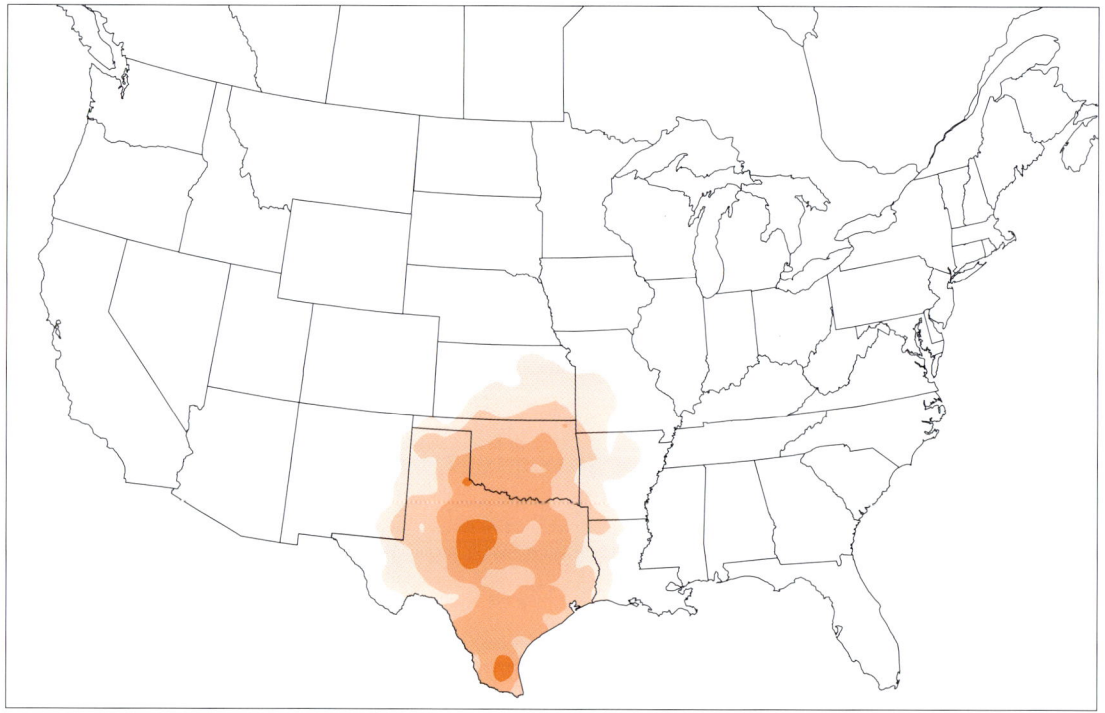

Horned Lark

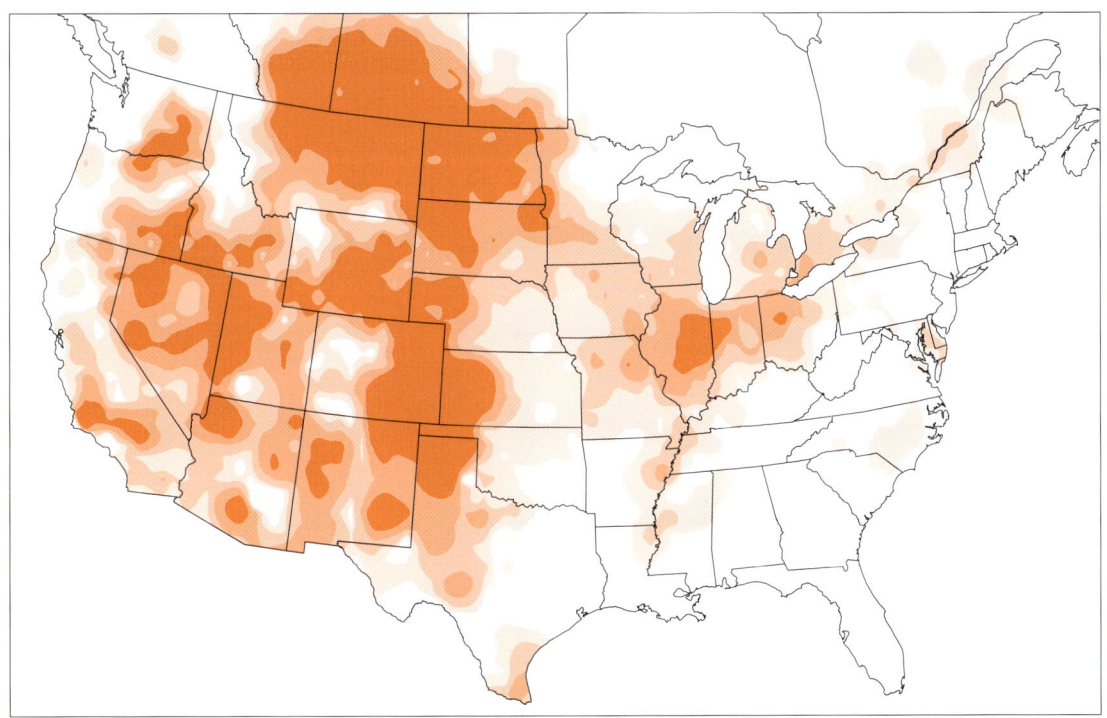

Purple Martin

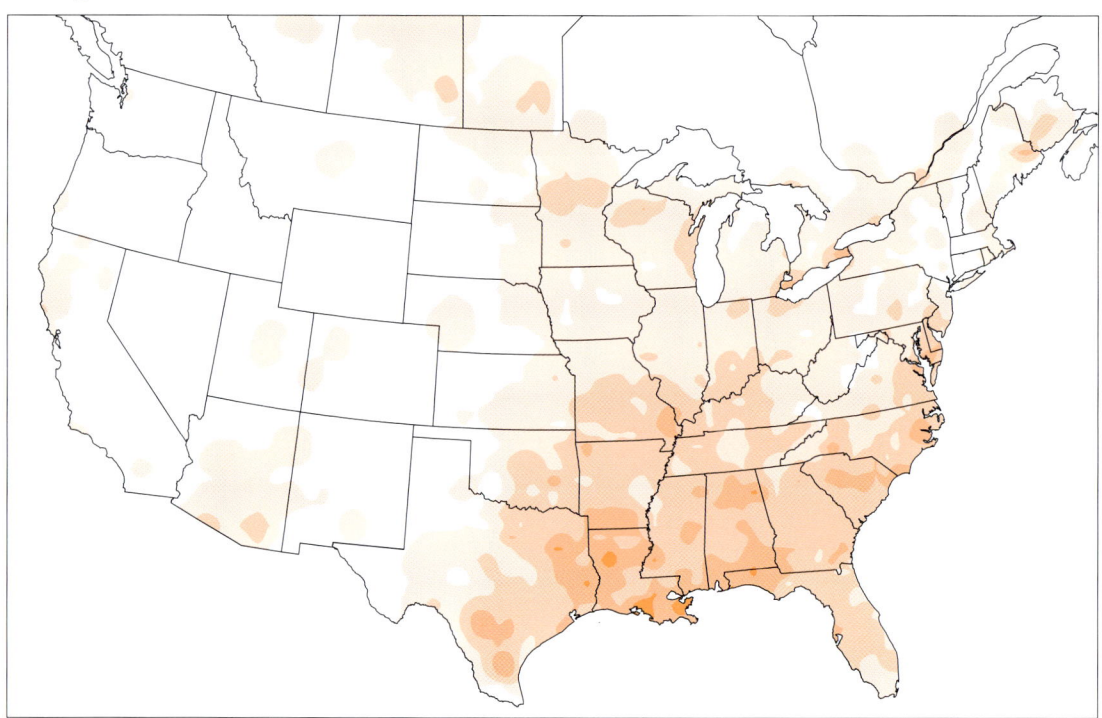

Tree Swallow

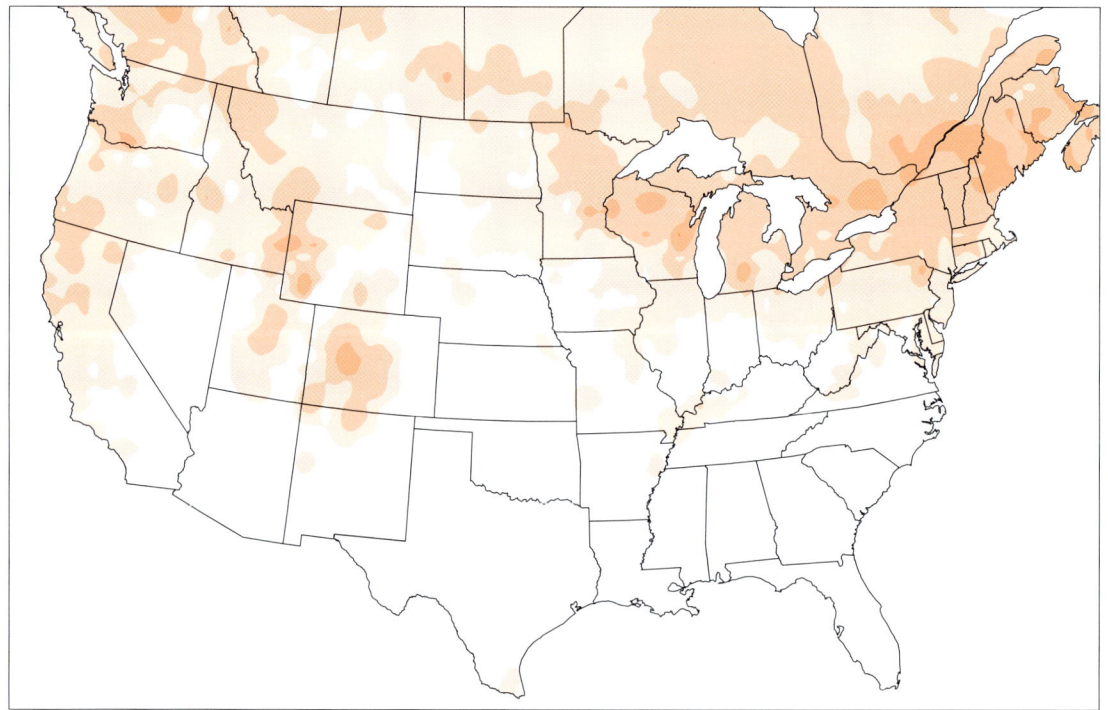

Violet-green Swallow

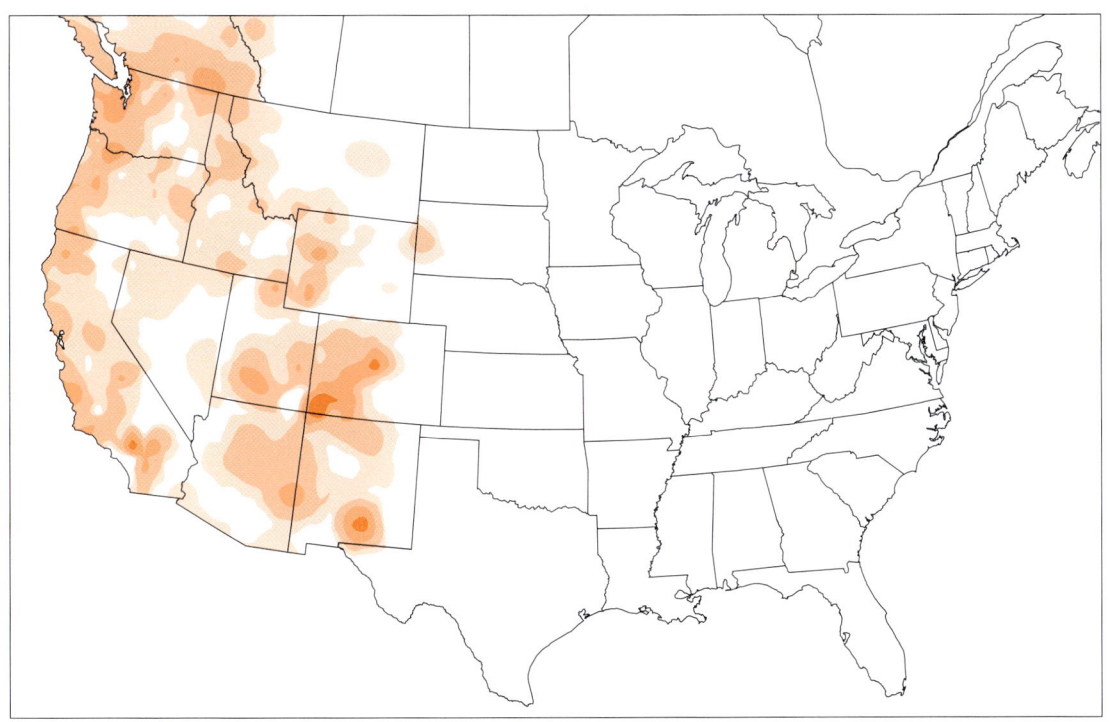

Northern Rough-winged Swallow

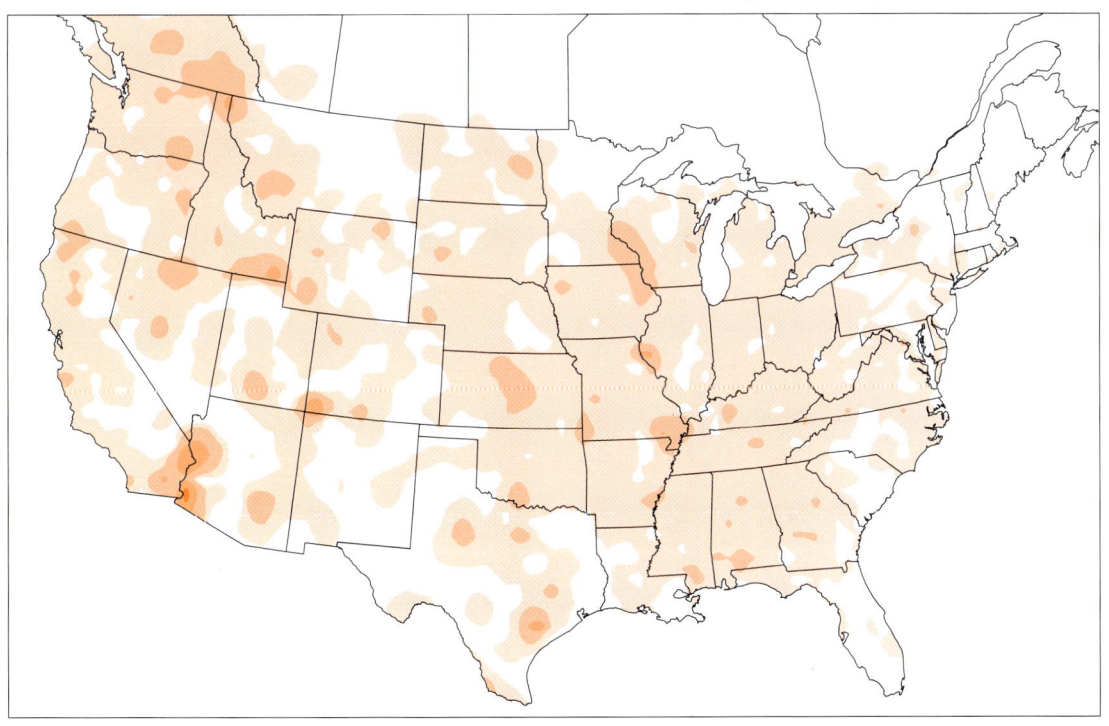

Bank Swallow

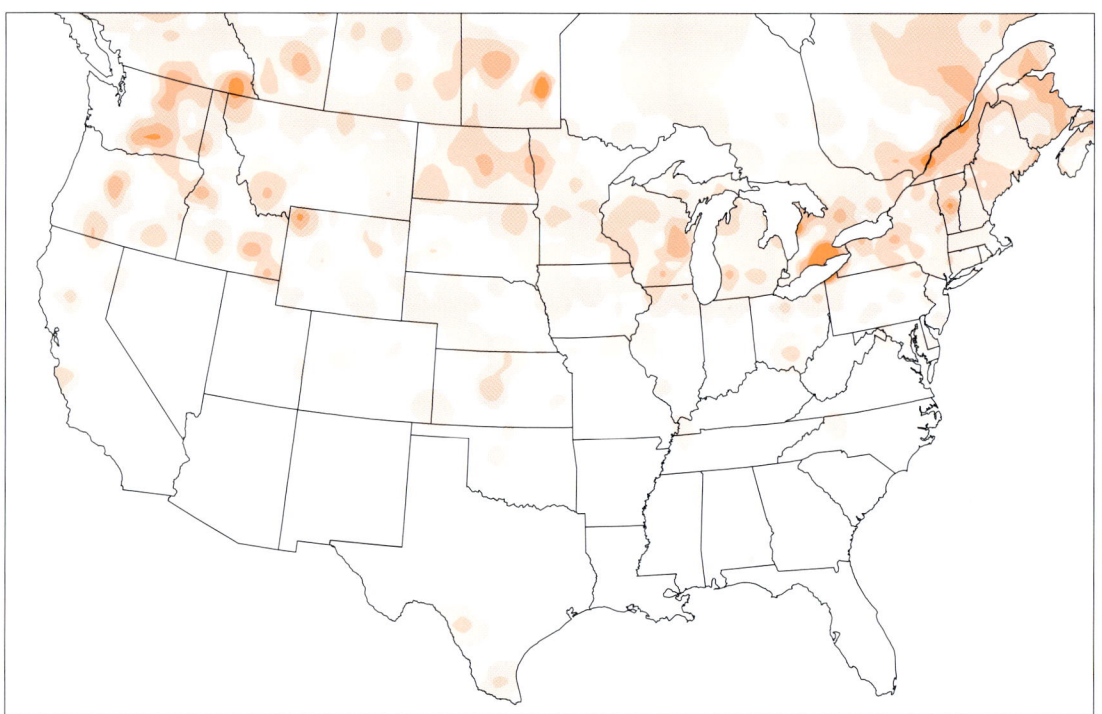

Cliff Swallow

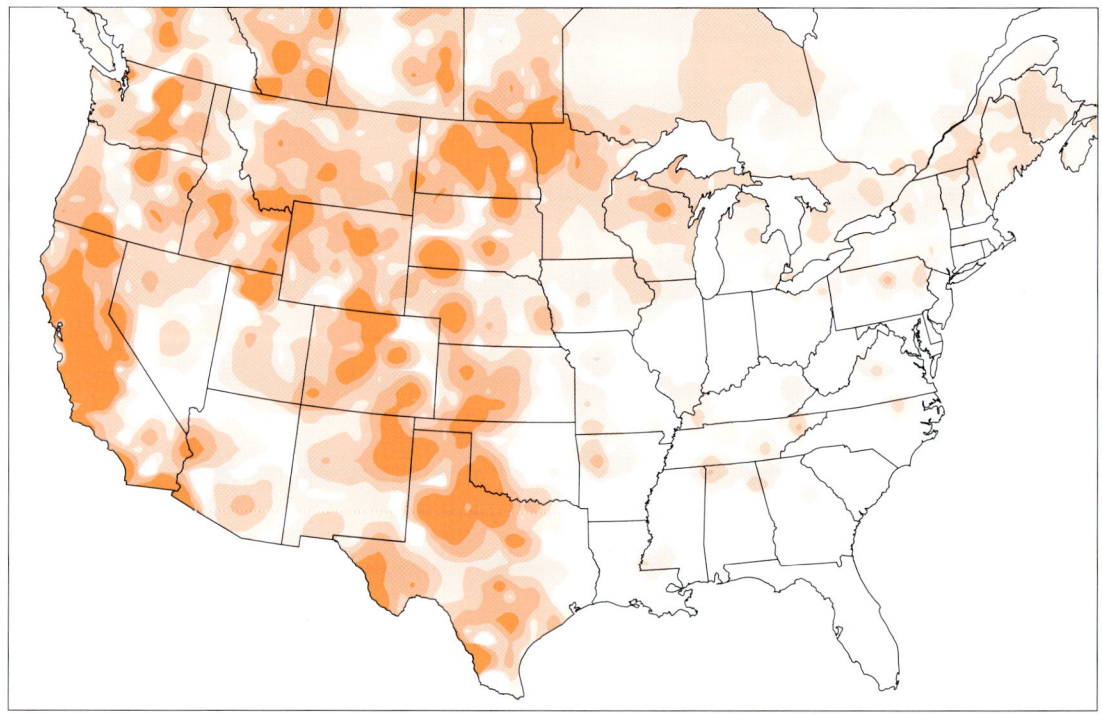

Cave Swallow

Barn Swallow

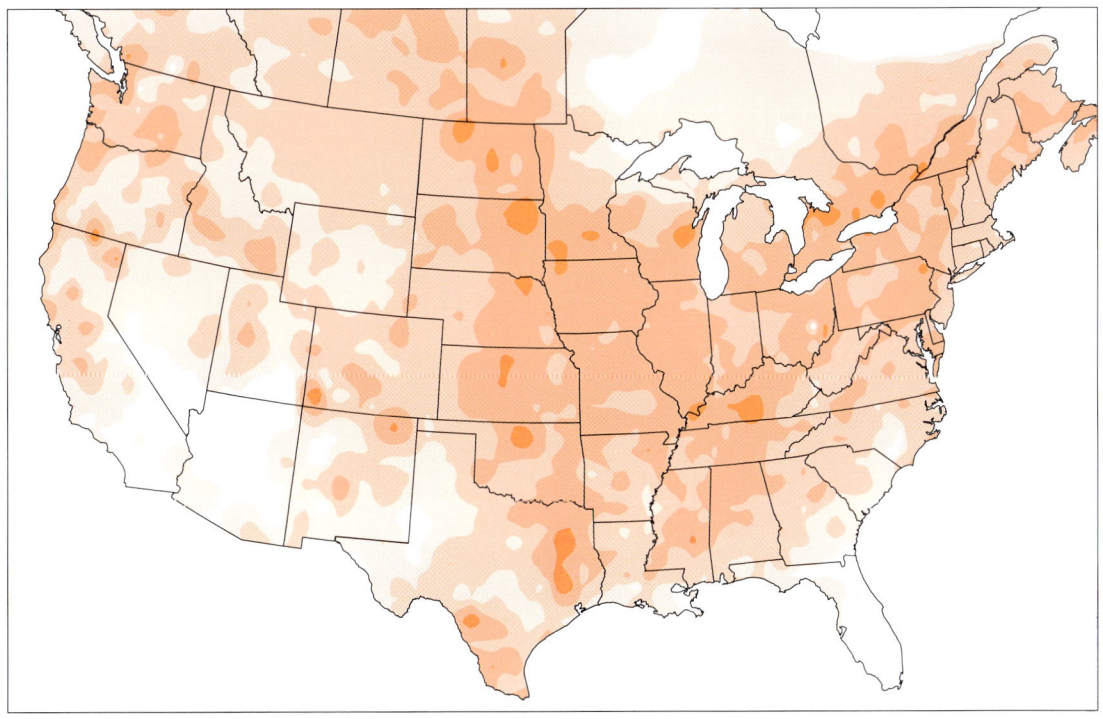

Gray Jay

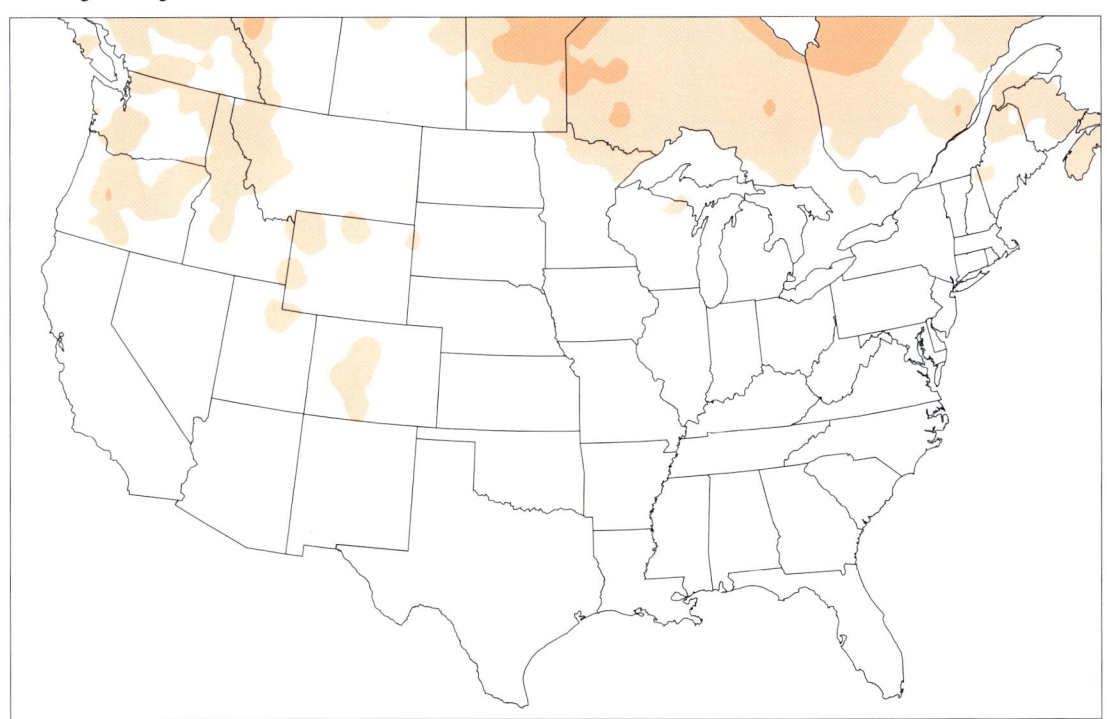

Steller's Jay

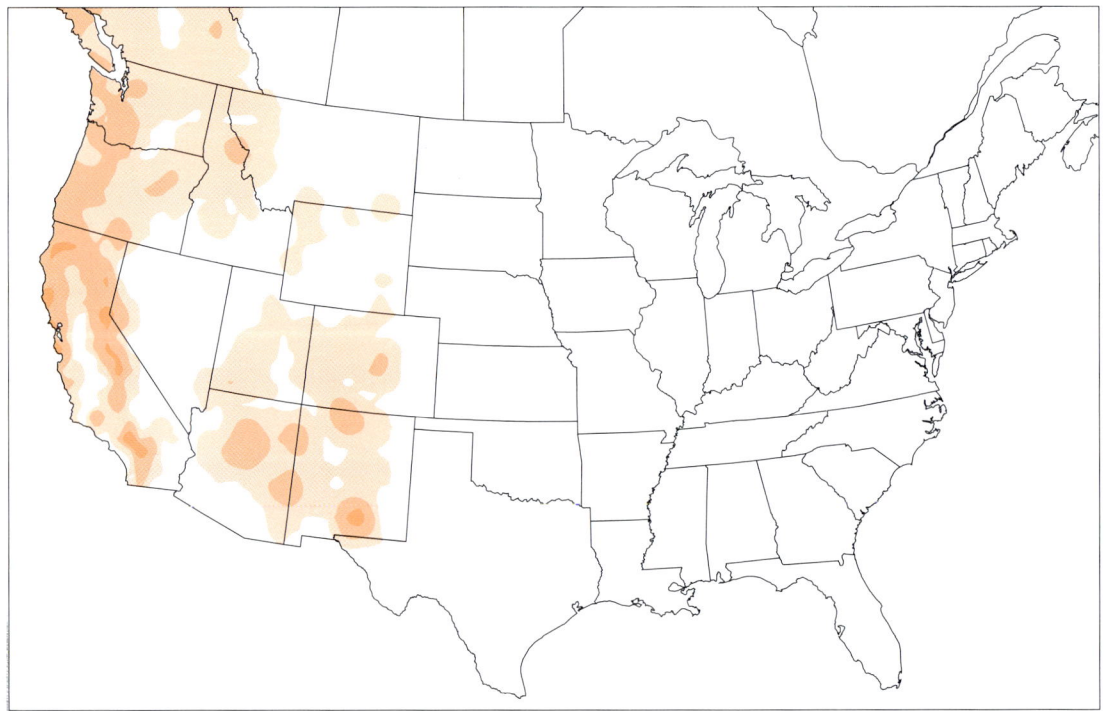

Blue Jay

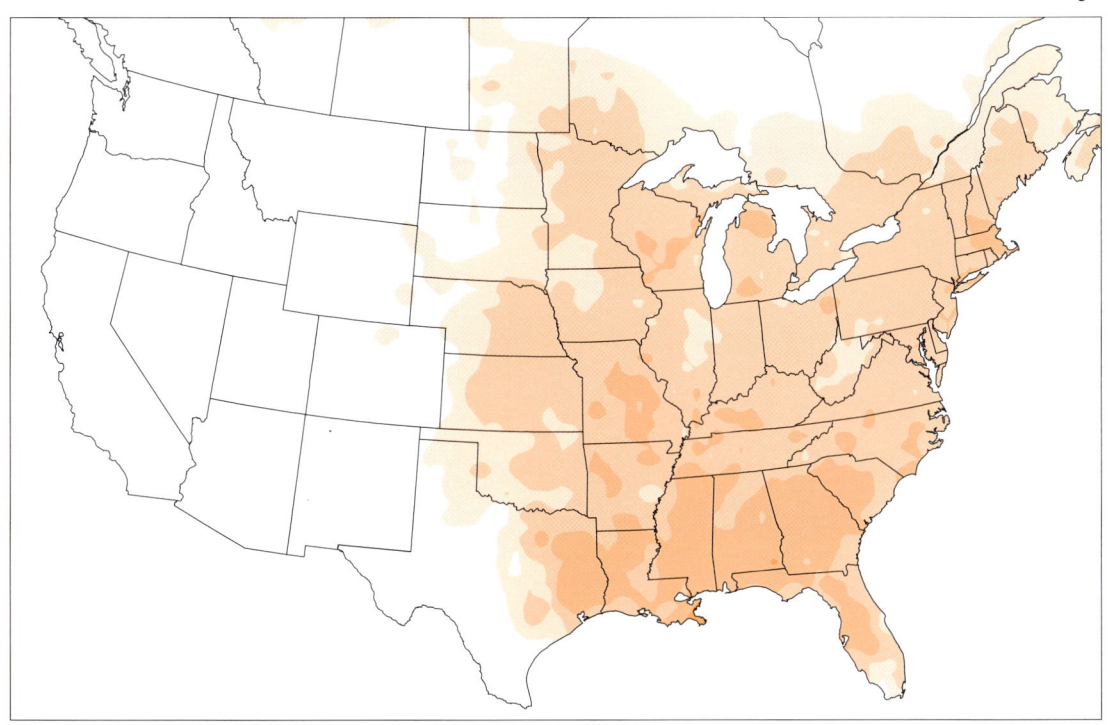

Green Jay

Scrub Jay

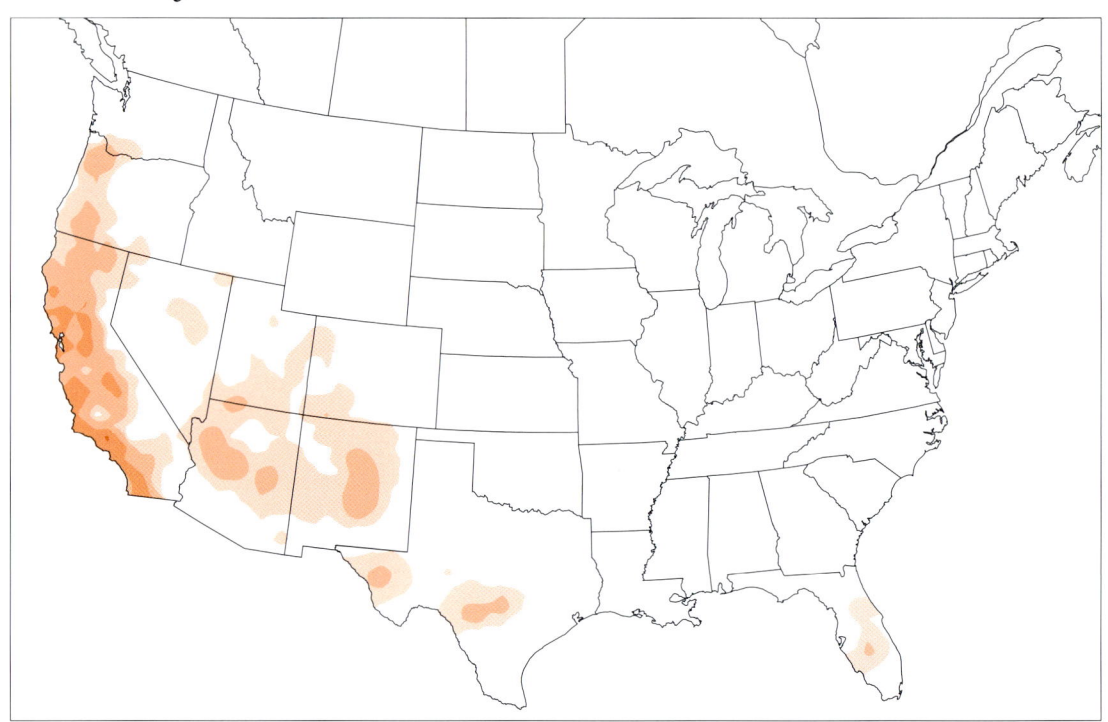

Scrub Jay (Florida)

Gray-breasted Jay

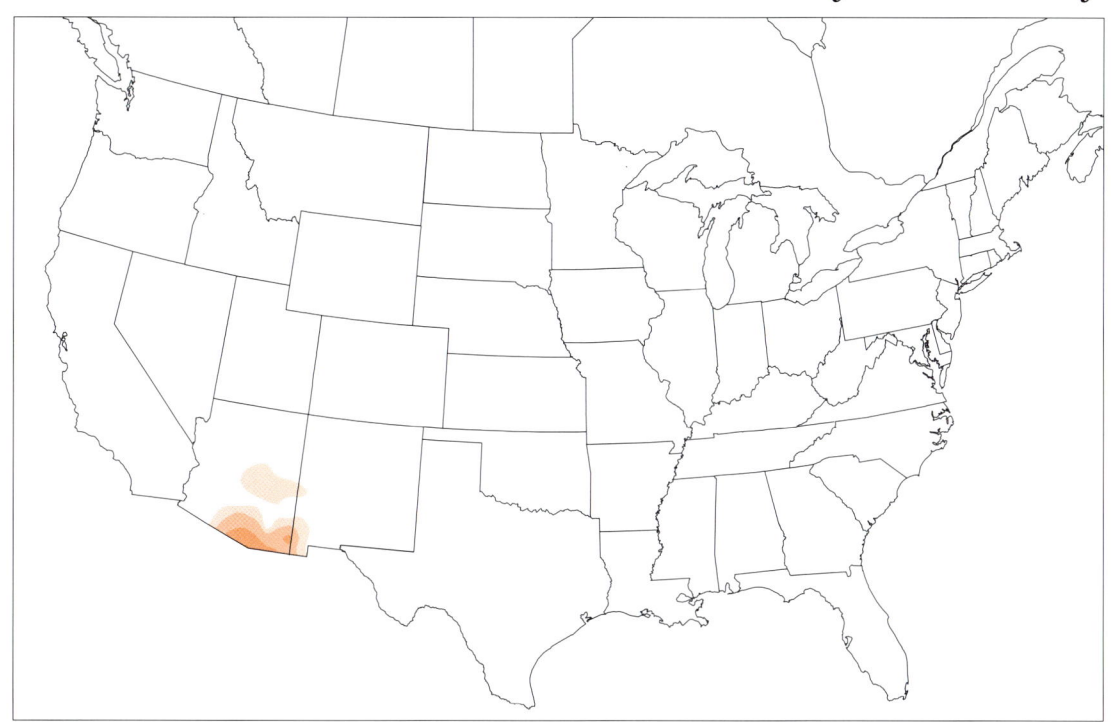

Pinyon Jay

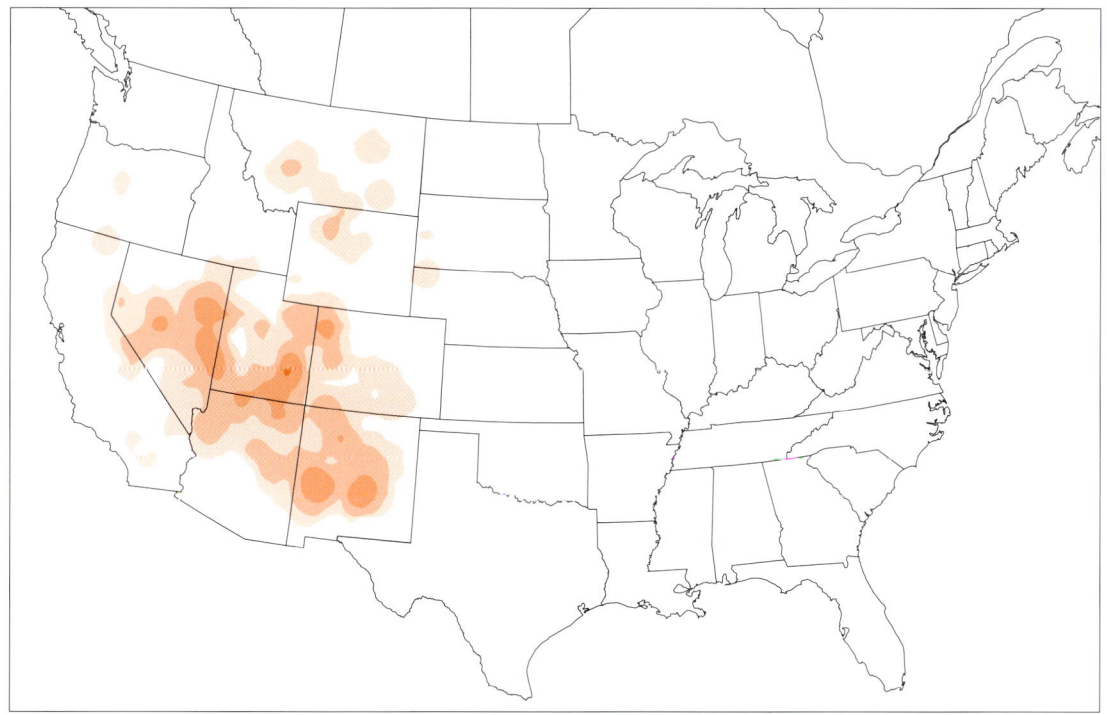

Clark's Nutcracker

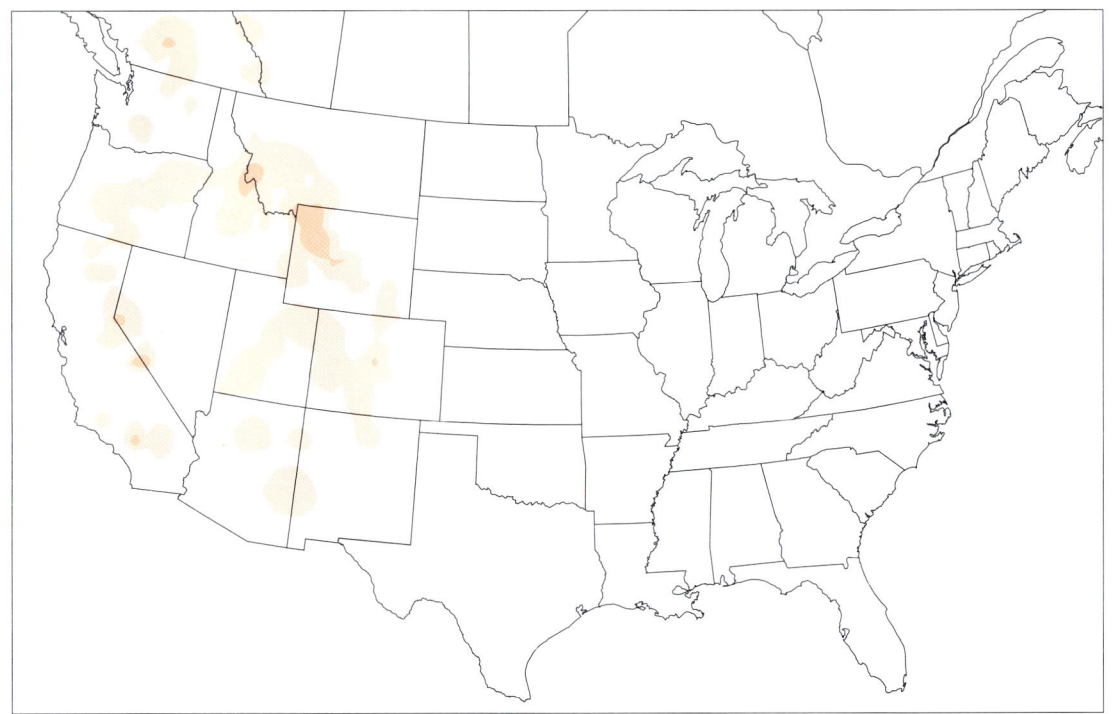

Black-billed Magpie

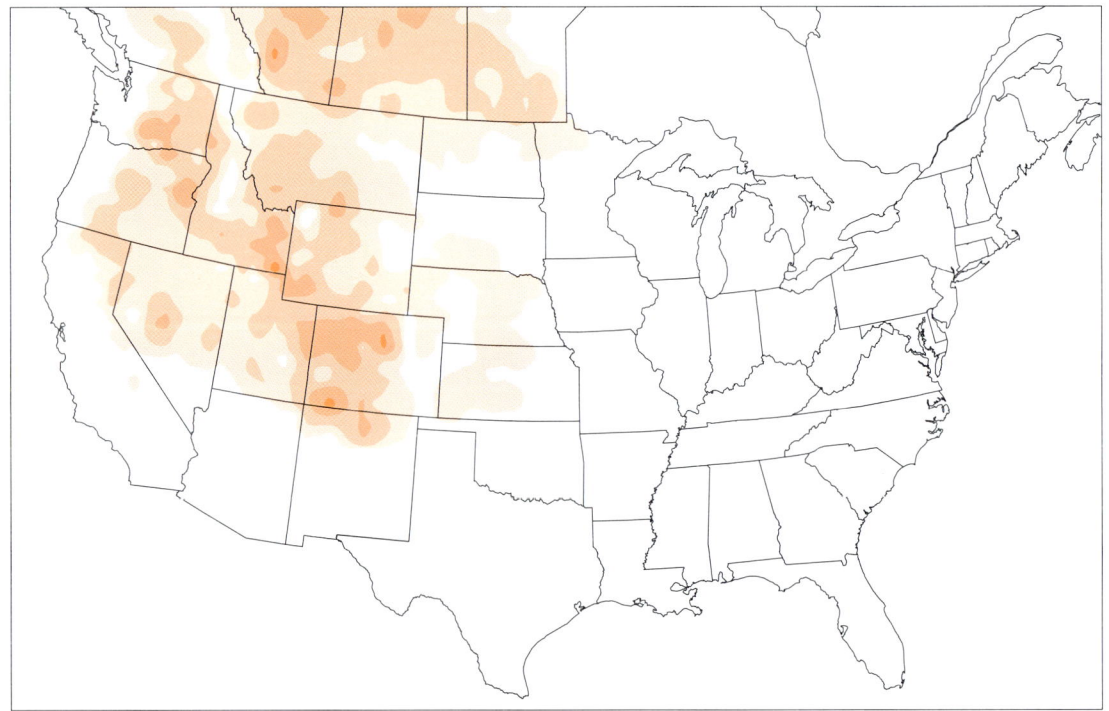

Yellow-billed Magpie

American Crow

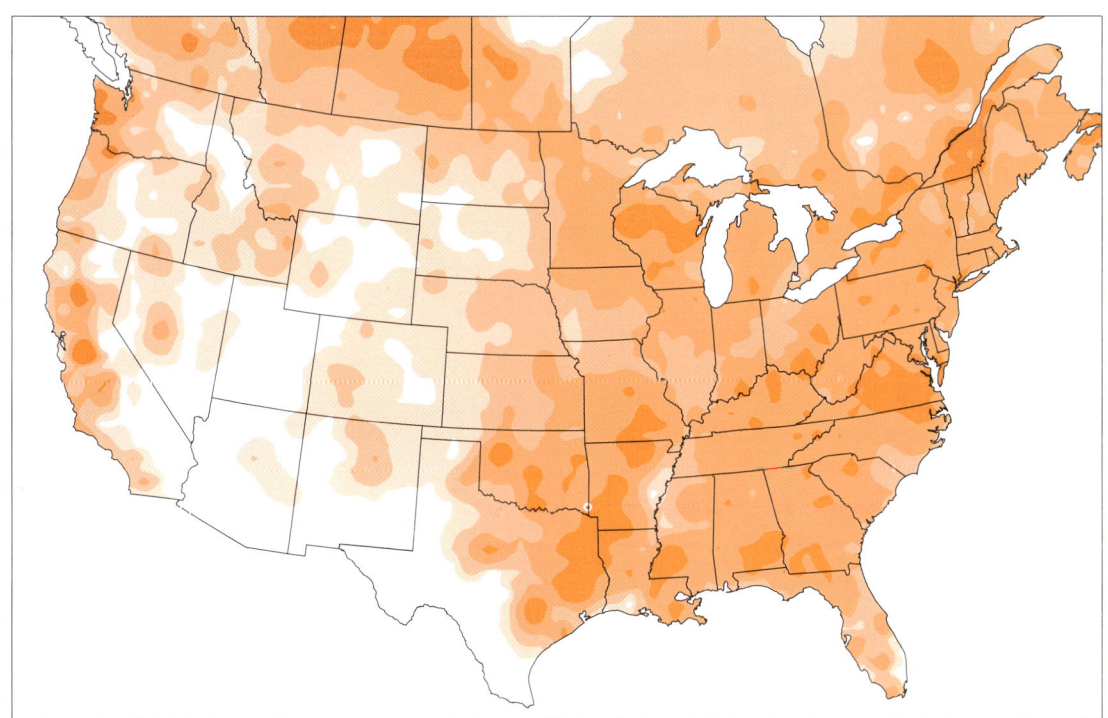

Northwestern Crow

Fish Crow

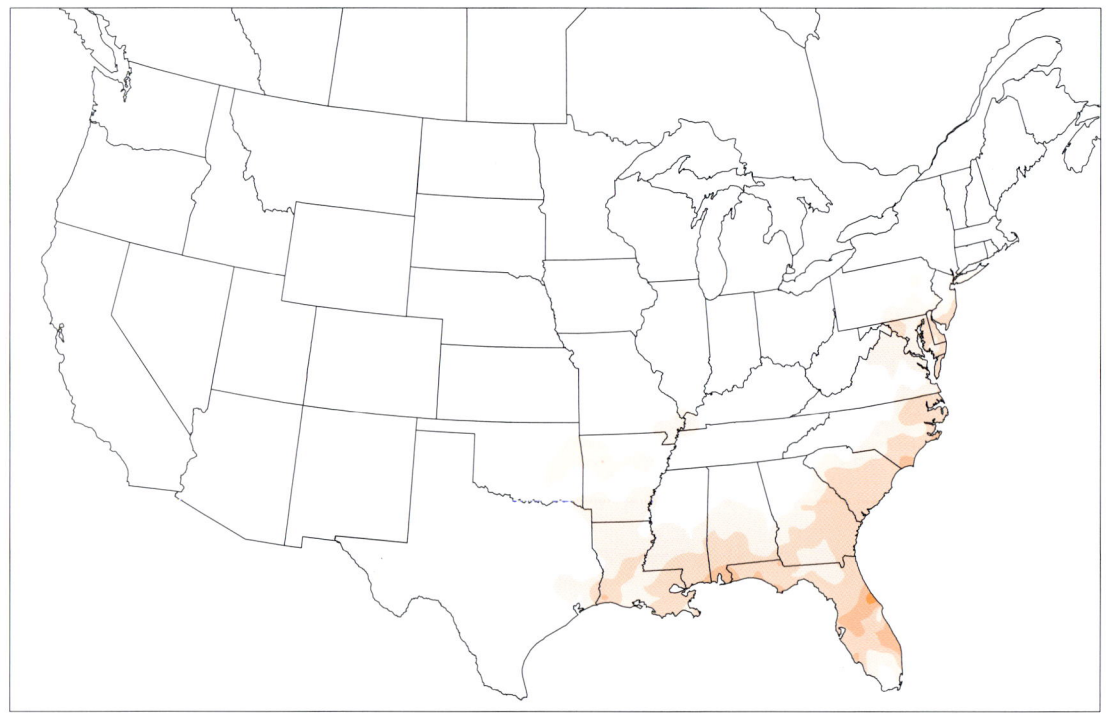

Chihuahuan Raven

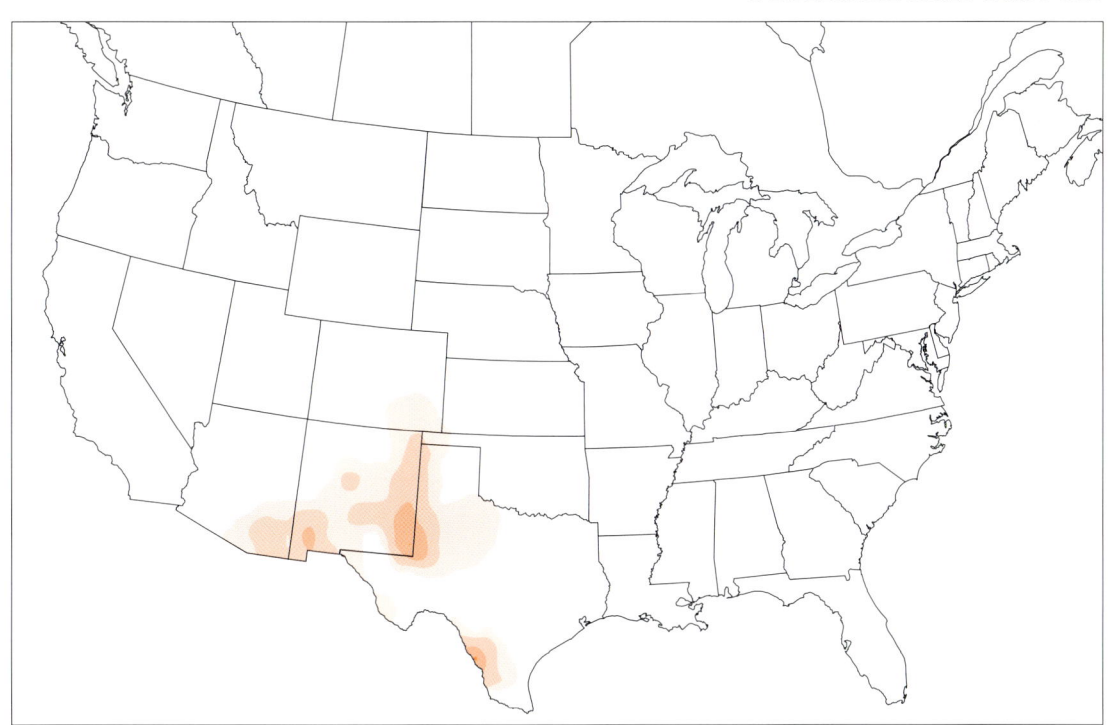

Common Raven

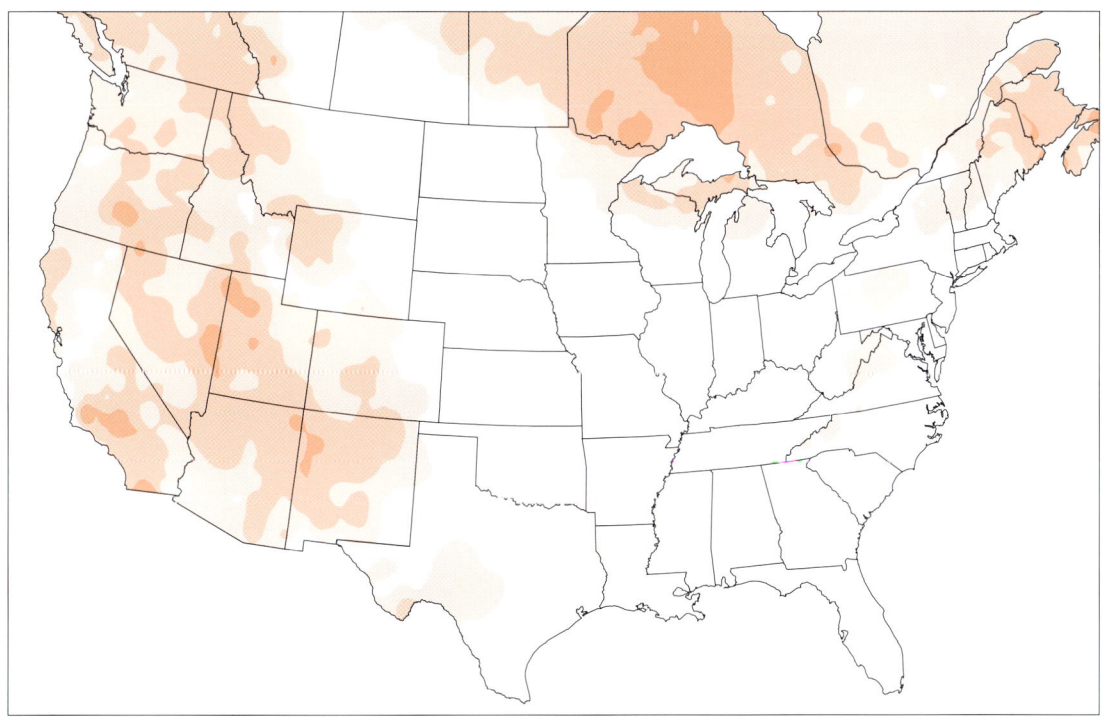

Black-capped Chickadee

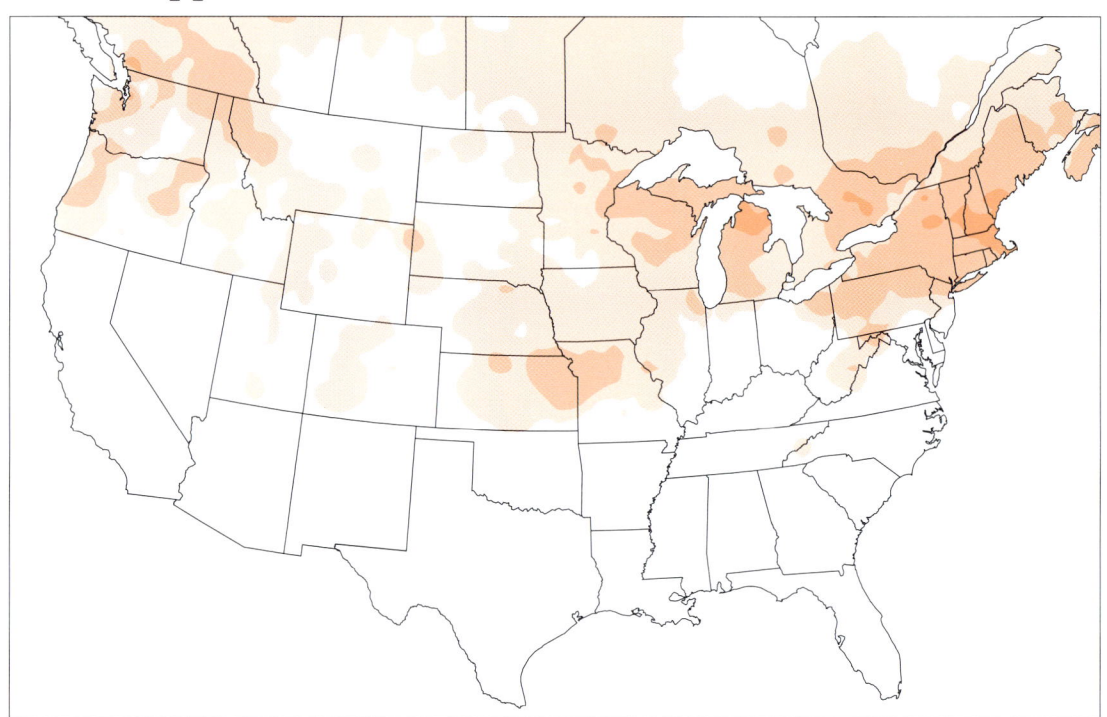

Carolina Chickadee

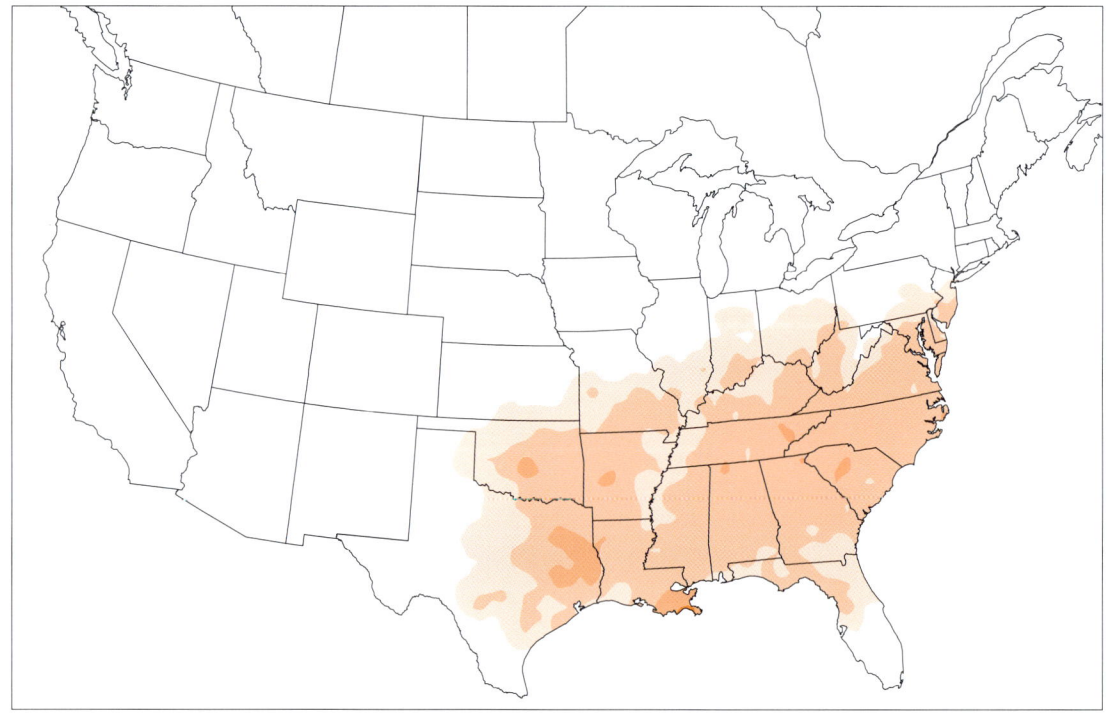

Mexican Chickadee

Mountain Chickadee

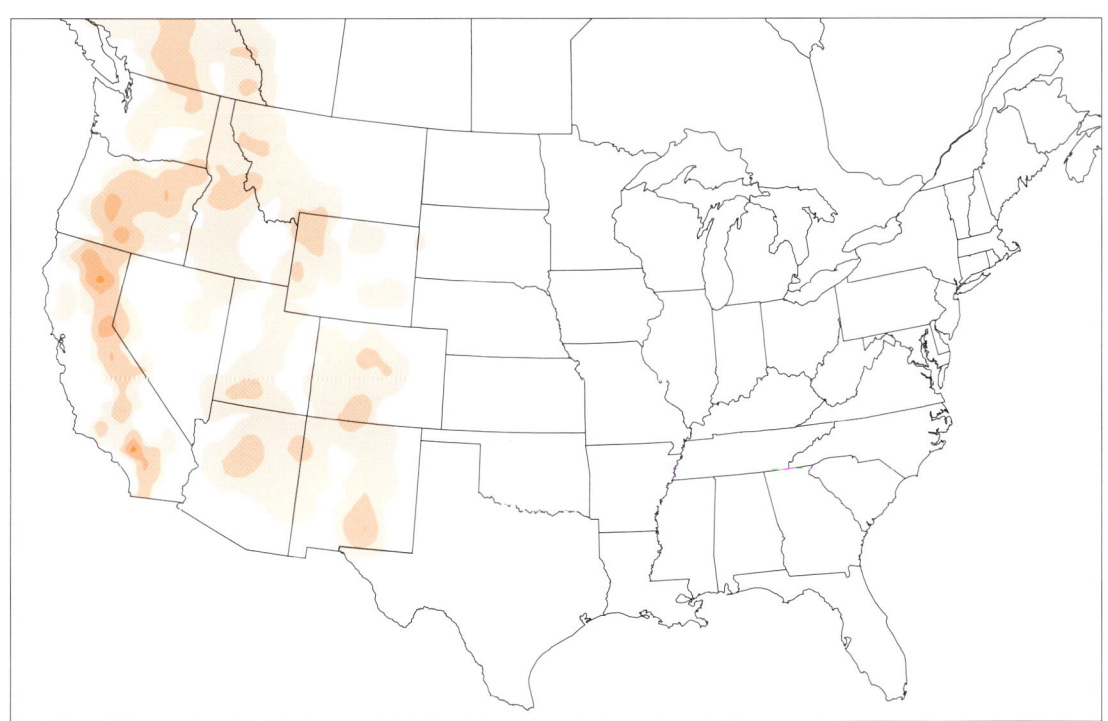

Boreal Chickadee

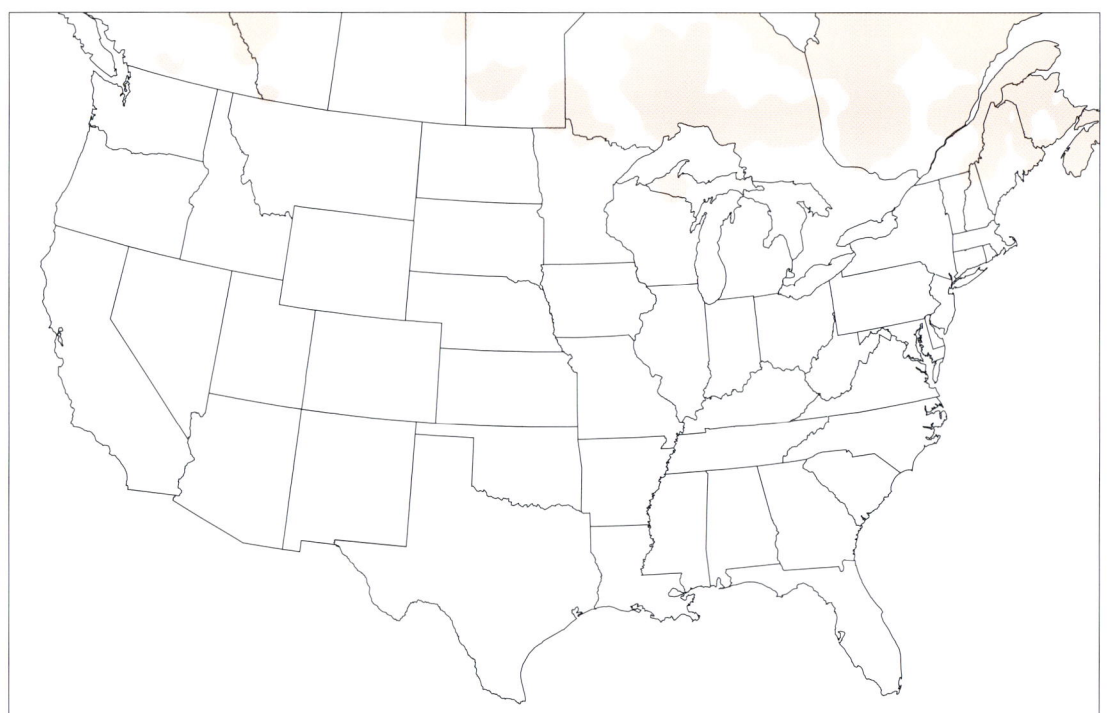

Chestnut-backed Chickadee

Bridled Titmouse

Plain Titmouse

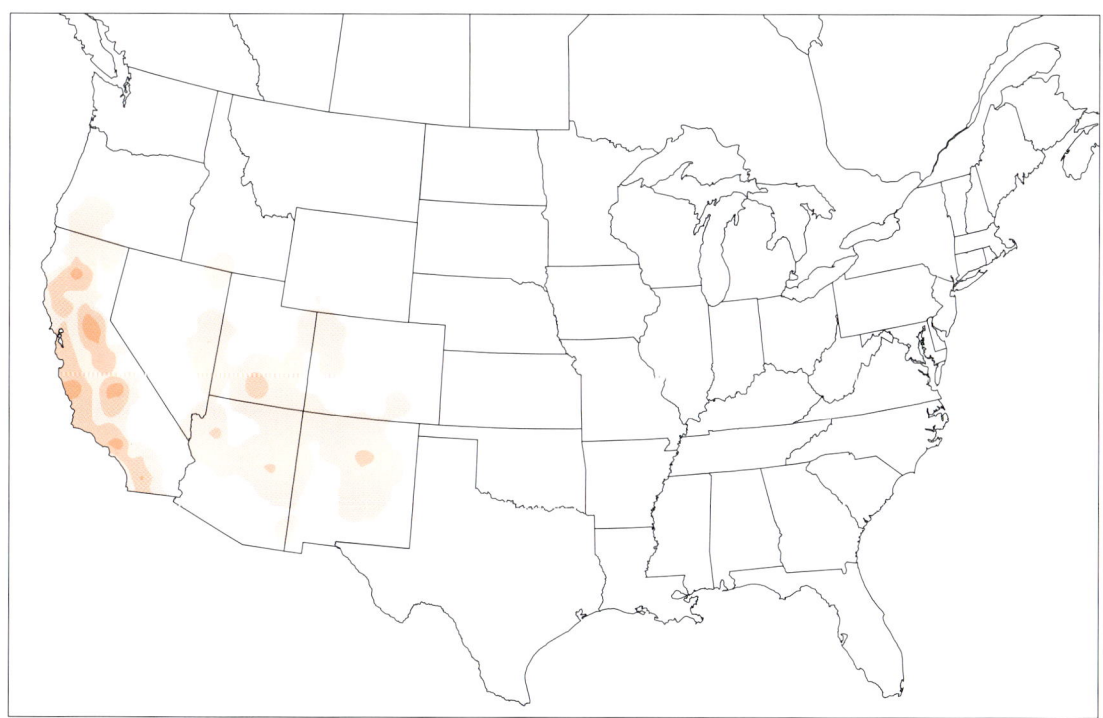

Tufted Titmouse

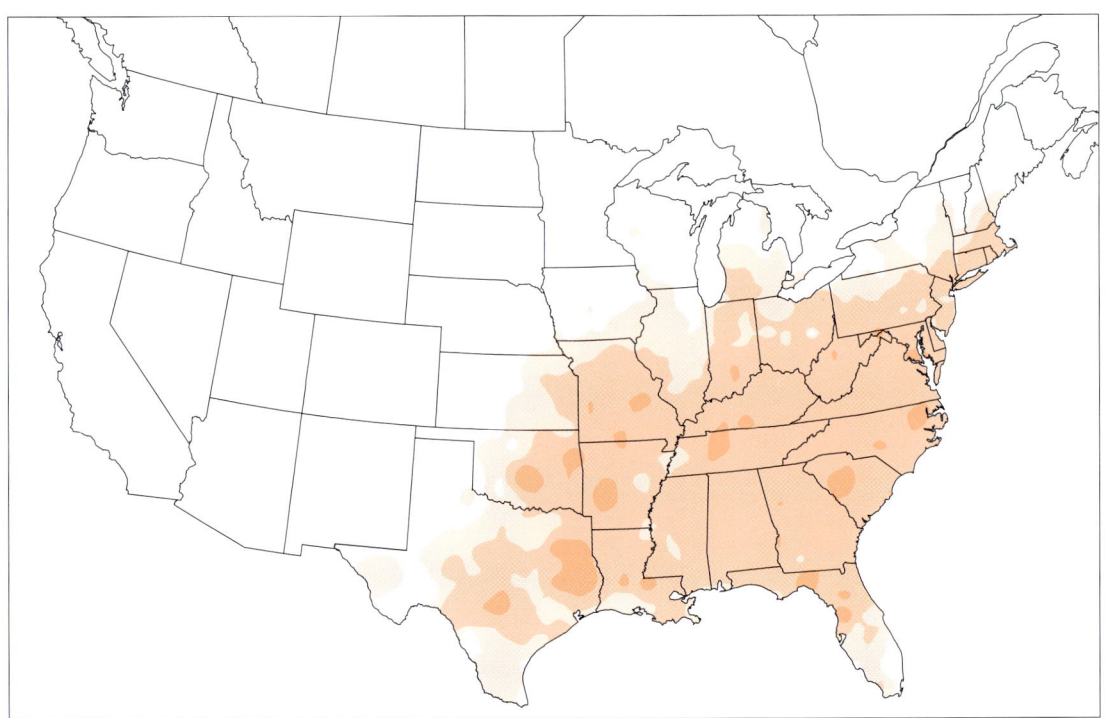

Tufted Titmouse (Black-crested)

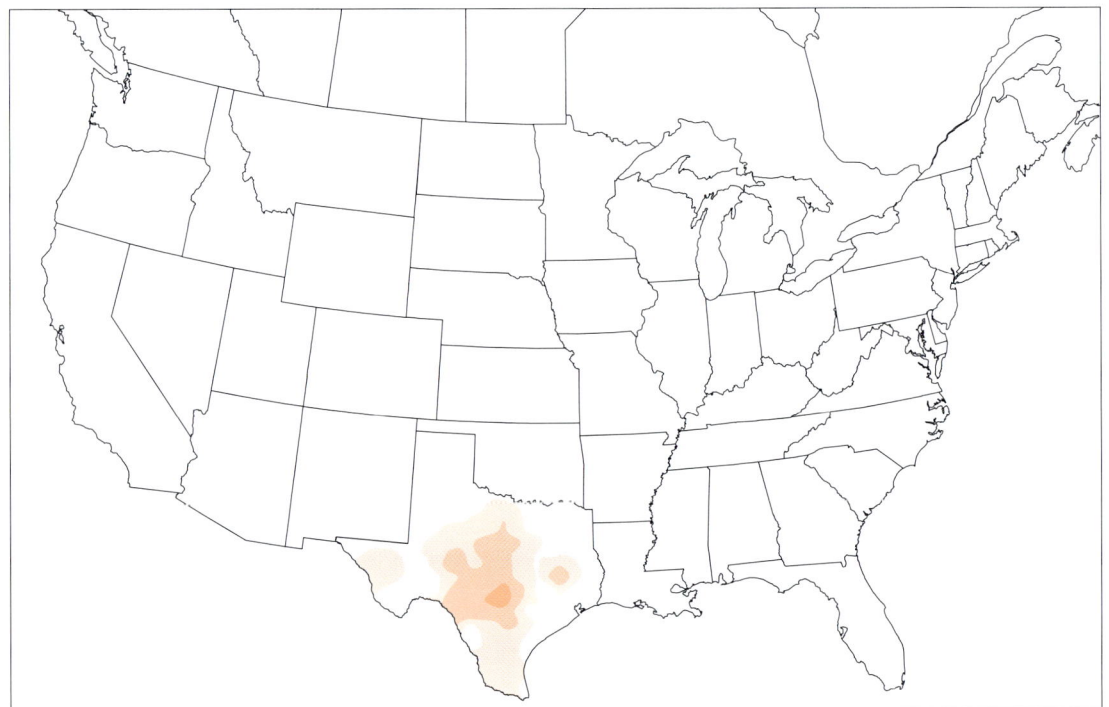

Verdin

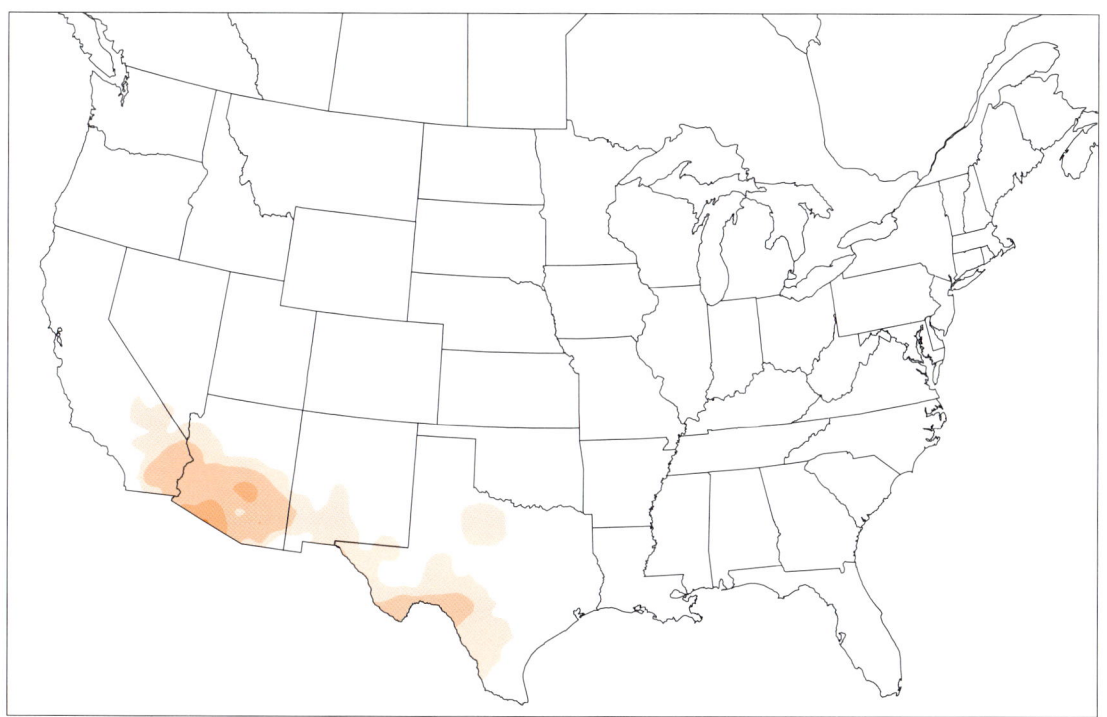

Bushtit

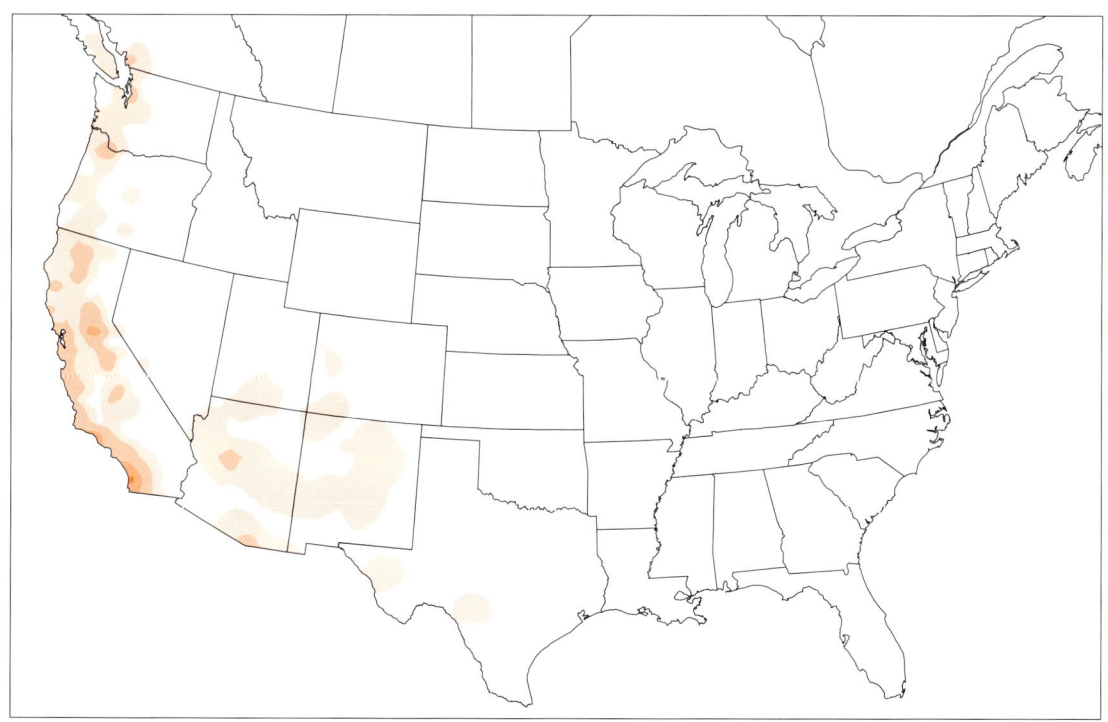

Red-breasted Nuthatch

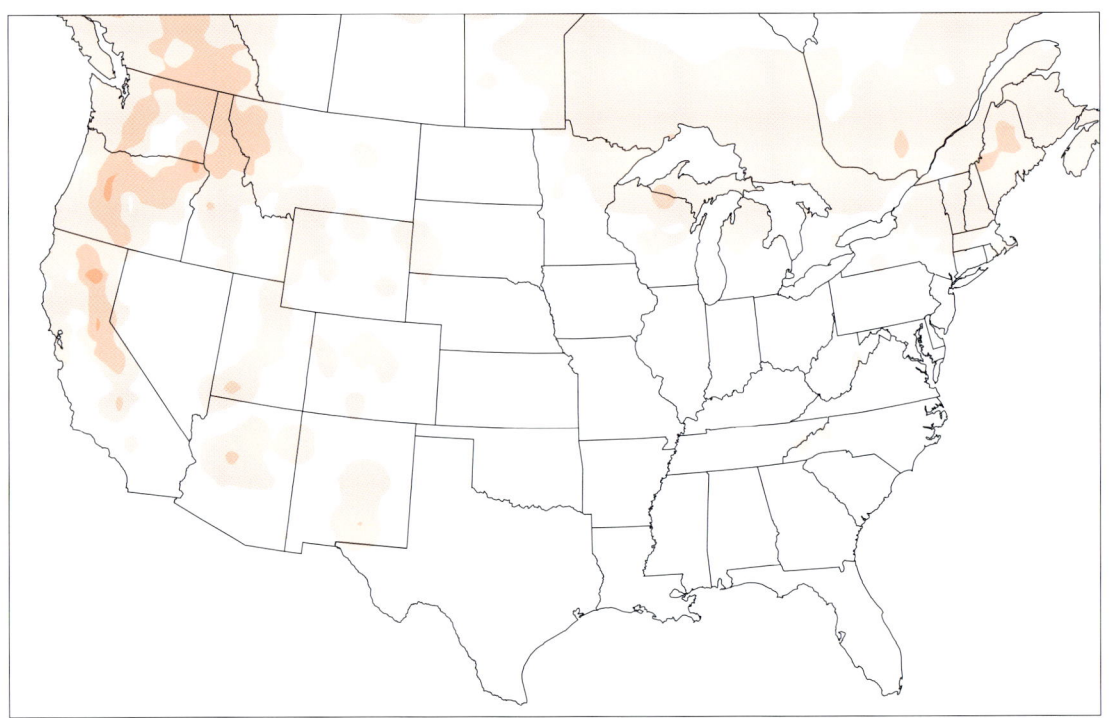

White-breasted Nuthatch

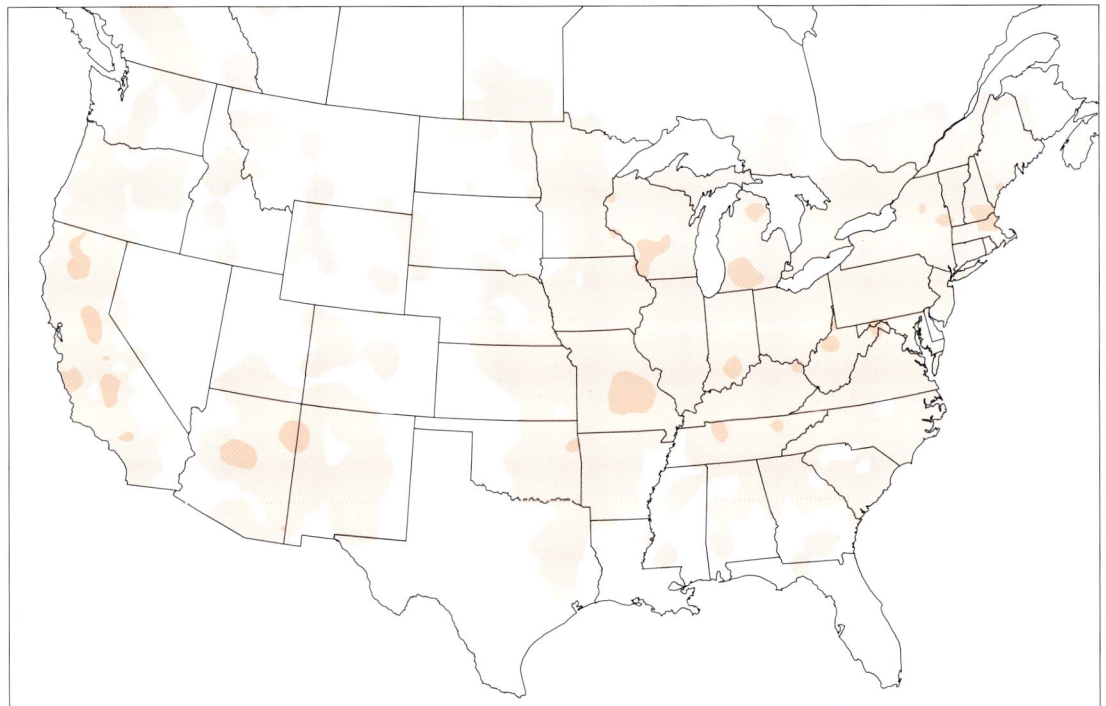

Pygmy Nuthatch

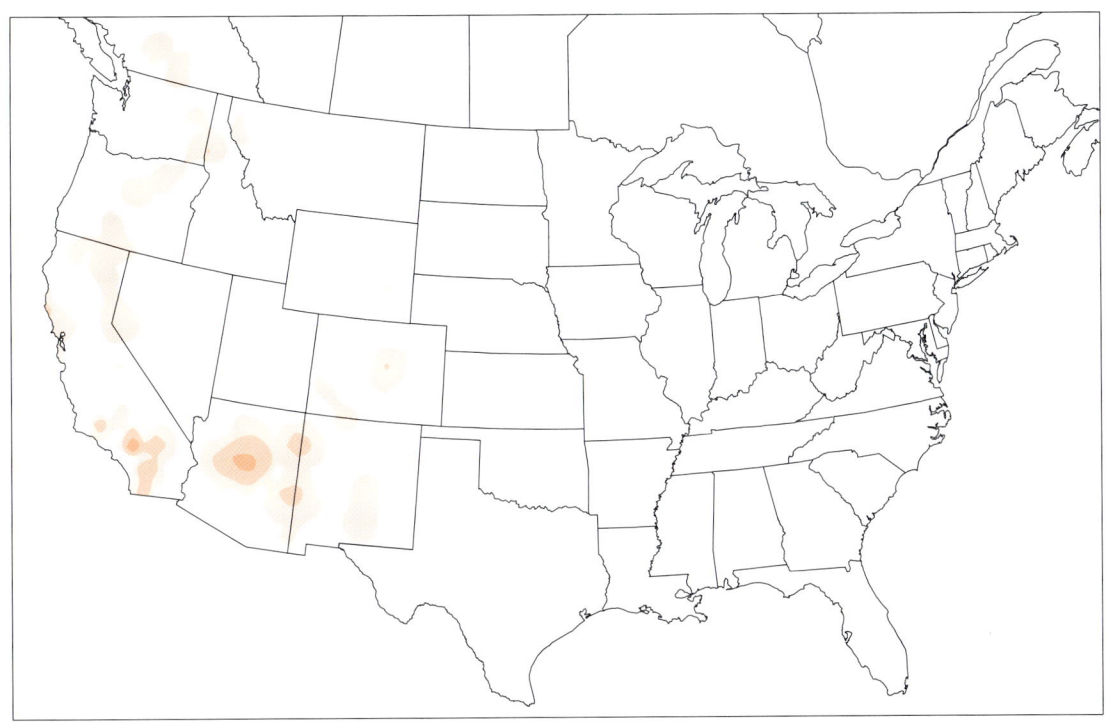

Brown-headed Nuthatch

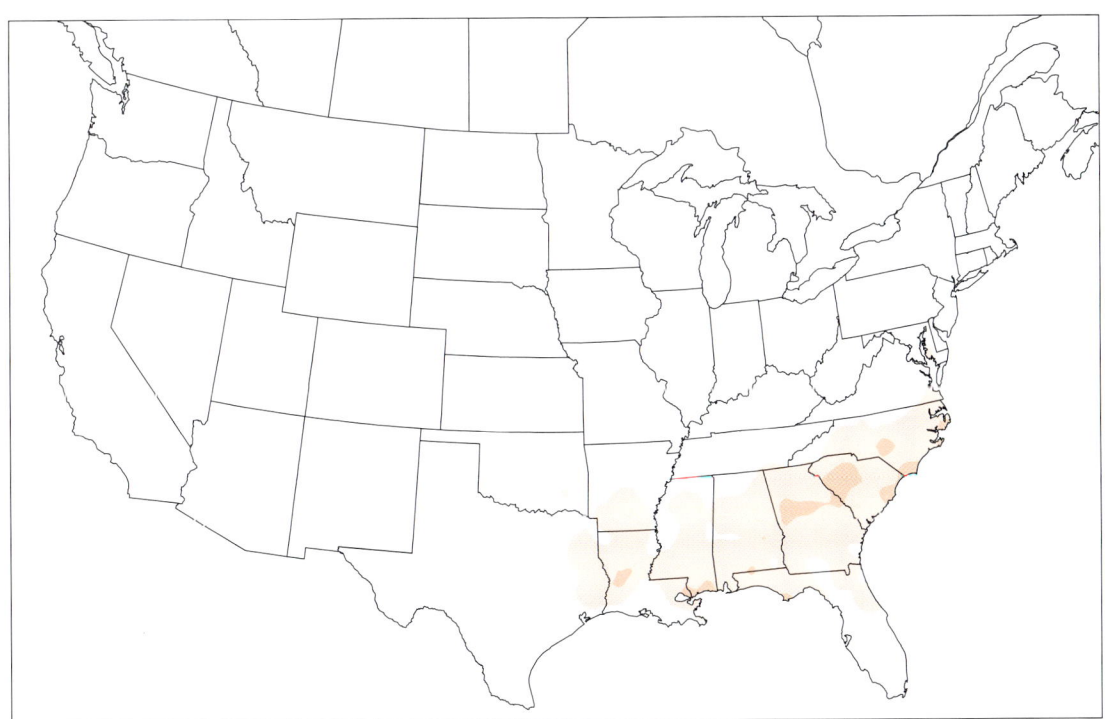

Brown Creeper

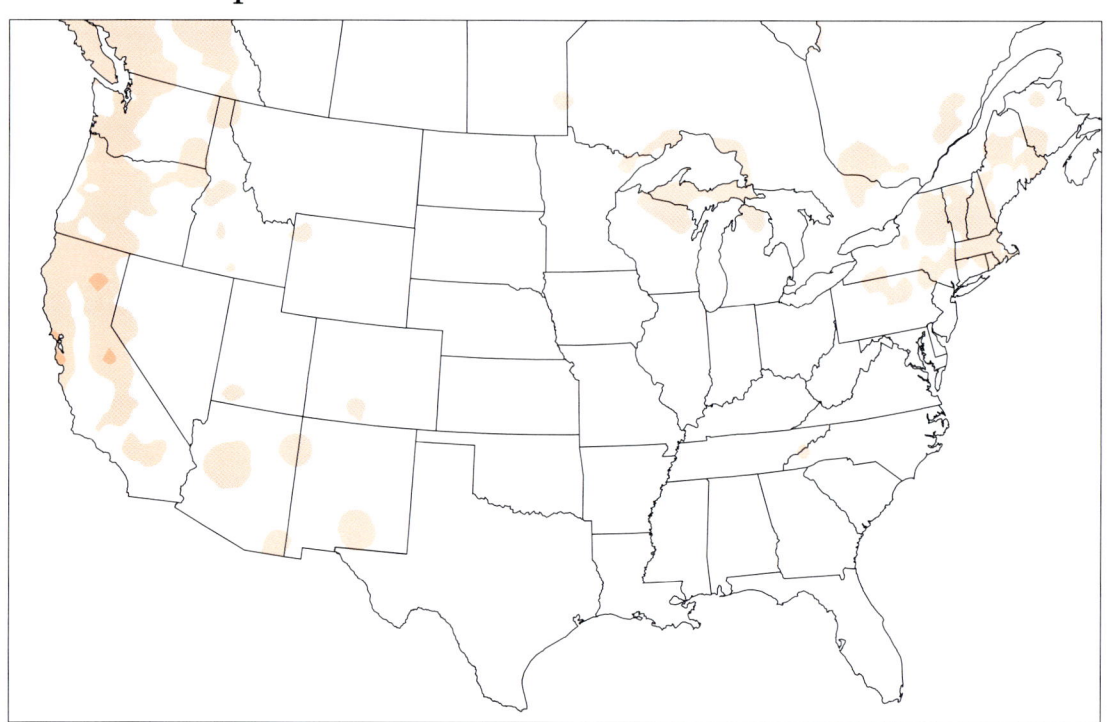

Cactus Wren

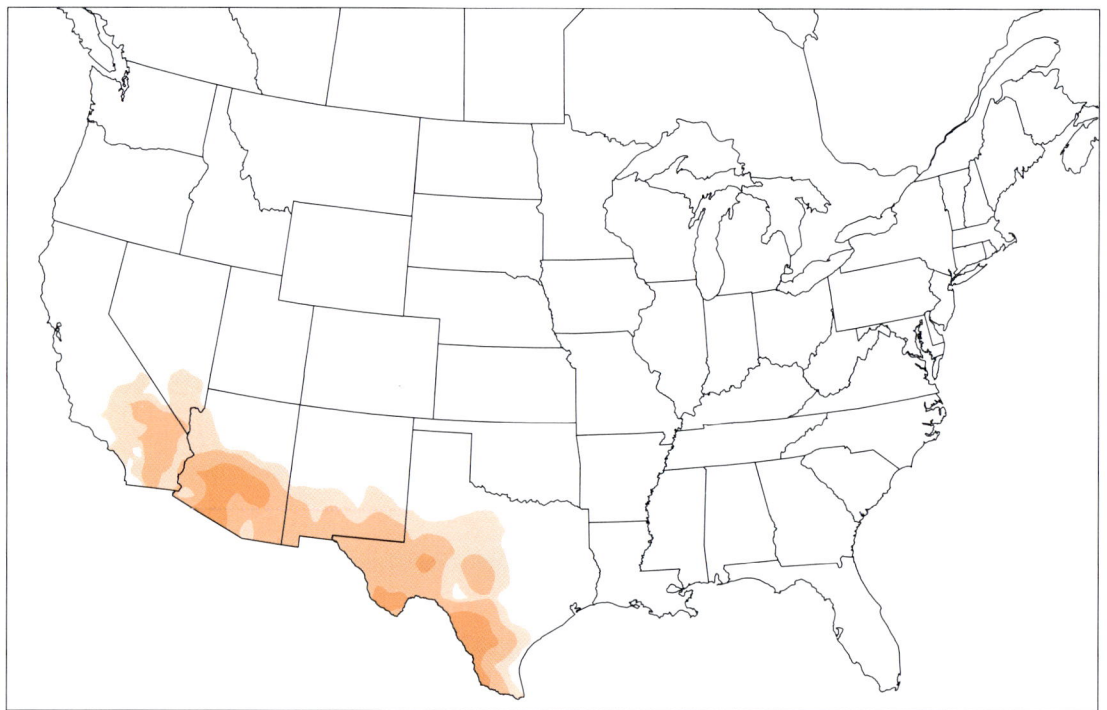

Rock Wren

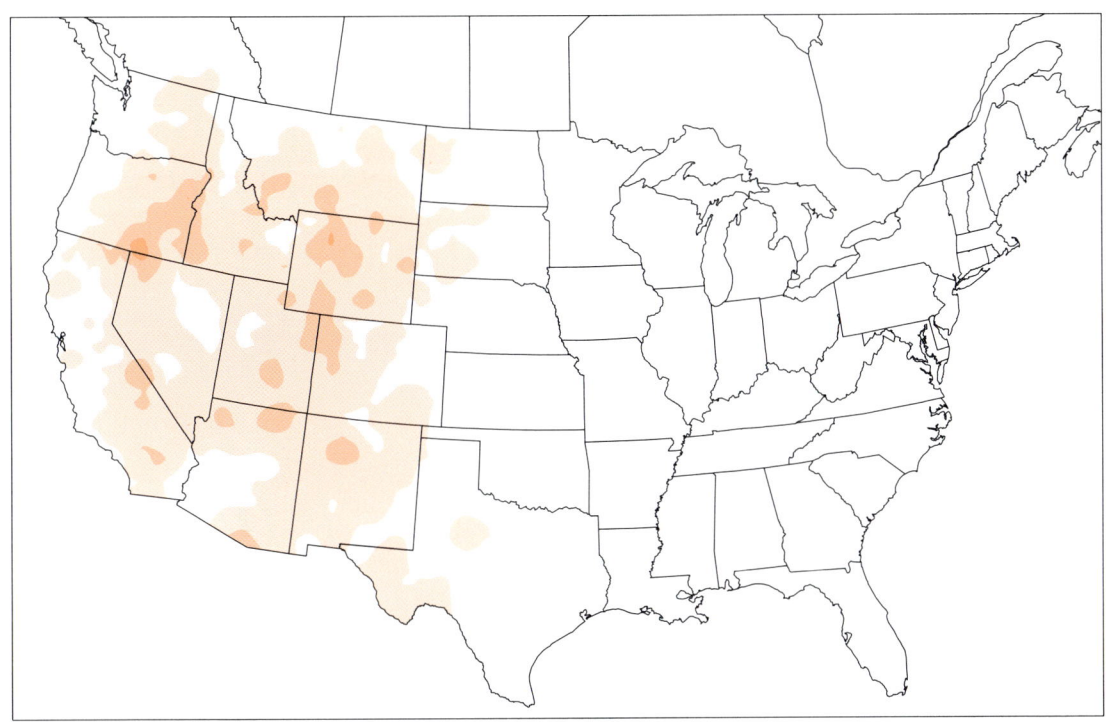

Canyon Wren

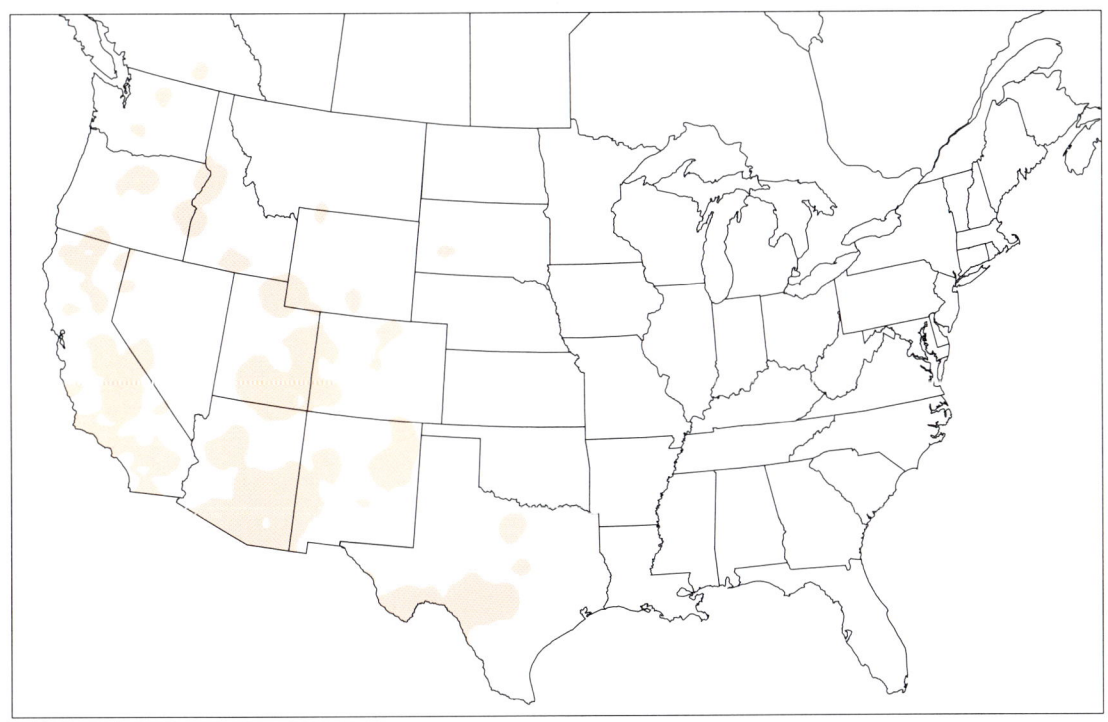

Carolina Wren

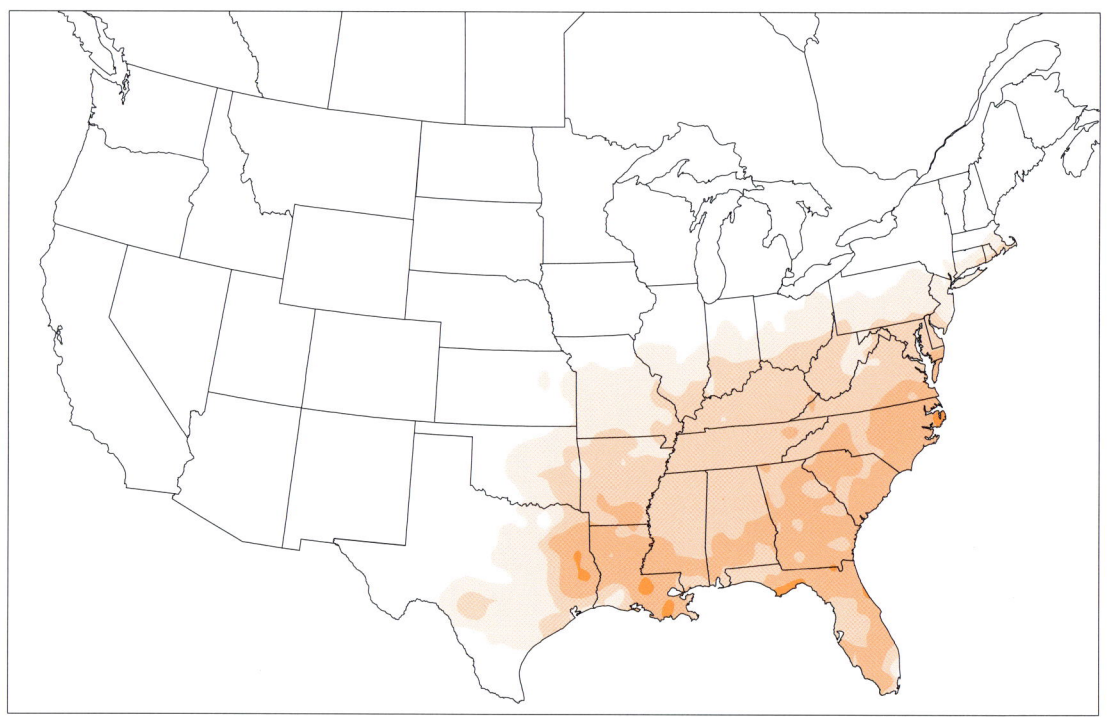

Bewick's Wren

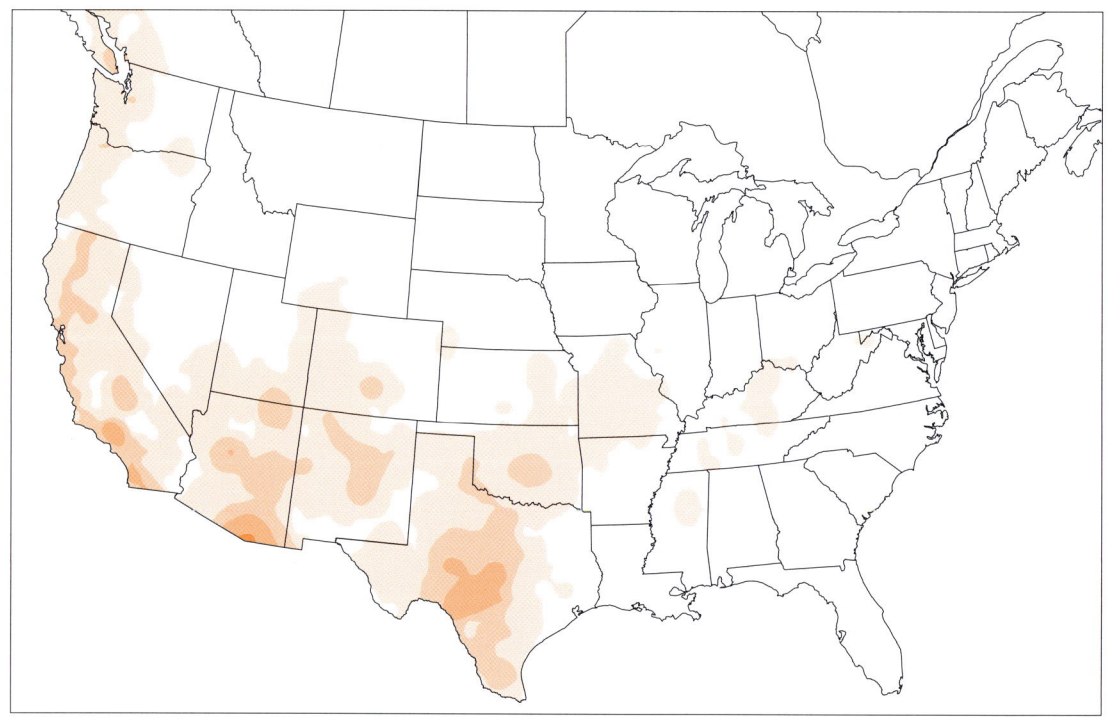

House Wren

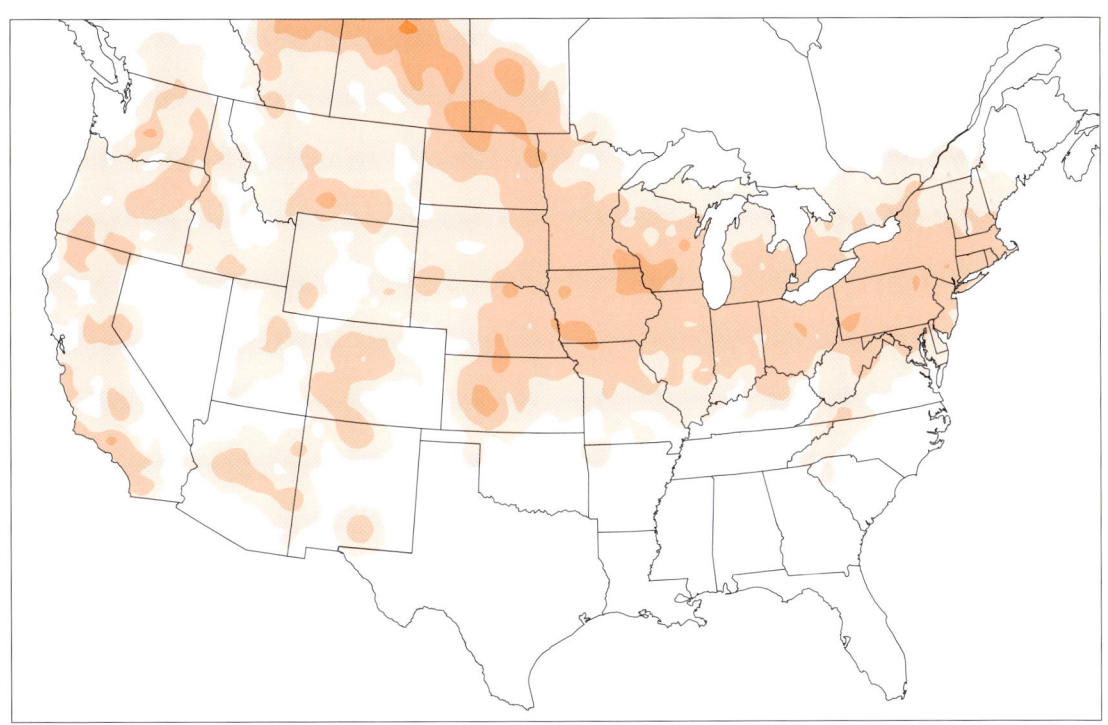

Winter Wren

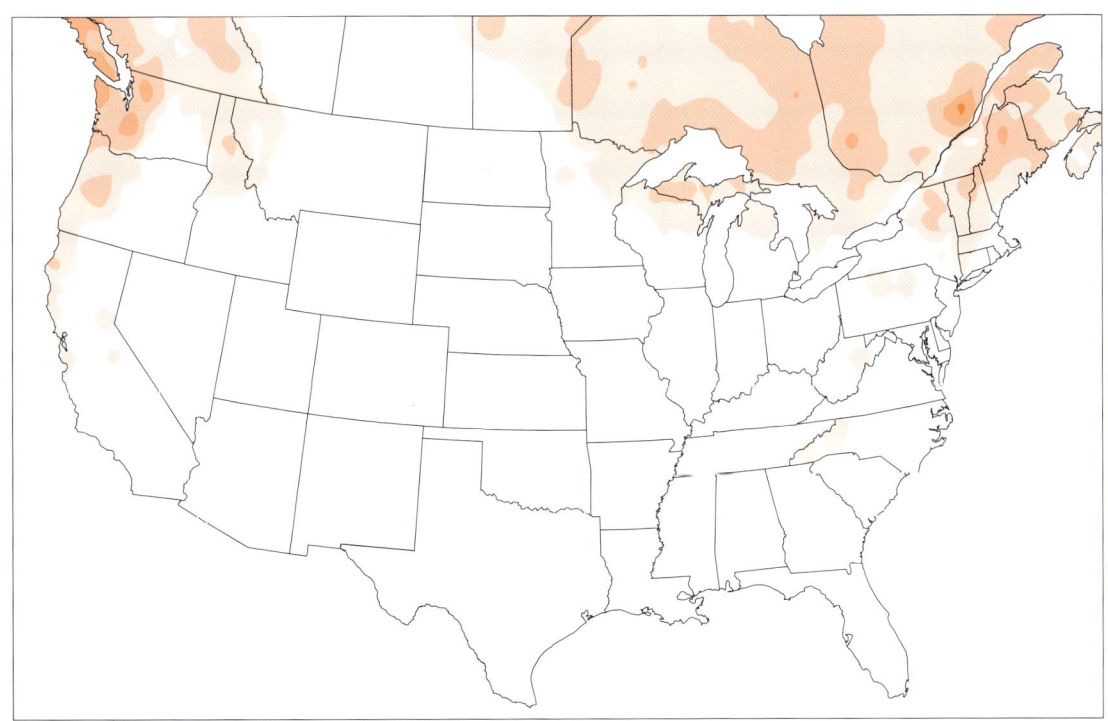

Sedge Wren

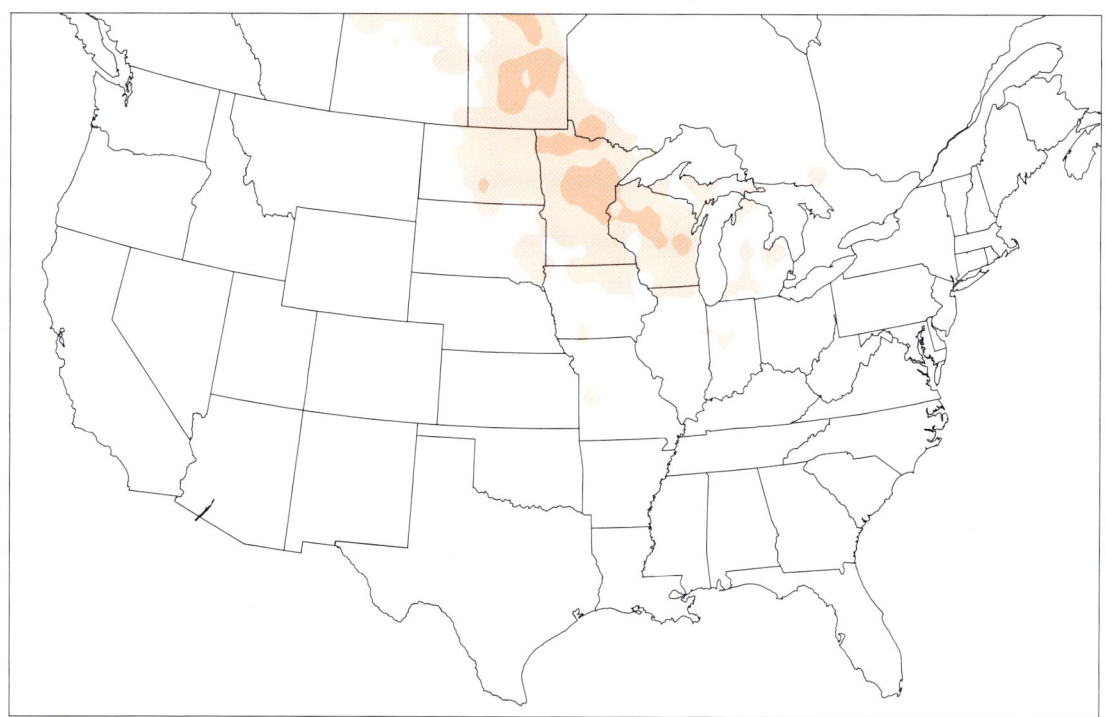

Marsh Wren

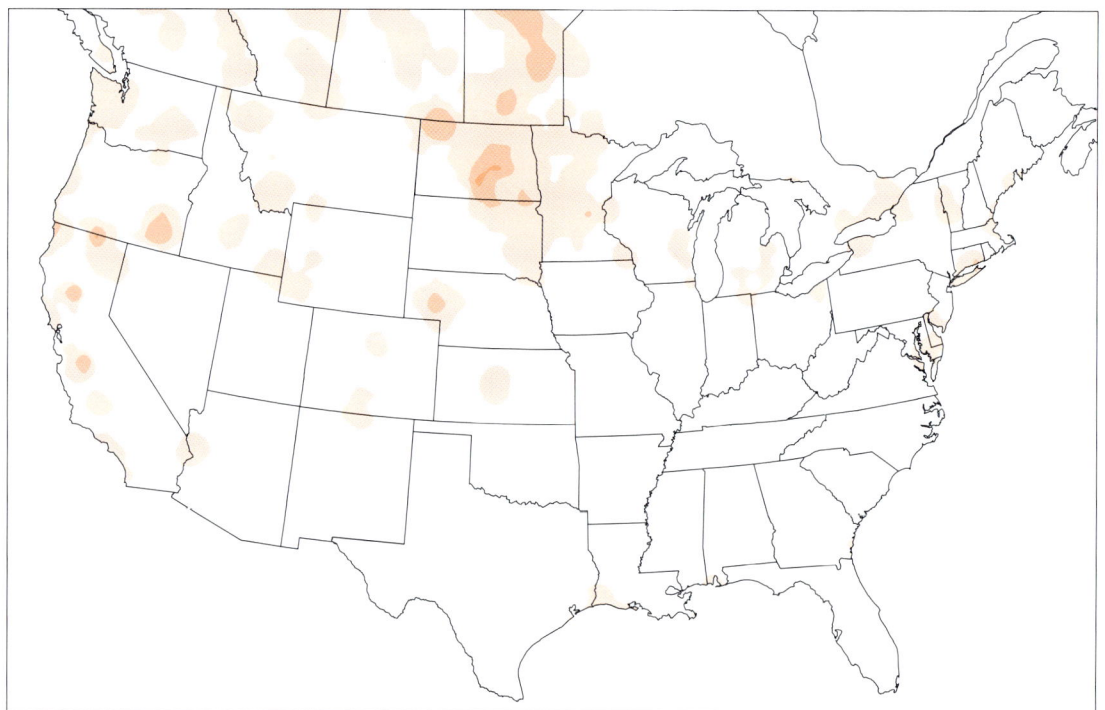

American Dipper

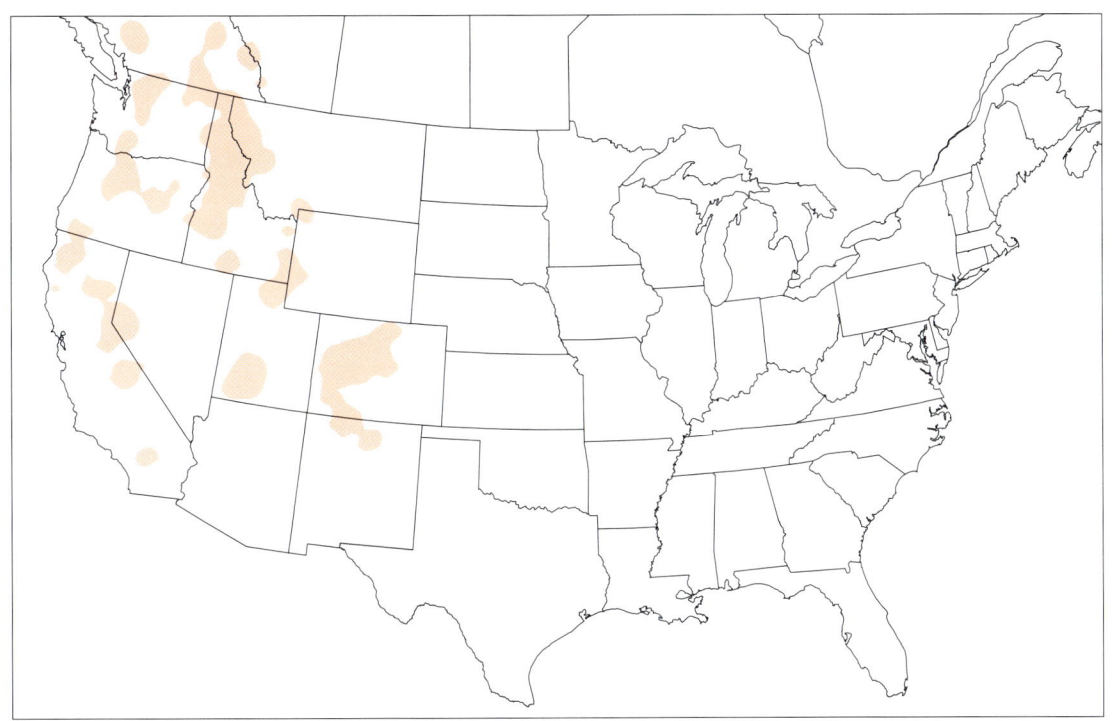

Golden-crowned Kinglet

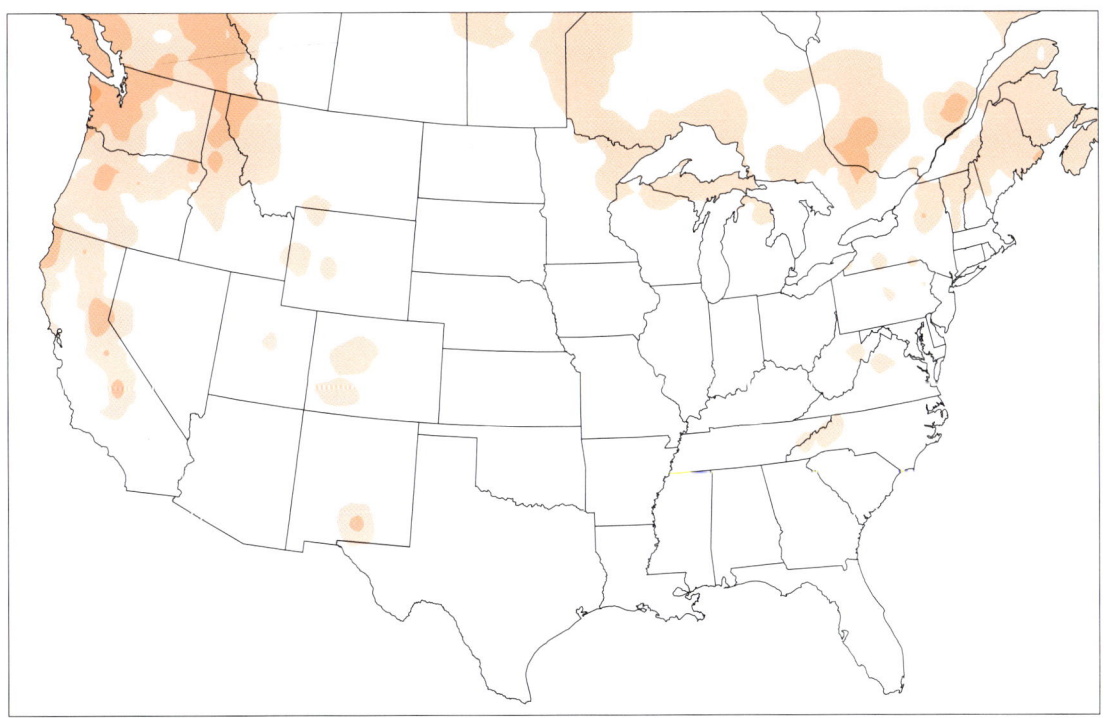

Ruby-crowned Kinglet

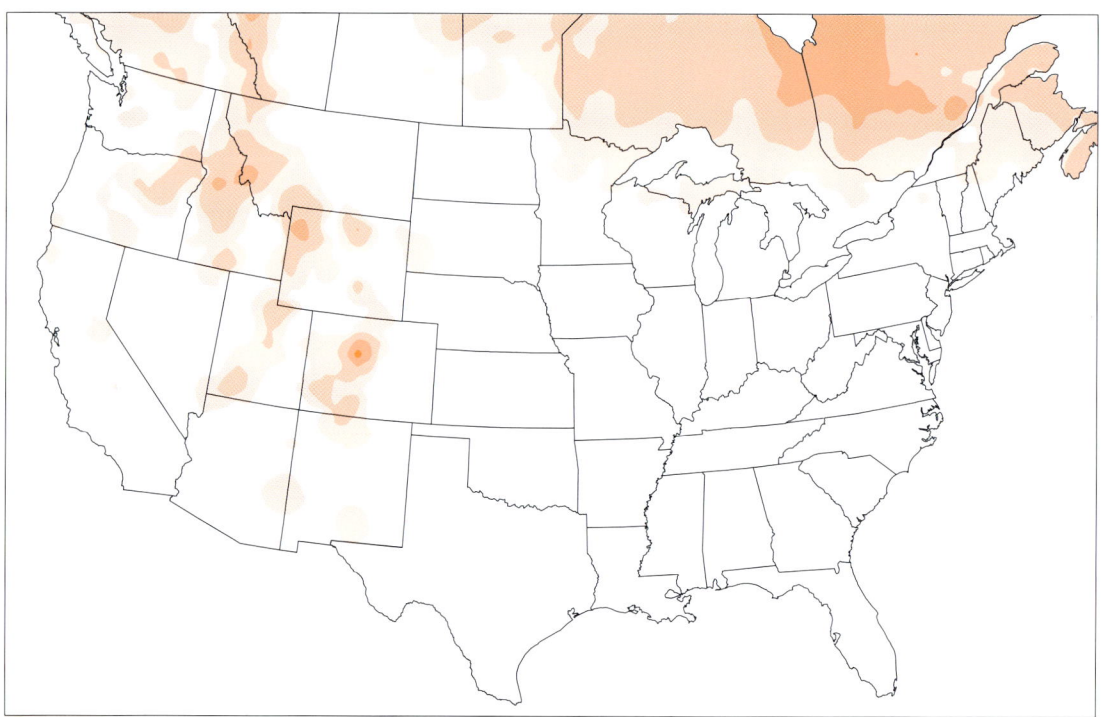

Blue-gray Gnatcatcher

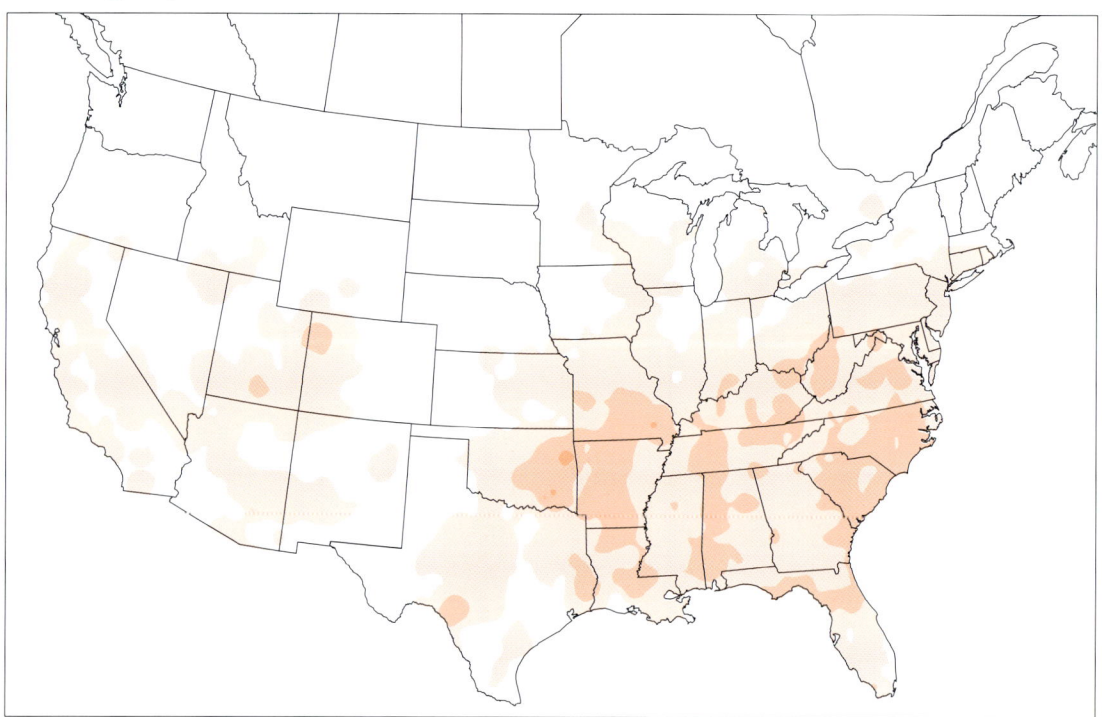

California Gnatcatcher

Black-tailed Gnatcatcher

Eastern Bluebird

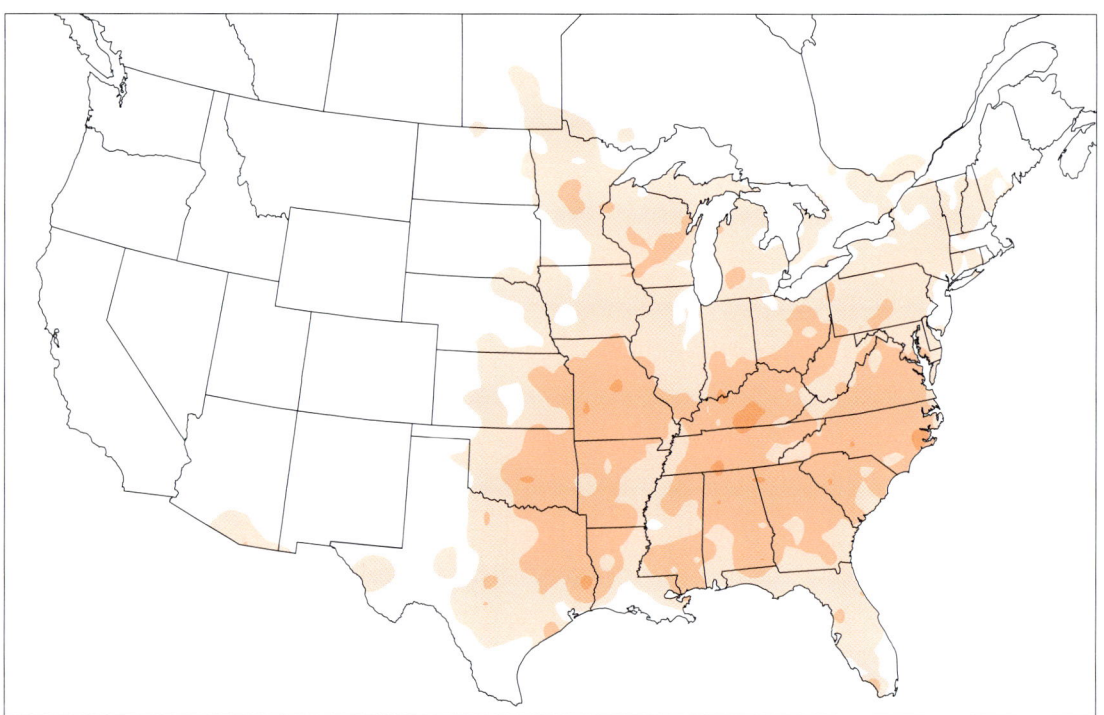

Western Bluebird

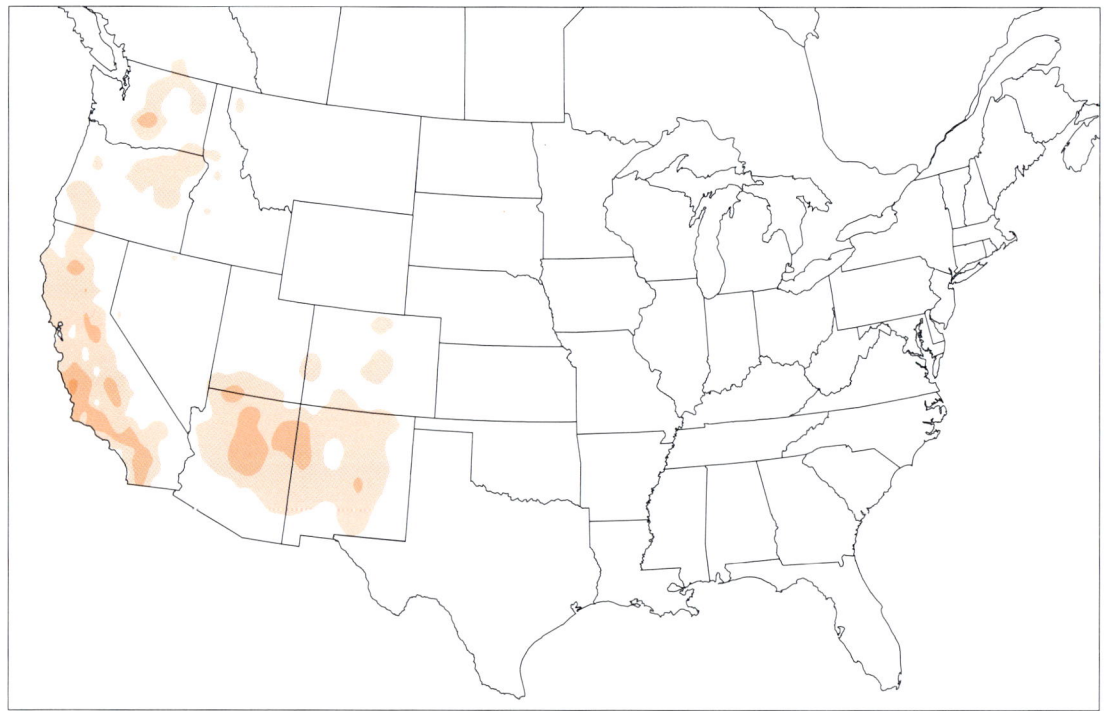

Mountain Bluebird

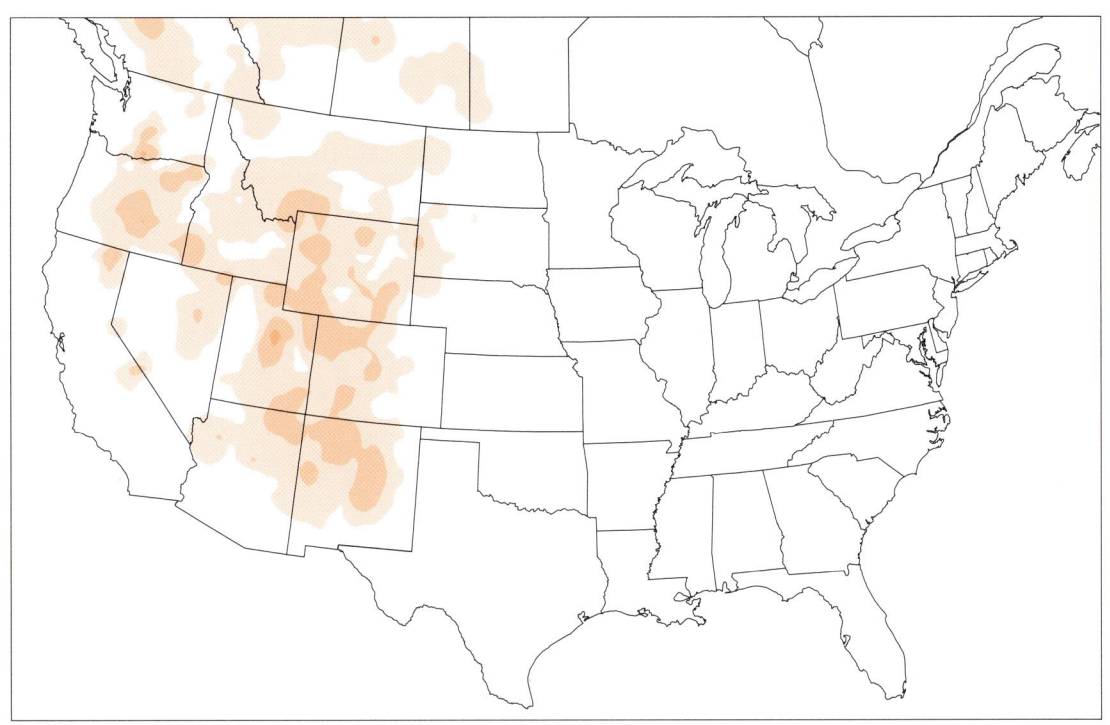

Townsend's Solitaire

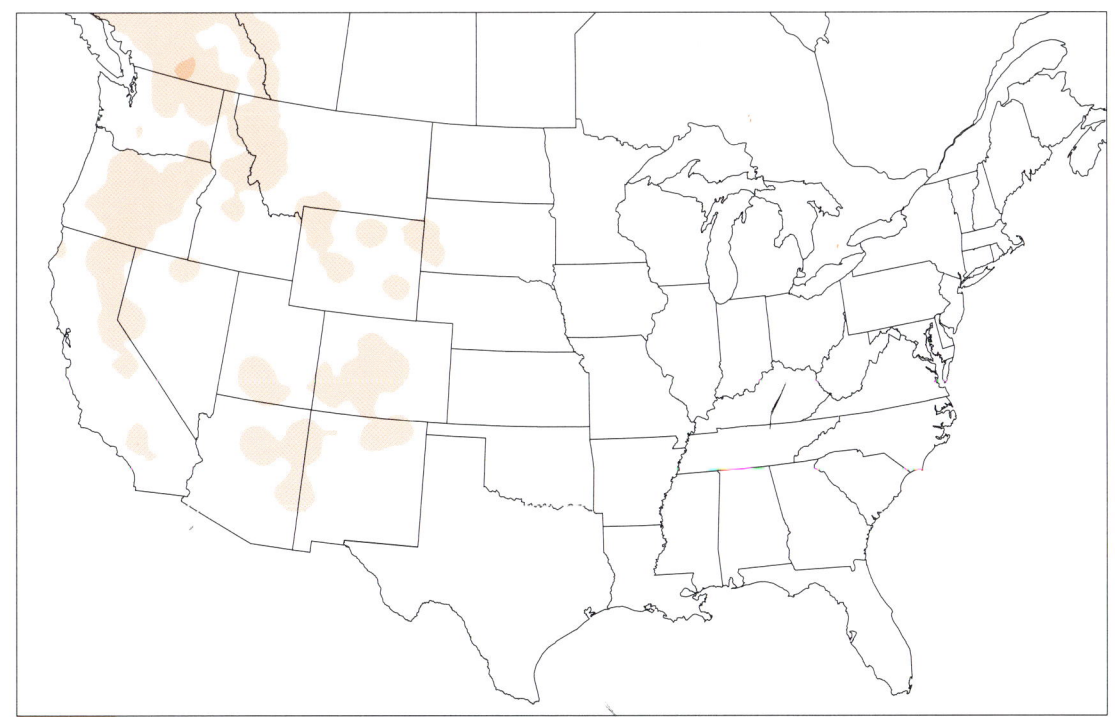

Veery

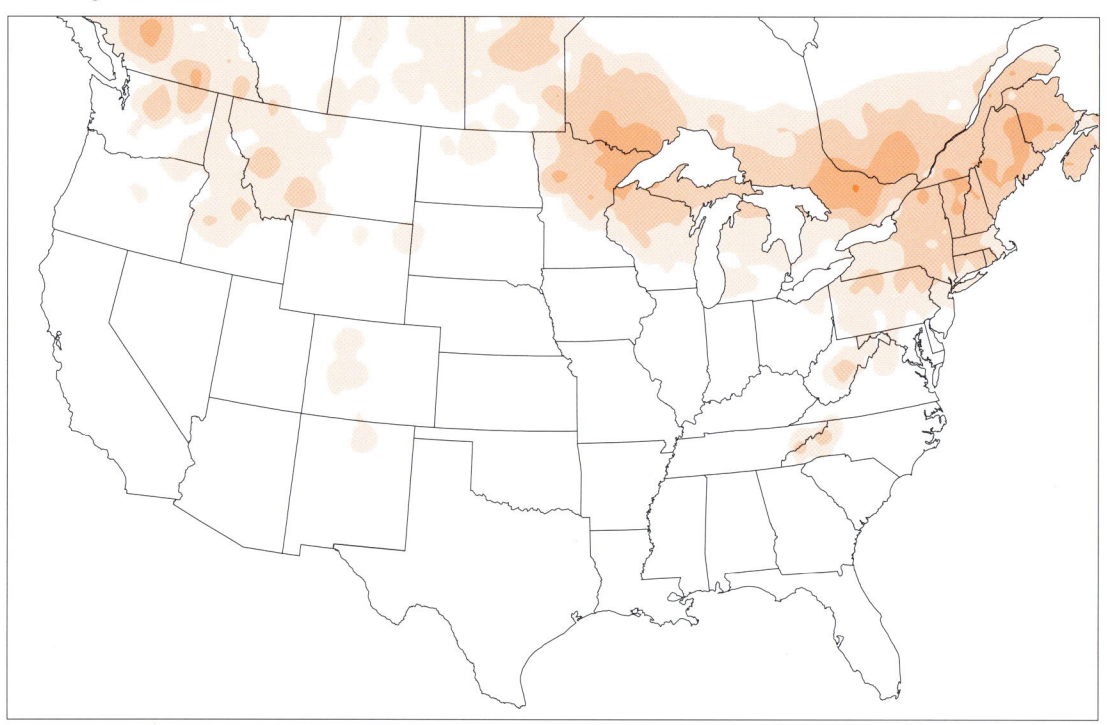

Gray-cheeked Thrush (Bicknell's)

Swainson's Thrush

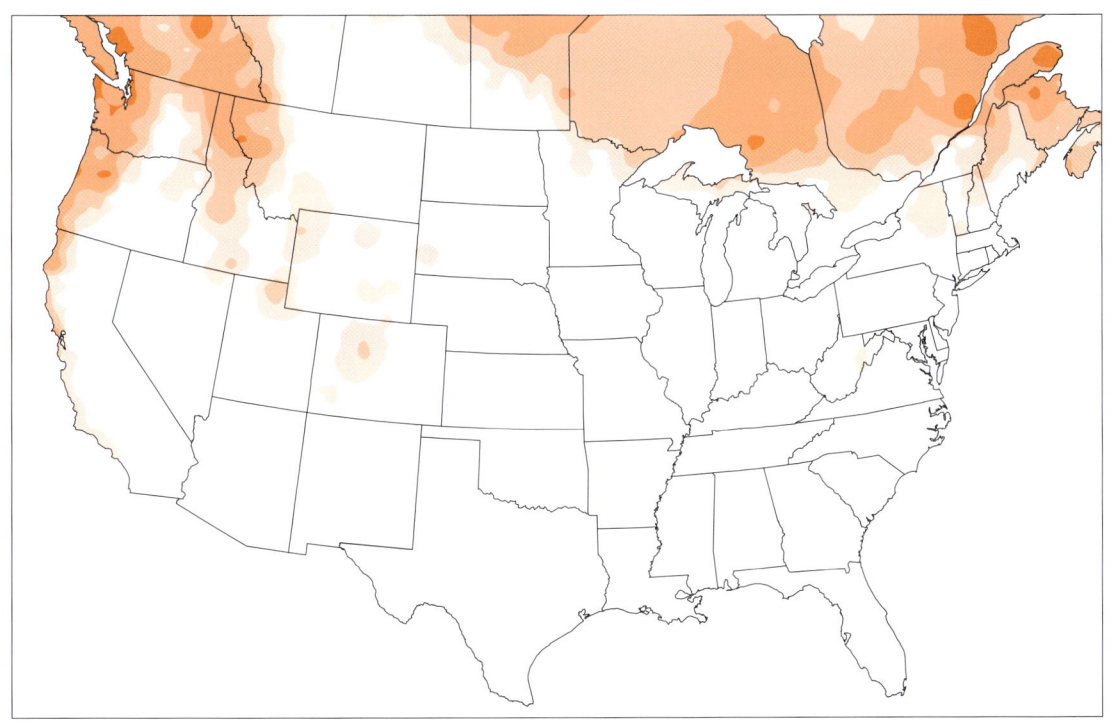

Hermit Thrush

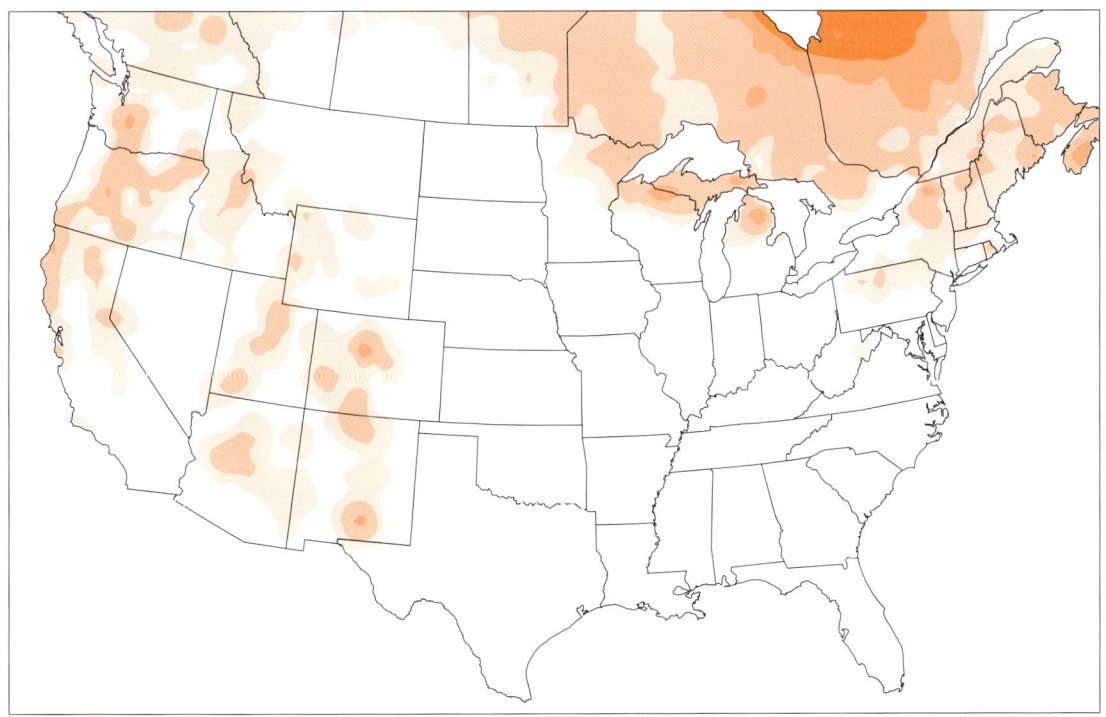

Wood Thrush

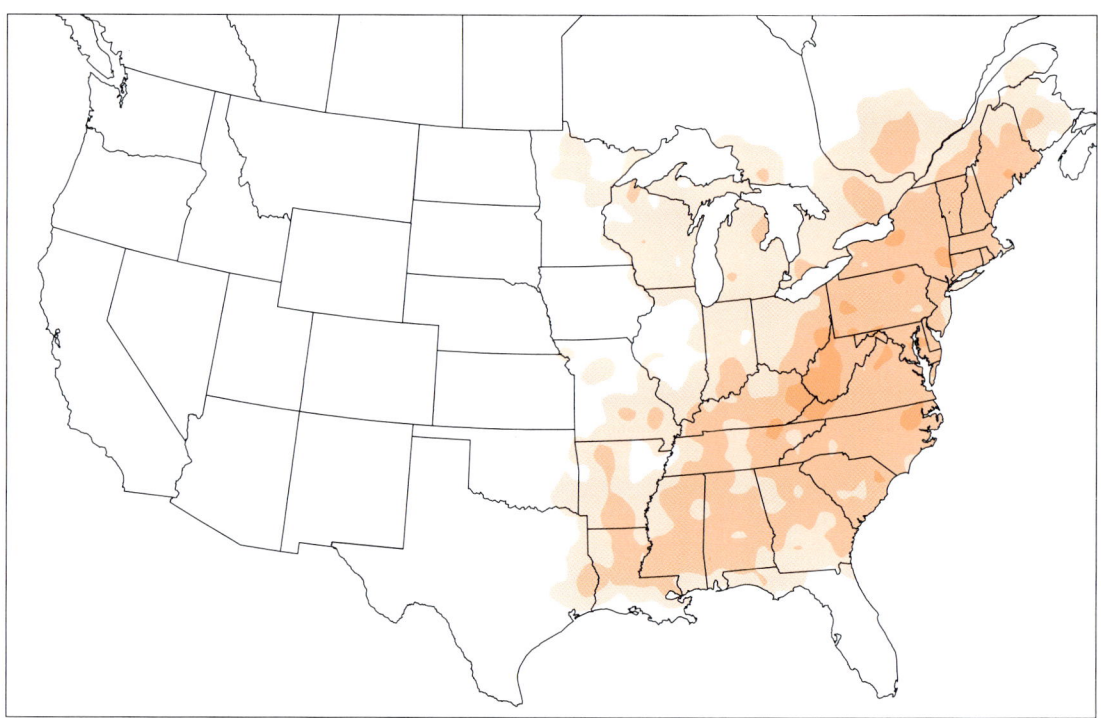

American Robin

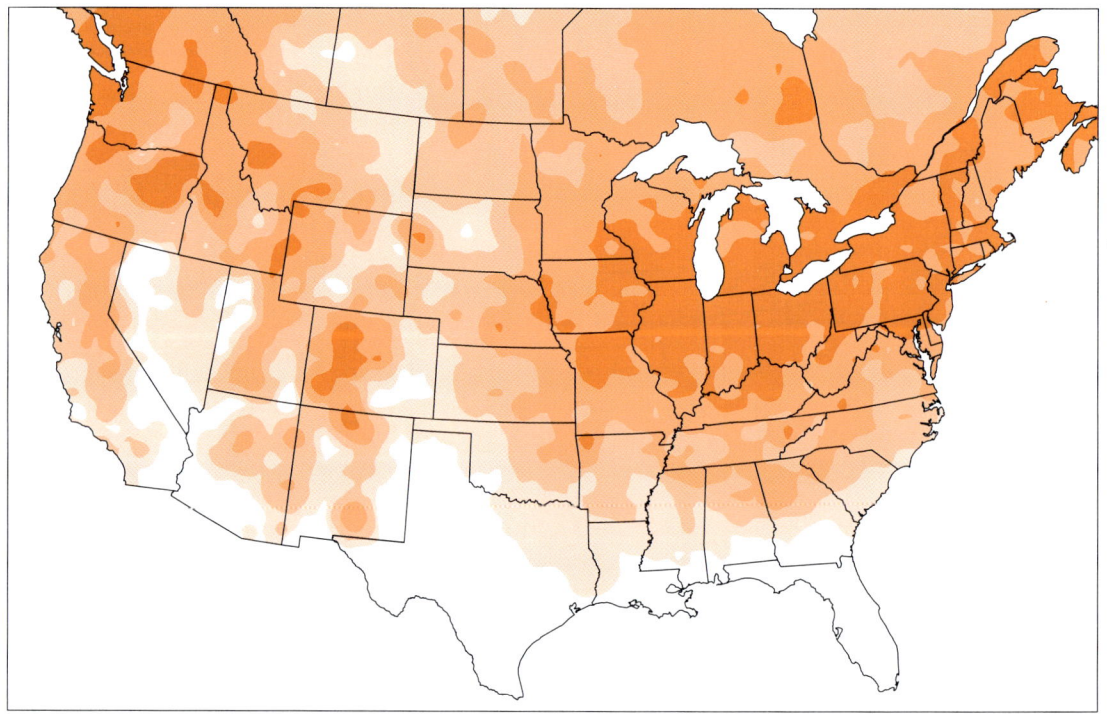

Varied Thrush

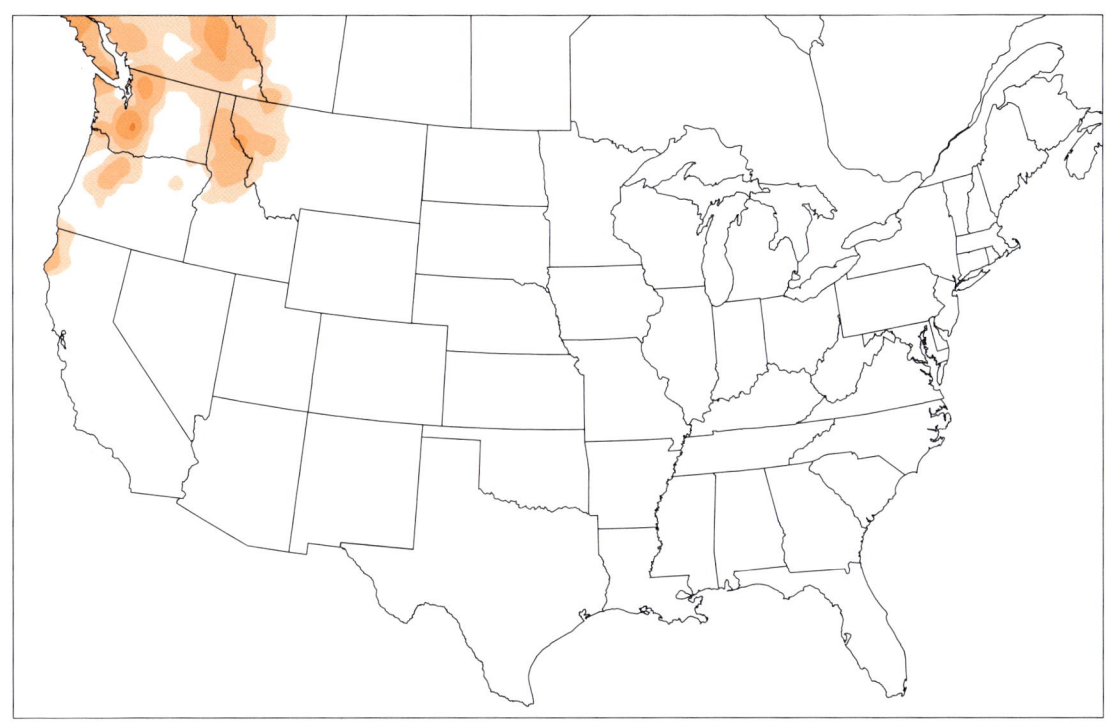

Wrentit

Gray Catbird

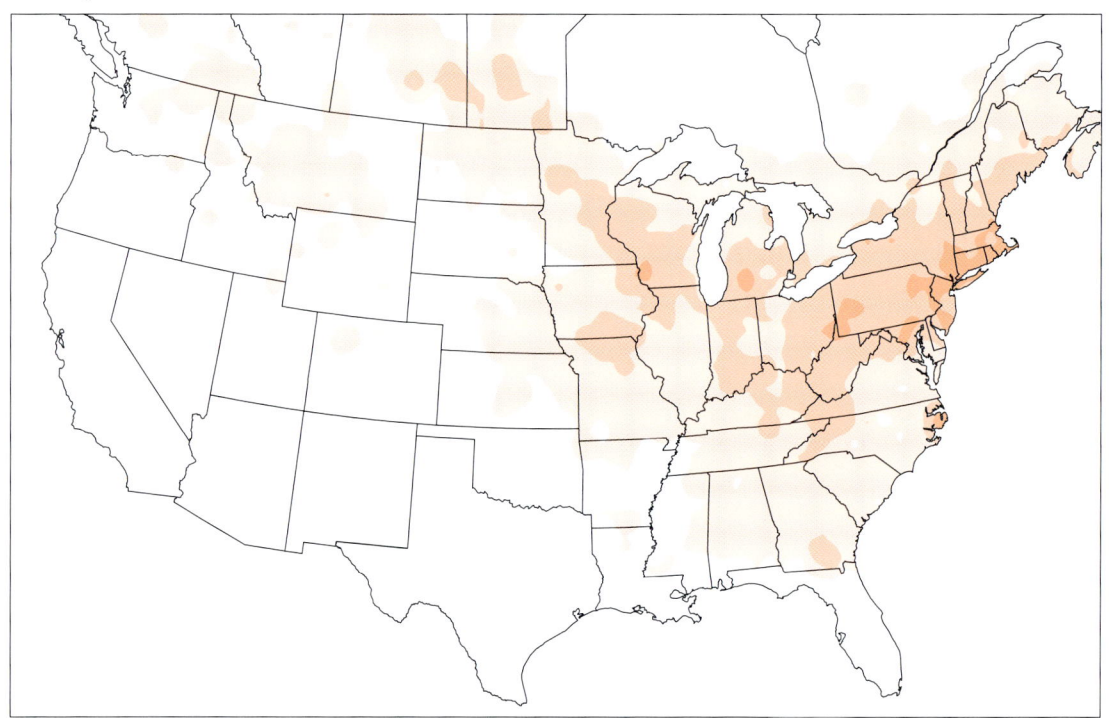

Northern Mockingbird

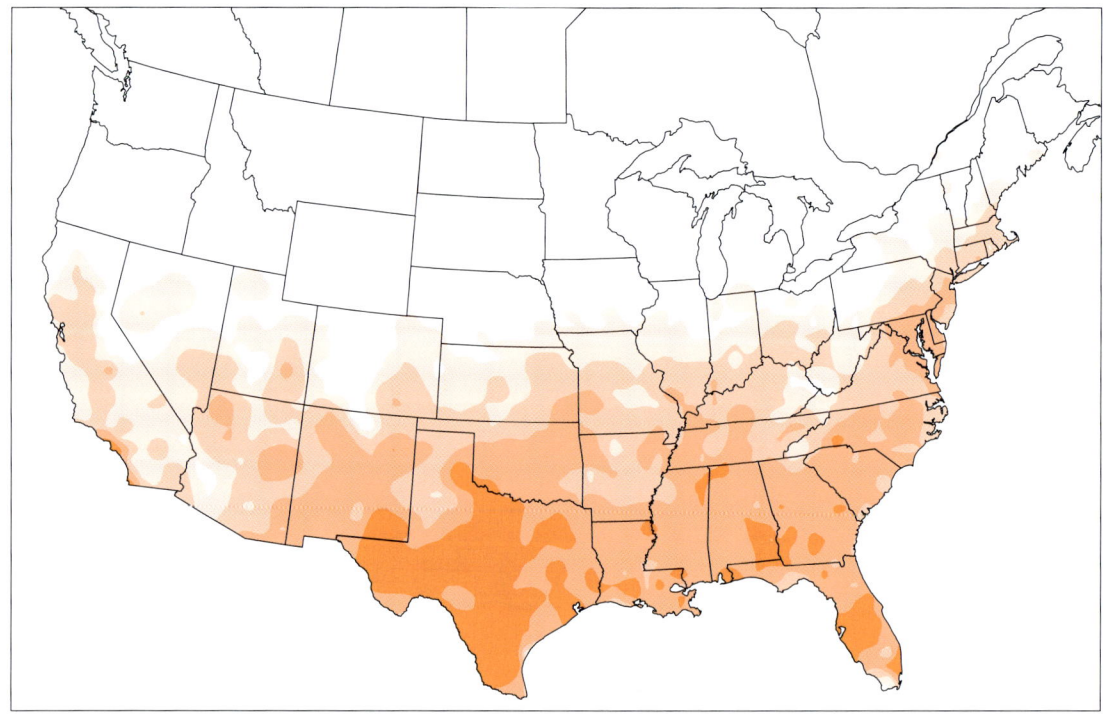

Sage Thrasher

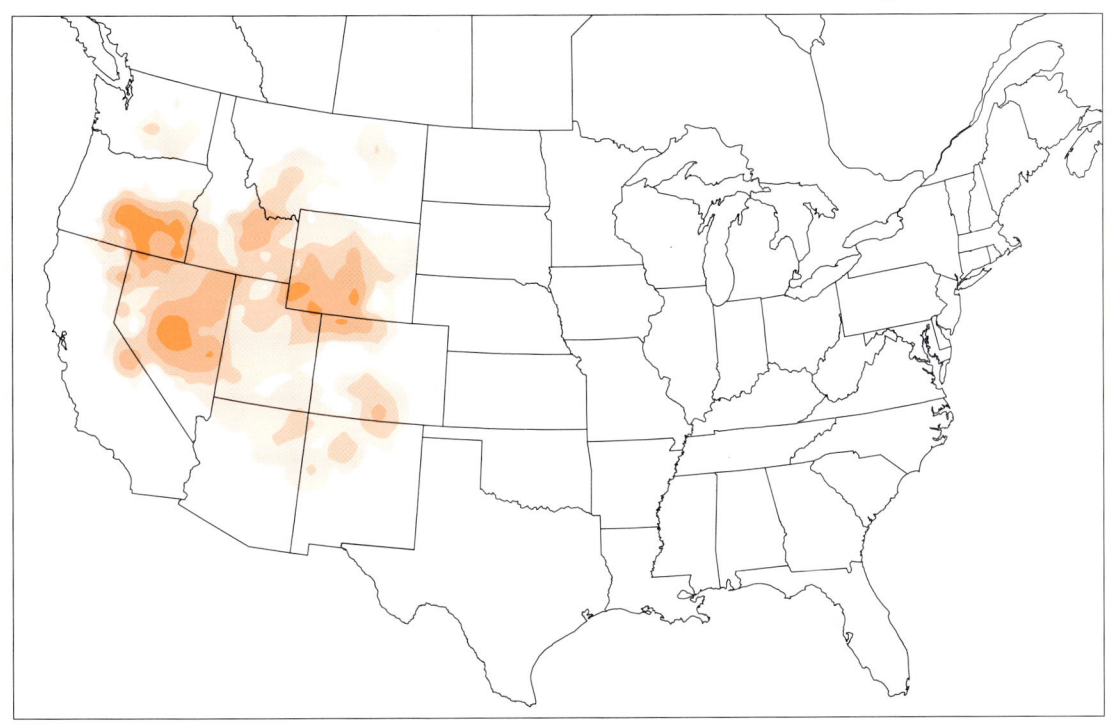

Brown Thrasher

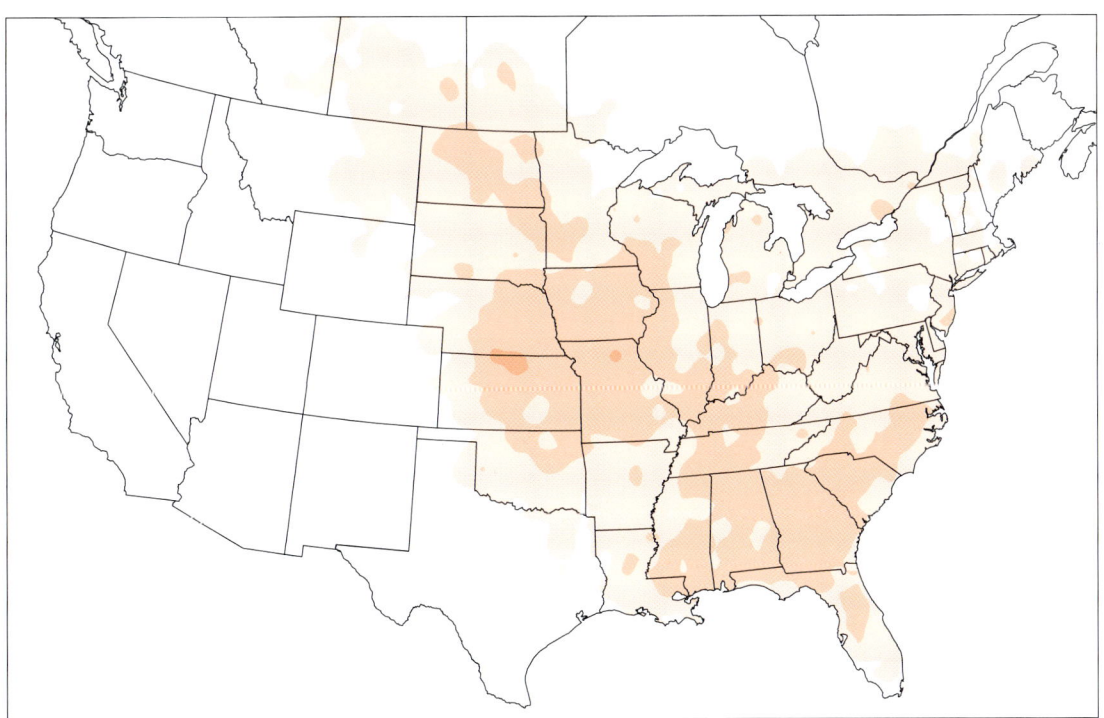

Long-billed Thrasher

Bendire's Thrasher

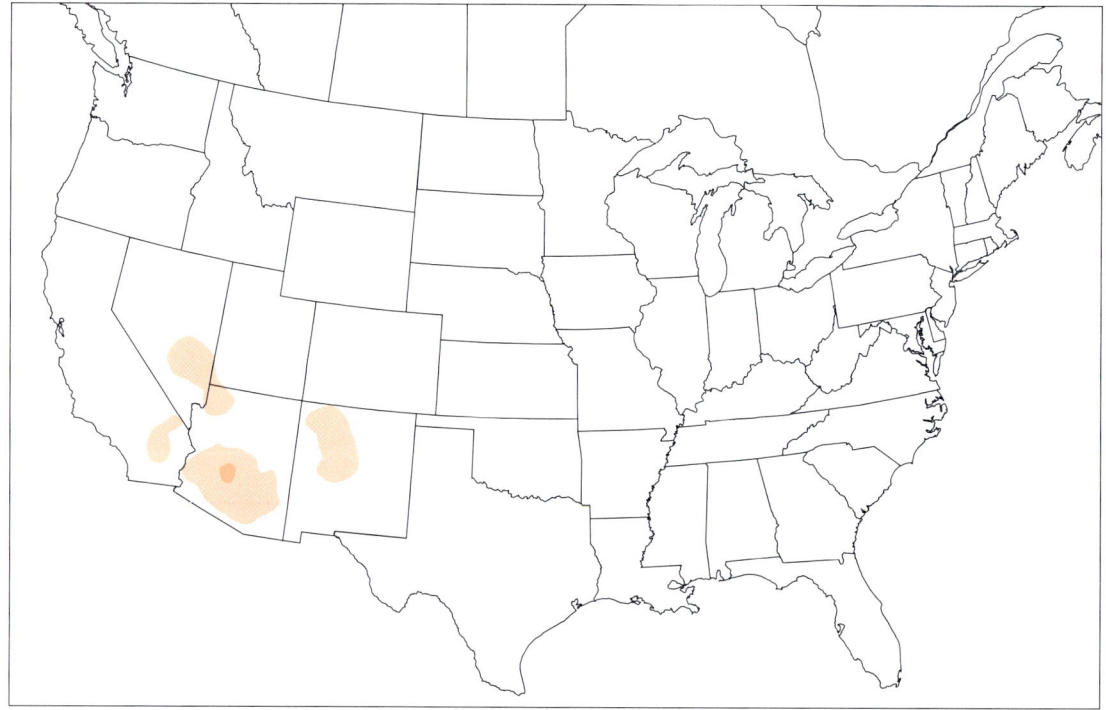

Curve-billed Thrasher

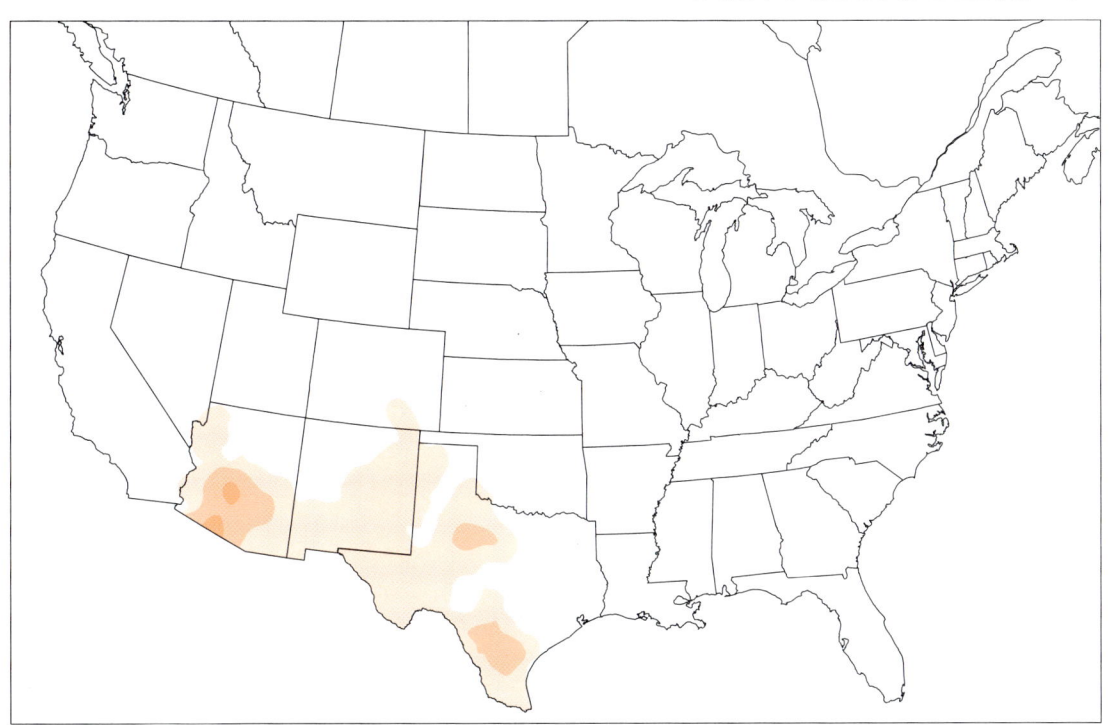

California Thrasher

Crissal Thrasher

Le Conte's Thrasher

Sprague's Pipit

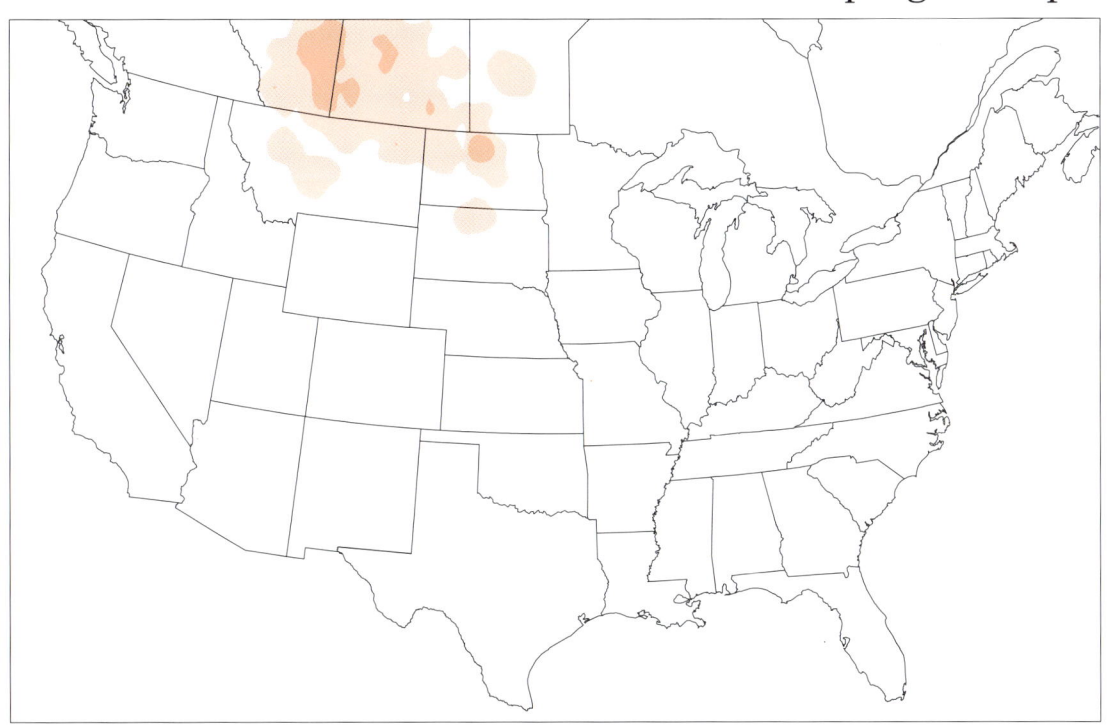

Cedar Waxwing

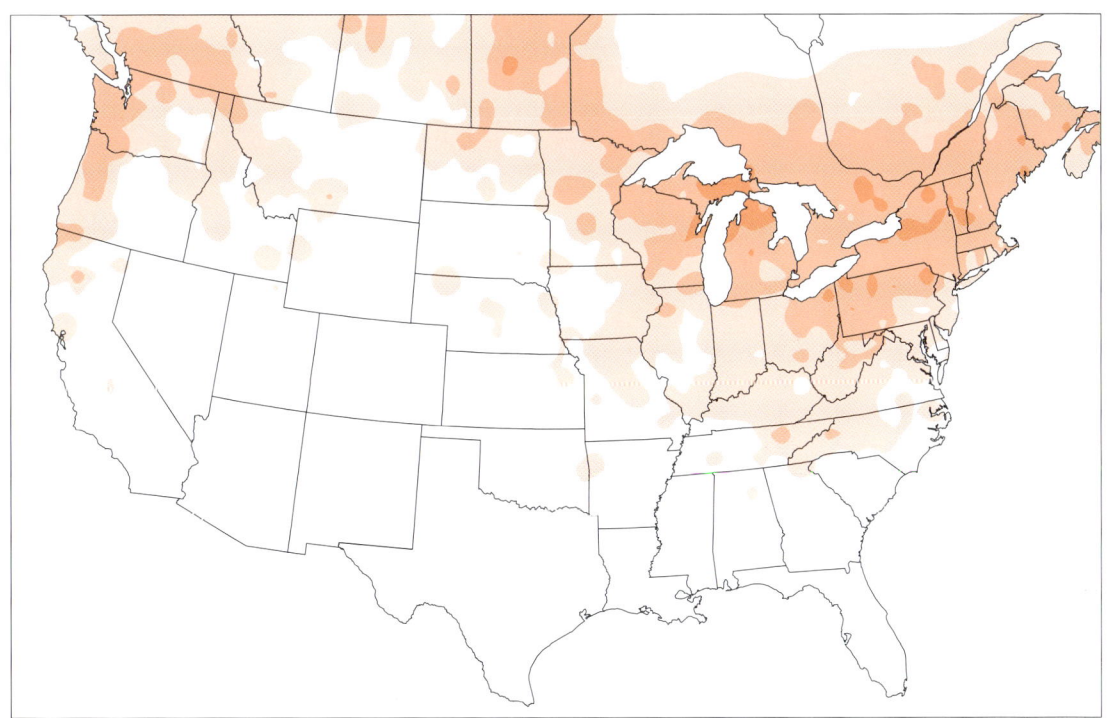

Phainopepla

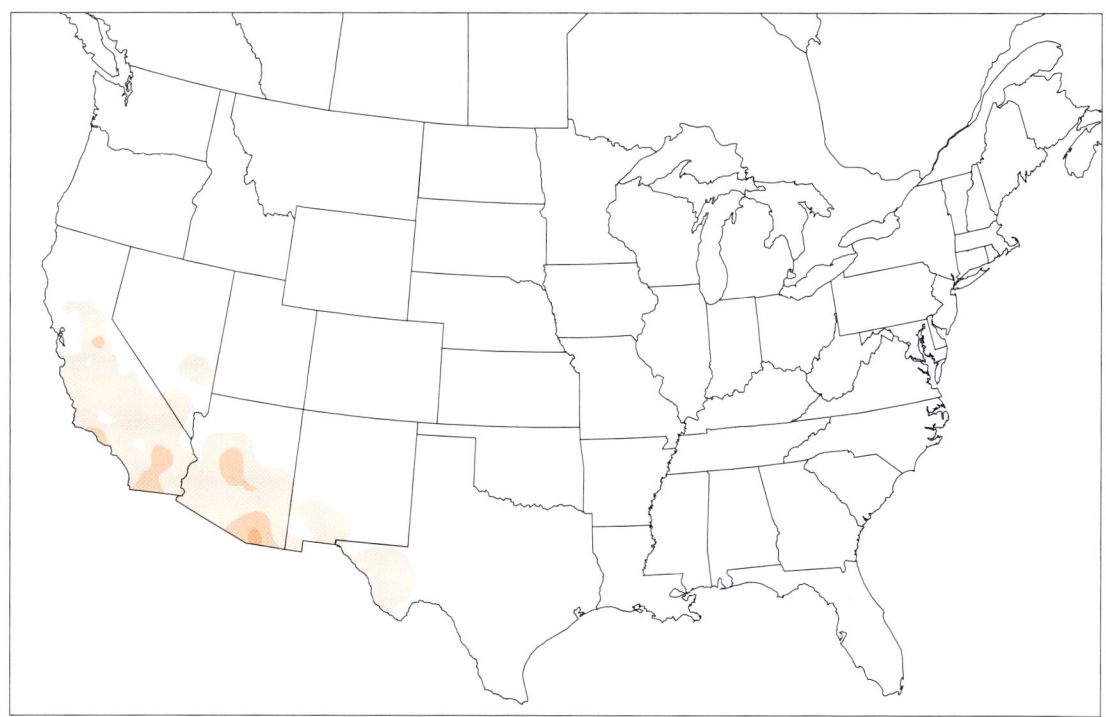

Loggerhead Shrike

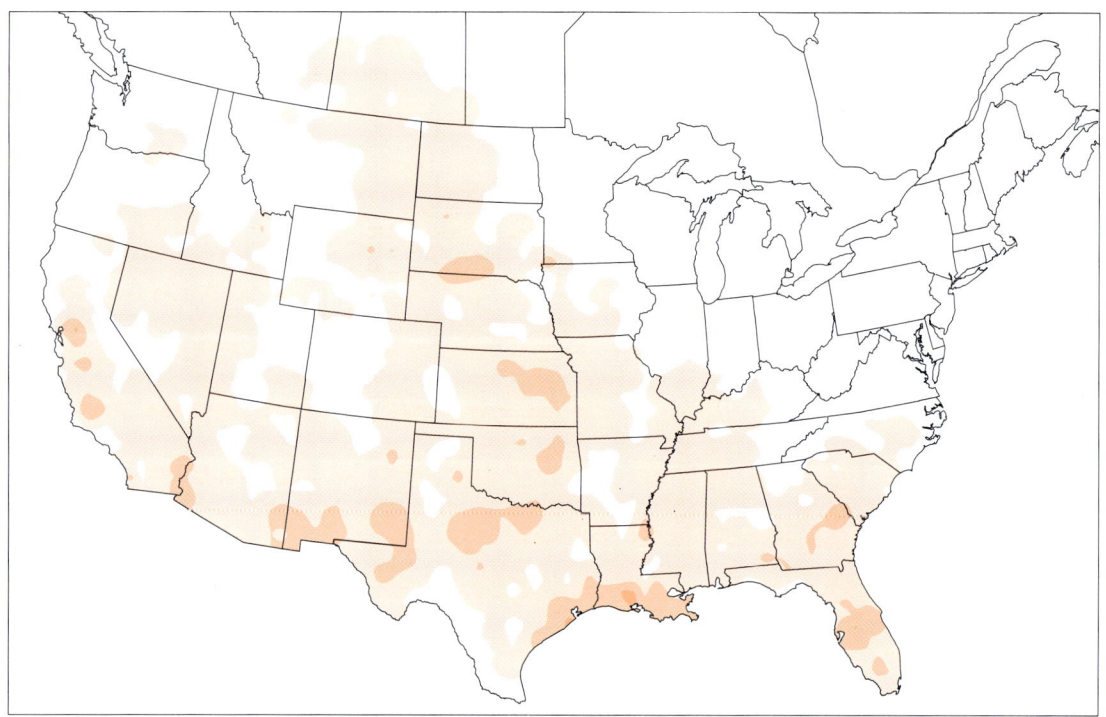

European Starling

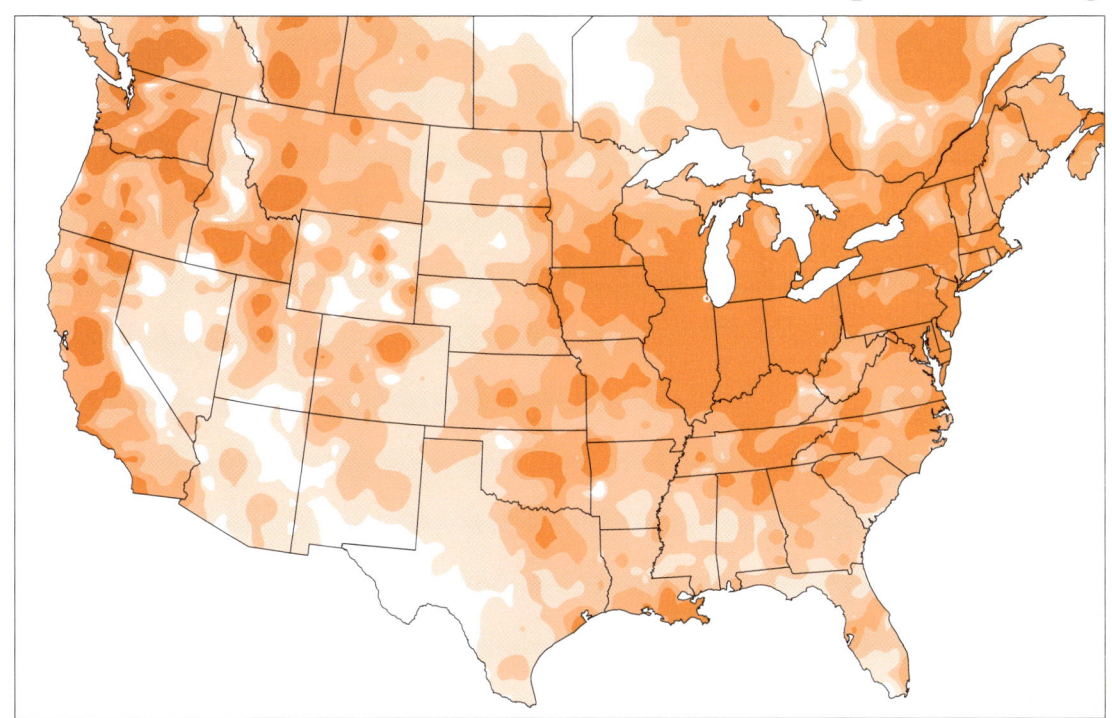

White-eyed Vireo

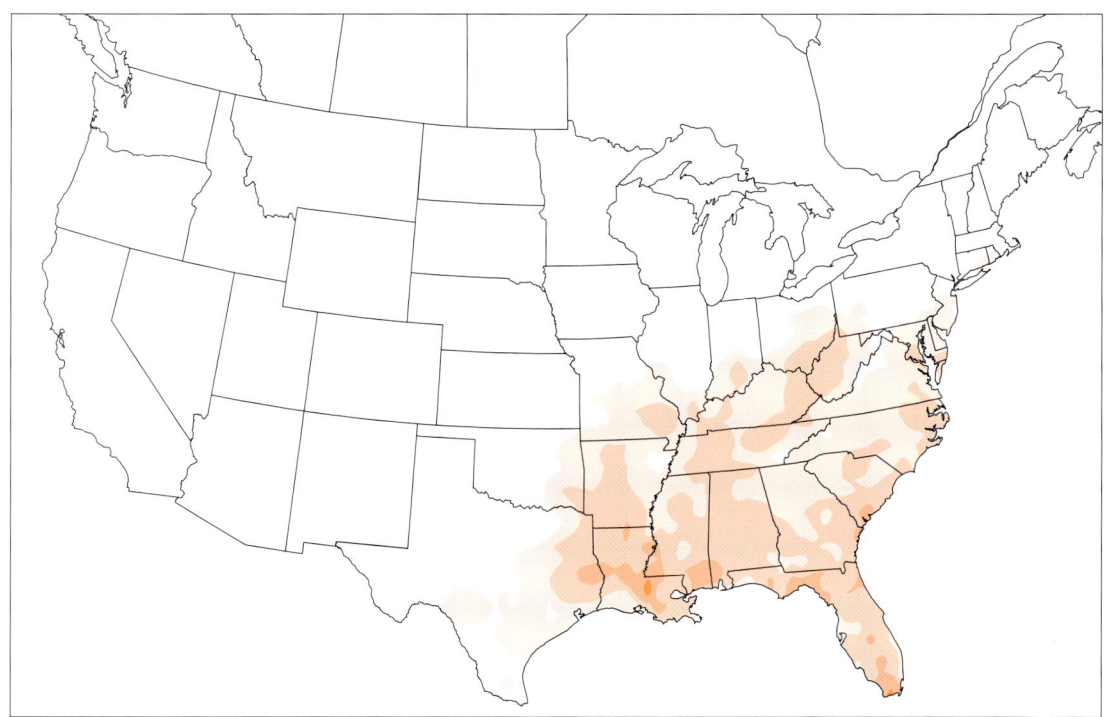

Bell's Vireo

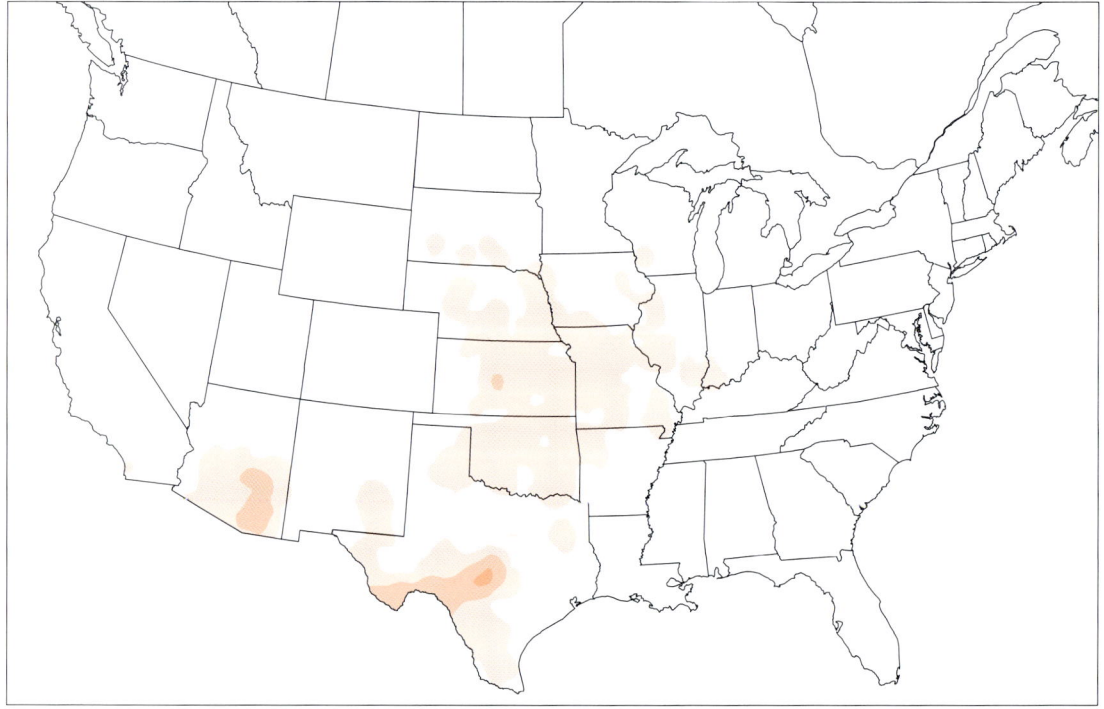

Black-capped Vireo

Gray Vireo

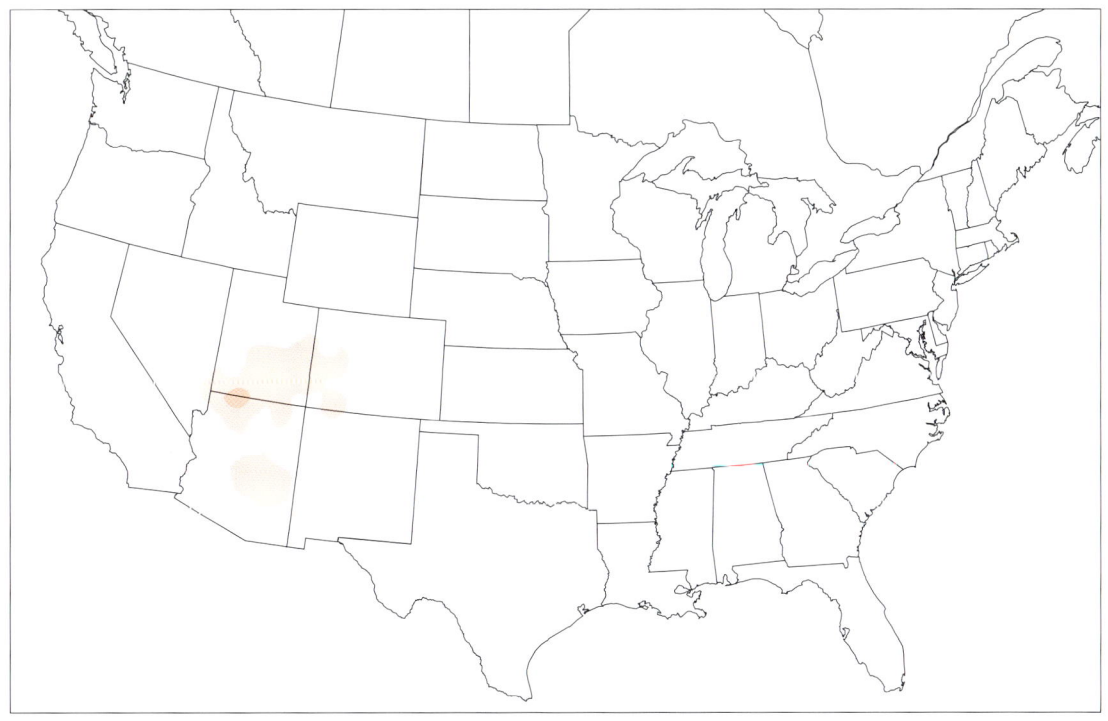

Solitary Vireo

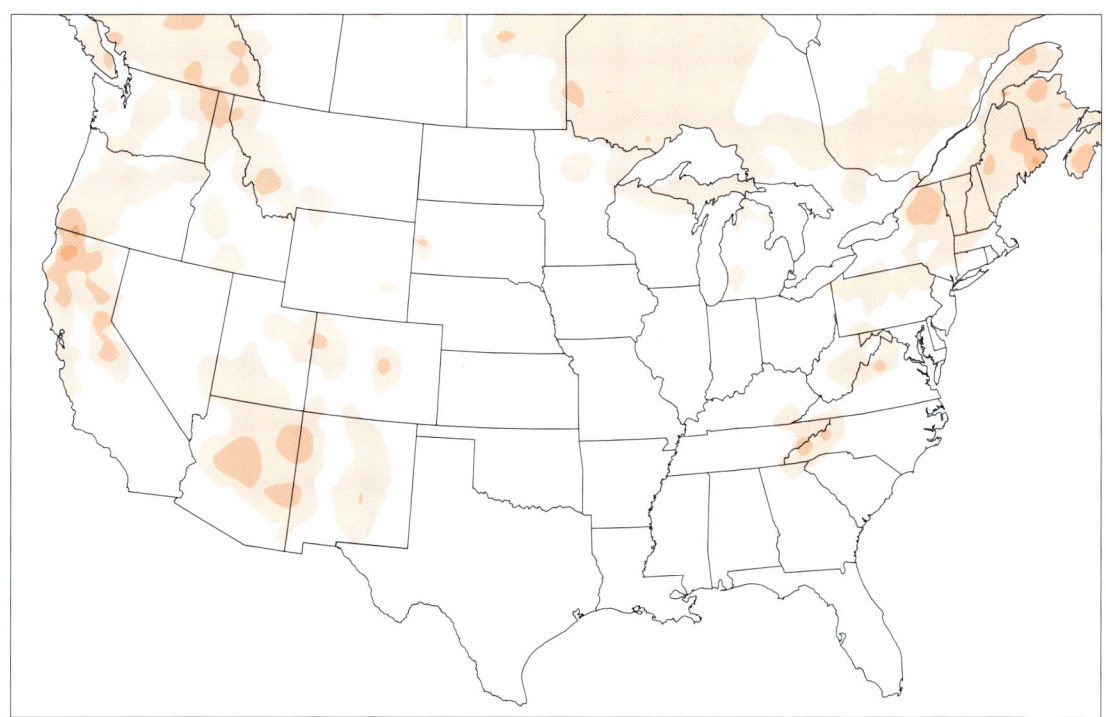

Yellow-throated Vireo

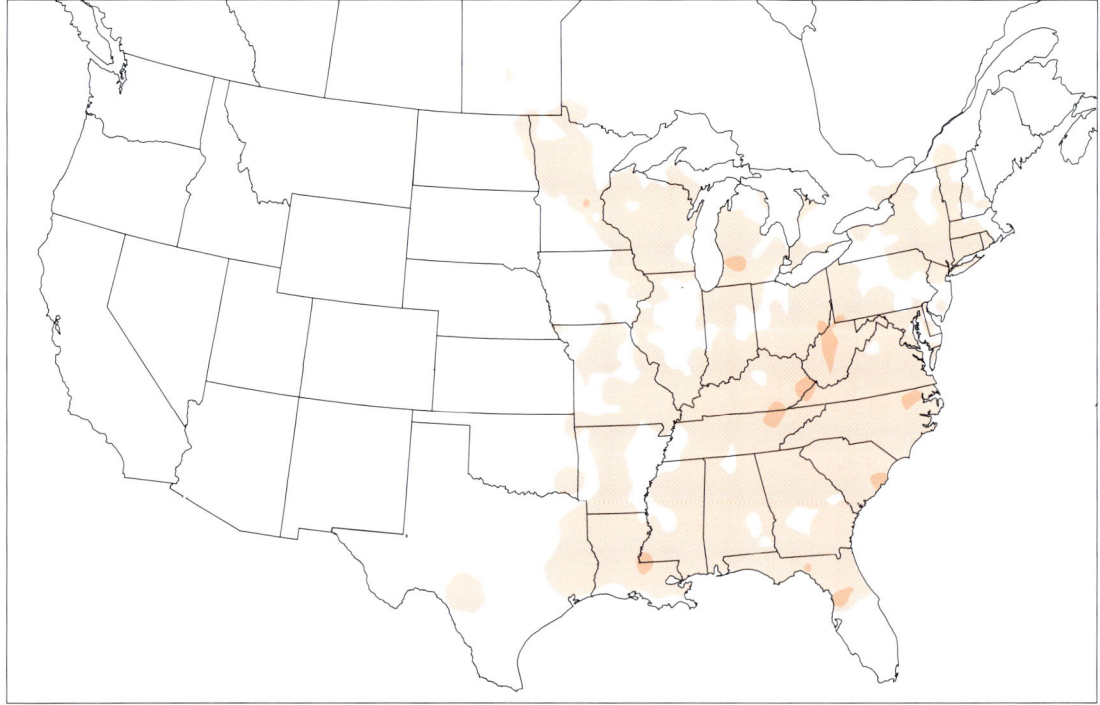

Hutton's Vireo

Warbling Vireo

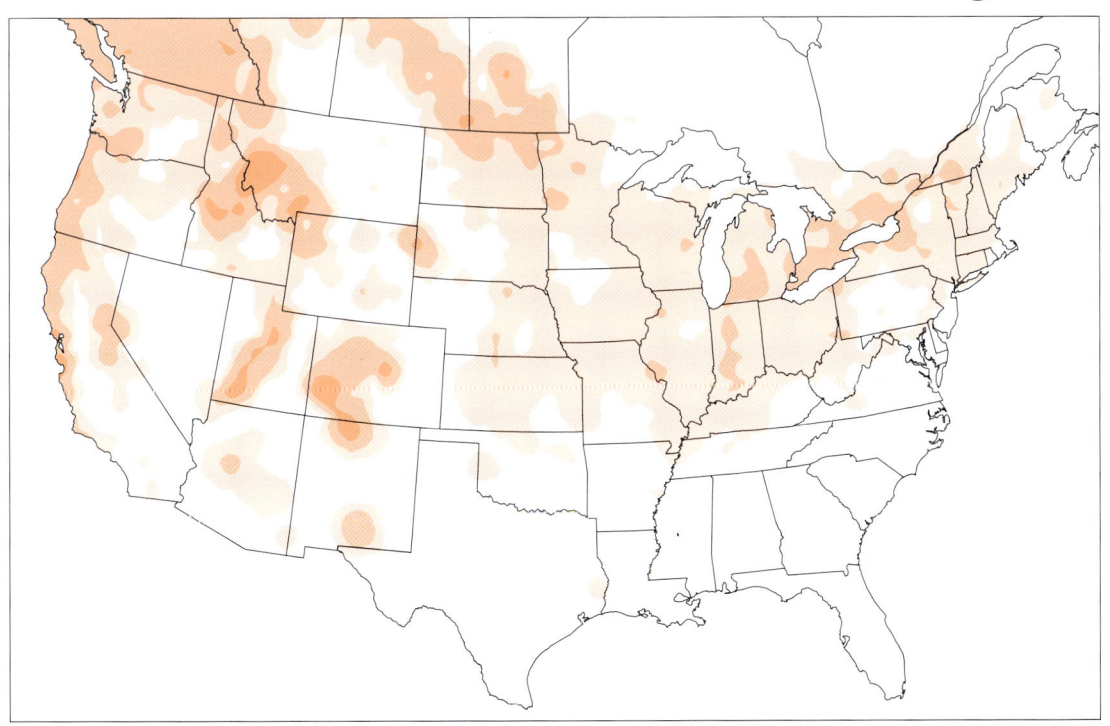

Philadelphia Vireo

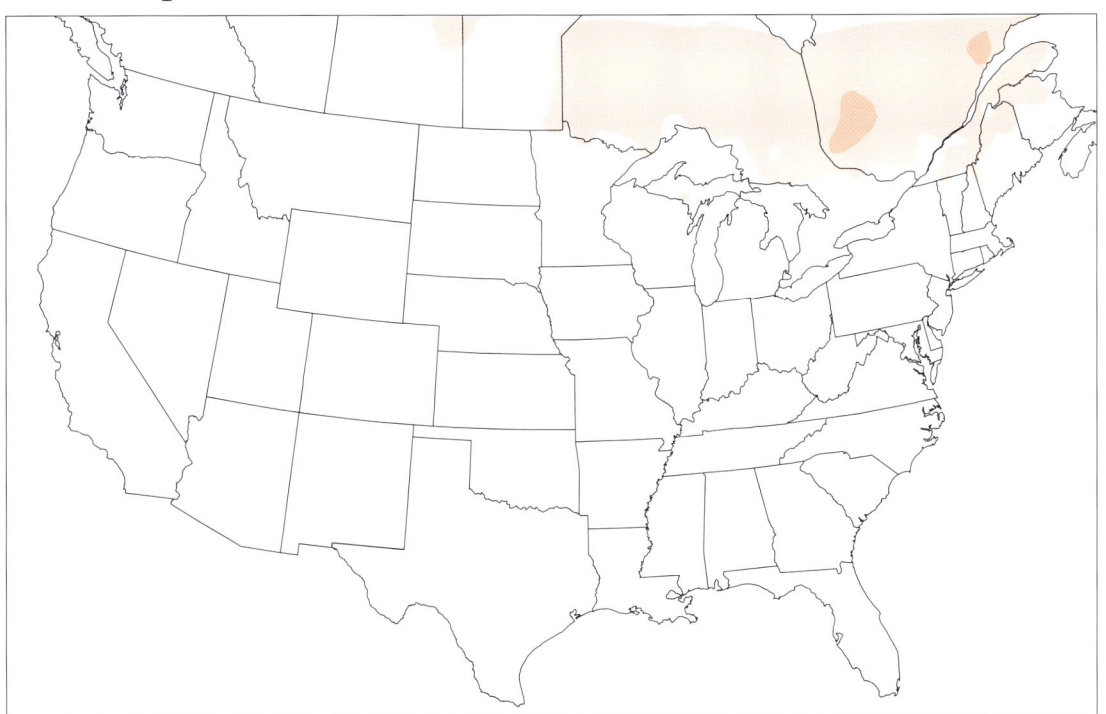

Red-eyed Vireo

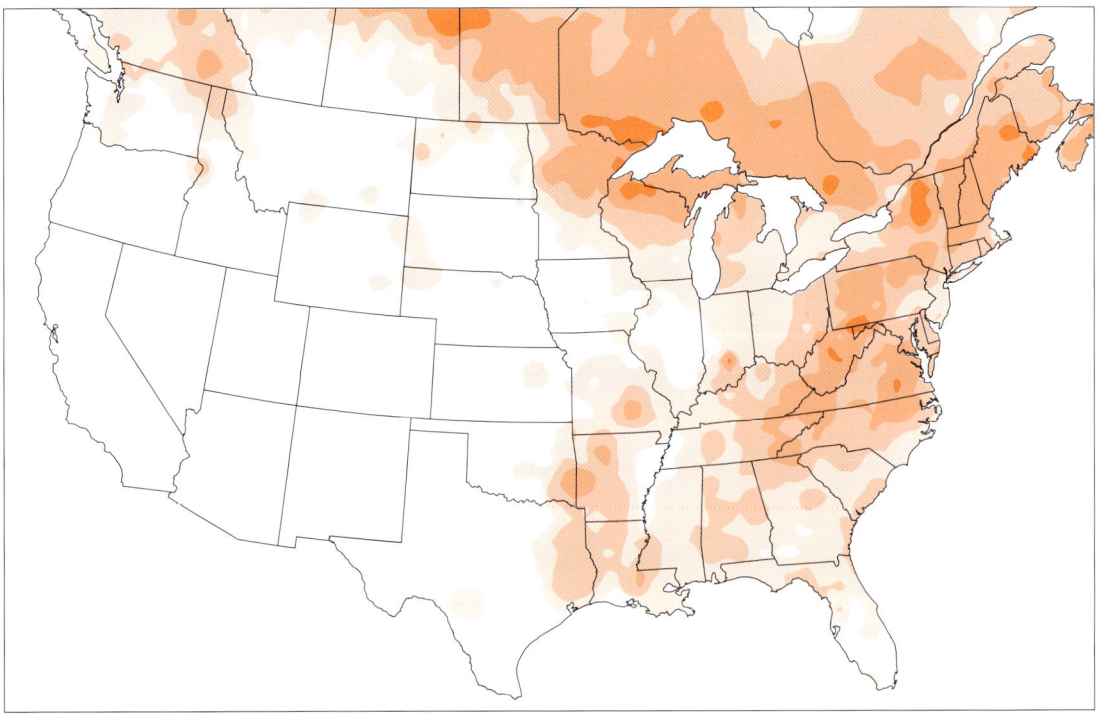

Black-whiskered Vireo

Blue-winged Warbler

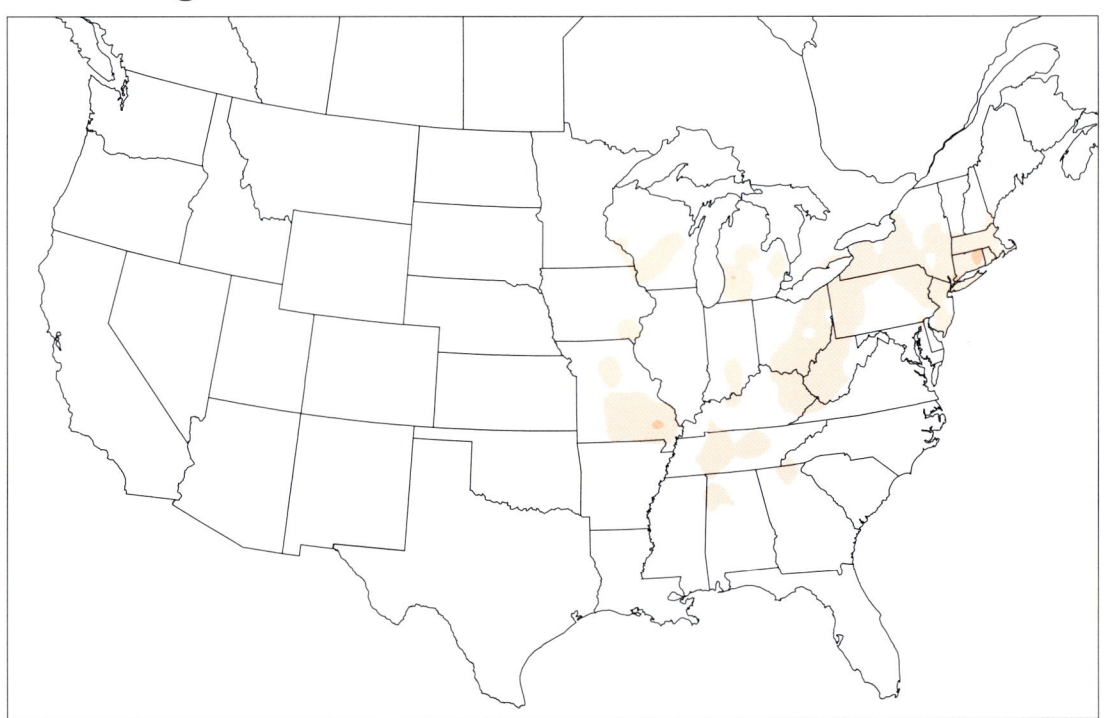

Golden-winged Warbler

Tennessee Warbler

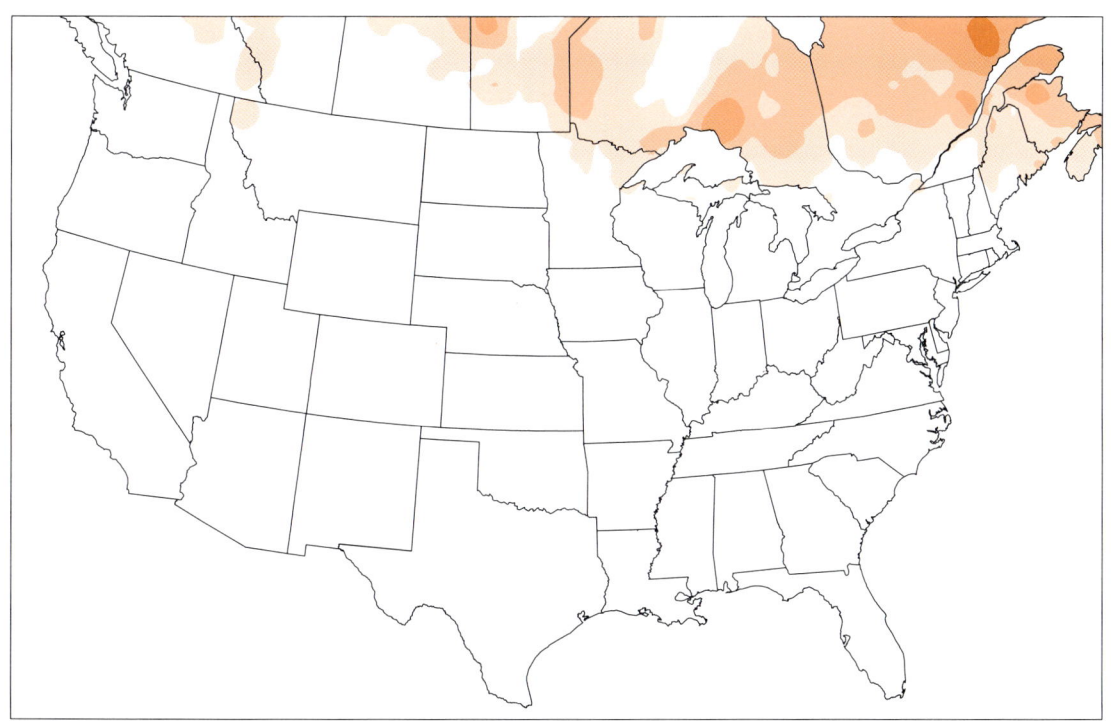

Orange-crowned Warbler

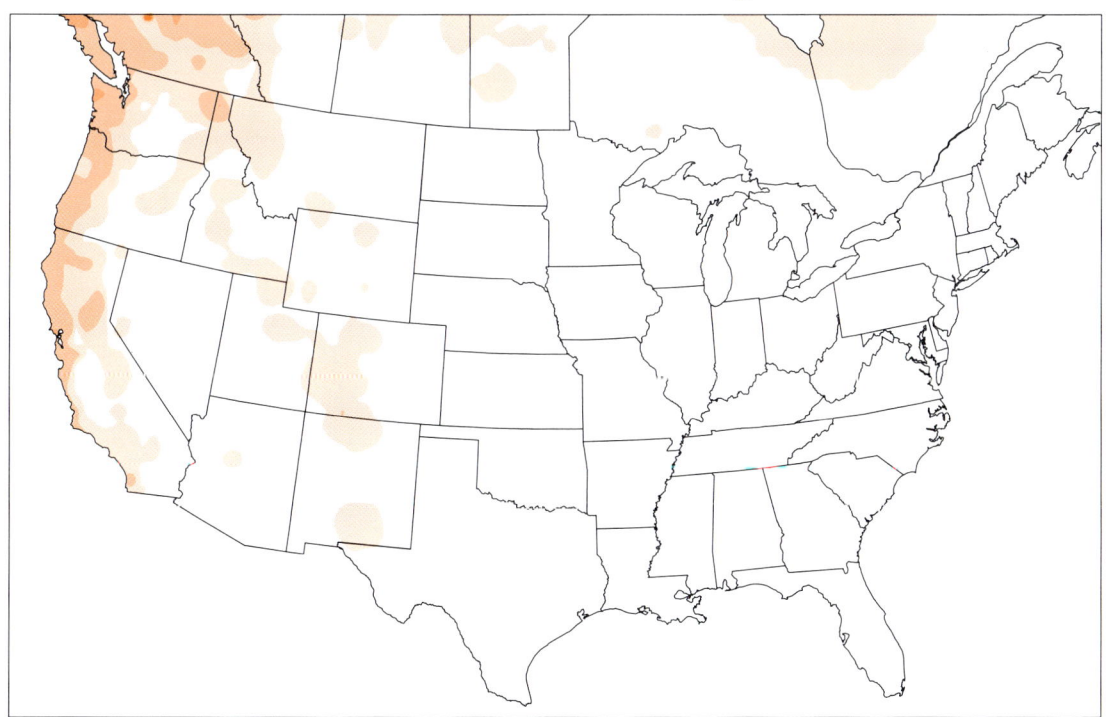

Nashville Warbler

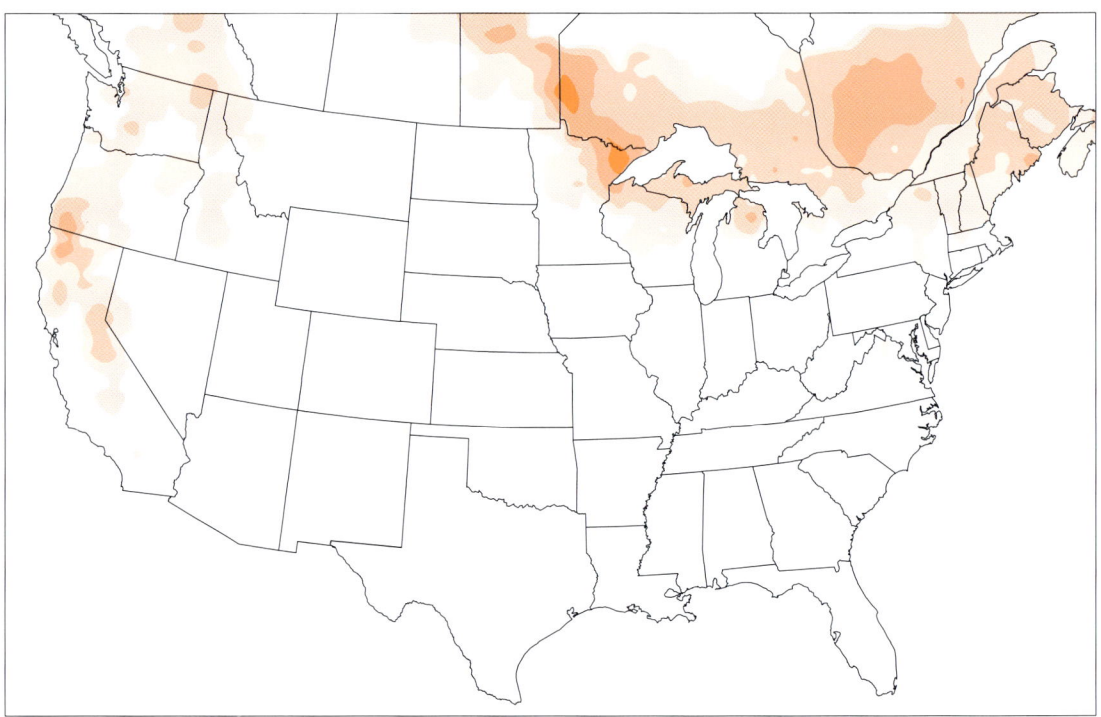

Virginia's Warbler

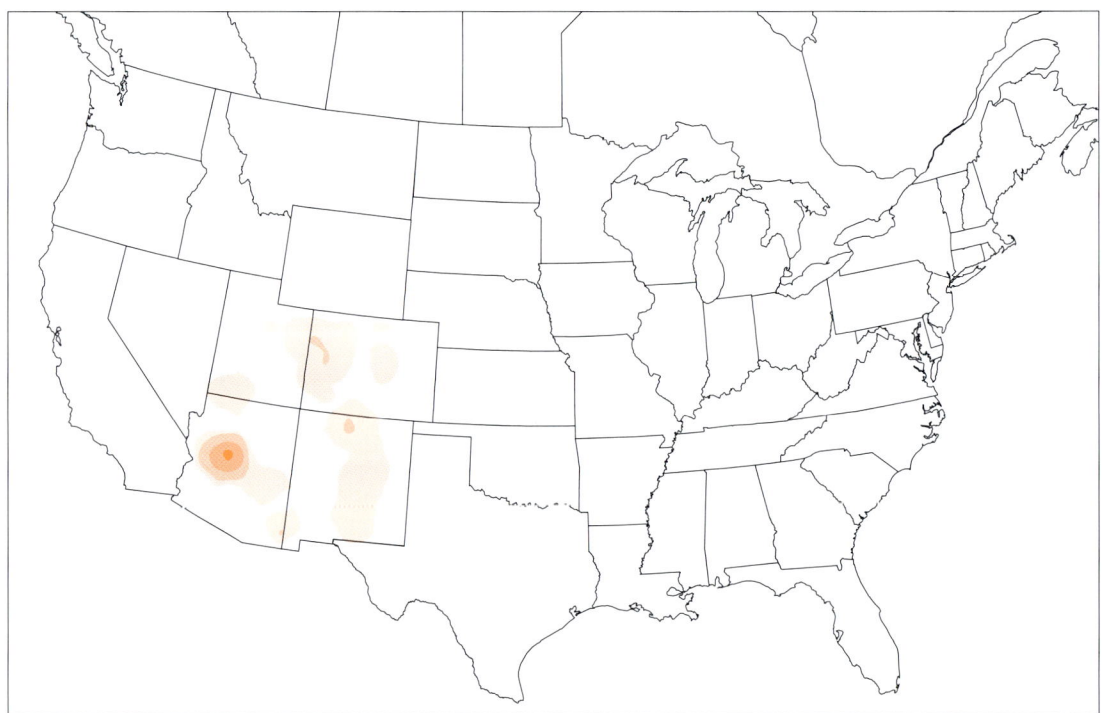

Lucy's Warbler

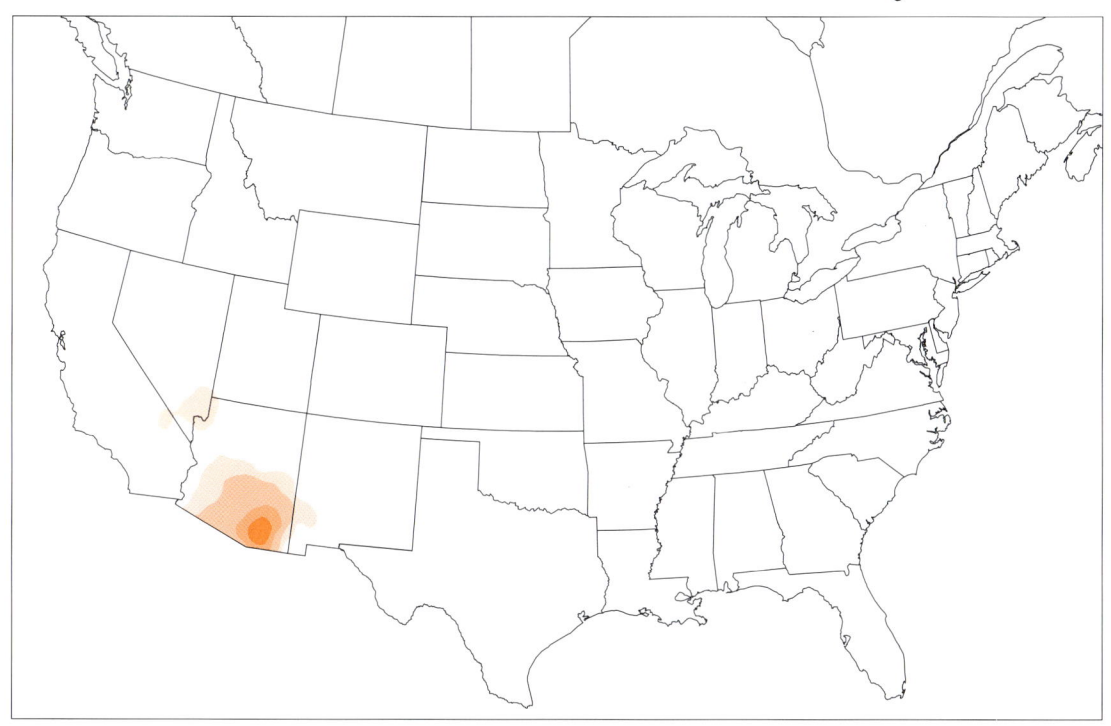

Northern Parula

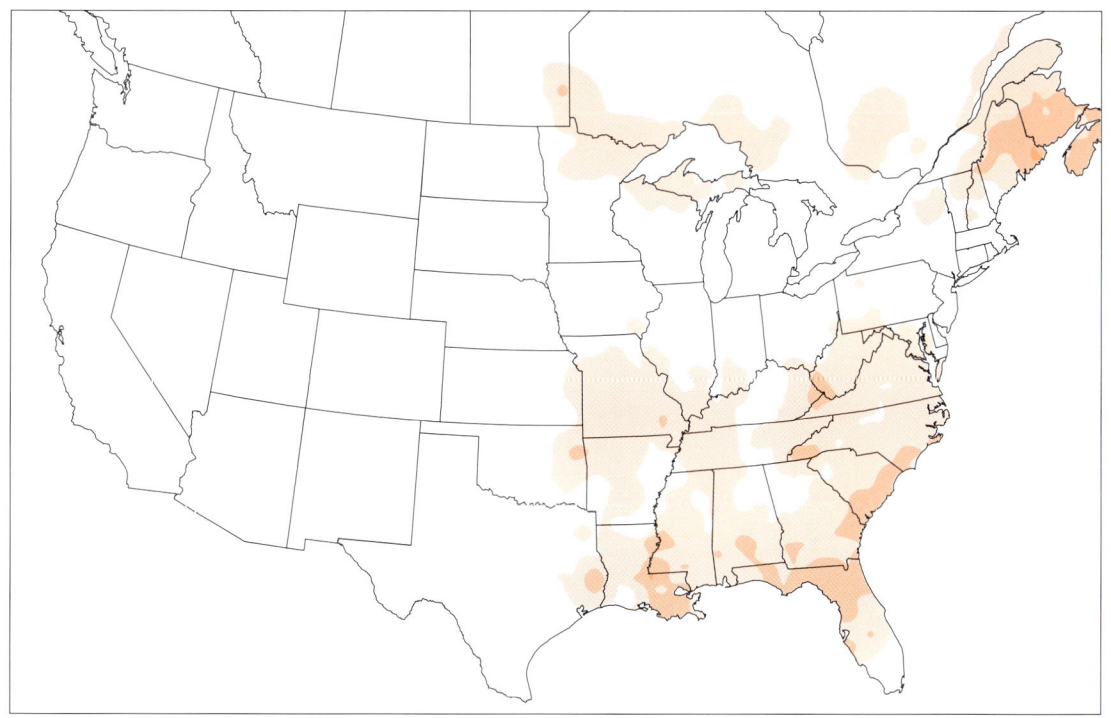

Yellow Warbler

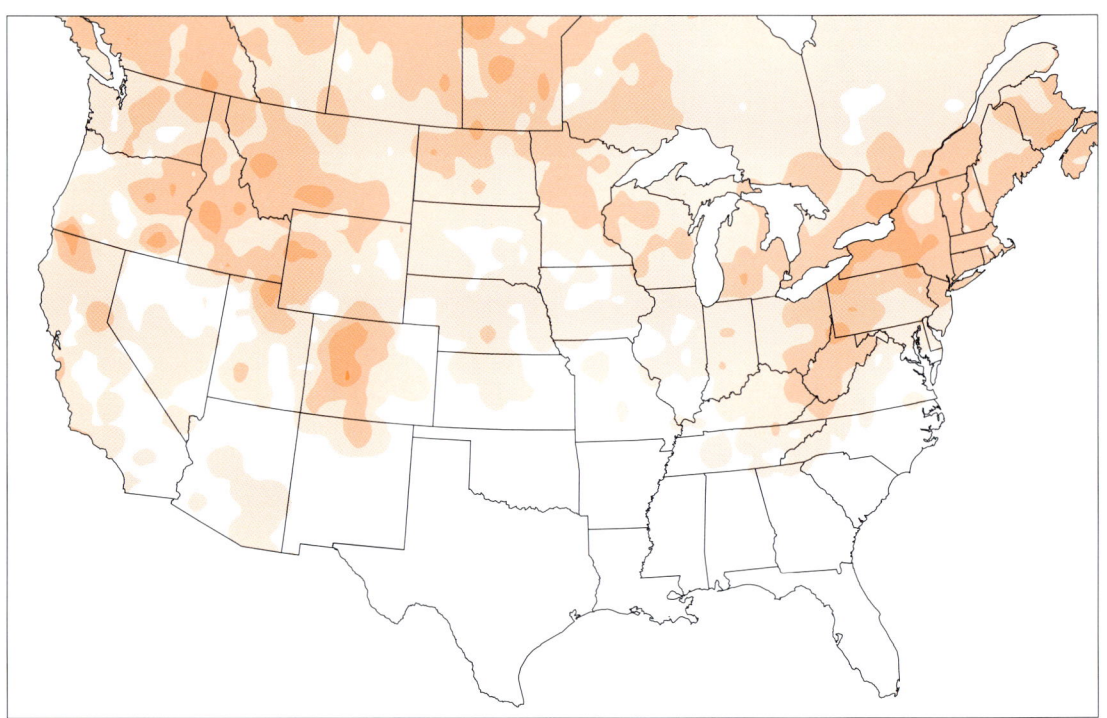

Chestnut-sided Warbler

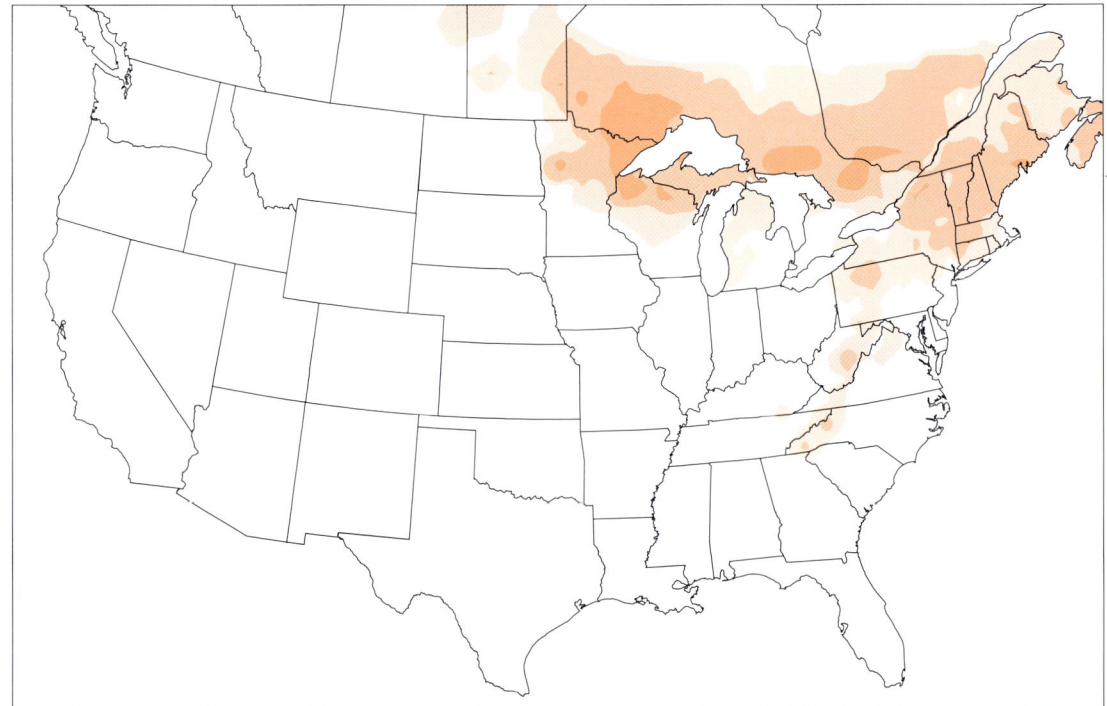

Magnolia Warbler

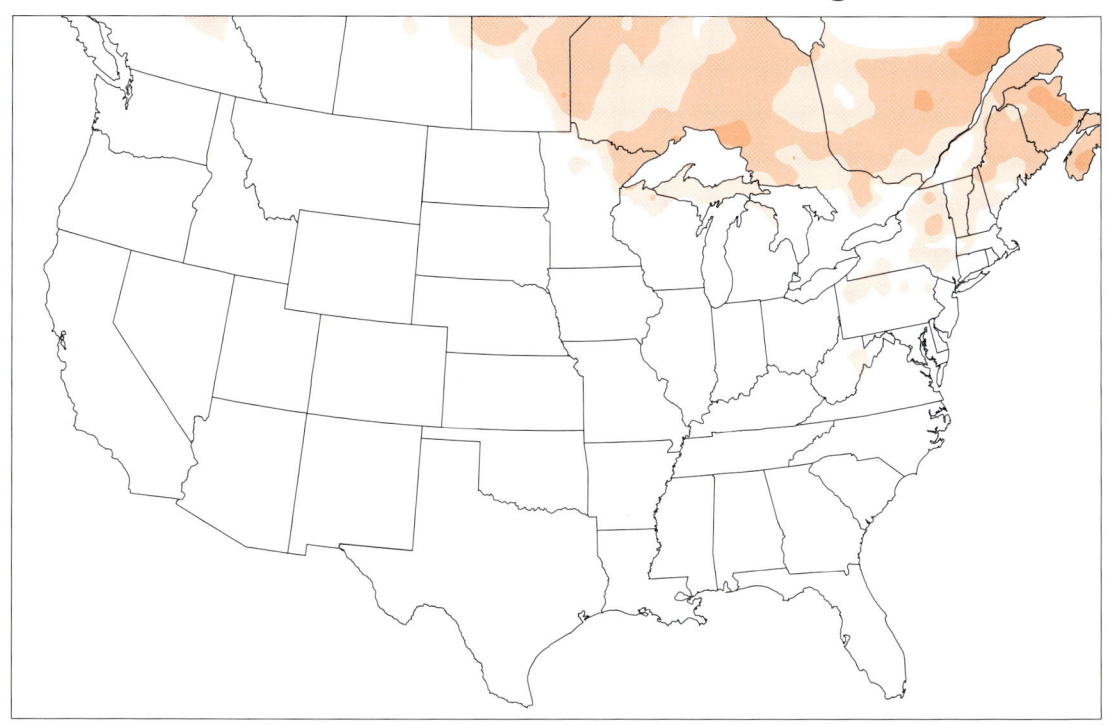

Cape May Warbler

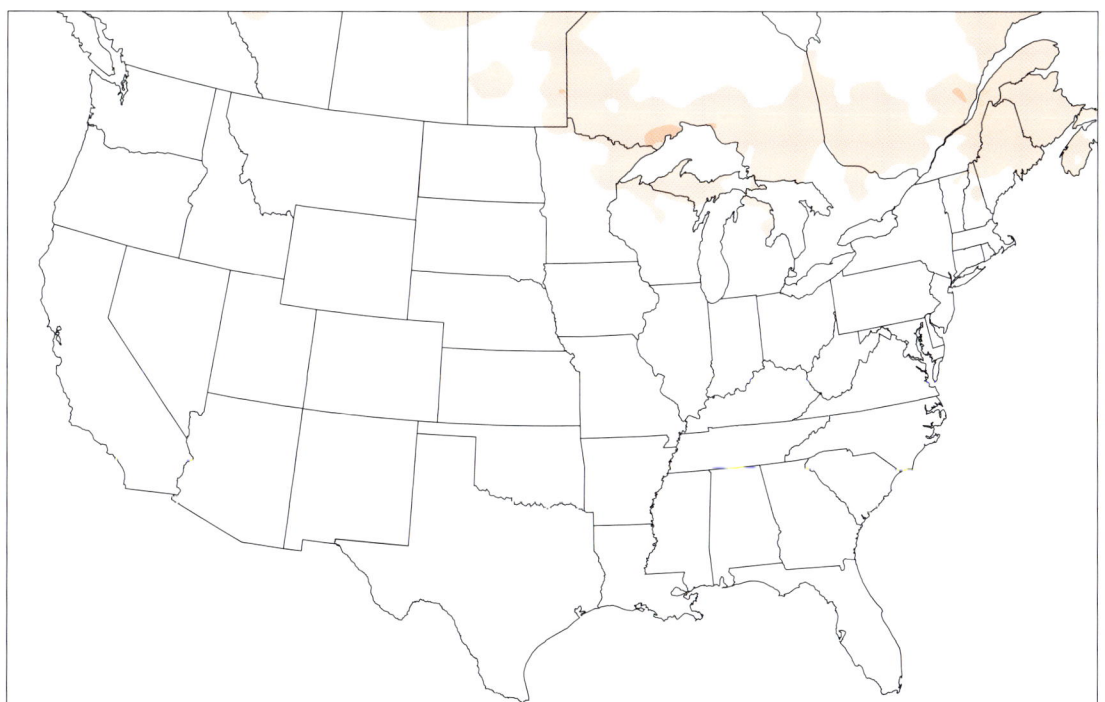

Black-throated Blue Warbler

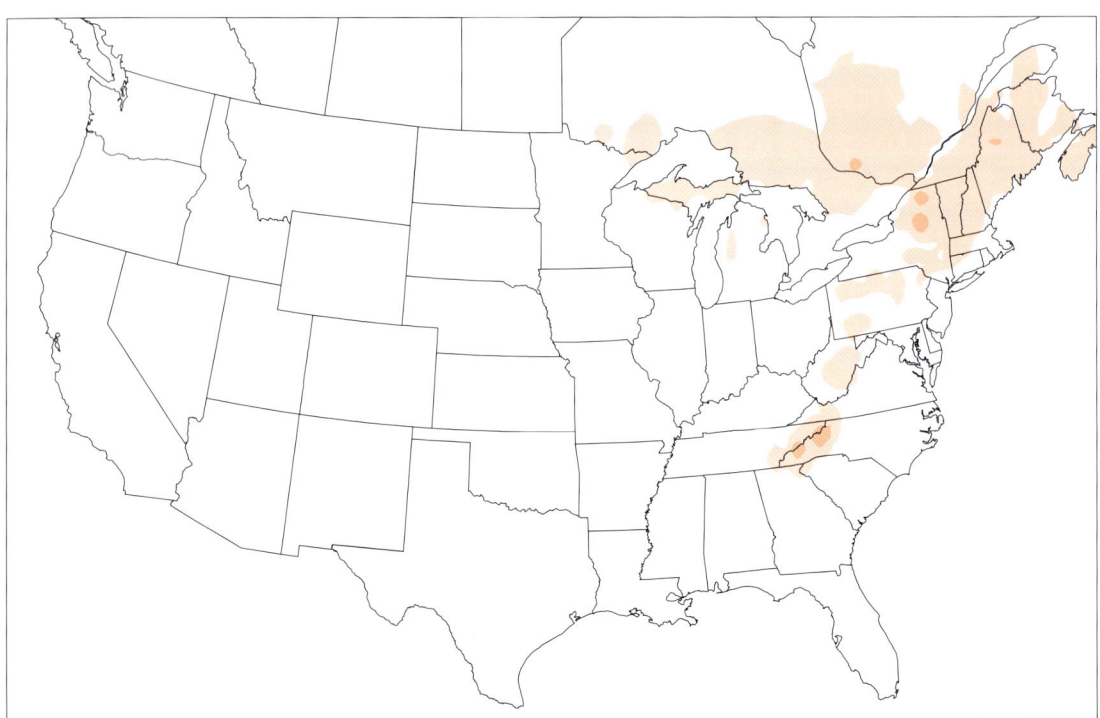

Yellow-rumped Warbler

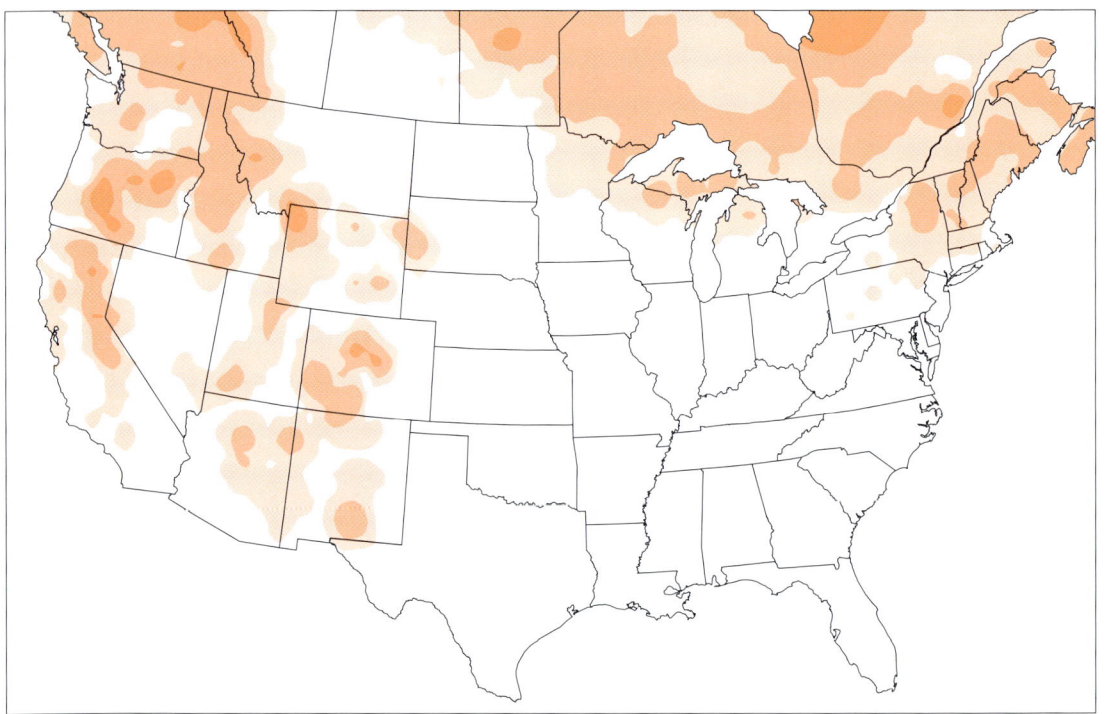

Yellow-rumped Warbler (Myrtle)

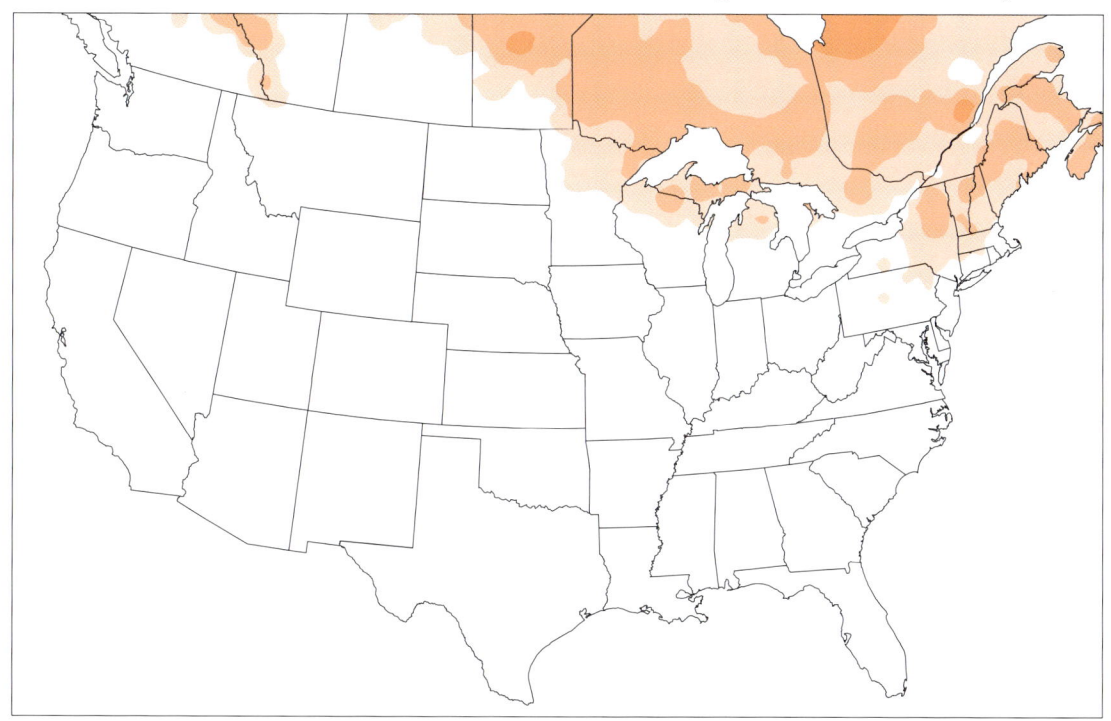

Yellow-rumped Warbler (Audubon's)

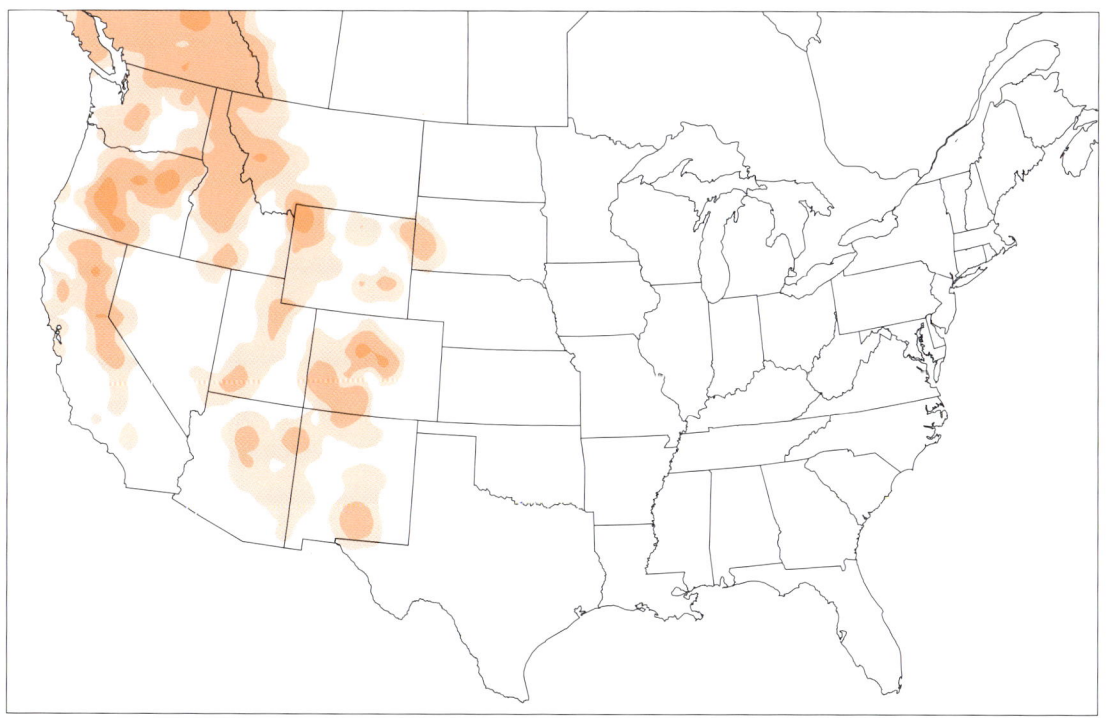

Black-throated Gray Warbler

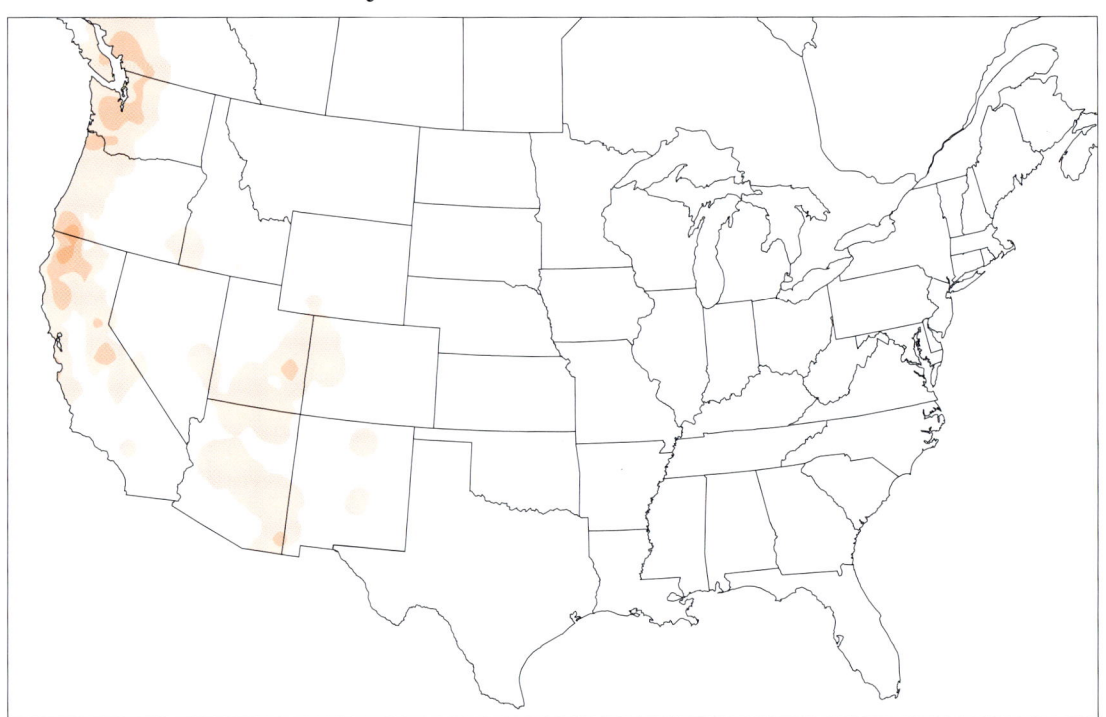

Townsend's Warbler

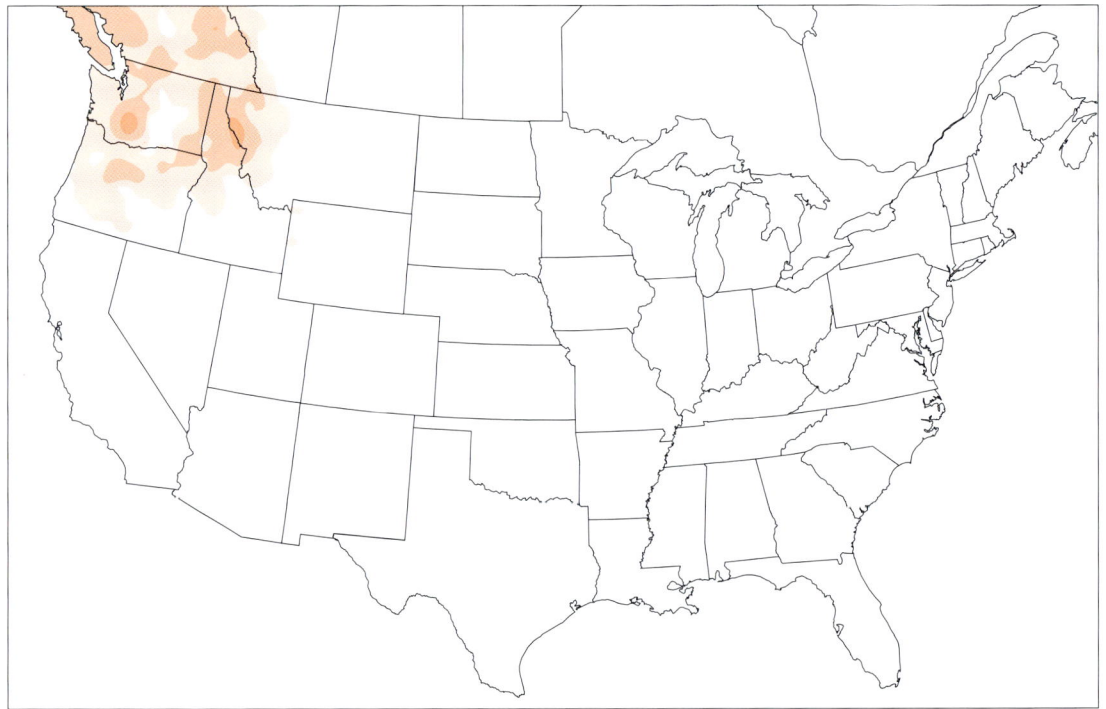

Hermit Warbler

Black-throated Green Warbler

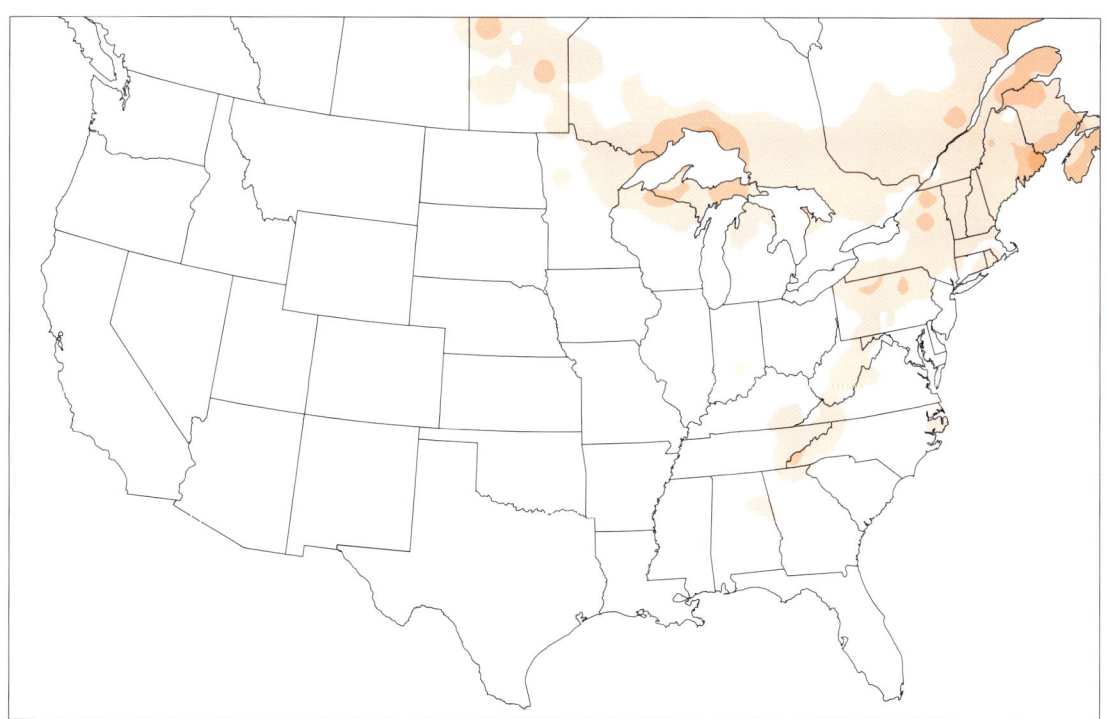

Blackburnian Warbler

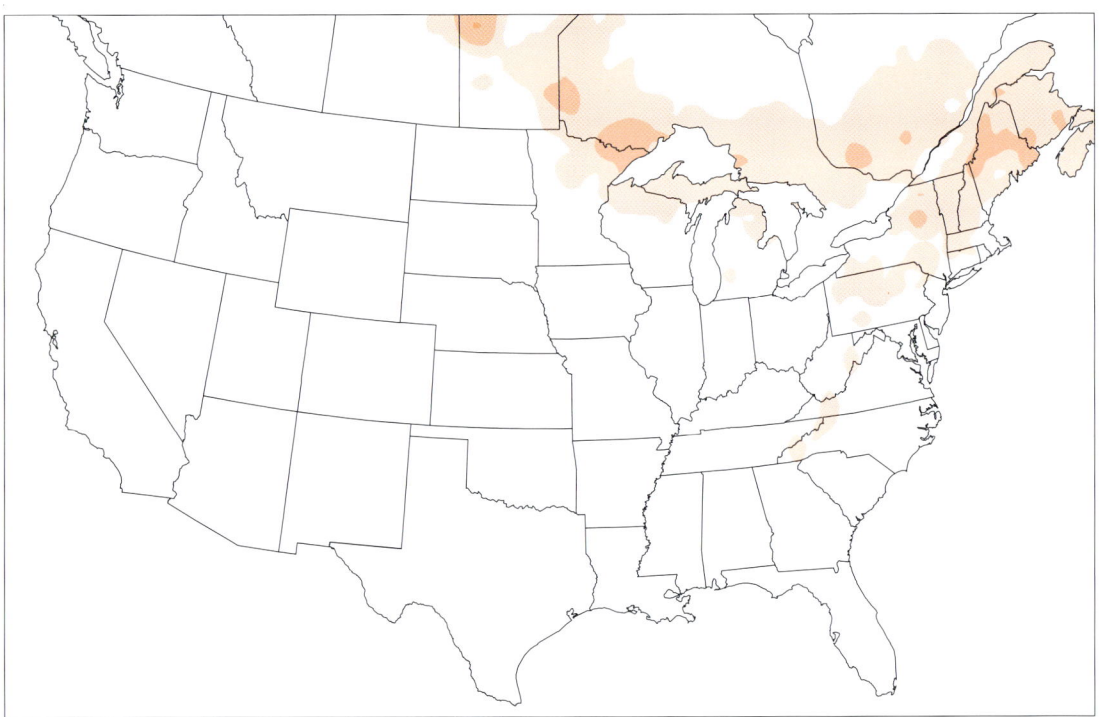

Yellow-throated Warbler

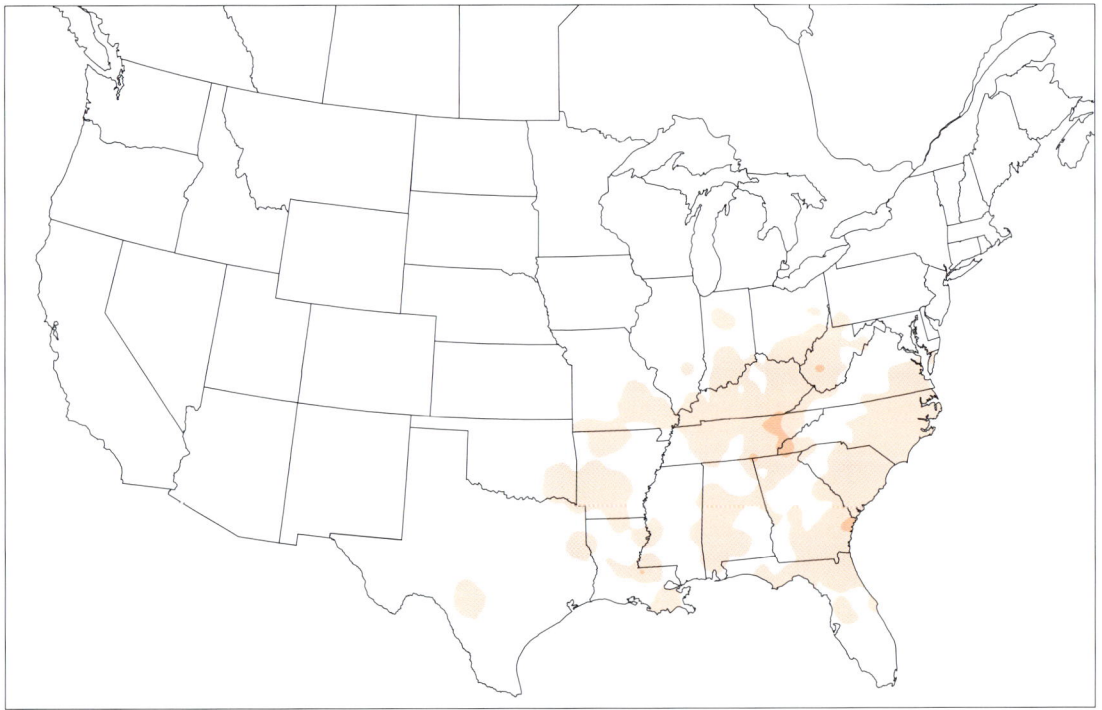

Grace's Warbler

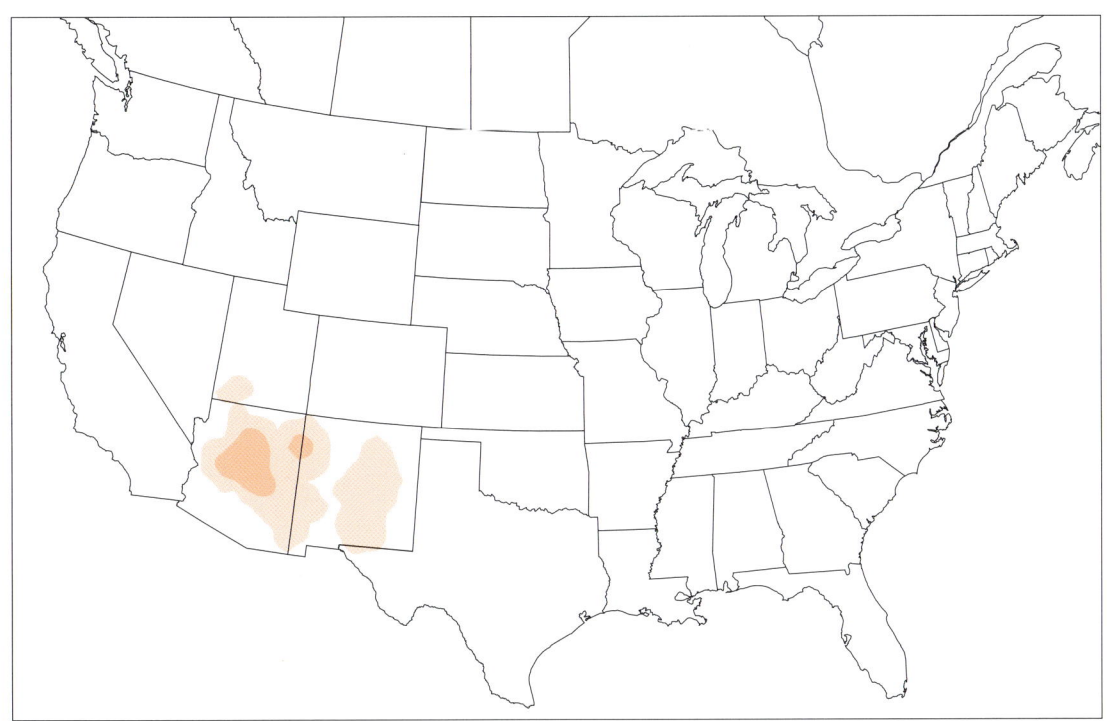

Pine Warbler

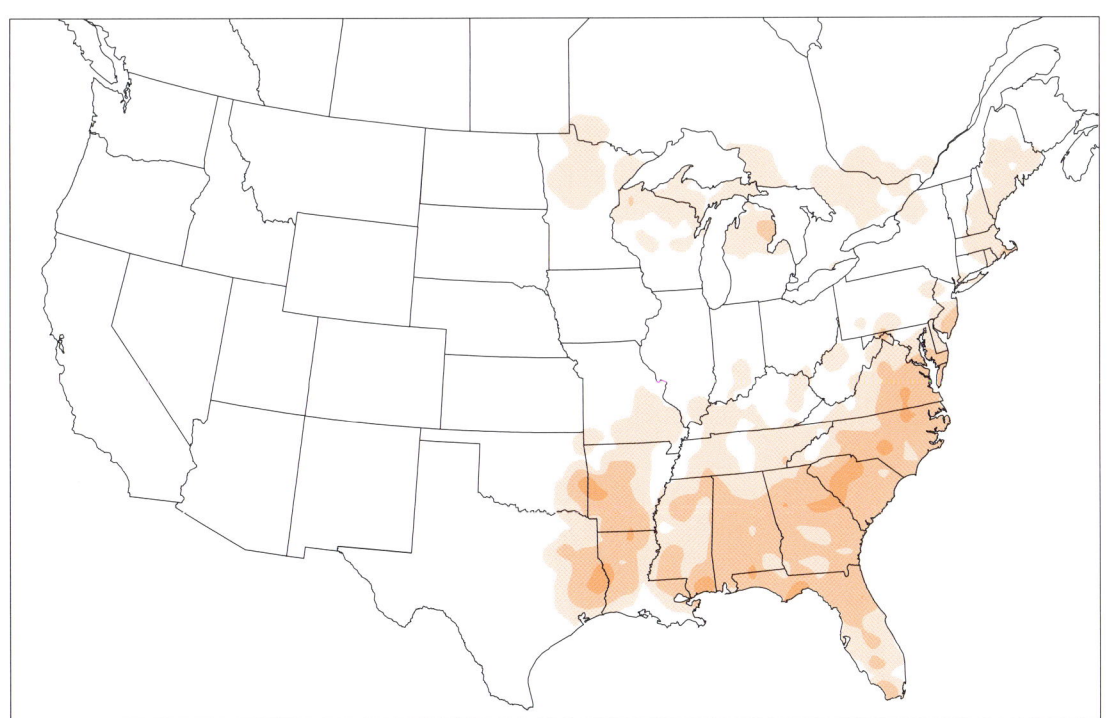

Prairie Warbler

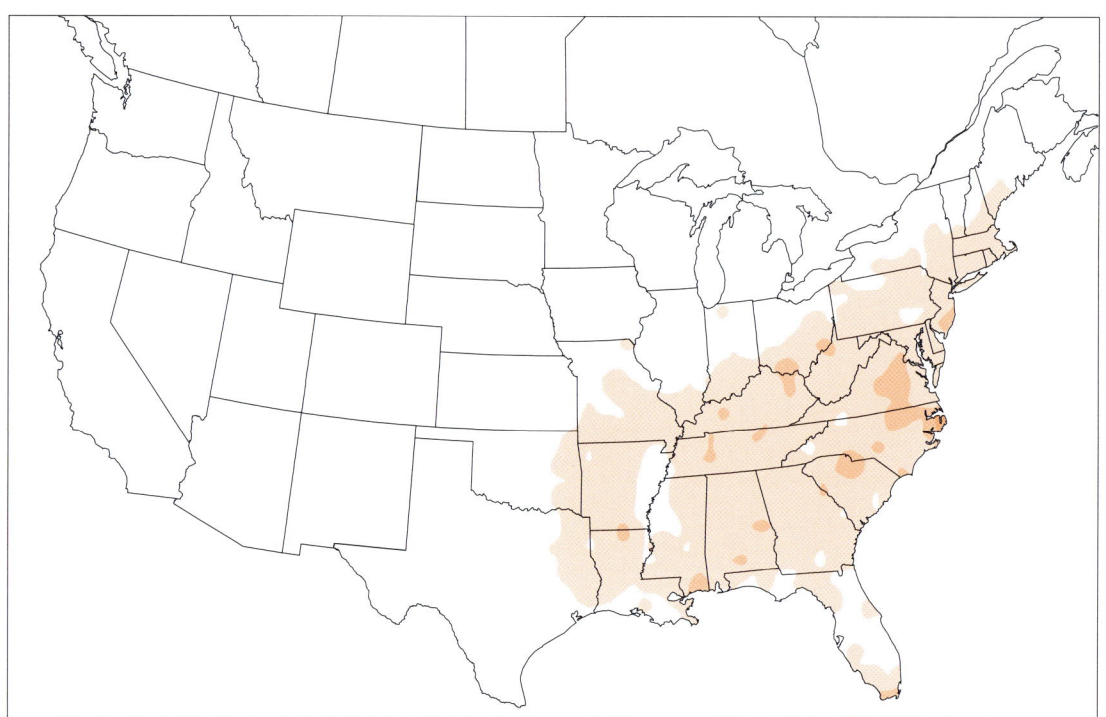

Palm Warbler

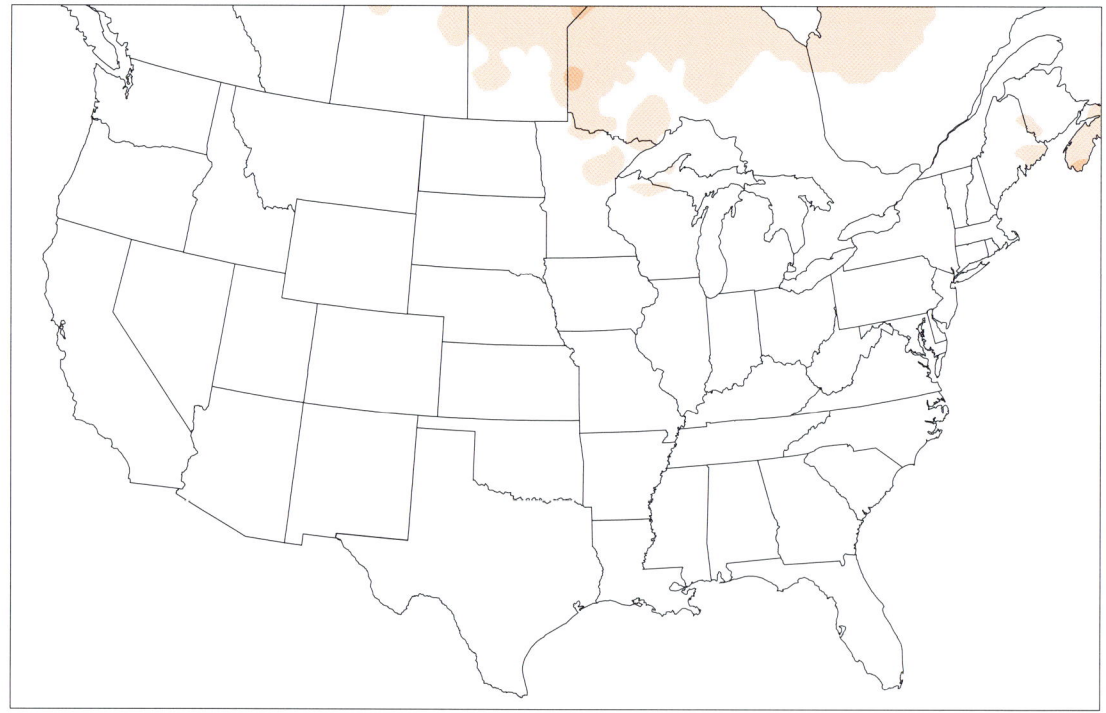

Bay-breasted Warbler

Blackpoll Warbler

Cerulean Warbler

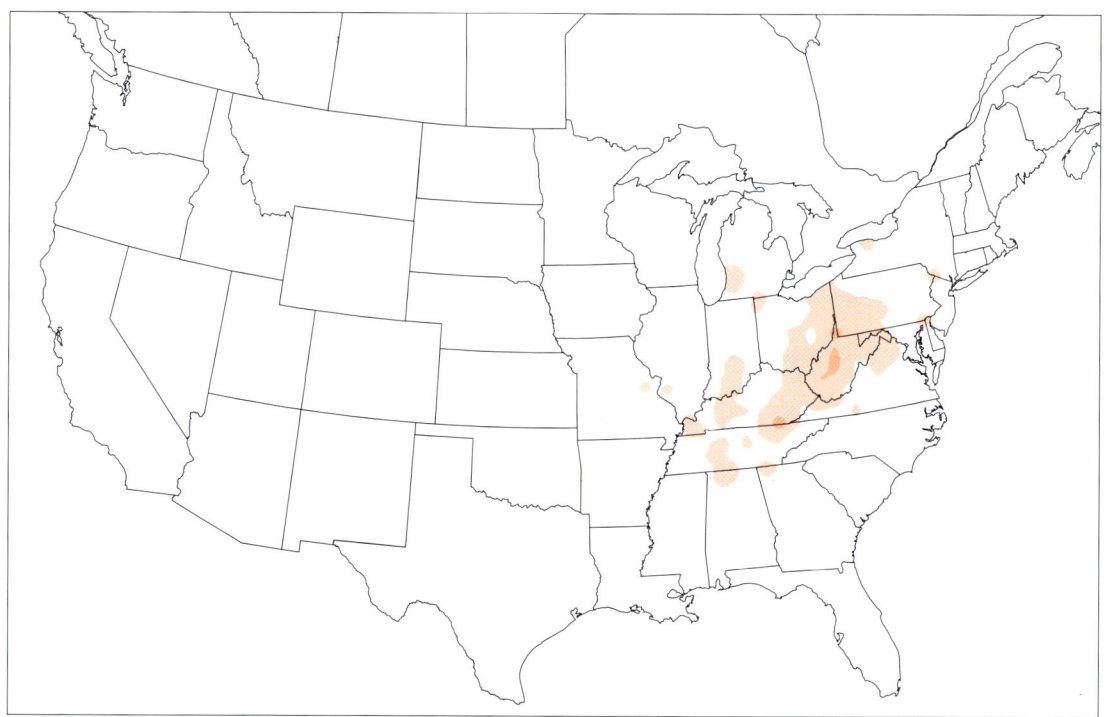

Black-and-white Warbler

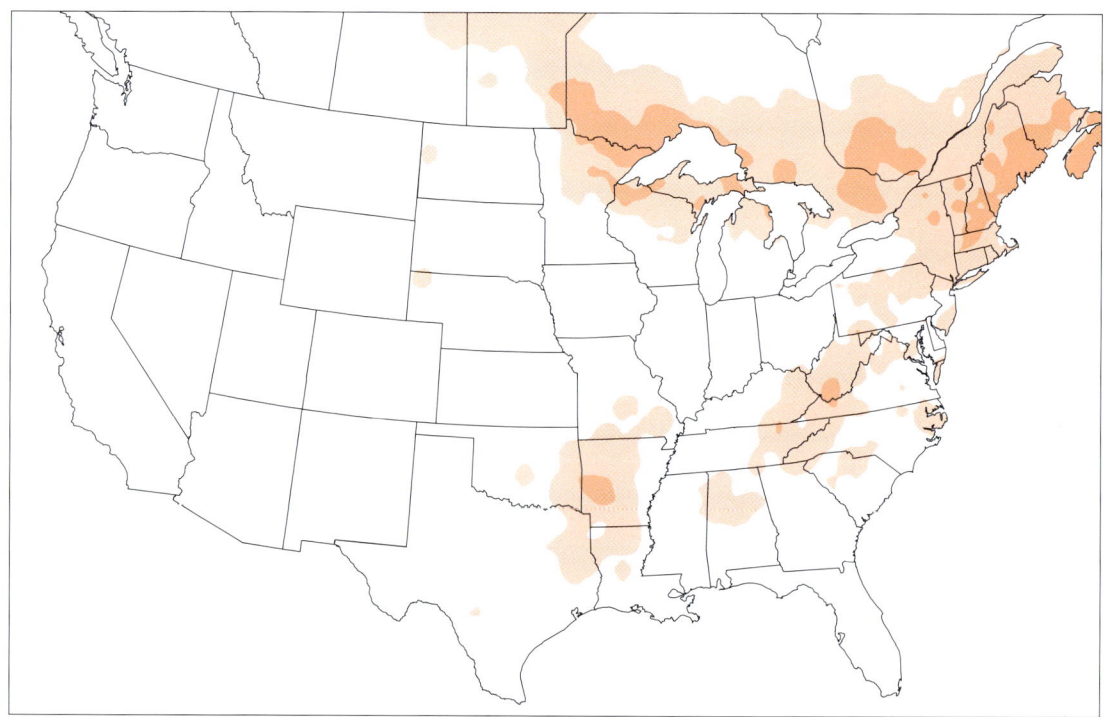

American Redstart

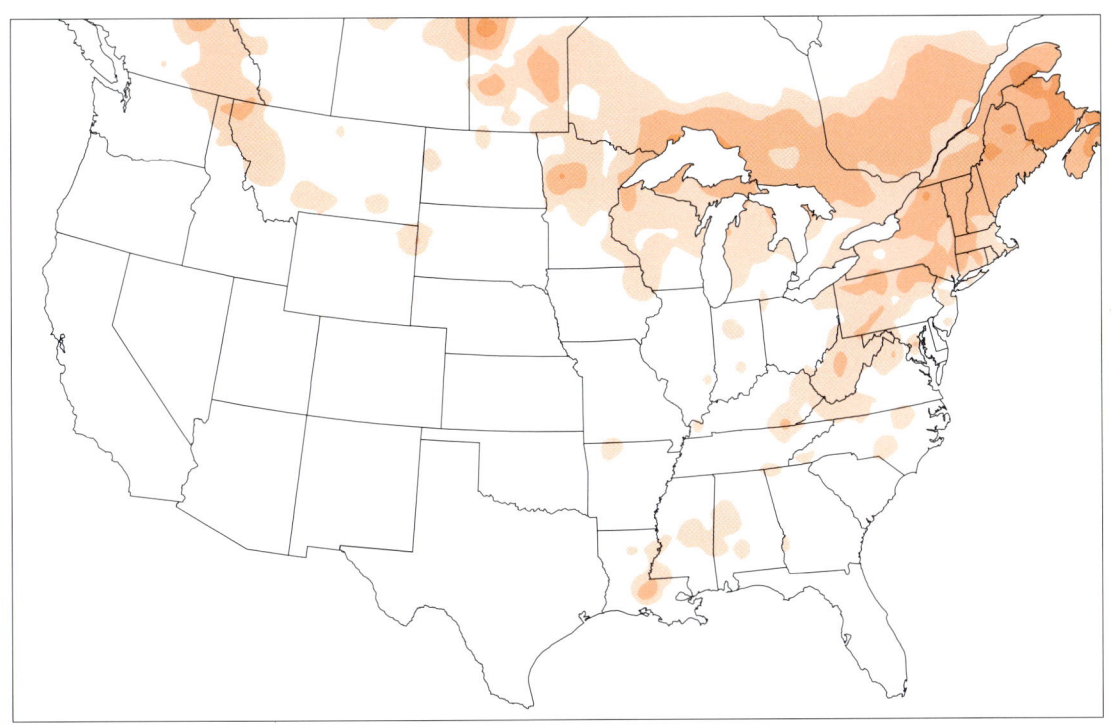

Prothonotary Warbler

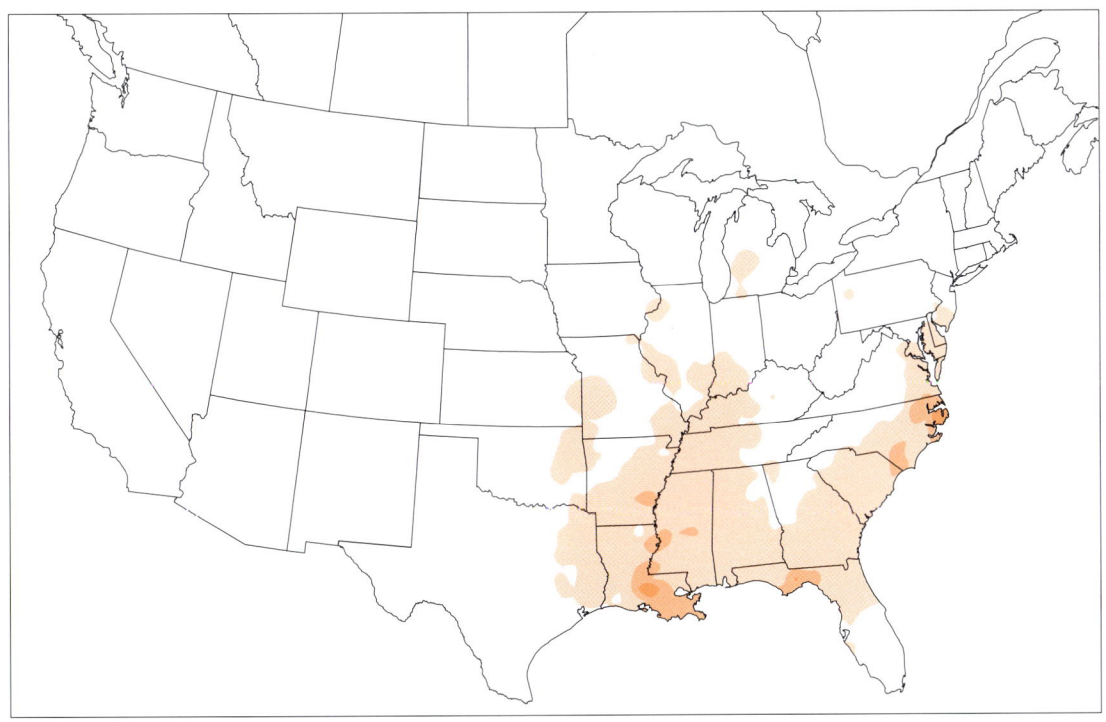

Worm-eating Warbler

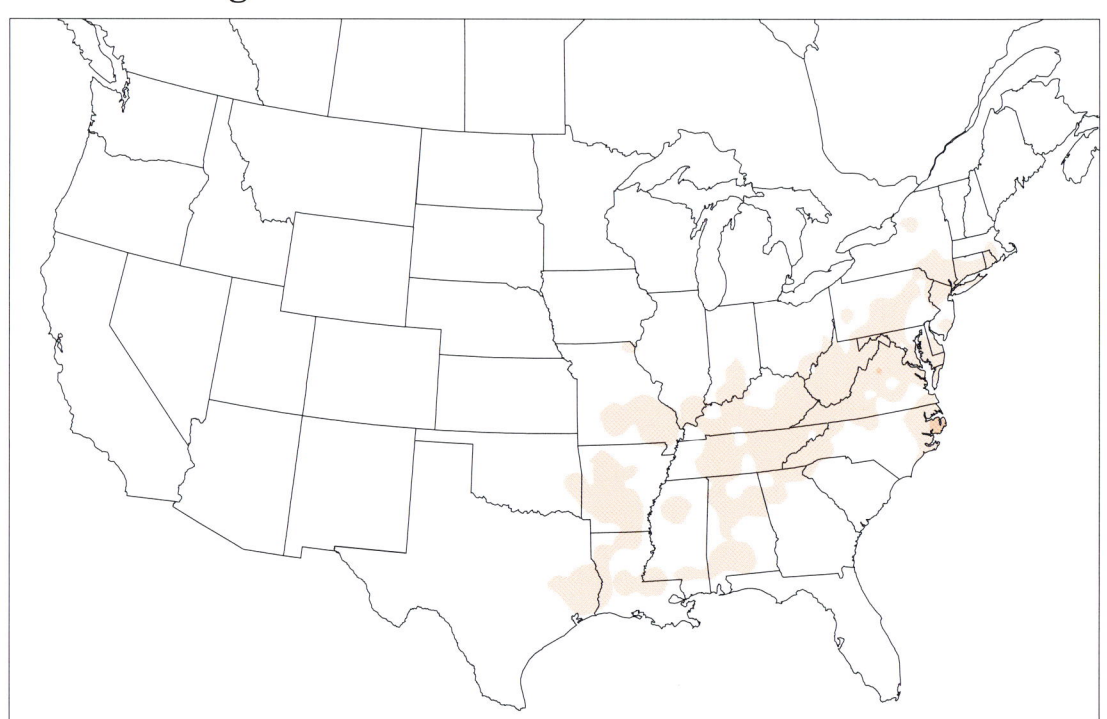

Swainson's Warbler

Ovenbird

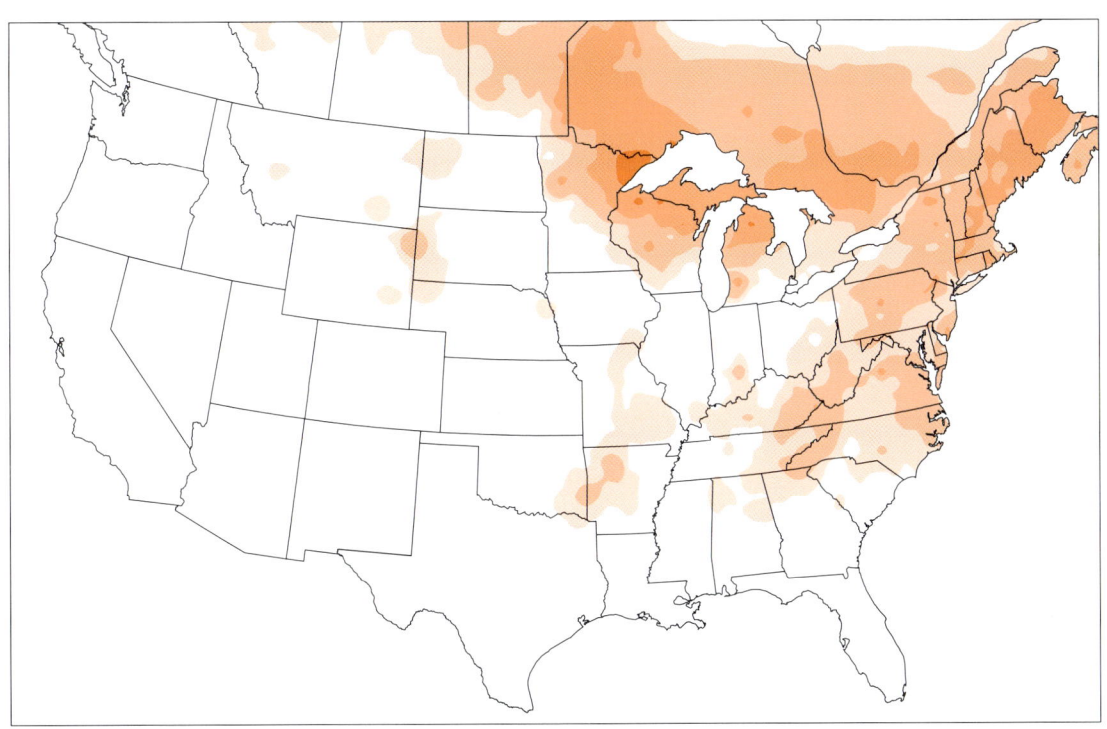

Northern Waterthrush

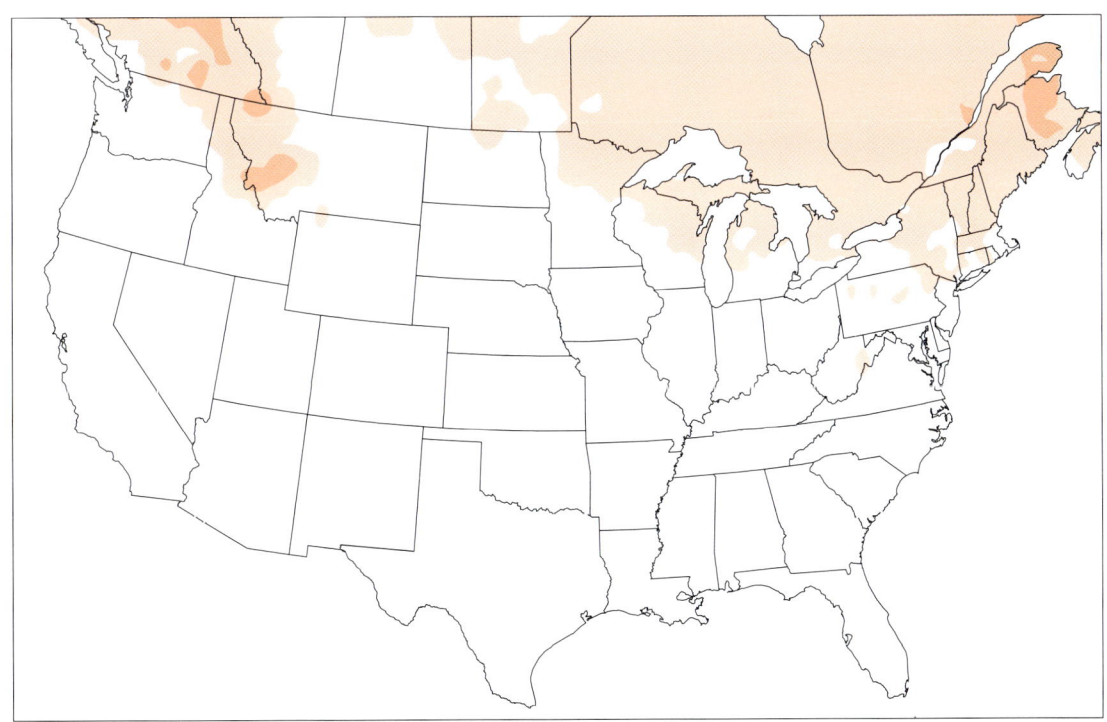

Louisiana Waterthrush

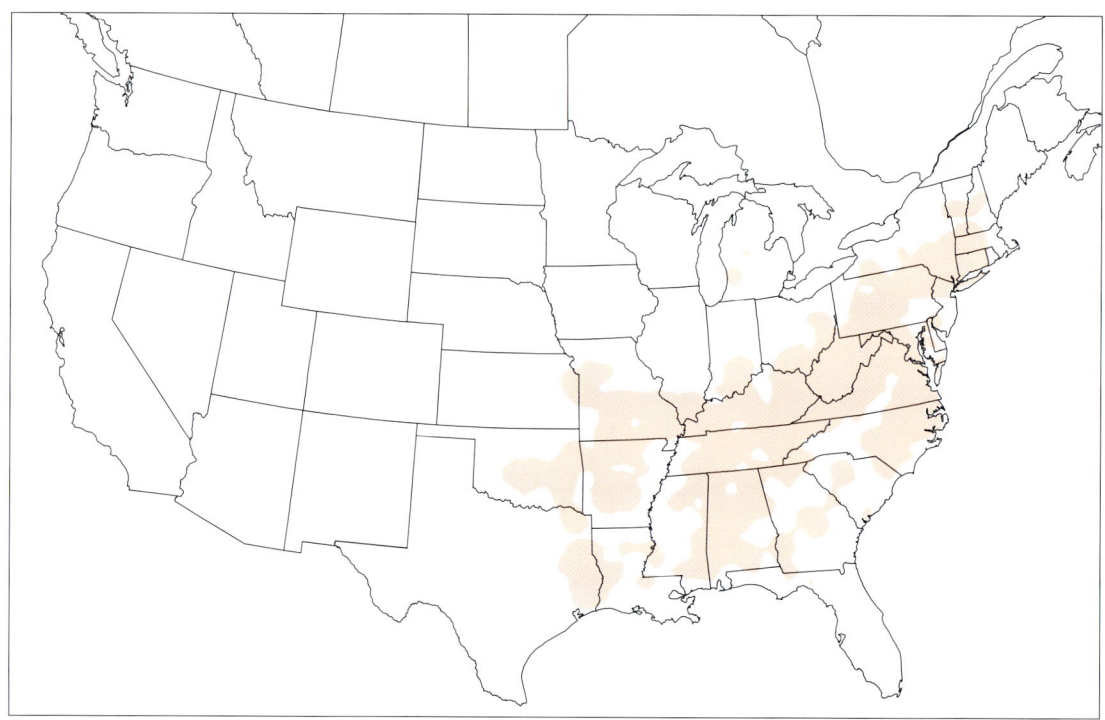

Kentucky Warbler

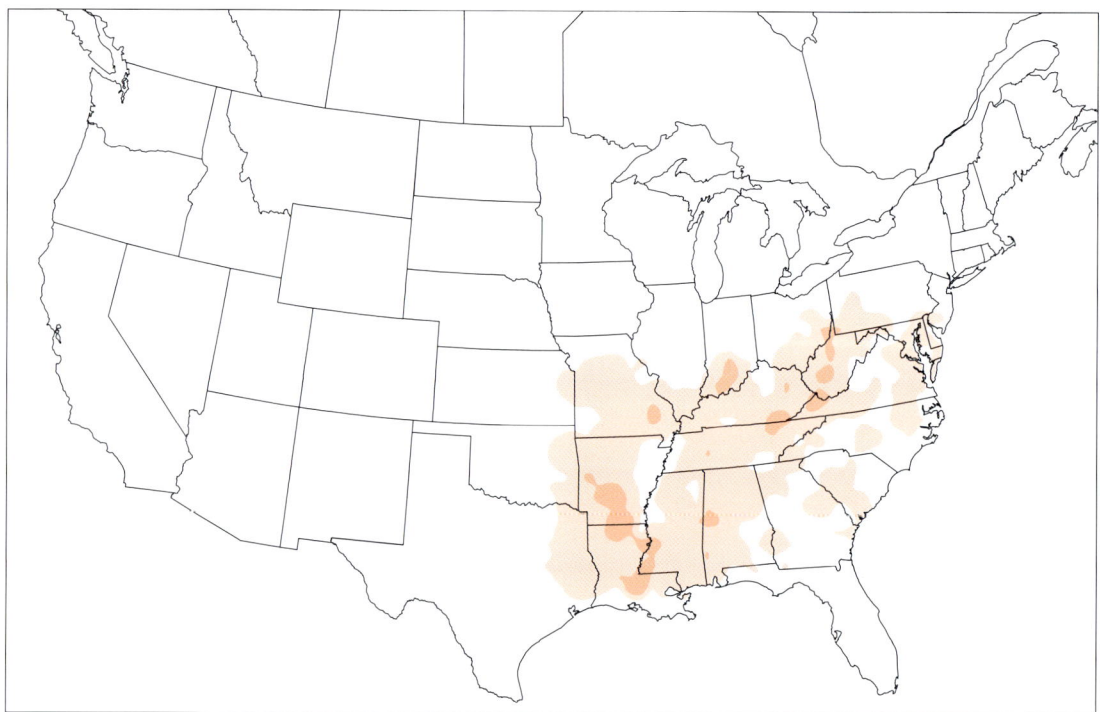

Warblers 199

Connecticut Warbler

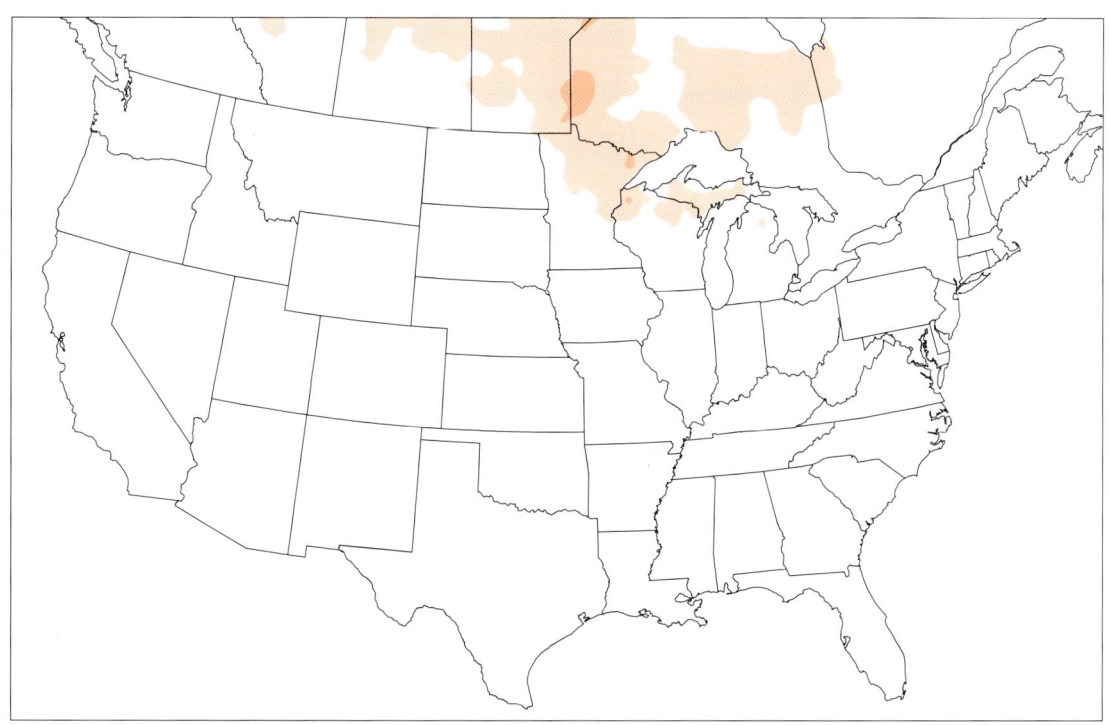

Mourning Warbler

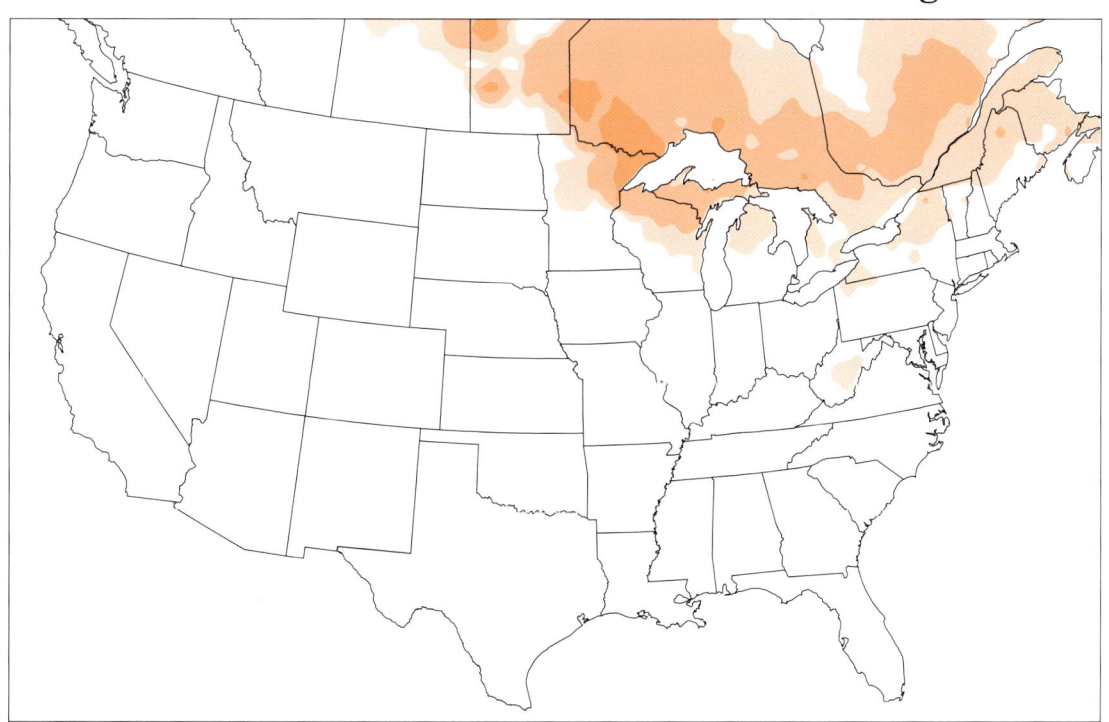

MacGillivray's Warbler

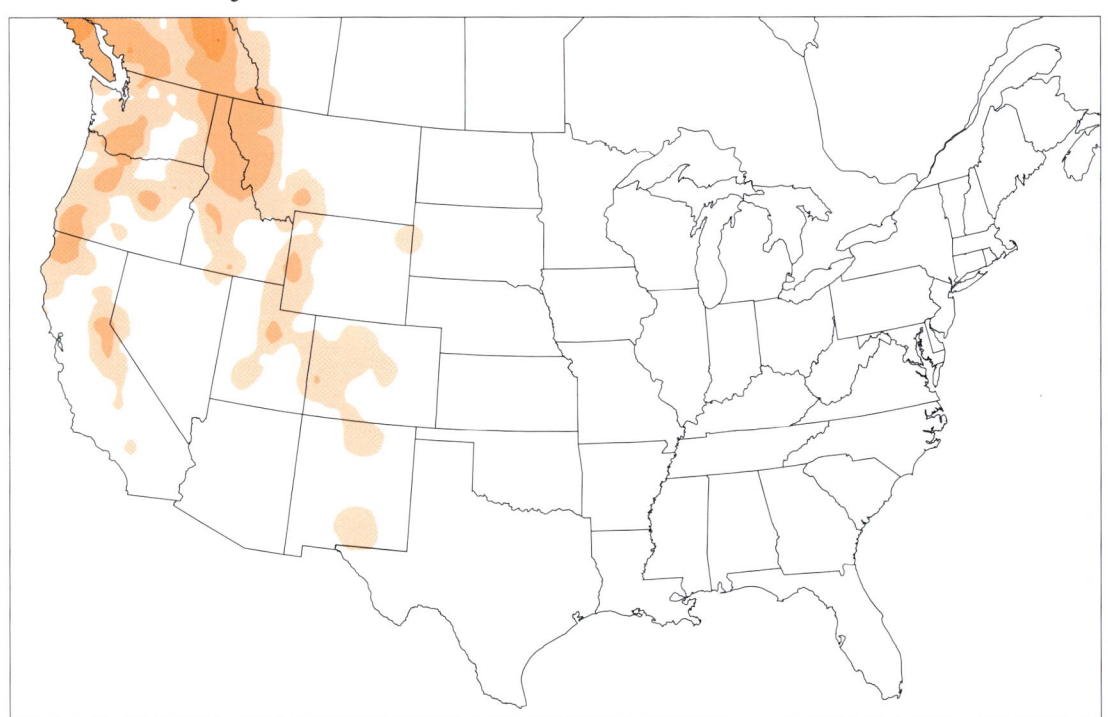

Common Yellowthroat

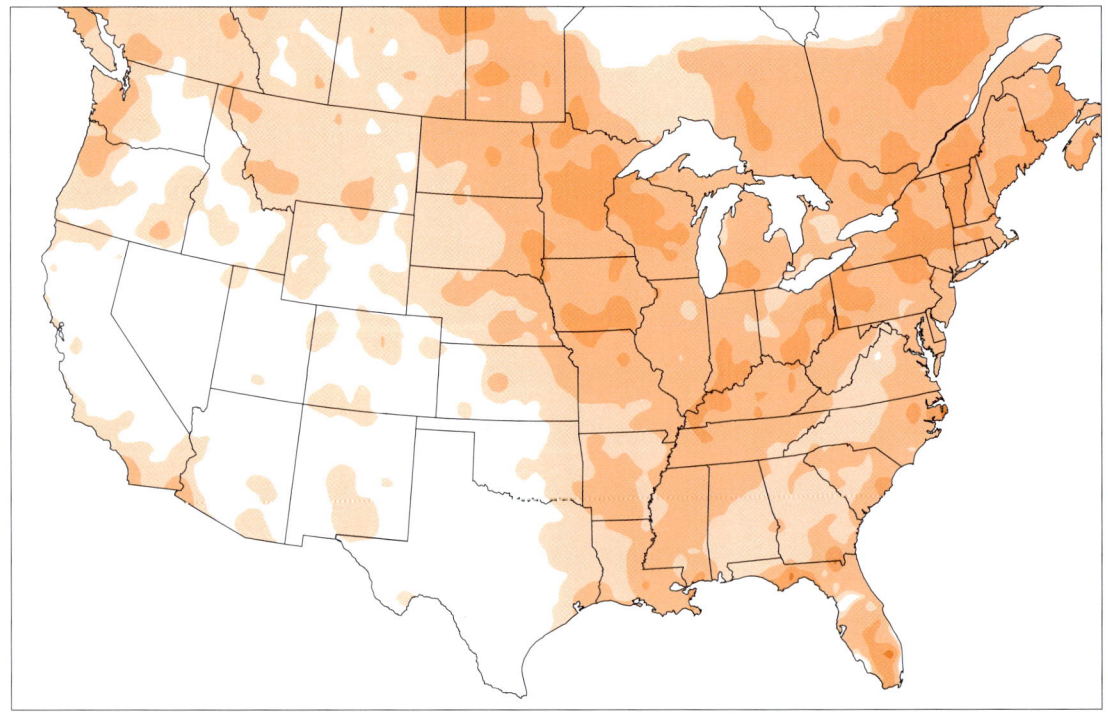

Hooded Warbler

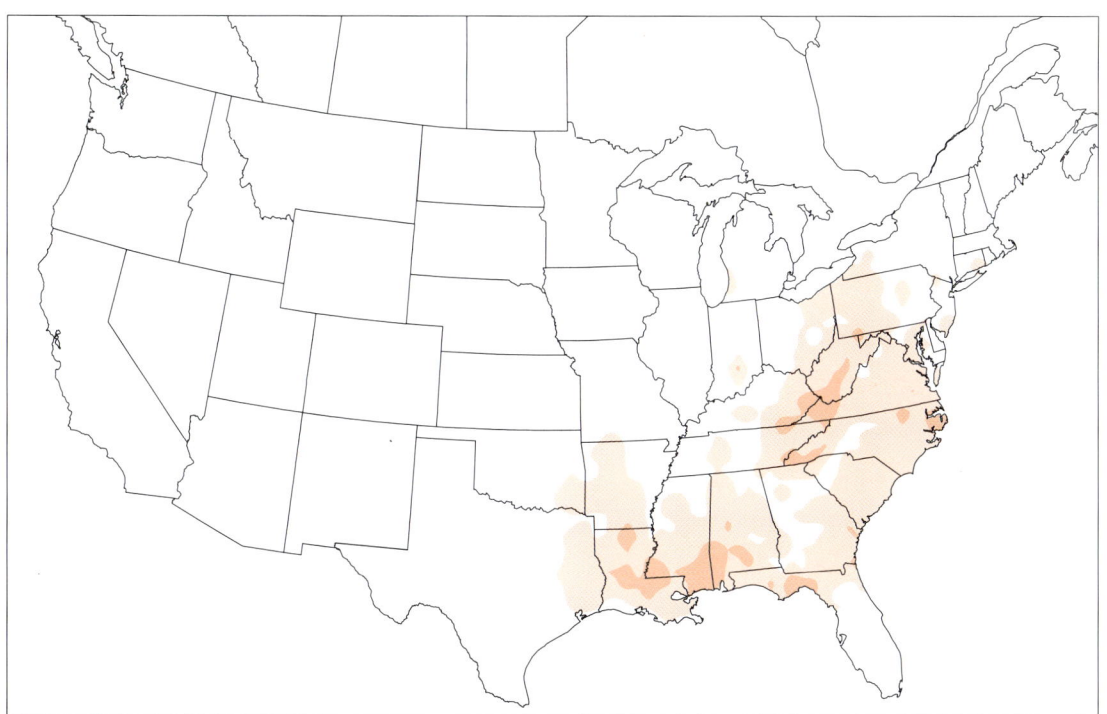

Wilson's Warbler

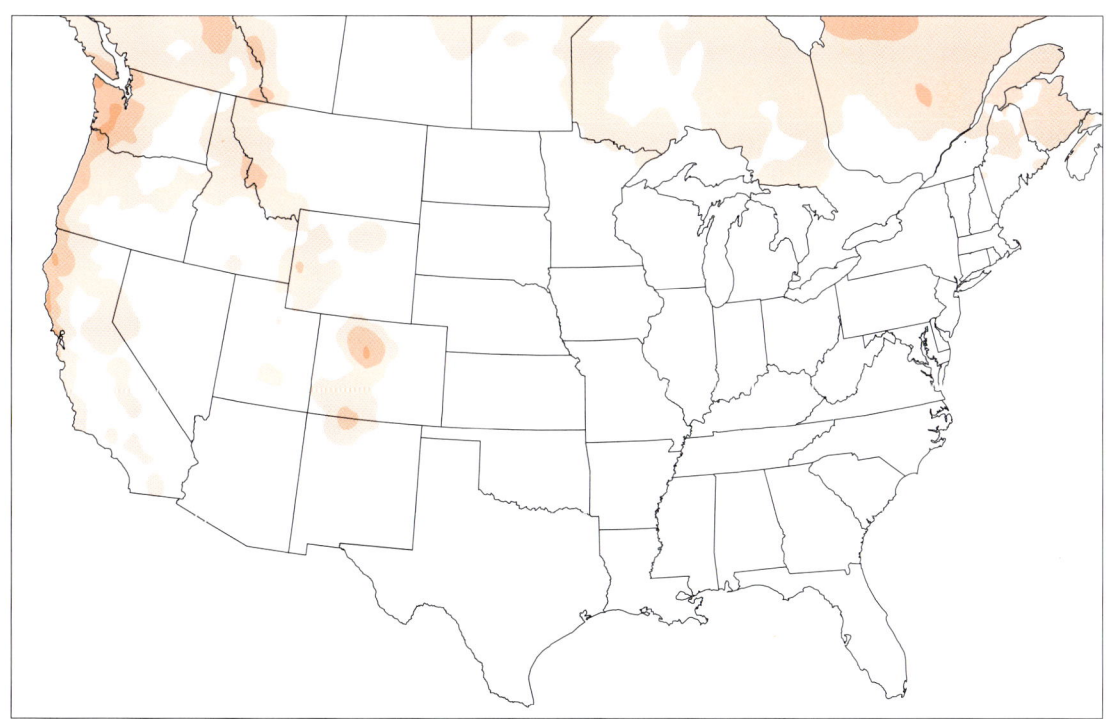

Canada Warbler

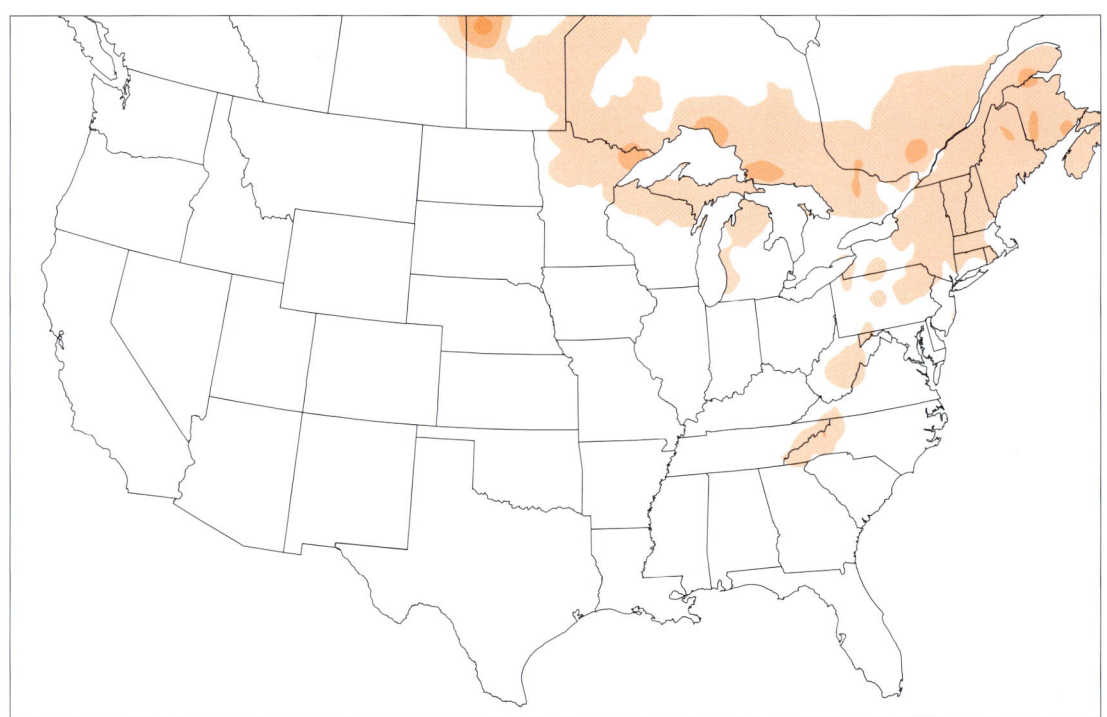

Red-faced Warbler

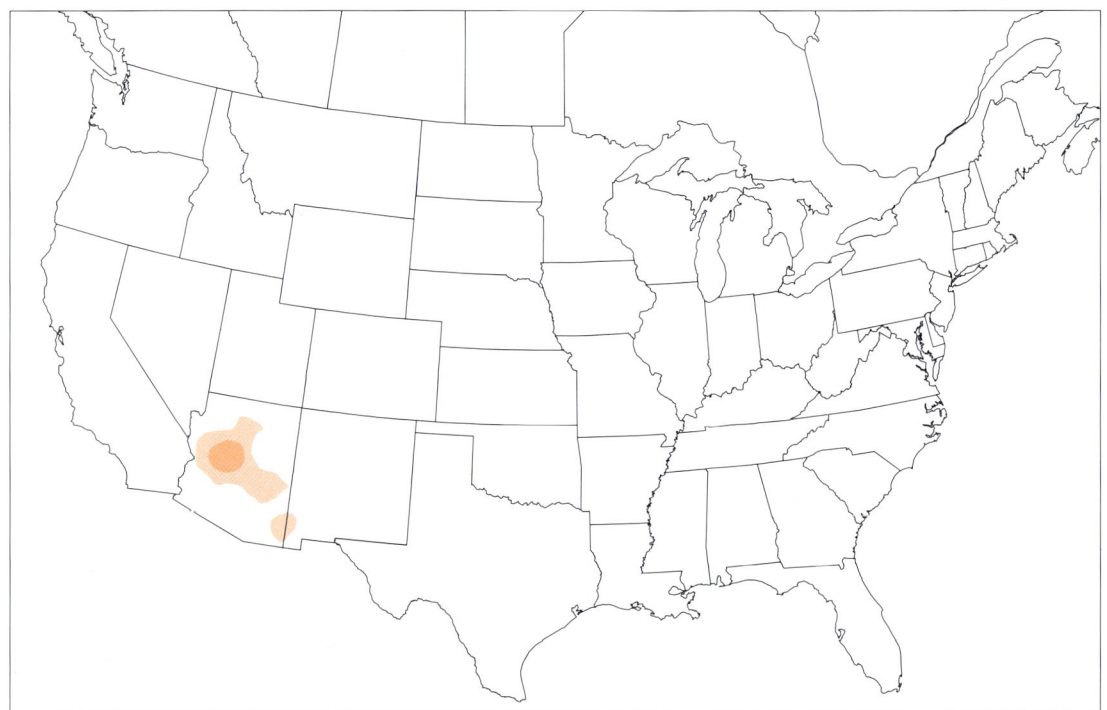

Painted Redstart

Yellow-breasted Chat

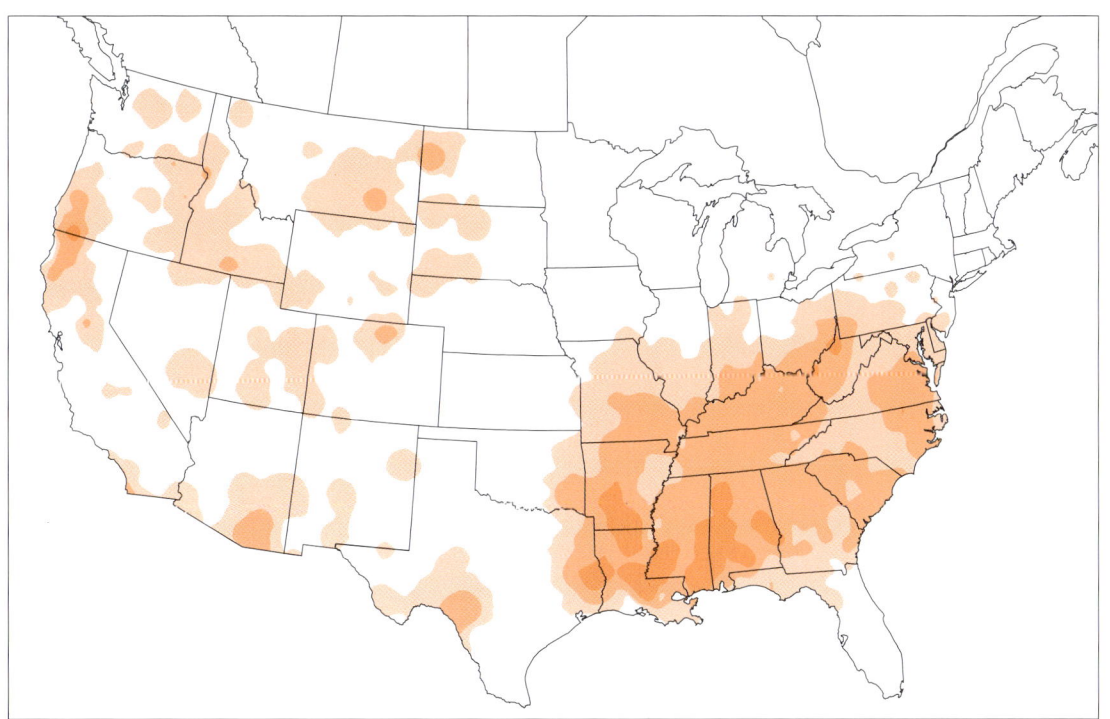

Olive Warbler

Hepatic Tanager

Summer Tanager

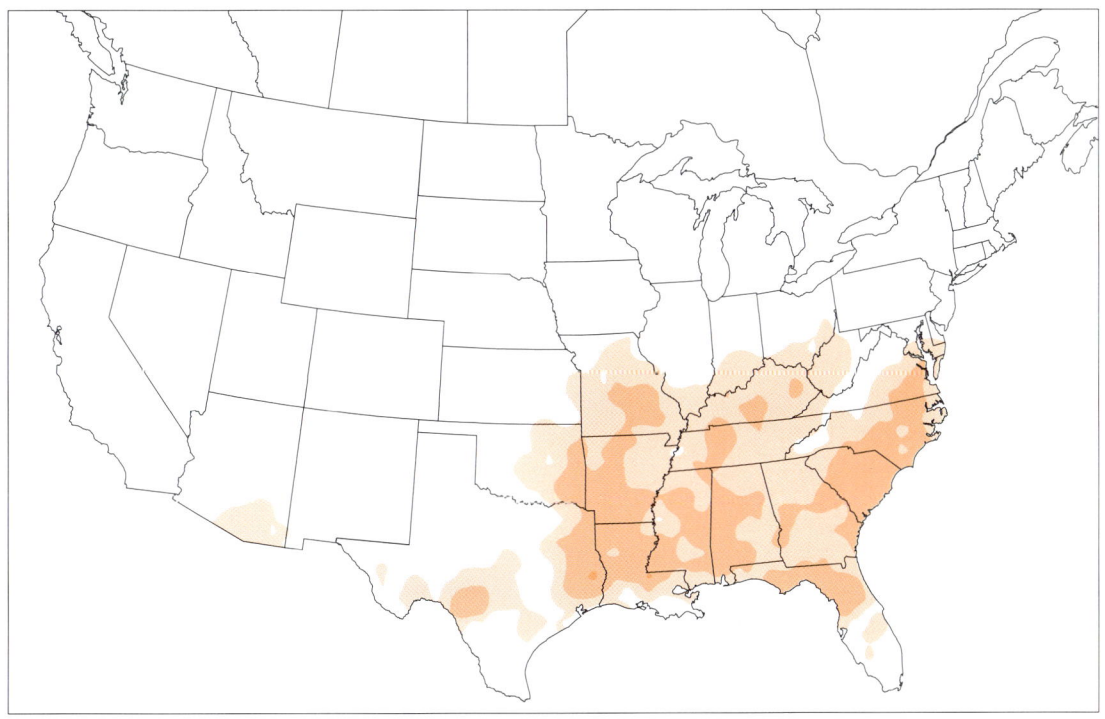

Scarlet Tanager

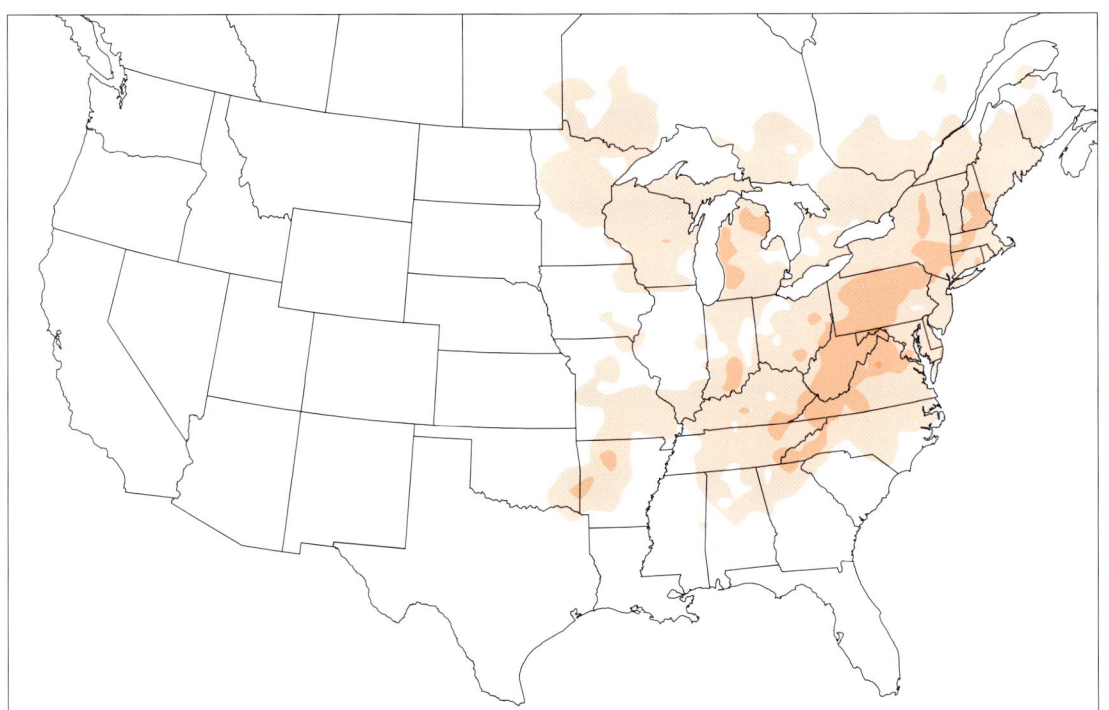

Western Tanager

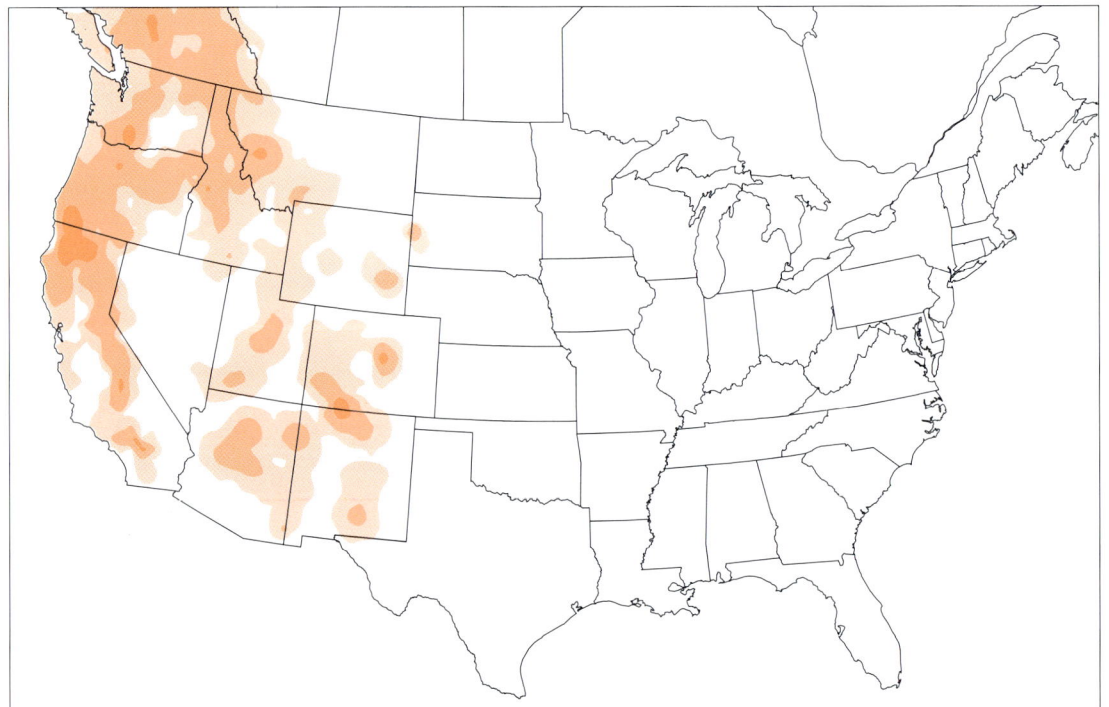

Northern Cardinal

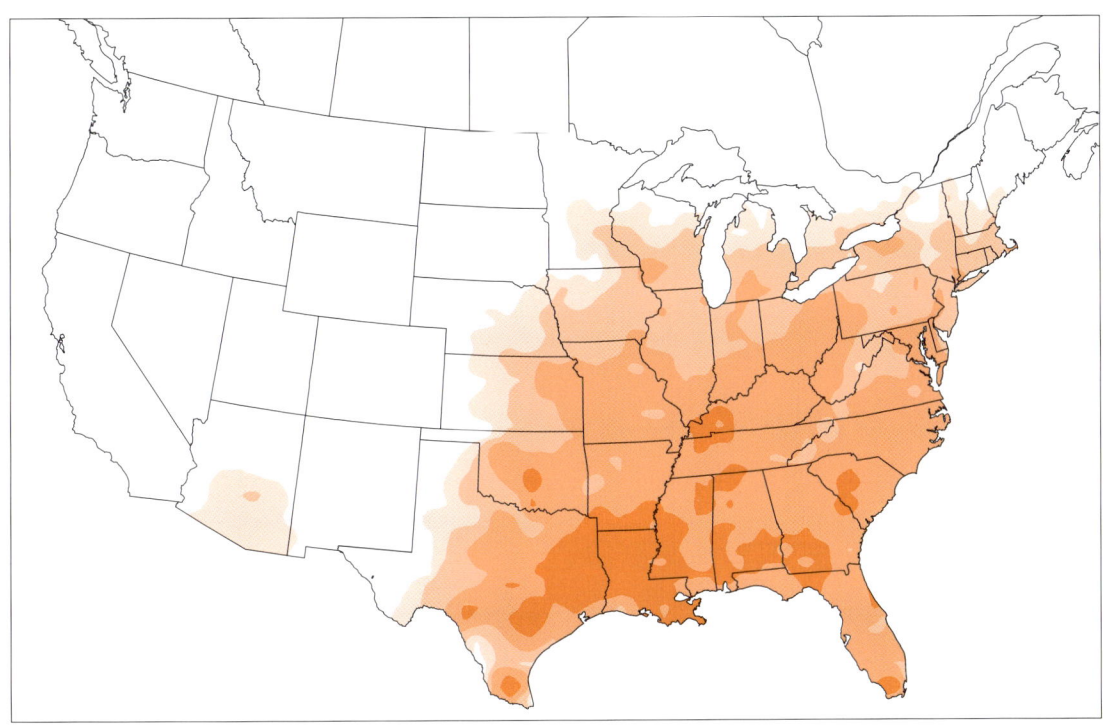

Pyrrhuloxia

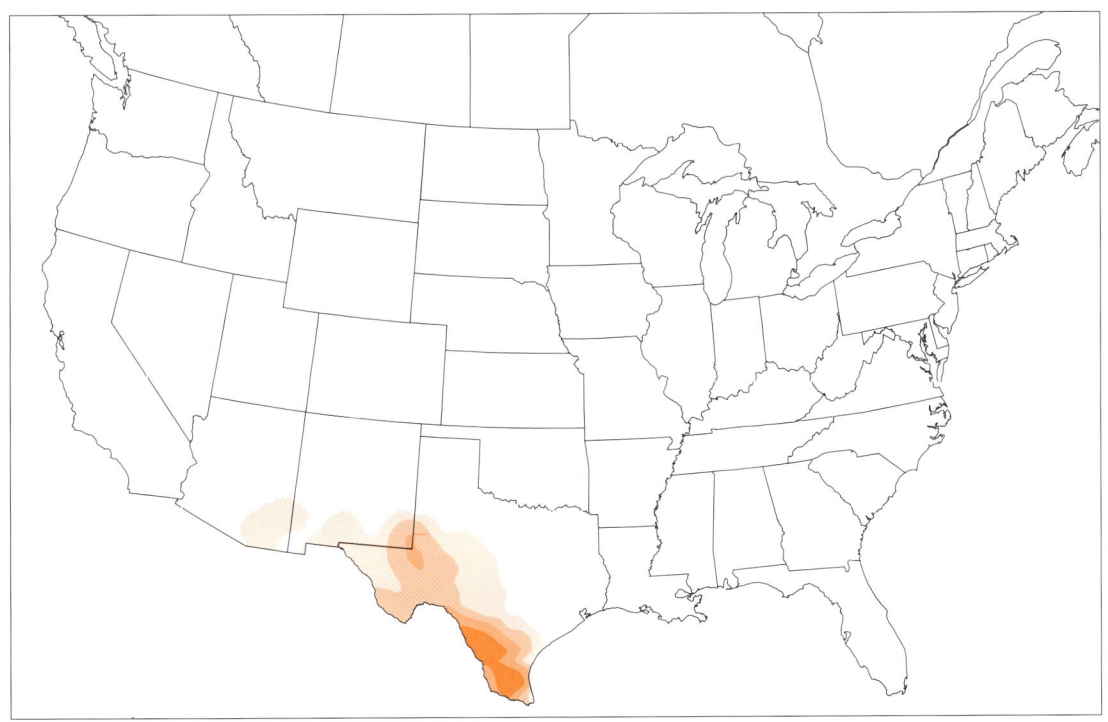

Rose-breasted Grosbeak

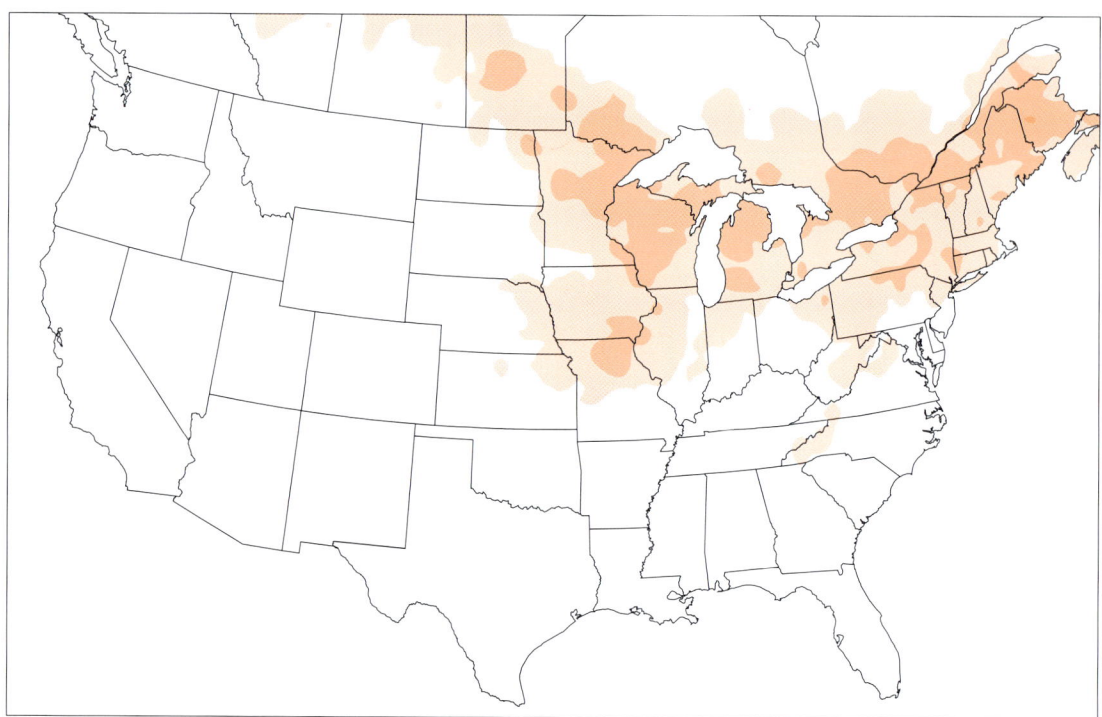

Black-headed Grosbeak

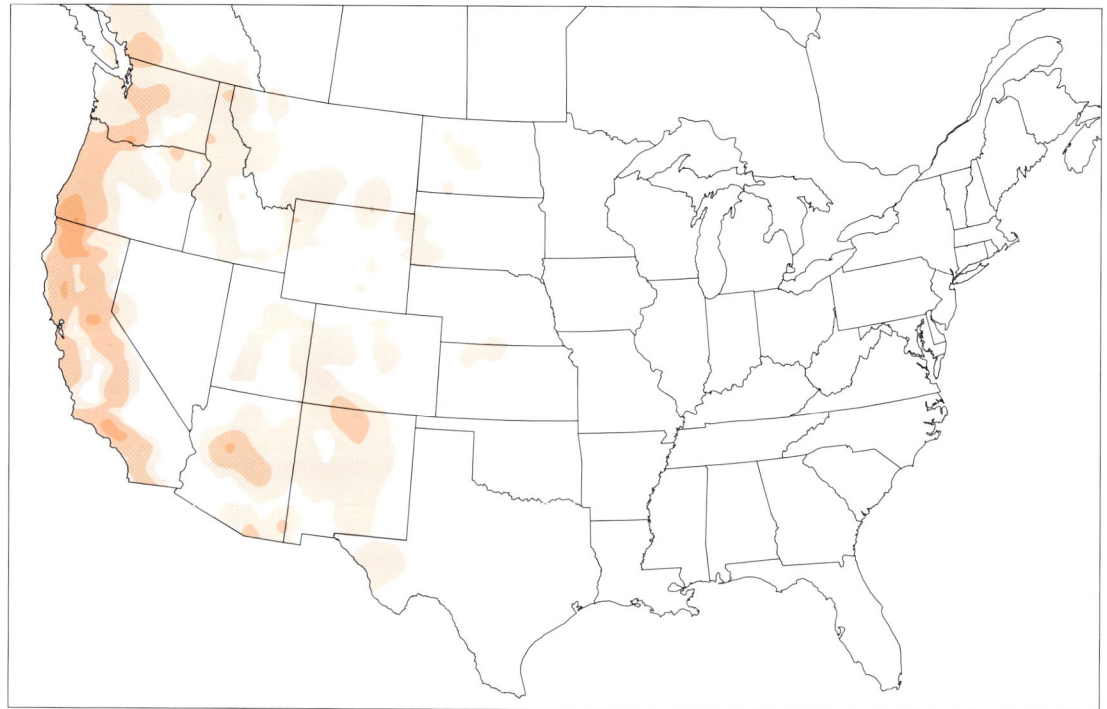

Blue Grosbeak

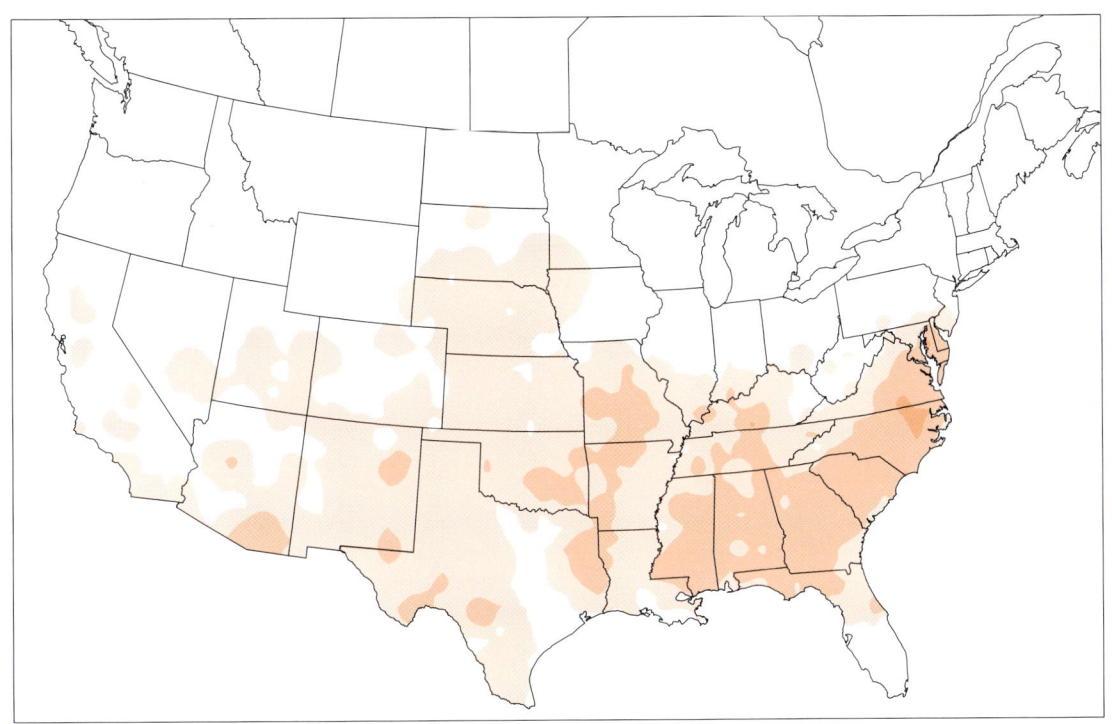

Lazuli Bunting

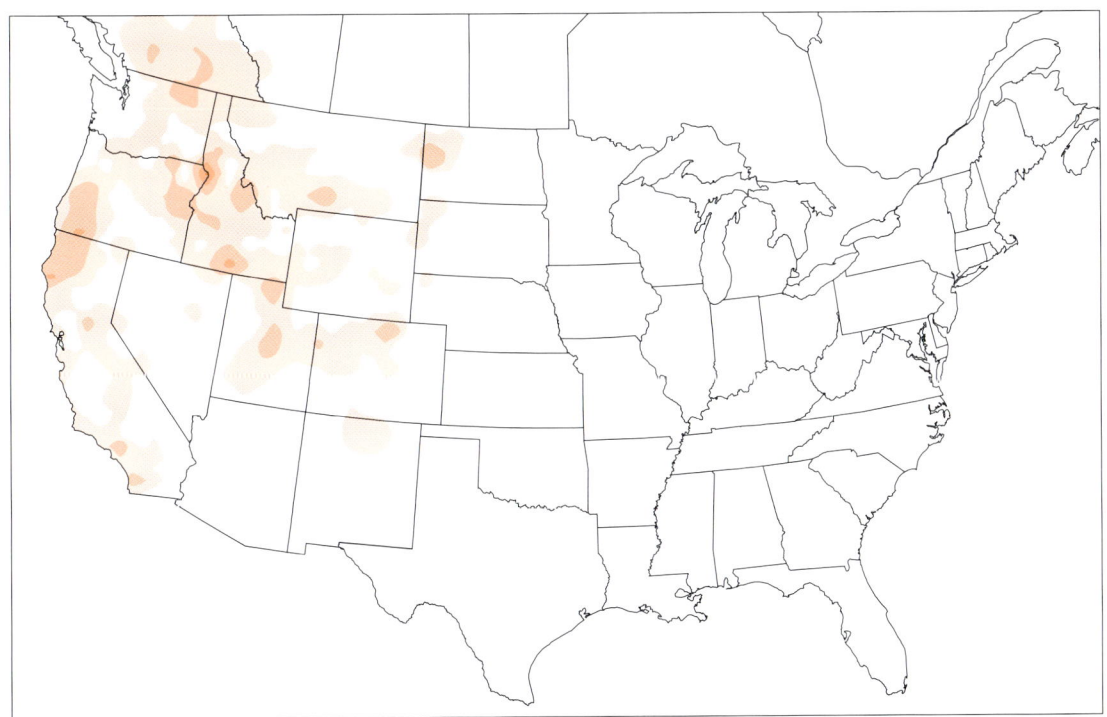

Indigo Bunting

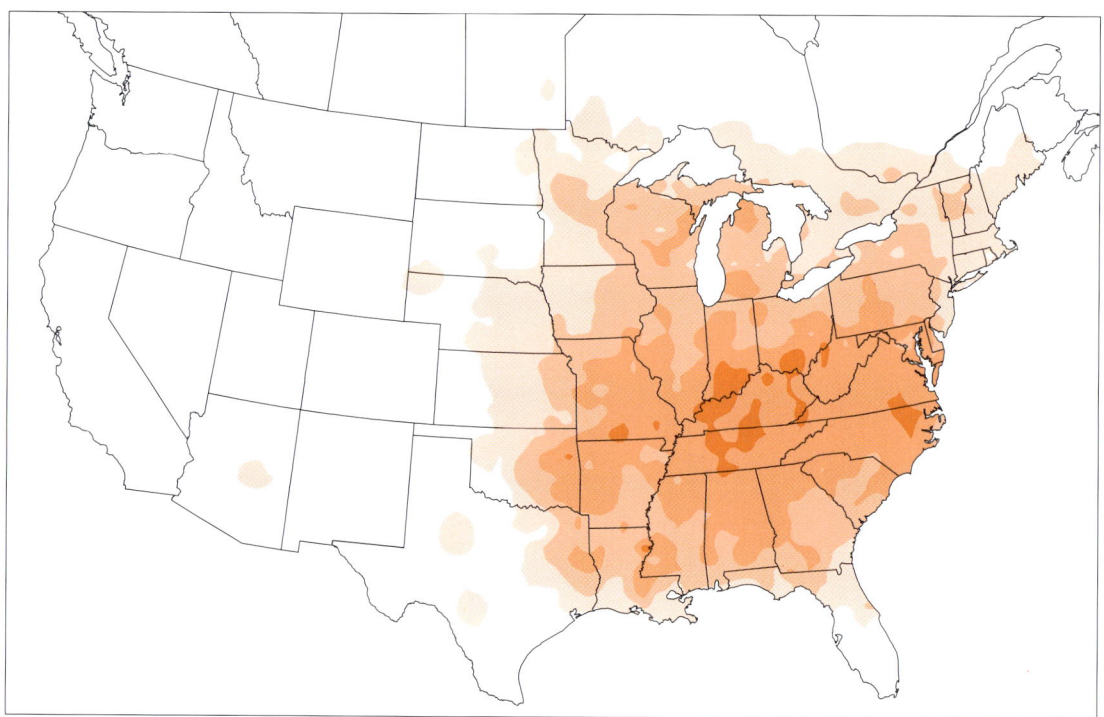

Varied Bunting

Painted Bunting

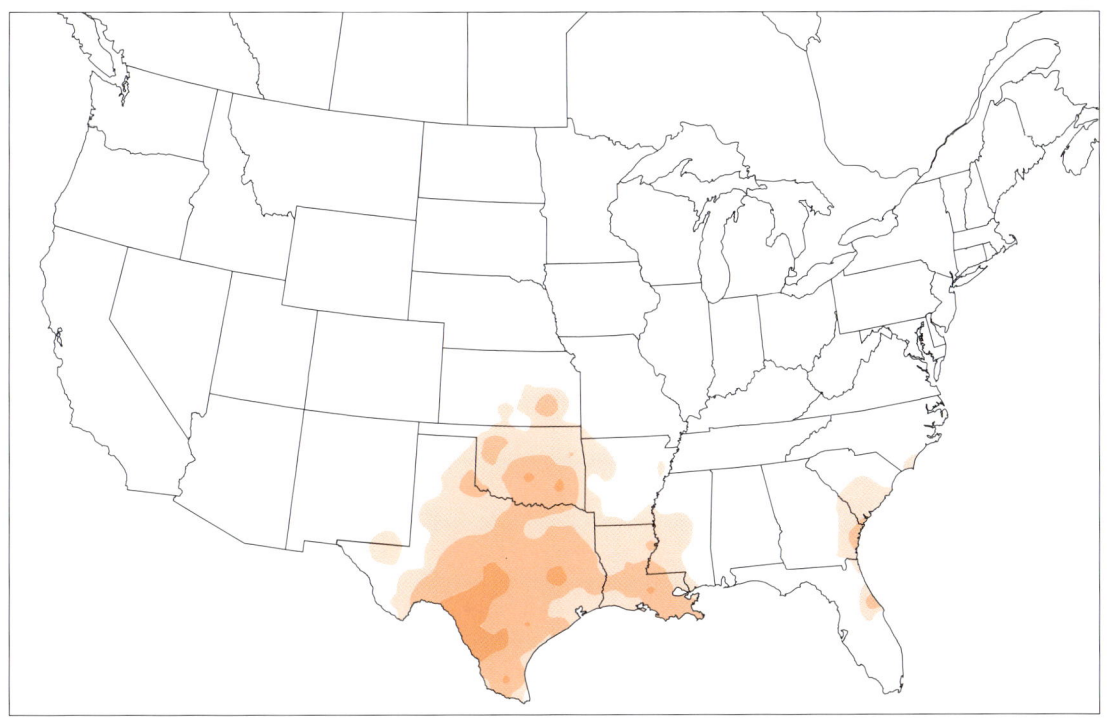

Dickcissel

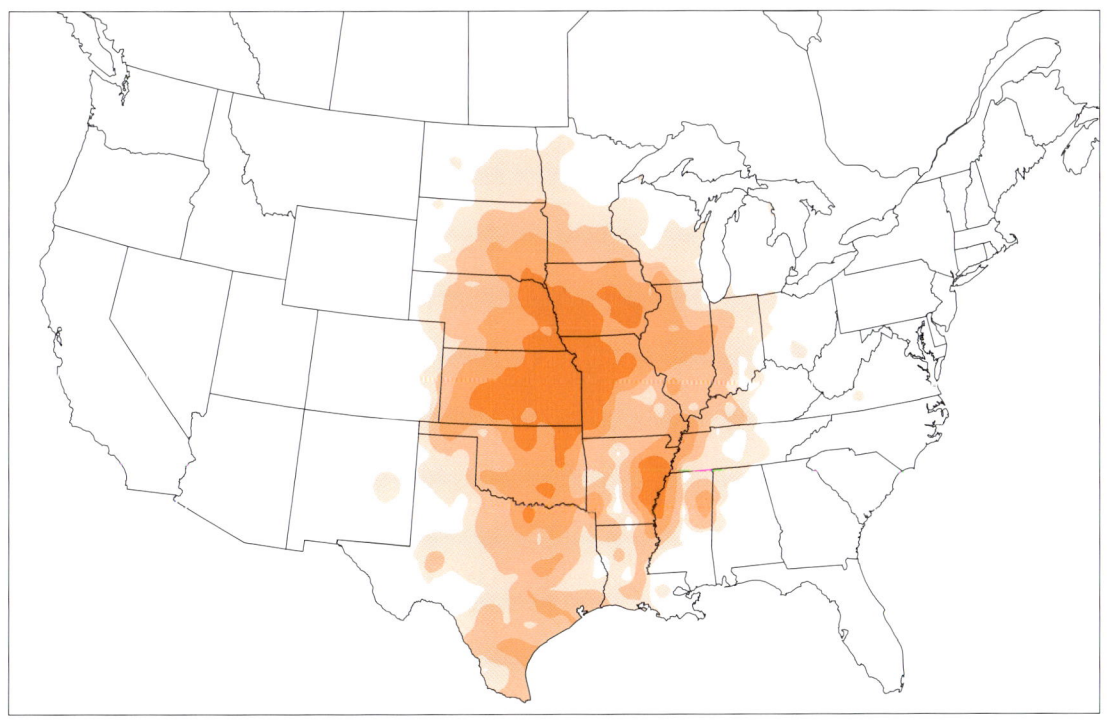

Olive Sparrow

Green-tailed Towhee

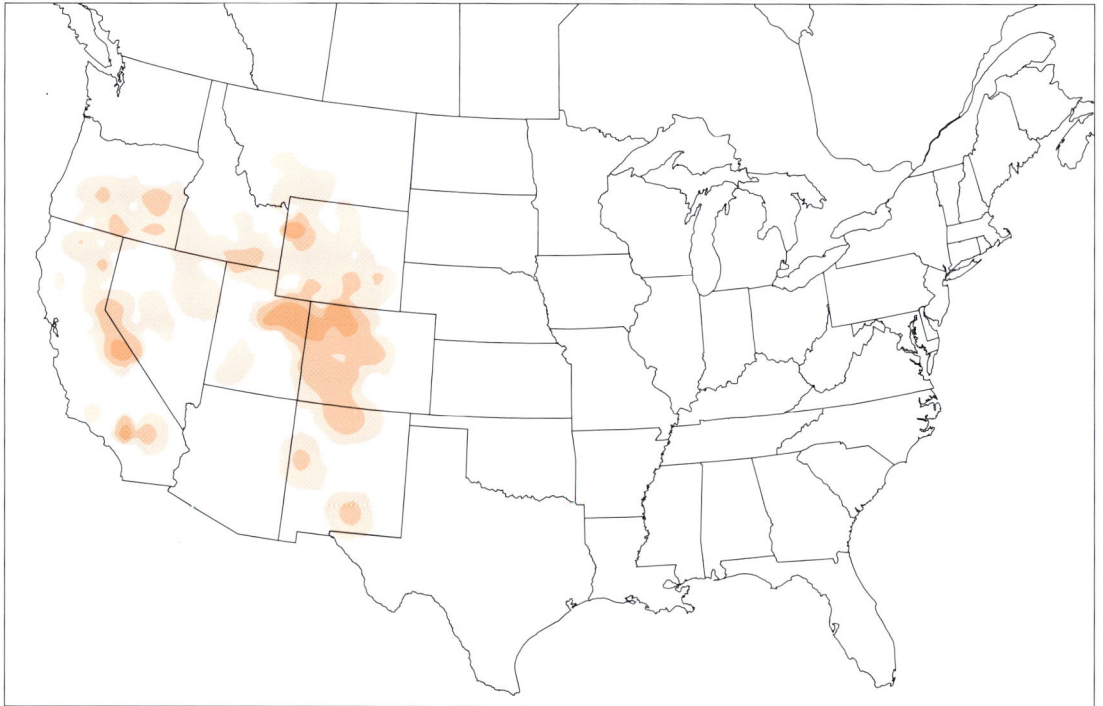

Rufous-sided Towhee

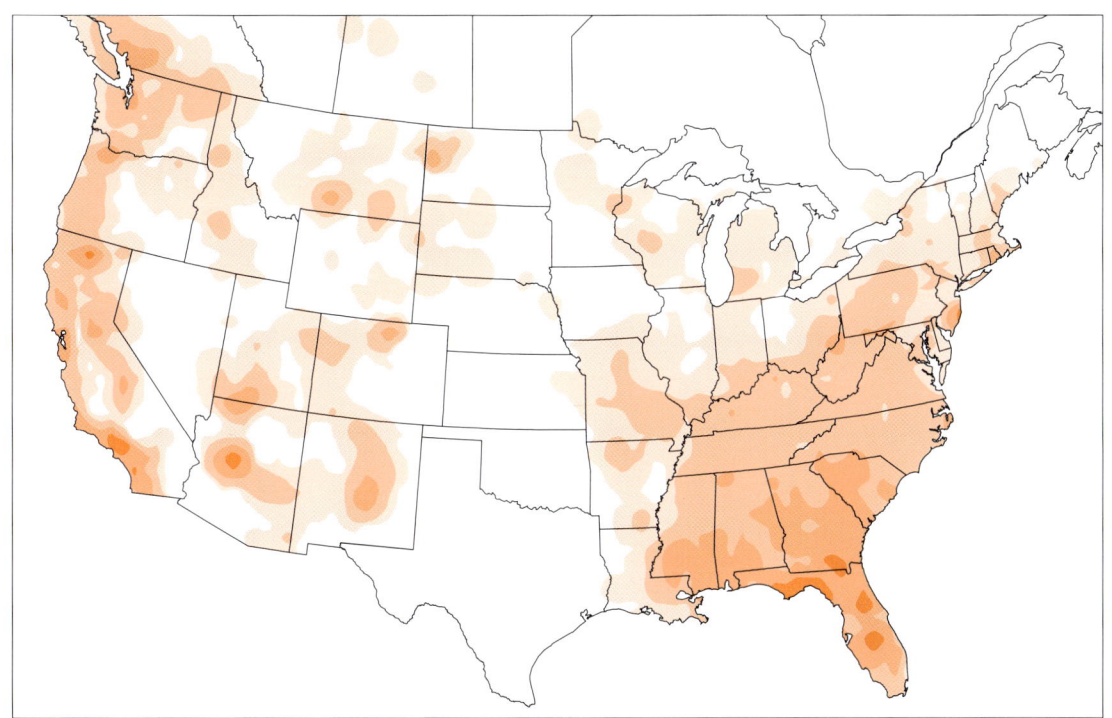

California Towhee

Canyon Towhee

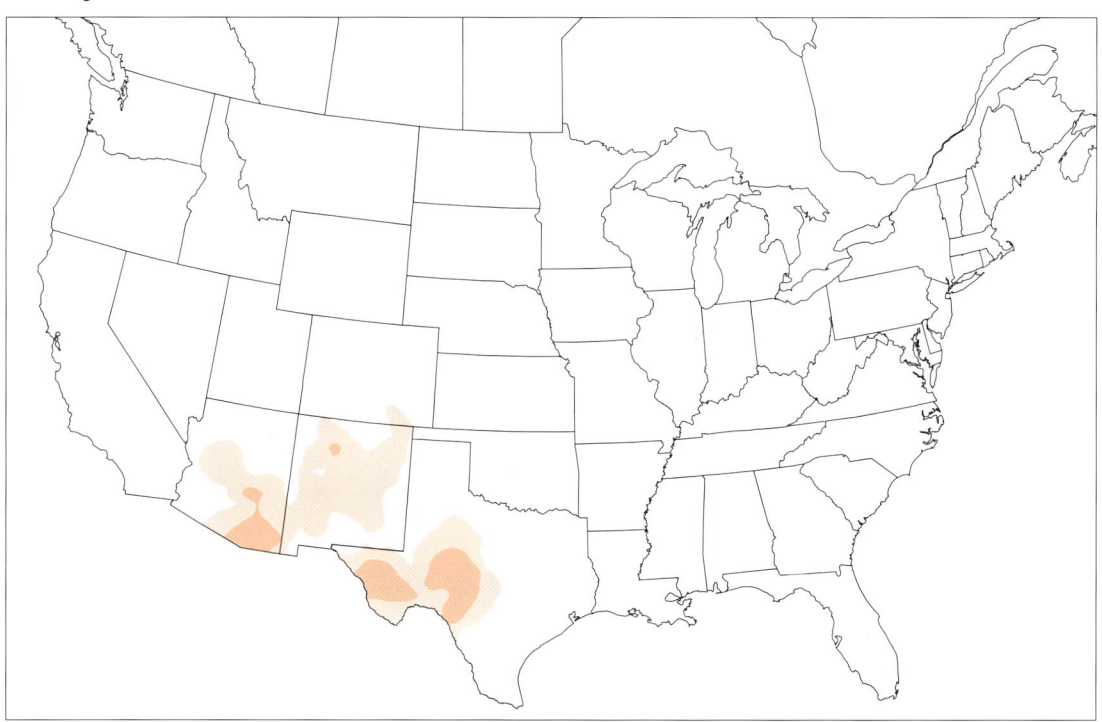

Abert's Towhee

Bachman's Sparrow

Botteri's Sparrow

Cassin's Sparrow

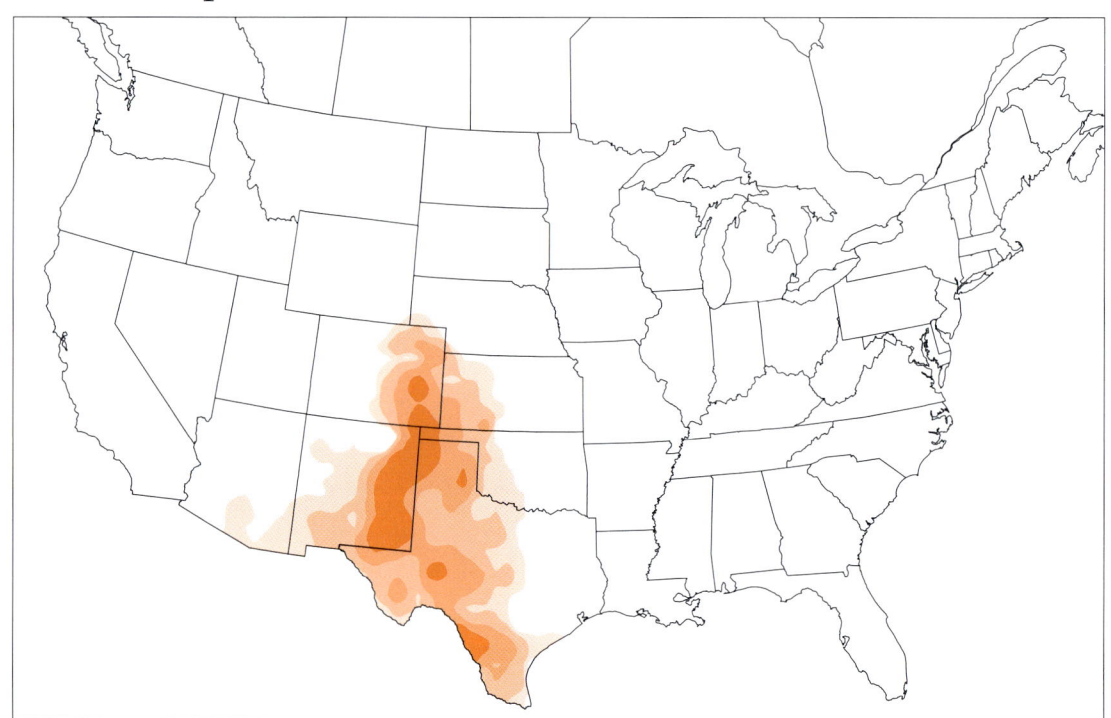

Rufous-crowned Sparrow

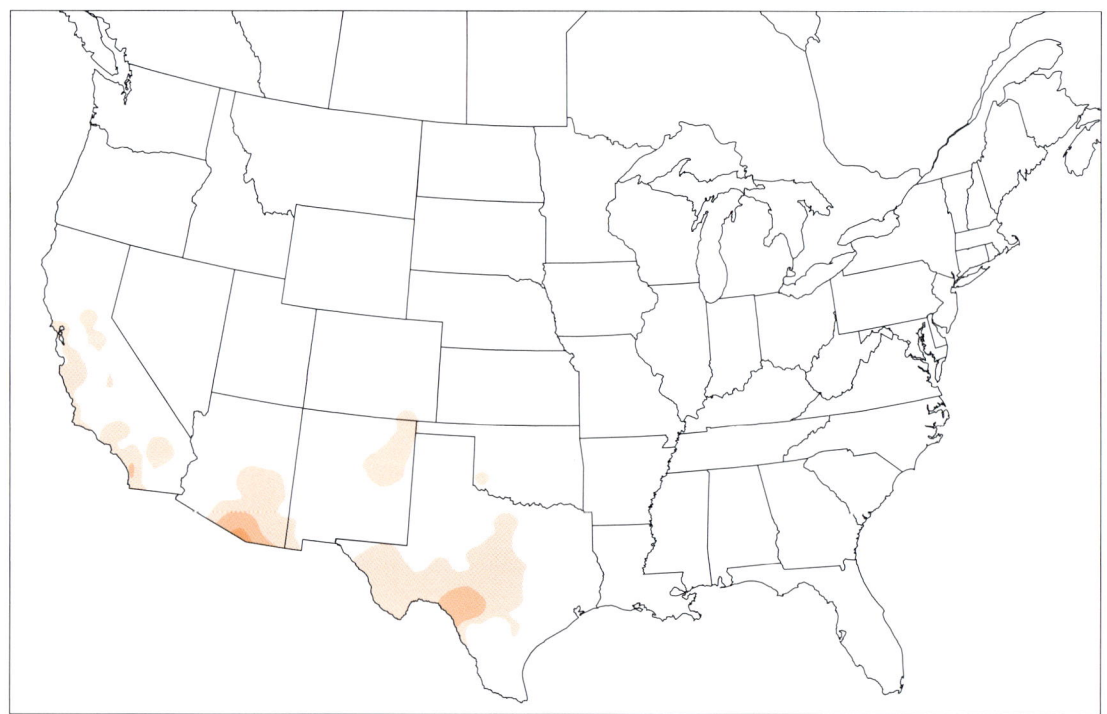

Chipping Sparrow

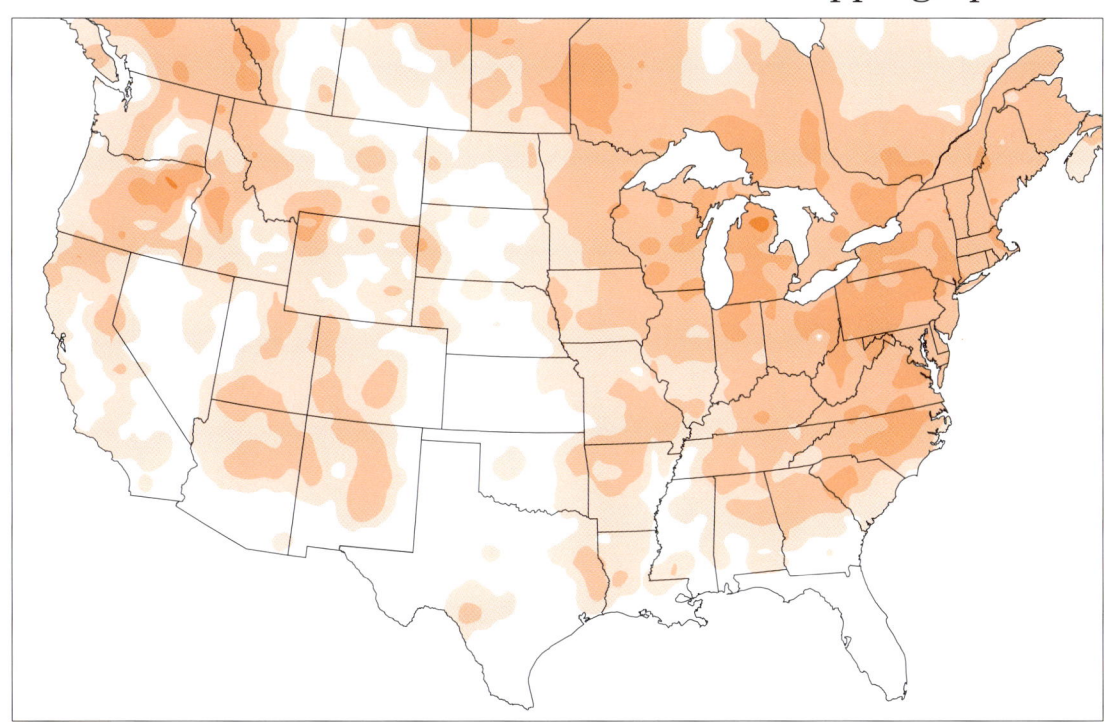

Clay-colored Sparrow

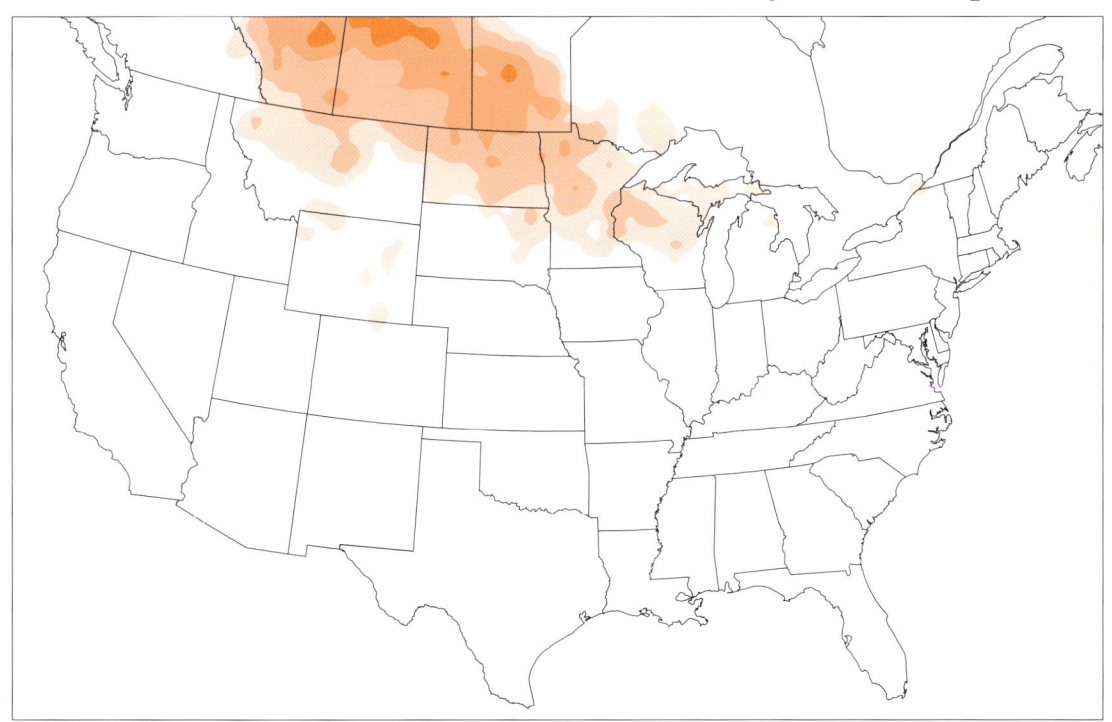

Brewer's Sparrow

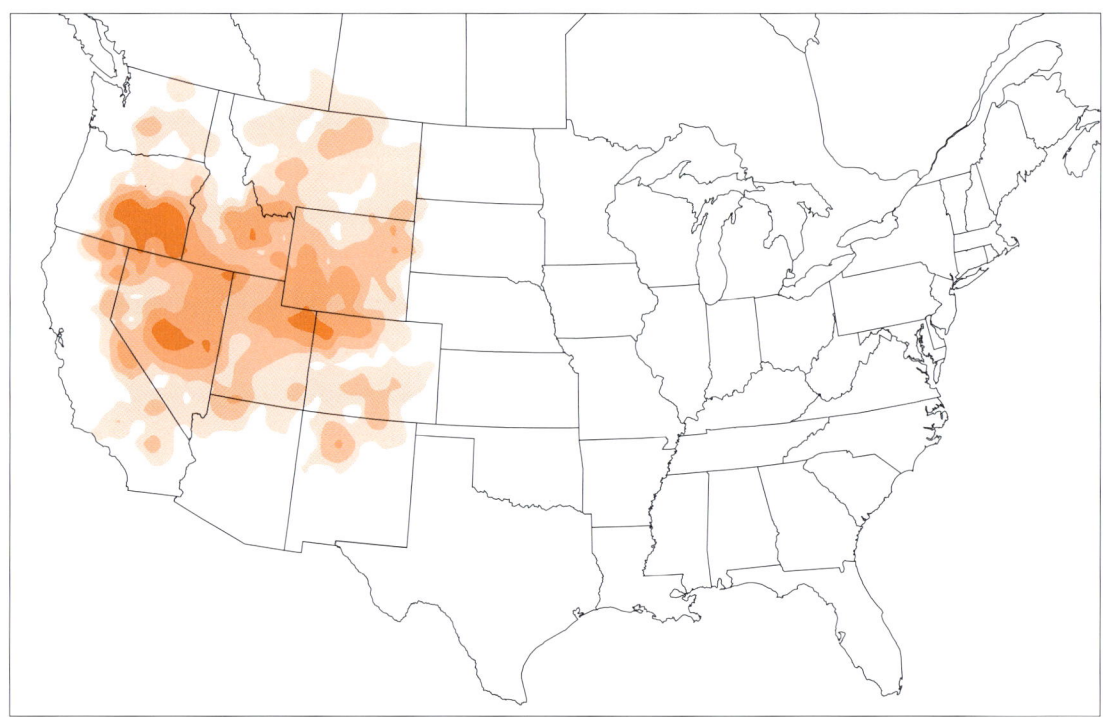

Field Sparrow

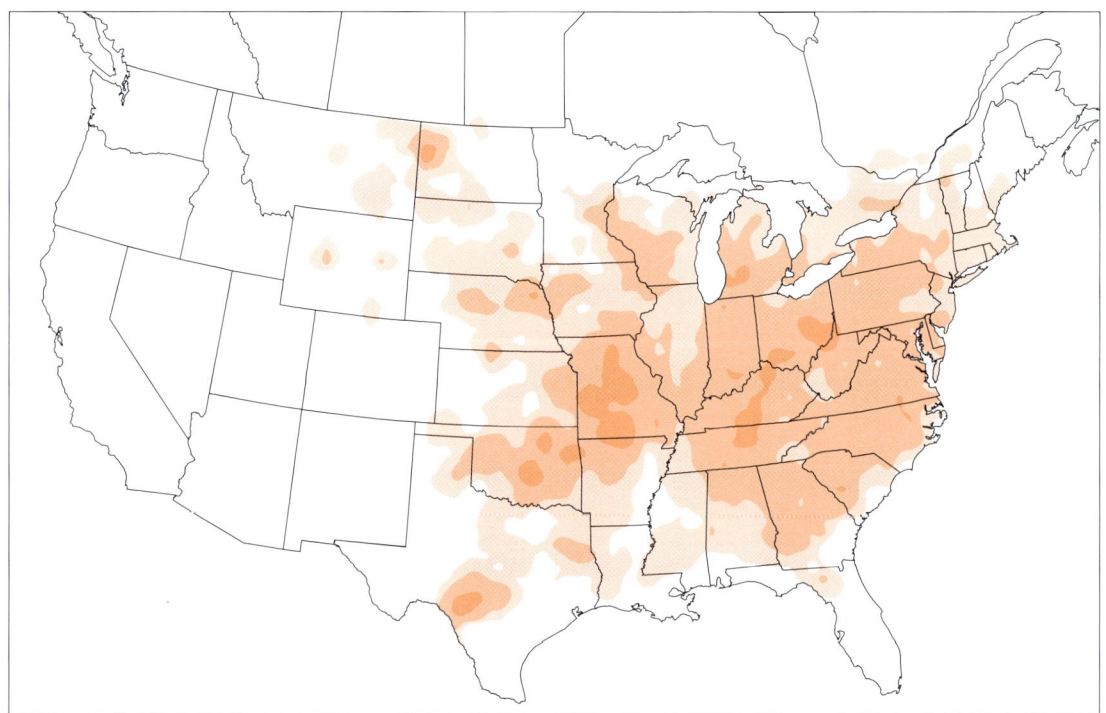

Black-chinned Sparrow

Vesper Sparrow

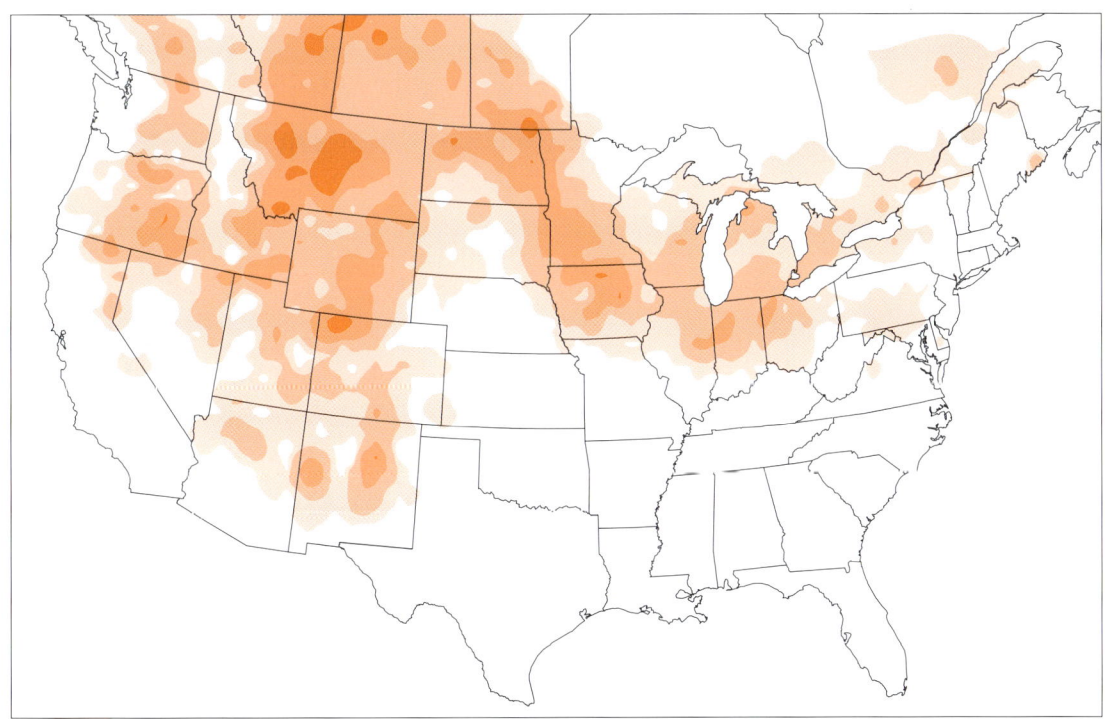

Lark Sparrow

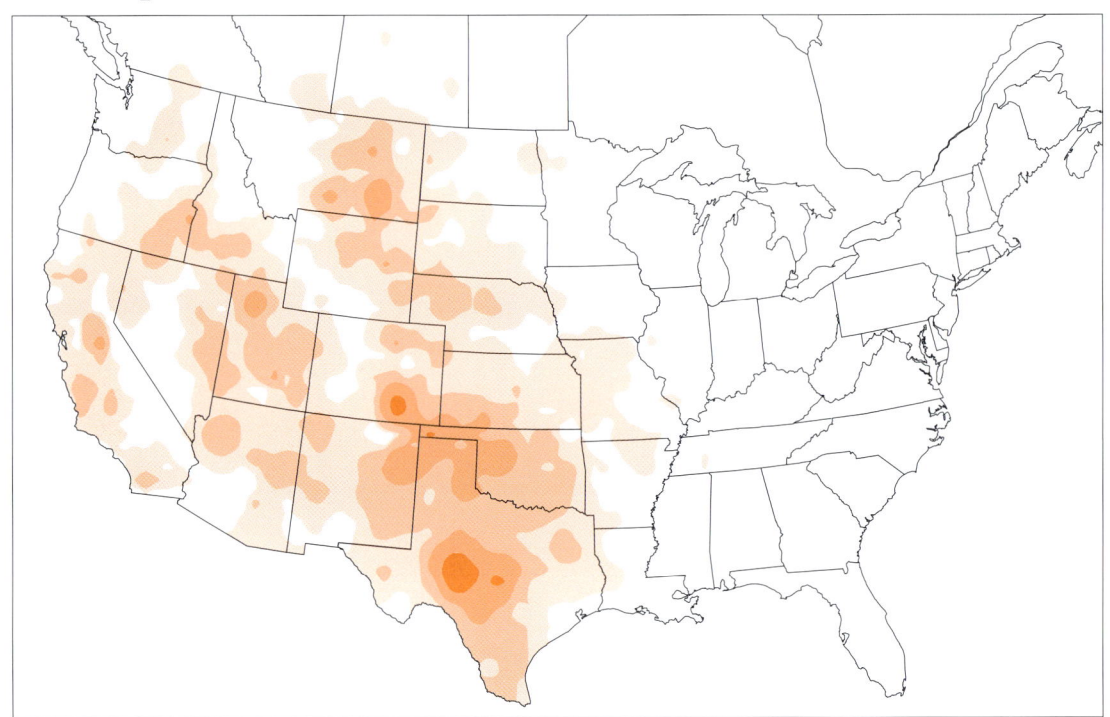

Black-throated Sparrow

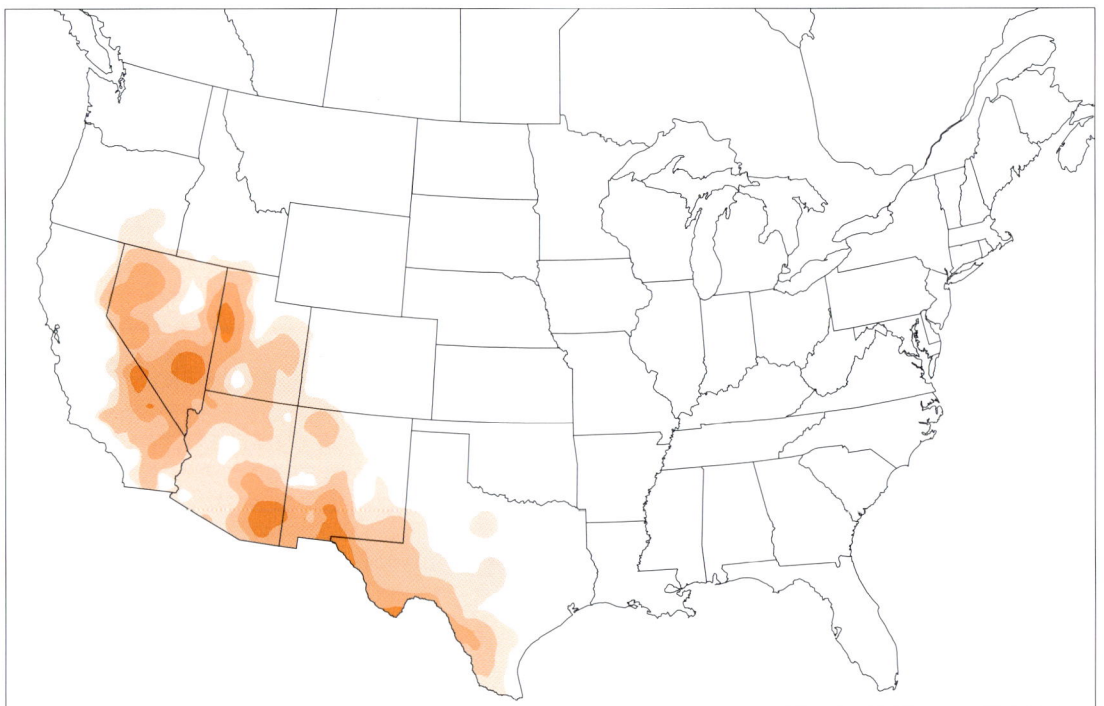

Sage Sparrow

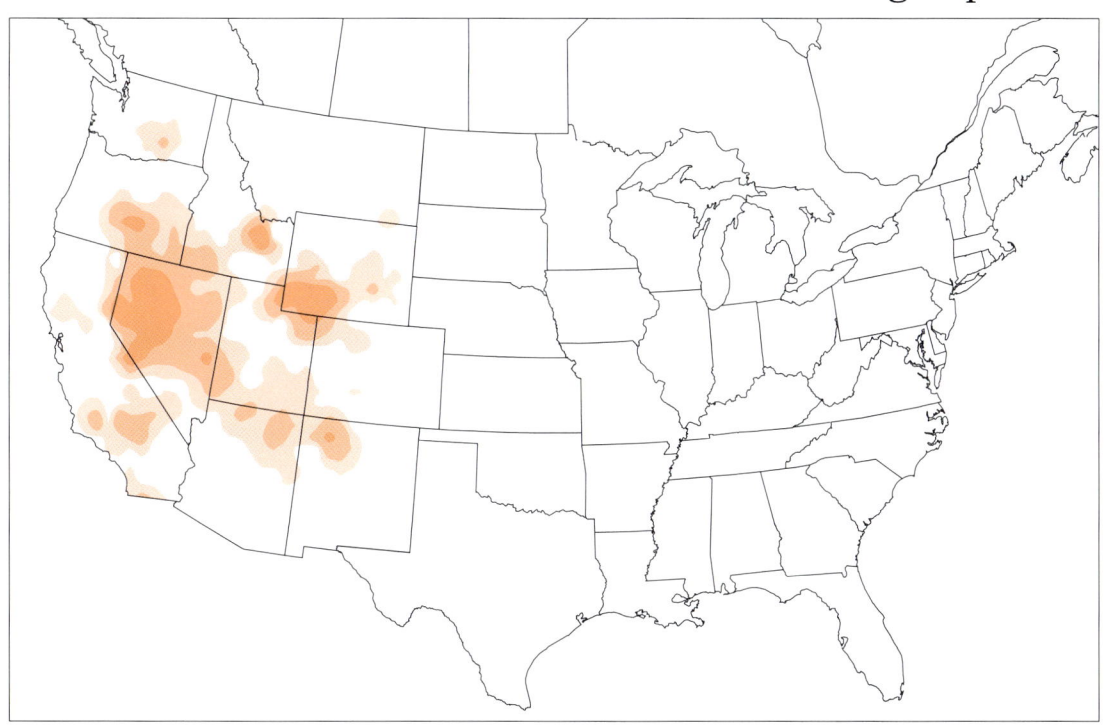

Lark Bunting

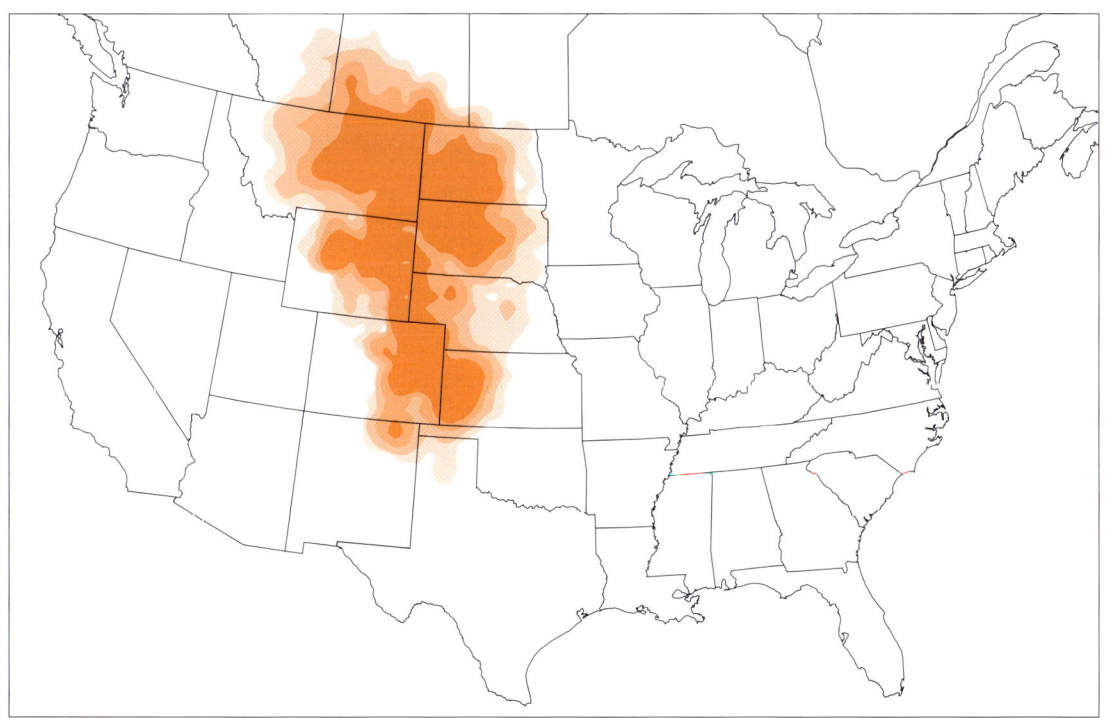

Savannah Sparrow

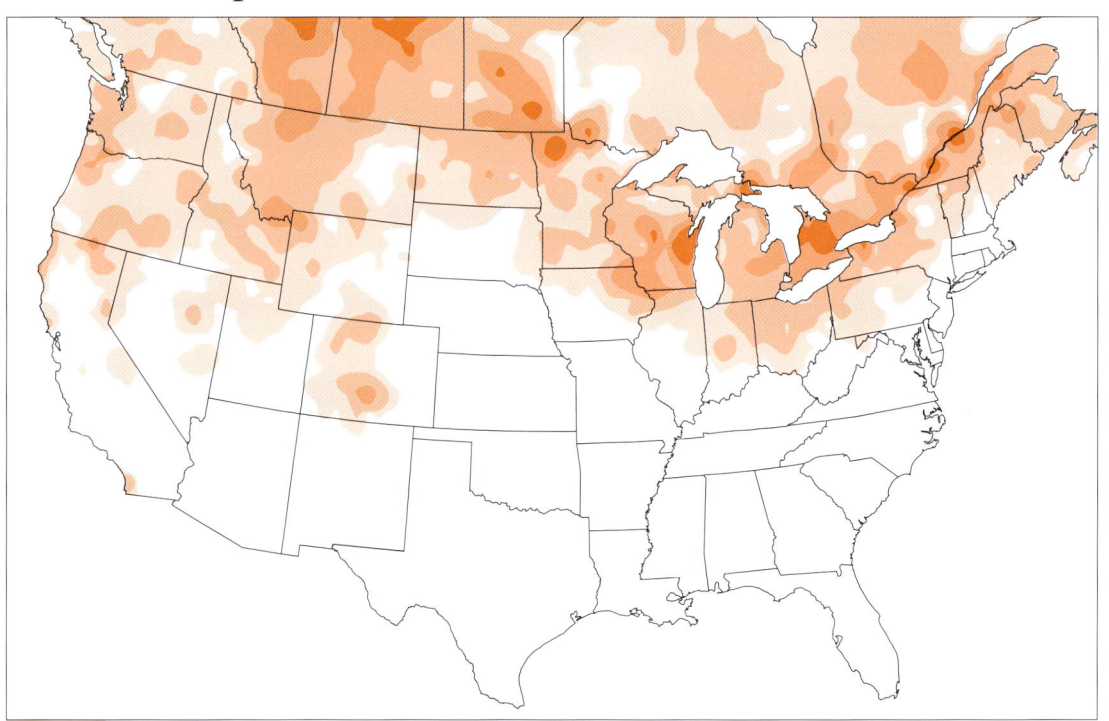

Baird's Sparrow

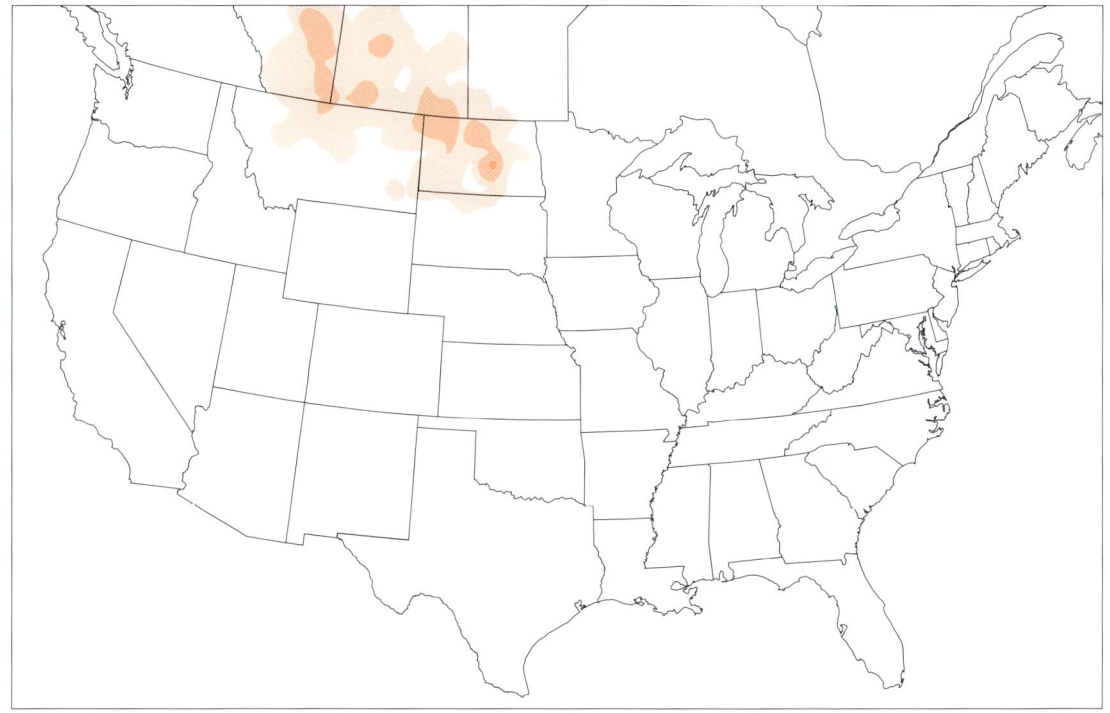

Grasshopper Sparrow

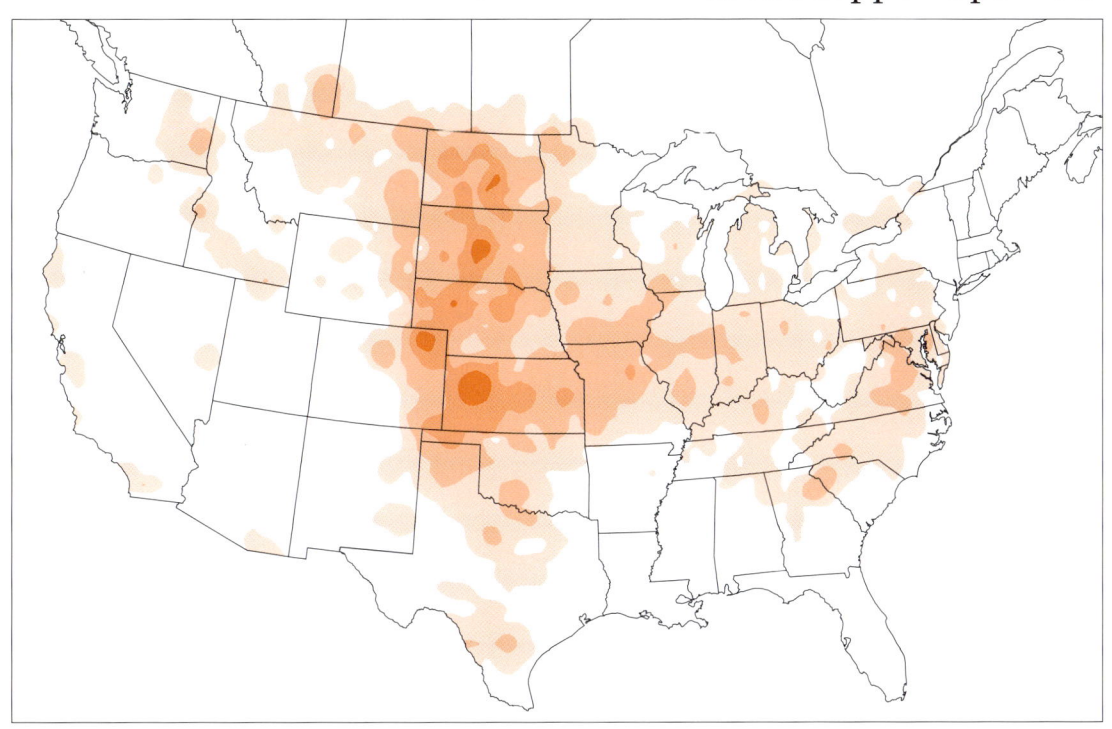

Le Conte's Sparrow

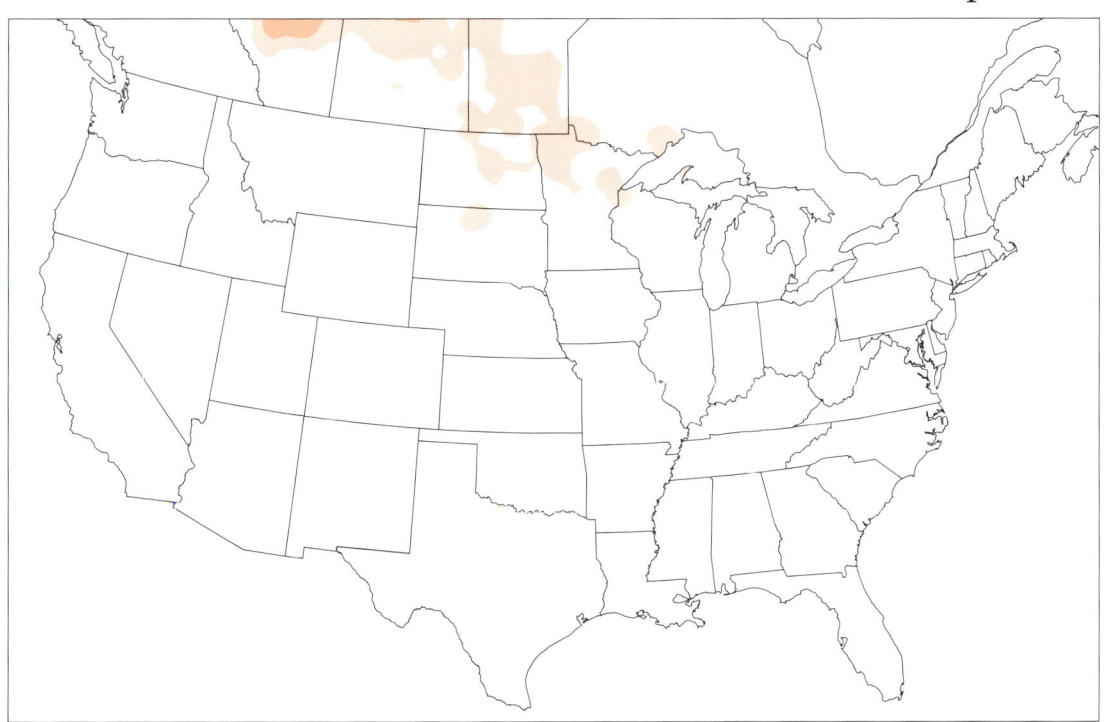

Sharp-tailed Sparrow

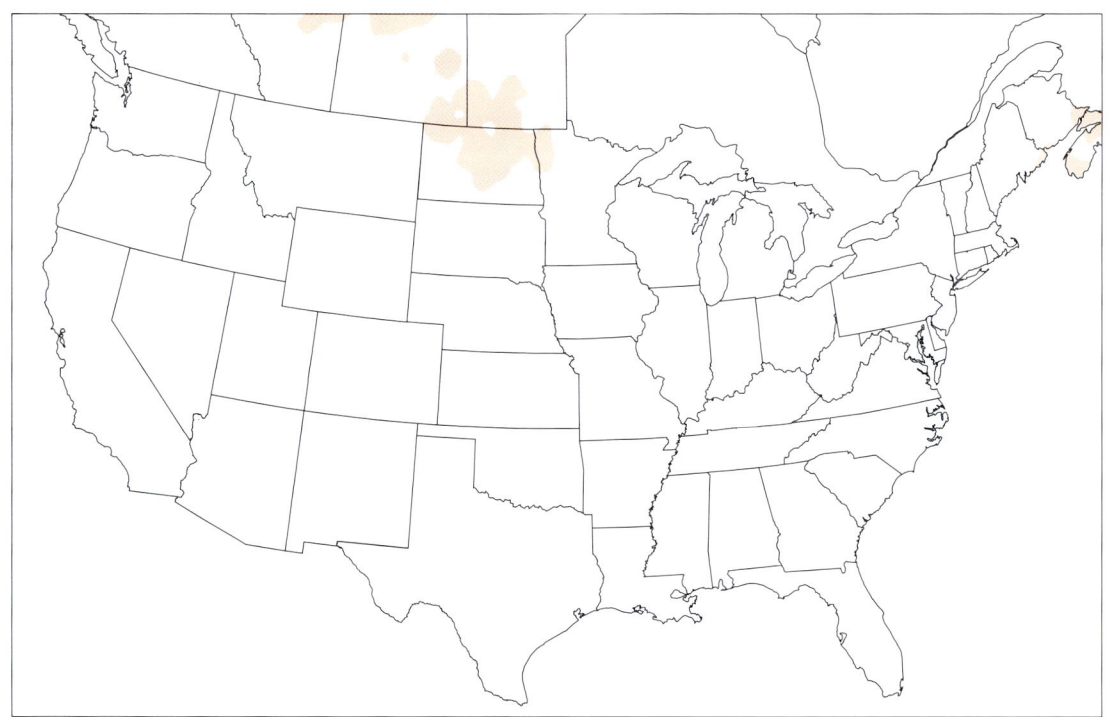

Seaside Sparrow

Fox Sparrow

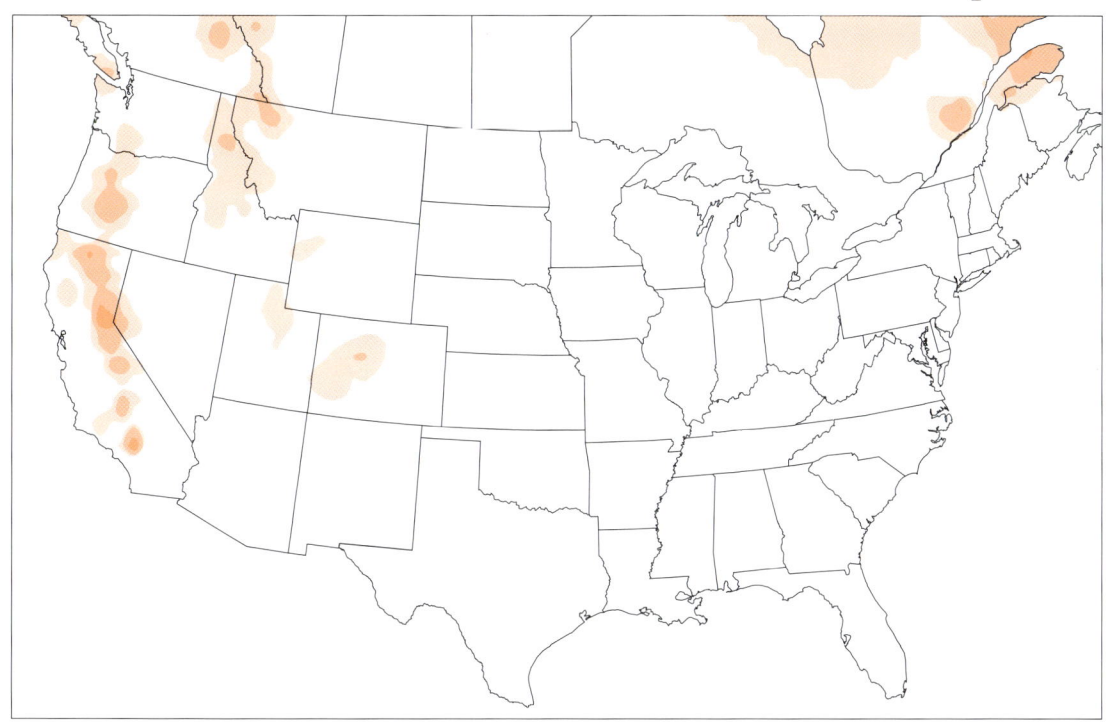

Song Sparrow

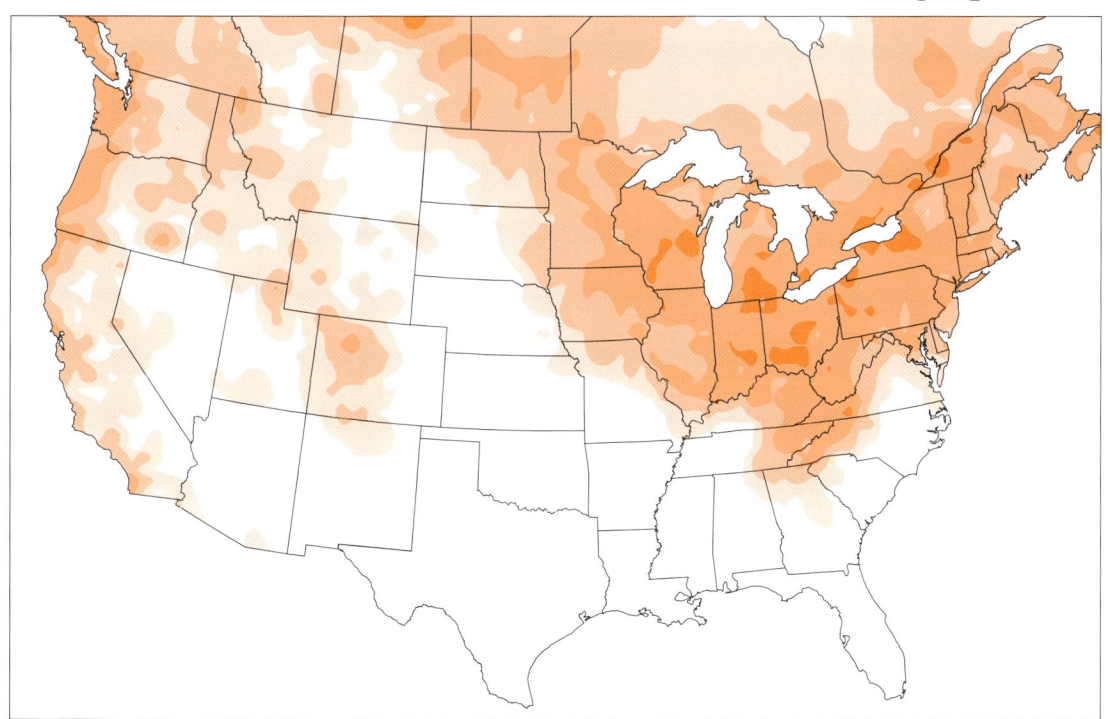

Lincoln's Sparrow

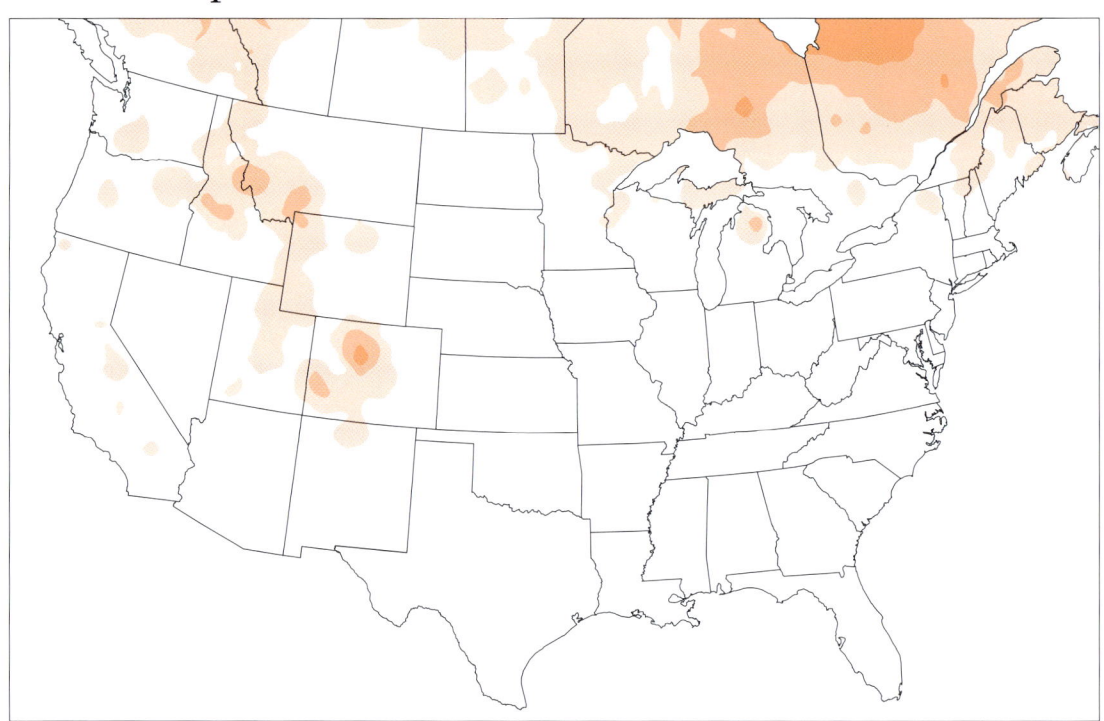

Swamp Sparrow

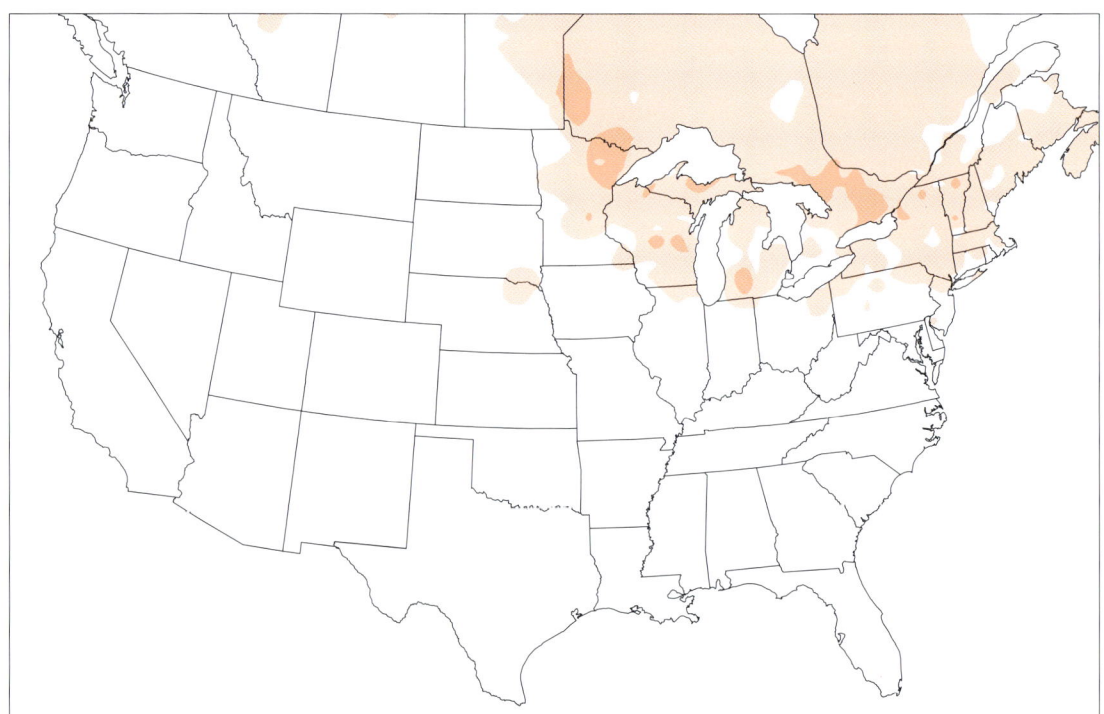

White-throated Sparrow

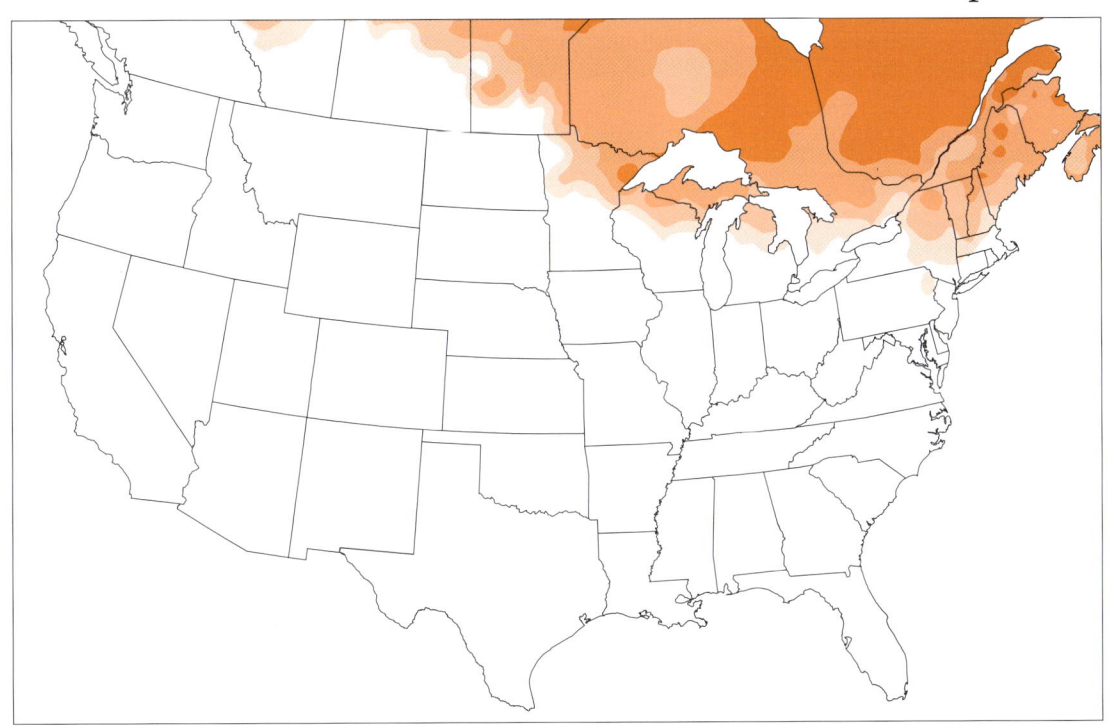

White-crowned Sparrow

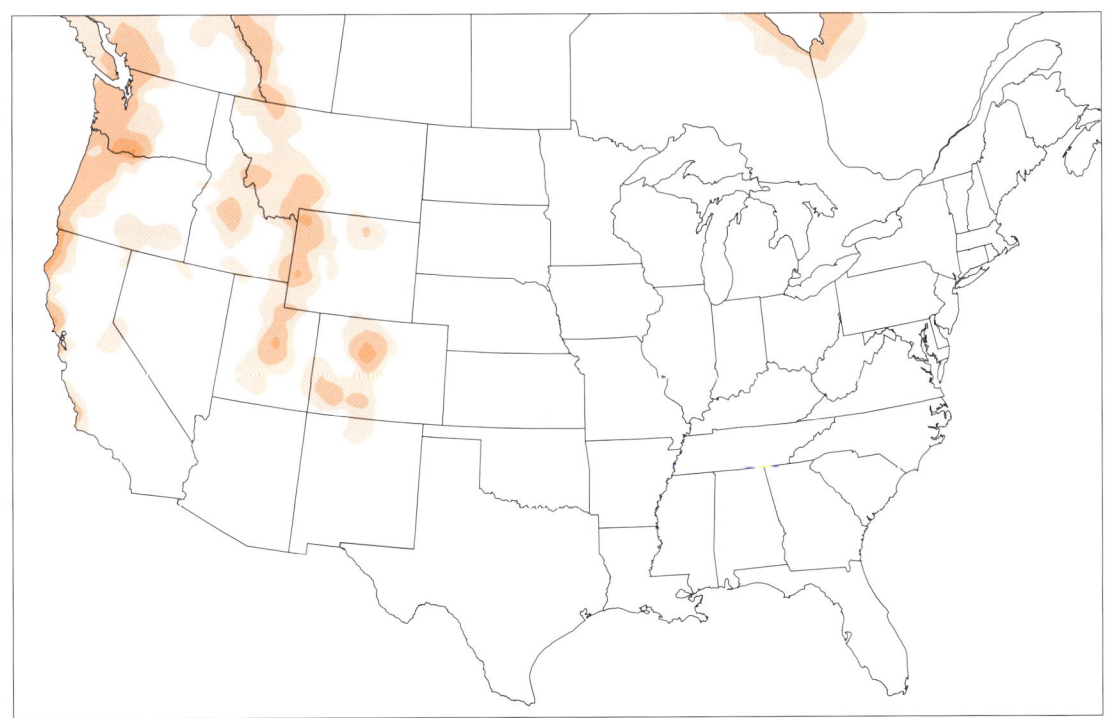

Dark-eyed Junco

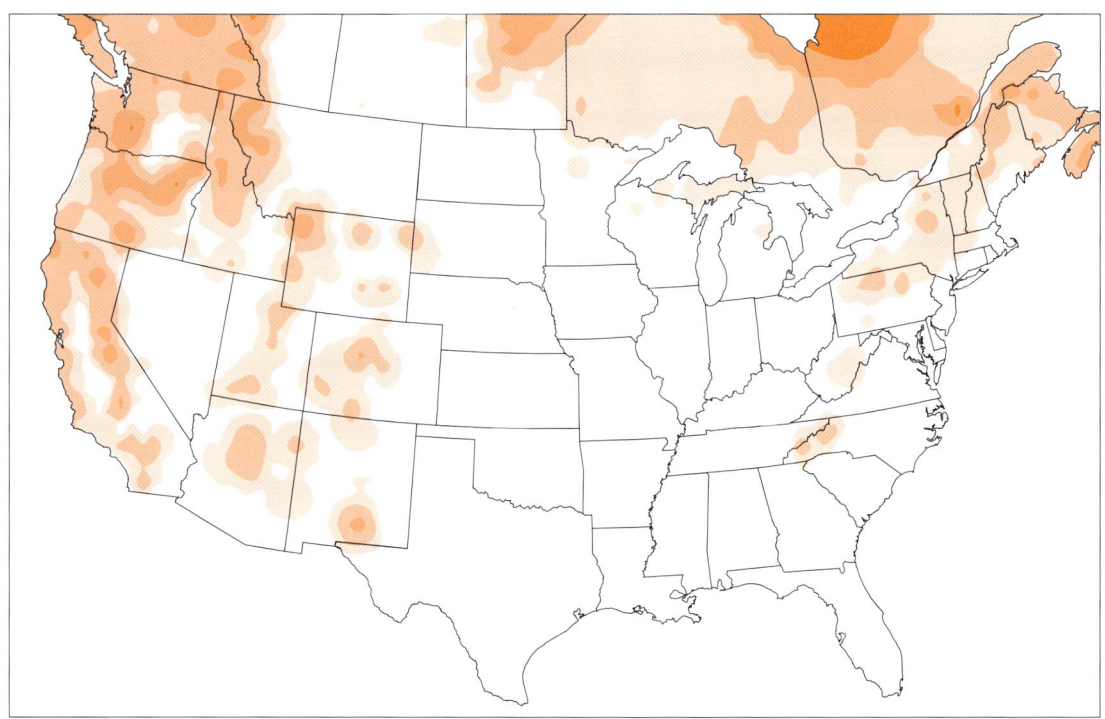

Dark-eyed Junco (Slate-colored)

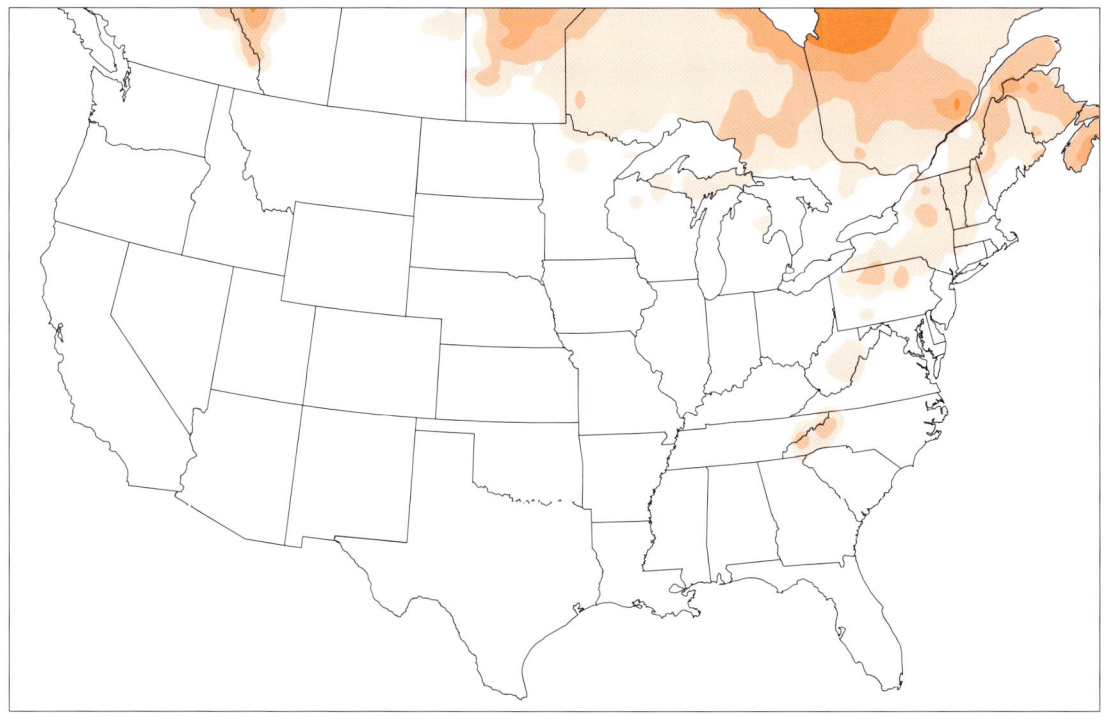

Dark-eyed Junco (Oregon)

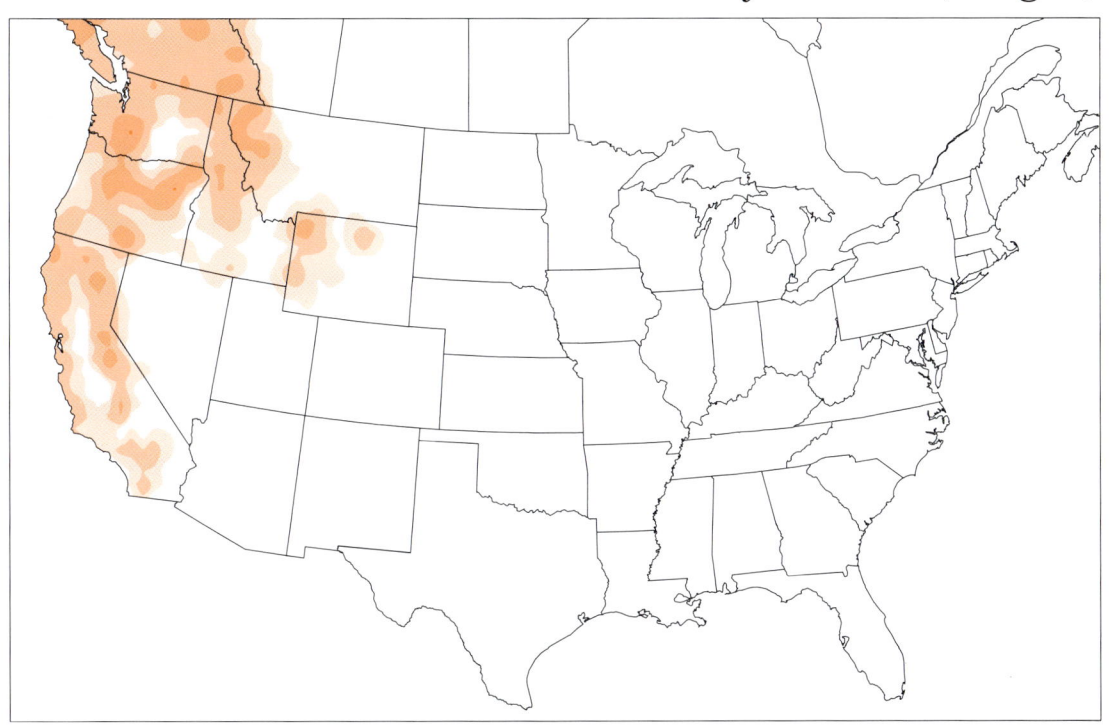

Dark-eyed Junco (White-winged)

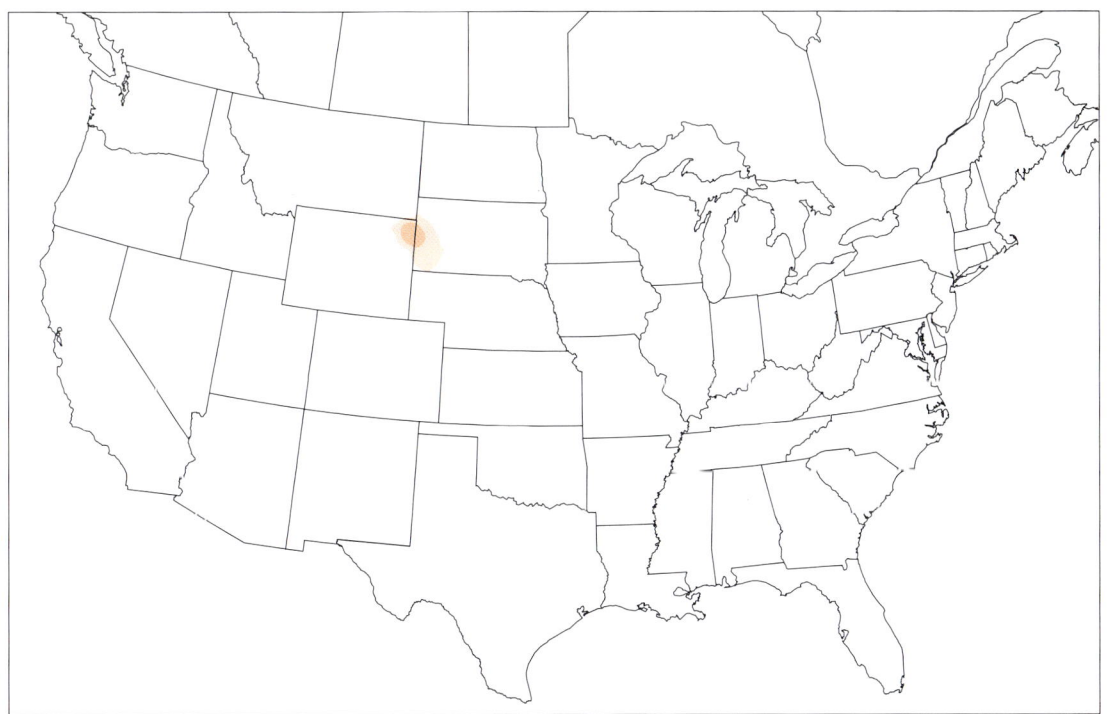

Dark-eyed Junco (Gray-headed)

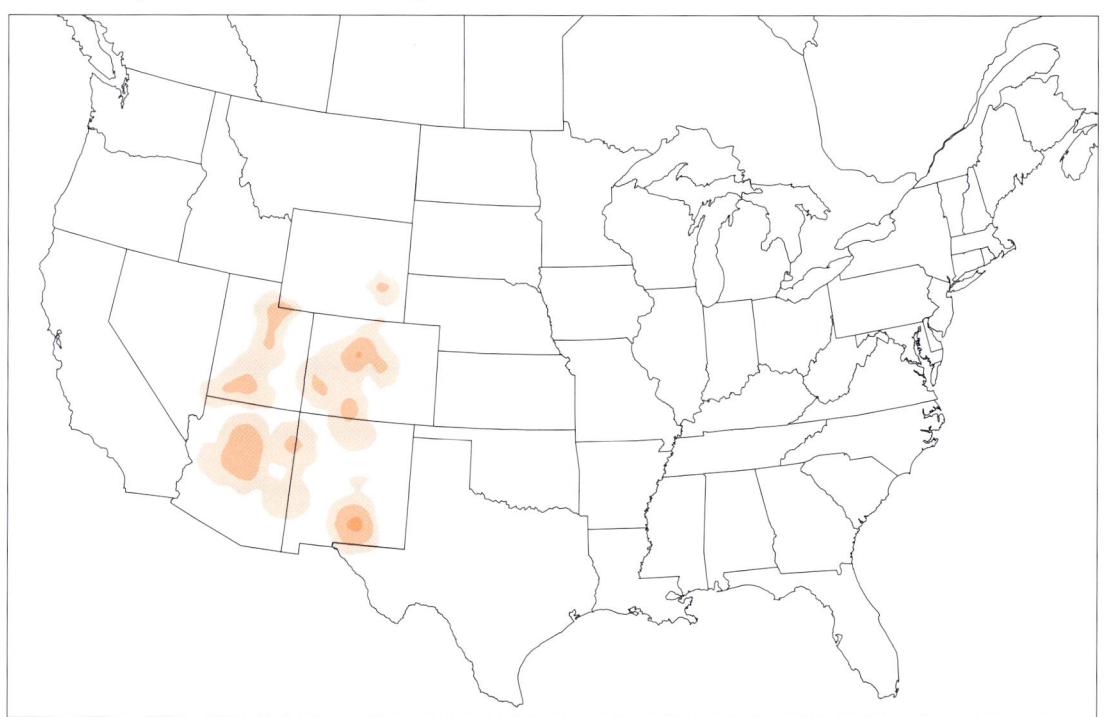

Yellow-eyed Junco

McCown's Longspur

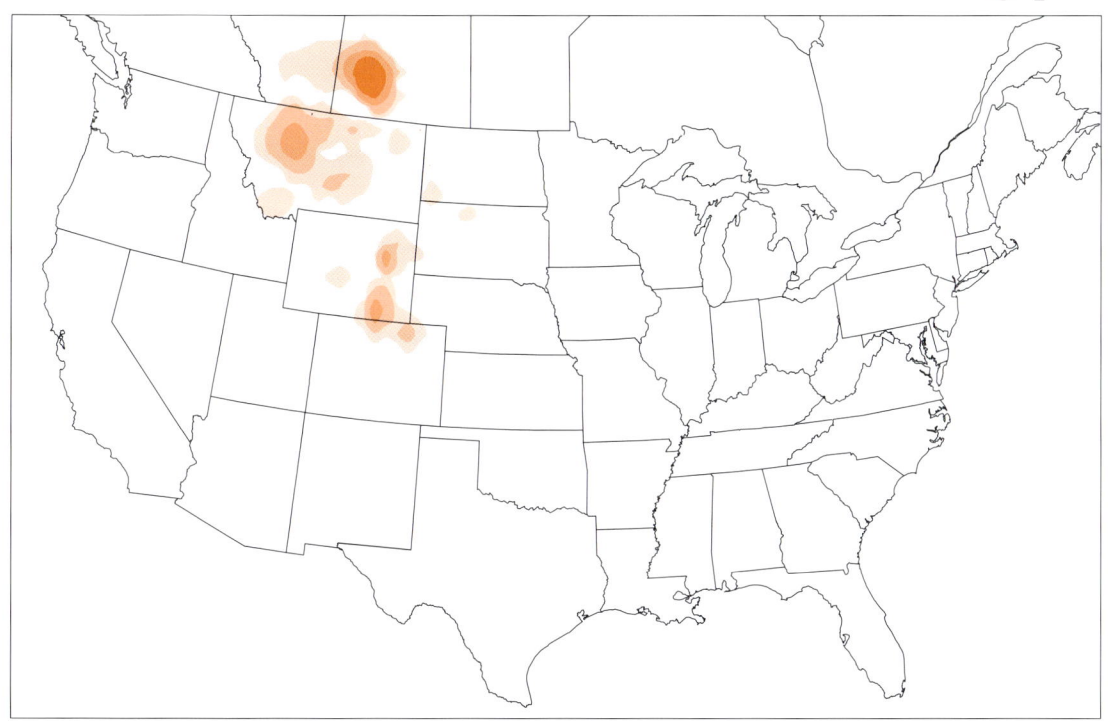

Chestnut-collared Longspur

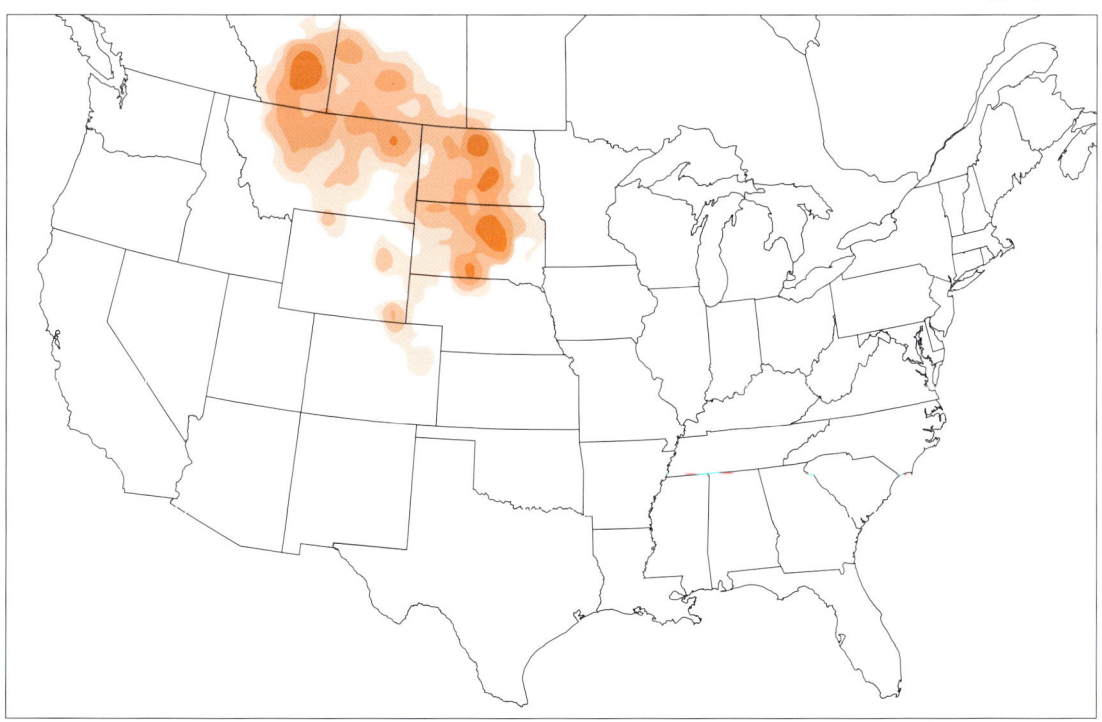

Bobolink

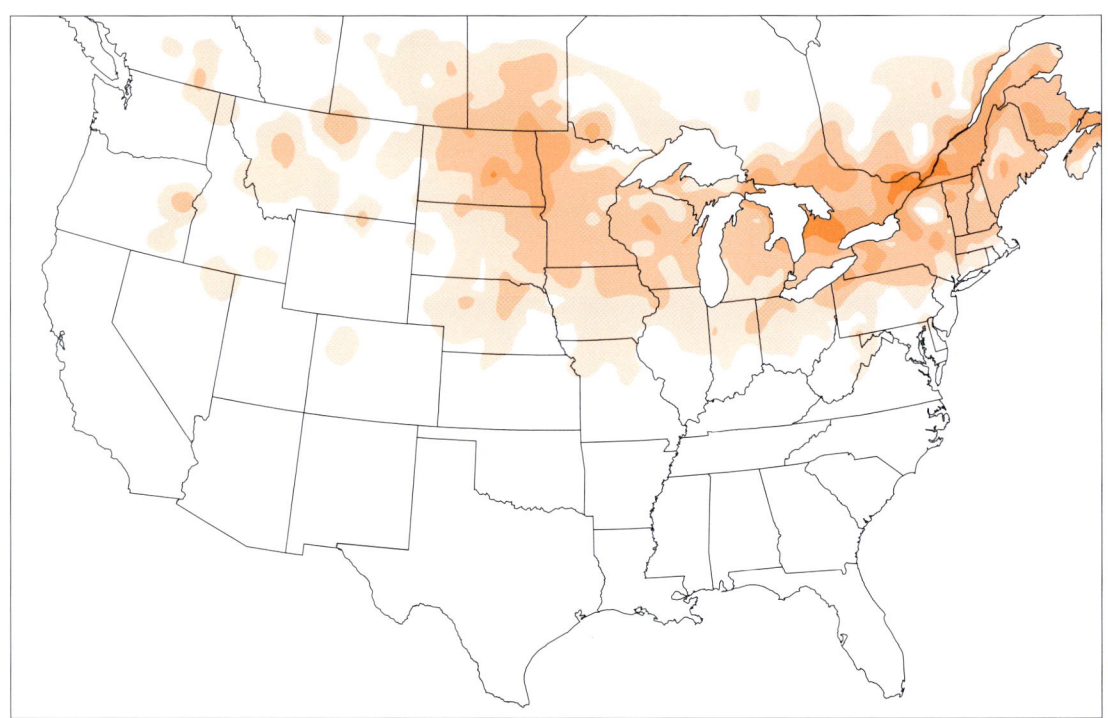

Red-winged Blackbird

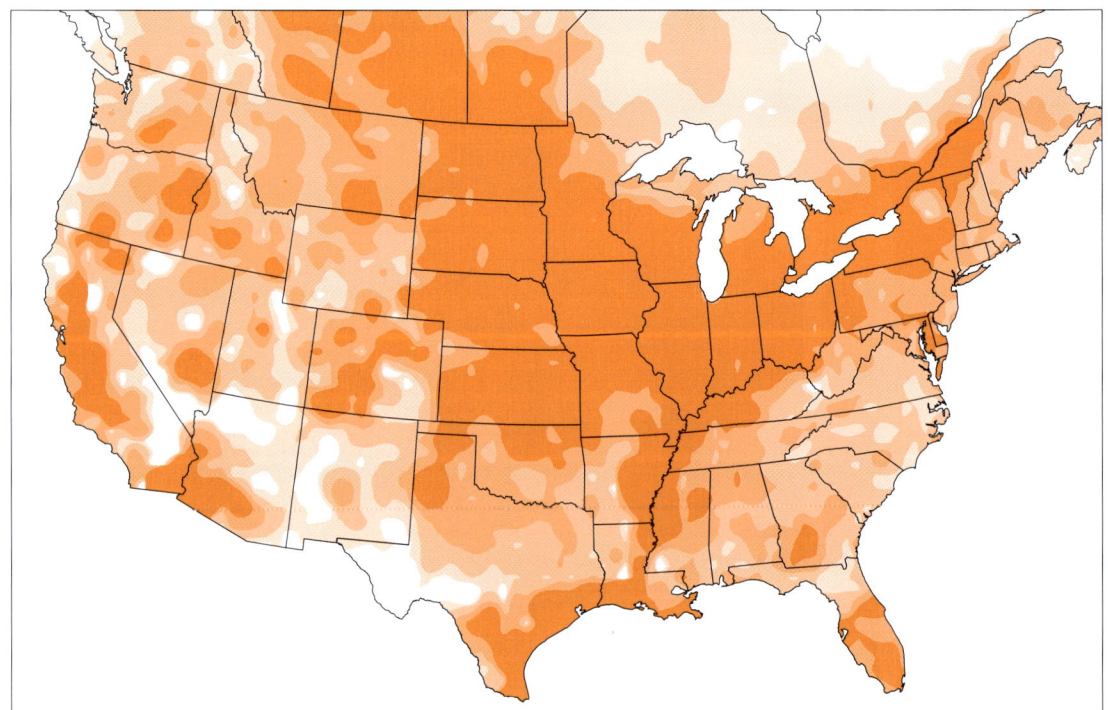

Tricolored Blackbird

Eastern Meadowlark

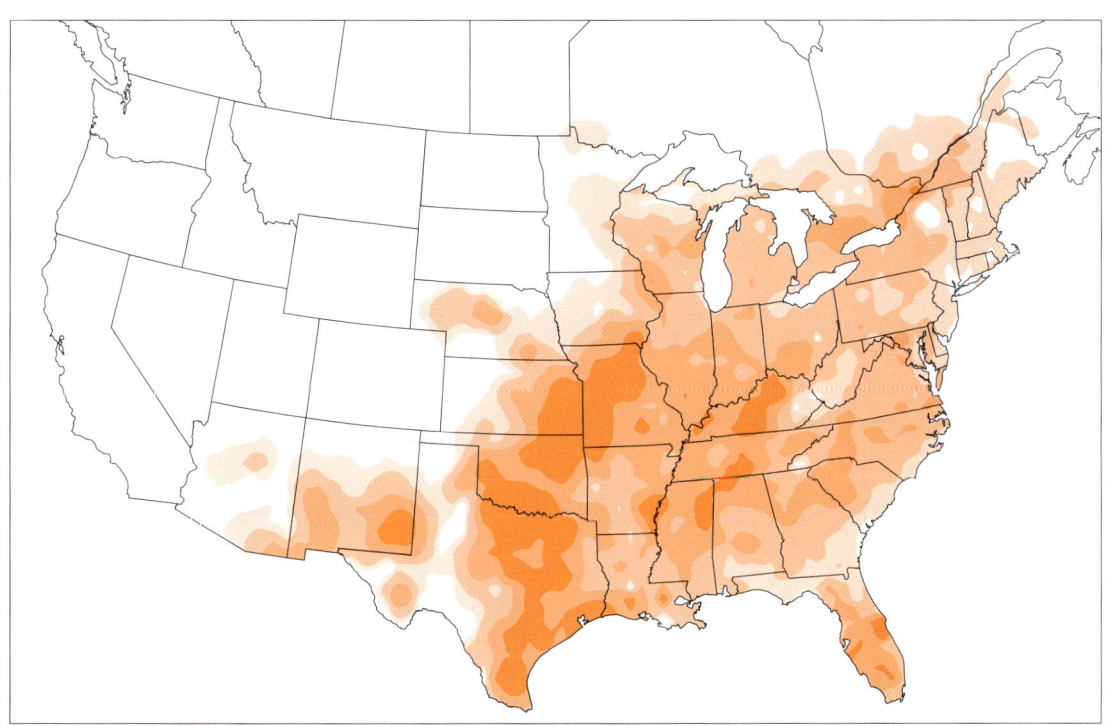

Western Meadowlark

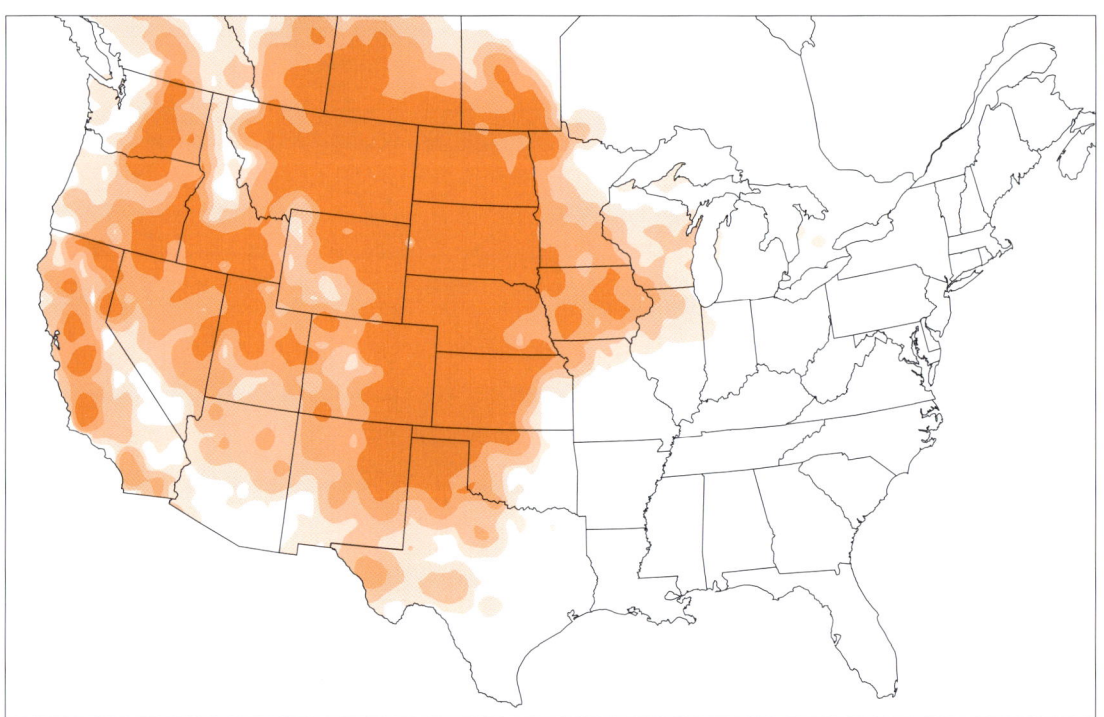

Yellow-headed Blackbird

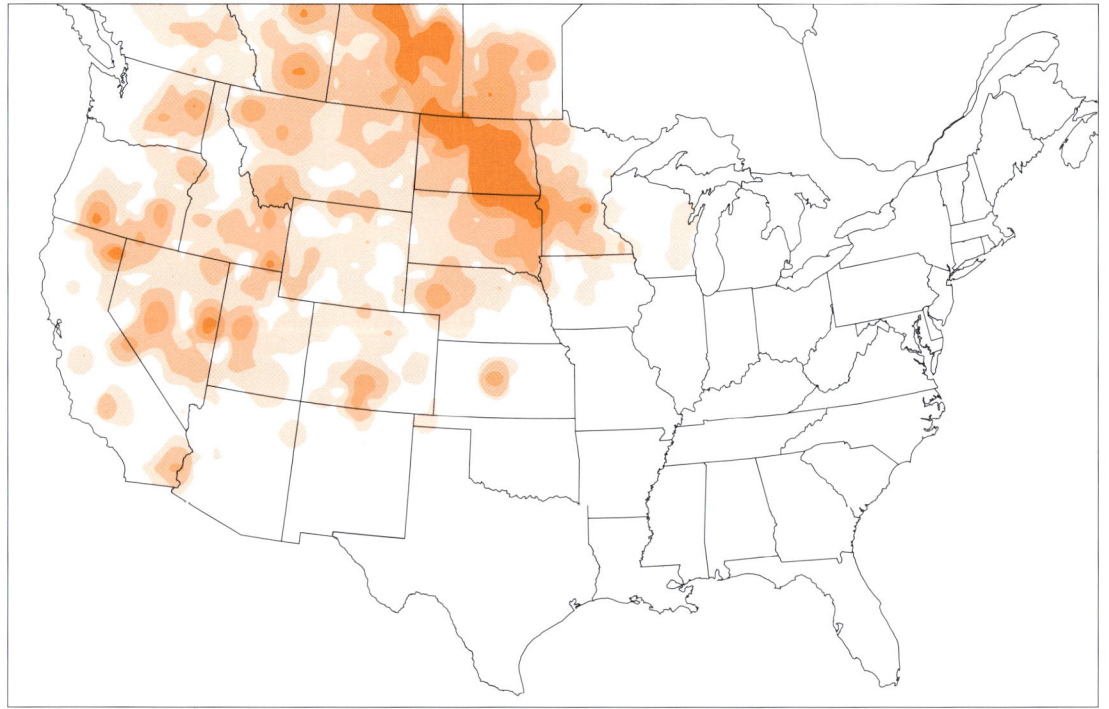

Brewer's Blackbird

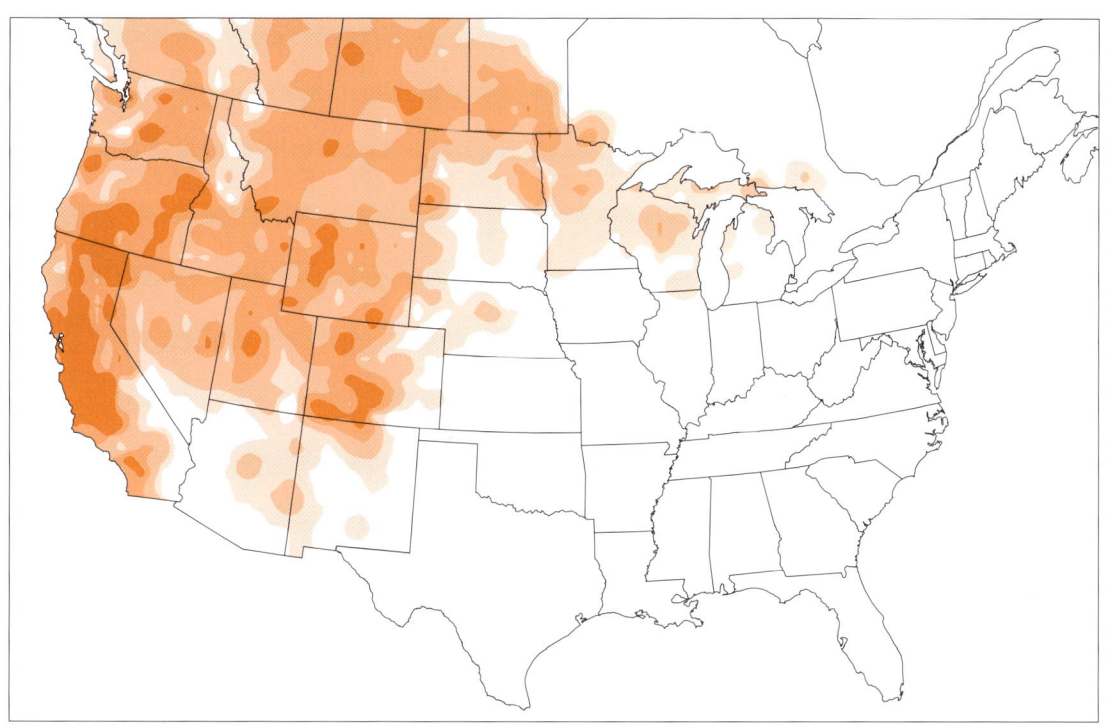

Great-tailed Grackle

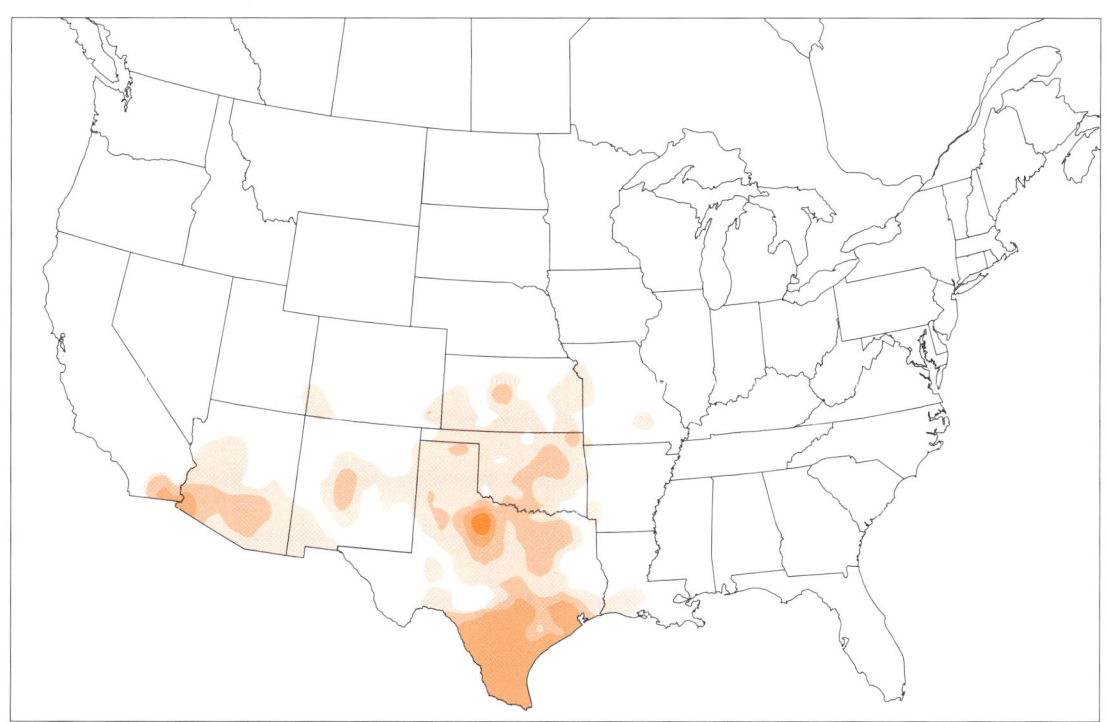

Boat-tailed Grackle

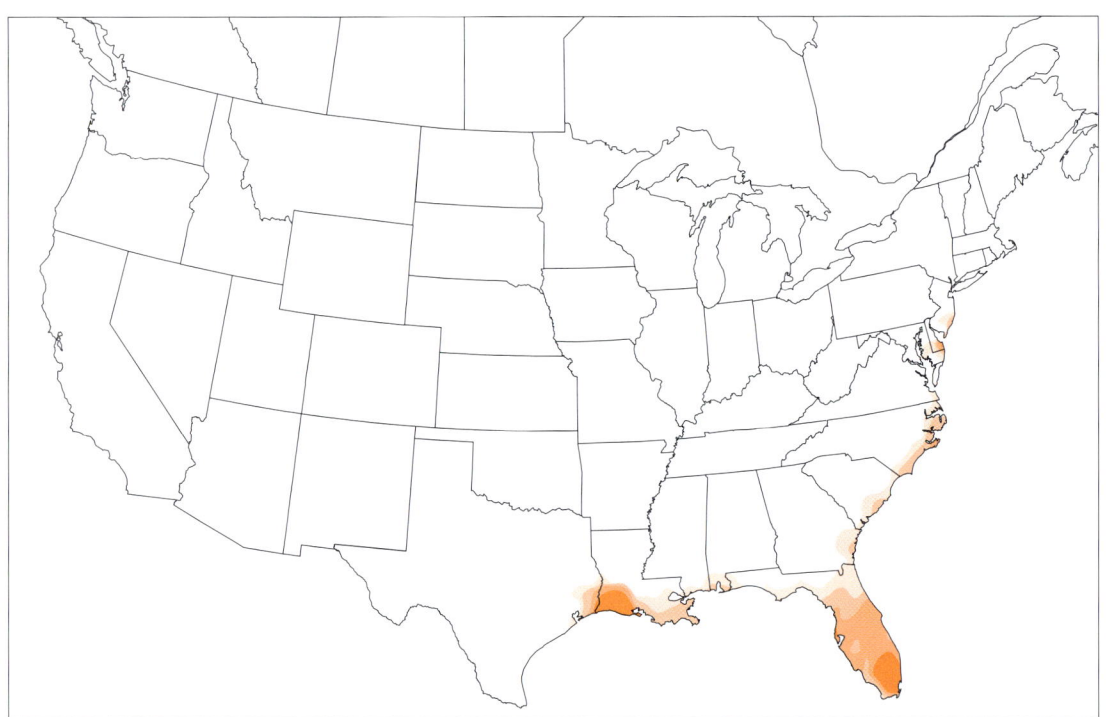

Common Grackle

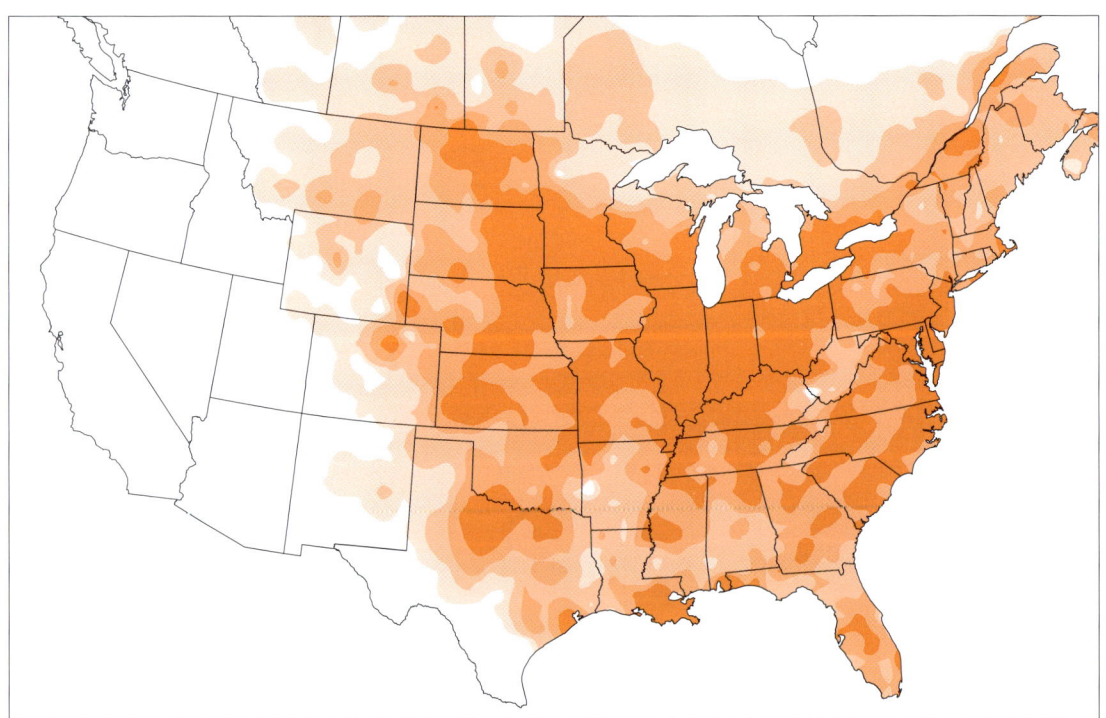

Bronzed Cowbird

Brown-headed Cowbird

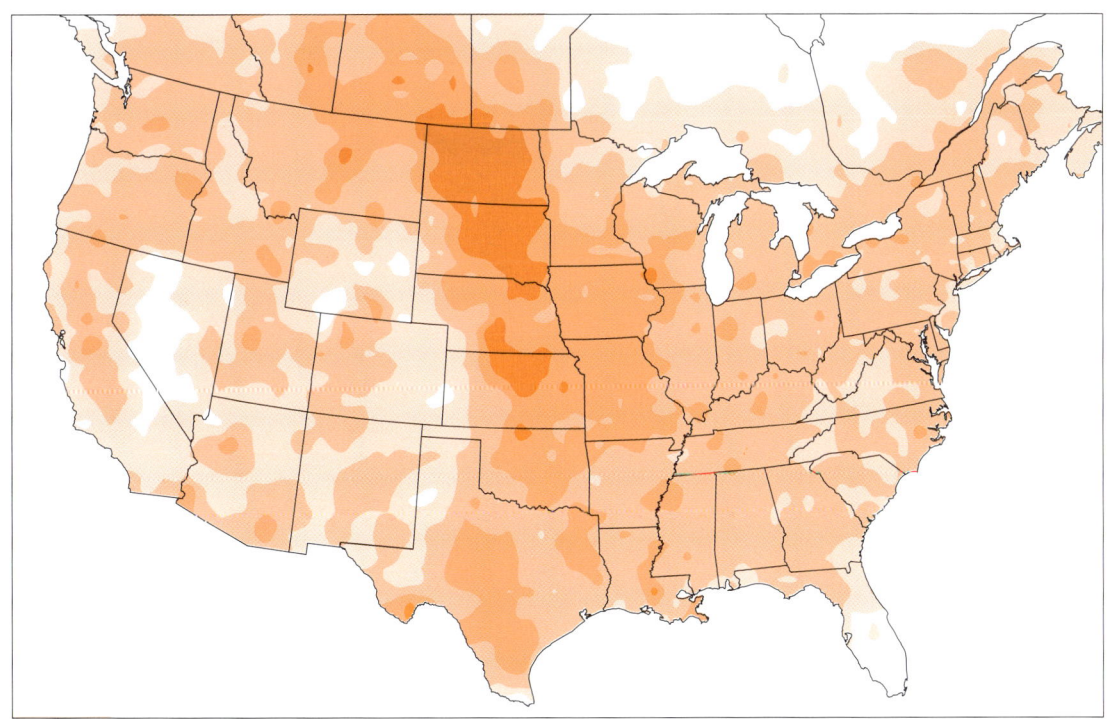

Orchard Oriole

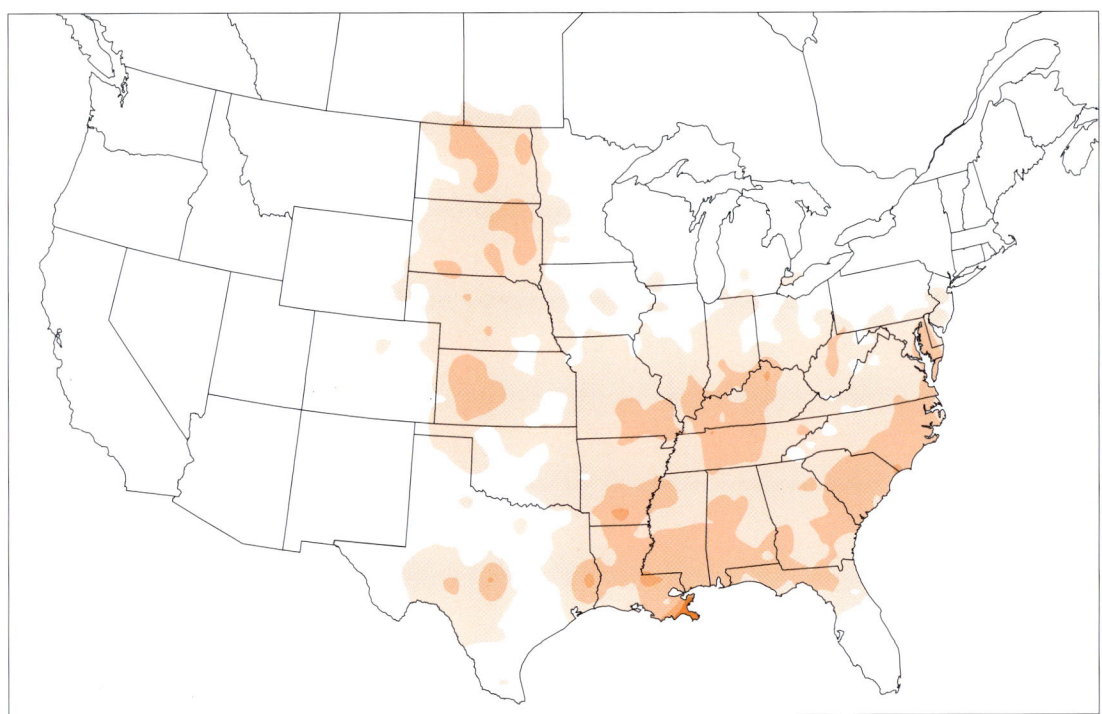

Hooded Oriole

Altamira Oriole

Audubon's Oriole

Northern Oriole

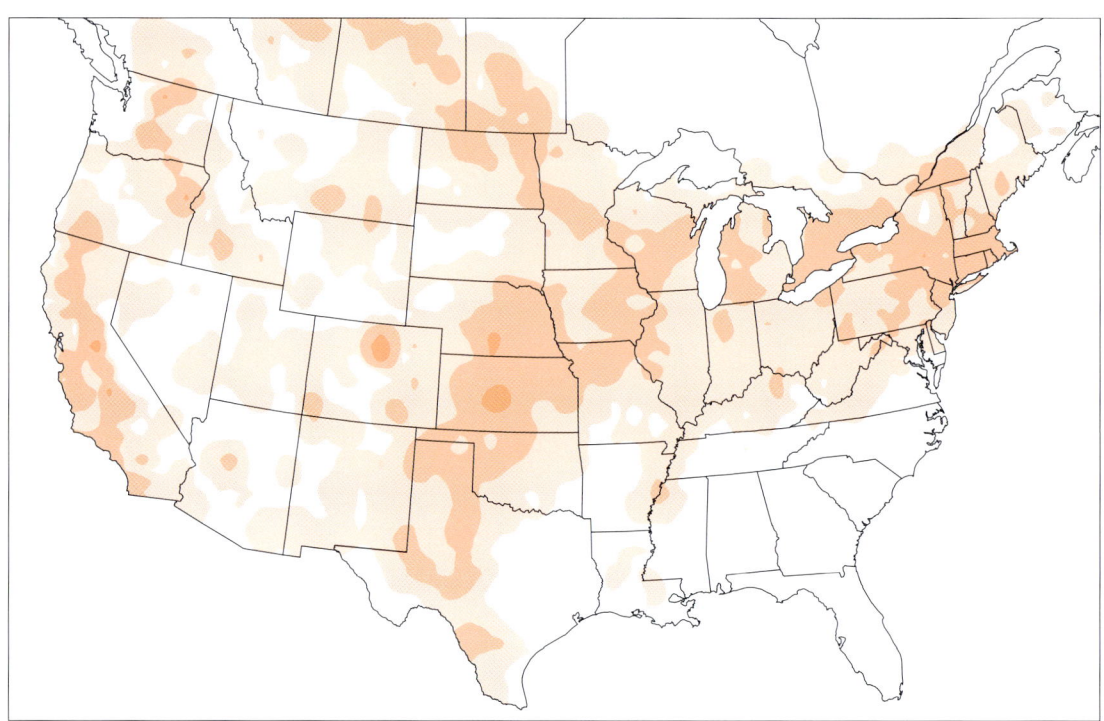

Northern Oriole (Baltimore)

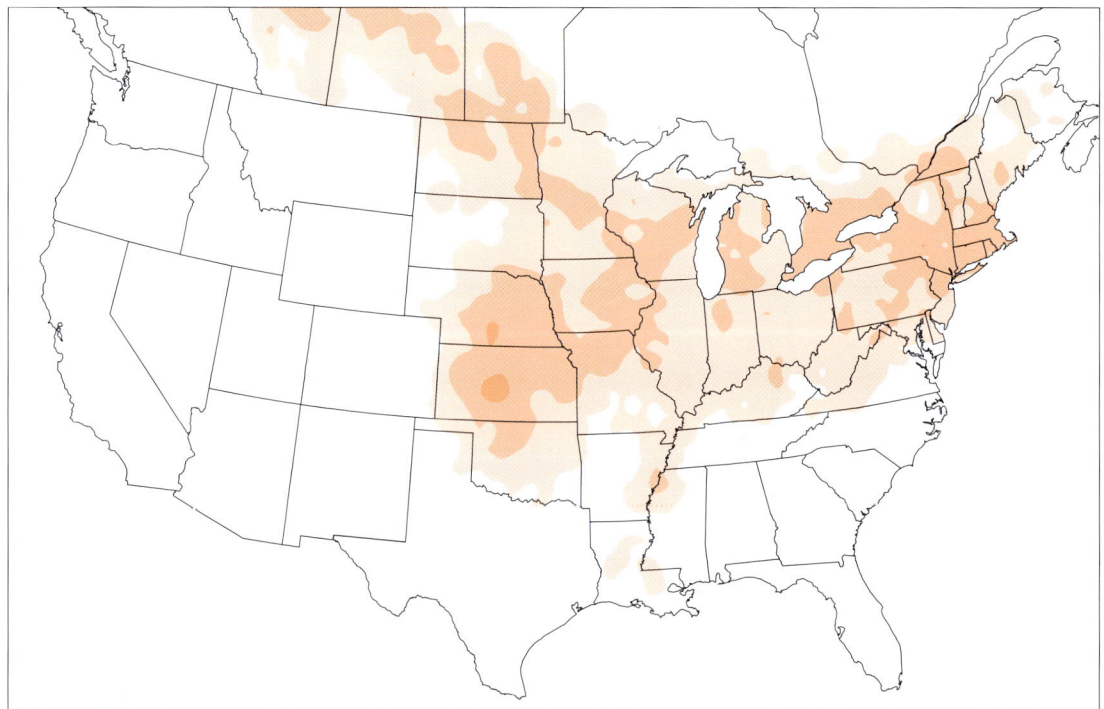

Northern Oriole (Bullock's)

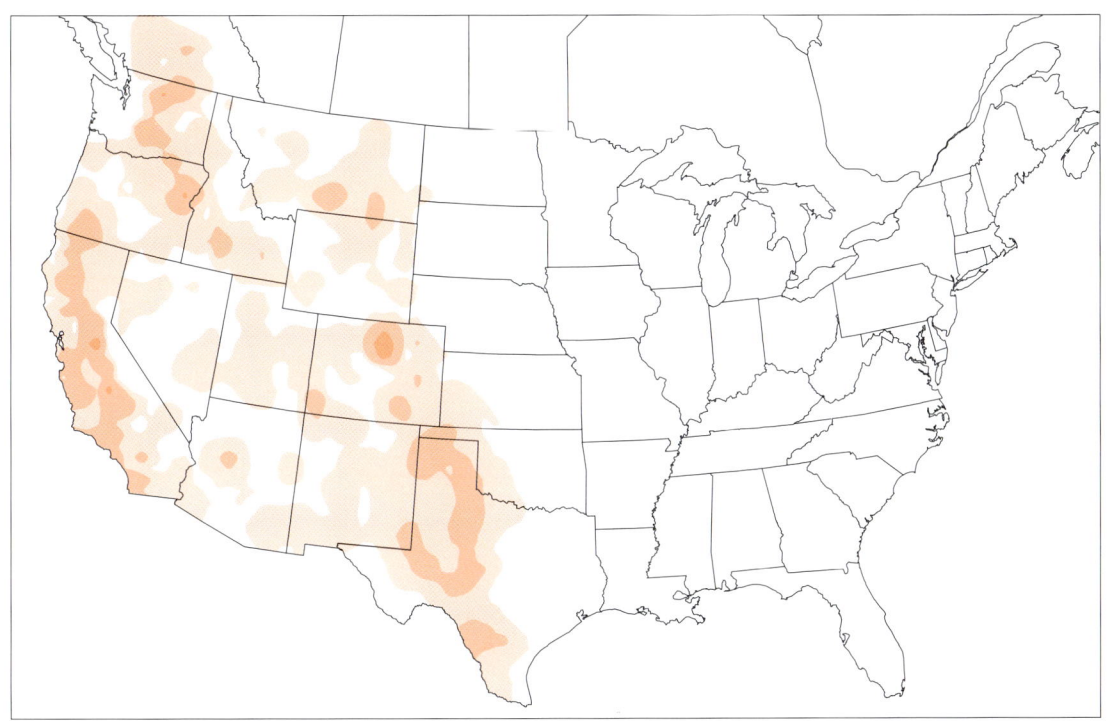

Scott's Oriole

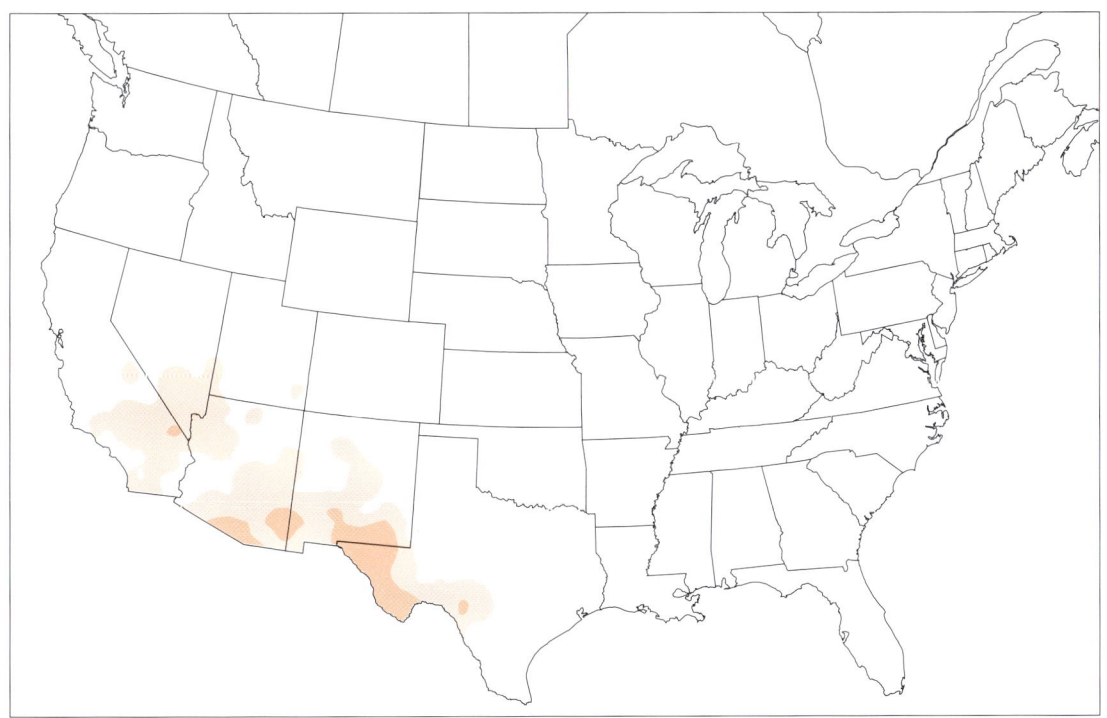

Purple Finch

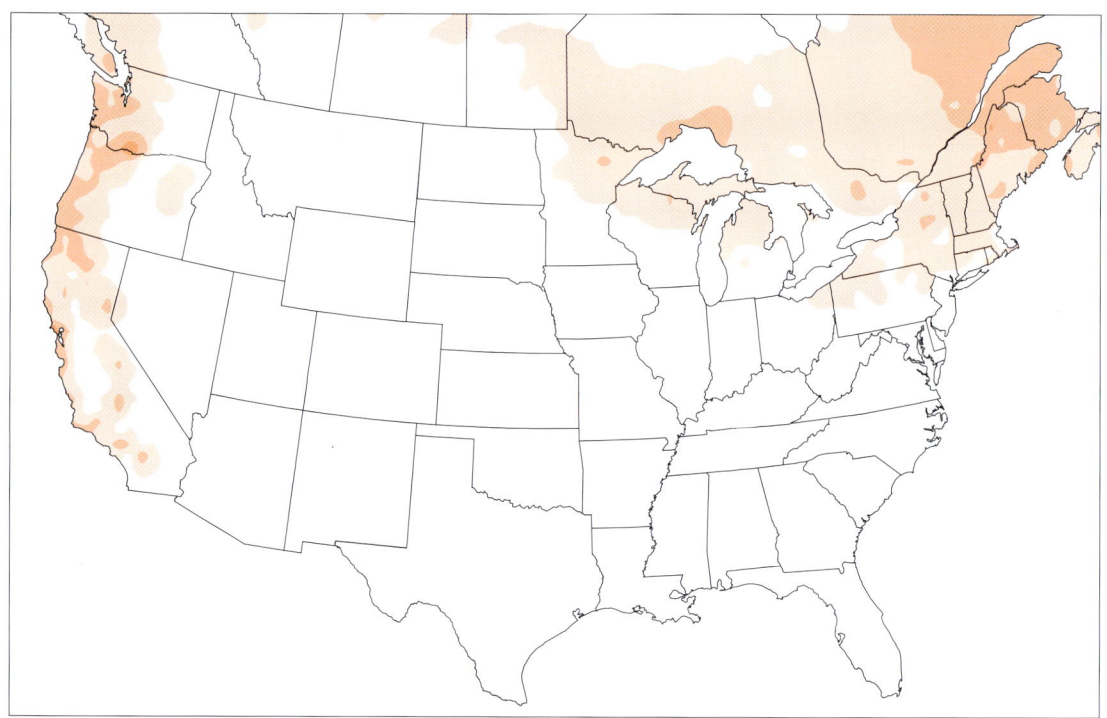

Cassin's Finch

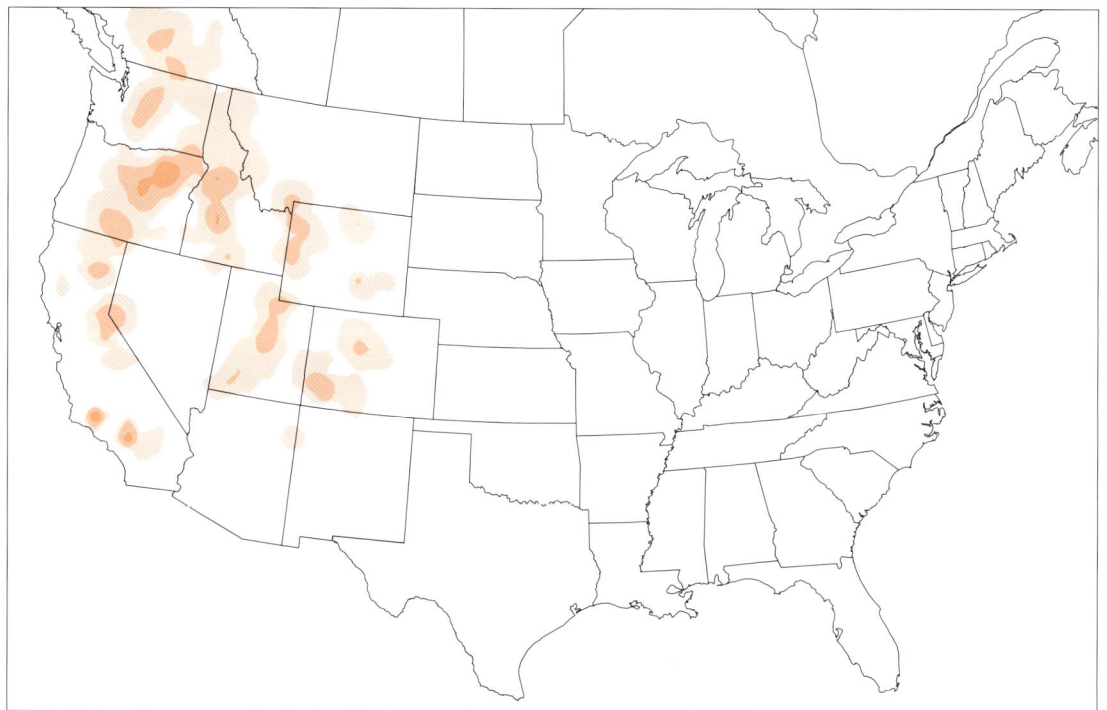

House Finch

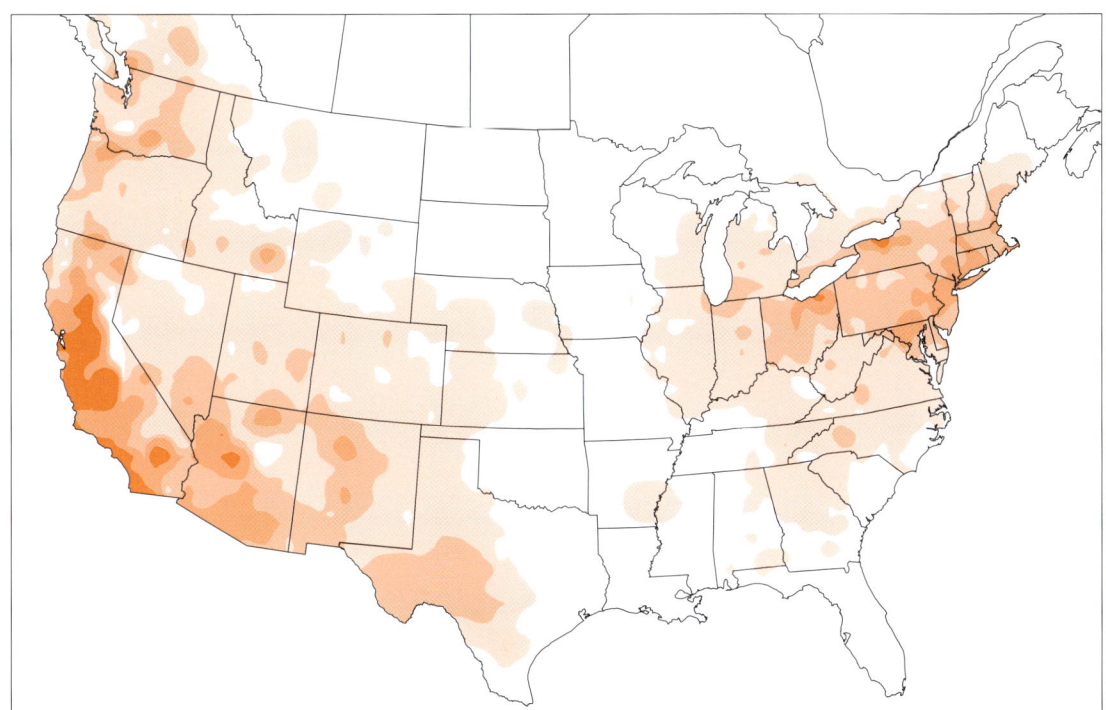

Red Crossbill

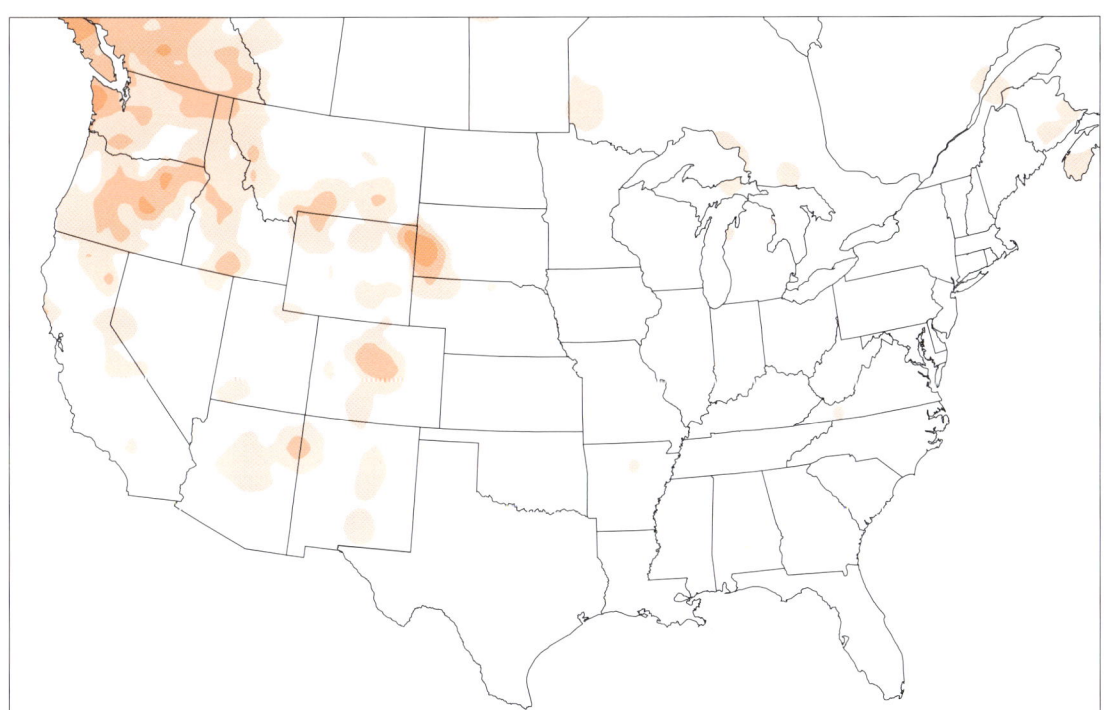

Pine Siskin

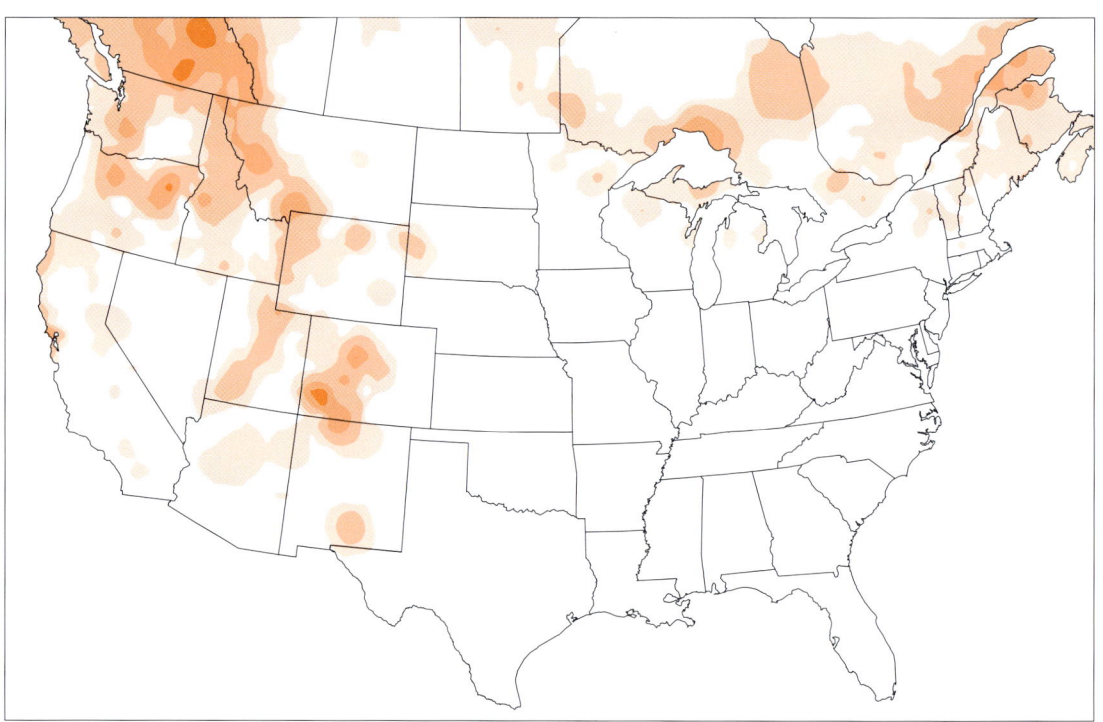

Lesser Goldfinch

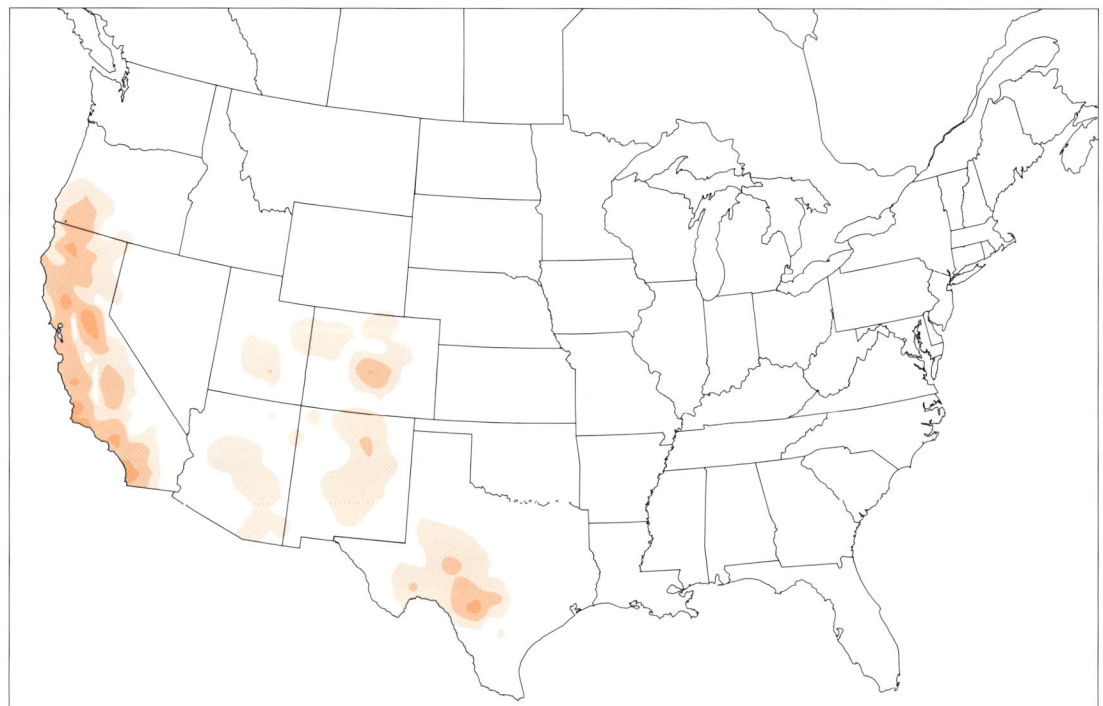

Lawrence's Goldfinch

American Goldfinch

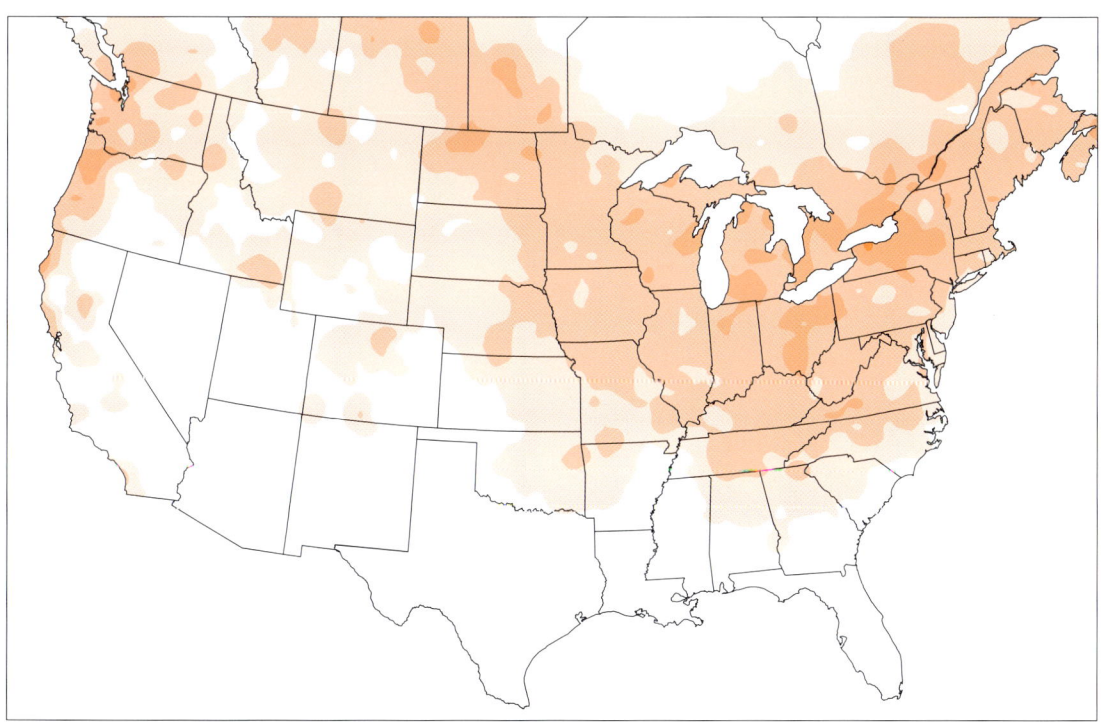

Evening Grosbeak

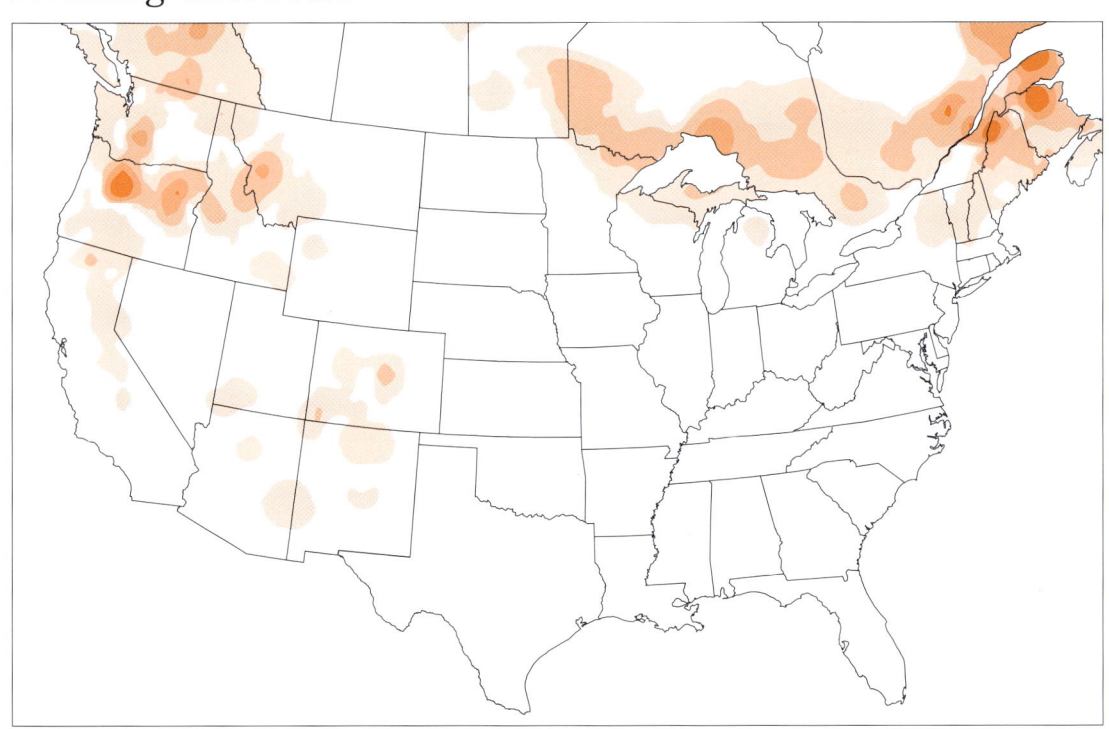

D. BEADLE

House Sparrow

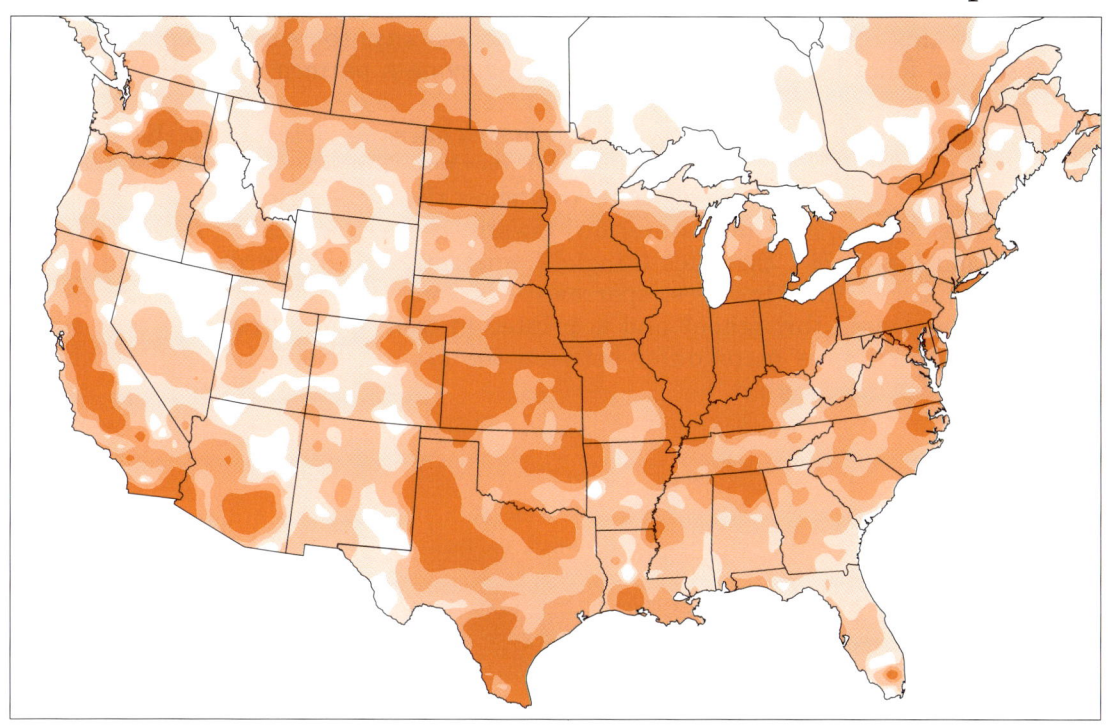

Eurasian Tree Sparrow

The previous maps all show the relative abundance of a single species. It is also often helpful to know approximately how many species can be found in a given area. While this is sometimes referred to as biodiversity, the correct term is species richness. The following maps show the species richness pattern for several different groups of birds.

The first map shows the overall species richness as detected by the Breeding Bird Survey (BBS). This is a measure of the average number of species detected per route per year. Other maps are provided that show the species richness of herons (bitterns, herons, egrets, and ibis); waterfowl (swans, geese, and ducks); flycatchers (flycatchers and kingbirds); thrushes (kinglets, gnatcatchers, bluebirds, and thrushes); warblers; and sparrows (towhees, sparrows, and longspurs). On previous maps the same scale was used throughout and is printed in front of the first map. The scales for the species richness maps differ between the groups, therefore each map has a separate scale printed with it.

Overall Species Richness

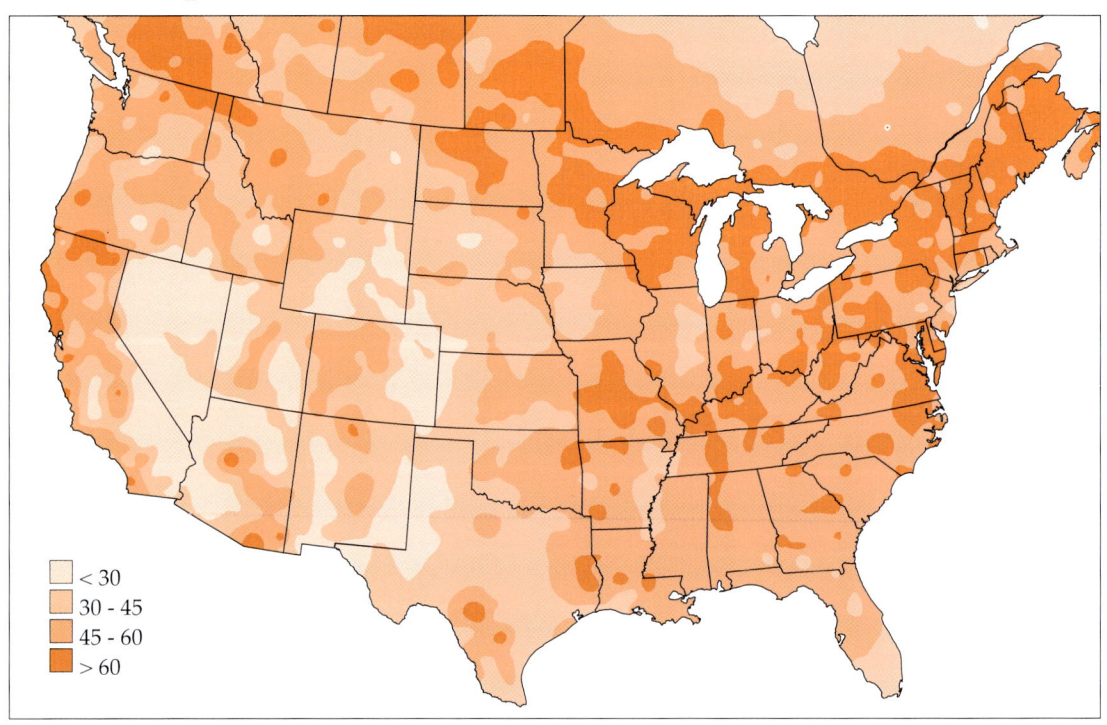

Heron Species Richness

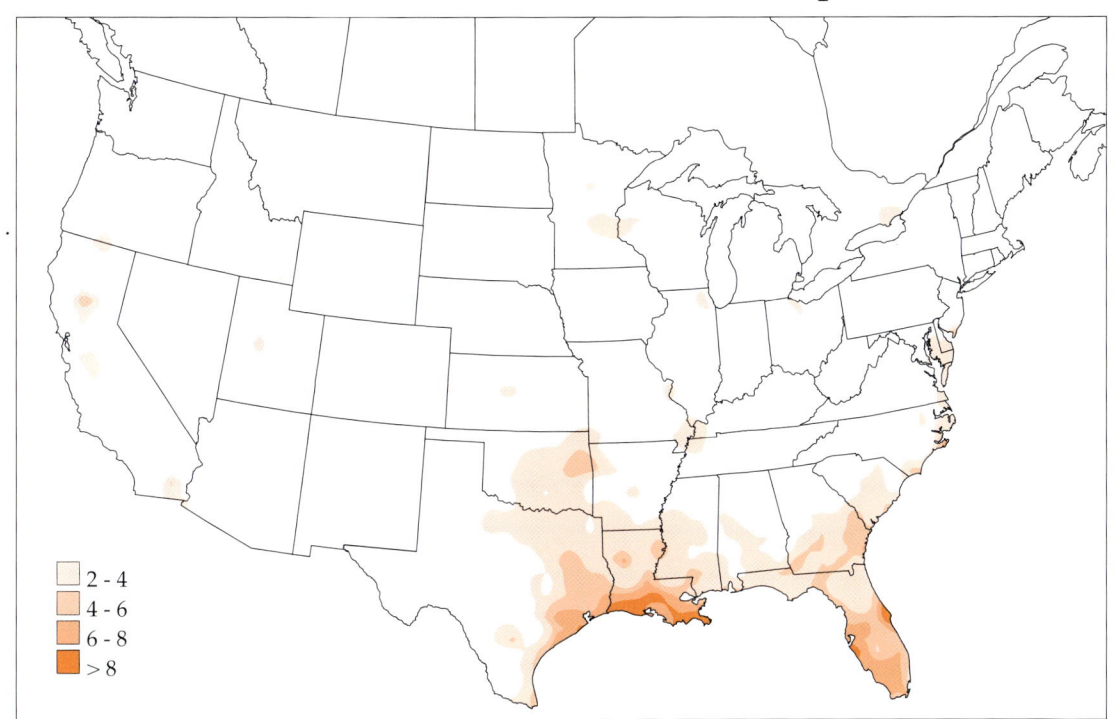

Waterfowl Species Richness

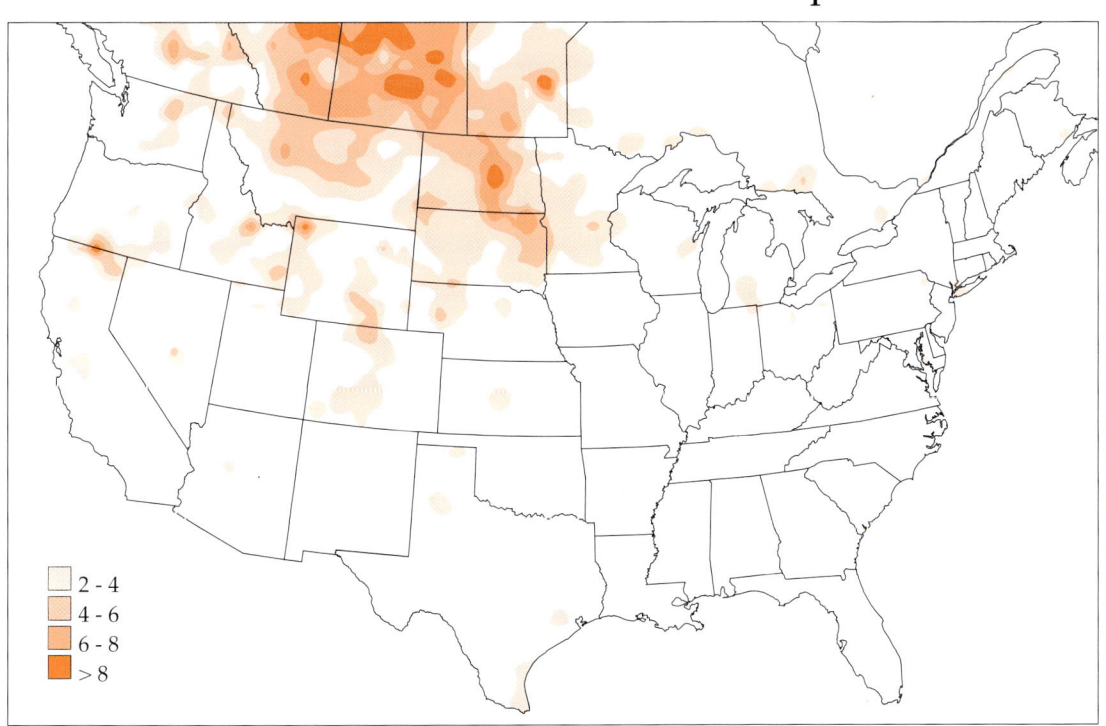

Flycatcher Species Richness

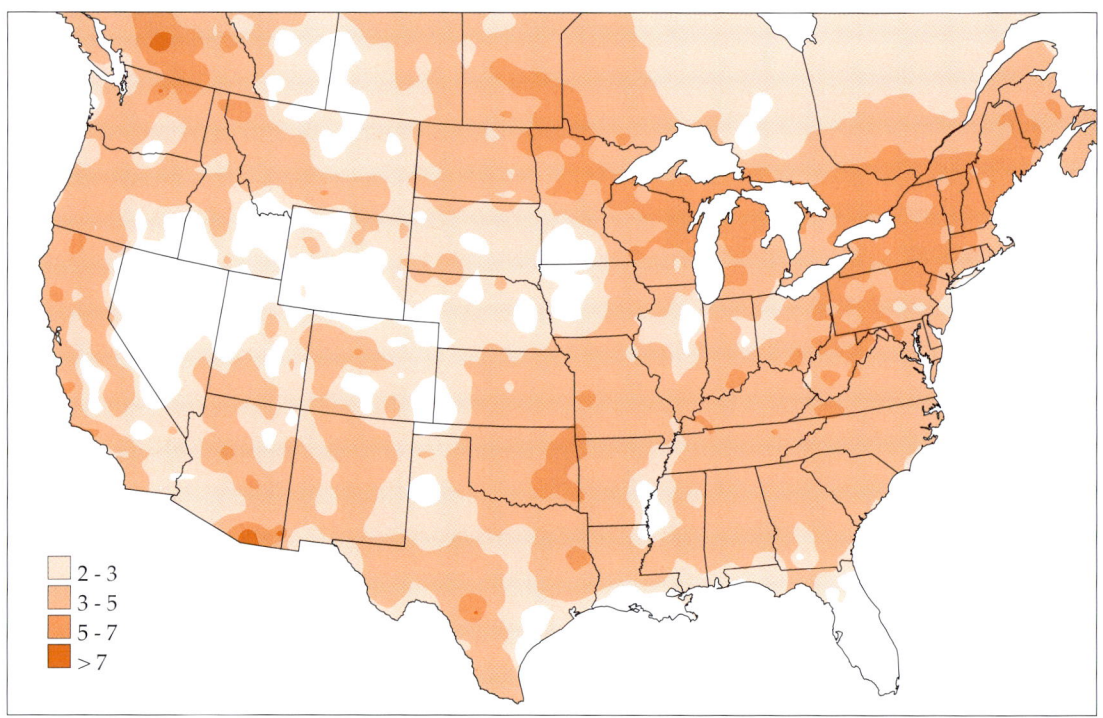

Thrush Species Richness

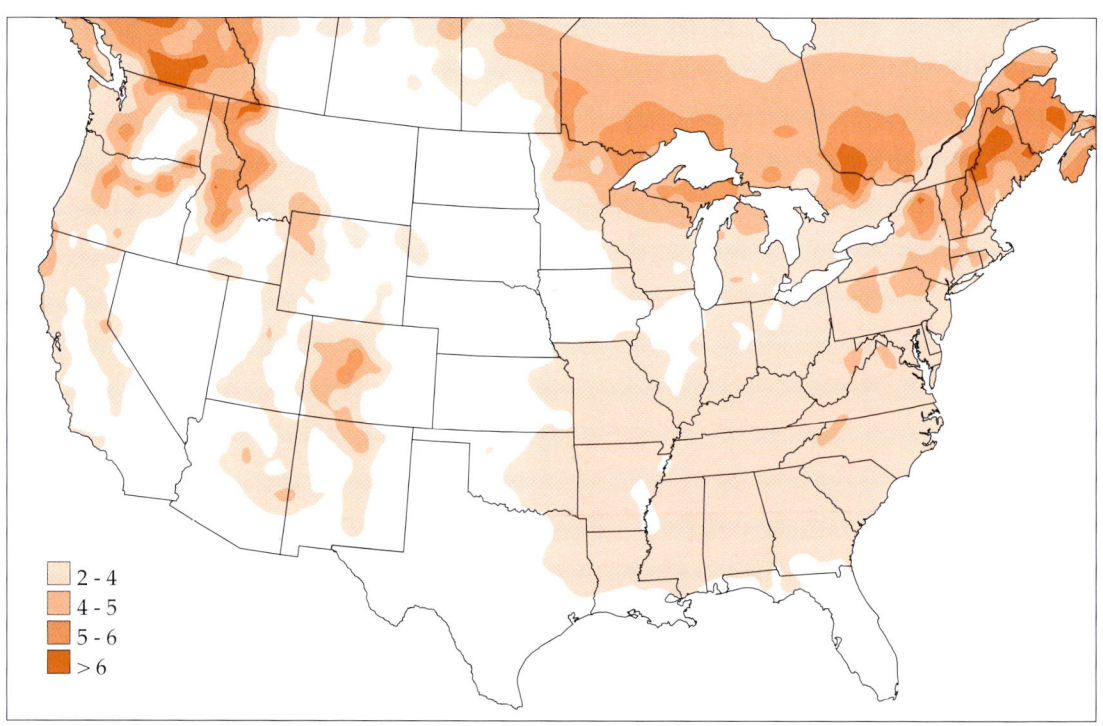

Warbler Species Richness

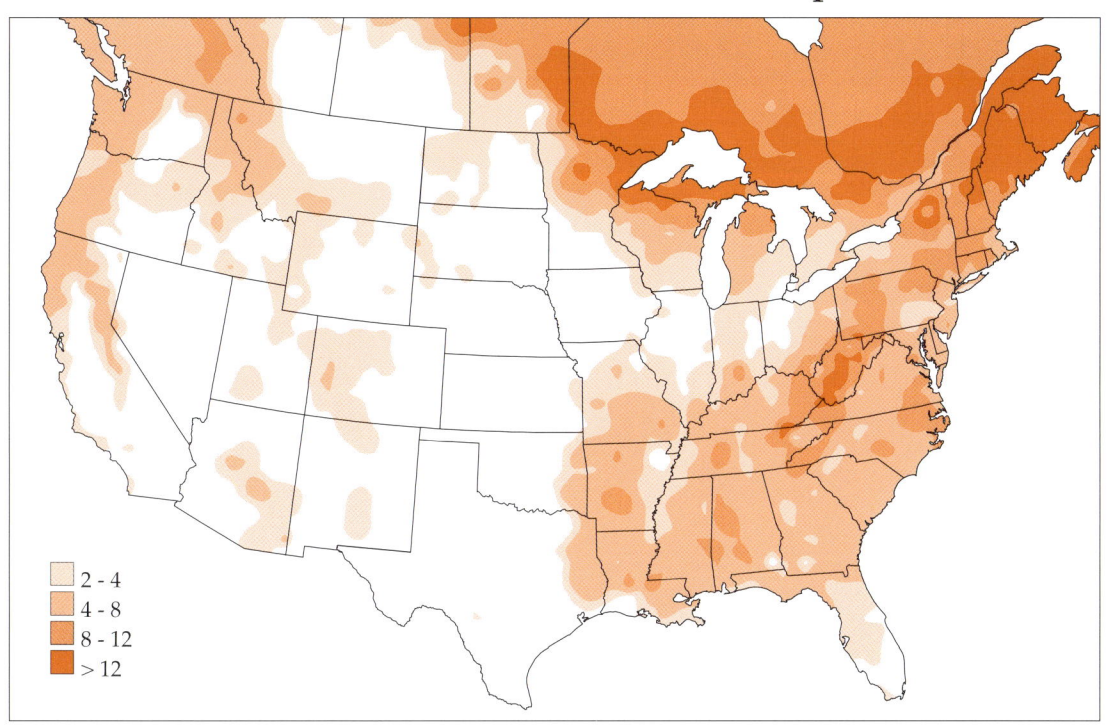

Sparrow Species Richness

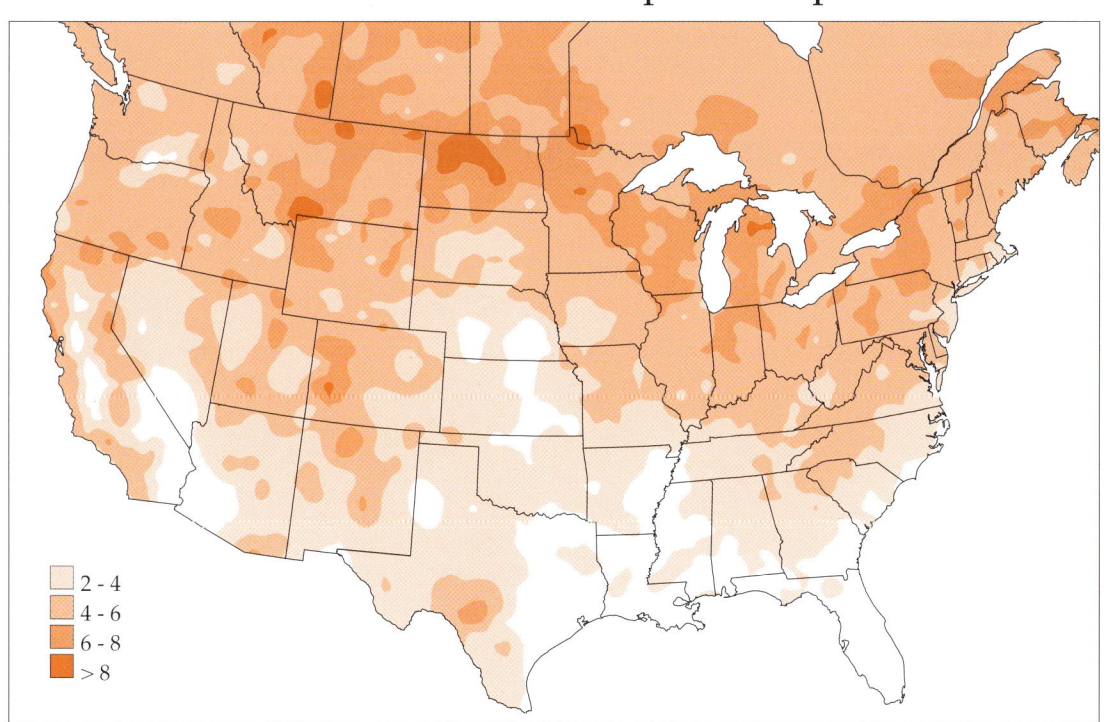

Annotated list of species, habitats, and areas with high relative abundance values

4

The maps in chapter 3 provide information on the relative abundance pattern of many species. However, there are many more species for which the data are too sparse to create a map. Even for those species that have maps, it can be difficult to determine the location of the peaks of abundance. The annotated list that follows includes data for all species for which maps have been prepared, as well as for most of the remaining species that have been detected on Breeding Bird Survey (BBS) routes. While the maps are limited to the conterminous United States and southern Canada, the list includes data from routes in Alaska and northern Canada as well.

This annotated list examines 531 species and identifiable forms that have been detected on BBS routes. Species are separated by family (subfamily in the case of the Emberizidae); the order and common names follow the sixth edition of the *American Ornithologists' Union Check-list of North American Birds* (1983) and supplements through 1993. Scientific names for these species can be found in appendix A.

A brief description of the habitats in which the species may be found follows the common name. This information has been compiled from the references listed below and from the authors' own experiences with the species. Following the habitat information is a listing of the locations of BBS routes that have regularly detected high numbers of individuals of that species. The routes chosen for the list were not necessarily those with the highest relative abundance. The data were carefully examined and those routes with the most current information and consistency of numbers were chosen for the list. Where possible, information on three routes is provided. If many routes had similar values, an effort was made to select routes from a cross-section of the species' range.

The first column of the list gives the average annual relative abundance for that BBS route. For some species not detected every year this value may be less than one. There are a number of reasons for a species having a low relative abundance. Rarity and vagrancy are two obvious causes. Truly rare breeding species are periodically detected on BBS routes, as are vagrants. As the BBS was designed to monitor breeding bird populations, efforts have been made to eliminate sightings of vagrants. Another possible reason for low relative abundance values is the detectability of a species. A BBS observer only spends three minutes at each stop. For a species to be detected at that stop it must either be vocalizing or in a position where it can be seen. The detectability of some species is so low on BBS routes that some relatively common birds are frequently missed. Nocturnal birds, such as owls and nightjars, and skulking species, like rails, are under-counted on these surveys. Finally, common but low density species, like raptors, would be expected to have a low relative abundance. Many of the species listed with low relative abundance may be difficult to find, but spending more time in the proper habitat in these areas will improve the chances for success.

Following the relative abundance value is the proportion of years the species was detected out of the total number of years of data that were used on that route. As with the maps, whenever possible the data for the list were drawn from the period of time 1985–1991. For this reason, even though some BBS routes have been run for over twenty years, the highest number in this column will be seven. Routes had to be run at least three of the seven years in order to be included in the list, so the smallest number appearing in this column would be three. There is an exception to this latter rule. Certain areas have only recently begun to be surveyed by the BBS. Because these may be the only data available for those areas, some routes have been included in the list that were only run in 1990 and 1991, or only in 1991. Those routes are indicated by either a two or a one in this column (chapter 2 provides more information on how the routes were selected).

REFERENCES: American Ornithologists' Union 1983; Bent 1939, 1946, 1949, 1953, 1958, 1968; Chandler 1989; Ehrlich *et al.* 1988; Hayman *et al.* 1986; Johnsgard 1979, 1986, 1988; Kessel 1989; Kricher 1993; Ouellet 1993; Palmer 1962, 1976, 1988a, 1988b.

Interpreting the Annotated List – The following example provides information on how to interpret the annotated list.

Black-billed Magpie *(common name)*
 Open country, grasslands, scattered trees, riparian woodland, fields *(habitat)*

				distance and direction
mean (frequency)	*route name: county, state*	*latitude*	*longitude*	*from the closest town*
91.5 (4/4)	PRESTON: Franklin, ID	42.13	111.92	3 mi NW Preston
82.7 (3/3)	OKOTOKS: AB	50.55	114.08	12 mi SW Okotoks
69.9 (7/7)	WAPATO: Yakima, WA	46.38	120.47	4 mi SE Harrah

mean — The average number of individuals detected on that BBS route per year.

frequency — The number of years the species was detected on that route out of the total number of years of data used on that route.

route name — The name of the BBS route. In many cases the name of the route is the same as that of the closest town, crossroads, or landmark.

county — The county (or equivalent) in which the route begins (United States routes only).

state — The state or province in which the route begins. The codes are as follows:

AB	Alberta	IN	Indiana	ND	North Dakota	RI	Rhode Island
AK	Alaska	KS	Kansas	NE	Nebraska	SC	South Carolina
AL	Alabama	KY	Kentucky	NF	Newfoundland	SD	South Dakota
AR	Arkansas	LA	Louisiana	NJ	New Jersey	SK	Saskatchewan
AZ	Arizona	MA	Massachusetts	NM	New Mexico	TN	Tennessee
BC	British Columbia	MB	Manitoba	NS	Nova Scotia	TX	Texas
CA	California	MD	Maryland	NT	Northwest Territories	UT	Utah
CO	Colorado	ME	Maine	NV	Nevada	VA	Virginia
CT	Connecticut	MI	Michigan	NY	New York	WA	Washington
DE	Delaware	MN	Minnesota	OH	Ohio	WV	West Virginia
FL	Florida	MO	Missouri	OK	Oklahoma	WI	Wisconsin
GA	Georgia	MS	Mississippi	ON	Ontario	WY	Wyoming
IA	Iowa	MT	Montana	OR	Oregon	YT	Yukon Territories
ID	Idaho	NB	New Brunswick	PA	Pennsylvania		
IL	Illinois	NC	North Carolina	PQ	Quebec		

latitude, longitude — The latitude and longitude of the starting point of that route as provided by the BBS. The coordinates are expressed as degrees and decimal degrees north latitude, degrees and decimal degrees west longitude. On some road (and other) maps, west longitude may be printed as a negative number.

distance — The straight-line distance, in miles, from the closest town to the starting point of the route. The towns chosen were those that could be identified in the index of state and provincial highway maps. In some cases the starting point of the route is actually in the town. With very few exceptions (noted in

direction The direction from the town to the starting point of the route. The direction refers to the general quadrant the route lies in, not a specific direction. For example, NW could be north, west, or anywhere in-between.

    In the example listed above, the PRESTON BBS route detected an average of 91.5 Black-billed Magpies per year, and the species was detected on all four of the years the route was run during the period 1985–1991. The starting point of the Preston route is located in Franklin County, Idaho at the coordinates of 42.13 degrees north latitude and 111.92 degrees west longitude. This starting point is located approximately 3 miles NW of the town of Preston, ID.

Annotated list of species detected on Breeding Bird Survey routes

GAVIIDAE – Loons
Red-throated Loon
  Ponds and small shallow lakes; coastal and alpine tundra, coastal flats
  3.0 (1/1)   PAXSON LAKE: Valdez-Cordova, AK   63.05 145.83   49 mi NE Gakona
  0.9 (3/7)   CRAIG: Pr. Wales-Out. Ketch., AK   55.52 133.17   3 mi NE Craig
  0.8 (2/4)   MITKOF ISLE: Wrangell-Petersburg, AK   56.62 132.72   16 mi SE Petersburg

Pacific Loon
  Larger, deeper lakes; tundra and taiga
  17.7 (3/3)   CHURCHILL: MB   58.63 93.78   18 mi SE Churchill
  3.5 (3/4)   INGRAHAM: NT   62.53 113.83   31 mi NE Yellowknife
  1.7 (2/3)   SOURDOUGH: Valdez-Cordova, AK   62.38 145.35   5 mi NE Gakona

Common Loon
  Larger, deeper lakes; coniferous forest to tundra
  12.3 (7/7)   BRIDGE LAKE: BC   51.40 120.67   4 mi SE Bridge Lake
  10.7 (7/7)   ATIKOKAN: ON   48.70 91.45   8 mi SE Atikokan
  9.3 (7/7)   SWAN LAKE RD: Kenai Peninsula, AK   60.62 150.78   19 mi SE Kenai

PODICIPEDIDAE – Grebes
Pied-billed Grebe
  Marshes and ponds with emergent vegetation
  17.3 (4/4)   HORSEHEAD LK: Kidder, ND   47.07 99.63   7 mi SW Pettibone
  5.9 (7/7)   DORRIS: Siskiyou, CA   41.98 121.90   1 mi NE Dorris
  5.4 (7/7)   VOLGA: Brookings, SD   44.23 96.95   5 mi SE Sinai

Horned Grebe
  Lakes, ponds and marshes with open water and aquatic vegetation, little or no emergent vegetation
  4.3 (4/4)   STAGG RIVER: NT   62.68 115.37   19 mi SE Rae-Edzo
  3.5 (4/4)   INGRAHAM: NT   62.53 113.83   31 mi NE Yellowknife
  3.3 (3/3)   BIRCH HILLS: SK   52.98 105.63   9 mi SW Birch Hills

Red-necked Grebe
  Medium to larger lakes, often with reeds or sedges
  19.5 (4/4)   STAGG RIVER: NT   62.68 115.37   19 mi SE Rae-Edzo
  10.0 (7/7)   LINDBROOK: AB   53.33 112.77   5 mi SE Lindbrook
  8.6 (7/7)   BRIDGE LAKE: BC   51.40 120.67   4 mi SE Bridge Lake

Eared Grebe
  Ponds, lakes and marshes
  281.0 (7/7)   DORRIS: Siskiyou, CA   41.98 121.90   1 mi NE Dorris
  49.3 (3/4)   HORSEHEAD LK: Kidder, ND   47.07 99.63   7 mi SW Pettibone
  44.9 (7/7)   MABEL LAKE: BC   50.42 118.77   16 mi NE Lumby

Western Grebe
  Lakes
  151.0 (7/7)   MODOC POINT: Klamath, OR   42.37 121.80   2 mi NE Algoma
  135.8 (6/6)   LUMSDEN: SK   50.63 104.93   2 mi SW Lumsden
  116.7 (7/7)   DORRIS: Siskiyou, CA   41.98 121.90   1 mi NE Dorris

Clark's Grebe
  Lakes
    9.0 (3/3)   IRON GATE: Siskiyou, CA   41.95 122.43   4 mi SW Copco
    7.0 (5/7)   DORRIS: Siskiyou, CA   41.98 121.90   1 mi NE Dorris
    2.0 (5/7)   MODOC POINT: Klamath, OR   42.37 121.80   2 mi NE Algoma

PELECANIDAE – Pelicans
American White Pelican
  Lakes with islands
    135.0 (7/7) DORRIS: Siskiyou, CA   41.98 121.90   1 mi NE Dorris
    82.7 (3/3)   SATTLEY: Sierra, CA   39.65 120.45   1 mi SW Calpine
    61.7 (6/6)   LUMSDEN: SK   50.63 104.93   2 mi SW Lumsden

Brown Pelican
  Coastal islands
    72.5 (6/6)   DAUPHIN IS: Mobile, AL   30.25   88.10   1 mi SE Dauphin Island
    33.5 (6/6)   FT WALTN BCH: Walton, FL   30.37   86.28   4 mi SW Santa Rosa Beach
    20.8 (5/6)   ALABAMA PT: Baldwin, AL   30.27   87.52   4 mi SE Orange Beach

PHALACROCORACIDAE – Cormorants
Double-crested Cormorant
  Lakes and coastal cliffs
    184.0 (3/3) IRON GATE: Siskiyou, CA   41.95 122.43   4 mi SW Copco
    131.4 (7/7) DORRIS: Siskiyou, CA   41.98 121.90   1 mi NE Dorris
    126.0 (7/7) PLANTATION K: Monroe, FL   24.97   80.58   4 mi NE Islamorada

Neotropic Cormorant
  Lakes, marshes and coastal areas
    12.7 (2/3)   ESTHER: Vermilion, LA   29.92   92.23   5 mi SW Perry
    7.3 (3/7)   HACKBERRY: Cameron, LA   30.02   93.42   5 mi NW Hackberry
    2.0 (2/5)   WEINERT: Haskell, TX   33.38   99.67   4 mi NE Weinert

Brandt's Cormorant
  Coastal rocky areas; areas with kelp
    4.3 (6/7)   FISH ROCK: Mendocino, CA   38.80 123.62   2 mi NW Anchor Bay

Pelagic Cormorant
  Coastal rocky areas; areas with rocky bottoms
    50.3 (7/7)   BODEGA BAY: Sonoma, CA   38.30 123.05   2 mi SW Bodega Bay
    9.4 (5/5)   ADAK: Aleutian Islands, AK   51.85 176.60   3 mi SE Adak
    7.3 (6/7)   LAYTONVILLE: Mendocino, CA   39.80 123.47   8 mi NE Laytonville

ANHINGIDAE – Anhingas
Anhinga
  Swamps and lagoons, primarily freshwater
    8.7 (3/3)   ATCHAFALAYA: St. Landry, LA   30.48   91.75   4 mi SE Krotz Springs
    8.4 (5/5)   SCOTTSMOOR: Brevard, FL   28.73   80.87   3 mi SE Scottsmoor
    7.8 (5/5)   LOVEDALE: Jackson, FL   30.88   85.00   5 mi NE Dellwood

FREGATIDAE – Frigatebirds
Magnificent Frigatebird
  Mangrove islands; pelagic
    4.6 (4/5)   KEY LARGO: Monroe, FL   25.20   80.35   8 mi NE Newport
    4.1 (7/7)   PLANTATION K: Monroe, FL   24.97   80.58   4 mi NE Islamorada

ARDEIDAE – Bitterns, Herons

American Bittern
   Marshes with abundant vegetation
17.0 (7/7)	GLENN: Glenn, CA	39.55	122.07	3 mi SW Bayliss
10.1 (7/7)	PENNINGTON: Sutter, CA	39.27	121.73	4 mi SE Pennington
10.1 (7/7)	ROBLIN: ON	44.35	77.07	1 mi SW Roblin

Least Bittern
   Marshes with abundant vegetation
6.3 (3/3)	ANDYTOWN: Broward, FL	26.07	80.75	30 mi SW Cooper City
3.2 (5/5)	LTL CHENIER: Cameron, LA	29.77	93.02	3 mi NW Grand Chenier
2.5 (6/6)	HONGA: Dorchester, MD	38.37	76.23	2 mi NW Honga

Great Blue Heron
   Freshwater and brackish marshes; lakes and other bodies of water
30.1 (7/7)	PAWPAW: Obion, TN	36.30	89.37	4 mi NW Elbridge
25.3 (7/7)	TIPTONVILLE: Lake, TN	36.42	89.43	4 mi NE Tiptonville
22.3 (7/7)	HERNER CRNS: Trumbull, OH	41.32	80.98	1 mi NW Southington

Great Egret
   Marshes, tidal flats, wet forests
318.3 (4/4)	MAURICE: Vermilion, LA	30.08	92.30	5 mi SW Indian Bayou
113.8 (5/5)	SCOTTSMOOR: Brevard, FL	28.73	80.87	3 mi SE Scottsmoor
104.2 (5/5)	BERWICK: St. Martin, LA	29.85	91.18	8 mi SW Bellewood

Snowy Egret
   Marshes, coastal areas, lakes and other bodies of water
53.7 (3/3)	JUNIOR: Plaquemines, LA	29.48	89.70	0 mi Port Sulphur
36.2 (5/5)	SCOTTSMOOR: Brevard, FL	28.73	80.87	3 mi SE Scottsmoor
20.3 (7/7)	NILAND: Imperial, CA	33.23	115.50	1 mi SE Niland

Little Blue Heron
   Marshes, ponds and other bodies of water
210.8 (4/4)	VILLE PLATTE: Evangeline, LA	30.67	92.27	1 mi SE Ville Platte
188.7 (3/3)	ATCHAFALAYA: St. Landry, LA	30.48	91.75	4 mi SE Krotz Springs
43.7 (6/6)	MAYFLOWER: Tensas, LA	31.97	91.45	5 mi NE Holly Ridge

Tricolored Heron
   Marshes, rivers, saltwater areas with mangroves
35.8 (5/5)	WEAVER STN: Collier, FL	25.97	81.52	5 mi SE Royal Palm Hamm.
25.2 (5/5)	SCOTTSMOOR: Brevard, FL	28.73	80.87	3 mi SE Scottsmoor
13.4 (5/5)	LTL CHENIER: Cameron, LA	29.77	93.02	3 mi NW Grand Chenier

Reddish Egret
   Coastal areas and brackish marshes
2.0 (6/6)	DAUPHIN IS: Mobile, AL	30.25	88.10	1 mi SE Dauphin Island
2.0 (3/5)	SCOTTSMOOR: Brevard, FL	28.73	80.87	3 mi SE Scottsmoor
0.9 (1/7)	LAG ATASCOSA: Cameron, TX	26.20	97.33	6 mi NE Bayview

Cattle Egret
   Pastures, freshwater and brackish marshes
792.2 (5/5)	PENNYWASH CR: Osceola, FL	28.27	80.97	11 mi NE Holopaw
741.1 (7/7)	MASSEY LAKE: Anderson, TX	31.80	95.87	3 mi SW Tennessee Colony
646.5 (4/4)	VILLE PLATTE: Evangeline, LA	30.67	92.27	1 mi SE Ville Platte

Green Heron
    Wooded ponds, rivers, freshwater and brackish marshes
24.5 (6/6)	TOWN BLUFF: Jasper, TX	30.80	94.10	9 mi NE Spurger
17.0 (3/3)	JUNIOR: Plaquemines, LA	29.48	89.70	0 mi Port Sulphur
10.0 (7/7)	SUNNILAND GR: Collier, FL	26.30	81.48	9 mi SW Immokalee

Black-crowned Night-Heron
    Wooded marshes, swamps, lakes and other bodies of water
48.2 (6/6)	OROVILLE: Butte, CA	39.60	121.62	4 mi SW Pentz
21.0 (7/7)	DORRIS: Siskiyou, CA	41.98	121.90	1 mi NE Dorris
15.7 (5/6)	JEFFERSN CTY: Grainger, TN	36.18	83.52	4 mi NW Jefferson City

Yellow-crowned Night-Heron
    Wooded marshes, swamps, lakes and other bodies of water
72.3 (3/3)	RAMAH: Iberville, LA	30.27	91.45	8 mi NW Indian Village
64.0 (5/5)	BERWICK: St. Martin, LA	29.85	91.18	8 mi SW Bellewood
62.7 (3/3)	ATCHAFALAYA: St. Landry, LA	30.48	91.75	4 mi SE Krotz Springs

THRESKIORNITHIDAE – Ibises, Spoonbills

White Ibis
    Wooded marshes, lagoons with mangroves
176.0 (4/4)	VILLE PLATTE: Evangeline, LA	30.67	92.27	1 mi SE Ville Platte
166.0 (7/7)	SHALLOTTE: Brunswick, NC	33.98	78.37	1 mi NE Shallotte
117.4 (7/7)	POLK CITY: Polk, FL	28.18	81.88	3 mi SW Polk City

Glossy Ibis
    Wooded marshes, swamps, lagoons and lakes
193.9 (7/7)	OCEAN CITY: Cape May, NJ	39.23	74.55	4 mi SE Ocean City
10.7 (5/7)	NEWARK: Worcester, MD	38.23	75.25	3 mi SE Newark
9.2 (5/5)	SCOTTSMOOR: Brevard, FL	28.73	80.87	3 mi SE Scottsmoor

White-faced Ibis
    Marshes, ponds and rivers
304.3 (4/4)	PRESTON: Franklin, ID	42.13	111.92	3 mi NW Preston
205.0 (7/7)	FISH LAKE: Harney, OR	42.62	118.60	11 mi NE Andrews
189.8 (4/4)	DELTA: Millard, UT	39.50	112.63	8 mi NE Sutherland

Roseate Spoonbill
    Marshes, ponds, rivers and lagoons
9.3 (2/4)	MAURICE: Vermilion, LA	30.08	92.30	5 mi SW Indian Bayou
2.7 (2/3)	ESTHER: Vermilion, LA	29.92	92.23	5 mi SW Perry
2.4 (4/7)	HACKBERRY: Cameron, LA	30.02	93.42	5 mi NW Hackberry

CICONIIDAE – Storks

Wood Stork
    Marshes, lagoons with mangroves
17.5 (3/4)	DALE MABRY: Hillsborough, FL	28.05	82.47	5 mi NW Temple Terrace
8.2 (3/5)	SCOTTSMOOR: Brevard, FL	28.73	80.87	3 mi SE Scottsmoor
4.9 (6/7)	KENANSVILLE: Brevard, FL	27.85	80.85	9 mi SE Kenansville

ANATIDAE – Swans, Geese, Ducks

Fulvous Whistling-Duck
    Freshwater and brackish marshes, lagoons, wet fields and woodlands, rice fields

58.8 (4/4)	MAURICE: Vermilion, LA	30.08	92.30	5 mi SW Indian Bayou
28.1 (6/7)	RAYMONDVILLE: Willacy, TX	26.53	97.70	4 mi NW San Perlita
25.8 (4/4)	VILLE PLATTE: Evangeline, LA	30.67	92.27	1 mi SE Ville Platte

Black-bellied Whistling-Duck
    Freshwater and brackish marshes, lagoons, woodlands and cultivated fields

50.2 (5/5)	KINGSVILLE: Kleberg, TX	27.53	97.93	5 mi NW Kingsville
49.0 (7/7)	RAYMONDVILLE: Willacy, TX	26.53	97.70	4 mi NW San Perlita
44.6 (7/7)	LAG ATASCOSA: Cameron, TX	26.20	97.33	6 mi NE Bayview

Tundra Swan
    Ponds, lakes and slow streams, with islets; tundra

9.5 (5/6)	COLD BAY: Aleutian Islands, AK	55.00	162.00	62 mi NW Squaw Harbor

Trumpeter Swan
    Freshwater ponds, lakes and marshes with reeds and sedges

6.0 (3/4)	RED ROCK: Beaverhead, MT	44.62	111.53	14 mi SE Lakeview
2.7 (2/3)	NABESNA ROAD: Valdez-Cordova, AK	62.55	143.35	17 mi NW Nabesna
2.3 (2/3)	MONAHAN: Matanuska-Susitna, AK	63.22	147.97	37 mi SE Cantwell

Mute Swan
    Freshwater lakes, ponds and marshes with open water and reeds

18.9 (7/7)	MONTEREY: Allegan, MI	42.60	85.83	4 mi SW Hopkins
15.9 (5/7)	PURDY: Westchester, NY	41.32	73.60	1 mi SE Salem Center
7.1 (7/7)	GALESBURG: Kalamazoo, MI	42.25	85.42	3 mi SE Galesburg

Canada Goose
    Lakes, marshes and other bodies of water; suburban parks

707.8 (4/4)	IRON SPRINGS: Custer, ID	44.32	113.58	16 mi SE Patterson
593.5 (4/4)	YELLOWSTONE: Park, WY	44.78	110.47	3 mi NE Canyon Junction
485.7 (6/6)	CLEAR LK RES: Modoc, CA	41.83	121.10	14 mi SE Newell

Wood Duck
    Wooded swamps, wet forests, along streams

12.6 (7/7)	KNAPP: Wright, MN	45.17	94.20	6 mi SE Kingston
12.2 (6/6)	TOWN BLUFF: Jasper, TX	30.80	94.10	9 mi NE Spurger
11.7 (6/7)	BAXLEY: Toombs, GA	31.92	82.23	12 mi NE Baxley

Green-winged Teal
    Lakes, marshes and other bodies of water with emergent vegetation

68.2 (5/5)	ADAK: Aleutian Islands, AK	51.85	176.60	3 mi SE Adak
11.1 (7/7)	LINDBROOK: AB	53.33	112.77	5 mi SE Lindbrook
6.1 (7/7)	DERWENT: AB	53.50	110.80	6 mi SW Clandonald

American Black Duck
    Wooded swamps, freshwater and brackish wetlands with emergent vegetation

12.0 (7/7)	HAMPTON: NB	45.63	65.72	0 mi Norton
4.8 (5/5)	BETHANY BCH: Sussex, DE	38.58	75.05	2 mi NW Sussex Shores
4.0 (6/7)	ROBLIN: ON	44.35	77.07	1 mi SW Roblin

Mottled Duck
    Freshwater and brackish coastal wetlands, fields
29.4 (5/5)	LTL CHENIER: Cameron, LA	29.77	93.02	3 mi NW Grand Chenier
18.0 (3/3)	JUNIOR: Plaquemines, LA	29.48	89.70	0 mi Port Sulphur
15.7 (3/3)	ESTHER: Vermilion, LA	29.92	92.23	5 mi SW Perry

Mallard
    Shallow ponds and other bodies of water, flooded fields
486.0 (7/7)	DORRIS: Siskiyou, CA	41.98	121.90	1 mi NE Dorris
195.0 (7/7)	WAKAW: SK	52.73	105.65	7 mi NE Wakaw
168.7 (7/7)	BISMARK: Huron, OH	41.15	82.80	2 mi NE Reedtown

Northern Pintail
    Lakes, marshes, prairie grasslands, tundra, open woodland, fields
64.0 (7/7)	DORRIS: Siskiyou, CA	41.98	121.90	1 mi NE Dorris
52.7 (3/3)	VANESTI: AB	53.27	110.62	9 mi SW Islay
35.6 (7/7)	RANIER: AB	50.38	112.02	5 mi NE Rainier

Blue-winged Teal
    Marshes, sloughs, sluggish streams
48.4 (7/7)	DERWENT: AB	53.50	110.80	6 mi SW Clandonald
31.0 (6/6)	LUMSDEN: SK	50.63	104.93	2 mi SW Lumsden
26.4 (7/7)	BREWSTER: Okanogan, WA	48.08	119.73	3 mi SE Brewster

Cinnamon Teal
    Shallow lakes and ponds, sluggish streams
104.1 (7/7)	DORRIS: Siskiyou, CA	41.98	121.90	1 mi NE Dorris
56.6 (7/7)	BREWSTER: Okanogan, WA	48.08	119.73	3 mi SE Brewster
18.9 (7/7)	GLENN: Glenn, CA	39.55	122.07	3 mi SW Bayliss

Northern Shoveler
    Muddy, sluggish bodies of water, shallow ponds
96.6 (7/7)	DORRIS: Siskiyou, CA	41.98	121.90	1 mi NE Dorris
76.7 (3/3)	KEHIWIN LAKE: AB	54.07	110.93	4 mi SW Hoselaw
32.0 (4/4)	ABERDEEN: SK	52.18	106.28	12 mi SW Aberdeen

Gadwall
    Freshwater and brackish marshes; grassy areas and islands
213.7 (7/7)	DORRIS: Siskiyou, CA	41.98	121.90	1 mi NE Dorris
44.3 (4/4)	BRADDOCK: Emmons, ND	46.58	100.10	0 mi Braddock
43.3 (4/4)	HORSEHEAD LK: Kidder, ND	47.07	99.63	7 mi SW Pettibone

American Wigeon
    Large marshes and lakes, open shorelines
29.0 (4/4)	YELLOWSTONE: Park, WY	44.78	110.47	3 mi NE Canyon Junction
26.7 (3/3)	HAYDEN VAL: Park, WY	44.67	110.67	5 mi SE Norris Junction
25.6 (7/7)	BREWSTER: Okanogan, WA	48.08	119.73	3 mi SE Brewster

Canvasback
    Freshwater marshes, ponds and lakes with emergent vegetation
14.0 (3/4)	BRADDOCK: Emmons, ND	46.58	100.10	0 mi Braddock
13.0 (6/6)	LUMSDEN: SK	50.63	104.93	2 mi SW Lumsden
9.0 (5/7)	MODOC POINT: Klamath, OR	42.37	121.80	2 mi NE Algoma

Redhead
Large freshwater marshes, lakes and lagoons

103.6 (7/7)	DORRIS: Siskiyou, CA	41.98	121.90	1 mi NE Dorris
61.8 (6/6)	LUMSDEN: SK	50.63	104.93	2 mi SW Lumsden
39.6 (7/7)	BREWSTER: Okanogan, WA	48.08	119.73	3 mi SE Brewster

Ring-necked Duck
Marshes, sloughs and bogs with dense vegetation

6.0 (7/7)	KENORA: ON	49.77	94.22	12 mi SE Kenora
5.3 (3/3)	HOLLAND: MB	49.55	98.73	4 mi SW Holland
4.8 (6/6)	SPILIMACHEEN: BC	50.85	116.47	9 mi SW Spillimacheen

Greater Scaup
Ponds and lakes; tundra and taiga

25.0 (4/5)	ADAK: Aleutian Islands, AK	51.85	176.60	3 mi SE Adak
18.3 (6/6)	COLD BAY: Aleutian Islands, AK	55.00	162.00	62 mi NW Squaw Harbor
5.0 (2/3)	CHURCHILL: MB	58.63	93.78	18 mi SE Churchill

Lesser Scaup
Ponds and small lakes; grassy areas

112.6 (7/7)	DORRIS: Siskiyou, CA	41.98	121.90	1 mi NE Dorris
86.6 (7/7)	BIGGAR: SK	52.25	107.85	15 mi NE Biggar
50.9 (7/7)	DERWENT: AB	53.50	110.80	6 mi SW Clandonald

Common Eider
Coastal; ponds and lagoons with access to the sea

216.7 (3/3)	MATANE: PQ	48.83	67.50	2 mi SE Matane
51.3 (4/4)	GRAND MANAN: NB	44.65	66.88	2 mi SW Seal Cove
14.0 (7/7)	LARRYS RIVER: NS	45.15	61.57	2 mi SW Coddle Harbour

Harlequin Duck
Mountain streams, forested and rocky coastal areas

21.7 (7/7)	CHINIAK: Kodiak Island, AK	57.53	152.43	17 mi SW Kodiak
5.8 (5/5)	ADAK: Aleutian Islands, AK	51.85	176.60	3 mi SE Adak
4.4 (5/7)	SITKA: Sitka, AK	57.07	135.37	1 mi NW Mount Edgecombe

Oldsquaw
Shallow lakes; taiga, tundra, and coastal

8.0 (3/3)	CHURCHILL: MB	58.63	93.78	18 mi SE Churchill
5.3 (3/3)	MONAHAN: Matanuska-Susitna, AK	63.22	147.97	37 mi SE Cantwell
1.7 (2/3)	MACLAREN: SE Fairbanks, AK	63.07	146.07	54 mi NW Gakona

Black Scoter
Lakes and pools; tundra with bushes and taiga

16.3 (6/6)	COLD BAY: Aleutian Islands, AK	55.00	162.00	62 mi NW Squaw Harbor

Surf Scoter
Bogs, ponds and sluggish streams in forested regions

11.0 (2/7)	SITKA: Sitka, AK	57.07	135.37	1 mi NW Mount Edgecombe
7.5 (4/4)	INGRAHAM: NT	62.53	113.83	31 mi NE Yellowknife
4.0 (1/3)	KLUANE LAKE: YT	61.05	138.52	16 mi SE Destruction Bay

White-winged Scoter
   Ponds, lakes and sluggish streams; tundra and forests
7.8 (3/6)	LAKE LABERGE: YT	61.25	135.47	37 mi NW Whitehorse
4.3 (1/3)	CHURCHILL: MB	58.63	93.78	18 mi SE Churchill

Common Goldeneye
   Lakes, rivers and coastal areas; areas with trees for nesting
7.3 (4/4)	WINAGAMI LK: AB	55.53	116.77	6 mi SE Kathleen
6.8 (6/6)	BEAR CREEK: Yukon-Koyukuk, AK	64.00	157.00	43 mi SW Galena
3.0 (4/5)	NAPLES: Boundary, ID	48.55	116.42	2 mi SW Naples

Barrow's Goldeneye
   Lakes, ponds, rivers and coastal areas with emergent vegetation
68.3 (4/4)	YELLOWSTONE: Park, WY	44.78	110.47	3 mi NE Canyon Junction
5.0 (7/7)	WILLIAMS LK: BC	52.17	122.07	1 mi NW Williams Lake
4.8 (5/5)	RISKE CREEK: BC	51.97	122.40	9 mi NE Riske Creek

Bufflehead
   Lakes, ponds and coastal areas; open forest
16.8 (4/4)	YELLOWSTONE: Park, WY	44.78	110.47	3 mi NE Canyon Junction
9.1 (6/7)	BIGGAR: SK	52.25	107.85	15 mi NE Biggar
4.4 (5/5)	TURTLE MTNS: Bottineau, ND	48.88	100.22	8 mi NW Dunseith

Hooded Merganser
   Forested areas near water, fast-moving streams
1.3 (4/6)	SPILIMACHEEN: BC	50.85	116.47	9 mi SW Spillimacheen
1.1 (4/7)	CATTARAUGUS: Cattaraugus, NY	42.28	78.90	4 mi SW Cattaraugus

Common Merganser
   Open clear water lakes; forests and mountainous regions
24.0 (4/4)	YELLOWSTONE: Park, WY	44.78	110.47	3 mi NE Canyon Junction
17.1 (7/7)	HORSE CREEK: Siskiyou, CA	41.92	123.07	8 mi NW Horse Creek
14.2 (6/6)	SYRINGA CR: BC	49.37	117.95	14 mi NW Castlegar

Red-breasted Merganser
   Lakes, ponds, and rivers with islands, low shrubs; also coastal
12.2 (5/5)	ADAK: Aleutian Islands, AK	51.85	176.60	3 mi SE Adak
11.7 (6/6)	KODIAK: Kodiak Island, AK	57.62	152.55	12 mi SW Kodiak
5.2 (5/5)	WASHINGTON I: Door, WI	45.38	86.95	16 mi NE Sister Bay

Ruddy Duck
   Marshes and lakes with dense emergent vegetation
155.3 (7/7)	DORRIS: Siskiyou, CA	41.98	121.90	1 mi NE Dorris
44.3 (7/7)	BREWSTER: Okanogan, WA	48.08	119.73	3 mi SE Brewster
24.3 (7/7)	MABEL LAKE: BC	50.42	118.77	16 mi NE Lumby

CATHARTIDAE – Vultures

Black Vulture
   Widespread in lowlands, dense woodland for nesting, open areas for foraging
38.2 (5/5)	SANDY: Sarasota, FL	27.25	82.30	5 mi SW Old Myakka
24.6 (7/7)	HINKLES FER: Brazoria, TX	28.90	95.62	5 mi NE Sargent
21.4 (6/7)	OLNEY: Montgomery, MD	39.15	77.08	1 mi SW Olney

Turkey Vulture
  Widespread throughout range, most commonly in lowlands, often roost near water
    79.8 (5/5)   KINGSVILLE: Kleberg, TX   27.53   97.93   5 mi NW Kingsville
    51.3 (7/7)   FISH LAKE: Harney, OR   42.62   118.60   11 mi NE Andrews
    46.4 (7/7)   VIENNA: Dorchester, MD   38.52   75.82   1 mi SE Reids Grove

ACCIPITRIDAE – Kites, Eagles, Hawks, and Allies
Osprey
  Rivers, lakes and coastal areas
    11.6 (5/5)   BETHANY BCH: Sussex, DE   38.58   75.05   2 mi NW Sussex Shores
    10.0 (7/7)   OCEAN CITY: Cape May, NJ   39.23   74.55   4 mi SE Ocean City
    9.0 (3/3)   IRON GATE: Siskiyou, CA   41.95   122.43   4 mi SW Copco

American Swallow-tailed Kite
  Swamps, lowland forest, open woodland, forest edge
    4.6 (5/5)   DEVILS GARDN: Hendry, FL   26.57   81.23   13 mi NE Felda
    3.8 (4/5)   GREEN SWAMP: Lake, FL   28.42   81.95   5 mi SW Bay Lake
    3.4 (4/5)   PALMDALE: Glades, FL   26.95   81.48   10 mi SW Palmdale

White-tailed Kite
  Lowlands, grasslands, open areas including fields
    3.3 (6/6)   CP PENDLETON: San Diego, CA   33.23   117.40   3 mi NW Oceanside
    2.3 (7/7)   MARK WEST: Sonoma, CA   38.57   122.72   5 mi SW Kellogg
    1.7 (5/6)   HOLLISTER: San Benito, CA   36.87   121.33   4 mi NE Hollister

Snail Kite
  Lowlands, large freshwater marshes
    4.0 (3/3)   ANDYTOWN: Broward, FL   26.07   80.75   30 mi SW Cooper City

Mississippi Kite
  Open and riparian woodlands, grasslands
    18.8 (6/6)   ERICK: Beckham, OK   35.27   99.87   4 mi NW Erick
    15.7 (3/3)   ATCHAFALAYA: St. Landry, LA   30.48   91.75   4 mi SE Krotz Springs
    12.3 (6/6)   GRIMES: Roger Mills, OK   35.47   99.73   6 mi SE Dempsey

Bald Eagle
  Large lakes and rivers, coastal areas; tall trees and cliffs
    39.6 (7/7)   SITKA: Sitka, AK   57.07   135.37   1 mi NW Mount Edgecombe
    30.0 (3/3)   KETCHIKAN: Ketchikan Gateway, AK   55.33   131.52   3 mi SE Saxman
    26.2 (5/5)   JUNEAU: Juneau, AK   58.43   134.72   14 mi NW Juneau

Northern Harrier
  Grasslands and marshes, wet meadows
    9.3 (7/7)   DORRIS: Siskiyou, CA   41.98   121.90   1 mi NE Dorris
    6.3 (6/6)   SUNBURST: Toole, MT   48.87   111.63   10 mi NE Ferdig
    6.3 (6/6)   VIRGELLE: Chouteau, MT   48.05   110.35   11 mi NE Loma

Cooper's Hawk
  Mature coniferous forest, mixed deciduous woodland, forest edge
    1.0 (2/3)   JUNIOR: Plaquemines, LA   29.48   89.70   0 mi Port Sulphur
    1.0 (4/7)   BARON: Cherokee, OK   35.82   94.87   4 mi SE Welling
    0.9 (5/7)   MERRIMAC: Taylor, KY   37.43   85.13   1 mi NW Merrimac

Northern Goshawk
  Deciduous and coniferous forest with openings; montane
  1.0 (3/3)   WASATCH NF: Summit, UT   40.95 110.65   30 mi SE Upton
  0.5 (2/4)   BECK: Utah, UT   40.05 111.27   6 mi NE Mill Fork
  0.5 (3/6)   SKYLINE DRIV: Sanpete, UT   39.70 111.33   5 mi SE Milburn

Harris' Hawk
  Cactus and mesquite scrub desert; riparian woodland
  6.3 (3/4)   GUERRA: Zapata, TX   26.95 99.03   6 mi SE Bustamante
  5.3 (3/4)   MIRANDO CITY: Webb, TX   27.32 98.87   7 mi SW Bruni
  4.0 (5/5)   ENCINAL: Webb, TX   27.97 99.27   7 mi SE Encinal

Gray Hawk
  Riparian woodland with cottonwoods, mesquite scrub
  0.4 (3/7)   PATAGONIA: Santa Cruz, AZ   31.52 110.80   3 mi SW Patagonia

Red-shouldered Hawk
  Wet forest, riparian woodland, forest edge and open areas
  18.2 (6/6)   TOWN BLUFF: Jasper, TX   30.80 94.10   9 mi NE Spurger
  14.4 (5/5)   DEVILS GARDN: Hendry, FL   26.57 81.23   13 mi NE Felda
  13.4 (5/5)   PENNYWASH CR: Osceola, FL   28.27 80.97   11 mi NE Holopaw

Broad-winged Hawk
  Deciduous and mixed woodland, dense vegetation
  2.3 (4/4)   SHANAGOLDEN: Ashland, WI   46.15 90.75   13 mi SW Mellen
  2.0 (3/3)   PEARL RIVER: St. Tammany, LA   30.37 89.92   2 mi SW Saint Tammany
  1.7 (7/7)   CRANDON: Forest, WI   45.48 88.75   10 mi SE Crandon

Short-tailed Hawk
  Mixed woodland and grassland, with adjacent open country
  0.2 (1/5)   ARIPEKA: Pasco, FL   28.35 82.72   2 mi SW Hudson
  0.2 (1/5)   ARBUCKLE: Polk, FL   27.75 81.48   3 mi NE Frostproof
  0.2 (1/5)   MILLER XRDS: Holmes, FL   30.93 85.90   2 mi SW New Hope

Swainson's Hawk
  Grasslands, shelterbelts
  17.7 (3/3)   OKOTOKS: AB   50.55 114.08   12 mi SW Okotoks
  10.3 (7/7)   MILK RIVER: AB   49.07 112.45   11 mi SW Milk River
  10.2 (5/5)   BEAVERHEAD: Beaverhead, MT   44.63 112.05   12 mi NW Lakeview

White-tailed Hawk
  Grasslands and scrub-live oak areas in coastal areas; mesquite and oak scrub in interior
  1.9 (6/7)   HINKLES FER: Brazoria, TX   28.90 95.62   5 mi NE Sargent
  1.2 (3/5)   KINGSVILLE: Kleberg, TX   27.53 97.93   5 mi NW Kingsville
  1.0 (4/7)   RACHAL: Brooks, TX   26.80 98.08   7 mi SE Rachal

Zone-tailed Hawk
  Canyons and mountains, riparian woodland
  0.3 (1/7)   PATAGONIA: Santa Cruz, AZ   31.52 110.80   3 mi SW Patagonia

Red-tailed Hawk
  Widespread, tall trees in open areas

18.0 (7/7)	MACDOEL: Siskiyou, CA	41.85	122.15	8 mi NW Macdoel
13.8 (6/6)	MESA GRANDE: San Diego, CA	33.20	116.82	3 mi NW Mesa Grande
11.7 (7/7)	JOSEPH: Wallowa, OR	45.28	117.22	5 mi SW Joseph

Ferruginous Hawk
  Arid or semi-arid grasslands; nest in riparian woodland and open areas

6.6 (7/7)	KYLE CANYON: Butte, ID	43.87	112.82	11 mi NE Howe
5.5 (4/4)	HORSEHEAD LK: Kidder, ND	47.07	99.63	7 mi SW Pettibone
5.0 (5/5)	BEAVERHEAD: Beaverhead, MT	44.63	112.05	12 mi NW Lakeview

Rough-legged Hawk
  Open coniferous forest, tundra and other barren country; areas with cliffs or trees for nesting

0.3 (2/6)	LAKE LABERGE: YT	61.25	135.47	37 mi NW Whitehorse

Golden Eagle
  Widespread, usually secluded regions with open areas for foraging and cliffs or trees for nesting

3.3 (3/3)	MAJORS PLACE: White Pine, NV	39.18	114.48	12 mi NE Majors Place
3.3 (7/7)	VENTUCOPA: Santa Barbara, CA	34.80	119.55	5 mi SW Ventucopa
3.0 (4/4)	HIGHLIGHT: Campbell, WY	43.65	105.45	8 mi SE Reno Junction

FALCONIDAE – Caracaras, Falcons

Crested Caracara
  Grasslands, open lowlands and pastures

9.8 (4/4)	GUERRA: Zapata, TX	26.95	99.03	6 mi SE Bustamante
8.8 (5/5)	KINGSVILLE: Kleberg, TX	27.53	97.93	5 mi NW Kingsville
4.9 (7/7)	RANDADO: Jim Hogg, TX	27.05	98.78	6 mi SE Randado

American Kestrel
  Widespread, open country and cropland

14.3 (3/3)	JOEL: Latah, ID	46.58	116.83	5 mi NE Genesee
11.3 (7/7)	LAUREL: Yellowstone, MT	45.55	108.73	5 mi SE Silesia
11.0 (6/6)	CP PENDLETON: San Diego, CA	33.23	117.40	3 mi NW Oceanside

Merlin
  Coniferous forest, discontinuous woodland patches

1.0 (2/3)	BRODERICK: SK	51.62	106.80	12 mi NE Broderick
1.0 (2/3)	HECLA ISLAND: MB	51.07	96.77	3 mi SW Hecla
1.0 (2/2)	HAY LAKES: AB	53.12	113.15	6 mi SW Hay Lakes

Peregrine Falcon
  Widespread in open areas with cliffs or similar nesting areas

0.8 (4/5)	ORLEANS: Humboldt, CA	41.22	123.47	7 mi SE Orleans
0.7 (1/3)	MOAB: Grand, UT	38.58	109.57	1 mi NW Moab
0.5 (2/4)	CHILLIWACK: BC	49.03	121.97	9 mi SE Chilliwack

Prairie Falcon
  Arid regions; deserts, foothills and mountain valleys

2.8 (5/5)	FISH SPRINGS: Juab, UT	39.63	113.27	30 mi SE Trout Creek
1.4 (6/7)	BLITZEN: Harney, OR	42.97	119.08	13 mi NW Frenchglen
1.3 (3/3)	SYBILLE CYN: Albany, WY	41.73	105.35	21 mi NE Bosler

CRACIDAE – Chachalacas

Plain Chachalaca

    Semi-arid regions; thickets and scrub, dense second growth

3.4 (4/7)	LAG ATASCOSA: Cameron, TX	26.20	97.33	6 mi NE Bayview

PHASIANIDAE – Partridges, Grouse, Turkeys, Quail

Gray Partridge

    Cultivated fields and pastures

9.8 (5/5)	ZEARING: Story, IA	42.13	93.33	3 mi SW Zearing
8.3 (7/7)	GAZA: O'Brien, IA	43.03	95.57	1 mi NE Gaza
7.1 (7/7)	ROCK VALLEY: Lyon, IA	43.27	96.28	2 mi SW Doon

Chukar

    Rocky hillsides, open desert, grassy and barren areas

34.3 (6/6)	ADRIAN: Malheur, OR	43.67	117.07	5 mi SW Adrian
7.7 (5/6)	BLIZZARD GAP: Lake, OR	42.02	119.50	23 mi SE Adel
6.0 (7/7)	ALVORD LAKE: Harney, OR	42.35	118.65	6 mi NE Fields

Ring-necked Pheasant

    Cultivated fields, woodland edge

114.6 (7/7)	PENNINGTON: Sutter, CA	39.27	121.73	4 mi SE Pennington
108.0 (7/7)	SURPRISE: Butler, NE	41.17	97.35	3 mi SW Rising City
99.2 (6/6)	FLATWILLOW: Petroleum, MT	46.82	108.12	13 mi SE Flatwillow

Spruce Grouse

    Coniferous forest, especially with spruce and pine, and a dense understory

1.0 (2/3)	CIRCLE: Yukon-Koyukuk, AK	65.72	144.33	11 mi SW Circle

Blue Grouse

    Coniferous forest with open areas, mixed woodland and shrubs

12.3 (6/6)	KITSUMKALUM: BC	54.83	128.87	7 mi NW Rosswood
5.7 (6/6)	KWINITSA: BC	54.33	129.30	29 mi SW Terrace
4.5 (4/4)	NO CASCADES: Whatcom, WA	48.70	121.08	3 mi SE Diablo

Willow Ptarmigan

    Arctic tundra dominated with grasses and mosses, especially with moist depressions and basins

41.8 (6/6)	COLD BAY: Aleutian Islands, AK	55.00	162.00	62 mi NW Squaw Harbor
10.0 (4/4)	SAVAGE: Yukon-Koyukuk, AK	63.73	149.28	14 mi SW Healy
9.5 (4/4)	TOKLAT: Yukon-Koyukuk, AK	63.47	150.07	41 mi NW Cantwell

Rock Ptarmigan

    Barren and rocky slopes, dry areas; tundra

12.0 (5/5)	ADAK: Aleutian Islands, AK	51.85	176.60	3 mi SE Adak
1.8 (2/4)	TOKLAT: Yukon-Koyukuk, AK	63.47	150.07	41 mi NW Cantwell

Ruffed Grouse

    Deciduous and mixed woodland

7.6 (7/7)	LINDBROOK: AB	53.33	112.77	5 mi SE Lindbrook
6.0 (3/3)	FOLEYET: ON	48.20	82.37	4 mi SE Foleyet
4.0 (4/4)	CRANE LAKE: St. Louis, MN	48.28	92.55	3 mi NW Crane Lake

Sage Grouse
Sagebrush regions
34.8 (6/6)	BEAR CREEK: Sweetwater, WY	42.22	108.63	19 mi SE South Pass City
11.7 (3/3)	BAIROIL: Sweetwater, WY	42.23	107.93	19 mi NW Bairoil
5.7 (7/7)	GREAT DIVIDE: Moffat, CO	40.80	107.70	21 mi NE Lay

Greater Prairie-Chicken
Tallgrass prairie, some fields
12.0 (4/4)	WAVERLY: Yuma, CO	40.25	102.52	10 mi NW Eckley
11.4 (6/7)	ABARR: Yuma, CO	39.88	102.63	5 mi SW Heartstrong
8.4 (4/7)	BARCLAY: Osage, KS	38.45	95.78	3 mi SW Olivet

Lesser Prairie-Chicken
Arid grassland with shrubs
2.0 (2/5)	CAPROCK: Lea, NM	33.38	103.58	8 mi SE Caprock
0.7 (1/6)	ASHLAND: Clark, KS	37.13	99.75	4 mi SE Ashland

Sharp-tailed Grouse
Grassland with woody patches, sagebrush regions, brushy hills
16.8 (5/5)	WILLOWBROOK: SK	51.18	102.88	2 mi SW Willowbrook
13.9 (7/7)	CLEVELAND: Blaine, MT	48.33	109.10	5 mi NE Cleveland
11.2 (4/5)	FARRERDALE: SK	51.58	105.85	16 mi SW Young

Wild Turkey
Deciduous and mixed woodland with open areas, riparian and mountainous regions
9.0 (4/6)	RED OAK: Oscoda, MI	44.83	84.22	6 mi SE Lewiston
5.9 (7/7)	STICKLERVILL: Adair, MO	40.07	92.50	4 mi SE Millard
5.0 (5/6)	MIDWAY: Holt, NE	42.65	98.70	13 mi NE Emmet

Montezuma Quail
Open woodland, pine-oak and oak scrub highlands
7.6 (6/7)	PENA BLANCA: Santa Cruz, AZ	31.38	111.08	9 mi NW Nogales
0.7 (2/3)	VALENTINE: Jeff Davis, TX	30.90	104.25	12 mi SW Kent

Northern Bobwhite
Fields and open woodland, especially woodland edge
209.6 (7/7)	RACHAL: Brooks, TX	26.80	98.08	7 mi SE Rachal
206.4 (5/5)	GRAYBACK: Wilbarger, TX	33.92	99.22	6 mi SW Grayback
147.9 (7/7)	RANDADO: Jim Hogg, TX	27.05	98.78	6 mi SE Randado

Scaled Quail
Desert grasslands, thorn scrub
37.2 (6/6)	HOT SPRINGS: Brewster, TX	29.18	103.02	15 mi SE Panther Junction
28.0 (4/4)	RANKIN: Upton, TX	31.18	101.95	3 mi SW Rankin
25.1 (7/7)	GAGE: Luna, NM	32.35	108.17	10 mi NW Gage

Gambel's Quail
Mesquite and yucca desert, adjacent fields
86.1 (7/7)	CARR MTN: Gila, AZ	33.80	110.88	17 mi NE Roosevelt
74.0 (3/3)	CASA GRANDE: Pinal, AZ	33.07	111.23	9 mi NE Cactus Forest
56.1 (7/7)	POMERENE: Cochise, AZ	32.03	110.30	2 mi NW Pomerene

California Quail
- Chaparral, fields, brushy and scrubby areas

93.4 (7/7)	COALINGA: Fresno, CA	36.15	120.55	11 mi NW Coalinga
63.3 (6/6)	OAK GROVE: San Diego, CA	33.40	116.80	5 mi SE Aguanga
52.5 (4/4)	ADELAIDA: San Luis Obispo, CA	35.60	120.83	8 mi NW Templeton

Mountain Quail
- Brushy mountainsides, woodland edge with dense undergrowth

31.3 (6/6)	RIVERTON: El Dorado, CA	38.85	120.45	6 mi NE Riverton
23.9 (7/7)	HULLVILLE: Mendocino, CA	39.55	122.93	13 mi SW Alder Springs
23.7 (7/7)	BARTLETT SPS: Lake, CA	39.10	122.72	4 mi SE Lucerne

RALLIDAE – Rails, Gallinules, Coots

Yellow Rail
- Wet meadows, bogs, fens, shallow marshes

0.4 (2/5)	CROLL: MB	49.32	100.12	7 mi NW Boissevain
0.3 (1/4)	HORSEHEAD LK: Kidder, ND	47.07	99.63	7 mi SW Pettibone

Clapper Rail
- Saltwater and brackish marshes, mangrove swamps

8.8 (5/5)	LTL CHENIER: Cameron, LA	29.77	93.02	3 mi NW Grand Chenier
8.4 (7/7)	OCEAN CITY: Cape May, NJ	39.23	74.55	4 mi SE Ocean City
6.7 (6/6)	DAUPHIN IS: Mobile, AL	30.25	88.10	1 mi SE Dauphin Island

King Rail
- Freshwater marshes

29.2 (5/5)	LTL CHENIER: Cameron, LA	29.77	93.02	3 mi NW Grand Chenier
4.5 (4/4)	KATY: Waller, TX	29.78	95.85	2 mi SW Katy
2.5 (4/4)	MAURICE: Vermilion, LA	30.08	92.30	5 mi SW Indian Bayou

Virginia Rail
- Freshwater and brackish marshes with extensive emergent vegetation

2.8 (5/6)	HONGA: Dorchester, MD	38.37	76.23	2 mi NW Honga
2.4 (7/7)	MADISON: Dorchester, MD	38.53	76.22	1 mi NW Madison
2.0 (6/7)	ALBERT: Barton, KS	38.45	98.97	2 mi SE Albert

Sora
- Marshes with grasses and sedges, mudflats

15.6 (7/7)	HALKIRK: AB	52.17	112.33	10 mi SW Halkirk
12.6 (7/7)	CLOUSTON: SK	53.08	105.83	9 mi SW Prince Albert
12.0 (3/3)	HOLLAND: MB	49.55	98.73	4 mi SW Holland

Purple Gallinule
- Marshes and lowlands with dense emergent and aquatic vegetation, rice fields

3.4 (4/5)	LTL CHENIER: Cameron, LA	29.77	93.02	3 mi NW Grand Chenier
2.0 (2/3)	SHAWANO: Palm Beach, FL	26.47	80.50	16 mi SE Okeelanta

Common Moorhen
- Marshes, ponds, and lakes with emergent vegetation and grassy edges

33.0 (5/5)	LTL CHENIER: Cameron, LA	29.77	93.02	3 mi NW Grand Chenier
32.0 (5/5)	LOVEDALE: Jackson, FL	30.88	85.00	5 mi NE Dellwood
16.6 (5/5)	SANDY: Sarasota, FL	27.25	82.30	5 mi SW Old Myakka

American Coot
   Lakes, ponds, marshes and other bodies of water with emergent vegetation
      184.4 (7/7)   DORRIS: Siskiyou, CA   41.98   121.90   1 mi NE Dorris
      126.4 (7/7)   MABEL LAKE: BC   50.42   118.77   16 mi NE Lumby
      86.8 (4/4)   HORSEHEAD LK: Kidder, ND   47.07   99.63   7 mi SW Pettibone

ARAMIDAE – Limpkins
Limpkin
   Swampy forest, lagoons and marshes with mangroves
      0.7 (1/3)   ANDYTOWN: Broward, FL   26.07   80.75   30 mi SW Cooper City
      0.4 (2/5)   CROOM: Hernando, FL   28.58   82.27   5 mi SE Nobleton

GRUIDAE – Cranes
Sandhill Crane
   Grasslands, marshes, lakes and ponds, wet meadows
      69.0 (4/4)   RED ROCK: Beaverhead, MT   44.62   111.53   14 mi SE Lakeview
      54.8 (5/5)   BEAVERHEAD: Beaverhead, MT   44.63   112.05   12 mi NW Lakeview
      32.6 (7/7)   ERIE: Pennington, MN   48.08   95.62   10 mi SE Goodridge

CHARADRIIDAE – Plovers
American Golden-Plover
   Arctic tundra
      13.3 (3/3)   CHURCHILL: MB   58.63   93.78   18 mi SE Churchill
      4.0 (3/3)   MACLAREN: SE Fairbanks, AK   63.07   146.07   54 mi NW Gakona
      3.8 (4/4)   TOKLAT: Yukon-Koyukuk, AK   63.47   150.07   41 mi NW Cantwell

Snowy Plover
   Beaches and other sandy shorelines, dry mudflats
      5.6 (3/7)   NILAND: Imperial, CA   33.23   115.50   1 mi SE Niland
      2.7 (3/7)   ALBERT: Barton, KS   38.45   98.97   2 mi SE Albert

Wilson's Plover
   Coastal areas, beaches, mudflats
      1.4 (3/5)   KINGSVILLE: Kleberg, TX   27.53   97.93   5 mi NW Kingsville

Semipalmated Plover
   Arctic tundra, sandy areas
      8.5 (6/6)   COLD BAY: Aleutian Islands, AK   55.00   162.00   62 mi NW Squaw Harbor
      4.0 (2/3)   MONAHAN: Matanuska-Susitna, AK   63.22   147.97   37 mi SE Cantwell
      3.0 (2/3)   CHURCHILL: MB   58.63   93.78   18 mi SE Churchill

Killdeer
   Widespread, fields and pastures, freshwater shorelines, prefers areas with gravel for nesting
      77.3 (7/7)   DORRIS: Siskiyou, CA   41.98   121.90   1 mi NE Dorris
      70.0 (7/7)   GLENN: Glenn, CA   39.55   122.07   3 mi SW Bayliss
      57.1 (7/7)   DUFRESNE: MB   49.72   96.72   0 mi Dufresne

Mountain Plover
   Open plains, shortgrass prairie
      9.5 (4/4)   LAMAR: Prowers, CO   38.15   102.52   5 mi SE Kornman
      7.3 (3/3)   RUSH: El Paso, CO   38.85   104.07   1 mi NE Rush
      5.0 (4/4)   HARMONY: Albany, WY   41.18   105.98   5 mi NE Woods Landing

HAEMATOPODIDAE – Oystercatchers

American Oystercatcher
   Rocky and sandy coastal areas
6.5 (6/6)	DAUPHIN IS: Mobile, AL	30.25	88.10	1 mi SE Dauphin Island
4.7 (6/7)	MERRIMON: Carteret, NC	34.95	76.67	4 mi SW South River
4.7 (6/7)	OCEAN CITY: Cape May, NJ	39.23	74.55	4 mi SE Ocean City

Black Oystercatcher
   Rocky coastal areas
4.5 (4/4)	VICTORIA: BC	48.42	123.37	2 mi SE Victoria
2.4 (5/5)	GIBSONS LDG: BC	49.40	123.53	0 mi Gibsons
1.3 (5/7)	SITKA: Sitka, AK	57.07	135.37	1 mi NW Mount Edgecombe

RECURVIROSTRIDAE – Stilts, Avocets

Black-necked Stilt
   Grassy marshes, mudflats, wet fields, alkaline lakes, rice fields
196.0 (7/7)	NILAND: Imperial, CA	33.23	115.50	1 mi SE Niland
82.1 (7/7)	DORRIS: Siskiyou, CA	41.98	121.90	1 mi NE Dorris
50.4 (7/7)	ARVIN: Kern, CA	35.23	118.88	2 mi SE Weed Patch

American Avocet
   Alkaline lakes, lowland marshes, open flats with grassy tufts
108.1 (7/7)	DORRIS: Siskiyou, CA	41.98	121.90	1 mi NE Dorris
25.0 (5/7)	NILAND: Imperial, CA	33.23	115.50	1 mi SE Niland
23.4 (7/7)	GLENN: Glenn, CA	39.55	122.07	3 mi SW Bayliss

SCOLOPACIDAE – Sandpipers, Phalaropes, and Allies

Greater Yellowlegs
   Tundra and muskeg
4.3 (6/6)	SEVEN LAKES: Kenai Peninsula, AK	60.45	150.25	31 mi SE Soldotna
4.0 (4/4)	ZIMOVIA STRT: Wrangell-Petersburg, AK	56.32	132.32	10 mi SW Wrangell
3.9 (6/7)	SWAN LAKE RD: Kenai Peninsula, AK	60.62	150.78	19 mi SE Kenai

Lesser Yellowlegs
   Tundra and muskeg
30.8 (4/4)	STAGG RIVER: NT	62.68	115.37	19 mi SE Rae-Edzo
28.0 (3/3)	LITL BUFFALO: NT	60.05	113.17	40 mi NW Fort Smith
23.3 (3/3)	CHURCHILL: MB	58.63	93.78	18 mi SE Churchill

Solitary Sandpiper
   Taiga and boreal forest
4.7 (3/3)	NORTHWAY: SE Fairbanks, AK	62.92	141.53	15 mi SE Northway
3.3 (4/6)	BEAR CREEK: Yukon-Koyukuk, AK	64.00	157.00	43 mi SW Galena
2.0 (3/3)	SOURDOUGH: Valdez-Cordova, AK	62.38	145.35	5 mi NE Gakona

Willet
   Marshy lakes and uplands in west; saltwater marshes in east
91.0 (5/5)	BETHANY BCH: Sussex, DE	38.58	75.05	2 mi NW Sussex Shores
62.0 (7/7)	OCEAN CITY: Cape May, NJ	39.23	74.55	4 mi SE Ocean City
42.6 (7/7)	DORRIS: Siskiyou, CA	41.98	121.90	1 mi NE Dorris

Spotted Sandpiper
   Widespread, nests near water in gravel or grass
   15.3 (4/4)   YELLOWSTONE: Park, WY   44.78   110.47   3 mi NE Canyon Junction
   14.9 (7/7)   GRAND FORKS: BC   49.37   118.48   14 mi NW Grand Forks
   12.4 (7/7)   HORSE CREEK: Siskiyou, CA   41.92   123.07   8 mi NW Horse Creek

Upland Sandpiper
   Grasslands, dry meadows and pastures
   60.1 (7/7)   LAPLAND: Greenwood, KS   37.87   96.35   5 mi NW Eureka
   59.0 (7/7)   DENBIGH: McHenry, ND   48.40   100.65   8 mi SW Bantry
   55.2 (5/5)   FORT PIERRE: Stanley, SD   44.38   100.50   7 mi NW Fort Pierre

Whimbrel
   Tundra with sedges and dwarf shrubs
   16.0 (3/3)   CHURCHILL: MB   58.63   93.78   18 mi SE Churchill
   2.0 (2/4)   TOKLAT: Yukon-Koyukuk, AK   63.47   150.07   41 mi NW Cantwell
   1.3 (1/3)   MONAHAN: Matanuska-Susitna, AK 63.22   147.97   37 mi SE Cantwell

Long-billed Curlew
   Shortgrass prairie, wet meadows, near water
   50.3 (7/7)   TIMPIE SPG: Tooele, UT   40.73   112.65   1 mi SE Timpie
   41.6 (7/7)   TEXLINE: Dallam, TX   36.38   102.90   7 mi SE Texline
   41.3 (3/3)   MAJORS PLACE: White Pine, NV   39.18   114.48   12 mi NE Majors Place

Hudsonian Godwit
   Arctic tundra, near water
   14.0 (3/3)   CHURCHILL: MB   58.63   93.78   18 mi SE Churchill

Marbled Godwit
   Mixedgrass prairie, near water
   29.0 (4/4)   HORSEHEAD LK: Kidder, ND   47.07   99.63   7 mi SW Pettibone
   26.7 (7/7)   BROOKS: AB   50.57   111.85   2 mi NE Brooks
   25.6 (7/7)   RANIER: AB   50.38   112.02   5 mi NE Rainier

Least Sandpiper
   Coastal and upland tundra, marshy areas in spruce forest
   4.2 (5/6)   COLD BAY: Aleutian Islands, AK 55.00   162.00   62 mi NW Squaw Harbor
   3.4 (6/7)   CHINIAK: Kodiak Island, AK   57.53   152.43   17 mi SW Kodiak
   1.3 (2/3)   MASSETT: BC   54.02   132.15   11 mi SE Masset

Rock Sandpiper
   Tundra with grasses and mosses, coastal regions
   68.3 (5/6)   COLD BAY: Aleutian Islands, AK 55.00   162.00   62 mi NW Squaw Harbor
   1.8 (3/5)   ADAK: Aleutian Islands, AK   51.85   176.60   3 mi SE Adak

Dunlin
   Wet coastal tundra
   3.0 (2/3)   CHURCHILL: MB   58.63   93.78   18 mi SE Churchill
   2.0 (5/6)   COLD BAY: Aleutian Islands, AK 55.00   162.00   62 mi NW Squaw Harbor

Short-billed Dowitcher
   Grassy and mossy tundra, wet meadows
6.3 (3/3)	CHURCHILL: MB	58.63	93.78	18 mi SE Churchill
1.7 (1/3)	THERIEN: AB	54.27	111.28	4 mi NW Therien
1.0 (1/3)	VANESTI: AB	53.27	110.62	9 mi SW Islay

Common Snipe
   Wet, grassy areas; fens, bogs, marshes
50.3 (7/7)	JOSEPH: Wallowa, OR	45.28	117.22	5 mi SW Joseph
43.2 (6/6)	BRIDGEPORT: Baker, OR	44.50	117.75	1 mi NW Bridgeport
39.1 (7/7)	LIKELY: Modoc, CA	41.23	120.30	11 mi SE Likely

American Woodcock
   Moist deciduous and mixed woodland, bogs
2.0 (3/7)	MORISSET STA: PQ	46.27	70.53	4 mi NE Morisset-Station
1.8 (5/6)	EAGLE DEPOT: PQ	46.23	76.32	19 mi SW Maniwaki
1.8 (3/6)	HIGHMARKET: Lewis, NY	43.65	75.62	10 mi SW Martinsburg

Wilson's Phalarope
   Wet meadows and freshwater marshes
43.6 (7/7)	DORRIS: Siskiyou, CA	41.98	121.90	1 mi NE Dorris
23.6 (7/7)	SHEYENNE LK: Wells, ND	47.63	100.03	10 mi NE Goodrich
22.3 (4/4)	HORSEHEAD LK: Kidder, ND	47.07	99.63	7 mi SW Pettibone

Red-necked Phalarope
   Ponds and lakes with emergent vegetation, bogs
8.6 (3/6)	KENNY LAKE: Valdez-Cordova, AK	61.72	144.93	11 mi NW Lower Tonsina
6.6 (5/5)	ADAK: Aleutian Islands, AK	51.85	176.60	3 mi SE Adak
5.0 (2/3)	CHURCHILL: MB	58.63	93.78	18 mi SE Churchill

LARIDAE – Jaegers, Gulls, Terns, Skimmers

Parasitic Jaeger
   Barren and dwarf shrub tundra, coastal areas
8.8 (5/5)	ADAK: Aleutian Islands, AK	51.85	176.60	3 mi SE Adak
1.7 (2/3)	CHURCHILL: MB	58.63	93.78	18 mi SE Churchill

Long-tailed Jaeger
   Dry, open tundra
5.0 (1/1)	KOBUK RIVER: Kobuk, AK	67.10	158.27	14 mi NW Ambler
1.8 (3/4)	TOKLAT: Yukon-Koyukuk, AK	63.47	150.07	41 mi NW Cantwell

Laughing Gull
   Sandy islands, coastal dunes
1201.1 (7/7)	QUINBY: Accomack, VA	37.53	75.67	4 mi SE Quinby
468.1 (7/7)	OCEAN CITY: Cape May, NJ	39.23	74.55	4 mi SE Ocean City
221.6 (7/7)	MERRIMON: Carteret, NC	34.95	76.67	4 mi SW South River

Franklin's Gull
   Prairie marshes
348.7 (3/3)	MUD LAKE: Jefferson, ID	43.87	112.53	3 mi NW Mud Lake
249.8 (6/6)	RIVERSIDE: MB	50.02	97.07	3 mi NW Birds Hill
249.4 (7/7)	GRYGLA: Beltrami, MN	48.30	95.57	2 mi SE Grygla

Annotated list of species, habitats and areas 275

Bonaparte's Gull
  Coniferous forest, near water
    20.7 (3/3)   CHURCHILL: MB   58.63   93.78   18 mi SE Churchill
    15.0 (4/4)   STAGG RIVER: NT   62.68   115.37   19 mi SE Rae-Edzo
    5.4 (7/7)   EDSON: AB   53.60   116.37   9 mi NW Edson

Heerman's Gull
  Coastal islands, especially rocky areas with scattered grass clumps
    4.0 (3/3)   HONEYDEW: Humboldt, CA   40.25   124.13   1 mi NW Honeydew
    1.3 (2/3)   MORRO BAY: San Luis Obispo, CA   35.27   120.75   5 mi NW San Luis Obispo

Mew Gull
  Coastal, lakes and rivers, rocky or sandy areas
    40.3 (6/6)   WIGAN: YT   60.65   135.03   7 mi SE Whitehorse
    29.2 (6/6)   KODIAK: Kodiak Island, AK   57.62   152.55   12 mi SW Kodiak
    9.2 (6/6)   COLD BAY: Aleutian Islands, AK   55.00   162.00   62 mi NW Squaw Harbor

Ring-billed Gull
  Widespread, fresh and saltwater, rocky or grassy islets, fields and plowed land
    403.1 (7/7)   DORRIS: Siskiyou, CA   41.98   121.90   1 mi NE Dorris
    350.0 (7/7)   MACDOEL: Siskiyou, CA   41.85   122.15   8 mi NW Macdoel
    348.4 (7/7)   E YOUNGSTOWN: Niagara, NY   43.25   78.98   4 mi NE Youngstown

California Gull
  Widespread, sandy or gravelly areas, lakes and ponds
    213.1 (7/7)   DORRIS: Siskiyou, CA   41.98   121.90   1 mi NE Dorris
    211.1 (7/7)   SPRINGFIELD: Bingham, ID   43.15   112.80   8 mi NW Springfield
    118.4 (7/7)   POCATELLO: Bannock, ID   42.85   112.48   2 mi SW Pocatello

Herring Gull
  Coastal, lakes and rivers; rocky and sandy areas, tundra
    279.2 (5/5)   SILVER ISLET: ON   48.32   88.82   19 mi SW Pass Lake
    195.5 (4/4)   GRAND MANAN: NB   44.65   66.88   2 mi SW Seal Cove
    150.1 (7/7)   KITTERY PT: York, ME   43.15   70.72   3 mi SW York Village

Western Gull
  Coastal, rocky islands and cliffs
    114.1 (7/7)   BODEGA BAY: Sonoma, CA   38.30   123.05   2 mi SW Bodega Bay
    73.8 (6/6)   SAN YSIDRO: San Diego, CA   32.55   117.17   4 mi SW Imperial Beach
    57.1 (7/7)   FISH ROCK: Mendocino, CA   38.80   123.62   2 mi NW Anchor Bay

Glaucous-winged Gull
  Coastal, cliffs and ledges, grassy slopes and barrens
    325.2 (5/5)   POINT GREY: BC   49.23   123.23   4 mi NW Vancouver
    228.0 (4/4)   VICTORIA: BC   48.42   123.37   2 mi SE Victoria
    136.6 (7/7)   PORT ANGELES: Clallam, WA   48.12   123.38   2 mi SE Port Angeles

Glaucous Gull
  Coastal, cliffs and rocky areas, tundra lakes
    5.0 (1/1)   KOBUK RIVER: Kobuk, AK   67.10   158.27   14 mi NW Ambler

Great Black-backed Gull
  Coastal and large lakes, rocky islands
    52.3 (4/4)   PEGGYS COVE: NS   44.50 63.75   2 mi NW Whites Lake
    49.7 (3/3)   MATANE: PQ   48.83 67.50   2 mi SE Matane
    25.3 (3/3)   ST JOHNS: NF   47.62 52.72   5 mi NW St. John's

Black-legged Kittiwake
  Coastal areas with steep cliffs
    319.7 (3/3)   ST JOHNS: NF   47.62 52.72   5 mi NW St. John's
    26.6 (3/5)   ADAK: Aleutian Islands, AK   51.85 176.60   3 mi SE Adak

Gull-billed Tern
  Gravelly or sandy beaches, saltwater marshes, lagoons
    10.3 (6/6)   DAUPHIN IS: Mobile, AL   30.25 88.10   1 mi SE Dauphin Island
    5.9 (5/7)   RAYMONDVILLE: Willacy, TX   26.53 97.70   4 mi NW San Perlita
    1.3 (4/7)   NILAND: Imperial, CA   33.23 115.50   1 mi SE Niland

Caspian Tern
  Gravelly or sandy beaches, coastal, islands
    65.0 (3/3)   IRON GATE: Siskiyou, CA   41.95 122.43   4 mi SW Copco
    13.4 (7/7)   DORRIS: Siskiyou, CA   41.98 121.90   1 mi NE Dorris
    8.0 (4/4)   TAHOLAH: Grays Harbor, WA   47.45 124.27   7 mi SE Queets

Royal Tern
  Sandy beaches, coastal
    22.0 (3/3)   MYRTLE GROVE: New Hanover, NC   34.15 77.93   5 mi SE Wilmington
    13.2 (6/6)   DAUPHIN IS: Mobile, AL   30.25 88.10   1 mi SE Dauphin Island
    5.4 (7/7)   MERRIMON: Carteret, NC   34.95 76.67   4 mi SW South River

Sandwich Tern
  Sandy beaches and flats
    1.9 (4/7)   DAUPHIN IS: Mobile, AL   30.25 88.10   1 mi SE Dauphin Island

Common Tern
  Beaches, grassy areas, islands
    71.0 (6/6)   LUMSDEN: SK   50.63 104.93   2 mi SW Lumsden
    12.4 (7/7)   OCEAN CITY: Cape May, NJ   39.23 74.55   4 mi SE Ocean City
    10.2 (5/5)   RICHIBUCTO: NB   46.73 64.97   0 mi St-Louis-de-Kent

Arctic Tern
  Coastal islands, tundra; rocky or grassy areas
    63.0 (3/3)   CHURCHILL: MB   58.63 93.78   18 mi SE Churchill
    20.2 (5/5)   ADAK: Aleutian Islands, AK   51.85 176.60   3 mi SE Adak
    5.3 (5/6)   KODIAK: Kodiak Island, AK   57.62 152.55   12 mi SW Kodiak

Forster's Tern
  Fresh and saltwater marshes with emergent vegetation
    57.7 (7/7)   DORRIS: Siskiyou, CA   41.98 121.90   1 mi NE Dorris
    15.0 (3/3)   JUNIOR: Plaquemines, LA   29.48 89.70   0 mi Port Sulphur
    13.9 (7/7)   MERRIMON: Carteret, NC   34.95 76.67   4 mi SW South River

Least Tern
  Sandy or gravelly beaches, rivers and lakes, coastal
    141.6 (5/5)   SANTA ROSA: Escambia, FL   30.37   86.92   4 mi SW Navarre
    64.5 (6/6)   FT WALTN BCH: Walton, FL   30.37   86.28   4 mi SW Santa Rosa Beach
    28.7 (6/6)   DAUPHIN IS: Mobile, AL   30.25   88.10   1 mi SE Dauphin Island

Aleutian Tern
  Offshore islands, grassy or mossy flats, spits and lagoons
    45.2 (5/5)   ADAK: Aleutian Islands, AK   51.85   176.60   3 mi SE Adak
    8.5 (6/6)   KODIAK: Kodiak Island, AK   57.62   152.55   12 mi SW Kodiak
    5.0 (4/5)   KACHEMAK: Kenai Peninsula, AK   59.00   151.00   39 mi SE Seldovia

Black Tern
  Marshes, sloughs and wet meadows
    54.0 (6/6)   LUMSDEN: SK   50.63   104.93   2 mi SW Lumsden
    39.8 (6/6)   MARCELIN: SK   52.97   106.75   3 mi NE Marcelin
    23.0 (7/7)   HALKIRK: AB   52.17   112.33   10 mi SW Halkirk

Black Skimmer
  Coastal, sandy beaches, islands and rivers
    41.2 (6/6)   DAUPHIN IS: Mobile, AL   30.25   88.10   1 mi SE Dauphin Island
    21.6 (6/7)   OCEAN CITY: Cape May, NJ   39.23   74.55   4 mi SE Ocean City
    3.6 (5/7)   MERRIMON: Carteret, NC   34.95   76.67   4 mi SW South River

ALCIDAE – Murres, Guillemots, Murrelets, Auklets
Common Murre
  Coastal areas with steep cliffs
    324.0 (3/3)   HONEYDEW: Humboldt, CA   40.25   124.13   1 mi NW Honeydew
    8.5 (2/4)   TAHOLAH: Grays Harbor, WA   47.45   124.27   7 mi SE Queets
    3.9 (5/7)   FISH ROCK: Mendocino, CA   38.80   123.62   2 mi NW Anchor Bay

Pigeon Guillemot
  Coastal areas with cliffs or rocky areas
    3.7 (7/7)   CHINIAK: Kodiak Island, AK   57.53   152.43   17 mi SW Kodiak
    3.0 (4/6)   KODIAK: Kodiak Island, AK   57.62   152.55   12 mi SW Kodiak
    2.4 (6/7)   WARM BEACH: Snohomish, WA   48.13   122.33   6 mi SW Silvana

Marbled Murrelet
  Coastal coniferous forest
    46.8 (5/5)   ADAK: Aleutian Islands, AK   51.85   176.60   3 mi SE Adak
    12.6 (6/7)   CHINIAK: Kodiak Island, AK   57.53   152.43   17 mi SW Kodiak
    9.5 (4/4)   MITKOF ISLE: Wrangell-Petersburg, AK 56.62 132.72   16 mi SE Petersburg

Rhinoceros Auklet
  Wooded or grassy islands
    22.3 (2/4)   VICTORIA: BC   48.42   123.37   2 mi SE Victoria
    7.4 (2/7)   OZETTE: Clallam, WA   48.12   124.67   15 mi NE La Push
    1.4 (4/7)   WARM BEACH: Snohomish, WA   48.13   122.33   6 mi SW Silvana

COLUMBIDAE – Pigeons, Doves

Rock Dove
    Cities, buildings and structures with ledges; near human habitation

291.3 (7/7)	BIRMINGHAM: Jefferson, AL	33.58	86.70	7 mi NE Birmingham
132.7 (6/6)	ST JOHNSBURG: Niagara, NY	43.08	78.85	2 mi SE Saint Johnsburg
122.9 (7/7)	COLLEGEVILLE: Montgomery, PA	40.15	75.47	2 mi NE Mont Clare

White-crowned Pigeon
    Mangrove swamps, hardwood hammocks

100.0 (5/5)	KEY LARGO: Monroe, FL	25.20	80.35	8 mi NE Newport
57.7 (7/7)	PLANTATION K: Monroe, FL	24.97	80.58	4 mi NE Islamorada

Band-tailed Pigeon
    Coniferous forest and oak woodlands

19.1 (7/7)	VALERMO: Los Angeles, CA	34.38	117.68	1 mi SE Big Pines
15.3 (4/4)	TAHOLAH: Grays Harbor, WA	47.45	124.27	7 mi SE Queets
14.0 (7/7)	CRESCENT CTY: Del Norte, CA	41.75	124.18	1 mi SE Crescent City

Spotted Dove
    Residential areas, cities

25.6 (7/7)	HARBOR LAKE: Los Angeles, CA	33.78	118.28	1 mi NW Wilmington

White-winged Dove
    Arid regions; riparian woodland, parks

185.5 (2/2)	ORGAN PIPE: Pima, AZ	31.97	112.92	9 mi NW Lukeville
129.3 (7/7)	IMPERIAL DAM: Imperial, CA	32.83	114.50	4 mi NE Bard
105.3 (6/6)	LAGUNA: Yuma, AZ	32.85	114.40	7 mi NW Dome

Mourning Dove
    Widespread, fields, open woodland, desert

231.1 (7/7)	ALBANY: Shackelford, TX	32.82	99.12	10 mi SE Fort Griffin
222.1 (7/7)	IMPERIAL DAM: Imperial, CA	32.83	114.50	4 mi NE Bard
210.2 (6/6)	PHILLIPSBURG: Phillips, KS	39.72	99.22	5 mi NE Glade

Inca Dove
    Arid or semi-arid regions; cities, parks and gardens

12.0 (7/7)	RACHAL: Brooks, TX	26.80	98.08	7 mi SE Rachal
5.6 (5/5)	KINGSVILLE: Kleberg, TX	27.53	97.93	5 mi NW Kingsville
4.3 (7/7)	DANBURY: Brazoria, TX	29.12	95.22	11 mi NE Oyster Creek

Common Ground-Dove
    Open areas with trees and bushes, fields; residential areas

70.4 (5/5)	SCOTTSMOOR: Brevard, FL	28.73	80.87	3 mi SE Scottsmoor
23.4 (5/5)	WEBB: Charlotte, FL	26.88	81.87	7 mi NW Tuckers Corner
14.0 (7/7)	SUNNILAND GR: Collier, FL	26.30	81.48	9 mi SW Immokalee

White-tipped Dove
    Arid or semi-arid regions; open woodland, clearings and second growth

1.7 (2/7)	RAYMONDVILLE: Willacy, TX	26.53	97.70	4 mi NW San Perlita
0.4 (2/7)	LAG ATASCOSA: Cameron, TX	26.20	97.33	6 mi NE Bayview

Annotated list of species, habitats and areas 279

CUCULIDAE – Cuckoos, Roadrunners, Anis
Black-billed Cuckoo
   Deciduous and coniferous woodland
   19.9 (6/7)   GRANADA: PQ   48.20   79.02   2 mi SE Rouyn-Noranda
   11.9 (7/7)   ERIE: Pennington, MN   48.08   95.62   10 mi SE Goodridge
   11.0 (6/7)   GRYGLA: Beltrami, MN   48.30   95.57   2 mi SE Grygla

Yellow-billed Cuckoo
   Riparian woodland in west; deciduous forest in east, thick undergrowth, near water
   39.3 (7/7)   BLANCO: Pittsburg, OK   34.75   95.77   0 mi Blanco
   33.4 (7/7)   BARON: Cherokee, OK   35.82   94.87   4 mi SE Welling
   31.0 (7/7)   ARDMORE: Carter, OK   34.13   97.18   4 mi SW Ardmore

Mangrove Cuckoo
   Forest edge, mangrove swamps
   0.8 (2/5)   KEY LARGO: Monroe, FL   25.20   80.35   8 mi NE Newport

Greater Roadrunner
   Desert scrub, chaparral, fields
   9.0 (7/7)   PATAGONIA: Santa Cruz, AZ   31.52 110.80   3 mi SW Patagonia
   6.4 (7/7)   POMERENE: Cochise, AZ   32.03 110.30   2 mi NW Pomerene
   5.0 (6/7)   ALBANY: Shackelford, TX   32.82   99.12   10 mi SE Fort Griffin

Smooth-billed Ani
   Brushy and scrubby areas with open areas, fields and clearings
   7.7 (3/3)   SHAWANO: Palm Beach, FL   26.47   80.50   16 mi SE Okeelanta
   3.0 (2/3)   ANDYTOWN: Broward, FL   26.07   80.75   30 mi SW Cooper City
   1.0 (2/3)   HOLEY LAND: Broward, FL   26.33   80.83   20 mi SW Okeelanta

Groove-billed Ani
   Scrubby areas with openings, thickets, second growth
   2.6 (4/7)   RAYMONDVILLE: Willacy, TX 26.53   97.70   4 mi NW San Perlita
   2.5 (3/4)   GUERRA: Zapata, TX   26.95   99.03   6 mi SE Bustamante
   2.0 (5/7)   RACHAL: Brooks, TX   26.80   98.08   7 mi SE Rachal

TYTONIDAE – Barn Owls
Barn Owl
   Open country, farm buildings, caves and crevices
   1.0 (4/6)   MONTESAND: Grays Harbor, WA 47.02 123.65   4 mi NW Montesano
   1.0 (3/3)   SHAWANO: Palm Beach, FL   26.47   80.50   16 mi SE Okeelanta
   0.6 (4/7)   GREENFIELD: Monterey, CA   36.32 121.47   7 mi SE Jamesburg

STRIGIDAE – Owls
Great Horned Owl
   Widespread, deciduous and coniferous forest with open areas and edge, parks
   7.3 (4/4)   ADELAIDA: San Luis Obispo, CA 35.60 120.83   8 mi NW Templeton
   5.3 (3/3)   CASA GRANDE: Pinal, AZ   33.07 111.23   9 mi NE Cactus Forest
   5.0 (7/7)   LINDBROOK: AB   53.33 112.77   5 mi SE Lindbrook

Northern Pygmy-Owl
   Coniferous and mixed woodland, especially with pine-oak; open areas for foraging
   2.0 (6/7)   DOWNIEVILLE: Sierra, CA   39.57 120.85   1 mi NW Downieville
   1.1 (4/7)   GLEN ELLEN: Sonoma, CA   38.38 122.52   1 mi NE Glen Ellen
   0.7 (4/7)   MARK WEST: Sonoma, CA   38.57 122.72   5 mi SW Kellogg

Burrowing Owl
　　Shortgrass prairie, grasslands, prairie dog towns, open areas and vacant lots
　　36.1 (7/7)　　　　ALAMO RIVER: Imperial, CA　　　32.83　115.45　　3 mi NE Anza
　　28.8 (6/6)　　　　BRAWLEY: Imperial, CA　　　　　32.92　115.55　　4 mi SW Brawley
　　28.4 (7/7)　　　　NILAND: Imperial, CA　　　　　 33.23　115.50　　1 mi SE Niland

Spotted Owl
　　Dense old-growth forest; mixed forest in southwestern canyons
　　0.4 (2/7)　　　　 GLEN ELLEN: Sonoma, CA　　　　 38.38　122.52　　1 mi NE Glen Ellen

Barred Owl
　　Dense coniferous and hardwood forest, swamps and wet areas
　　6.8 (4/4)　　　　 TENSAS NWR: Madison, LA　　　　 32.28　91.43　　 10 mi NE Crowville
　　5.4 (7/7)　　　　 FREETOWN: Assumption, LA　　　 29.90　90.95　　 2 mi SE Rosedale
　　4.6 (7/7)　　　　 PLETTENBERG: West Feliciana, LA 30.78　91.52　　 5 mi NE Labarre

Short-eared Owl
　　Open country, grasslands, meadows, marshes
　　8.0 (3/6)　　　　 POWDERVILLE: Custer, MT　　　　 45.98　105.47　　14 mi NE Volborg
　　6.1 (3/7)　　　　 TRACTOR FLAT: Bingham, ID　　　 43.52　112.65　　10 mi NE Atomic City
　　3.8 (2/4)　　　　 CRANE CREEK: Washington, ID　　 44.32　116.55　　14 mi SE Midvale

CAPRIMULGIDAE – Nightjars
Lesser Nighthawk
　　Arid regions; open country, desert, scrub, grasslands and fields
　　37.3 (3/3)　　　　COACHELLA CN: Riverside, CA　　 33.48　115.63　　14 mi SE Chiriaco Summit
　　35.7 (7/7)　　　　POMERENE: Cochise, AZ　　　　　 32.03　110.30　　2 mi NW Pomerene
　　22.8 (6/6)　　　　LAGUNA: Yuma, AZ　　　　　　　　32.85　114.40　　7 mi NW Dome

Common Nighthawk
　　Widespread, cities, grasslands and fields
　　137.4 (5/5)　　　 KINGSVILLE: Kleberg, TX　　　　 27.53　97.93　　 5 mi NW Kingsville
　　86.1 (7/7)　　　　ALBANY: Shackelford, TX　　　　 32.82　99.12　　 10 mi SE Fort Griffin
　　52.8 (5/5)　　　　KENDALL: Dade, FL　　　　　　　 25.65　80.48　　 7 mi NW Richmond
Heights

Pauraque
　　Open woodland, edge and clearings, roadsides
　　1.0 (1/3)　　　　 AGUA NUEVA: Jim Hogg, TX　　　 26.90　98.43　　 10 mi NE Santa Elena
　　0.7 (3/7)　　　　 LAG ATASCOSA: Cameron, TX　　　 26.20　97.33　　 6 mi NE Bayview
　　0.6 (2/7)　　　　 RANDADO: Jim Hogg, TX　　　　　 27.05　98.78　　 6 mi SE Randado

Common Poorwill
　　Arid and semi-arid regions; pinyon-juniper woodland and grassland, scrubby rocky areas
　　4.0 (7/7)　　　　 COTTONWOOD: Callahan, TX　　　 32.22　99.27　　 9 mi NW Cross Plains
　　3.4 (5/5)　　　　 TUJUNGA: Los Angeles, CA　　　 34.28　118.10　　7 mi NE Altadena
　　3.2 (5/5)　　　　 CLAUNCH: Lincoln, NM　　　　　 34.05　105.82　　9 mi NW Luna

Chuck-will's-widow
　　Deciduous woodland, especially pine-oak and live-oak
　　14.1 (7/7)　　　　MAYNARD: Randolph, AR　　　　　 36.45　90.93　　 1 mi SW Middlebrook
　　13.0 (6/6)　　　　SAFFELL: Lawrence, AR　　　　　 35.90　91.35　　 4 mi SW Saffell
　　10.1 (7/7)　　　　BLAKELY: Garland, AR　　　　　　34.70　93.08　　 1 mi NW Blakely

Whip-poor-will
  Widespread, open woodland
  6.4 (5/5)   FRIENDSHIP: Burlington, NJ   39.75   74.47   4 mi NE Speedwell
  5.3 (7/7)   DELWOOD: Saline, IL   37.60   88.52   3 mi SW Rudement
  5.0 (7/7)   CENTERTOWN: Moniteau, MO   38.57   92.45   3 mi SE McGirk

APODIDAE – Swifts
Black Swift
  Montane forest, cliffs and canyons, near waterfalls
  17.3 (2/4)   NO CASCADES: Whatcom, WA   48.70   121.08   3 mi SE Diablo
  14.7 (3/3)   SQUAMISH: BC   49.50   123.23   12 mi SW Squamish
  13.0 (3/4)   RONALD: Kittitas, WA   47.22   121.02   1 mi SW Ronald

Chimney Swift
  Cities, open woodlands, chimneys
  99.3 (7/7)   BIRMINGHAM: Jefferson, AL   33.58   86.70   7 mi NE Birmingham
  72.6 (7/7)   HERNER CRNS: Trumbull, OH   41.32   80.98   1 mi NW Southington
  72.6 (5/5)   BEATTYVILLE: Lee, KY   37.63   83.80   4 mi SW Mount Olive

Vaux's Swift
  Forested regions, near water; forages over open country
  8.7 (6/7)   COUGAR: Cowlitz, WA   46.05   122.43   4 mi NW Yale
  8.6 (5/7)   GLACIER: Whatcom, WA   48.85   121.88   4 mi SE Glacier
  6.8 (4/4)   NO CASCADES: Whatcom, WA   48.70   121.08   3 mi SE Diablo

White-throated Swift
  Mountainous regions, cliffs and canyons
  66.7 (3/3)   MOAB: Grand, UT   38.58   109.57   1 mi NW Moab
  62.2 (6/6)   ADRIAN: Malheur, OR   43.67   117.07   5 mi SW Adrian
  47.7 (7/7)   MOSKEE: Crook, WY   44.35   104.12   6 mi NE Moskee

TROCHILIDAE – Hummingbirds
Broad-billed Hummingbird
  Arid regions; open deciduous woodland and scrub
  0.9 (4/7)   PATAGONIA: Santa Cruz, AZ   31.52   110.80   3 mi SW Patagonia
  0.7 (4/7)   PENA BLANCA: Santa Cruz, AZ   31.38   111.08   9 mi NW Nogales

Blue-throated Hummingbird
  Deciduous woodland, especially pine-oak with open and shrubby areas
  1.0 (3/4)   PORTAL: Cochise, AZ   31.98   109.20   3 mi NE Paradise

Ruby-throated Hummingbird
  Deciduous and mixed woodland, parks, meadows and gardens
  20.5 (6/6)   TOWN BLUFF: Jasper, TX   30.80   94.10   9 mi NE Spurger
  7.4 (7/7)   ARDMORE: Carter, OK   34.13   97.18   4 mi SW Ardmore
  7.0 (4/4)   CANADIAN: Pittsburg, OK   35.17   95.63   1 mi SE Canadian

Black-chinned Hummingbird
  Scrub, desert washes, riparian woodland, parks and gardens
  4.4 (7/7)   BOERNE: Kendall, TX   29.88   98.65   8 mi NE Boerne
  3.3 (6/6)   SELDEN: Erath, TX   32.17   98.05   10 mi SE Stephenville
  2.9 (7/7)   COTTONWOOD: Callahan, TX   32.22   99.27   9 mi NW Cross Plains

Anna's Hummingbird
    Open woodland, scrubby areas, gardens and meadows

14.8 (6/6)	SAN YSIDRO: San Diego, CA	32.55	117.17	4 mi SW Imperial Beach
9.8 (5/5)	TUJUNGA: Los Angeles, CA	34.28	118.10	7 mi NE Altadena
8.4 (7/7)	CARMEL VAL: Monterey, CA	36.45	121.67	4 mi SE Carmel Valley

Costa's Hummingbird
    Desert and semi-desert, foothills and chaparral

8.6 (4/5)	LAKE CACHUMA: Santa Barbara, CA	34.68	119.65	15 mi SW Ventucopa
6.4 (4/5)	TUJUNGA: Los Angeles, CA	34.28	118.10	7 mi NE Altadena
4.9 (6/7)	FOSTER PARK: Ventura, CA	34.35	119.25	4 mi SE Oak View

Calliope Hummingbird
    Montane forest, mountain meadows, willow-alder thickets

4.0 (6/7)	WILSON: Teton, WY	43.47	110.77	1 mi SW Jackson
3.7 (3/3)	FEATHERVILLE: Elmore, ID	43.75	115.25	7 mi SW Atlanta
3.3 (6/7)	CENTERVILLE: Boise, ID	43.75	115.95	8 mi SW Idaho City

Broad-tailed Hummingbird
    Open pinyon-juniper and pine-oak woodland, brush and thickets

52.8 (5/5)	PARLIN: Gunnison, CO	38.55	106.75	4 mi NW Parlin
39.0 (5/5)	CLOUDCROFT: Otero, NM	32.88	105.67	7 mi SE Cloudcroft
22.7 (6/6)	CHEESMAN LK: Douglas, CO	39.18	105.28	6 mi SW Deckers

Rufous Hummingbird
    Coniferous forest, second growth, thickets and brushy hillsides, meadows

25.6 (7/7)	PORT RENFREW: BC	48.43	124.03	5 mi SE Jordan River
11.3 (7/7)	NEWHALEM: Whatcom, WA	48.75	121.22	4 mi NW Diablo
7.6 (7/7)	KENDALL: Whatcom, WA	48.97	122.15	4 mi NE Kendall

Allen's Hummingbird
    Chaparral, thickets and brushy hillsides, open coniferous woodland

8.2 (6/6)	POINT REYES: Marin, CA	38.03	122.88	5 mi SW Point Reyes Station
7.3 (7/7)	FISH ROCK: Mendocino, CA	38.80	123.62	2 mi NW Anchor Bay
6.4 (7/7)	FAIRFAX: Marin, CA	37.98	122.58	1 mi SE Fairfax

TROGONIDAE – Trogons
Elegant Trogon
    Riparian canyons with sycamores, pine-oak woodland

1.0 (2/4)	PORTAL: Cochise, AZ	31.98	109.20	3 mi NE Paradise

ALCEDINIDAE – Kingfishers
Belted Kingfisher
    Fresh and marine watercourses

6.8 (6/6)	TOWN BLUFF: Jasper, TX	30.80	94.10	9 mi NE Spurger
4.6 (7/7)	SITKA: Sitka, AK	57.07	135.37	1 mi NW Mount Edgecombe
4.5 (4/4)	ZIMOVIA STRT: Wrangell-Petersburg, AK	56.32	132.32	10 mi SW Wrangell

Green Kingfisher
    Streams, rivers, marshes and swamps

0.7 (2/3)	UTOPIA: Uvalde, TX	29.53	99.53	6 mi SW Utopia

PICIDAE – Woodpeckers

Lewis' Woodpecker
    Coniferous forest, logged or burned areas, ponderosa pine and oak woodlands
6.0 (6/6)	BRIDGEPORT: Baker, OR	44.50	117.75	1 mi NW Bridgeport
6.0 (7/7)	TWISP: Okanogan, WA	48.35	120.20	4 mi NW Twisp
5.9 (6/7)	IMNAHA: Wallowa, OR	45.72	116.62	15 mi NE Imnaha

Red-headed Woodpecker
    Deciduous woodland, aspen, beech and oak forest with openings, parks
26.5 (6/6)	WINSIDE: Wayne, NE	42.20	97.15	2 mi NE Winside
23.5 (6/6)	MIDWAY: Holt, NE	42.65	98.70	13 mi NE Emmet
19.2 (6/6)	EAGLE CREEK: Holt, NE	42.77	98.60	5 mi SW Bristow

Acorn Woodpecker
    Open oak and pine-oak woodland
104.6 (7/7)	LOCKWOOD: Monterey, CA	35.93	121.08	1 mi SW Lockwood
84.3 (4/4)	ADELAIDA: San Luis Obispo, CA	35.60	120.83	8 mi NW Templeton
65.6 (7/7)	ORANGE COVE: Tulare, CA	36.65	119.28	3 mi NE Orange Cove

Gila Woodpecker
    Saguaro desert, riparian woodland, residential areas
76.5 (2/2)	ORGAN PIPE: Pima, AZ	31.97	112.92	9 mi NW Lukeville
40.0 (3/3)	CASA GRANDE: Pinal, AZ	33.07	111.23	9 mi NE Cactus Forest
15.5 (6/6)	QUARTZSITE: La Paz, AZ	33.55	114.10	11 mi SE Quartzsite

Golden-fronted Woodpecker
    Open woodland, especially mesquite scrub and semi-desert regions; parks and residential areas
28.0 (3/3)	AGUA NUEVA: Jim Hogg, TX	26.90	98.43	10 mi NE Santa Elena
25.9 (7/7)	RACHAL: Brooks, TX	26.80	98.08	7 mi SE Rachal
23.5 (4/4)	GUERRA: Zapata, TX	26.95	99.03	6 mi SE Bustamante

Red-bellied Woodpecker
    Open deciduous woodland, second growth, swamps, residential areas
58.5 (4/4)	TENSAS NWR: Madison, LA	32.28	91.43	10 mi NE Crowville
41.4 (7/7)	FOWLSTOWN: Decatur, GA	30.82	84.53	6 mi NW Attapulgus
38.7 (7/7)	MICCOSUKEE: Levy, FL	30.58	84.03	1 mi NE Concord

Yellow-bellied Sapsucker
    Deciduous and mixed woodland
25.1 (7/7)	ST REGIS FLS: Franklin, NY	44.55	74.48	9 mi SE Saint Regis Falls
20.7 (6/6)	HERON LAKE: Piscataquis, ME	46.40	69.28	19 mi SE Clayton Lake
20.3 (6/6)	NEPISIQUIT: NB	47.40	66.52	22 mi NW Heath Steele

Red-naped Sapsucker
    Coniferous forest, aspen groves
9.1 (7/7)	GRAND FORKS: BC	49.37	118.48	14 mi NW Grand Forks
7.6 (7/7)	OLIVER: BC	49.07	119.27	6 mi NW Bridesville
7.0 (6/6)	CABARTON: Valley, ID	44.42	116.03	7 mi SW Cascade

Red-breasted Sapsucker
    Coniferous forest, aspen-pine woodland, humid coastal regions
26.3 (3/3)	MASSETT: BC	54.02	132.15	11 mi SE Masset
20.3 (4/4)	MITKOF ISLE: Wrangell-Petersburg, AK	56.62	132.72	16 mi SE Petersburg
5.7 (7/7)	VALERMO: Los Angeles, CA	34.38	117.68	1 mi SE Big Pines

Williamson's Sapsucker
    Montane coniferous forest, including fir and lodgepole pine
    7.0 (5/5)   ALBEE: Umatilla, OR   45.23   118.88   2 mi NE Albee
    5.7 (7/7)   SUMMIT PR: Crook, OR   44.35   120.47   22 mi SW Mitchell
    2.4 (6/7)   RIMROCK: Yakima, WA   46.55   121.37   14 mi SW Rimrock

Ladder-backed Woodpecker
    Desert; riparian, pinyon-juniper and pine-oak woodland
    11.7 (7/7)   BOERNE: Kendall, TX   29.88   98.65   8 mi NE Boerne
    7.8 (4/4)   VALLEY SPGS: Llano, TX   30.90   98.75   5 mi NE Valley Spring
    5.9 (6/7)   PENA BLANCA: Santa Cruz, AZ   31.38   111.08   9 mi NW Nogales

Nuttall's Woodpecker
    Oak woodland, chaparral, willow-cottonwood riparian woodland
    11.6 (7/7)   GOLD HILL: El Dorado, CA   38.75   120.93   3 mi NW Cold Springs
    11.1 (7/7)   LOCKWOOD: Monterey, CA   35.93   121.08   1 mi SW Lockwood
    10.4 (7/7)   PENNINGTON: Sutter, CA   39.27   121.73   4 mi SE Pennington

Downy Woodpecker
    Deciduous and mixed woodland, parks, orchards
    17.1 (7/7)   ATHENS: Henderson, TX   32.18   95.75   5 mi NW New York
    14.0 (5/5)   LAFITTE: Jefferson, LA   29.68   90.03   3 mi SW Naomi
    12.6 (7/7)   BARON: Cherokee, OK   35.82   94.87   4 mi SE Welling

Hairy Woodpecker
    Deciduous and coniferous forest, open areas with trees
    8.5 (6/6)   DELL SPRING: Klamath, OR   43.57   121.70   6 mi NE Gilchrist
    6.0 (6/6)   TOWN BLUFF: Jasper, TX   30.80   94.10   9 mi NE Spurger
    6.0 (7/7)   ST REGIS FLS: Franklin, NY   44.55   74.48   9 mi SE Saint Regis Falls

Strickland's Woodpecker
    Open oak and pine-oak woodland
    1.6 (7/7)   PENA BLANCA: Santa Cruz, AZ   31.38   111.08   9 mi NW Nogales
    1.3 (6/7)   PATAGONIA: Santa Cruz, AZ   31.52   110.80   3 mi SW Patagonia
    0.8 (2/4)   PORTAL: Cochise, AZ   31.98   109.20   3 mi NE Paradise

Red-cockaded Woodpecker
    Open mature pine woodland, especially with longleaf pine
    6.2 (6/6)   JAMESTOWN: Berkeley, SC   33.23   79.68   4 mi SE Jamestown
    3.4 (5/5)   BLOXHAM: Levy, FL   30.32   84.52   11 mi NW Arran
    2.0 (3/4)   APALACHICOLA: Liberty, FL   30.17   84.70   14 mi SE Telogia

White-headed Woodpecker
    Montane coniferous forest, especially with pine and fir
    9.9 (7/7)   VALERMO: Los Angeles, CA   34.38   117.68   1 mi SE Big Pines
    4.8 (6/6)   RIVERTON: El Dorado, CA   38.85   120.45   6 mi NE Riverton
    4.7 (7/7)   GREENHORN MT: Kern, CA   35.78   118.63   2 mi SE Balance Rock

Three-toed Woodpecker
    Coniferous forest, especially burned spruce forest
    0.9 (3/7)   BLUE: Greenlee, AZ   33.70   109.13   6 mi NW Blue
    0.8 (2/6)   RANCHERIA: YT   60.08   130.87   12 mi NE Swift River
    0.7 (3/7)   MARTEN RIVER: AB   55.52   114.88   9 mi NW Slave Lake

Annotated list of species, habitats and areas 285

Black-backed Woodpecker
    Coniferous forest, burns and windfalls, standing dead trees
4.5 (6/6)	HERON LAKE: Piscataquis, ME	46.40	69.28	19 mi SE Clayton Lake
3.6 (5/5)	ELK LAKE: Lane, OR	43.98	121.88	17 mi SE Belknap Springs
1.8 (3/4)	GANDER RIVER: NF	48.83	55.52	8 mi SE Grand Falls

Northern Flicker
    Widespread, woodland for nesting, open areas for foraging
32.3 (6/6)	MIDWAY: Holt, NE	42.65	98.70	13 mi NE Emmet
26.7 (6/6)	EAGLE CREEK: Holt, NE	42.77	98.60	5 mi SW Bristow
24.2 (5/5)	GRANITE: Grant, OR	44.92	118.40	15 mi NE Greenhorn

Northern Flicker (Yellow-shafted)
    Widespread, open country and sparse woodland
32.3 (6/6)	MIDWAY: Holt, NE	42.65	98.70	13 mi NE Emmet
26.7 (6/6)	EAGLE CREEK: Holt, NE	42.77	98.60	5 mi SW Bristow
15.9 (7/7)	DINORWIC: ON	49.60	92.48	9 mi SE Dinorwic

Northern Flicker (Red-shafted)
    Widespread, open country and sparse woodland, coniferous forest
24.2 (5/5)	GRANITE: Grant, OR	44.92	118.40	15 mi NE Greenhorn
19.3 (6/6)	WICKIUP: Grant, OR	44.15	118.62	12 mi NE Van
18.2 (6/6)	LOGDELL: Grant, OR	44.20	119.23	12 mi NE Izee

Northern Flicker (Gilded)
    Desert with saguaro and other large cacti
16.5 (2/2)	ORGAN PIPE: Pima, AZ	31.97	112.92	9 mi NW Lukeville
10.0 (3/3)	CASA GRANDE: Pinal, AZ	33.07	111.23	9 mi NE Cactus Forest
3.3 (6/6)	QUARTZSITE: La Paz, AZ	33.55	114.10	11 mi SE Quartzsite

Pileated Woodpecker
    Mature deciduous and coniferous forest
22.5 (6/6)	TOWN BLUFF: Jasper, TX	30.80	94.10	9 mi NE Spurger
20.1 (7/7)	YELLOW SPG: Hampshire, WV	39.18	78.48	2 mi NE Yellow Spring
16.1 (7/7)	W AUGUSTA: Highland, VA	38.25	79.47	3 mi SW Liberty

TYRANNIDAE – Tyrant Flycatchers

Northern Beardless-Tyrannulet
    Arid scrub, mesquite thickets, near water
0.4 (3/7)	PATAGONIA: Santa Cruz, AZ	31.52	110.80	3 mi SW Patagonia
0.3 (2/7)	PENA BLANCA: Santa Cruz, AZ	31.38	111.08	9 mi NW Nogales

Olive-sided Flycatcher
    Coniferous and mixed woodland, burned areas, taiga, bogs
20.7 (7/7)	HAT CREEK: Shasta, CA	40.80	121.58	4 mi NW Hat Creek
18.0 (7/7)	COOL CAMP: Linn, OR	44.48	122.20	15 mi NE Cascadia
16.3 (6/6)	POINT REYES: Marin, CA	38.03	122.88	5 mi SW Point Reyes Station

Greater Pewee
    Montane coniferous forest, especially with pine and pine-oak; forest edge
3.5 (4/4)	PORTAL: Cochise, AZ	31.98	109.20	3 mi NE Paradise

Western Wood-Pewee
   Coniferous and mixed forest, riparian woodland, forest edge
   58.9 (7/7)   SUMMIT PR: Crook, OR   44.35   120.47   22 mi SW Mitchell
   56.9 (7/7)   VALERMO: Los Angeles, CA   34.38   117.68   1 mi SE Big Pines
   47.3 (7/7)   ELLENSBURG: Yakima, WA   46.90   120.68   9 mi SW Ellensburg

Eastern Wood-Pewee
   Deciduous and mixed woodland, parks and open areas
   34.0 (6/6)   SOUTH MTN: Adams, PA   39.90   77.43   4 mi NE Mount Union
   23.1 (7/7)   JAMESVILLE: Martin, NC   35.75   76.97   6 mi SW Jamesville
   22.9 (7/7)   WESCO: Crawford, MO   37.90   91.45   6 mi NW Cook Station

Yellow-bellied Flycatcher
   Boreal coniferous forest, including spruce, fir, jack pine and tamarack
   23.3 (4/4)   GANDER RIVER: NF   48.83   55.52   8 mi SE Grand Falls
   16.0 (7/7)   SAWBILL LNDG: Lake, MN   47.68   91.50   8 mi NW Isabella
   14.9 (7/7)   PARC CARTIER: PQ   47.28   71.25   16 mi NE Saint-Adolphe

Acadian Flycatcher
   Mature river-bottom deciduous forest, thickets, wet second growth
   34.8 (4/4)   DRESDEN: Muskingum, OH   40.15   81.80   0 mi Maysville
   31.3 (4/4)   TENSAS NWR: Madison, LA   32.28   91.43   10 mi NE Crowville
   30.2 (6/6)   CEDARVILLE: Gilmer, WV   38.85   80.82   1 mi NW Cedarville

Alder Flycatcher
   Deciduous forest edge, damp alder thickets, brushy areas
   94.5 (4/4)   COTTONWOOD: Matanuska-Susitna, AK 61.52   149.62   8 mi NW Wasilla
   69.5 (4/4)   STAGG RIVER: NT   62.68   115.37   19 mi SE Rae-Edzo
   58.4 (7/7)   STEWIACKE: NS   45.30   63.43   1 mi SW Beaver Brook

Willow Flycatcher
   Swampy willow thickets, scrubby and brushy areas, grasslands
   43.1 (7/7)   FISH LAKE: Harney, OR   42.62   118.60   11 mi NE Andrews
   31.0 (4/4)   CARNATION: King, WA   47.65   121.92   0 mi Carnation
   30.1 (7/7)   MENDOTA: Lewis, WA   46.72   122.82   4 mi SW Tono

Least Flycatcher
   Deciduous woodland, scrub, edge and brushy areas
   84.0 (3/3)   CRANE RIVER: MB   51.47   99.15   4 mi SE Crane River
   43.6 (7/7)   LINDBROOK: AB   53.33   112.77   5 mi SE Lindbrook
   34.0 (7/7)   THUNDER LAKE: AB   54.08   114.75   6 mi SW Tiger Lilly

Hammond's Flycatcher
   Cool mature montane coniferous forest, especially with dense fir
   40.5 (6/6)   PAISLEY: Lake, OR   42.63   120.70   9 mi SW Paisley
   31.0 (7/7)   CREIGHTON V: BC   50.22   118.73   9 mi NE Lumby
   21.6 (7/7)   NEWHALEM: Whatcom, WA   48.75   121.22   4 mi NW Diablo

Dusky Flycatcher
   Open coniferous forest, aspen-willow thickets, near water
   34.2 (6/6)   DELL SPRING: Klamath, OR   43.57   121.70   6 mi NE Gilchrist
   31.3 (3/3)   ADAMS LAKE: BC   51.40   119.45   12 mi SE Vavenby
   21.1 (7/7)   SUMMIT PR: Crook, OR   44.35   120.47   22 mi SW Mitchell

Gray Flycatcher
   Open woodland, especially with pinyon-juniper; arid regions with sagebrush
   58.3 (3/3)   CLOVER CREEK: Crook, OR   43.83   120.20   11 mi NE Hampton
   27.2 (5/6)   WAGONTIRE: Harney, OR   43.33   119.52   15 mi SW Riley
   19.3 (7/7)   BLITZEN: Harney, OR   42.97   119.08   13 mi NW Frenchglen

Pacific-slope Flycatcher
   Coastal forest with redwood or pine, also pine-oak grassland and giant sequoia forest; near streams
   46.3 (7/7)   KAMILCHE: Mason, WA   47.12   123.13   2 mi SW Kamilche
   42.9 (7/7)   NAVARRO: Mendocino, CA   39.18   123.65   5 mi NE Elk
   38.5 (6/6)   POINT REYES: Marin, CA   38.03   122.88   5 mi SW Point Reyes Station

Cordilleran Flycatcher
   Montane pine forest, also aspen and cottonwood forest; riparian woodland, canyon bottoms
   25.8 (6/6)   PRESCOTT: Yavapai, AZ   34.67   112.38   6 mi NW Prescott Valley
   20.2 (5/5)   CLOUDCROFT: Otero, NM   32.88   105.67   7 mi SE Cloudcroft
   13.0 (6/6)   NAVAJO LAKE: Washington, UT   37.42   112.92   17 mi SE Kanarraville

Black Phoebe
   Near water, rocky canyon walls, coastal cliffs
   8.0 (7/7)   RED BLUFF: Tehama, CA   40.35   122.28   2 mi SW Cottonwood
   7.0 (7/7)   GOLD HILL: El Dorado, CA   38.75   120.93   3 mi NW Cold Springs
   6.9 (7/7)   RUMSEY: Colusa, CA   38.97   122.27   6 mi NW Rumsey

Eastern Phoebe
   Open woodland, farmlands, cliffs, structures with ledges, near water
   18.1 (7/7)   CASCADE: Wayne, MO   37.25   90.45   4 mi SW Coldwater
   17.0 (7/7)   HONESDALE: Wayne, PA   41.55   75.23   2 mi SW Bethel
   16.6 (5/5)   NICUT: Fayette, WV   38.02   81.05   2 mi NW Cunard

Say's Phoebe
   Arid regions; desert, cliffs and buildings
   13.3 (4/4)   TORREON: Sandoval, NM   35.77   107.13   20 mi SW Cuba
   12.2 (6/6)   BOULDER: Garfield, UT   37.93   111.18   23 mi SE Grover
   12.0 (3/3)   NOTOM: Garfield, UT   38.13   111.07   14 mi SW Caineville

Vermilion Flycatcher
   Arid regions; desert and riparian scrub, mesquite grasslands
   7.9 (7/7)   PATAGONIA: Santa Cruz, AZ   31.52   110.80   3 mi SW Patagonia
   4.4 (7/7)   POMERENE: Cochise, AZ   32.03   110.30   2 mi NW Pomerene
   4.3 (7/7)   PENA BLANCA: Santa Cruz, AZ   31.38   111.08   9 mi NW Nogales

Dusky-capped Flycatcher
   Oak woodland, riparian woodland, semi-arid scrub
   17.6 (7/7)   PENA BLANCA: Santa Cruz, AZ   31.38   111.08   9 mi NW Nogales
   7.1 (7/7)   PATAGONIA: Santa Cruz, AZ   31.52   110.80   3 mi SW Patagonia
   3.5 (4/4)   PORTAL: Cochise, AZ   31.98   109.20   3 mi NE Paradise

Ash-throated Flycatcher
   Desert and thorn scrub, pinyon-juniper, oak and riparian woodland
   57.2 (5/5)   TUJUNGA: Los Angeles, CA   34.28   118.10   7 mi NE Altadena
   48.9 (7/7)   POMERENE: Cochise, AZ   32.03   110.30   2 mi NW Pomerene
   45.5 (2/2)   ORGAN PIPE: Pima, AZ   31.97   112.92   9 mi NW Lukeville

Great Crested Flycatcher
Deciduous forest, open areas, parks and orchards

42.6 (7/7)	SHALLOTTE: Brunswick, NC	33.98	78.37	1 mi NE Shallotte
39.1 (7/7)	FT GADSDEN: Franklin, FL	29.98	84.90	5 mi SE Sumatra
32.4 (5/5)	ROMEO: Marion, FL	29.17	82.40	3 mi SE Romeo

Brown-crested Flycatcher
Arid or semi-arid regions; open and riparian woodland, areas with scattered trees or cacti

52.9 (7/7)	RANDADO: Jim Hogg, TX	27.05	98.78	6 mi SE Randado
49.4 (7/7)	RACHAL: Brooks, TX	26.80	98.08	7 mi SE Rachal
28.7 (3/3)	CASA GRANDE: Pinal, AZ	33.07	111.23	9 mi NE Cactus Forest

Great Kiskadee
Woodland, partly open areas with scattered trees, near water

2.6 (5/7)	LAG ATASCOSA: Cameron, TX	26.20	97.33	6 mi NE Bayview
2.0 (5/5)	KINGSVILLE: Kleberg, TX	27.53	97.93	5 mi NW Kingsville
1.0 (3/7)	RAYMONDVILLE: Willacy, TX	26.53	97.70	4 mi NW San Perlita

Sulphur-bellied Flycatcher
Open riparian woodland, especially canyons with sycamores

2.5 (3/4)	PORTAL: Cochise, AZ	31.98	109.20	3 mi NE Paradise
0.6 (3/7)	PATAGONIA: Santa Cruz, AZ	31.52	110.80	3 mi SW Patagonia

Couch's Kingbird
Scattered trees, open and riparian woodland, residential areas

8.0 (4/4)	GUERRA: Zapata, TX	26.95	99.03	6 mi SE Bustamante
2.0 (4/7)	RACHAL: Brooks, TX	26.80	98.08	7 mi SE Rachal
1.9 (4/7)	RAYMONDVILLE: Willacy, TX	26.53	97.70	4 mi NW San Perlita

Cassin's Kingbird
Dry grasslands, pinyon-juniper woodland, scrub, open areas

34.4 (7/7)	PATAGONIA: Santa Cruz, AZ	31.52	110.80	3 mi SW Patagonia
27.3 (6/7)	PENA BLANCA: Santa Cruz, AZ	31.38	111.08	9 mi NW Nogales
25.2 (6/6)	PRESCOTT: Yavapai, AZ	34.67	112.38	6 mi NW Prescott Valley

Thick-billed Kingbird
Arid regions; riparian woodland, open areas with trees

1.1 (4/7)	PENA BLANCA: Santa Cruz, AZ	31.38	111.08	9 mi NW Nogales
0.6 (3/7)	PATAGONIA: Santa Cruz, AZ	31.52	110.80	3 mi SW Patagonia

Western Kingbird
Open country, fields, grasslands, scattered trees, residential areas

111.8 (4/4)	HORSEHEAD LK: Kidder, ND	47.07	99.63	7 mi SW Pettibone
94.9 (7/7)	ALBERT: Barton, KS	38.45	98.97	2 mi SE Albert
88.0 (7/7)	ST JOHN: Stafford, KS	37.97	98.87	6 mi SW Saint John

Eastern Kingbird
Woodland edge, open areas with trees, fencerows, parks

70.3 (4/4)	HORSEHEAD LK: Kidder, ND	47.07	99.63	7 mi SW Pettibone
58.1 (7/7)	LORAINE: Renville, ND	48.87	101.55	1 mi SE Loraine
53.6 (7/7)	SHEYENNE LK: Wells, ND	47.63	100.03	10 mi NE Goodrich

Annotated list of species, habitats and areas   289

Gray Kingbird
    Coastal woodland, mangrove swamps
        20.4 (5/5)   KEY LARGO: Monroe, FL   25.20 80.35   8 mi NE Newport
        12.4 (7/7)   PLANTATION K: Monroe, FL   24.97 80.58   4 mi NE Islamorada
        2.2 (4/5)   ALLIGATOR PT: Wakulla, FL   30.00 84.52   5 mi SW Sopchoppy

Scissor-tailed Flycatcher
    Open country, dry grasslands, fields
        112.6 (7/7)   COTTONWOOD: Callahan, TX   32.22 99.27   9 mi NW Cross Plains
        99.9 (7/7)   RACHAL: Brooks, TX   26.80 98.08   7 mi SE Rachal
        52.7 (7/7)   ALBANY: Shackelford, TX   32.82 99.12   10 mi SE Fort Griffin

ALAUDIDAE – Larks
Horned Lark
    Grassland, stubble and cultivated fields, tundra
        534.9 (7/7)   PINNEO: Washington, CO   40.18 103.42   11 mi NW Akron
        467.6 (5/5)   CIRCLE: McCone, MT   47.60 105.73   19 mi NW Circle
        419.7 (6/6)   VIRGELLE: Chouteau, MT   48.05 110.35   11 mi NE Loma

HIRUNDINIDAE – Swallows
Purple Martin
    Widespread, open and partly open areas, near water
        188.3 (3/3)   CARLISLE: Plaquemines, LA   29.68 89.88   4 mi NE Bellevue
        77.4 (5/5)   LAFITTE: Jefferson, LA   29.68 90.03   3 mi SW Naomi
        72.7 (7/7)   CHANDLER: Henderson, TX   32.22 95.52   5 mi SE New Hope

Tree Swallow
    Open areas, streams, lakes, marshes and other bodies of water, trees
        99.9 (7/7)   OMRO: Winnebago, WI   44.05 88.68   3 mi NE Omro
        72.3 (7/7)   PHILLIPS: Price, WI   45.63 90.20   7 mi NE Prentice
        50.8 (6/6)   PRINCE GEORG: BC   53.93 122.80   14 mi NE Prince George

Violet-green Swallow
    Open woodland and forest, highlands, cliffs, trees
        145.0 (7/7)   VALERMO: Los Angeles, CA   34.38 117.68   1 mi SE Big Pines
        61.4 (7/7)   CAMAS: Clark, WA   45.70 122.42   4 mi SE Hockinson
        60.9 (7/7)   WARM BEACH: Snohomish, WA 48.13 122.33   6 mi SW Silvana

Northern Rough-winged Swallow
    Open areas, watercourses with steep banks, roadside cuts
        72.0 (4/5)   CORTEZ: Montezuma, CO   37.42 108.52   4 mi SW Dolores
        52.7 (7/7)   MELROSE: Adams, IL   39.90 91.28   2 mi SW Burton
        36.8 (5/5)   NAPLES: Boundary, ID   48.55 116.42   2 mi SW Naples

Bank Swallow
    Open areas, sand, dirt or gravel banks near flowing water
        406.8 (6/6)   PORT DOVER: ON   42.65 80.33   1 mi SW Normandale
        131.4 (7/7)   DERWENT: AB   53.50 110.80   6 mi SW Clandonald
        108.6 (7/7)   VERCHERES: PQ   45.72 73.40   4 mi SW Vercheres

Cliff Swallow
    Open areas, cliffs, bridges, caves, dams and buildings, near water

977.4 (7/7)	DORRIS: Siskiyou, CA		41.98	121.90	1 mi NE Dorris
709.4 (7/7)	HUGHSON: Stanislaus, CA		37.58	120.83	2 mi SE Hughson
673.7 (7/7)	BREWSTER: Okanogan, WA		48.08	119.73	3 mi SE Brewster

Cave Swallow
    Open areas, caves, sinkholes and culverts, near water

217.0 (4/4)	GUERRA: Zapata, TX		26.95	99.03	6 mi SE Bustamante
163.3 (3/3)	CAMPBELLTON: Atascosa, TX		28.65	98.40	8 mi NW Whitsett
106.1 (7/7)	RANDADO: Jim Hogg, TX		27.05	98.78	6 mi SE Randado

Barn Swallow
    Open areas, buildings, bridges and caves, near water

121.3 (7/7)	HONESDALE: Wayne, PA		41.55	75.23	2 mi SW Bethel
118.6 (7/7)	OMRO: Winnebago, WI		44.05	88.68	3 mi NE Omro
104.3 (7/7)	WOODFORD: ON		44.60	80.73	0 mi Woodford

CORVIDAE – Jays, Magpies, Crows, Ravens

Gray Jay
    Boreal coniferous and mixed forest, especially with spruce; open areas and bogs

29.7 (3/3)	FREEMAN LAKE: AB		54.75	115.52	5 mi NW Swan Hills
22.3 (3/3)	NORTHWAY: SE Fairbanks, AK		62.92	141.53	15 mi SE Northway
18.0 (3/3)	SOURDOUGH: Valdez-Cordova, AK		62.38	145.35	5 mi NE Gakona

Steller's Jay
    Coniferous and mixed forest, pine-oak woodland

64.0 (7/7)	VALERMO: Los Angeles, CA		34.38	117.68	1 mi SE Big Pines
40.3 (7/7)	WATERMAN GAP: Santa Cruz, CA		37.20	122.15	3 mi NE Wildwood
39.4 (7/7)	FISH ROCK: Mendocino, CA		38.80	123.62	2 mi NW Anchor Bay

Blue Jay
    Forest, open woodland, parks and residential areas

73.7 (3/3)	JUNIOR: Plaquemines, LA		29.48	89.70	0 mi Port Sulphur
61.7 (7/7)	SAXEVILLE: Waushara, WI		44.20	89.03	9 mi SW Fremont
59.3 (7/7)	FOWLSTOWN: Decatur, GA		30.82	84.53	6 mi NW Attapulgus

Green Jay
    Humid woodland, riparian thickets, dense second growth

2.8 (4/5)	KINGSVILLE: Kleberg, TX		27.53	97.93	5 mi NW Kingsville
1.8 (3/4)	GUERRA: Zapata, TX		26.95	99.03	6 mi SE Bustamante
1.6 (5/7)	RACHAL: Brooks, TX		26.80	98.08	7 mi SE Rachal

Scrub Jay
    Scrub, oak, pinyon and juniper woodland, brush and chaparral

69.0 (7/7)	COALINGA: Fresno, CA		36.15	120.55	11 mi NW Coalinga
62.0 (4/4)	ADELAIDA: San Luis Obispo, CA		35.60	120.83	8 mi NW Templeton
58.2 (6/6)	JACUMBA: San Diego, CA		32.62	116.22	2 mi NW Jacumba

Scrub Jay (Florida)
    Scrub thickets, open scrub oak woodland, myrtle and saw palmetto scrub

8.3 (7/7)	CHILDS: Highlands, FL		27.27	81.48	7 mi SW Lake Placid
6.0 (5/5)	PALMDALE: Glades, FL		26.95	81.48	10 mi SW Palmdale
5.2 (5/5)	ARBUCKLE: Polk, FL		27.75	81.48	3 mi NE Frostproof

Gray-breasted Jay
Oak, pine-oak and juniper woodland
62.3 (7/7)	PENA BLANCA: Santa Cruz, AZ	31.38	111.08	9 mi NW Nogales
32.8 (4/4)	PORTAL: Cochise, AZ	31.98	109.20	3 mi NE Paradise
31.3 (7/7)	PATAGONIA: Santa Cruz, AZ	31.52	110.80	3 mi SW Patagonia

Pinyon Jay
Pinyon-juniper woodland
52.0 (5/5)	HORSE SPGS: Catron, NM	33.90	108.12	6 mi SE Old Horse Springs
42.4 (5/5)	BERYL: Iron, UT	37.88	113.78	7 mi NW Beryl
40.4 (5/5)	HORSE MTN: Socorro, NM	33.75	107.42	25 mi NE Monticello

Clark's Nutcracker
Montane coniferous forest, open areas, forest edge
17.6 (7/7)	VALERMO: Los Angeles, CA	34.38	117.68	1 mi SE Big Pines
16.7 (7/7)	HORSE CREEK: Fremont, WY	43.65	109.65	8 mi NE Dubois
13.8 (6/6)	DUBOIS: Fremont, WY	43.35	109.55	13 mi SE Dubois

Black-billed Magpie
Open country, grasslands, scattered trees, riparian woodland, fields
91.5 (4/4)	PRESTON: Franklin, ID	42.13	111.92	3 mi NW Preston
82.7 (3/3)	OKOTOKS: AB	50.55	114.08	12 mi SW Okotoks
69.9 (7/7)	WAPATO: Yakima, WA	46.38	120.47	4 mi SE Harrah

Yellow-billed Magpie
Oak woodland with fields, grassland, open riparian woodland
72.6 (5/5)	WESTLEY: Stanislaus, CA	37.48	121.25	6 mi SW Westley
43.6 (7/7)	HUGHSON: Stanislaus, CA	37.58	120.83	2 mi SE Hughson
40.4 (7/7)	ORLAND: Glenn, CA	39.77	122.25	3 mi NW Orland

American Crow
Forest and woodland for roosting and nesting; open country, residential areas
181.3 (7/7)	HUGHSON: Stanislaus, CA	37.58	120.83	2 mi SE Hughson
158.4 (5/5)	WESTLEY: Stanislaus, CA	37.48	121.25	6 mi SW Westley
153.0 (7/7)	ORLAND: Glenn, CA	39.77	122.25	3 mi NW Orland

Northwestern Crow
Coniferous forest near tidelands; fields, residential areas
159.6 (5/5)	POINT GREY: BC	49.23	123.23	4 mi NW Vancouver
113.5 (4/4)	VICTORIA: BC	48.42	123.37	2 mi SE Victoria
106.4 (7/7)	ALBION: BC	49.18	122.52	1 mi SE Albion

Fish Crow
Beaches, bays, lagoons and swamps, woodlands near major watercourses
106.2 (5/5)	SCOTTSMOOR: Brevard, FL	28.73	80.87	3 mi SE Scottsmoor
61.8 (5/5)	LAKE BUFFUM: Polk, FL	27.75	81.70	6 mi NE Fort Meade
56.2 (6/6)	DAUPHIN IS: Mobile, AL	30.25	88.10	1 mi SE Dauphin Island

Chihuahuan Raven
Arid and semi-arid regions; Yucca-mesquite grassland
53.0 (5/5)	SAN SIMON: Lea, NM	32.47	103.27	2 mi SW Oil Center
36.3 (7/7)	GAGE: Luna, NM	32.35	108.17	10 mi NW Gage
35.6 (5/5)	CAPROCK: Lea, NM	33.38	103.58	8 mi SE Caprock

Common Raven
- Coniferous forest; cliffs in mountainous regions

79.0 (6/6)	JACUMBA: San Diego, CA	32.62	116.22	2 mi NW Jacumba
73.1 (7/7)	STEWIACKE: NS	45.30	63.43	1 mi SW Beaver Brook
42.4 (7/7)	SITKA: Sitka, AK	57.07	135.37	1 mi NW Mount Edgecombe

PARIDAE – Chickadees, Titmice

Black-capped Chickadee
- Deciduous and mixed woodland, parks, residential areas

53.0 (3/3)	CAPE COD NS: Barnstable, MA	41.95	70.00	2 mi NE Wellfleet
51.2 (6/6)	PLEASANT VAL: Antrim, MI	45.05	85.17	1 mi SW Pleasant Valley
47.3 (6/6)	WELLFLEET: Barnstable, MA	41.97	70.05	2 mi SE Truro

Carolina Chickadee
- Deciduous woodland, clearings and edge, swamps and thickets, residential areas

56.8 (5/5)	LAFITTE: Jefferson, LA	29.68	90.03	3 mi SW Naomi
47.3 (7/7)	CALEDONIA: Rusk, TX	31.88	94.52	3 mi SE Caledonia
44.7 (7/7)	NOBLE: Cleveland, OK	35.18	97.43	3 mi SE Norman

Mexican Chickadee
- Montane pine woodland, spruce-fir forest

1.3 (2/4)	PORTAL: Cochise, AZ	31.98	109.20	3 mi NE Paradise

Mountain Chickadee
- Montane coniferous forest, especially with pine and spruce-fir

105.1 (7/7)	VALERMO: Los Angeles, CA	34.38	117.68	1 mi SE Big Pines
65.6 (5/5)	LASSEN PARK: Shasta, CA	40.50	121.33	5 mi NE Drakesbad
58.6 (7/7)	HAT CREEK: Shasta, CA	40.80	121.58	4 mi NW Hat Creek

Boreal Chickadee
- Boreal forest, spruce bogs

6.0 (3/3)	CIRCLE: Yukon-Koyukuk, AK	65.72	144.33	11 mi SW Circle
4.9 (6/7)	SWAN LAKE RD: Kenai Peninsula, AK	60.62	150.78	19 mi SE Kenai
4.3 (6/6)	KENNY LAKE: Valdez-Cordova, AK	61.72	144.93	11 mi NW Lower Tonsina

Chestnut-backed Chickadee
- Humid coniferous and mixed forest

52.3 (6/6)	POINT REYES: Marin, CA	38.03	122.88	5 mi SW Point Reyes Station
31.9 (7/7)	NANAIMO RIV: BC	49.18	124.17	9 mi NW Nanaimo
31.7 (7/7)	WATERMAN GAP: Santa Cruz, CA	37.20	122.15	3 mi NE Wildwood

Bridled Titmouse
- Pine-oak and oak woodland

9.3 (7/7)	PENA BLANCA: Santa Cruz, AZ	31.38	111.08	9 mi NW Nogales
6.0 (6/6)	PRESCOTT: Yavapai, AZ	34.67	112.38	6 mi NW Prescott Valley
4.1 (6/7)	PATAGONIA: Santa Cruz, AZ	31.52	110.80	3 mi SW Patagonia

Plain Titmouse
- Pinyon-juniper and oak woodland

48.3 (7/7)	LOCKWOOD: Monterey, CA	35.93	121.08	1 mi SW Lockwood
47.0 (6/6)	MESA GRANDE: San Diego, CA	33.20	116.82	3 mi NW Mesa Grande
45.3 (7/7)	GOLD HILL: El Dorado, CA	38.75	120.93	3 mi NW Cold Springs

Tufted Titmouse
   Variety of deciduous forests and woodlands, scrub, parks and residential areas
   66.6 (7/7)   NOBLE: Cleveland, OK   35.18   97.43   3 mi SE Norman
   47.0 (7/7)   ATHENS: Henderson, TX   32.18   95.75   5 mi NW New York
   39.7 (7/7)   PLETTENBERG: West Feliciana, LA   30.78   91.52   5 mi NE Labarre

Tufted Titmouse (Black-crested)
   Deciduous woodland, old lagoon beds, mesquite scrub
   37.1 (7/7)   BOERNE: Kendall, TX   29.88   98.65   8 mi NE Boerne
   35.7 (5/6)   DRIPPING SPG: Hays, TX   30.20   98.08   1 mi NE Dripping Springs
   24.6 (7/7)   INDIAN MTN: Edwards, TX   29.65   100.42   18 mi SE Carta Valley

REMIZIDAE – Verdins
Verdin
   Arid regions; desert, mesquite and creosotebush shrubland
   47.3 (3/3)   CASA GRANDE: Pinal, AZ   33.07   111.23   9 mi NE Cactus Forest
   24.6 (7/7)   POMERENE: Cochise, AZ   32.03   110.30   2 mi NW Pomerene
   21.3 (7/7)   IMPERIAL DAM: Imperial, CA   32.83   114.50   4 mi NE Bard

AEGITHALIDAE – Bushtits
Bushtit
   Oak scrub, pinyon-juniper and pine-oak woodland, chaparral
   37.9 (7/7)   HIGGINS CORN: Nevada, CA   39.05   121.02   3 mi NW Weimar
   33.7 (6/6)   CP PENDLETON: San Diego, CA   33.23   117.40   3 mi NW Oceanside
   29.1 (7/7)   FOSTER PARK: Ventura, CA   34.35   119.25   4 mi SE Oak View

SITTIDAE – Nuthatches
Red-breasted Nuthatch
   Coniferous and mixed forest, especially with spruce, fir, or aspen
   46.4 (5/5)   LASSEN PARK: Shasta, CA   40.50   121.33   5 mi NE Drakesbad
   33.8 (5/5)   ELK LAKE: Lane, OR   43.98   121.88   17 mi SE Belknap Springs
   32.8 (6/6)   RIVERTON: El Dorado, CA   38.85   120.45   6 mi NE Riverton

White-breasted Nuthatch
   Deciduous and mixed forest with openings
   31.0 (7/7)   LOCKWOOD: Monterey, CA   35.93   121.08   1 mi SW Lockwood
   19.4 (7/7)   GOLD HILL: El Dorado, CA   38.75   120.93   3 mi NW Cold Springs
   19.3 (7/7)   TEHAMA: Tehama, CA   40.23   121.95   8 mi SW Paynes Creek

Pygmy Nuthatch
   Ponderosa pine forest and pinyon-juniper woodland
   75.4 (7/7)   VALERMO: Los Angeles, CA   34.38   117.68   1 mi SE Big Pines
   34.6 (5/5)   HAPPY JACK: Coconino, AZ   34.73   111.45   3 mi SW Happy Jack
   22.8 (6/6)   PRESCOTT: Yavapai, AZ   34.67   112.38   6 mi NW Prescott Valley

Brown-headed Nuthatch
   Open pine forest and pine-oak woodland
   17.6 (7/7)   SHALLOTTE: Brunswick, NC   33.98   78.37   1 mi NE Shallotte
   11.7 (7/7)   JULIETTE: Monroe, GA   33.10   83.82   1 mi SW Juliette
   10.5 (6/6)   JAMESTOWN: Berkeley, SC   33.23   79.68   4 mi SE Jamestown

CERTHIIDAE – Creepers

Brown Creeper
    Coniferous and deciduous forest, montane regions
17.0 (5/5)	LASSEN PARK: Shasta, CA	40.50	121.33	5 mi NE Drakesbad
15.0 (6/6)	POINT REYES: Marin, CA	38.03	122.88	5 mi SW Point Reyes Station
12.0 (7/7)	WATERMAN GAP: Santa Cruz, CA	37.20	122.15	3 mi NE Wildwood

TROGLODYTIDAE – Wrens

Cactus Wren
    Cholla or yucca desert, mesquite scrub, residential areas
44.7 (3/3)	CASA GRANDE: Pinal, AZ	33.07	111.23	9 mi NE Cactus Forest
41.5 (2/2)	ORGAN PIPE: Pima, AZ	31.97	112.92	9 mi NW Lukeville
40.3 (4/4)	GUERRA: Zapata, TX	26.95	99.03	6 mi SE Bustamante

Rock Wren
    Arid and semi-arid regions with exposed rocks, canyons or cliffs
41.8 (6/6)	BLIZZARD GAP: Lake, OR	42.02	119.50	23 mi SE Adel
29.0 (7/7)	BUCHANAN: Harney, OR	43.68	118.68	4 mi NW Buchanan
21.0 (5/5)	ROCK SPRINGS: Sweetwater, WY	41.57	109.22	2 mi SW Rock Springs

Canyon Wren
    Arid regions with cliffs and steep canyons, rocks and boulders
5.0 (6/6)	BOULDER: Garfield, UT	37.93	111.18	23 mi SE Grover
3.4 (7/7)	INDIAN MTN: Edwards, TX	29.65	100.42	18 mi SE Carta Valley
3.0 (6/7)	PENA BLANCA: Santa Cruz, AZ	31.38	111.08	9 mi NW Nogales

Carolina Wren
    Open deciduous woodland, undergrowth and thickets, parks and residential areas
117.3 (3/3)	ATCHAFALAYA: St. Landry, LA	30.48	91.75	4 mi SE Krotz Springs
77.6 (5/5)	LAFITTE: Jefferson, LA	29.68	90.03	3 mi SW Naomi
71.1 (7/7)	SHALLOTTE: Brunswick, NC	33.98	78.37	1 mi NE Shallotte

Bewick's Wren
    Open country, thickets and scrub; riparian, pine-oak and pinyon-juniper woodland
62.1 (7/7)	PENA BLANCA: Santa Cruz, AZ	31.38	111.08	9 mi NW Nogales
58.3 (7/7)	PATAGONIA: Santa Cruz, AZ	31.52	110.80	3 mi SW Patagonia
49.9 (7/7)	INDIAN MTN: Edwards, TX	29.65	100.42	18 mi SE Carta Valley

House Wren
    Open woodland, farmland, brushy areas, residential areas
71.7 (7/7)	CLOUSTON: SK	53.08	105.83	9 mi SW Prince Albert
52.1 (7/7)	DERWENT: AB	53.50	110.80	6 mi SW Clandonald
50.6 (7/7)	GRAY: Hodgeman, KS	38.17	99.58	3 mi SW Burdett

Winter Wren
    Coniferous forest with spruce or fir and dense understory, near water, bogs
66.0 (5/5)	LAURENTIDES: PQ	47.78	71.28	14 mi SE Mont-Apica
58.4 (7/7)	CRAIG: Pr. Wales-Out. Ketch., AK	55.52	133.17	3 mi NE Craig
43.0 (7/7)	PORT RENFREW: BC	48.43	124.03	5 mi SE Jordan River

Sedge Wren
   Wet, boggy grasslands, marshes with sedges
32.9 (7/7)	BACKUS: Cass, MN	46.80	94.50	2 mi SE Backus
24.9 (7/7)	UNITY: Clark, WI	44.80	90.38	5 mi SW Unity
22.8 (6/6)	GILMAN: Taylor, WI	45.15	90.78	2 mi SE Gilman

Marsh Wren
   Freshwater and brackish marshes with cattails, tules and reeds
37.0 (4/4)	BRADDOCK: Emmons, ND	46.58	100.10	0 mi Braddock
33.6 (7/7)	DORRIS: Siskiyou, CA	41.98	121.90	1 mi NE Dorris
28.0 (7/7)	FISH LAKE: Harney, OR	42.62	118.60	11 mi NE Andrews

CINCLIDAE – Dippers
American Dipper
   Swiftly flowing mountain streams
4.6 (5/5)	ORLEANS: Humboldt, CA	41.22	123.47	7 mi SE Orleans
3.3 (7/7)	ST REGIS: Mineral, MT	47.37	115.15	5 mi NW Saint Regis
2.1 (7/7)	AVERY: Shoshone, ID	47.03	115.78	15 mi SW Avery

MUSCICAPIDAE – Old World Warblers, Kinglets, Gnatcatchers, Thrushes
Arctic Warbler
   Medium height willow thickets
65.7 (3/3)	MACLAREN: SE Fairbanks, AK	63.07	146.07	54 mi NW Gakona
21.3 (3/3)	MONAHAN: Matanuska-Susitna, AK	63.22	147.97	37 mi SE Cantwell
7.0 (3/4)	TOKLAT: Yukon-Koyukuk, AK	63.47	150.07	41 mi NW Cantwell

Golden-crowned Kinglet
   Coniferous forest, especially with spruce-fir
39.5 (4/4)	TAHOLAH: Grays Harbor, WA	47.45	124.27	7 mi SE Queets
20.8 (6/6)	RIVERTON: El Dorado, CA	38.85	120.45	6 mi NE Riverton
17.9 (7/7)	CRESCENT CTY: Del Norte, CA	41.75	124.18	1 mi SE Crescent City

Ruby-crowned Kinglet
   Coniferous and mixed forest, montane parks, muskeg
68.0 (3/3)	RED CLIFF: Eagle, CO	39.52	106.37	1 mi NW Redcliff
46.7 (7/7)	ROMAN VALLEY: NS	45.38	61.82	2 mi SE Giant Lake
43.1 (7/7)	P GR JARDINS: PQ	47.60	70.98	21 mi NW Saint-Urbain

Blue-gray Gnatcatcher
   Deciduous woodland, open areas and second growth, chaparral, pinyon and oak-juniper woodland
34.7 (7/7)	BLANCO: Pittsburg, OK	34.75	95.77	0 mi Blanco
32.1 (7/7)	BARON: Cherokee, OK	35.82	94.87	4 mi SE Welling
30.0 (7/7)	CASCADE: Wayne, MO	37.25	90.45	4 mi SW Coldwater

California Gnatcatcher
   Coastal sagebrush regions
1.7 (5/6)	CP PENDLETON: San Diego, CA	33.23	117.40	3 mi NW Oceanside

Black-tailed Gnatcatcher
   Desert scrub with mesquite and creosotebush
30.5 (2/2)	ORGAN PIPE: Pima, AZ	31.97	112.92	9 mi NW Lukeville
14.0 (3/3)	BLACK GAP: Brewster, TX	29.58	102.98	22 mi NE Panther Junction
6.1 (7/7)	CARR MTN: Gila, AZ	33.80	110.88	17 mi NE Roosevelt

Eastern Bluebird
   Forest edge, open woodland with scattered trees
35.1 (7/7)	MERRIMAC: Taylor, KY	37.43	85.13	1 mi NW Merrimac
35.0 (7/7)	LINWOOD: Walker, GA	34.67	85.35	4 mi NW Walnut Grove
30.7 (7/7)	CENTERTOWN: Moniteau, MO	38.57	92.45	3 mi SE McGirk

Western Bluebird
   Open coniferous, deciduous and mixed forest
28.9 (7/7)	VALERMO: Los Angeles, CA	34.38	117.68	1 mi SE Big Pines
25.8 (4/4)	ADELAIDA: San Luis Obispo, CA	35.60	120.83	8 mi NW Templeton
25.3 (7/7)	COALINGA: Fresno, CA	36.15	120.55	11 mi NW Coalinga

Mountain Bluebird
   Coniferous forest with open areas, sub-alpine meadows
50.3 (7/7)	BICKLETON: Klickitat, WA	45.97	120.25	3 mi SE Bickleton
34.0 (6/6)	SKYLINE DRIV: Sanpete, UT	39.70	111.33	5 mi SE Milburn
31.6 (7/7)	INGALLS: Modoc, CA	41.62	120.73	13 mi NW Alturas

Townsend's Solitaire
   Montane and sub-alpine coniferous forest, cliffs, thickets
16.1 (7/7)	SUMMERLAND: BC	49.60	119.72	2 mi NW Summerland
10.3 (7/7)	VALERMO: Los Angeles, CA	34.38	117.68	1 mi SE Big Pines
7.9 (7/7)	BARTLE: Siskiyou, CA	41.25	121.83	1 mi SW Bartle

Veery
   Moist areas with shrubby understory, poplar and aspen woodland, tamarack bogs, near water
59.5 (6/6)	WHITNEY: ON	45.35	78.17	7 mi NW Lake St. Peter
57.1 (7/7)	BARRY BAY: ON	45.52	77.78	6 mi NW Barry's Bay
57.0 (6/6)	CLOVERDALE: NB	46.35	67.53	1 mi SE Peel

Gray-cheeked Thrush
   Mature coniferous forest, especially with dwarf birch; tall shrubby areas in taiga
56.3 (3/3)	SOURDOUGH: Valdez-Cordova, AK	62.38	145.35	5 mi NE Gakona
43.7 (3/3)	MONAHAN: Matanuska-Susitna, AK	63.22	147.97	37 mi SE Cantwell
20.7 (7/7)	CHINIAK: Kodiak Island, AK	57.53	152.43	17 mi SW Kodiak

Gray-cheeked Thrush (Bicknell's)
   Krummholz, coniferous forest, deciduous and mixed second-growth forest
0.6 (4/7)	PARC CARTIER: PQ	47.28	71.25	16 mi NE Saint-Adolphe
0.6 (3/5)	SOUTH ARM: Oxford, ME	44.73	70.85	2 mi SE South Arm

Swainson's Thrush
   Coniferous forest, moist dense thickets
103.1 (7/7)	KENDALL: Whatcom, WA	48.97	122.15	4 mi NE Kendall
84.5 (6/6)	KENNY LAKE: Valdez-Cordova, AK	61.72	144.93	11 mi NW Lower Tonsina
80.3 (7/7)	ST URBAIN: PQ	47.65	70.62	8 mi NW Saint-Urbain

Hermit Thrush
   Open moist coniferous and mixed forest
68.9 (7/7)	CHINIAK: Kodiak Island, AK	57.53	152.43	17 mi SW Kodiak
57.7 (7/7)	GABRIELS: Franklin, NY	44.45	74.18	4 mi NE Paul Smiths
54.0 (6/6)	KODIAK: Kodiak Island, AK	57.62	152.55	12 mi SW Kodiak

Wood Thrush
Mature deciduous forest and woodland, moist areas or near water
49.7 (7/7)	ISOM: Dickenson, VA	37.23	82.50	6 mi NW Georges Fork
46.0 (6/6)	CEDARVILLE: Gilmer, WV	38.85	80.82	1 mi NW Cedarville
45.5 (6/6)	WASHBURN: Ritchie, WV	39.08	81.03	2 mi SW Hazelgreen

American Robin
Variety of open woodland, parks, gardens, and residential areas
205.0 (6/6)	WICKIUP: Grant, OR	44.15	118.62	12 mi NE Van
190.6 (7/7)	ORLEANS: Ontario, NY	42.90	77.12	2 mi NW Seneca Castle
178.0 (7/7)	STEWIACKE: NS	45.30	63.43	1 mi SW Beaver Brook

Varied Thrush
Mature humid montane coniferous forest with understory
50.0 (4/4)	MITKOF ISLE: Wrangell-Petersburg, AK	56.62	132.72	16 mi SE Petersburg
49.6 (7/7)	PORT RENFREW: BC	48.43	124.03	5 mi SE Jordan River
43.7 (7/7)	GLACIER: Whatcom, WA	48.85	121.88	4 mi SE Glacier

Wrentit
Chaparral and brushy areas
66.4 (5/5)	LAKE CACHUMA: Santa Barbara, CA	34.68	119.65	15 mi SW Ventucopa
64.0 (5/5)	TUJUNGA: Los Angeles, CA	34.28	118.10	7 mi NE Altadena
38.4 (7/7)	FISH ROCK: Mendocino, CA	38.80	123.62	2 mi NW Anchor Bay

MIMIDAE – Mockingbirds, Thrashers

Gray Catbird
Thickets, dense shrubs, undergrowth of woodland edge
79.0 (5/5)	BLOCK ISLAND: Washington, RI	41.15	71.57	2 mi SW New Shoreham
56.4 (7/7)	HOMETOWN: Schuylkill, PA	40.82	75.97	1 mi SE Hometown
53.6 (7/7)	BACHMAN MILL: Carroll, MD	39.73	76.97	3 mi NE Deep Run

Northern Mockingbird
Thickets and edge, fields, gardens, and residential areas
224.4 (7/7)	GRAFORD: Palo Pinto, TX	32.98	98.35	7 mi NW Graford
163.2 (5/5)	ENCINAL: Webb, TX	27.97	99.27	7 mi SE Encinal
147.4 (5/5)	GRAYBACK: Wilbarger, TX	33.92	99.22	6 mi SW Grayback

Sage Thrasher
Sagebrush regions
158.2 (5/5)	FANDANGO CAN: Lake, OR	43.15	120.63	6 mi SW Christmas Valley
101.3 (4/4)	LOOKOUT LAKE: Malheur, OR	42.20	117.18	31 mi NE McDermitt
99.7 (6/6)	BLIZZARD GAP: Lake, OR	42.02	119.50	23 mi SE Adel

Brown Thrasher
Deciduous woodlands, clearings and edge, gardens and thickets
30.8 (6/6)	JEWELL: Jewell, KS	39.67	98.10	3 mi SE Jewell
29.8 (6/6)	PHILLIPSBURG: Phillips, KS	39.72	99.22	5 mi NE Glade
29.6 (5/5)	FRIENDSHIP: Burlington, NJ	39.75	74.47	4 mi NE Speedwell

Long-billed Thrasher
Willow and mesquite brush and shrubs, especially bottomlands with stagnant water
2.3 (3/3)	CAMPBELLTON: Atascosa, TX	28.65	98.40	8 mi NW Whitsett
1.4 (3/7)	RANDADO: Jim Hogg, TX	27.05	98.78	6 mi SE Randado
0.7 (4/7)	RACHAL: Brooks, TX	26.80	98.08	7 mi SE Rachal

Bendire's Thrasher
    Cholla, creosotebush and yucca desert; arid and sparsely vegetated regions
7.6 (6/7)	CERRO VERDE: Valencia, NM	34.87	107.25	9 mi SE El Rito
4.2 (5/5)	NAGEESI: San Juan, NM	36.15	107.78	8 mi SW Nageezi
2.8 (6/6)	QUARTZSITE: La Paz, AZ	33.55	114.10	11 mi SE Quartzsite

Curve-billed Thrasher
    Semi-desert and desert with mesquite and cholla; thorn scrub, residential areas
39.0 (2/2)	ORGAN PIPE: Pima, AZ	31.97	112.92	9 mi NW Lukeville
21.3 (3/3)	CASA GRANDE: Pinal, AZ	33.07	111.23	9 mi NE Cactus Forest
9.3 (7/7)	ALBANY: Shackelford, TX	32.82	99.12	10 mi SE Fort Griffin

California Thrasher
    Lowland and coastal chaparral, riparian thickets
19.6 (5/5)	TUJUNGA: Los Angeles, CA	34.28	118.10	7 mi NE Altadena
19.5 (6/6)	JACUMBA: San Diego, CA	32.62	116.22	2 mi NW Jacumba
17.5 (6/6)	MESA GRANDE: San Diego, CA	33.20	116.82	3 mi NW Mesa Grande

Crissal Thrasher
    Mesquite desert scrub, riparian brush
1.8 (5/5)	JORNADA: Dona Ana, NM	32.38	106.72	5 mi SE Dona Ana
1.4 (6/7)	PENA BLANCA: Santa Cruz, AZ	31.38	111.08	9 mi NW Nogales
0.9 (5/7)	TECOPA: Inyo, CA	35.80	116.20	4 mi SE Tecopa

Le Conte's Thrasher
    Desert scrub, creosotebush flatland
14.3 (4/4)	BARSTOW: San Bernardino, CA	34.57	117.03	9 mi NW Lucerne Valley
11.5 (6/6)	GOLDSTONE: San Bernardino, CA	35.32	116.93	26 mi NE Calico
2.9 (6/7)	GREENWATER V: Inyo, CA	36.05	116.50	14 mi NW Shoshone

MOTACILLIDAE – Pipits
American Pipit
    Tundra, alpine meadows, rocky slopes
23.2 (6/6)	COLD BAY: Aleutian Islands, AK	55.00	162.00	62 mi NW Squaw Harbor
2.0 (2/4)	TOKLAT: Yukon-Koyukuk, AK	63.47	150.07	41 mi NW Cantwell

Sprague's Pipit
    Short to mixedgrass prairie, moist meadows, especially near alkaline lakes
22.1 (7/7)	DENBIGH: McHenry, ND	48.40	100.65	8 mi SW Bantry
18.3 (4/4)	CZAR: AB	52.43	110.72	5 mi SE Czar
16.0 (3/3)	BRODERICK: SK	51.62	106.80	12 mi NE Broderick

BOMBYCILLIDAE – Waxwings
Bohemian Waxwing
    Coniferous and deciduous forest, muskeg
20.0 (3/3)	KLUANE LAKE: YT	61.05	138.52	16 mi SE Destruction Bay
5.7 (3/3)	SOURDOUGH: Valdez-Cordova, AK	62.38	145.35	5 mi NE Gakona
5.0 (3/3)	EAGLE RIVER: YT	66.53	136.42	81 mi SW Ft McPherson, NT

Cedar Waxing
    Variety of open woodlands, edge, second growth, parks
74.3 (7/7)	GREENTOWN: Pike, PA	41.35	75.25	3 mi NE Greentown
51.0 (7/7)	SPECULATOR: Hamilton, NY	43.55	74.38	4 mi NW Speculator
49.9 (7/7)	BEAR LAKE: Manistee, MI	44.43	86.12	2 mi NE Bear Lake

PTILOGONATIDAE – Silky-flycatchers
Phainopepla
    Desert scrub, especially mesquite and paloverde with mistletoe berries; riparian woodland

39.3 (7/7)	PATAGONIA: Santa Cruz, AZ	31.52	110.80	3 mi SW Patagonia
27.8 (6/6)	JACUMBA: San Diego, CA	32.62	116.22	2 mi NW Jacumba
15.1 (7/7)	COPPEROPOLIS: Calaveras, CA	37.93	120.55	4 mi NW Yosemite Junction

LANIIDAE – Shrikes
Loggerhead Shrike
    Open country and desert scrub with scattered trees, poles and fences

44.5 (4/4)	MAURICE: Vermilion, LA	30.08	92.30	5 mi SW Indian Bayou
28.1 (7/7)	DANBURY: Brazoria, TX	29.12	95.22	11 mi NE Oyster Creek
28.0 (5/5)	LAKE BUFFUM: Polk, FL	27.75	81.70	6 mi NE Fort Meade

STURNIDAE – Starlings
European Starling
    Widespread, cultivated fields and urban areas

496.1 (7/7)	QUINBY: Accomack, VA	37.53	75.67	4 mi SE Quinby
481.2 (5/5)	MOUNT JOY: Lancaster, PA	40.10	76.50	1 mi SE Mount Joy
461.8 (4/4)	CHILLIWACK: BC	49.03	121.97	9 mi SE Chilliwack

VIREONIDAE – Vireos
White-eyed Vireo
    Thickets, undergrowth, wooded bottomland, near water

95.0 (3/3)	ATCHAFALAYA: St. Landry, LA	30.48	91.75	4 mi SE Krotz Springs
60.3 (6/6)	BENNDALE: Jackson, MS	30.73	88.72	6 mi SE Benndale
58.4 (7/7)	PLETTENBERG: West Feliciana, LA	30.78	91.52	5 mi NE Labarre

Bell's Vireo
    Arid regions; mesquite thickets, scrub oak and riparian woodland

33.3 (6/6)	HARPER: Gillespie, TX	30.35	99.18	5 mi NE Harper
23.0 (7/7)	POMERENE: Cochise, AZ	32.03	110.30	2 mi NW Pomerene
21.9 (7/7)	CARR MTN: Gila, AZ	33.80	110.88	17 mi NE Roosevelt

Black-capped Vireo
    Oak-juniper thickets, rocky hillsides

14.1 (7/7)	INDIAN MTN: Edwards, TX	29.65	100.42	18 mi SE Carta Valley

Gray Vireo
    Mesquite scrub, chaparral, pinyon-juniper foothills

15.6 (4/5)	MOQUITH MTN: Kane, UT	37.10	112.72	9 mi SW Mount Carmel Jct.
3.1 (7/7)	HOUSE ROCK: Mohave, AZ	36.72	112.05	9 mi SE Jacob Lake

Solitary Vireo
    Variety of coniferous, deciduous and mixed forest and woodland

52.4 (5/5)	ORLEANS: Humboldt, CA	41.22	123.47	7 mi SE Orleans
39.4 (7/7)	HORSE CREEK: Siskiyou, CA	41.92	123.07	8 mi NW Horse Creek
24.0 (3/4)	SAWMILL: Apache, AZ	35.65	109.15	3 mi NW Saint Michaels

Yellow-throated Vireo
    Coniferous and deciduous forest with open areas, riparian woodland

14.0 (6/6)	CEDARVILLE: Gilmer, WV	38.85	80.82	1 mi NW Cedarville
13.8 (5/5)	NICUT: Fayette, WV	38.02	81.05	2 mi NW Cunard
12.0 (7/7)	ELK VALLEY: Scott, TN	36.53	84.32	7 mi SE Winfield

Hutton's Vireo
    Oak, pine-oak and riparian woodland, low trees and scrub
11.9 (7/7)	FISH ROCK: Mendocino, CA	38.80	123.62	2 mi NW Anchor Bay
8.9 (7/7)	CARMEL VAL: Monterey, CA	36.45	121.67	4 mi SE Carmel Valley
7.5 (6/6)	POINT REYES: Marin, CA	38.03	122.88	5 mi SW Point Reyes Station

Warbling Vireo
    Deciduous and mixed woodland with open areas, riparian woodland, thickets
62.2 (6/6)	POINT REYES: Marin, CA	38.03	122.88	5 mi SW Point Reyes Station
53.8 (6/6)	SULA: Ravalli, MT	45.85	113.97	1 mi NE Sula
48.2 (6/6)	CLINTON: Granite, MT	46.70	113.65	6 mi SE Clinton

Philadelphia Vireo
    Deciduous forest, willow-alder thickets and aspen groves, riparian woodland
5.7 (7/7)	P GR JARDINS: PQ	47.60	70.98	21 mi NW Saint-Urbain
5.5 (2/2)	BARRAGE: PQ	47.15	79.38	4 mi SW Fabre

Red-eyed Vireo
    Deciduous woodland, second growth, thickets and scrub
151.7 (7/7)	ST REGIS FLS: Franklin, NY	44.55	74.48	9 mi SE Saint Regis Falls
124.2 (5/5)	OLD FORGE: Herkimer, NY	43.58	74.85	11 mi SE Old Forge
117.0 (7/7)	GABRIELS: Franklin, NY	44.45	74.18	4 mi NE Paul Smiths

Black-whiskered Vireo
    Mangrove swamps, hardwood hammocks
54.6 (5/5)	KEY LARGO: Monroe, FL	25.20	80.35	8 mi NE Newport
14.0 (7/7)	PLANTATION K: Monroe, FL	24.97	80.58	4 mi NE Islamorada
8.4 (5/5)	WEAVER STN: Collier, FL	25.97	81.52	5 mi SE Royal Palm Hamm.

EMBERIZIDAE (Parulinae) – Wood Warblers

Blue-winged Warbler
    Brushy hillsides, second growth with openings, borders of swamps and streams
9.9 (5/7)	CASCADE: Wayne, MO	37.25	90.45	4 mi SW Coldwater
9.1 (7/7)	MT MORRIS: Livingston, NY	42.70	77.95	3 mi SE Perry
8.7 (7/7)	WILLIMANTIC: Windham, CT	41.77	72.13	0 mi South Chaplin

Golden-winged Warbler
    Open deciduous woodland with dense understory, second growth, brushy pastures
6.3 (7/7)	CHAFFEY: Douglas, WI	46.32	92.23	4 mi NW Moose Junction
6.0 (7/7)	COUDERAY: Sawyer, WI	45.83	91.23	4 mi NW Radisson
5.7 (7/7)	AMBERG: Marinette, WI	45.47	88.03	8 mi NW Wausaukee

Tennessee Warbler
    Coniferous and deciduous forest, willow-alder thickets, tamarack and cedar bogs
82.3 (3/3)	FORT LIARD: NT	60.45	123.40	16 mi NW Fort Liard
54.2 (6/6)	NEPISIQUIT: NB	47.40	66.52	22 mi NW Heath Steele
40.1 (7/7)	ST URBAIN: PQ	47.65	70.62	8 mi NW Saint-Urbain

Orange-crowned Warbler
    Deciduous and mixed woodland, chaparral, riparian thickets
80.4 (5/5)	ANCHOR RIVER: Kenai Peninsula, AK	59.50	149.50	38 mi SW Seward
72.0 (5/5)	KACHEMAK: Kenai Peninsula, AK	59.00	151.00	39 mi SE Seldovia
34.0 (7/7)	FOLSOM: El Dorado, CA	38.75	121.05	6 mi SW Pilot Hill

Annotated list of species, habitats and areas 301

Nashville Warbler
    Open deciduous and coniferous woodland, second growth, tamarack bogs
87.3 (7/7)	SAWBILL LNDG: Lake, MN	47.68	91.50	8 mi NW Isabella
72.3 (3/3)	SPRINGER LK: MB	50.62	95.45	14 mi NE Pointe du Bois
68.3 (7/7)	KENORA: ON	49.77	94.22	12 mi SE Kenora

Virginia's Warbler
    Arid montane woodland; canyons with scrub oak, pinyon-juniper scrub; thickets
76.3 (6/6)	PRESCOTT: Yavapai, AZ	34.67	112.38	6 mi NW Prescott Valley
10.7 (6/6)	DOUGLAS PASS: Garfield, CO	39.42	108.78	14 mi NE Mack
6.7 (7/7)	DELTA: Delta, CO	38.70	108.15	5 mi SW Delta

Lucy's Warbler
    Desert and riparian woodland, mesquite scrub
109.9 (7/7)	POMERENE: Cochise, AZ	32.03	110.30	2 mi NW Pomerene
51.6 (7/7)	PATAGONIA: Santa Cruz, AZ	31.52	110.80	3 mi SW Patagonia
31.0 (7/7)	CARR MTN: Gila, AZ	33.80	110.88	17 mi NE Roosevelt

Northern Parula
    Open deciduous and coniferous forest with lichen; swamps, tamarack bogs
36.2 (5/5)	LAFITTE: Jefferson, LA	29.68	90.03	3 mi SW Naomi
27.8 (5/5)	HIXTOWN SWMP: Madison, FL	30.38	83.47	7 mi SW Madison
25.0 (6/6)	MICANOPY: Alachua, FL	29.55	82.30	3 mi NW Micanopy

Yellow Warbler
    Open scrub, second growth woodland, often near water; riparian woodland in west
70.1 (7/7)	HORSE CREEK: Siskiyou, CA	41.92	123.07	8 mi NW Horse Creek
66.6 (7/7)	FISH LAKE: Harney, OR	42.62	118.60	11 mi NE Andrews
63.9 (7/7)	ORLEANS: Ontario, NY	42.90	77.12	2 mi NW Seneca Castle

Chestnut-sided Warbler
    Open deciduous woodland, edge, second growth and brushy areas
62.4 (5/5)	LOCKPORT: Cook, MN	47.73	90.68	6 mi NW Lutsen
52.1 (7/7)	HART LAKE: St. Louis, MN	47.07	91.80	5 mi SW Stewart
47.0 (6/6)	MINONG: Washburn, WI	46.05	91.80	4 mi SE Minong

Magnolia Warbler
    Open coniferous and mixed forest, especially with spruce and fir; second growth, coniferous bogs
52.6 (7/7)	ROMAN VALLEY: NS	45.38	61.82	2 mi SE Giant Lake
42.5 (6/6)	NEPISIQUIT: NB	47.40	66.52	22 mi NW Heath Steele
37.7 (6/6)	WHITNEY: ON	45.35	78.17	7 mi NW Lake St. Peter

Cape May Warbler
    Boreal coniferous forest, birch and hemlock woodland, edge and open areas
9.6 (5/5)	SILVER ISLET: ON	48.32	88.82	19 mi SW Pass Lake
5.9 (7/7)	BIRD RIVER: MB	50.42	95.70	7 mi NW Pointe du Bois
5.7 (6/6)	MARATHON: ON	48.75	86.48	5 mi NW Marathon

Black-throated Blue Warbler
    Deciduous and mixed woodland, understory, second growth
21.0 (5/5)	OLD FORGE: Herkimer, NY	43.58	74.85	11 mi SE Old Forge
13.7 (3/3)	NEWFOUND GAP: Sevier, TN	35.62	83.43	3 mi SW Mascot
10.4 (7/7)	INLET: Hamilton, NY	43.72	74.78	2 mi SE Inlet

Yellow-rumped Warbler
    A variety of coniferous, deciduous and mixed forest
64.3 (3/3)	FREEMAN LAKE: AB	54.75	115.52	5 mi NW Swan Hills
56.5 (6/6)	DELL SPRING: Klamath, OR	43.57	121.70	6 mi NE Gilchrist
47.7 (6/6)	KENNY LAKE: Valdez-Cordova, AK	61.72	144.93	11 mi NW Lower Tonsina

Yellow-rumped Warbler (Myrtle)
    Widespread, coniferous and deciduous forest
64.3 (3/3)	FREEMAN LAKE: AB	54.75	115.52	5 mi NW Swan Hills
54.0 (4/4)	COTTONWOOD: Matanuska-Susitna, AK	61.52	149.62	8 mi NW Wasilla
51.3 (3/3)	MALIGNE LAKE: AB	52.73	117.67	19 mi SE Jasper

Yellow-rumped Warbler (Audubon's)
    Coniferous forest, including pine, fir and spruce
56.5 (6/6)	DELL SPRING: Klamath, OR	43.57	121.70	6 mi NE Gilchrist
51.4 (5/5)	ELK LAKE: Lane, OR	43.98	121.88	17 mi SE Belknap Springs
50.0 (3/3)	ADAMS LAKE: BC	51.40	119.45	12 mi SE Vavenby

Black-throated Gray Warbler
    Pinyon-juniper and pine-oak woodland with brushy undergrowth
65.4 (5/5)	ORLEANS: Humboldt, CA	41.22	123.47	7 mi SE Orleans
63.3 (7/7)	HORSE CREEK: Siskiyou, CA	41.92	123.07	8 mi NW Horse Creek
34.6 (7/7)	HULLVILLE: Mendocino, CA	39.55	122.93	13 mi SW Alder Springs

Townsend's Warbler
    Tall coniferous and mixed montane forest
49.3 (3/3)	MASSETT: BC	54.02	132.15	11 mi SE Masset
46.0 (7/7)	RIMROCK: Yakima, WA	46.55	121.37	14 mi SW Rimrock
41.7 (7/7)	PACKWOOD: Skamania, WA	46.35	121.58	18 mi SW Packwood

Hermit Warbler
    Mature coniferous forest
48.2 (6/6)	RIVERTON: El Dorado, CA	38.85	120.45	6 mi NE Riverton
45.0 (7/7)	SHELLROCK: Clackamas, OR	45.05	121.88	19 mi SW Government Camp
36.0 (7/7)	COOL CAMP: Linn, OR	44.48	122.20	15 mi NE Cascadia

Black-throated Green Warbler
    Open coniferous and mixed forest with balsam fir and white pine, edge
28.0 (6/6)	MARATHON: ON	48.75	86.48	5 mi NW Marathon
23.7 (7/7)	MARSH HILL: Lycoming, PA	41.48	76.90	12 mi SE Liberty
23.0 (5/5)	SILVER ISLET: ON	48.32	88.82	19 mi SW Pass Lake

Blackburnian Warbler
    Mature coniferous forest with balsam fir and swampy areas; occasionally open woodland and mixed forest
20.8 (5/5)	OLD FORGE: Herkimer, NY	43.58	74.85	11 mi SE Old Forge
17.1 (7/7)	BIRD RIVER: MB	50.42	95.70	7 mi NW Pointe du Bois
12.1 (7/7)	INLET: Hamilton, NY	43.72	74.78	2 mi SE Inlet

Yellow-throated Warbler
    Swampy hardwood forest, southern wet coniferous forest with pine or sycamore-baldcypress
20.7 (3/3)	FONTANA: Swain, NC	35.47	83.80	3 mi NE Fontana Village
16.4 (7/7)	SIGNAL MTN: Hamilton, TN	35.10	85.35	2 mi SW Signal Mountain
13.3 (7/7)	SMOKEY JCT: Scott, TN	36.28	84.42	4 mi NE Lone Mountain

Grace's Warbler
Montane coniferous forest, pine and pine-oak parkland
21.0 (6/6)	PRESCOTT: Yavapai, AZ	34.67	112.38	6 mi NW Prescott Valley
18.5 (4/4)	FLAGSTAFF: Coconino, AZ	35.38	111.70	13 mi NW Flagstaff
15.4 (5/5)	HAPPY JACK: Coconino, AZ	34.73	111.45	3 mi SW Happy Jack

Pine Warbler
Open pine forest and woodland
81.0 (5/5)	FRIENDSHIP: Burlington, NJ	39.75	74.47	4 mi NE Speedwell
44.6 (7/7)	SALEM XRD: Fairfield, SC	34.45	81.28	2 mi NE Salem Crossroads
41.1 (7/7)	GROVETOWN: Columbia, GA	33.52	82.22	5 mi NW Grovetown

Prairie Warbler
Second growth, brushy areas and dry scrub, low pine-juniper woodland
47.4 (5/5)	FRIENDSHIP: Burlington, NJ	39.75	74.47	4 mi NE Speedwell
20.8 (6/6)	ARCOLA: Halifax, NC	36.25	77.98	1 mi SW Essex
19.6 (7/7)	ROME: Adams, OH	38.67	83.42	5 mi SE Wrightsville

Palm Warbler
Tamarack and cedar bogs, near water, open boreal coniferous forest
26.5 (4/4)	STAGG RIVER: NT	62.68	115.37	19 mi SE Rae-Edzo
13.7 (3/3)	SPRINGER LK: MB	50.62	95.45	14 mi NE Pointe du Bois
5.3 (7/7)	SHELBURNE: NS	43.80	65.25	1 mi SW Jordan Falls

Bay-breasted Warbler
Boreal coniferous forest, mixed forest in swampy areas
31.5 (6/6)	NEPISIQUIT: NB	47.40	66.52	22 mi NW Heath Steele
18.0 (3/3)	GREEN RIVER: NB	47.57	68.25	15 mi NE Edmundston
14.8 (5/5)	SILVER ISLET: ON	48.32	88.82	19 mi SW Pass Lake

Blackpoll Warbler
Boreal coniferous forest, including spruce, second growth and alder thickets, mixed woodland
40.0 (3/3)	ST JOHNS: NF	47.62	52.72	5 mi NW St. John's
39.3 (3/3)	PARC LAUREN: PQ	47.93	71.33	4 mi SE Mont-Apica
35.0 (3/3)	PT SAUNDERS: NF	50.70	57.30	4 mi NW Port Saunders

Cerulean Warbler
Moist mature deciduous forest with little understory
15.2 (6/6)	CEDARVILLE: Gilmer, WV	38.85	80.82	1 mi NW Cedarville
12.0 (7/7)	ELK VALLEY: Scott, TN	36.53	84.32	7 mi SE Winfield
8.0 (6/6)	MOUNDSVILLE: Marshall, WV	39.93	80.75	1 mi NW Moundsville

Black-and-white Warbler
Deciduous and mixed forest and woodlands, scrubby areas, ravines
16.8 (6/6)	WHITNEY: ON	45.35	78.17	7 mi NW Lake St. Peter
16.8 (5/5)	AURORA: Hancock, ME	44.80	68.17	6 mi SW Beddington
15.3 (7/7)	N ORANGE: Franklin, MA	42.62	72.28	1 mi SW North Orange

American Redstart
Moist deciduous and mixed woodland, open areas and second growth
44.1 (7/7)	STEWIACKE: NS	45.30	63.43	1 mi SW Beaver Brook
40.4 (7/7)	SPECULATOR: Hamilton, NY	43.55	74.38	4 mi NW Speculator
37.4 (7/7)	PENOBSQUIS: NB	45.77	65.05	1 mi NW Hillside

Prothonotary Warbler
　　Swamps and wet lowland forest
　　75.0 (3/3)　　　ATCHAFALAYA: St. Landry, LA　　　30.48　91.75　　　4 mi SE Krotz Springs
　　44.6 (5/5)　　　BERWICK: St. Martin, LA　　　　　29.85　91.18　　　8 mi SW Bellewood
　　33.8 (4/4)　　　APALACHICOLA: Liberty, FL　　　　30.17　84.70　　　14 mi SE Telogia

Worm-eating Warbler
　　Deciduous forest with undergrowth; damp, brushy ravines
　　9.0 (2/2)　　　　HOOSIER: Jackson, IN　　　　　　39.03　86.28　　　3 mi SW Elkinsville
　　6.8 (5/5)　　　　SLEEPY CREEK: Morgan, WV　　　 39.60　78.13　　　5 mi SW Sleepy Creek
　　4.6 (7/7)　　　　INDIANTOWN: Worcester, MD　　　 38.08　75.52　　　2 mi NW Goodwill

Swainson's Warbler
　　Moist lowland forest with undergrowth; swamps and canebrakes; rhododendron thickets at higher elevations
　　8.0 (3/3)　　　　ATCHAFALAYA: St. Landry, LA　　　30.48　91.75　　　4 mi SE Krotz Springs
　　1.9 (7/7)　　　　BICKHAM: Washington, LA　　　　　30.88　90.25　　　5 mi SW Clifton
　　1.9 (7/7)　　　　ROSELAND: Tangipahoa, LA　　　　 30.70　90.52　　　2 mi SW Amite

Ovenbird
　　Mature deciduous forest
　　89.1 (7/7)　　　SAWBILL LNDG: Lake, MN　　　　　47.68　91.50　　　8 mi NW Isabella
　　75.6 (7/7)　　　HART LAKE: St. Louis, MN　　　　 47.07　91.80　　　5 mi SW Stewart
　　70.6 (7/7)　　　COUDERAY: Sawyer, WI　　　　　　 45.83　91.23　　　4 mi NW Radisson

Northern Waterthrush
　　Near standing water, thickets, swamps and bogs with woody borders
　　93.7 (3/3)　　　O'REGANS: NF　　　　　　　　　　47.88　59.22　　　1 mi NE O'Regan's
　　90.3 (3/3)　　　ST PAULS: NF　　　　　　　　　　 49.73　57.68　　　11 mi SE St. Pauls
　　84.0 (3/3)　　　ST ANTHONY: NF　　　　　　　　　 51.52　55.50　　　10 mi NE St. Anthony

Louisiana Waterthrush
　　Woodland in ravines and along streams, humid forest, swamps
　　4.8 (5/5)　　　　LAUREL HILL: Somerset, PA　　　　40.10　79.18　　　8 mi NW Somerset
　　4.1 (7/7)　　　　ELK VALLEY: Scott, TN　　　　　　36.53　84.32　　　7 mi SE Winfield
　　4.0 (7/7)　　　　YELLOW SPG: Hampshire, WV　　　 39.18　78.48　　　2 mi NE Yellow Spring

Kentucky Warbler
　　Humid deciduous forest, dense second growth, swamps
　　24.7 (3/3)　　　ATCHAFALAYA: St. Landry, LA　　　30.48　91.75　　　4 mi SE Krotz Springs
　　19.5 (4/4)　　　MARION: Union, LA　　　　　　　　32.80　92.23　　　4 mi SW Linville
　　12.3 (7/7)　　　CLEAR SPRING: Jackson, IN　　　　38.92　86.17　　　2 mi SE Clear Spring

Connecticut Warbler
　　Spruce and tamarack bogs, poplar woodland, muskeg
　　19.3 (3/3)　　　SPRINGER LK: MB　　　　　　　　　50.62　95.45　　　14 mi NE Pointe du Bois
　　11.4 (7/7)　　　BRIGHTSAND: SK　　　　　　　　　 53.50　108.67　　 15 mi NE Turtleford
　　9.7 (6/6)　　　　MINONG: Washburn, WI　　　　　　46.05　91.80　　　4 mi SE Minong

Mourning Warbler
　　Deciduous forest, shrubs and bushes, bog and marsh edges
　　35.7 (7/7)　　　CHAFFEY: Douglas, WI　　　　　　 46.32　92.23　　　4 mi NW Moose Junction
　　33.3 (7/7)　　　HART LAKE: St. Louis, MN　　　　 47.07　91.80　　　5 mi SW Stewart
　　29.4 (5/5)　　　SUOMI: ON　　　　　　　　　　　　48.13　90.22　　　14 mi SW Suomi

MacGillivray's Warbler
Riparian thickets, coniferous forest undergrowth and edge

35.7 (3/3)	SCOTCH CREEK: BC	51.18	119.15	7 mi SW Seymour Arm
30.3 (4/4)	LOGAN PASS: Glacier, MT	48.73	113.73	10 mi NE Lake McDonald
23.0 (3/3)	MARBLE CREEK: Shoshone, ID	47.12	116.10	10 mi NE Clarkia

Common Yellowthroat
Marshes with cattails, brushy pastures and fields, near water

83.0 (5/5)	GREEN SWAMP: Lake, FL	28.42	81.95	5 mi SW Bay Lake
82.3 (4/4)	APALACHICOLA: Liberty, FL	30.17	84.70	14 mi SE Telogia
72.2 (5/5)	OSCEOLA: Baker, FL	30.35	82.43	10 mi NW Olustee

Hooded Warbler
Mature deciduous forest, streams and ravine edges, thickets and swamps

23.3 (6/6)	BENNDALE: Jackson, MS	30.73	88.72	6 mi SE Benndale
21.7 (7/7)	PLETTENBERG: West Feliciana, LA	30.78	91.52	5 mi NE Labarre
17.0 (5/5)	BLOXHAM: Levy, FL	30.32	84.52	11 mi NW Arran

Wilson's Warbler
Shrubby and brushy areas, willow-alder thickets, near water, riparian woodland

60.5 (6/6)	KODIAK: Kodiak Island, AK	57.62	152.55	12 mi SW Kodiak
60.3 (7/7)	CHINIAK: Kodiak Island, AK	57.53	152.43	17 mi SW Kodiak
45.2 (6/6)	POINT REYES: Marin, CA	38.03	122.88	5 mi SW Point Reyes Station

Canada Warbler
Forest undergrowth, aspen-poplar groves, bogs, riparian woodland

16.7 (7/7)	HAMPTON: NB	45.63	65.72	0 mi Norton
16.4 (5/5)	LOCKPORT: Cook, MN	47.73	90.68	6 mi NW Lutsen
9.5 (6/6)	MARATHON: ON	48.75	86.48	5 mi NW Marathon

Red-faced Warbler
Montane forest with fir, pine, pine-oak or aspen

21.3 (5/6)	PRESCOTT: Yavapai, AZ	34.67	112.38	6 mi NW Prescott Valley
2.8 (3/4)	PORTAL: Cochise, AZ	31.98	109.20	3 mi NE Paradise

Painted Redstart
Oak and pine forest, pinyon-juniper woodland, montane riparian woodland

6.0 (5/6)	PRESCOTT: Yavapai, AZ	34.67	112.38	6 mi NW Prescott Valley
1.3 (2/4)	SUNIZONA: Cochise, AZ	31.82	109.70	7 mi NE Courtland
0.8 (2/4)	PORTAL: Cochise, AZ	31.98	109.20	3 mi NE Paradise

Yellow-breasted Chat
Second growth and undergrowth, thickets and brushy areas, ravines and steamsides

70.7 (3/3)	ATCHAFALAYA: St. Landry, LA	30.48	91.75	4 mi SE Krotz Springs
53.4 (7/7)	PLETTENBERG: West Feliciana, LA	30.78	91.52	5 mi NE Labarre
52.0 (7/7)	HORSE CREEK: Siskiyou, CA	41.92	123.07	8 mi NW Horse Creek

Olive Warbler
Open coniferous forest with ponderosa pine

2.0 (3/4)	PORTAL: Cochise, AZ	31.98	109.20	3 mi NE Paradise

EMBERIZIDAE (Thraupinae) – Tanagers

Hepatic Tanager
    Coniferous forest with pine and pine-oak; pinyon-juniper and riparian woodland
6.2 (6/6)	PRESCOTT: Yavapai, AZ	34.67	112.38	6 mi NW Prescott Valley
3.6 (4/5)	CARRIZOZO: Lincoln, NM	33.57	105.82	6 mi SE Carrizozo
2.0 (7/7)	CARR MTN: Gila, AZ	33.80	110.88	17 mi NE Roosevelt

Summer Tanager
    Deciduous forest, especially with pine-oak; riparian woodland
24.4 (7/7)	PLETTENBERG: West Feliciana, LA	30.78	91.52	5 mi NE Labarre
24.2 (6/6)	TOWN BLUFF: Jasper, TX	30.80	94.10	9 mi NE Spurger
19.3 (6/6)	HARDEEVILLE: Jasper, SC	32.25	81.03	4 mi SE Hardeeville

Scarlet Tanager
    Mature deciduous forest
34.1 (7/7)	OLDTOWN: Allegany, MD	39.55	78.60	1 mi NE Oldtown
32.4 (5/5)	MILL RUN: Fayette, PA	39.87	79.52	9 mi SE Dunbar
26.6 (7/7)	WARRENS MILL: Somerset, PA	39.78	78.97	10 mi SE Berlin

Western Tanager
    Mountainous regions, open coniferous and mixed woodland
58.1 (7/7)	HORSE CREEK: Siskiyou, CA	41.92	123.07	8 mi NW Horse Creek
46.4 (7/7)	RIMROCK: Yakima, WA	46.55	121.37	14 mi SW Rimrock
44.3 (3/3)	GAZELLE: Siskiyou, CA	41.43	122.65	9 mi SW Gazelle

EMBERIZIDAE (Cardinalinae) – Cardinals, Grosbeaks, and Allies

Northern Cardinal
    Thickets, brushy areas, edges and clearings, riparian woodland, parks and residential areas
138.1 (7/7)	RACHAL: Brooks, TX	26.80	98.08	7 mi SE Rachal
131.3 (6/6)	DIBOLL: Angelina, TX	31.18	94.85	4 mi SW Diboll
118.5 (6/6)	LIVINGSTON: Polk, TX	30.70	94.93	1 mi SE Livingston

Pyrrhuloxia
    Arid brush, thorn scrub with mesquite, fields and riparian thickets
179.1 (7/7)	RACHAL: Brooks, TX	26.80	98.08	7 mi SE Rachal
124.4 (7/7)	RANDADO: Jim Hogg, TX	27.05	98.78	6 mi SE Randado
102.8 (5/5)	CATARINA: Webb, TX	28.15	99.78	17 mi SW Catarina

Rose-breasted Grosbeak
    Open deciduous forest, especially with poplar and aspen groves; second growth
32.8 (6/6)	CLOVERDALE: NB	46.35	67.53	1 mi SE Peel
24.4 (7/7)	MATHER: Jackson, WI	44.22	90.37	9 mi NE Warrens
20.6 (7/7)	SAXEVILLE: Waushara, WI	44.20	89.03	9 mi SW Fremont

Black-headed Grosbeak
    Deciduous woodland, including pine-oak, oak scrub and pinyon-juniper
68.6 (7/7)	HORSE CREEK: Siskiyou, CA	41.92	123.07	8 mi NW Horse Creek
48.7 (7/7)	SHASTA LAKE: Shasta, CA	40.88	122.30	4 mi SE Lakehead
43.4 (7/7)	SECRET VAL: Josephine, OR	42.42	123.67	8 mi NW Wonder

Blue Grosbeak
  Riparian woodland, weedy fields, open areas with trees, thickets
  35.3 (6/6)   SPEED: Edgecombe, NC   35.98   77.42   2 mi NE Speed
  34.3 (7/7)   BRODNAX: Brunswick, VA   36.60   78.00   2 mi NW Ebony
  30.7 (6/6)   NASHVILLE: Berrien, GA   31.20   83.27   1 mi SW Nashville

Lazuli Bunting
  Arid brush, canyons, riparian thickets, chaparral
  65.9 (7/7)   IMNAHA: Wallowa, OR   45.72   116.62   15 mi NE Imnaha
  31.4 (5/5)   MAGIC MTN: Cassia, ID   42.23   114.27   17 mi SE Rogerson
  28.3 (7/7)   HORSE CREEK: Siskiyou, CA   41.92   123.07   8 mi NW Horse Creek

Indigo Bunting
  Deciduous edge, clearings and open areas, second growth
  113.1 (7/7)   CLEAR SPRING: Jackson, IN   38.92   86.17   2 mi SE Clear Spring
  97.6 (7/7)   CELESTINE: Dubois, IN   38.40   86.82   2 mi NW Celestine
  96.3 (7/7)   CUMBACK: Daviess, IN   38.57   87.18   2 mi NW Cumback

Varied Bunting
  Arid regions; washes, scrub, brush and thickets
  4.3 (3/3)   BLACK GAP: Brewster, TX   29.58   102.98   22 mi NE Panther Junction
  2.7 (6/7)   PATAGONIA: Santa Cruz, AZ   31.52   110.80   3 mi SW Patagonia
  1.2 (4/6)   HOT SPRINGS: Brewster, TX   29.18   103.02   15 mi SE Panther Junction

Painted Bunting
  Riparian thickets, open areas with brush and trees, weedy areas
  39.3 (7/7)   INDIAN MTN: Edwards, TX   29.65   100.42   18 mi SE Carta Valley
  36.4 (7/7)   RACHAL: Brooks, TX   26.80   98.08   7 mi SE Rachal
  32.3 (7/7)   BLANCO: Pittsburg, OK   34.75   95.77   0 mi Blanco

Dickcissel
  Tallgrass prairie; alfalfa, timothy and clover fields
  182.2 (5/5)   STET: Carroll, MO   39.40   93.75   2 mi SE Stet
  170.7 (6/6)   WINSIDE: Wayne, NE   42.20   97.15   2 mi NE Winside
  168.7 (7/7)   HUMBOLDT: Allen, KS   37.85   95.43   3 mi NE Humboldt

EMBERIZIDAE (Emberizinae) – Towhees, Sparrows, and Allies
Olive Sparrow
  Undergrowth, thickets and second growth, mesquite scrub, riparian woodland
  7.9 (7/7)   LAG ATASCOSA: Cameron, TX   26.20   97.33   6 mi NE Bayview
  5.6 (5/5)   KINGSVILLE: Kleberg, TX   27.53   97.93   5 mi NW Kingsville
  2.1 (6/7)   RAYMONDVILLE: Willacy, TX   26.53   97.70   4 mi NW San Perlita

Green-tailed Towhee
  Thickets, chaparral and riparian scrub in mountainous regions
  84.4 (7/7)   MOOSE: Teton, WY   43.65   110.70   1 mi SE Moose
  84.4 (7/7)   VALERMO: Los Angeles, CA   34.38   117.68   1 mi SE Big Pines
  67.6 (7/7)   GREAT DIVIDE: Moffat, CO   40.80   107.70   21 mi NE Lay

Rufous-sided Towhee
  Thickets, open and riparian woodland, edge and second growth, parks and residential areas
  206.0 (5/5)   FRIENDSHIP: Burlington, NJ   39.75   74.47   4 mi NE Speedwell
  109.7 (6/6)   PORT ST JOE: Gulf, FL   29.78   85.30   2 mi SE Port Saint Joe
  109.2 (5/5)   TUJUNGA: Los Angeles, CA   34.28   118.10   7 mi NE Altadena

California Towhee
  Broken chaparral, brushy and riparian woodland, hedgerows
  51.5 (6/6)   MESA GRANDE: San Diego, CA   33.20   116.82   3 mi NW Mesa Grande
  47.7 (7/7)   HARBOR LAKE: Los Angeles, CA   33.78   118.28   1 mi NW Wilmington
  41.5 (6/6)   JACUMBA: San Diego, CA   32.62   116.22   2 mi NW Jacumba

Canyon Towhee
  Dense brush, arid scrub, riparian thickets, rocky areas
  13.0 (7/7)   CARR MTN: Gila, AZ   33.80   110.88   17 mi NE Roosevelt
  12.3 (7/7)   POMERENE: Cochise, AZ   32.03   110.30   2 mi NW Pomerene
  10.3 (7/7)   INDIAN MTN: Edwards, TX   29.65   100.42   18 mi SE Carta Valley

Abert's Towhee
  Desert scrub, riparian woodland, undergrowth and thickets
  9.9 (7/7)   IMPERIAL DAM: Imperial, CA   32.83   114.50   4 mi NE Bard
  7.0 (3/3)   CASA GRANDE: Pinal, AZ   33.07   111.23   9 mi NE Cactus Forest
  6.2 (5/6)   BRAWLEY: Imperial, CA   32.92   115.55   4 mi SW Brawley

Bachman's Sparrow
  Open pine woods with open, grassy cover; brushy, overgrown hillsides and fields
  26.2 (5/5)   BLACKWATER: Santa Rosa, FL   30.85   86.83   3 mi SE Munson
  21.6 (5/5)   BLOXHAM: Levy, FL   30.32   84.52   11 mi NW Arran
  21.3 (4/4)   LATIMER: Jackson, MS   30.65   88.78   11 mi SW Benndale

Botteri's Sparrow
  Arid grassland with scattered bushes and scrub
  3.0 (6/7)   PENA BLANCA: Santa Cruz, AZ   31.38   111.08   9 mi NW Nogales
  0.9 (5/7)   PATAGONIA: Santa Cruz, AZ   31.52   110.80   3 mi SW Patagonia

Cassin's Sparrow
  Arid shortgrass prairie or grasslands with scattered sagebrush, mesquite or yucca
  179.0 (5/5)   LAKEWOOD: Eddy, NM   32.70   104.53   10 mi SW Atoka
  132.2 (5/5)   COOLEY LAKE: De Baca, NM   34.12   104.23   24 mi SW Fort Sumner
  120.8 (5/5)   LOGAN: Harding, NM   35.42   103.52   7 mi NW Logan

Rufous-crowned Sparrow
  Arid regions; rocky and hilly areas with scattered scrub and oaks
  40.6 (7/7)   PENA BLANCA: Santa Cruz, AZ   31.38   111.08   9 mi NW Nogales
  18.6 (7/7)   INDIAN MTN: Edwards, TX   29.65   100.42   18 mi SE Carta Valley
  13.1 (7/7)   PATAGONIA: Santa Cruz, AZ   31.52   110.80   3 mi SW Patagonia

American Tree Sparrow
  Willow thickets, scrub conifers and bogs, low shrubs
  81.7 (3/3)   MACLAREN: SE Fairbanks, AK   63.07   146.07   54 mi NW Gakona
  77.8 (4/4)   SAVAGE: Yukon-Koyukuk, AK   63.73   149.28   14 mi SW Healy
  60.0 (4/4)   TOKLAT: Yukon-Koyukuk, AK   63.47   150.07   41 mi NW Cantwell

Chipping Sparrow
  Open coniferous and deciduous forest, second growth, forest edge, parks and residential areas
  104.8 (6/6)   RED OAK: Oscoda, MI   44.83   84.22   6 mi SE Lewiston
  77.4 (7/7)   HONESDALE: Wayne, PA   41.55   75.23   2 mi SW Bethel
  71.8 (5/5)   ALBEE: Umatilla, OR   45.23   118.88   2 mi NE Albee

Annotated list of species, habitats and areas

Clay-colored Sparrow
  Shrubby areas and thickets, near water, brushy open areas, small trees
  77.3 (3/3)   CRANE RIVER: MB   51.47   99.15   4 mi SE Crane River
  73.1 (7/7)   BIGGAR: SK   52.25   107.85   15 mi NE Biggar
  61.7 (7/7)   CLOUSTON: SK   53.08   105.83   9 mi SW Prince Albert

Brewer's Sparrow
  Shortgrass prairie, sagebrush regions
  131.4 (7/7)   BUCHANAN: Harney, OR   43.68   118.68   4 mi NW Buchanan
  126.5 (6/6)   MALHEUR NWR: Harney, OR   43.23   118.77   10 mi SW New Princeton
  124.8 (6/6)   CROWLEY: Malheur, OR   43.28   117.78   26 mi SE Riverside

Field Sparrow
  Overgrown fields and pastures, hillsides, edge, shrubs and low trees
  52.3 (6/6)   SWEDEN: Douglas, MO   36.87   92.53   5 mi NE Squires
  49.3 (7/7)   HARVEYSBURG: Warren, OH   39.50   84.03   1 mi SW Harveysburg
  42.9 (7/7)   ROOSEVELT PK: McKenzie, ND   47.55   103.50   19 mi SW Arnegard

Black-chinned Sparrow
  Arid regions; chaparral, sagebrush regions, brushy hillsides
  51.0 (5/5)   TUJUNGA: Los Angeles, CA   34.28   118.10   7 mi NE Altadena
  13.0 (3/3)   ANGELUS OAKS: San Bernardino, CA 34.13 116.98 5 mi NW Forest Falls
  7.0 (6/6)   JACUMBA: San Diego, CA   32.62   116.22   2 mi NW Jacumba

Vesper Sparrow
  Grasslands, weedy pastures, fields and clearings, sagebrush regions, montane parklands
  114.1 (7/7)   LEROY: Blaine, MT   47.75   109.43   13 mi NW Winifred
  104.0 (5/5)   BEAVERHEAD: Beaverhead, MT   44.63   112.05   12 mi NW Lakeview
  96.9 (7/7)   BUCHANAN: Harney, OR   43.68   118.68   4 mi NW Buchanan

Lark Sparrow
  Open areas with scattered bushes, grasslands, edge, fields
  117.8 (4/4)   CONE MTN: Las Animas, CO   37.63   104.28   11 mi NW Thatcher
  54.2 (6/6)   ASHLAND: Clark, KS   37.13   99.75   4 mi SE Ashland
  51.7 (7/7)   EAGLE CITY: Blaine, OK   35.90   98.60   2 mi SW Eagle City

Black-throated Sparrow
  Desert scrub with mesquite
  102.1 (7/7)   SLAUGHTER: El Paso, TX   31.53   106.10   4 mi NE Fabens
  100.9 (7/7)   POMERENE: Cochise, AZ   32.03   110.30   2 mi NW Pomerene
  92.1 (7/7)   GREENWATER V: Inyo, CA   36.05   116.50   14 mi NW Shoshone

Sage Sparrow
  Sagebrush regions, chaparral
  67.9 (7/7)   LOST RIVER: Butte, ID   43.57   113.05   10 mi SE Butte City
  54.7 (7/7)   TWIN BUTTES: Bingham, ID   43.48   112.80   3 mi NE Atomic City
  54.0 (7/7)   TRACTOR FLAT: Bingham, ID   43.52   112.65   10 mi NE Atomic City

Lark Bunting
  Areas with mixed short grasses and sagebrush; weedy roadsides, alfalfa and clover fields
  463.0 (4/4)   CARSON: Grant, ND   46.43   101.65   4 mi NW Leith
  373.5 (6/6)   ALBION: Carter, MT   45.23   104.38   14 mi NE Alzada
  338.1 (7/7)   BOWMAN: Bowman, ND   46.22   103.43   2 mi NW Bowman

Savannah Sparrow
    Tallgrass and mixedgrass prairie, grasslands, wet meadows, saltwater marshes, tundra
164.7 (6/6)	CASCO: Kewaunee, WI	44.58	87.65	2 mi NW Casco
123.3 (7/7)	VERCHERES: PQ	45.72	73.40	4 mi SW Vercheres
122.3 (7/7)	PICKFORD: Chippewa, MI	46.22	84.35	3 mi NW Stirlingville

Baird's Sparrow
    Mixedgrass prairie, scattered low bushes, wet meadows, some hayfields
34.8 (4/4)	HORSEHEAD LK: Kidder, ND	47.07	99.63	7 mi SW Pettibone
19.3 (7/7)	DENBIGH: McHenry, ND	48.40	100.65	8 mi SW Bantry
14.1 (7/7)	STANLEY: Mountrail, ND	48.27	102.42	5 mi SW Stanley

Grasshopper Sparrow
    Mixedgrass prairie, grasslands and fields
141.9 (7/7)	GOVE: Gove, KS	38.90	100.23	11 mi SW Collyer
100.8 (5/5)	FORT PIERRE: Stanley, SD	44.38	100.50	7 mi NW Fort Pierre
78.8 (4/4)	HORSEHEAD LK: Kidder, ND	47.07	99.63	7 mi SW Pettibone

Henslow's Sparrow
    Open fields and meadows, weedy areas, damp, low-lying areas
4.0 (6/7)	NASHVILLE: Barry, MI	42.60	85.13	2 mi SW Nashville
3.7 (7/7)	OHIO: St. Clair, MO	38.20	93.85	6 mi SW Deepwater
3.3 (7/7)	JAMESVILLE: Martin, NC	35.75	76.97	6 mi SW Jamesville

Le Conte's Sparrow
    Sedge meadows, moist areas, edges of marshes and bogs, fens
13.3 (7/7)	DERWENT: AB	53.50	110.80	6 mi SW Clandonald
11.6 (7/7)	THUNDER LAKE: AB	54.08	114.75	6 mi SW Tiger Lilly
11.0 (7/7)	RONAN: AB	53.78	115.25	13 mi SE Mayerthorpe

Sharp-tailed Sparrow
    Marshes and wet meadows, fens, saltwater marshes
1.3 (3/4)	HORSEHEAD LK: Kidder, ND	47.07	99.63	7 mi SW Pettibone
1.0 (5/7)	WARBURG: AB	53.12	114.25	3 mi SE Warburg

Seaside Sparrow
    Saltwater marshes, rushes and tidal reeds
12.4 (7/7)	MADISON: Dorchester, MD	38.53	76.22	1 mi NW Madison
8.7 (6/6)	HONGA: Dorchester, MD	38.37	76.23	2 mi NW Honga
8.0 (7/7)	MERRIMON: Carteret, NC	34.95	76.67	4 mi SW South River

Fox Sparrow
    Undergrowth, thickets, forest, riparian woodland, montane brushland
125.7 (6/6)	KODIAK: Kodiak Island, AK	57.62	152.55	12 mi SW Kodiak
107.7 (7/7)	CHINIAK: Kodiak Island, AK	57.53	152.43	17 mi SW Kodiak
72.3 (7/7)	VALERMO: Los Angeles, CA	34.38	117.68	1 mi SE Big Pines

Song Sparrow
    Brushy, shrubby areas, riparian woodland, marshes, forest edge, bogs
198.4 (7/7)	ORLEANS: Ontario, NY	42.90	77.12	2 mi NW Seneca Castle
117.7 (7/7)	VERCHERES: PQ	45.72	73.40	4 mi SW Vercheres
105.6 (7/7)	MANAWA: Waupaca, WI	44.42	88.95	3 mi SW Manawa

Lincoln's Sparrow
   Bogs and wet meadows, riparian thickets, montane regions
   41.3 (4/4)   GANDER RIVER: NF   48.83   55.52   8 mi SE Grand Falls
   38.7 (3/3)   RED CLIFF: Eagle, CO   39.52 106.37   1 mi NW Redcliff
   33.8 (4/4)   SWAN RIVER: AB   55.13 115.33   12 mi SE Kinuso

Swamp Sparrow
   Near bodies of water with emergent vegetation; bogs, fens and wet meadows
   29.7 (3/3)   ST JOHNS: NF   47.62   52.72   5 mi NW St. John's
   27.2 (6/6)   WHITNEY: ON   45.35   78.17   7 mi NW Lake St. Peter

White-throated Sparrow
   Coniferous and mixed forest with clearings, brushy areas
   156.7 (7/7)   ST URBAIN: PQ   47.65   70.62   8 mi NW Saint-Urbain
   109.2 (6/6)   HERON LAKE: Piscataquis, ME   46.40 69.28   19 mi SE Clayton Lake
   103.0 (7/7)   P GR JARDINS: PQ   47.60   70.98   21 mi NW Saint-Urbain

Golden-crowned Sparrow
   Montane thickets, dwarf conifers, stunted willows, scree slopes
   63.9 (7/7)   CHINIAK: Kodiak Island, AK   57.53 152.43 17 mi SW Kodiak
   58.2 (6/6)   KODIAK: Kodiak Island, AK   57.62 152.55 12 mi SW Kodiak
   25.8 (5/5)   KACHEMAK: Kenai Peninsula, AK 59.00 151.00 39 mi SE Seldovia

White-crowned Sparrow
   Brushy areas, stunted trees, wet meadows, willow thickets, edge, coniferous forest, aspen groves
   108.7 (3/3)   MONAHAN: Matanuska-Susitna, AK   63.22 147.97   37 mi SE Cantwell
   103.5 (4/4)   SAVAGE: Yukon-Koyukuk, AK   63.73 149.28   14 mi SW Healy
   68.4 (7/7)   SNOWDEN: Klickitat, WA   45.83 121.35   4 mi NW Appleton

Harris' Sparrow
   Coniferous forest-tundra regions, shrubs and stunted trees, taiga
   1.3 (2/3)   CHURCHILL: MB   58.63   93.78   18 mi SE Churchill

Dark-eyed Junco
   Coniferous and deciduous forest, clearings, brushy areas
   76.0 (6/6)   KENNY LAKE: Valdez-Cordova, AK   61.72 144.93   11 mi NW Lower Tonsina
   69.8 (6/6)   LAKE LABERGE: YT   61.25 135.47   37 mi NW Whitehorse
   63.7 (7/7)   SITKA: Sitka, AK   57.07 135.37   1 mi NW Mount Edgecombe

Dark-eyed Junco (Slate-colored)
   Coniferous forest, open northern spruce woodlands
   69.8 (6/6)   LAKE LABERGE: YT   61.25 135.47   37 mi NW Whitehorse
   68.9 (7/7)   P GR JARDINS: PQ   47.60   70.98   21 mi NW Saint-Urbain
   68.7 (6/6)   MCQUESTEN: YT   63.57 137.42   28 mi NW Stuart Crossing

Dark-eyed Junco (Oregon)
   Coniferous forest edge, aspen groves
   62.8 (5/5)   GRANITE: Grant, OR   44.92 118.40   15 mi NE Greenhorn
   59.0 (6/6)   PAISLEY: Lake, OR   42.63 120.70   9 mi SW Paisley
   53.3 (7/7)   GREENHORN MT: Kern, CA   35.78 118.63   2 mi SE Balance Rock

Dark-eyed Junco (White-winged)
    Coniferous forest with pine, spruce, or aspen
    19.7 (7/7)   SUNDANCE: Crook, WY   44.42   104.42   2 mi NW Sundance
    9.3 (7/7)   MOSKEE: Crook, WY   44.35   104.12   6 mi NE Moskee
    7.0 (7/7)   CUSTER: Custer, SD   43.82   103.63   4 mi NW Custer

Dark-eyed Junco (Gray-headed)
    Coniferous forest, thickets bordering open areas
    36.8 (5/5)   CLOUDCROFT: Otero, NM   32.88   105.67   7 mi SE Cloudcroft
    25.3 (3/3)   RED CLIFF: Eagle, CO   39.52   106.37   1 mi NW Redcliff
    22.0 (4/4)   FLAGSTAFF: Coconino, AZ   35.38   111.70   13 mi NW Flagstaff

Yellow-eyed Junco
    Open coniferous forest, including pine-oak woodland
    8.0 (4/4)   PORTAL: Cochise, AZ   31.98   109.20   3 mi NE Paradise

McCown's Longspur
    Sparse shortgrass prairie, stubble fields, bare earth
    47.8 (6/6)   GREAT FALLS: Cascade, MT   47.48   111.28   2 mi SE Great Falls
    26.4 (7/7)   AUGUSTA: Lewis and Clark, MT 47.32   112.42   12 mi SW Augusta
    20.8 (4/4)   HAY LAKE: Glacier, MT   48.83   112.25   9 mi NE Santa Rita

Lapland Longspur
    Arctic tundra with grassy tussocks
    248.8 (5/5)   ADAK: Aleutian Islands, AK   51.85   176.60   3 mi SE Adak
    68.7 (6/6)   COLD BAY: Aleutian Islands, AK 55.00 162.00   62 mi NW Squaw Harbor
    17.3 (4/4)   TOKLAT: Yukon-Koyukuk, AK   63.47   150.07   41 mi NW Cantwell

Smith's Longspur
    Tundra with dry grassy and hummocky areas
    9.3 (3/3)   CHURCHILL: MB   58.63   93.78   18 mi SE Churchill

Chestnut-collared Longspur
    Shortgrass and mixedgrass prairie, pastures
    235.6 (7/7)   BROOKS: AB   50.57   111.85   2 mi NE Brooks
    133.9 (7/7)   DENBIGH: McHenry, ND   48.40   100.65   8 mi SW Bantry
    120.0 (4/4)   HORSEHEAD LK: Kidder, ND   47.07   99.63   7 mi SW Pettibone

Snow Bunting
    Rocky areas, shores and cliffs, dry tundra
    6.2 (5/5)   ADAK: Aleutian Islands, AK   51.85   176.60   3 mi SE Adak

EMBERIZIDAE (Icterinae) – Blackbirds, Meadowlarks, Orioles
Bobolink
    Tallgrass prairie, grasslands, wet meadows; hayfields, alfalfa and clover fields
    123.3 (6/6)   BOURGET: ON   45.42   75.27   1 mi NW Cheney
    101.7 (7/7)   VERCHERES: PQ   45.72   73.40   4 mi SW Vercheres
    95.4 (7/7)   WOODFORD: ON   44.60   80.73   0 mi Woodford

Red-winged Blackbird
    Freshwater and brackish marshes, upland cultivated fields, wet meadows, hayfields
    2071.6 (7/7)   GLENN: Glenn, CA   39.55   122.07   3 mi SW Bayliss
    1489.3 (6/6)   BRAWLEY: Imperial, CA   32.92   115.55   4 mi SW Brawley
    1296.2 (6/6)   LAGUNA: Yuma, AZ   32.85   114.40   7 mi NW Dome

Tricolored Blackbird
    Freshwater marshes with cattails, tules, bulrushes and sedges; cropland
1144.1 (7/7)	GLENN: Glenn, CA	39.55	122.07	3 mi SW Bayliss
1104.0 (7/7)	PENNINGTON: Sutter, CA	39.27	121.73	4 mi SE Pennington
196.6 (7/7)	YREKA: Siskiyou, CA	41.75	122.67	2 mi NW Yreka

Eastern Meadowlark
    Grasslands, fields and pastures, wet meadows
231.6 (5/5)	PENNYWASH CR: Osceola, FL	28.27	80.97	11 mi NE Holopaw
207.6 (7/7)	HENRIETTA: Clay, TX	33.80	98.23	2 mi SW Henrietta
156.7 (7/7)	GAINESVILLE: Cooke, TX	33.55	97.27	4 mi NE Era

Western Meadowlark
    Grasslands, fields and pastures, sagebrush regions
701.0 (5/5)	RIVERVIEW: Niobrara, WY	43.45	104.20	5 mi NE Mule Creek Junction
664.6 (5/5)	LUSK: Niobrara, WY	42.87	104.38	8 mi NE Lusk
467.1 (7/7)	PINNEO: Washington, CO	40.18	103.42	11 mi NW Akron

Yellow-headed Blackbird
    Deep marshes with cattails, tules and bulrushes
811.0 (4/4)	HORSEHEAD LK: Kidder, ND	47.07	99.63	7 mi SW Pettibone
248.5 (4/4)	BRADDOCK: Emmons, ND	46.58	100.10	0 mi Braddock
224.1 (7/7)	SHEYENNE LK: Wells, ND	47.63	100.03	10 mi NE Goodrich

Rusty Blackbird
    Moist coniferous forest, bogs, wooded watercourses, beaver ponds
11.5 (6/6)	BEAR CREEK: Yukon-Koyukuk, AK	64.00	157.00	43 mi SW Galena
8.0 (7/7)	P GR JARDINS: PQ	47.60	70.98	21 mi NW Saint-Urbain
5.0 (3/3)	NORTHWAY: SE Fairbanks, AK	62.92	141.53	15 mi SE Northway

Brewer's Blackbird
    Shrubby areas near water, riparian woodland, fields, marshes, residential areas
500.4 (7/7)	ARVIN: Kern, CA	35.23	118.88	2 mi SE Weed Patch
407.0 (7/7)	LIKELY: Modoc, CA	41.23	120.30	11 mi SE Likely
391.8 (6/6)	HOLLISTER: San Benito, CA	36.87	121.33	4 mi NE Hollister

Great-tailed Grackle
    Residential areas, parks, open areas with scattered trees
1229.1 (7/7)	RAYMONDVILLE: Willacy, TX	26.53	97.70	4 mi NW San Perlita
934.6 (7/7)	LAG ATASCOSA: Cameron, TX	26.20	97.33	6 mi NE Bayview
574.2 (5/5)	KINGSVILLE: Kleberg, TX	27.53	97.93	5 mi NW Kingsville

Boat-tailed Grackle
    Brackish marshes, coastal and open areas, pastures and fields
319.6 (5/5)	LTL CHENIER: Cameron, LA	29.77	93.02	3 mi NW Grand Chenier
168.8 (5/5)	KENDALL: Dade, FL	25.65	80.48	7 mi NW Richmond Heights
136.1 (7/7)	HACKBERRY: Cameron, LA	30.02	93.42	5 mi NW Hackberry

Common Grackle
    Residential areas, parks, open areas with scattered trees, woodland edge
846.9 (7/7)	QUINBY: Accomack, VA	37.53	75.67	4 mi SE Quinby
661.3 (7/7)	EVANSVILLE: Vanderburgh, IN	37.98	87.47	3 mi SW Stevenson
548.8 (5/5)	HARRINGTON: Kent, DE	38.95	75.53	1 mi SW Melvins Crossroads

Bronzed Cowbird
  Open areas, fields and pastures, parks
    75.4 (7/7)   RAYMONDVILLE: Willacy, TX   26.53   97.70   4 mi NW San Perlita
    52.8 (5/5)   KINGSVILLE: Kleberg, TX   27.53   97.93   5 mi NW Kingsville
    33.0 (7/7)   LAG ATASCOSA: Cameron, TX   26.20   97.33   6 mi NE Bayview

Brown-headed Cowbird
  Grassland, fields, brushy thickets, deciduous woodland, forest edge
    289.9 (7/7)   LORAINE: Renville, ND   48.87   101.55   1 mi SE Loraine
    275.3 (4/4)   HORSEHEAD LK: Kidder, ND   47.07   99.63   7 mi SW Pettibone
    262.3 (7/7)   SHEYENNE LK: Wells, ND   47.63   100.03   10 mi NE Goodrich

Orchard Oriole
  Scrub, second growth, brushy hillsides, orchards
    34.1 (7/7)   LOCUST BAYOU: Calhoun, AR   33.58   92.70   2 mi NW Locust Bayou
    33.4 (7/7)   PLETTENBERG: West Feliciana, LA   30.78   91.52   5 mi NE Labarre
    33.0 (6/6)   TOWN BLUFF: Jasper, TX   30.80   94.10   9 mi NE Spurger

Hooded Oriole
  Riparian woodland, arid mesquite scrub, residential areas
    7.0 (6/6)   SAN YSIDRO: San Diego, CA   32.55   117.17   4 mi SW Imperial Beach
    4.7 (5/6)   CP PENDLETON: San Diego, CA   33.23   117.40   3 mi NW Oceanside
    4.6 (7/7)   POMERENE: Cochise, AZ   32.03   110.30   2 mi NW Pomerene

Altamira Oriole
  Deciduous forest, arid scrub and semi-desert, second growth
    0.8 (3/4)   GUERRA: Zapata, TX   26.95   99.03   6 mi SE Bustamante

Audubon's Oriole
  Mesquite scrub, riparian thickets
    1.8 (3/5)   ENCINAL: Webb, TX   27.97   99.27   7 mi SE Encinal
    0.5 (2/4)   GUERRA: Zapata, TX   26.95   99.03   6 mi SE Bustamante

Northern Oriole
  Deciduous forest, open and edge areas, riparian woodland, orchards
    50.3 (7/7)   ALBERT: Barton, KS   38.45   98.97   2 mi SE Albert
    49.0 (7/7)   GOLD HILL: El Dorado, CA   38.75   120.93   3 mi NW Cold Springs
    47.1 (7/7)   ORANGE COVE: Tulare, CA   36.65   119.28   3 mi NE Orange Cove

Northern Oriole (Baltimore)
  Orchards, deciduous forest, wooded river bottoms, residential areas
    50.3 (7/7)   ALBERT: Barton, KS   38.45   98.97   2 mi SE Albert
    36.0 (6/6)   KEARNEY: Kearney, NE   40.63   98.83   8 mi SE Gibbon
    35.9 (7/7)   ST JOHN: Stafford, KS   37.97   98.87   6 mi SW Saint John

Northern Oriole (Bullock's)
  Deciduous forest, including cottonwood and willow; riparian woodland, field edge, mesquite scrub
    49.0 (7/7)   GOLD HILL: El Dorado, CA   38.75   120.93   3 mi NW Cold Springs
    47.1 (7/7)   ORANGE COVE: Tulare, CA   36.65   119.28   3 mi NE Orange Cove
    43.6 (7/7)   COPPEROPOLIS: Calaveras, CA   37.93   120.55   4 mi NW Yosemite Junction

Scott's Oriole
   Arid and semi-arid regions with yucca, palms, pinyon-juniper or oak scrub
   18.9 (7/7)   CORNUDAS: Hudspeth, TX   31.77   105.38   5 mi SE Cornudas
   18.3 (7/7)   PENA BLANCA: Santa Cruz, AZ   31.38   111.08   9 mi NW Nogales
   14.0 (3/3)   BLACK GAP: Brewster, TX   29.58   102.98   22 mi NE Panther Junction

EMBERIZIDAE (Carduelinae) – Finches

Gray-crowned Rosy-Finch
   Barren, rocky or grassy areas, cliffs; tundra or above timberline
   15.6 (5/5)   ADAK: Aleutian Islands, AK   51.85   176.60   3 mi SE Adak

Pine Grosbeak
   Coniferous forest and forest edge
   7.3 (3/3)   RED CLIFF: Eagle, CO   39.52   106.37   1 mi NW Redcliff
   6.7 (5/6)   KENNY LAKE: Valdez-Cordova, AK   61.72   144.93   11 mi NW Lower Tonsina

Purple Finch
   Coniferous forest with fir and spruce, edge and open areas
   45.7 (7/7)   SNOWDEN: Klickitat, WA   45.83   121.35   4 mi NW Appleton
   44.5 (6/6)   POINT REYES: Marin, CA   38.03   122.88   5 mi SW Point Reyes Station
   19.3 (7/7)   FAIRFAX: Marin, CA   37.98   122.58   1 mi SE Fairfax

Cassin's Finch
   Dry coniferous forest, open areas in ponderosa pine forest
   59.9 (7/7)   VALERMO: Los Angeles, CA   34.38   117.68   1 mi SE Big Pines
   46.2 (5/5)   ALBEE: Umatilla, OR   45.23   118.88   2 mi NE Albee
   35.4 (7/7)   SUMMIT PR: Crook, OR   44.35   120.47   22 mi SW Mitchell

House Finch
   Arid scrub, residential areas, open woodland, fields
   251.5 (6/6)   SAN YSIDRO: San Diego, CA   32.55   117.17   4 mi SW Imperial Beach
   198.3 (6/6)   GRAVESBORO: Fresno, CA   36.80   119.43   3 mi SW Piedra
   181.3 (7/7)   HUGHSON: Stanislaus, CA   37.58   120.83   2 mi SE Hughson

Red Crossbill
   Coniferous and mixed forest, pine-oak woodland
   75.6 (7/7)   CUSTER: Custer, SD   43.82   103.63   4 mi NW Custer
   57.9 (7/7)   SUNDANCE: Crook, WY   44.42   104.42   2 mi NW Sundance
   57.6 (7/7)   ROUBAIX LK: Lawrence, SD   44.22   103.65   4 mi NW Greenwood

White-winged Crossbill
   Coniferous forest, especially with spruce, fir and larch; forest edge
   32.2 (4/5)   LAURENTIDES: PQ   47.78   71.28   14 mi SE Mont-Apica
   23.6 (6/7)   PARC CARTIER: PQ   47.28   71.25   16 mi NE Saint-Adolphe
   20.4 (5/5)   ANCHOR RIVER: Kenai Peninsula, AK 59.50   149.50   38 mi SW Seward

Common Redpoll
   Sub-arctic forest, tundra with bushes or dwarf trees; shrubby areas
   42.7 (3/3)   EAGLE RIVER: YT   66.53   136.42   81 mi SW Ft McPherson, NT
   42.7 (3/3)   MONAHAN: Matanuska-Susitna, AK   63.22   147.97   37 mi SE Cantwell
   40.0 (3/3)   MACLAREN: SE Fairbanks, AK   63.07   146.07   54 mi NW Gakona

Pine Siskin
  Coniferous and mixed forest, parks, residential areas
    92.1 (7/7)   BEAVERDELL: BC   49.45   119.05   1 mi SE Beaverdell
    73.8 (5/5)   GRANITE: Grant, OR   44.92   118.40   15 mi NE Greenhorn
    70.0 (6/6)   POINT REYES: Marin, CA   38.03   122.88   5 mi SW Point Reyes Station

Lesser Goldfinch
  Open areas with scattered trees, second growth, fields, riparian and pine-oak woodland, sagebrush regions
    62.6 (7/7)   FOLSOM: El Dorado, CA   38.75   121.05   6 mi SW Pilot Hill
    53.7 (7/7)   GOLD HILL: El Dorado, CA   38.75   120.93   3 mi NW Cold Springs
    48.4 (7/7)   RUMSEY: Colusa, CA   38.97   122.27   6 mi NW Rumsey

Lawrence's Goldfinch
  Oak, pinyon-juniper and riparian woodland, chaparral, weedy areas
    10.6 (5/5)   LAKE CACHUMA: Santa Barbara, CA   34.68   119.65   15 mi SW Ventucopa
    5.9 (7/7)   CARMEL VAL: Monterey, CA   36.45   121.67   4 mi SE Carmel Valley
    5.7 (7/7)   GREENHORN MT: Kern, CA   35.78   118.63   2 mi SE Balance Rock

American Goldfinch
  Weedy fields, especially with thistle; second growth woodland, roadsides
    81.9 (7/7)   ORLEANS: Ontario, NY   42.90   77.12   2 mi NW Seneca Castle
    79.4 (7/7)   WARM BEACH: Snohomish, WA   48.13   122.33   6 mi SW Silvana
    66.4 (7/7)   ALDER CREEK: Oneida, NY   43.40   75.25   2 mi SW Alder Creek

Evening Grosbeak
  Coniferous and mixed woodland, especially with spruce and fir; second growth
    219.2 (5/5)   CAMP SHERMAN: Jefferson, OR 44.48   121.75   13 mi SE Marion Forks
    176.3 (6/6)   NEPISIQUIT: NB   47.40   66.52   22 mi NW Heath Steele
    76.9 (7/7)   SHELLROCK: Clackamas, OR   45.05   121.88   19 mi SW Government Camp

PASSERIDAE – Old World Sparrows

House Sparrow
  Urban areas, cultivated fields
    678.0 (5/5)   KINGSVILLE: Kleberg, TX   27.53   97.93   5 mi NW Kingsville
    584.8 (6/6)   WEST LIBERTY: Muscatine, IA 41.57   91.27   0 mi West Liberty
    572.0 (7/7)   ARVIN: Kern, CA   35.23   118.88   2 mi SE Weed Patch

Eurasian Tree Sparrow
  Cultivated fields, open woodland, residential areas
    11.3 (7/7)   ATHENSVILLE: Greene, IL   39.43   90.17   6 mi NE Greenfield
    4.8 (5/5)   CONCORD: Morgan, IL   39.80   90.42   3 mi NW Chapin
    1.6 (4/7)   STILLWELL: Hancock, IL   40.22   91.18   5 mi NE Loraine

Conservation issues and population trends 5

The Breeding Bird Survey (BBS) was established to track the population trends of North American birds. Changes in bird populations and the patterns of changes among groups of birds reflect the well-being of North American environments as well as the health of the individual species' populations (Temple and Wiens 1989). Each species has a unique set of nesting requirements, food preferences, climatic comfort zones, susceptibility to disease, and vulnerability to predators. Changes in populations reflect how well the environment provides for each of these needs. Studying the causes of population changes helps to identify situations that could lead to a species becoming endangered.

The status of bird populations also reflects the relative health of the environment. Humans in most parts of the world have so compartmentalized their environment that they are neither individually nor collectively dependent on the productivity, biodiversity, or health of their local environments. Food, raw materials, and energy are readily transported to any spot in the world, allowing human populations to increase beyond the capacity of the local environment to sustain them. Medical expertise prolongs life and has removed many of the constraints that formerly kept populations in balance with the local carrying capacity. Consequently, local population changes in human numbers are a poor reflection of the quality of the local environment.

Birds have no such support system. If a region does not contain the factors necessary for survival, birds either die or leave. Thus, bird population trends mirror the cumulative impact on the local environment. Bird populations change whenever water quality declines, land use shifts, or the climate changes. Investigating the patterns of these changes helps us to begin to understand not only how the birds' environments have changed but ours as well.

For many birds, especially the most abundant landbirds, the BBS is thought to track population trends well; for others, such as pelagics and night birds, it is less accurate. It has been difficult to completely substantiate how well the BBS performs. Because the BBS is designed to measure population trends at the scale of a state or a major physiographic region, it has, so far, been impossible to validate the survey by comparing BBS indices with populations of known size. There is indirect evidence that BBS trends are good measures of population change. Comparisons with trends from independent surveys such as the U.S. Fish and Wildlife Service's waterfowl and dove surveys (Sauer *et al.* 1994), National Audubon Society's Christmas Bird Counts (Butcher *et al.* 1990), migration banding stations (Pyle *et al.* 1994), state quail and pheasant surveys, and checklist projects from Quebec (Cyr and Larivee 1993) and Wisconsin (Temple and Cary 1990) all provide corroboration for the trends of many species. The harsh winters of 1976 and 1977 also provide evidence that the BBS is a reasonable measure of population changes. During those winters, ornithologists and birders documented a widespread crash in populations of semi-hardy birds wintering at the northern edges of their ranges. Data from the BBS documented those declines and subsequent recoveries (Droege and Sauer 1990, Sauer and Droege 1990b).

The table that follows lists the continental population trends for birds from 1966–1993 and 1984–1993. To calculate those trends, all BBS routes from the southern portions of the Yukon Territories south were used. Routes from Alaska were not included because coverage in Alaska is not uniformly distributed. Of the over 3500 BBS routes that have ever been run, Killdeer, Mourning Dove, Barn Swallow, European Starling, Red-winged Blackbird and Brown-headed Cowbird occur on the most routes (over 2800), though this ranking is influenced by the much greater density of eastern routes. American Crow, American Robin and House Sparrow rank just below these species, occurring on over 2600 routes.

The following sections present some of the patterns of increase and decrease found in groups, or guilds, of birds. Information about consistent patterns of population increase or decrease existing in groups of birds with similar characteristics (e.g., migratory patterns, habitat use) increases our ability to identify broadfront conservation problems that may be affecting entire plant and animal communities.

Scrub Nesters

There are strong indications that some birds breeding in successional and scrub habitats are in decline (Askins 1993). In the East, populations of

Northern Bobwhite, Brown Thrasher, Golden-winged Warbler, Prairie Warbler, Painted Bunting and Field Sparrow have declined dramatically. In the West, Scaled Quail, Curve-billed Thrasher, California Thrasher, Bell's Vireo, Clay-colored Sparrow, Brewer's Sparrow, Black-chinned Sparrow, Lark Sparrow, Black-throated Sparrow and White-crowned Sparrow are the populations showing the greatest declines. On a continent-wide basis, Common Ground-Dove, Loggerhead Shrike, and Rufous-sided Towhee populations are all decreasing. Few scrub nesting species are showing significant increases. Those that are, are often associated with more savannah-like habitats or with forest edges (e.g., Ash-throated Flycatcher, House Wren, and Cedar Waxwing).

Environmental disturbances such as burns and droughts, plus man-made disturbances such as farm abandonment, logging, and agriculture, create and maintain most scrub habitats. The extent of scrub environments in any landscape will be determined by that environment's past disturbance history. Perhaps more than any other habitat type today, the scrub or successional habitat lacks a contingent championing its conservation. These habitats are often viewed as wastelands, land waiting to be converted to better uses. Scrub-creating fires are suppressed, permitting trees to invade; sage and mesquite lands are dragged with chains in order to create a more open rangeland; farmers eliminate hedgerows to increase crop acreage; and landowners mow, plant, and clear scrub in the name of tidiness. Even logging usually provides only a relatively brief opportunity for a limited number of successional species. Modern forestry endeavors to create a brush suppressing, closed canopy environment as quickly as possible in order to maximize commercial tree growth.

Farm abandonment during the early part of this century created brush and successional environments throughout much of the East. These grassy pastures have gradually yielded to invading woody vegetation. This former mosaic of grasslands interspersed and grading to forest has now largely changed to closed canopy forests, agriculture, or has been cleared and built upon for homes, industries, and shopping malls. The pattern and extent of brushland is now largely determined by man not nature. Maintaining healthy populations of many scrub nesting species may soon require active management for these successional stages and a change in the way these transitory habitats are viewed.

Open-water and Wetland Species

A number of birds that forage in the rivers, lakes, and other open-water areas of North America have increased dramatically during the past quarter-century (e.g., Common Loon, Double-crested Cormorant, Great Blue Heron, Mute Swan, Canada Goose, Wood Duck, Osprey, Bald Eagle, Laughing Gull, and Ring-billed Gull). These gains can be interpreted as possible signs of improved water quality and decreases in ambient levels of long-lived pesticides and other contaminants. When the BBS was established, the use of chlorinated hydrocarbons and polychlorinated biphenyls (PCBs) were at their unregulated peak. Populations of many fish-eating species had declined due to the heavy contamination in many bodies of water. Following the ban of the worst pesticides and contaminants, some populations began to recover. Many of the species showing the greatest increases are those that have also benefited from the formation of man-made lakes and ponds (e.g., Double-crested Cormorant, Mute Swan, Canada Goose, and many of the gulls).

Not all of the wetland species have undergone population increases (e.g., rails, bitterns, gallinules). The BBS does a relatively poor job of surveying crepuscular and cryptic marsh dwellers, so it is difficult to determine their status using these data (with the possible exception of American Bittern, detected on over 700 BBS routes and significantly declining). With wetland loss still occurring at an estimated rate of 260,000 wetland acres/year, the impacts must be severe.

City Birds

House Sparrow, Rock Dove, and European Starling are among the most common city birds. Even these tolerant species have shown declines, with European Starling and House Sparrow populations both significantly down during the past quarter-century. The causes for these changes remain unclear. The amount of preferred habitat, both urban area and agriculture, has certainly increased. Although, changes in these species do not rank among the most critical conservation issues, it would be interesting to investigate what processes are associated with these patterns.

Backyard Birds

Backyard birds, or birds tolerant of suburban lifestyles, should benefit as suburban landscapes expand and natural habitats are modified into lawns and gardens. Birds best suited to living in such altered habitats occur commonly in both man-made and natural habitats, thus population changes in these habitat generalists are affected by changes in both suburban and rural landscapes. Consequently, it is difficult to pinpoint the causes behind the large increases in House Wren and American Robin populations; decreases in Blue Jay, Northern Mockingbird, Song Sparrow, White-crowned Sparrow, Brewer's Blackbird and Common Grackle; or the relative stability of Northern Cardinal. Could it be that there are more worms available for American Robins, but fewer acorns for Blue Jays? Are Song Sparrow declines primarily a phenomenon of rural landscapes, suburban landscapes, or both?

Despite their recent eastern colonizations, the House Finch has not shown a significant overall increase in long-term population size. Examination of regional trends demonstrated that the overall population trend is formed by a balance between rapidly increasing eastern populations

Figure 3. Changes in the relative abundance pattern of the House Finch from 1970–1991. This species, native to western North America, was introduced on Long Island, New York in 1940. Population growth was slow at first, and by the early 1970s the species had moved only as far west as Pennsylvania. Fig. 3a shows the relative abundance of the House Finch, as detected on Breeding Bird Survey (BBS) routes, for the period 1970–1976. By the early 1990s the eastern population had rapidly spread south and west. Fig. 3b shows the relative abundance of the House Finch, as detected on BBS routes, for the period 1985–1991. Only BBS routes that had been run at least twice in each time period were used in the creation of these maps.

3a

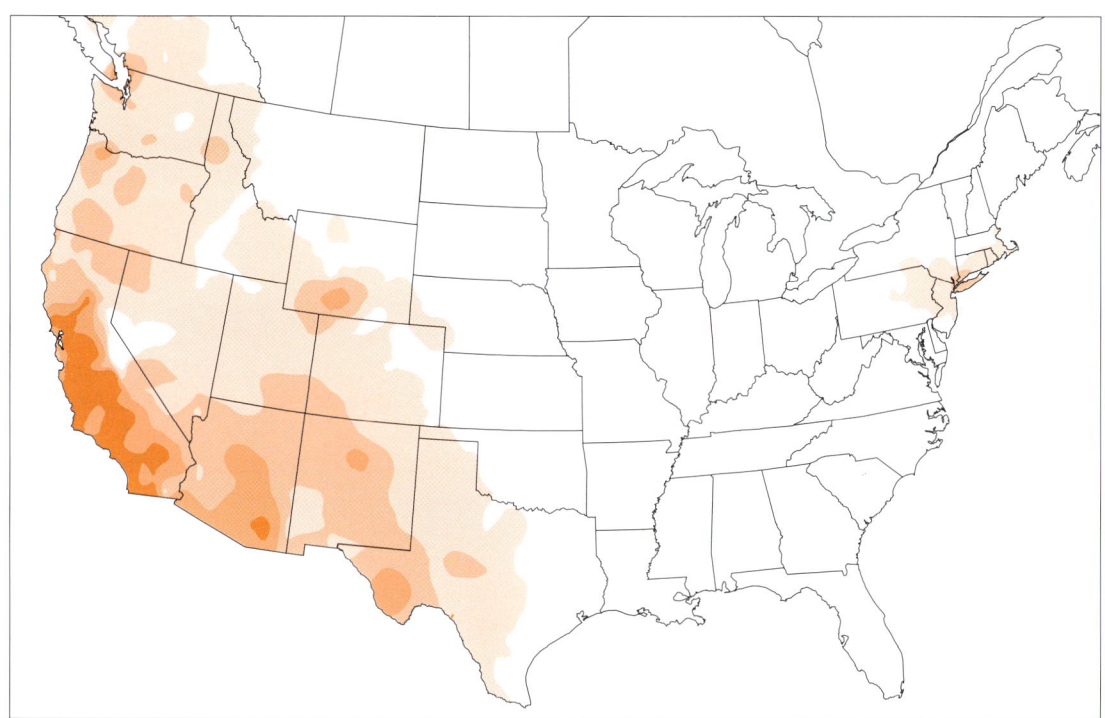

3b

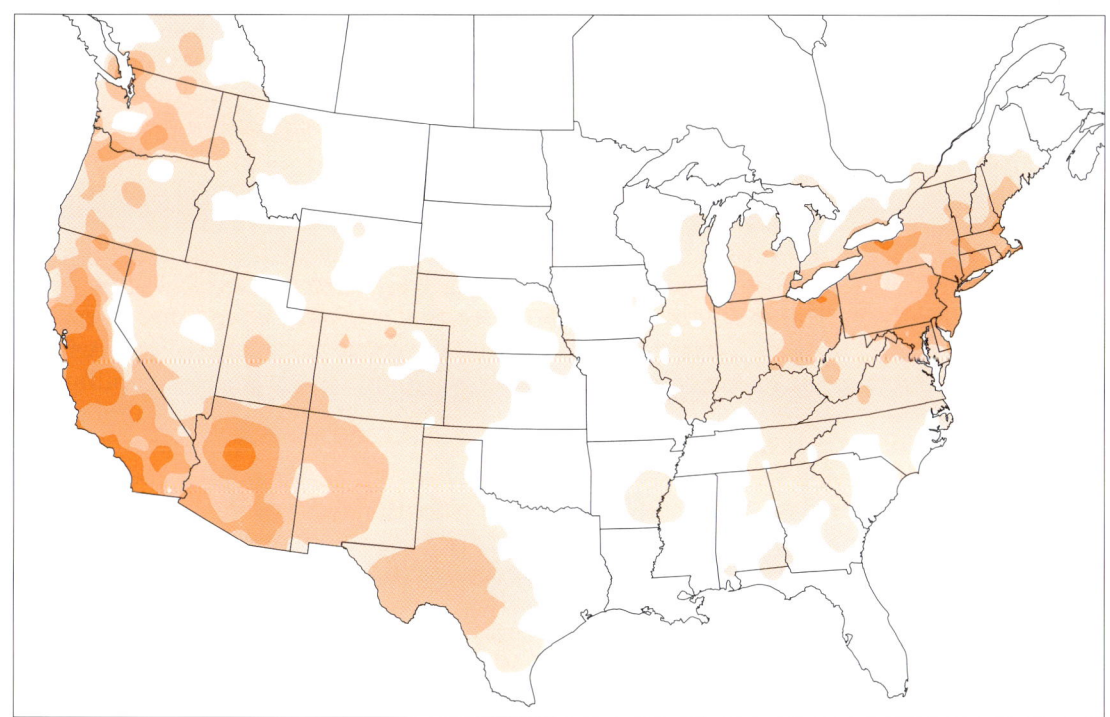

and declines in the more geographically extensive western populations. Figure 3 shows the range expansion of the House Finch over the last twenty years.

Feeder Birds

Unlike the National Audubon Society's Christmas Bird Counts or the Cornell Laboratory of Ornithology's Project Feederwatch, the BBS does not incorporate observers who count birds at feeders. However, many of the birds that appear at winter feeders occur commonly as breeders on BBS routes. Because feeding birds is now an increasingly popular activity, it is reasonable to speculate that feeder species would have increased over the past several decades. However, that does not appear to be the case. Among the jays: Scrub Jays have increased, Steller's Jays have remained steady, and Blue Jays have declined. Among the chickadees and titmice: Black-capped Chickadee and Tufted Titmouse numbers are up; Mountain Chickadee and Chestnut-backed Chickadee populations appear relatively stable; and Carolina Chickadees, Boreal Chickadees, and Plain Titmice are all significantly declining. Most of the long-term trends in finch populations appear to be relatively stable (with the exception of declines in goldfinches). However, trends during the last ten years have been uniformly negative. Populations vary so much from year to year that BBS data do not provide a clear portrait of population changes for the irruptive finches. Many, if not most, of the towhee (e.g., Rufous-sided) and sparrow (e.g., Field, Song, and White-throated) populations appear to be declining. This is probably due more to the quality and quantity of breeding habitat rather than a lack of feeder opportunities.

Grassland Nesters

More than in any other North American habitat, birds of prairies, meadows, and hayfields have declined during the past several decades. In this case the causes appear to be clear. In the East, the acreage of human maintained grasslands have declined. The small, relatively unmechanized farms that dominated that landscape in the late 19th century were abandoned through the early 1900s as large flatland farms made them uncompetitive. Farther west, in the original prairie ecoregions of North America, bird population declines can be attributed to intensification of agricultural practices. Hayfields and grazed lands are now managed so intensely that most species no longer have the opportunity to complete their nesting cycle before the fields are mowed or harvested. Worse, conversion of prairie to row crops excludes breeding by all but the Horned Lark.

Of the 28 grassland nesting species that the BBS monitors, only 7 (Ferruginous Hawk, Sharp-tailed Grouse, Upland Sandpiper, Sedge Wren, Le Conte's Sparrow, McCown's Longspur, and Chestnut-collared Longspur) have positive trends. Within that group, only the trends of the Ferruginous Hawk, Upland Sandpiper, Sedge Wren, and McCown's Longspur are statistically significant. All of the remaining grassland species show declines, many of them significant. Although most of these species are still quite common, the pattern of consistent decline raises the specter of serious problems ahead. Currently, Sprague's Pipit, Baird's Sparrow, and Henslow's Sparrow are all uncommon enough that immediate conservation efforts need to be undertaken.

The Black Tern, a prairie wetland breeder, shows a steep population decline. Insects associated with shallow prairie wetlands normally provide the bulk of this species' diet. As an insect feeder living in an agricultural landscape, this species is directly and indirectly susceptible to the applications of pesticides. Over the past 26 years, as much as 70% of the population of this species may have disappeared. This rate of decline is not sustainable and the population must stabilize soon or the species will probably become a candidate for the endangered species list.

Neotropical Migrants

The Breeding Bird Survey was designed to function as an early warning system. As unusual patterns of species declines were detected, researchers would investigate those patterns and, based on the conclusions of that research, the conservation community would design a management strategy. In reality, population declines and increases are either ignored by managers and other decision makers, or they are unaware that these population changes are occurring. The situation often becomes one of where a population decline goes undetected until the species is nearly extirpated. This then limits conservation options to those that are often expensive and disruptive. An exception to that situation is the case of neotropical migrants (birds that breed in North America, but winter from Mexico south).

In 1989, the BBS office, along with researchers from the U.S. Fish and Wildlife Service (now National Biological Service) and the Smithsonian Institution published a paper that first outlined a pattern of consistent declines in eastern forest dwelling neotropical migrants (Robbins *et al.* 1989). That paper, and numerous subsequent ones (Hagan and Johnston 1992; Finch and Stangel 1993), indicated that population declines were concentrated in the northeastern portions of the continent and that the greatest declines occurred during the 1980s. In some states and provinces in this region, populations of more than 80% of the neotropical migratory bird species were declining. There was also an indication that these declines were greatest in those species that winter in Central and South America. That pattern of broadscale decline stimulated the conservation community into uniting federal, state, and private groups interested in the conservation of these species and resulted in the formation of Partners in Flight. Partners in Flight's ultimate aim is to alleviate the problems facing neotropical migrants and to prevent those populations from moving onto the endangered species list (Stangel 1993).

Because of the complex patterns of changes in spatial and temporal populations of neotropical migrants, there are relatively few species from this group with consistent continental declines. Some of the woodland nesting species with the greatest declines include Yellow-billed Cuckoo, Eastern Wood-Pewee, Veery, Wood Thrush, and Cerulean Warbler. Not all woodland nesting species have declined however. Solitary, Warbling, and Red-eyed Vireo have all significantly increased throughout the period, as have Yellow-bellied Flycatcher and Magnolia Warbler. Figures 4–6 show the relative numbers of species of different groups of neotropical migrants in different parts of the United States and southern Canada.

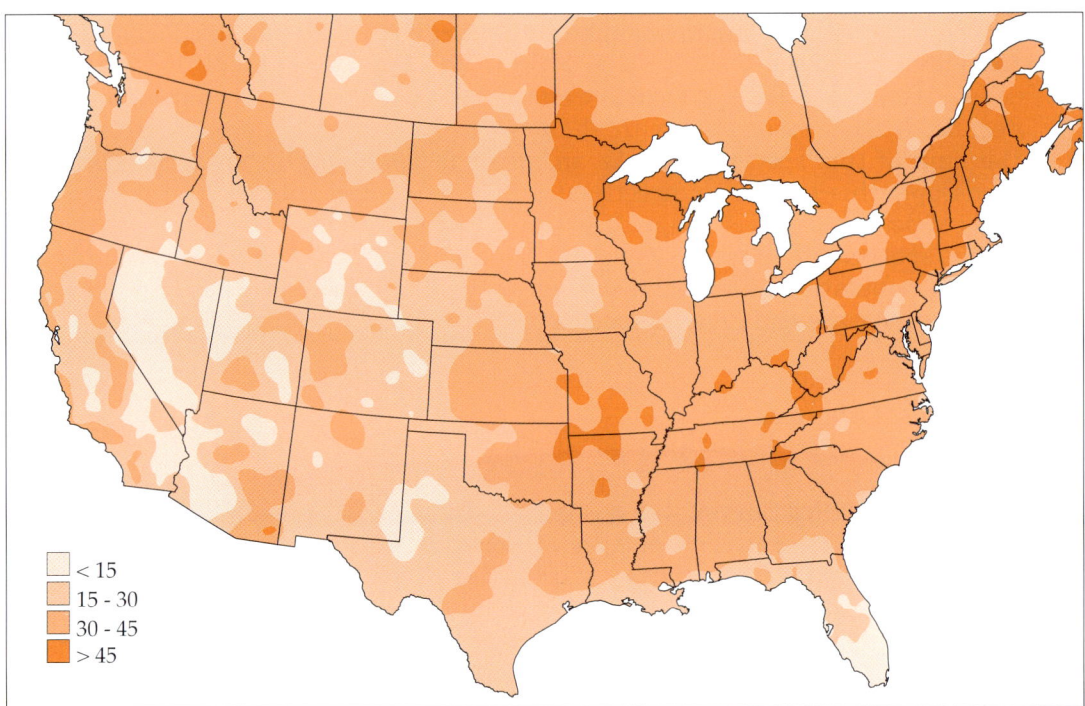

Figure 4. Annual average number of code A neotropical migrant landbird species detected on Breeding Bird Survey (BBS) routes. These are species that breed in North America and spend their nonbreeding period primarily south of the United States. This map is based on the species list developed by Partners in Flight. Routes used in creating this map were the same as used for all other maps; see chapters 2 or 3 for more details.

Some Other Species Groups

All but three of the diurnal raptors have increased throughout the period. Of the declining species, only Harris' Hawk shows a significant decline. Black Vulture, Osprey, Bald Eagle, Red-shouldered Hawk, Red-tailed Hawk, and Crested Caracara have all increased. Recovery from the pesticide era, an increase in the overall amount of wooded cover, and a decrease in illegal shooting are all likely contributors to these increases.

Two of the 'big tree' woodpeckers, Hairy and Pileated, are showing significant increases; while open country woodpeckers such as Red-headed and Ladder-backed Woodpeckers, and Northern Flicker are showing steep declines. Even Downy Woodpecker populations are showing some recent declines.

The bluebirds show a range of trends. Eastern and Mountain Bluebird populations are up and Western is down. Eastern Bluebirds are an especially interesting example of the short-term impacts weather can have on birds. During the winters of 1976 and 1977 a series of heavy winter storms accompanied by a prolonged cold snap hit much of the East and Upper Midwest. While snow remained on the ground, bluebirds were forced to rely on residual berries and what overwintering insects could be gleaned from exposed trees and bushes. During that time populations of Eastern

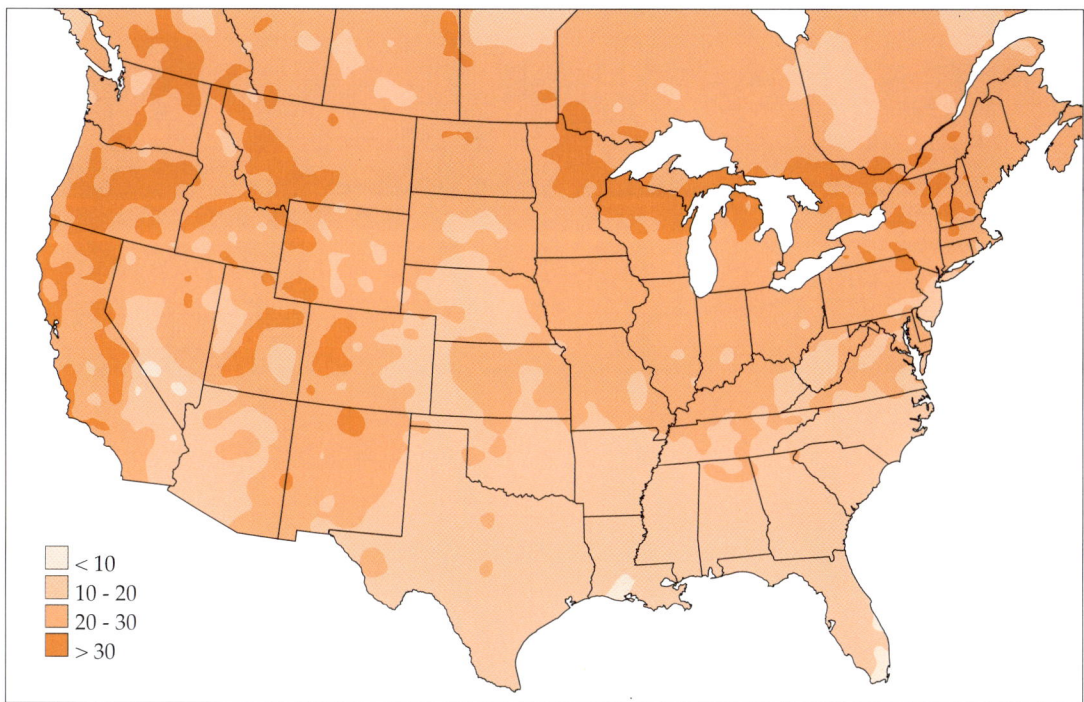

Figure 5. Annual average number of code B neotropical migrant landbird species detected on Breeding Bird Survey (BBS) routes. These are species that breed and winter in North America, although some populations winter and spend their nonbreeding period primarily south of the United States. This map is based on the species list developed by Partners in Flight. Routes used in creating this map were the same as used for all other maps; see chapters 2 or 3 for more details.

Bluebirds and other semi-hardy species (e.g., Northern Bobwhite, Hermit Thrush, Winter Wren) plummeted, but have since recovered.

Data collected by the BBS demonstrates the expansion and population increases of Brown-headed Cowbird into the West and the Deep South. Interestingly, increases in the West have been counterbalanced by large decreases in portions of the East. Even with these increases in range, the overall populations of both Brown-headed and Bronzed Cowbird have significantly declined. Shiny Cowbird, a species which has recently colonized Florida, has just begun to be detected on BBS routes. Although there are not enough data yet to calculate any trends, it will be interesting to see how quickly this species becomes established.

Summary

The information highlighted here is only a portion of what the BBS data can provide about changing bird populations. Each species is connected directly to its environment via the food it eats, the habitats in which it lives, and its climatic adaptations. As such, these species act as sentinels to environmental change, both beneficial and adverse.

As landscapes change, so do the populations of birds. Some birds will benefit whereas others will not. While landscape change is a natural

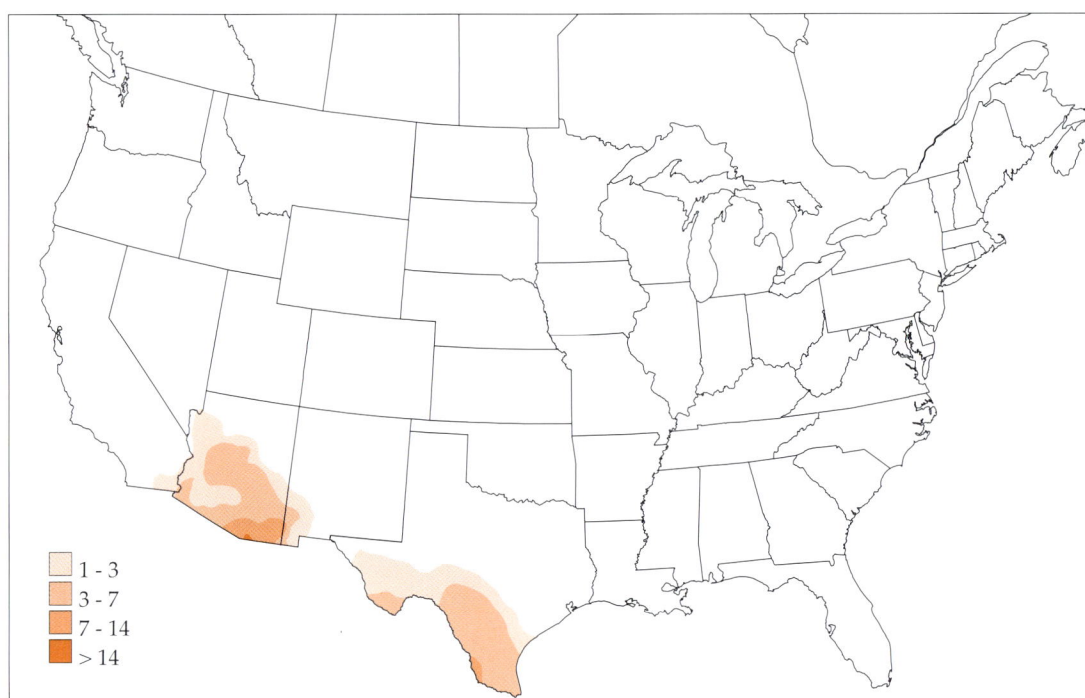

Figure 6. Annual average number of code C neotropical migrant landbird species detected on Breeding Bird Survey (BBS) routes. These are species that breed primarily south of the United States but that have small populations breeding in the United States. Code D (not shown) is restricted to those tropical species that have a portion of their breeding range in Florida. This map is based on the species list developed by Partners in Flight. Routes used in creating this map were the same as used for all other maps; see chapters 2 or 3 for more details.

process, the types of changes occurring today are unprecedented – in rate, magnitude, and type – in the evolutionary history of birds and mankind. Consider the Great Plains. One-hundred and fifty years ago this system was a continuous expanse of grasslands, broken only by wetlands, streams, and rivers. Trees were rare and even the riparian areas were mostly devoid of the large cottonwoods that dominate those areas today. Migrating herds of buffalo and other grazers occurred at high densities, and prairie dog towns were widespread. Today, this system has been configured to support high intensity agriculture. Over 50% of the wetlands have been drained, woody vegetation is now widespread, and almost all of the native grazers are gone. As a consequence of these changes, the community of prairie bird species and their populations are drastically different from that of the recent past. During an extraordinarily brief period of time, the Whooping Crane was nearly lost, and the abundance of most species has been greatly reduced.

What about the environment of the Great Plains today? Current land-use practices seem to be pushing several species toward critically low populations. In this chapter, several possible endangered species candidates (e.g., Black Tern, Sprague's Pipit, Baird's and Henslow's Sparrows) have been listed. Information from the BBS and other sources now provides the ability to directly track changes in bird populations. Such monitoring tools permit the detection of declines before they become critical. To be effectively used, birders and conservationists must train themselves to use these tools

Interpreting the Trends

The following pages contain the population changes for some of the species discussed in this book. Trend analyses are presented for two time periods. The first trend is for the entire length of time the Breeding Bird Survey (BBS) has been run (1966–1993). The second is for the last ten years (1984–1993). Trends from 1966–1993 are calculated from routes that began in the eastern states and provinces in 1966, the central states and provinces in 1967, and the western states and provinces in 1968. The geographic coverage of the analyses include the southern portions of Canada and the entire lower 48 states. These data are provided courtesy of the National Biological Service.

The table lists the species, the overall percentage of population increase or decrease for that time period, the significance of the trend, and the number of routes used in calculating the trend. The overall percentage change is based on the median population trend estimate provided by the BBS. Positive values represent population increases and negative values represent population decreases.

The asterisks (*) indicate whether that particular population change is statistically significant. If there are no asterisks following the value, then there has been no statistically significant change in the population. The level of significance is as follows: * $p<0.10$; ** $p<0.05$; *** $p<0.01$. The more asterisks (the smaller the p value) the less likely it is that that particular value could have occurred by random chance alone (e.g., *** indicates that there is a less than 1% probability that that value could have been obtained by chance alone).

These trends represent estimates of the true population trends for these species. As such, they are subject to the sampling problems inherent in the technique used by the BBS. Individual estimates are affected by how variable the data are, low sample sizes, and any biases in how the data were collected. Consequently, it is difficult to use the estimated figures to rank species by how much they are declining or increasing. In fact, the species with the largest estimated increases and decreases are the ones most likely to be the farthest from the truth. The calculation of statistical significance helps identify those species most likely to be declining, but large declines could be masked by BBS data for some species if those species are inadequately sampled. Consequently, while statistical significance does imply that a species is increasing or decreasing (assuming there is no bias) the lack of a trend does not imply that a species has a stable population.

The sample size is the number of routes used in calculating the trend. These are *not* the same number of routes used in creating the maps. Caution should be used in interpreting any population change that was calculated based on fewer than 50 BBS routes.

For example
American Bittern   −38.9** (743)   −25.5*(440)

American Bittern has undergone a 38.9% decline during the period 1966–1993. This is based on BBS data collected on 743 routes and is statistically significant at the $p<0.05$ level. For the period 1984–1993, the decline has been less severe (25.5%). This value is significant at the $p<0.10$ level, but was based on fewer (440) BBS routes.

In terms of conservation it is important to look at both the long-term (1966–1993) and short-term (1984–1993) population changes. For many species there may be an overall long-term increase but a substantial short-term decline. The BBS trends provide an early warning system that a species might be in trouble. Hopefully, this warning allows conservation action to be taken before the species is classified as threatened or endangered.

Population stability is difficult to define. All species fluctuate in numbers within and among years. To define stability one has to define a threshold trend (e.g., 1% change per year) that above which constitutes a population increase and below which constitutes a population decline. Having defined a threshold, it would be possible to test for stability. This type of test is not presented here, but BBS data are available, in various formats, from the BBS offices in the U.S. and Canada for those interested (see chapter 1 for addresses of the BBS offices).

Population trends of some North American birds

Species	Population Trend (% change)			
	1966–1993		1984–1993	
Common Loon	95.4***	(460)	26.2***	(333)
Pied-billed Grebe	−41.3***	(624)	−48.6***	(385)
Horned Grebe	−28.0	(107)	−42.4**	(64)
Red-necked Grebe	49.8	(81)	−6.6	(59)
Eared Grebe	255.0**	(177)	49.4	(104)
American White Pelican	109.0**	(167)	4.6	(134)
Brown Pelican	252.6	(36)	14.6	(32)
Double-crested Cormorant	210.7***	(533)	−14.6	(437)
Anhinga	−39.5	(118)	−54.1***	(96)
American Bittern	−38.9**	(743)	−25.5*	(440)
Least Bittern	16.4	(77)	−42.6**	(38)
Great Blue Heron	47.0***	(2179)	6.7	(1858)
Great Egret	52.0	(537)	38.2**	(448)
Snowy Egret	221.7**	(284)	77.5*	(218)
Little Blue Heron	−29.1	(449)	−17.5	(346)
Tricolored Heron	27.4	(117)	20.1	(75)
Cattle Egret	43.2*	(509)	−9.4	(433)
Green Heron	−7.6	(1654)	−9.8	(1324)
Black-crowned Night-Heron	42.8	(510)	−22.8	(301)
Yellow-crowned Night-Heron	72.0*	(269)	51.3*	(153)
White Ibis	208.6	(178)	−5.0	(146)
Glossy Ibis	564.6	(57)	−12.8	(35)
Wood Stork	13.1	(85)	−28.5	(56)
Black-bellied Whistling-Duck	563.1**	(31)	−59.2	(25)
Mute Swan	1946.3***	(41)	42.5***	(32)
Canada Goose	499.8***	(1197)	89.7***	(1032)
Wood Duck	112.8***	(1365)	36.8**	(1040)
Green-winged Teal	−25.5*	(440)	−20.5	(274)
American Black Duck	−27.1	(448)	−5.5	(210)
Mottled Duck	−78.8**	(68)	−46.3	(52)
Mallard	36.9*	(2013)	27.3*	(1686)
Northern Pintail	−76.4***	(512)	−24.8	(328)
Blue-winged Teal	−16.8	(833)	−31.5**	(526)
Cinnamon Teal	112.6	(298)	−38.5**	(210)
Northern Shoveler	31.8	(397)	9.7	(274)
Gadwall	190.8***	(418)	77.6***	(322)
American Wigeon	−11.3	(343)	−20.0	(240)
Canvasback	−28.6	(166)	−62.1***	(109)
Redhead	211.3**	(264)	5.9	(189)
Ring-necked Duck	57.0	(184)	40.3*	(123)
Lesser Scaup	42.2	(277)	10.9	(183)
Common Goldeneye	−14.6	(154)	26.3	(92)
Barrow's Goldeneye	149.5	(50)	29.2	(35)
Bufflehead	36.5	(90)	48.2	(67)
Hooded Merganser	71.8*	(144)	40.4***	(94)
Common Merganser	59.5**	(435)	31.6**	(315)
Red-breasted Merganser	−56.7*	(49)	−8.6	(25)
Ruddy Duck	14.3	(256)	−45.2**	(172)

contd.

Species	Population Trend (% change)			
	1966–1993		1984–1993	
Black Vulture	114.4*	(554)	12.8	(442)
Turkey Vulture	17.9	(1805)	4.4	(1524)
Osprey	109.2***	(479)	44.2***	(354)
American Swallow-tailed Kite	89.2**	(55)	218.1	(46)
White-tailed Kite	31.2	(96)	−10.1	(58)
Mississippi Kite	26.8	(188)	−9.5	(153)
Bald Eagle	353.3***	(217)	78.8***	(160)
Northern Harrier	−9.2	(1155)	25.3**	(821)
Cooper's Hawk	16.7***	(868)	16.4***	(549)
Northern Goshawk	−3.7	(204)	−12.2***	(121)
Harris' Hawk	−64.6***	(40)	−53.1	(27)
Red-shouldered Hawk	58.5**	(949)	9.8	(664)
Broad-winged Hawk	16.4	(1002)	−8.6	(664)
Swainson's Hawk	44.2*	(678)	5.2	(518)
Red-tailed Hawk	76.1***	(2592)	30.6***	(2216)
Ferruginous Hawk	55.0**	(276)	64.8***	(208)
Golden Eagle	20.1	(384)	40.9*	(268)
Crested Caracara	268.1***	(35)	133.9*	(32)
American Kestrel	14.0*	(2365)	5.9	(1822)
Merlin	48.9**	(175)	26.4	(109)
Peregrine Falcon	25.7	(39)	93.2**	(25)
Prairie Falcon	9.4	(296)	−15.8	(192)
Gray Partridge	51.6	(313)	−7.0	(246)
Chukar	−84.2**	(88)	−56.6**	(55)
Ring-necked Pheasant	−29.4**	(1314)	24.3***	(1012)
Blue Grouse	−72.3**	(107)	13.8	(71)
Ruffed Grouse	−14.4	(745)	19.6	(444)
Sage Grouse	269.7	(108)	−27.9	(74)
Greater Prairie-Chicken	−85.3	(54)	182.3	(34)
Sharp-tailed Grouse	32.7	(187)	18.7	(132)
Wild Turkey	78.5***	(701)	92.2***	(605)
Northern Bobwhite	−48.7***	(1385)	−19.3***	(1158)
Scaled Quail	−61.6***	(118)	−27.2	(96)
Gambel's Quail	52.0*	(101)	3.2	(72)
California Quail	19.1	(275)	119.7***	(224)
Mountain Quail	46.3	(118)	41.4	(91)
Clapper Rail	97.9	(51)	1.4	(37)
King Rail	10.3	(63)	44.9	(31)
Virginia Rail	−2.1	(195)	−10.1*	(96)
Sora	−44.4**	(569)	−29.2*	(414)
Purple Gallinule	53.0	(34)	141.5	(17)
Common Moorhen	115.9	(178)	−7.6	(111)
American Coot	−41.1	(656)	−56.7***	(434)
Limpkin	−89.7*	(27)	49.3	(17)
Sandhill Crane	230.3***	(284)	26.9	(250)
Killdeer	−12.1**	(2818)	−26.6***	(2451)
Mountain Plover	−61.3***	(46)	51.7	(32)
Black-necked Stilt	70.6	(129)	−34.1	(95)
American Avocet	2.8	(277)	34.8	(211)
Greater Yellowlegs	31.9	(35)	−17.5	(22)
Lesser Yellowlegs	−72.9***	(76)	−62.4***	(46)

contd.

Species	Population Trend (% change)			
	1966–1993		1984–1993	
Solitary Sandpiper	0.9	(47)	32.8	(22)
Willet	−15.2	(314)	−14.1	(243)
Spotted Sandpiper	2.7	(1184)	9.9	(737)
Upland Sandpiper	103.4***	(709)	−5.5	(509)
Long-billed Curlew	−36.5	(253)	−46.4***	(194)
Marbled Godwit	22.0	(196)	19.8	(158)
Common Snipe	−0.6	(1040)	−30.3***	(802)
American Woodcock	−3.5	(442)	7.8	(198)
Wilson's Phalarope	−2.1	(369)	−41.0***	(263)
Laughing Gull	428.1***	(129)	78.8**	(102)
Franklin's Gull	26.7	(231)	15.6	(154)
Bonaparte's Gull	−7.8	(34)	−46.5	(14)
Ring-billed Gull	535.2***	(711)	11.4	(557)
California Gull	−24.7	(242)	−38.8	(186)
Herring Gull	−21.8	(456)	−41.7	(301)
Glaucous-winged Gull	286.5**	(41)	41.2	(29)
Great Black-backed Gull	−21.1	(109)	−35.3*	(70)
Caspian Tern	85.9*	(123)	55.5	(88)
Royal Tern	−31.0	(45)	−8.1	(27)
Common Tern	−5.4	(188)	−67.0*	(103)
Forster's Tern	129.3	(167)	35.3	(118)
Least Tern	−69.4	(92)	−14.5	(58)
Black Tern	−71.6***	(381)	8.8	(234)
Black Skimmer	−91.4*	(48)	2.5	(32)
Rock Dove	18.4*	(2340)	−11.5**	(1956)
Band-tailed Pigeon	−60.9***	(199)	−39.6*	(145)
White-winged Dove	6.5	(94)	12.2	(71)
Mourning Dove	−1.4	(2881)	7.3***	(2560)
Inca Dove	20.8	(72)	21.3	(56)
Common Ground-Dove	−51.9**	(199)	41.2*	(163)
Black-billed Cuckoo	−2.5	(1326)	−3.0	(939)
Yellow-billed Cuckoo	−31.2***	(1681)	−12.2***	(1338)
Greater Roadrunner	15.6	(289)	−10.6	(200)
Barn Owl	−10.5	(89)	−18.2	(44)
Great Horned Owl	16.8	(1645)	−12.6	(1203)
Northern Pygmy-Owl	9.2	(102)	−6.0	(63)
Burrowing Owl	5.0	(379)	18.6	(240)
Barred Owl	22.8**	(914)	−5.1	(632)
Short-eared Owl	−14.3	(285)	−13.1	(143)
Lesser Nighthawk	337.1**	(130)	−46.8	(85)
Common Nighthawk	−13.3	(1701)	−28.7***	(1225)
Common Poorwill	37.6	(178)	10.6	(107)
Chuck-will's-widow	−21.4*	(544)	−2.9	(459)
Whip-poor-will	−20.5	(649)	6.1	(372)
Black Swift	49.0	(82)	31.5	(55)
Chimney Swift	−21.0***	(1838)	−19.9***	(1593)
Vaux's Swift	−29.4	(159)	−26.5	(121)
White-throated Swift	−67.1*	(210)	−33.7	(148)
Ruby-throated Hummingbird	44.4*	(1513)	6.9	(1181)
Black-chinned Hummingbird	28.3	(219)	−22.2	(149)
Anna's Hummingbird	−15.9	(142)	15.3	(105)

contd.

Species	Population Trend (% change)			
	1966–1993		1984–1993	
Costa's Hummingbird	292.5**	(77)	267.2***	(50)
Calliope Hummingbird	53.6	(118)	−28.1**	(90)
Broad-tailed Hummingbird	26.3	(142)	19.4	(116)
Rufous Hummingbird	−59.4***	(198)	−22.0	(153)
Allen's Hummingbird	−10.6	(45)	−45.5**	(27)
Belted Kingfisher	−20.3***	(2097)	−9.4**	(1601)
Lewis' Woodpecker	−40.4	(122)	−28.8	(71)
Red-headed Woodpecker	−38.4***	(1286)	−10.3*	(1027)
Acorn Woodpecker	31.8**	(144)	23.4**	(104)
Gila Woodpecker	45.3	(30)	7.5	(24)
Golden-fronted Woodpecker	−44.4	(57)	−32.6**	(45)
Red-bellied Woodpecker	16.0***	(1301)	15.5***	(1168)
Red-naped Sapsucker	17.0	(199)	111.0***	(171)
Yellow-bellied Sapsucker	−17.7	(614)	46.7***	(481)
Red-breasted Sapsucker	6.7	(155)	53.4	(116)
Williamson's Sapsucker	65.8	(75)	−28.5*	(60)
Ladder-backed Woodpecker	−45.2***	(171)	−13.9	(136)
Nuttall's Woodpecker	35.0	(96)	−10.5	(72)
Downy Woodpecker	0.1	(2296)	−8.6***	(1952)
Hairy Woodpecker	28.0***	(2120)	1.8	(1666)
Red-cockaded Woodpecker	−24.5	(51)	−34.9***	(17)
White-headed Woodpecker	121.5**	(61)	47.1	(40)
Three-toed Woodpecker	−1.4	(47)	5.3	(33)
Black-backed Woodpecker	22.5	(134)	−65.0***	(83)
Yellow-shafted Flicker	−51.1***	(2102)	−9.1***	(1793)
Red-shafted Flicker	−18.6	(759)	7.2	(637)
Pileated Woodpecker	33.2***	(1571)	5.3	(1322)
Olive-sided Flycatcher	−48.8***	(764)	−24.5***	(528)
Western Wood-Pewee	−19.9	(703)	−18.7***	(575)
Eastern Wood-Pewee	−35.6***	(1765)	−13.5***	(1524)
Yellow-bellied Flycatcher	239.3***	(243)	42.8***	(142)
Acadian Flycatcher	15.5*	(887)	3.2	(705)
Least Flycatcher	−12.8	(1174)	−9.3*	(887)
Hammond's Flycatcher	33.8	(244)	9.9	(213)
Dusky Flycatcher	25.7	(298)	−14.9*	(254)
Gray Flycatcher	228.2*	(113)	122.8**	(90)
Black Phoebe	51.7*	(166)	−34.5***	(120)
Eastern Phoebe	21.7**	(1710)	59.0***	(1430)
Say's Phoebe	19.4	(560)	19.1	(437)
Vermilion Flycatcher	−54.0*	(62)	75.4	(37)
Ash-throated Flycatcher	94.0***	(413)	15.2*	(320)
Great Crested Flycatcher	1.3	(1860)	−0.7	(1640)
Brown-crested Flycatcher	423.8***	(55)	74.9***	(38)
Cassin's Kingbird	−42.3	(159)	−16.1	(110)
Western Kingbird	48.8***	(1024)	2.1	(837)
Eastern Kingbird	−3.1	(2347)	2.9	(2041)
Scissor-tailed Flycatcher	−0.1	(264)	2.2	(223)
Horned Lark	−17.3**	(1830)	−8.1**	(1379)
Purple Martin	14.0	(1652)	−26.8***	(1250)
Tree Swallow	40.8***	(1775)	-7.7	(1471)
Violet-green Swallow	24.1	(557)	10.3	(442)

contd.

Species	Population Trend (% change)			
	1966–1993		1984–1993	
Northern Rough-winged Swallow	26.5	(2202)	1.6	(1730)
Bank Swallow	−12.6	(1344)	−32.5***	(888)
Cliff Swallow	34.2**	(1819)	−6.6	(1459)
Barn Swallow	7.1	(2830)	−24.1***	(2470)
Gray Jay	−0.6	(371)	51.8***	(247)
Steller's Jay	10.8	(364)	11.4**	(300)
Blue Jay	−35.9***	(2045)	−5.0**	(1805)
Scrub Jay	45.5***	(290)	8.0	(235)
Pinyon Jay	9.7	(156)	93.8**	(120)
Clark's Nutcracker	98.3*	(208)	−4.8	(169)
Black-billed Magpie	−31.3***	(628)	19.9**	(525)
Yellow-billed Magpie	−13.4	(37)	28.9	(28)
American Crow	26.1***	(2678)	12.9***	(2316)
Northwestern Crow	69.9**	(29)	−0.8	(19)
Fish Crow	106.1***	(487)	−2.5	(416)
Chihuahuan Raven	−62.8	(102)	−32.7	(67)
Common Raven	162.4***	(1269)	37.0***	(1065)
Black-capped Chickadee	58.5***	(1466)	8.5*	(1259)
Carolina Chickadee	−17.4**	(890)	−23.9***	(794)
Mountain Chickadee	1.8	(328)	4.7	(275)
Boreal Chickadee	−64.0***	(195)	3.4	(104)
Chestnut-backed Chickadee	−30.1	(142)	−13.4	(120)
Plain Titmouse	−45.5***	(194)	−7.6	(149)
Tufted Titmouse	22.0***	(1337)	20.3***	(1163)
Black-crested Titmouse	65.7***	(65)	−24.8	(51)
Verdin	−33.1	(118)	−22.2	(86)
Bushtit	−22.8	(269)	−7.7	(196)
Red-breasted Nuthatch	102.5***	(937)	52.2***	(761)
White-breasted Nuthatch	66.6***	(1732)	4.5	(1421)
Pygmy Nuthatch	83.0**	(122)	58.1*	(84)
Brown-headed Nuthatch	−28.4	(298)	−27.6**	(256)
Brown Creeper	13.3	(609)	−18.9	(436)
Cactus Wren	−22.1	(154)	−37.5***	(123)
Rock Wren	−39.4***	(564)	−18.8**	(452)
Canyon Wren	−20.7	(193)	−12.2	(128)
Carolina Wren	29.2***	(1174)	37.0***	(1025)
Bewick's Wren	−5.2	(628)	−17.7	(425)
House Wren	55.5***	(2018)	28.8***	(1697)
Winter Wren	101.1	(677)	33.5***	(528)
Sedge Wren	83.3**	(402)	−2.1	(294)
Marsh Wren	84.0*	(448)	49.8*	(307)
American Dipper	−14.0	(128)	−33.4	(89)
Golden-crowned Kinglet	−12.3	(562)	9.3	(433)
Ruby-crowned Kinglet	−23.8	(671)	46.1***	(465)
Blue-gray Gnatcatcher	34.9*	(1304)	32.2***	(1101)
Black-tailed Gnatcatcher	−18.3	(69)	23.4	(43)
Eastern Bluebird	97.4***	(1691)	53.2***	(1485)
Western Bluebird	−35.7***	(268)	−22.3	(197)
Mountain Bluebird	51.0**	(484)	102.8***	(399)
Townsend's Solitaire	70.9	(268)	−13.6	(220)
Veery	−29.4***	(984)	−19.6***	(782)

contd.

Species	Population Trend (% change)			
	1966–1993		1984–1993	
Swainson's Thrush	11.6	(725)	−7.8	(511)
Hermit Thrush	91.0***	(931)	32.4***	(738)
Wood Thrush	−38.6***	(1549)	3.8	(1295)
American Robin	29.4***	(2702)	4.0***	(2383)
Varied Thrush	63.3**	(155)	−28.9**	(123)
Wrentit	−30.5	(117)	−11.2	(94)
Gray Catbird	−7.9	(1997)	9.3***	(1689)
Northern Mockingbird	−23.1***	(1794)	3.4	(1499)
Sage Thrasher	36.1	(272)	3.8	(223)
Brown Thrasher	−27.1***	(1974)	−1.9	(1682)
Bendire's Thrasher	−67.7	(43)	−28.8	(24)
Curve-billed Thrasher	−61.8***	(113)	2.2	(80)
California Thrasher	−66.2**	(84)	−20.3	(56)
Crissal Thrasher	99.2**	(43)	−22.3**	(29)
Le Conte's Thrasher	−11.7	(42)	15.0	(26)
Sprague's Pipit	−63.1***	(142)	−46.9**	(100)
Cedar Waxwing	74.4***	(1689)	4.3	(1437)
Phainopepla	70.5*	(114)	−19.8	(88)
Loggerhead Shrike	−54.7***	(1437)	1.3	(1082)
European Starling	−23.6***	(2836)	−8.9***	(2474)
White-eyed Vireo	−0.5	(979)	18.6***	(810)
Bell's Vireo	−40.4***	(315)	−26.3***	(201)
Solitary Vireo	145.5***	(1011)	59.0***	(789)
Yellow-throated Vireo	20.4**	(1234)	6.4	(974)
Hutton's Vireo	20.4	(140)	−19.9	(104)
Warbling Vireo	42.0***	(1825)	7.2*	(1476)
Philadelphia Vireo	54.6	(189)	66.7*	(110)
Red-eyed Vireo	42.0***	(2081)	7.9**	(1737)
Black-whiskered Vireo	43.5	(8)	−23.5	(6)
Blue-winged Warbler	-3.5	(511)	−7.5	(360)
Golden-winged Warbler	−44.0***	(341)	10.5	(208)
Tennessee Warbler	171.0	(332)	−69.3***	(208)
Orange-crowned Warbler	−13.9	(376)	25.3**	(304)
Nashville Warbler	58.9	(692)	−21.5**	(524)
Virginia's Warbler	108.6	(49)	13.2	(40)
Lucy's Warbler	−22.5	(41)	−29.3	(32)
Northern Parula	22.9	(1005)	1.8	(780)
Yellow Warbler	25.4***	(2231)	1.1	(1800)
Chestnut-sided Warbler	−13.3	(803)	4.8	(613)
Magnolia Warbler	100.9***	(524)	18.6*	(381)
Cape May Warbler	73.4	(242)	−51.1**	(143)
Black-throated Blue Warbler	11.3	(464)	−3.5	(329)
Myrtle Warbler	68.0***	(569)	35.0*	(445)
Audubon's Warbler	3.3	(431)	−4.9	(340)
Black-throated Gray Warbler	61.1	(212)	−23.7	(170)
Townsend's Warbler	37.2	(156)	7.4	(127)
Hermit Warbler	−5.6	(90)	−47.5**	(73)
Black-throated Green Warbler	−1.1	(644)	11.0	(492)
Blackburnian Warbler	28.3	(517)	48.1***	(375)
Yellow-throated Warbler	6.2	(538)	1.8	(405)
Grace's Warbler	−18.6	(29)	not enough data	

contd.

Species	Population Trend (% change)			
	1966–1993		1984–1993	
Pine Warbler	64.6***	(825)	30.3***	(693)
Prairie Warbler	−44.0***	(790)	−5.2	(611)
Palm Warbler	74.1	(81)	13.0	(44)
Bay-breasted Warbler	0.3	(215)	−61.9*	(121)
Blackpoll Warbler	70.9	(143)	−68.6***	(48)
Cerulean Warbler	−49.5***	(326)	−17.2	(196)
Black-and-white Warbler	23.3	(1133)	−7.2	(841)
American Redstart	−13.0	(1307)	−7.6	(937)
Prothonotary Warbler	−17.6	(474)	−12.0	(356)
Worm-eating Warbler	6.7	(401)	−3.7	(290)
Swainson's Warbler	24.0	(121)	−25.6	(81)
Ovenbird	20.0**	(1302)	9.3**	(1037)
Northern Waterthrush	19.8	(601)	−5.8	(409)
Louisiana Waterthrush	5.8	(626)	−4.1	(459)
Kentucky Warbler	−17.9	(703)	−20.2***	(533)
Connecticut Warbler	52.1*	(109)	−28.0	(72)
Mourning Warbler	−0.3	(530)	−17.0**	(397)
MacGillivray's Warbler	−7.1	(337)	2.6	(264)
Common Yellowthroat	−10.9**	(2441)	−7.6***	(2089)
Hooded Warbler	56.1*	(625)	15.5	(477)
Wilson's Warbler	18.7	(526)	−25.8***	(344)
Canada Warbler	−18.0	(512)	−21.9**	(346)
Yellow-breasted Chat	−8.7	(1327)	8.0*	(1011)
Summer Tanager	−3.4	(787)	−7.6	(640)
Scarlet Tanager	4.0	(1287)	6.0	(1039)
Western Tanager	0.5	(523)	16.1*	(413)
Northern Cardinal	−4.3	(1654)	9.0***	(1486)
Pyrrhuloxia	−16.6	(67)	−14.3	(55)
Rose-breasted Grosbeak	−9.9	(1174)	−16.5***	(971)
Black-headed Grosbeak	1.1	(552)	7.5	(455)
Blue Grosbeak	59.0***	(1068)	2.0	(899)
Lazuli Bunting	12.9	(452)	−0.3	(351)
Indigo Bunting	−15.3***	(1782)	−11.0***	(1519)
Painted Bunting	−59.5***	(284)	7.5	(233)
Dickcissel	−35.8***	(817)	−5.1	(701)
Green-tailed Towhee	17.0	(240)	3.7	(197)
Rufous-sided Towhee	−39.1***	(2042)	−1.0	(1711)
Bachman's Sparrow	−28.2	(210)	−33.0**	(135)
Cassin's Sparrow	−50.1***	(190)	42.0***	(155)
Rufous-crowned Sparrow	34.4	(114)	2.6	(84)
Chipping Sparrow	1.1	(2414)	3.5	(2015)
Clay-colored Sparrow	−27.8***	(464)	3.2	(358)
Brewer's Sparrow	−61.8***	(402)	−28.2***	(333)
Field Sparrow	−57.0***	(1626)	−11.7***	(1334)
Black-chinned Sparrow	−87.1***	(60)	39.0	(32)
Vesper Sparrow	−7.6	(1548)	7.4	(1127)
Lark Sparrow	−61.2***	(1013)	−26.6***	(772)
Black-throated Sparrow	−56.7**	(253)	9.5	(193)
Sage Sparrow	−29.8	(235)	63.4*	(160)
Lark Bunting	−44.1*	(390)	38.0**	(295)
Savannah Sparrow	−13.3	(1502)	−3.7	(1173)

contd.

Species	Population Trend (% change)			
	1966–1993		1984–1993	
Baird's Sparrow	−37.9	(138)	5.5	(97)
Grasshopper Sparrow	−67.8***	(1540)	−0.3	(1176)
Henslow's Sparrow	−74.7**	(253)	−56.3**	(113)
Le Conte's Sparrow	81.5	(169)	29.8*	(135)
Sharp-tailed Sparrow	19.5	(98)	25.8	(67)
Seaside Sparrow	130.6*	(28)	4.2	(22)
Fox Sparrow	27.3	(213)	−17.9	(142)
Song Sparrow	−17.6***	(2162)	6.6***	(1830)
Lincoln's Sparrow	229.5**	(430)	17.8	(311)
Swamp Sparrow	14.9	(786)	9.6	(586)
White-throated Sparrow	−28.2***	(625)	−12.9***	(481)
White-crowned Sparrow	−33.4**	(288)	4.5	(201)
Slate-colored Junco	−14.2	(539)	−3.7	(397)
Oregon Junco	−30.8***	(362)	−30.3***	(301)
Gray-headed Junco	95.8	(68)	57.8	(58)
McCown's Longspur	570.2***	(72)	124.3**	(46)
Chestnut-collared Longspur	12.7	(157)	32.2**	(115)
Bobolink	−34.2***	(1170)	−38.5***	(962)
Red-winged Blackbird	−26.5***	(2894)	−19.3***	(2540)
Tricolored Blackbird	466.9	(68)	−88.3**	(38)
Eastern Meadowlark	−46.0***	(1807)	−20.3***	(1537)
Western Meadowlark	−13.1*	(1424)	0.8	(1148)
Yellow-headed Blackbird	68.3	(690)	−33.2***	(535)
Rusty Blackbird	−79.9*	(160)	−32.0	(57)
Brewer's Blackbird	−29.4***	(1072)	−28.2***	(884)
Great-tailed Grackle	639.2***	(229)	−14.0	(200)
Boat-tailed Grackle	65.2	(124)	5.2	(94)
Common Grackle	−32.4***	(2284)	−15.9***	(2011)
Bronzed Cowbird	−1.6	(56)	−55.2**	(42)
Brown-headed Cowbird	−21.1***	(2939)	−1.4	(2583)
Orchard Oriole	−32.9***	(1357)	−17.2***	(1129)
Hooded Oriole	46.0	(78)	7.4	(49)
Baltimore Oriole	0.9	(1648)	−12.8***	(1368)
Bullock's Oriole	−17.6	(653)	1.5	(519)
Scott's Oriole	77.2	(131)	−16.2	(103)
Pine Grosbeak	−25.5	(134)	22.4	(69)
Purple Finch	−25.9**	(920)	−27.5**	(693)
Cassin's Finch	48.5*	(262)	10.1	(213)
House Finch	9.6	(1585)	60.8***	(1411)
Red Crossbill	67.5*	(458)	−13.0	(331)
White-winged Crossbill	−75.5	(144)	−78.1***	(90)
Pine Siskin	−2.4	(823)	−45.0***	(638)
Lesser Goldfinch	−38.7*	(302)	−24.3**	(230)
Lawrence's Goldfinch	−21.4	(66)	−13.7	(38)
American Goldfinch	−24.3***	(2249)	−8.9***	(1920)
Evening Grosbeak	60.8	(621)	−45.4	(474)
House Sparrow	−39.5***	(2665)	−30.7***	(2273)

Notes:
Values represent the overall percentage population change for that species during that time period.
Statistical significance of the population change: * $p<0.10$, ** $p<0.05$, *** $p<0.01$.
Numbers in parentheses indicate the number of BBS routes used in calculating the trend (the sample size).

APPENDIX A

Common and scientific names

Common and scientific names follow the *American Ornithologists' Union Check-list of North American Birds*, sixth edition (1983) with supplements through 1993. British common names (in parentheses) follow the *British Birds* List of English Names of Western Palearctic Birds (1993). Those entries that are indented represent subspecies or identifiable forms that have been included in the maps or in chapter 4.

Red-throated Loon (Red-throated Diver)/*Gavia stellata*
Pacific Loon/*Gavia pacifica*
Common Loon (Great Northern Diver)/*Gavia immer*
Pied-billed Grebe/*Podilymbus podiceps*
Horned Grebe (Slavonian Grebe)/*Podiceps auritus*
Red-necked Grebe/*Podiceps grisegena*
Eared Grebe (Black-necked Grebe)/*Podiceps nigricollis*
Western Grebe/*Aechmophorus occidentalis*
Clark's Grebe/*Aechmophorus clarkii*
American White Pelican/*Pelecanus erythrorhynchos*
Brown Pelican/*Pelecanus occidentalis*
Double-crested Cormorant/*Phalacrocorax auritus*
Neotropic Cormorant/*Phalacrocorax brasilianus*
Brandt's Cormorant/*Phalacrocorax penicillatus*
Pelagic Cormorant/*Phalacrocorax pelagicus*
Anhinga/*Anhinga anhinga*
Magnificent Frigatebird/*Fregata magnificens*
American Bittern/*Botaurus lentiginosus*
Least Bittern/*Ixobrychus exilis*
Great Blue Heron/*Ardea herodias*
Great Egret/*Casmerodius albus*
Snowy Egret/*Egretta thula*
Little Blue Heron/*Egretta caerulea*
Tricolored Heron/*Egretta tricolor*
Reddish Egret/*Egretta rufescens*
Cattle Egret/*Bubulcus ibis*
Green Heron/*Butorides virescens*
Black-crowned Night-Heron (Night Heron)/*Nycticorax nycticorax*
Yellow-crowned Night-Heron/*Nyctanassa violacea*
White Ibis/*Eudocimus albus*
Glossy Ibis/*Plegadis falcinellus*
White-faced Ibis/*Plegadis chihi*
Roseate Spoonbill/*Ajaia ajaja*
Wood Stork/*Mycteria americana*
Fulvous Whistling-Duck/*Dendrocygna bicolor*
Black-bellied Whistling-Duck/*Dendrocygna autumnalis*
Tundra Swan/*Cygnus columbianus*
Trumpeter Swan/*Cygnus buccinator*
Mute Swan/*Cygnus olor*
Canada Goose/*Branta canadensis*
Wood Duck/*Aix sponsa*
Green-winged Teal (Common Teal)/*Anas crecca*
American Black Duck/*Anas rubripes*
Mottled Duck/*Anas fulvigula*
Mallard/*Anas platyrhynchos*
Northern Pintail/*Anas acuta*

Blue-winged Teal/*Anas discors*
Cinnamon Teal/*Anas cyanoptera*
Northern Shoveler/*Anas clypeata*
Gadwall/*Anas strepera*
American Wigeon/*Anas americana*
Canvasback/*Aythya valisineria*
Redhead/*Aythya americana*
Ring-necked Duck/*Aythya collaris*
Greater Scaup/*Aythya marila*
Lesser Scaup/*Aythya affinis*
Common Eider/*Somateria mollissima*
Harlequin Duck/*Histrionicus histrionicus*
Oldsquaw (Long-tailed Duck)/*Clangula hyemalis*
Black Scoter (Common Scoter)/*Melanitta nigra*
Surf Scoter/*Melanitta perspicillata*
White-winged Scoter (Velvet Scoter)/*Melanitta fusca*
Common Goldeneye/*Bucephala clangula*
Barrow's Goldeneye/*Bucephala islandica*
Bufflehead/*Bucephala albeola*
Hooded Merganser/*Lophodytes cucullatus*
Common Merganser (Goosander)/*Mergus merganser*
Red-breasted Merganser/*Mergus serrator*
Ruddy Duck/*Oxyura jamaicensis*
Black Vulture/*Coragyps atratus*
Turkey Vulture/*Cathartes aura*
Osprey/*Pandion haliaetus*
American Swallow-tailed Kite/*Elanoides forficatus*
White-tailed Kite/*Elanus leucurus*
Snail Kite/*Rostrhamus sociabilis*
Mississippi Kite/*Ictinia mississippiensis*
Bald Eagle/*Haliaeetus leucocephalus*
Northern Harrier (Hen Harrier)/*Circus cyaneus*
Cooper's Hawk/*Accipiter cooperii*
Northern Goshawk/*Accipiter gentilis*
Harris' Hawk/*Parabuteo unicinctus*
Gray Hawk/*Buteo nitidus*
Red-shouldered Hawk/*Buteo lineatus*
Broad-winged Hawk/*Buteo platypterus*
Short-tailed Hawk/*Buteo brachyurus*
Swainson's Hawk/(Swainson's Buzzard) *Buteo swainsoni*
White-tailed Hawk/*Buteo albicaudatus*
Zone-tailed Hawk/*Buteo albonotatus*
Red-tailed Hawk/*Buteo jamaicensis*
Ferruginous Hawk/*Buteo regalis*
Rough-legged Hawk (Rough-legged Buzzard)/*Buteo lagopus*

Golden Eagle/*Aquila chrysaetos*
Crested Caracara/*Caracara plancus*
American Kestrel/*Falco sparverius*
Merlin/*Falco columbarius*
Peregrine Falcon/*Falco peregrinus*
Prairie Falcon/*Falco mexicanus*
Plain Chachalaca/*Ortalis vetula*
Gray Partridge/*Perdix perdix*
Chukar (Chukar Partridge)/*Alectoris chukar*
Ring-necked Pheasant (Common Pheasant)/*Phasianus colchicus*
Spruce Grouse/*Dendragapus canadensis*
Blue Grouse/*Dendragapus obscurus*
Willow Ptarmigan (Willow Grouse/Red Grouse)/*Lagopus lagopus*
Rock Ptarmigan (Ptarmigan)/*Lagopus mutus*
Ruffed Grouse/*Bonasa umbellus*
Sage Grouse/*Centrocercus urophasianus*
Greater Prairie-Chicken/*Tympanuchus cupido*
Lesser Prairie-Chicken/*Tympanuchus pallidicinctus*
Sharp-tailed Grouse/*Tympanuchus phasianellus*
Wild Turkey/*Meleagris gallopavo*
Montezuma Quail/*Cyrtonyx montezumae*
Northern Bobwhite/*Colinus virginianus*
Scaled Quail/*Callipepla squamata*
Gambel's Quail/*Callipepla gambelii*
California Quail/*Callipepla californica*
Mountain Quail/*Oreortyx pictus*
Yellow Rail/*Coturnicops noveboracensis*
Clapper Rail/*Rallus longirostris*
King Rail/*Rallus elegans*
Virginia Rail/*Rallus limicola*
Sora (Sora Crake)/*Porzana carolina*
Purple Gallinule (American Purple Gallinule)/*Porphyrula martinica*
Common Moorhen (Moorhen)/*Gallinula chloropus*
American Coot/*Fulica americana*
Limpkin/*Aramus guarauna*
Sandhill Crane/*Grus canadensis*
American Golden-Plover/*Pluvialis dominica*
Snowy Plover (Kentish Plover)/*Charadrius alexandrinus*
Wilson's Plover/*Charadrius wilsonia*
Semipalmated Plover/*Charadrius semipalmatus*
Killdeer (Killdeer Plover)/*Charadrius vociferus*
Mountain Plover/*Charadrius montanus*
American Oystercatcher/*Haematopus palliatus*
Black Oystercatcher/*Haematopus bachmani*
Black-necked Stilt/*Himantopus mexicanus*
American Avocet/*Recurvirostra americana*
Greater Yellowlegs/*Tringa melanoleuca*
Lesser Yellowlegs/*Tringa flavipes*
Solitary Sandpiper/*Tringa solitaria*
Willet/*Catoptrophorus semipalmatus*
Spotted Sandpiper/*Actitis macularia*
Upland Sandpiper/*Bartramia longicauda*
Whimbrel/*Numenius phaeopus*
Long-billed Curlew/*Numenius americanus*
Hudsonian Godwit/*Limosa haemastica*
Marbled Godwit/*Limosa fedoa*
Least Sandpiper/*Calidris minutilla*
Rock Sandpiper/*Calidris ptilocnemis*
Dunlin/*Calidris alpina*
Short-billed Dowitcher/*Limnodromus griseus*
Common Snipe/*Gallinago gallinago*

American Woodcock/*Scolopax minor*
Wilson's Phalarope/*Phalaropus tricolor*
Red-necked Phalarope/*Phalaropus lobatus*
Parasitic Jaeger (Arctic Skua)/*Stercorarius parasiticus*
Long-tailed Jaeger (Long-tailed Skua)/*Stercorarius longicaudus*
Laughing Gull/*Larus atricilla*
Franklin's Gull/*Larus pipixcan*
Bonaparte's Gull/*Larus philadelphia*
Heermann's Gull/*Larus heermanni*
Mew Gull (Common Gull)/*Larus canus*
Ring-billed Gull/*Larus delawarensis*
California Gull/*Larus californicus*
Herring Gull/*Larus argentatus*
Western Gull/*Larus occidentalis*
Glaucous-winged Gull/*Larus glaucescens*
Glaucous Gull/*Larus hyperboreus*
Great Black-backed Gull/*Larus marinus*
Black-legged Kittiwake (Kittiwake)/*Rissa tridactyla*
Gull-billed Tern/*Sterna nilotica*
Caspian Tern/*Sterna caspia*
Royal Tern/*Sterna maxima*
Sandwich Tern/*Sterna sandvicensis*
Common Tern/*Sterna hirundo*
Arctic Tern/*Sterna paradisaea*
Forster's Tern/*Sterna forsteri*
Least Tern/*Sterna antillarum*
Aleutian Tern/*Sterna aleutica*
Black Tern/*Chlidonias niger*
Black Skimmer/*Rynchops niger*
Common Murre (Common Guillemot)/*Uria aalge*
Pigeon Guillemot/*Cepphus columba*
Marbled Murrelet/*Brachyramphus marmoratus*
Rhinoceros Auklet/*Cerorhinca monocerata*
Rock Dove/*Columba livia*
White-crowned Pigeon/*Columba leucocephala*
Band-tailed Pigeon/*Columba fasciata*
Spotted Dove/*Streptopelia chinensis*
White-winged Dove/*Zenaida asiatica*
Mourning Dove/*Zenaida macroura*
Inca Dove/*Columbina inca*
Common Ground-Dove/*Columbina passerina*
White-tipped Dove/*Leptotila verreauxi*
Black-billed Cuckoo/*Coccyzus erythropthalmus*
Yellow-billed Cuckoo/*Coccyzus americanus*
Mangrove Cuckoo/*Coccyzus minor*
Greater Roadrunner/*Geococcyx californianus*
Smooth-billed Ani/*Crotophaga ani*
Groove-billed Ani/*Crotophaga sulcirostris*
Barn Owl/*Tyto alba*
Great Horned Owl/*Bubo virginianus*
Northern Pygmy-Owl/*Glaucidium gnoma*
Burrowing Owl/*Speotyto cunicularia*
Spotted Owl/*Strix occidentalis*
Barred Owl/*Strix varia*
Short-eared Owl/*Asio flammeus*
Lesser Nighthawk/*Chordeiles acutipennis*
Common Nighthawk/*Chordeiles minor*
Pauraque/*Nyctidromus albicollis*
Common Poorwill/*Phalaenoptilus nuttallii*
Chuck-will's-widow/*Caprimulgus carolinensis*
Whip-poor-will/*Caprimulgus vociferus*
Black Swift/*Cypseloides niger*
Chimney Swift/*Chaetura pelagica*
Vaux's Swift/*Chaetura vauxi*

White-throated Swift/*Aeronautes saxatalis*
Broad-billed Hummingbird/*Cynanthus latirostris*
Blue-throated Hummingbird/*Lampornis clemenciae*
Ruby-throated Hummingbird/*Archilochus colubris*
Black-chinned Hummingbird/*Archilochus alexandri*
Anna's Hummingbird/*Calypte anna*
Costa's Hummingbird/*Calypte costae*
Calliope Hummingbird/*Stellula calliope*
Broad-tailed Hummingbird/*Selasphorus platycercus*
Rufous Hummingbird/*Selasphorus rufus*
Allen's Hummingbird/*Selasphorus sasin*
Elegant Trogon/*Trogon elegans*
Belted Kingfisher/*Ceryle alcyon*
Green Kingfisher/*Chloroceryle americana*
Lewis' Woodpecker/*Melanerpes lewis*
Red-headed Woodpecker/*Melanerpes erythrocephalus*
Acorn Woodpecker/*Melanerpes formicivorus*
Gila Woodpecker/*Melanerpes uropygialis*
Golden-fronted Woodpecker/*Melanerpes aurifrons*
Red-bellied Woodpecker/*Melanerpes carolinus*
Yellow-bellied Sapsucker/*Sphyrapicus varius*
Red-naped Sapsucker/*Sphyrapicus nuchalis*
Red-breasted Sapsucker/*Sphyrapicus ruber*
Williamson's Sapsucker/*Sphyrapicus thyroideus*
Ladder-backed Woodpecker/*Picoides scalaris*
Nuttall's Woodpecker/*Picoides nuttallii*
Downy Woodpecker/*Picoides pubescens*
Hairy Woodpecker/*Picoides villosus*
Strickland's Woodpecker/*Picoides stricklandi*
Red-cockaded Woodpecker/*Picoides borealis*
White-headed Woodpecker/*Picoides albolarvatus*
Three-toed Woodpecker/*Picoides tridactylus*
Black-backed Woodpecker/*Picoides arcticus*
Northern Flicker/*Colaptes auratus*
    Yellow-shafted Flicker/*C. a. auratus*
      Red-shafted Flicker/*C. a. cafer*
        Gilded Flicker/*C. a. chrysoides*
Pileated Woodpecker/*Dryocopus pileatus*
Northern Beardless-Tyrannulet/*Camptostoma imberbe*
Olive-sided Flycatcher/*Contopus borealis*
Greater Pewee/*Contopus pertinax*
Western Wood-Pewee/*Contopus sordidulus*
Eastern Wood-Pewee/*Contopus virens*
Yellow-bellied Flycatcher/*Empidonax flaviventris*
Acadian Flycatcher/*Empidonax virescens*
Alder Flycatcher/*Empidonax alnorum*
Willow Flycatcher/*Empidonax traillii*
Least Flycatcher/*Empidonax minimus*
Hammond's Flycatcher/*Empidonax hammondii*
Dusky Flycatcher/*Empidonax oberholseri*
Gray Flycatcher/*Empidonax wrightii*
Pacific-slope Flycatcher/*Empidonax difficilis*
Cordilleran Flycatcher/*Empidonax occidentalis*
Black Phoebe/*Sayornis nigricans*
Eastern Phoebe/*Sayornis phoebe*
Say's Phoebe/*Sayornis saya*
Vermilion Flycatcher/*Pyrocephalus rubinus*
Dusky-capped Flycatcher/*Myiarchus tuberculifer*
Ash-throated Flycatcher/*Myiarchus cinerascens*
Great Crested Flycatcher/*Myiarchus crinitus*
Brown-crested Flycatcher/*Myiarchus tyrannulus*
Great Kiskadee/*Pitangus sulphuratus*
Sulphur-bellied Flycatcher/*Myiodynastes luteiventris*
Couch's Kingbird/*Tyrannus couchii*
Cassin's Kingbird/*Tyrannus vociferans*
Thick-billed Kingbird/*Tyrannus crassirostris*
Western Kingbird/*Tyrannus verticalis*
Eastern Kingbird/*Tyrannus tyrannus*
Gray Kingbird/*Tyrannus dominicensis*
Scissor-tailed Flycatcher/*Tyrannus forficatus*
Horned Lark/*Eremophila alpestris*
Purple Martin/*Progne subis*
Tree Swallow/*Tachycineta bicolor*
Violet-green Swallow/*Tachycineta thalassina*
Northern Rough-winged Swallow/*Stelgidopteryx serripennis*
Bank Swallow (Sand Martin)/*Riparia riparia*
Cliff Swallow/*Hirundo pyrrhonota*
Cave Swallow/*Hirundo fulva*
Barn Swallow/*Hirundo rustica*
Gray Jay/*Perisoreus canadensis*
Steller's Jay/*Cyanocitta stelleri*
Blue Jay/*Cyanocitta cristata*
Green Jay/*Cyanocorax yncas*
Scrub Jay/*Aphelocoma coerulescens*
    Florida Jay/*A. c. coerulescens*
Gray-breasted Jay/*Aphelocoma ultramarina*
Pinyon Jay/*Gymnorhinus cyanocephalus*
Clark's Nutcracker/*Nucifraga columbiana*
Black-billed Magpie (Magpie)/*Pica pica*
Yellow-billed Magpie/*Pica nuttalli*
American Crow/*Corvus brachyrhynchos*
Northwestern Crow/*Corvus caurinus*
Fish Crow/*Corvus ossifragus*
Chihuahuan Raven/*Corvus cryptoleucus*
Common Raven/*Corvus corax*
Black-capped Chickadee/*Parus atricapillus*
Carolina Chickadee/*Parus carolinensis*
Mexican Chickadee/*Parus sclateri*
Mountain Chickadee/*Parus gambeli*
Boreal Chickadee/*Parus hudsonicus*
Chestnut-backed Chickadee/*Parus rufescens*
Bridled Titmouse/*Parus wollweberi*
Plain Titmouse/*Parus inornatus*
Tufted Titmouse/*Parus bicolor*
    Black-crested Titmouse/*P. b. atricristatus*
Verdin/*Auriparus flaviceps*
Bushtit/*Psaltriparus minimus*
Red-breasted Nuthatch/*Sitta canadensis*
White-breasted Nuthatch/*Sitta carolinensis*
Pygmy Nuthatch/*Sitta pygmaea*
Brown-headed Nuthatch/*Sitta pusilla*
Brown Creeper/*Certhia americana*
Cactus Wren/*Campylorhynchus brunneicapillus*
Rock Wren/*Salpinctes obsoletus*
Canyon Wren/*Catherpes mexicanus*
Carolina Wren/*Thryothorus ludovicianus*
Bewick's Wren/*Thryomanes bewickii*
House Wren/*Troglodytes aedon*
Winter Wren (Wren)/*Troglodytes troglodytes*
Sedge Wren/*Cistothorus platensis*
Marsh Wren/*Cistothorus palustris*
American Dipper/*Cinclus mexicanus*
Arctic Warbler/*Phylloscopus borealis*
Golden-crowned Kinglet/*Regulus satrapa*
Ruby-crowned Kinglet/*Regulus calendula*
Blue-gray Gnatcatcher/*Polioptila caerulea*
California Gnatcatcher/*Polioptila californica*
Black-tailed Gnatcatcher/*Polioptila melanura*
Eastern Bluebird/*Sialia sialis*

Western Bluebird/*Sialia mexicana*
Mountain Bluebird/*Sialia currucoides*
Townsend's Solitaire/*Myadestes townsendi*
Veery/*Catharus fuscescens*
Gray-cheeked Thrush/*Catharus minimus*
    Bicknell's Thrush/*C. m. bicknelli*
Swainson's Thrush/*Catharus ustulatus*
Hermit Thrush/*Catharus guttatus*
Wood Thrush/*Hylocichla mustelina*
American Robin/*Turdus migratorius*
Varied Thrush/*Ixoreus naevius*
Wrentit/*Chamaea fasciata*
Gray Catbird/*Dumetella carolinensis*
Northern Mockingbird/*Mimus polyglottos*
Sage Thrasher/*Oreoscoptes montanus*
Brown Thrasher/*Toxostoma rufum*
Long-billed Thrasher/*Toxostoma longirostre*
Bendire's Thrasher/*Toxostoma bendirei*
Curve-billed Thrasher/*Toxostoma curvirostre*
California Thrasher/*Toxostoma redivivum*
Crissal Thrasher/*Toxostoma crissale*
Le Conte's Thrasher/*Toxostoma lecontei*
American Pipit (Buff-bellied Pipit)/*Anthus rubescens*
Sprague's Pipit/*Anthus spragueii*
Bohemian Waxwing/*Bombycilla garrulus*
Cedar Waxwing/*Bombycilla cedrorum*
Phainopepla/*Phainopepla nitens*
Loggerhead Shrike/*Lanius ludovicianus*
European Starling (Common Starling)/*Sturnus vulgaris*
White-eyed Vireo/*Vireo griseus*
Bell's Vireo/*Vireo bellii*
Black-capped Vireo/*Vireo atricapillus*
Gray Vireo/*Vireo vicinior*
Solitary Vireo/*Vireo solitarius*
Yellow-throated Vireo/*Vireo flavifrons*
Hutton's Vireo/*Vireo huttoni*
Warbling Vireo/*Vireo gilvus*
Philadelphia Vireo/*Vireo philadelphicus*
Red-eyed Vireo/*Vireo olivaceus*
Black-whiskered Vireo/*Vireo altiloquus*
Blue-winged Warbler/*Vermivora pinus*
Golden-winged Warbler/*Vermivora chrysoptera*
Tennessee Warbler/*Vermivora peregrina*
Orange-crowned Warbler/*Vermivora celata*
Nashville Warbler/*Vermivora ruficapilla*
Virginia's Warbler/*Vermivora virginiae*
Lucy's Warbler/*Vermivora luciae*
Northern Parula/*Parula americana*
Yellow Warbler/*Dendroica petechia*
Chestnut-sided Warbler/*Dendroica pensylvanica*
Magnolia Warbler/*Dendroica magnolia*
Cape May Warbler/*Dendroica tigrina*
Black-throated Blue Warbler/*Dendroica caerulescens*
Yellow-rumped Warbler/*Dendroica coronata*
    Myrtle Warbler/*D. c. coronata*
    Audubon's Warbler/*D. c. auduboni*
Black-throated Gray Warbler/*Dendroica nigrescens*
Townsend's Warbler/*Dendroica townsendi*
Hermit Warbler/*Dendroica occidentalis*
Black-throated Green Warbler/*Dendroica virens*
Blackburnian Warbler/*Dendroica fusca*
Yellow-throated Warbler/*Dendroica dominica*
Grace's Warbler/*Dendroica graciae*
Pine Warbler/*Dendroica pinus*
Prairie Warbler/*Dendroica discolor*
Palm Warbler/*Dendroica palmarum*
Bay-breasted Warbler/*Dendroica castanea*
Blackpoll Warbler/*Dendroica striata*
Cerulean Warbler/*Dendroica cerulea*
Black-and-white Warbler/*Mniotilta varia*
American Redstart/*Setophaga ruticilla*
Prothonotary Warbler/*Protonotaria citrea*
Worm-eating Warbler/*Helmitheros vermivorus*
Swainson's Warbler/*Limnothlypis swainsonii*
Ovenbird/*Seiurus aurocapillus*
Northern Waterthrush/*Seiurus noveboracensis*
Louisiana Waterthrush/*Seiurus motacilla*
Kentucky Warbler/*Oporornis formosus*
Connecticut Warbler/*Oporornis agilis*
Mourning Warbler/*Oporornis philadelphia*
MacGillivray's Warbler/*Oporornis tolmiei*
Common Yellowthroat/*Geothlypis trichas*
Hooded Warbler/*Wilsonia citrina*
Wilson's Warbler/*Wilsonia pusilla*
Canada Warbler/*Wilsonia canadensis*
Red-faced Warbler/*Cardellina rubrifrons*
Painted Redstart/*Myioborus pictus*
Yellow-breasted Chat/*Icteria virens*
Olive Warbler/*Peucedramus taeniatus*
Hepatic Tanager/*Piranga flava*
Summer Tanager/*Piranga rubra*
Scarlet Tanager/*Piranga olivacea*
Western Tanager/*Piranga ludoviciana*
Northern Cardinal/*Cardinalis cardinalis*
Pyrrhuloxia/*Cardinalis sinuatus*
Rose-breasted Grosbeak/*Pheucticus ludovicianus*
Black-headed Grosbeak/*Pheucticus melanocephalus*
Blue Grosbeak/*Guiraca caerulea*
Lazuli Bunting/*Passerina amoena*
Indigo Bunting/*Passerina cyanea*
Varied Bunting/*Passerina versicolor*
Painted Bunting/*Passerina ciris*
Dickcissel/*Spiza americana*
Olive Sparrow/*Arremonops rufivirgatus*
Green-tailed Towhee/*Pipilo chlorurus*
Rufous-sided Towhee/*Pipilo erythrophthalmus*
California Towhee/*Pipilo crissalis*
Canyon Towhee/*Pipilo fuscus*
Abert's Towhee/*Pipilo aberti*
Bachman's Sparrow/*Aimophila aestivalis*
Botteri's Sparrow/*Aimophila botterii*
Cassin's Sparrow/*Aimophila cassinii*
Rufous-crowned Sparrow/*Aimophila ruficeps*
American Tree Sparrow/*Spizella arborea*
Chipping Sparrow/*Spizella passerina*
Clay-colored Sparrow/*Spizella pallida*
Brewer's Sparrow/*Spizella breweri*
Field Sparrow/*Spizella pusilla*
Black-chinned Sparrow/*Spizella atrogularis*
Vesper Sparrow/*Pooecetes gramineus*
Lark Sparrow/*Chondestes grammacus*
Black-throated Sparrow/*Amphispiza bilineata*
Sage Sparrow/*Amphispiza belli*
Lark Bunting/*Calamospiza melanocorys*
Savannah Sparrow/*Passerculus sandwichensis*
Baird's Sparrow/*Ammodramus bairdii*
Grasshopper Sparrow/*Ammodramus savannarum*
Henslow's Sparrow/*Ammodramus henslowii*
Le Conte's Sparrow/*Ammodramus leconteii*

Sharp-tailed Sparrow/*Ammodramus caudacutus*
Seaside Sparrow/*Ammodramus maritimus*
Fox Sparrow/*Passerella iliaca*
Song Sparrow/*Melospiza melodia*
Lincoln's Sparrow/*Melospiza lincolnii*
Swamp Sparrow/*Melospiza georgiana*
White-throated Sparrow/*Zonotrichia albicollis*
Golden-crowned Sparrow/*Zonotrichia atricapilla*
White-crowned Sparrow/*Zonotrichia leucophrys*
Harris' Sparrow/*Zonotrichia querula*
Dark-eyed Junco/*Junco hyemalis*
    Slate-colored Junco/*J. h. hyemalis*
    Oregon Junco/*J. h. oreganus*
    White-winged Junco/*J. h. aikeni*
    Gray-headed Junco/*J. h. caniceps*
Yellow-eyed Junco/*Junco phaeonotus*
McCown's Longspur/*Calcarius mccownii*
Lapland Longspur/*Calcarius lapponicus*
Smith's Longspur/*Calcarius pictus*
Chestnut-collared Longspur/*Calcarius ornatus*
Snow Bunting/*Plectrophenax nivalis*
Bobolink/*Dolichonyx oryzivorus*
Red-winged Blackbird/*Agelaius phoeniceus*
Tricolored Blackbird/*Agelaius tricolor*
Eastern Meadowlark/*Sturnella magna*
Western Meadowlark/*Sturnella neglecta*
Yellow-headed Blackbird/*Xanthocephalus xanthocephalus*
Rusty Blackbird/*Euphagus carolinus*
Brewer's Blackbird/*Euphagus cyanocephalus*

Great-tailed Grackle/*Quiscalus mexicanus*
Boat-tailed Grackle/*Quiscalus major*
Common Grackle/*Quiscalus quiscula*
Bronzed Cowbird/*Molothrus aeneus*
Brown-headed Cowbird/*Molothrus ater*
Orchard Oriole/*Icterus spurius*
Hooded Oriole/*Icterus cucullatus*
Altamira Oriole/*Icterus gularis*
Audubon's Oriole/*Icterus graduacauda*
Northern Oriole/*Icterus galbula*
    Baltimore Oriole/*I. g. galbula*
    Bullock's Oriole/*I. g. bullockii*
Scott's Oriole/*Icterus parisorum*
Gray-crowned Rosy-Finch/*Leucosticte tephrocotis*
Pine Grosbeak/*Pinicola enucleator*
Purple Finch/*Carpodacus purpureus*
Cassin's Finch/*Carpodacus cassinii*
House Finch/*Carpodacus mexicanus*
Red Crossbill (Common Crossbill)/*Loxia curvirostra*
White-winged Crossbill (Two-barred Crossbill)/*Loxia leucoptera*
Common Redpoll/*Carduelis flammea*
Pine Siskin/*Carduelis pinus*
Lesser Goldfinch/*Carduelis psaltria*
Lawrence's Goldfinch/*Carduelis lawrencei*
American Goldfinch/*Carduelis tristis*
Evening Grosbeak/*Coccothraustes vespertinus*
House Sparrow/*Passer domesticus*
Eurasian Tree Sparrow (Tree Sparrow)/*Passer montanus*

APPENDIX B

Selected bird-finding guides, breeding bird atlases, and other references

The maps in chapter 3 are the most effective means for identifying general areas where a given species might be found. For more detailed regional information there are a number of bird-finding guides and breeding bird atlases available. The following is a selected list of some of these references. Not all of them are still in print but many of them should be available in libraries and second-hand bookstores. There are numerous other books available with more being published on a regular basis.

Two Sources of Publications on Birds and Birding:
American Birding Association Sales. P.O. Box 6599, Colorado Springs, CO 80934-6599, USA. Telephone 800-634-7736, US and Canada (International 719-578-0607).
Fax: 800-247-3329, US and Canada (International 719-471-4722).
Natural History Book Service Ltd. 2–3 Wills Road, Devon TQ9 5XN, UK. Telephone: 01803 865913 (International +44 803 865913).
Fax: 01803 865280 (International +44 803 865280). Internet: nhbs@gn.apc.org.

General:
American Birding Association. 1990. *ABA Checklist: Birds of the Continental United States and Canada*, 4th ed. American Birding Association, Colorado Springs, CO.
American Ornithologists' Union. 1983. *Check-list of North American Birds*, 6th ed. American Ornithologists' Union, Washington, DC.
Ehrlich, P., D.S. Dobkin, and D. Wheye. 1988. *The Birder's Handbook: A Field Guide to the Natural History of North American Birds*. Simon and Schuster, New York.
Root, T. 1988. *Atlas of Wintering North American Birds*. University of Chicago Press, Chicago.

Identification:
Farrand, J., Jr. (ed.) 1983. *The Audubon Society Master Guide to Birding*. Knopf, New York.
Kaufman, K. 1990. *A Field Guide to Advanced Birding*. Houghton Mifflin, Boston.
National Geographic Society. 1987. *Field Guide to the Birds of North America*, 2nd ed. National Geographic Society, Washington, DC.
Peterson, R.T. 1980. *A Field Guide to the Birds*, 4th ed. Houghton Mifflin, Boston.
Peterson, R.T. 1990. *A Field Guide to Western Birds*, 3rd ed. Houghton Mifflin, Boston.
Robbins, C., B. Bruun, and H.S. Zim. 1983. *A Guide to Field Identification: Birds of North America*, 2nd ed. Golden Press, New York.

Censusing:
Bibby, C.J., N.D. Burgess, and D.A. Hill. 1992. *Bird Census Techniques*. Academic Press, London.

Ralph, C.J., and J.M. Scott. 1981. Estimating numbers of terrestrial birds. *Studies in Avian Biology* 6:1–630.

Conservation:
Ehrlich, P.R., D.S. Dobkin, and D. Wheye. 1992. *Birds in Jeopardy: The Imperiled and Extinct Birds of the United States and Canada*. Stanford University Press, Stanford, CA.
Hagan, J.M., III, and D. Johnston (eds.) 1992. *Ecology and Conservation of Neotropical Migrant Land Birds*. Smithsonian Institution Press, Washington, DC.
Terborgh, J. 1990. *Where Have All the Birds Gone?* Princeton University Press, Princeton, NJ.

Regional:
American Birding Association, and U.S. Forest Service. 1994. *Birdfinding in Forty National Forests and Grasslands*. American Birding Association, Colorado Springs, CO.
Riley, L., and W. Riley. 1993. *Guide to the National Wildlife Refuges*. Collier Books, New York.
Wauer, R. 1992. *Visitor's Guide to the Birds of the Eastern National Parks*. John Muir, Santa Fe, NM.
Wauer, R. 1993. *Visitor's Guide to the Birds of the Rocky Mountain National Parks*. John Muir, Santa Fe, NM.
Wauer, R. 1994. *Visitor's Guide to the Birds of the Central National Parks*. John Muir, Santa Fe, NM.

Alabama:
Imhof, T. 1976. *Alabama Birds*. University of Alabama Press, Tuscaloosa.
Vaughan, R. 1993. *Birder's Guide to Alabama and Mississippi*. Gulf, Houston, TX.

Alaska:
Armstrong, R.H. 1990. *Guide to the Birds of Alaska*, 3rd ed. Alaska Northwest, Anchorage.
Isleib, M.E., and B. Kessel. 1989. *Birds of the North Gulf Coast – Prince William Sound Region, Alaska*. University of Alaska Press, Fairbanks.
Kessel, B. 1989. *Birds of the Seward Peninsula, Alaska: Their Biogeography, Seasonality and Natural History*. University of Alaska Press, Fairbanks.

Kessel, B., and D.G. Gibson. 1978. Status and distribution of Alaska birds. *Studies in Avian Biology* 1:1–100.
Springer, M.I. 1993. *Birdwatching in Eastcentral Alaska*. Falco, Fairbanks, AK.
West, G.C. 1994. *A Birder's Guide to the Kenai Peninsula*. Pratt Museum, Homer, AK.

Arizona:
Carr, J.N. 1992. *Arizona Wildlife Viewing Guide*. Falcon Press, Helena, MT.
Davis, W.A., and S.M. Russell. 1990. *Birds in Southeastern Arizona*, 3rd ed. Tucson Audubon Society, Tucson, AZ.
Holt, H.R. 1989. *A Birder's Guide to Southeastern Arizona*. American Birding Association, Colorado Springs, CO.
Jacobs, B. 1986. *Birding on the Navajo and Hopi Reservations*. Jacobs, Sycamore, MO.
Monson, G., and A.R. Phillips. 1981. *Annotated Checklist of the Birds of Arizona*, 2nd ed. University of Arizona Press, Tucson.
Phillips, A., J. Marshall, and G. Monson. 1964. *The Birds of Arizona*. University of Arizona Press, Tucson.

Arkansas:
James, D.A., and J.C. Neal. 1986. *Arkansas Birds, Their Distribution and Abundance*. University of Arkansas Press, Fayetteville.

California:
Clark, J.L. 1992. *California Wildlife Viewing Guide*. Falcon Press, Helena, MT.
Gaines, D. 1992. *Birds of Yosemite and the East Slope*. Artemisia Press, Lee Vining, CA.
Garrett, K., and J. Dunn. 1981. *Birds of Southern California*. Los Angeles Audubon Society, West Hollywood, CA.
Holt, H.R. 1990. *A Birder's Guide to Southern California*. American Birding Association, Colorado Springs, CO.
Lehman, P. 1994. *Birds of Santa Barbara County, CA*. Santa Barbara Museum of Natural History, Santa Barbara, CA.
Roberson, D., and C. Tenney. 1993. *Atlas of the Breeding Birds of Monterey County*. Monterey Peninsula Audubon Society, Carmel, CA.
Shuford, W.D. 1993. *The Marin County Breeding Bird Atlas*. Bushtit, Bolinas, CA.
Small, A. 1994. *California Birds: Their status and distribution*. Ibis, Vista, CA.
Unitt, P. 1984. *The Birds of San Diego County*. San Diego Society of Natural History, San Diego, CA.
Westrich, L., and J. Westrich. 1991. *Birder's Guide to Northern California*. Gulf, Houston, TX.

Colorado:
Andrews, R., and R. Righter. 1992. *Colorado Birds, A Reference to Their Distribution and Habitat*. Denver Museum of Natural History, Denver, CO.
Gray, M.T. 1992. *Colorado Wildlife Viewing Guide*. Falcon Press, Helena, MT
Holt, H.R., and J.A. Lane. 1988. *A Birder's Guide to Colorado*. American Birding Association, Colorado Springs, CO.
Johnsgard, P.A. 1986. *Birds of the Rocky Mountains*. Colorado Associated University Press, Boulder.

Connecticut:
Bevier, L.R. (ed.) 1994. *The Atlas of Breeding Birds of Connecticut*. DEP, Hartford, CT.
Walton, R.K. 1988. *Bird Finding in New England*. David R. Godine, Boston, MA.
Zeranski, J.D., and T.R. Baptist. 1990. *Connecticut Birds*. University of New England Press, Hanover, NH.

Delaware:
Harding, J.J., and J.J. Harding. 1980. *Birding the Delaware Valley Region*. Temple University Press, Philadelphia, PA.
Wilds, C. 1992. *Finding Birds in the National Capital Area*. Smithsonian Institution Press, Washington, DC.

Florida:
Cerulean, S. 1993. *Florida Wildlife Viewing Guide*. Falcon Press, Helena, MT.
Holt, H.R. 1989. *A Birder's Guide to Florida*. American Birding Association, Colorado Springs, CO.
Robertson, W.B., Jr., and G.E. Woolfenden. 1992. *Florida Bird Species: An Annotated List*. Florida Ornithological Society, Maitland.
Stevenson, H.M., and B.H. Anderson. 1994. *The Birdlife of Florida*. University of Florida Press, Gainesville.
Toops, C., and W.E. Dilley. 1986. *Birds of South Florida, An Interpretive Guide*. River Road Press, Conway, AR.

Georgia:
Blackshaw, K.T., and J.R. Hitt (eds.) 1992. *A Birder's Guide to Georgia*, 4th ed. Georgia Ornithological Society, Atlanta.
Georgia Ornithological Society. 1986. *Annotated Checklist of Georgia Birds*. Georgia Ornithological Society, Atlanta.

Idaho:
Burleigh, T.D. 1972. *Birds of Idaho*. Caxton, Caldwell, ID.
Carpenter, L.B. 1990. *Idaho Wildlife Viewing Guide*. Falcon Press, Helena, MT.
Johnsgard, P.A. 1986. *Birds of the Rocky Mountains*. Colorado Associated University Press, Boulder.
Roberts, H.B. 1993. *Birds of East Central Idaho*. H.B. Roberts, Salmon, ID.
Stephens, D.A., and S.H. Sturts. 1991. Idaho bird distribution. *Special Publication No. 11*, Idaho Museum of Natural History, Pocatello.

Illinois:
Bohlen, D.H. 1989. *The Birds of Illinois*. Indiana University Press, Bloomington.

Indiana:
Keller, C.E., S.A. Keller, and T.C. Keller. 1986. *Indiana Birds and Their Haunts*. Indiana University Press, Bloomington.
Mumford, R.E., and C.E. Keller. 1984. *The Birds of Indiana*. Indiana University Press, Bloomington.
Seng, P.T. 1992. *Indiana Wildlife Viewing Guide*. Falcon Press, Helena, MT.

Iowa:
Dinsmore, J.J. 1984. *Iowa Birds*. Iowa State University Press, Ames.
Petersen, P.C. (ed.) 1986. *Birding Areas of Iowa*. Petersen, Davenport, IA.

Kansas:
Johnsgard, P.A. 1979. *Birds of the Great Plains*. University of Nebraska Press, Lincoln.
Thompson, M., and C. Ely. 1989. *Birds in Kansas, Vol. I*. University of Kansas Museum of Natural History, Lawrence.
Thompson, M., and C. Ely. 1992. *Birds in Kansas, Vol. II*. University of Kansas Museum of Natural History, Lawrence.
Zimmerman, J.L., and S. Patti. 1988. *A Guide to Bird Finding in Kansas and Western Missouri*. University Press of Kansas, Lawrence.

Kentucky:
Lynn, C.H. 1994. *Kentucky Wildlife Viewing Guide*. Falcon Press, Helena, MT.
Monroe, B.L., Jr., A.L. Stamm, and B.L. Palmer-Ball, Jr. 1988. *Annotated Checklist of the Birds of Kentucky*. Kentucky Ornithological Society, Louisville.
Monroe, B.L., Jr. 1994. *The Birds of Kentucky*. Indiana University Press, Bloomington.

Louisiana:
Lowery, G.H., Jr. 1974. *Louisiana Birds*, 3rd ed. Louisiana State University Press, Baton Rouge.
Purrington, D., A. Smalley, G. Smalley, R.J. Stein, and J. Whelan. 1987. *A Bird Finder's Guide to SE Louisiana*. Orleans Audubon Society, New Orleans, LA.

Maine:
Adamus, P.R., compiler. 1987. *Atlas of Breeding Birds in Maine 1978–1983*. Maine Department of Inland Fisheries and Wildlife, Augusta.
Pierson, E.C., and J.E. Pierson. 1981. *A Birder's Guide to the Coast of Maine*. Down East Books, Camden, ME.
Walton, R.K. 1988. *Bird Finding in New England*. David R. Godine, Boston, MA.

Maryland:
Robbins, C.S. (ed.) In press. *Atlas of the Breeding Birds of Maryland and the District of Columbia*. University of Pittsburgh Press, Pittsburgh, PA.
Wilds, C. 1992. *Finding Birds in the National Capital Area*. Smithsonian Institution Press, Washington, DC.

Massachusetts:
Bird Observer of Eastern Massachusetts. 1994. *A Birder's Guide to Eastern Massachusetts*. American Birding Association, Colorado Springs, CO.
Veit, R., and W. Petersen. 1993. *Birds of Massachusetts*. Massachusetts Audubon Society, Lincoln.
Walton, R.K. 1988. *Bird Finding in New England*. David R. Godine, Boston, MA.

Michigan:
Brewer, R., G.A. McPeek, and R.J. Adams, Jr. 1991. *The Atlas of Breeding Birds of Michigan*. Michigan State University Press, Lansing.
McPeek, G.A. (ed.) 1994. *The Birds of Michigan*. Indiana University Press, Bloomington.
Michigan Audubon Society. 1989. *Enjoying Birds in Michigan*. Michigan Audubon Society, Kalamazoo.
Payne, R.B. 1983. A distributional checklist of the birds of Michigan. *Miscellaneous Publications Museum of Zoology #164*, University of Michigan Press, Ann Arbor.
Smith, R.C. (ed.) 1994. *Bird Finding Guide to Michigan*. Michigan Audubon Society, Lansing.

Minnesota:
Eckert, K.R. 1994. *A Birder's Guide to Minnesota*, 3rd ed. Minnesota Ornithologists' Union, Minneapolis.
Janssen, R.B. 1987. *Birds in Minnesota*. University of Minnesota Press, Minneapolis.

Mississippi:
Toups, J.A., and J.A. Jackson. 1987. *Birds and Birding on the Mississippi Coast*. University Press of Mississippi, Jackson.
Vaughan, R. 1993. *Birder's Guide to Alabama and Mississippi*. Gulf, Houston, TX.

Missouri:
Palmer, K. 1993. *A Guide to the Birding Areas of Missouri*. Audubon Society of Missouri, Columbia.
Robbins, M.B., and D.A. Easterla. 1992. *Birds of Missouri: Their Distribution and Abundance*. University of Missouri Press, Columbia.
Zimmerman, J.L., and S. Patti. 1988. *A Guide to Bird Finding in Kansas and Western Missouri*. University Press of Kansas, Lawrence.

Montana:
Fischer, C., and H. Fischer. 1990. *Montana Wildlife Viewing Guide*. Falcon Press, Helena, MT.
Johnsgard, P.A. 1986. *Birds of the Rocky Mountains*. Colorado University Associated Press, Boulder.
McEneaney, T. 1993. *The Birder's Guide to Montana*. Falcon Press, Helena, MT.
Skaar, D., D. Flath, and L.S. Thompson. 1985. P.D. Skaar's Montana bird distribution. *Supplement to the Proceedings, Vol. 44, Monograph #3*, Montana Academy of Sciences, Bozeman.

Nebraska:
Ducey, J.E. 1988. *Nebraska Birds: Breeding Status and Distribution*. Simmons-Boardman, Omaha, NE.
Johnsgard, P.A. 1979. *Birds of the Great Plains*. University of Nebraska Press, Lincoln.

Nevada:
Alcorn, J.R. 1988. *The Birds of Nevada*. Fairview West, Fallon, NV.
Clark, J.L. 1993. *Nevada Wildlife Viewing Guide*. Falcon Press, Helena, MT.
Ryser, F.A., Jr. 1985. *Birds of the Great Basin*. University of Nevada Press, Reno.
Titus, C.K. 1991. *Southern Nevada Birds, A Seeker's Guide*. Red Rock Audubon, Las Vegas, NV.

New Hampshire:
Walton, R.K. 1988. *Bird Finding in New England*. David R. Godine, Boston, MA.

New Jersey:
Boyle, W.J., Jr. 1989. *A Guide to Bird Finding in New Jersey*. Rutgers University Press, New Brunswick, NJ.
Harding, J.J., and J.J. Harding. 1980. *Birding the Delaware Valley Region*. Temple University Press, Philadelphia, PA.
Leck, C. 1984. *Status and Distribution of New Jersey Birds*. Rutgers University Press, New Brunswick, NJ.

New Mexico:
MacCarter, J.S. 1994. *New Mexico Wildlife Viewing Guide*. Falcon Press, Helena, MT.

Zimmerman, D.A., M.A. Zimmerman, and J.N. Durrie. 1992. *New Mexico Bird-finding Guide*. New Mexico Ornithological Society, Santa Fe.

New York:

Andrle, R.F., and J.R. Carroll (eds.) 1988. *Atlas of Breeding Birds in New York State*. Cornell University Press, Ithaca, NY.

Bessette, A. *et al.* 1993. *Birds of the Adirondacks*. North Country, Utica, NY.

Bull, J. 1986. *Birds of New York State*. Cornell University Press, Ithaca, NY.

Drennan, S.R. 1981. *Where to Find Birds in New York State: Top 500 Sites*. Syracuse University Press, Syracuse, NY.

North Carolina:

Alsop, F.J., III. 1991. *Birds of the Smokies*. Great Smoky Mountain Natural History Association, Gatlinburg, TN.

Fussell, J.O., III. 1994. *A Birder's Guide to Coastal North Carolina*. University of North Carolina Press, Chapel Hill.

Potter, E.F., J.F. Parnell, and R.P. Teulings. 1980. *Birds of the Carolinas*. University of North Carolina Press, Chapel Hill.

Roe, C.E. 1992. *North Carolina Wildlife Viewing Guide*. Falcon Press, Helena, MT.

Simpson, M.B., Jr. 1992. *Birds of the Blue Ridge Mountains*. University of North Carolina Press, Chapel Hill.

North Dakota:

Johnsgard, P.A. 1979. *Birds of the Great Plains*. University of Nebraska Press, Lincoln.

Knue, J. 1992. *North Dakota Wildlife Viewing Guide*. Falcon Press, Helena, MT.

Stewart, R. 1975. *Breeding Birds of North Dakota*. Tri-College Center for Environmental Studies, Fargo, ND.

Zimmer, K.J. 1979. *A Birder's Guide to North Dakota*. L&P Press, Denver, CO.

Ohio:

Peterjohn, B.G. 1989. *The Birds of Ohio*. Indiana University Press, Bloomington.

Peterjohn, B.G., and D.L. Rice. 1991. *The Ohio Breeding Bird Atlas*. Ohio Department of Natural Resources, Columbus.

Thomson, T. 1994. *Birding in Ohio*, 2nd ed. Indiana University Press, Bloomington.

Oklahoma:

Baumgartner, F.M., and M. Baumgartner. 1992. *Oklahoma Bird Life*. University of Oklahoma Press, Norman.

Johnsgard, P.A. 1979. *Birds of the Great Plains*. University of Nebraska Press, Lincoln.

Oklahoma Department of Wildlife Conservation. 1994. *Oklahoma Wildlife Viewing Guide*. Falcon Press, Helena, MT.

Tulsa Audubon Society. 1986. *Guide to Birding in Oklahoma*. Tulsa Audubon Society, Tulsa, OK.

Wood, D.S., and G.D. Schnell. 1984. *Distribution of Oklahoma Birds*. University of Oklahoma Press, Norman.

Oregon:

Evanich, J.E., Jr. 1990. *The Birder's Guide to Oregon*. Portland Audubon Society, Portland, OR.

Ryser, F.A., Jr. 1985. *Birds of the Great Basin*. University of Nevada Press, Reno.

Yuskavitch, J.A. 1994. *Oregon Wildlife Viewing Guide*. Falcon Press, Helena, MT.

Pennsylvania:

Brauning, D.W. (ed.) 1992. *Atlas of Breeding Birds in Pennsylvania*. University of Pittsburgh Press, Pittsburgh, PA.

Harding, J.J., and J.J. Harding. 1980. *Birding the Delaware Valley Region*. Temple University Press, Philadelphia, PA.

Rhode Island:

Enser, R.W. 1992. *Atlas of Breeding Birds in Rhode Island*. Rhode Island Department of Environmental Management, Providence.

Fry, A.J. 1992. *Bird Walks in Rhode Island*. Backcountry, Woodstock, VT.

Walton, R.K. 1988. *Bird Finding in New England*. David R. Godine, Boston, MA.

South Carolina:

Carter, R.M. 1992. *Finding Birds in South Carolina*. University of South Carolina Press, Columbia.

McNair, D.B., and W. Post. 1993. Status and distribution of South Carolina birds, supplement. *Contributions from the Charleston Museum #18*, Charleston, SC.

Post, W., S.A. Gauthreax, Jr. 1989. Status and distribution of South Carolina birds. *Contributions from the Charleston Museum #18*, Charleston, SC.

Potter, E.F., J.F. Parnell, and R.P. Teulings. 1980. *Birds of the Carolinas*. University of North Carolina Press, Chapel Hill.

South Dakota:

Johnsgard, P.A. 1979. *Birds of the Great Plains*. University of Nebraska Press, Lincoln.

Peterson, R.A. 1993. *A Birdwatcher's Guide to the Black Hills and Adjacent Plains*. PC, Vermillion, SD.

South Dakota Ornithologists' Union. 1991. *The Birds of South Dakota*. South Dakota Ornithologists' Union, Aberdeen.

Tennessee:

Alsop, F.J., III. 1991. *Birds of the Smokies*. Great Smoky Mountain Natural History Association, Gatlinburg, TN.

Bierly, M.L. 1980. *Bird-finding in Tennessee*. Bierly, Nashville, TN.

Hamel, P. 1993. *Tennessee Wildlife Viewing Guide*. Falcon Press, Helena, MT.

Robinson, J.C. 1990. *An Annotated Checklist for Birds of Tennessee*. University of Tennessee Press, Knoxville.

Texas:

Arnold, K.A. 1984. *T.O.S. Checklist of Birds of Texas*. Texas Ornithological Society, Houston.

Graham, G.L. 1992. *Texas Wildlife Viewing Guide*. Falcon Press, Helena, MT.

Holt, H.R. 1992. *A Birder's Guide to the Rio Grande Valley of Texas*. American Birding Association, Colorado Springs, CO.

Holt, H.R. 1993. *A Birder's Guide to the Texas Coast*. American Birding Association, Colorado Springs, CO.

Kutac, E.A. 1989. *Birder's Guide to Texas*. Gulf, Houston, TX.

Pulich, W.M. 1988. *The Birds of North Central Texas*. Texas A&M, Galveston.

Rappole, J.H., and G.W. Blacklock. 1985. *Birds of the Texas Coastal Bend: Abundance and Distribution*. Texas A&M, Galveston.

Rappole, J.H., and G.W. Blacklock. 1994. *Birds of Texas: A Field Guide*. Texas A&M, Galveston.

Wauer, R.H. 1985. *Field Guide to Birds of the Big Bend*. Texas Monthly Press, Austin.

Utah:

Behle, W.H., E.D. Sorensen, and C.M. White. 1985. *Utah Birds: A Revised Checklist*. Utah Museum of Natural History, Salt Lake City.

Cole, J. 1990. *Utah Wildlife Viewing Guide*. Falcon Press, Helena, MT.

Ryser, F.A., Jr. 1985. *Birds of the Great Basin*. University of Nevada Press, Reno.

Vermont:

Killgore-Brown, C. 1994. *Vermont Wildlife Viewing Guide*. Falcon Press, Helena, MT.

Laughlin, S.B., and D.P. Kibbe (eds.) 1985. *Atlas of Breeding Birds of Vermont*. University Press of New England, Hanover, NH.

Walton, R.K. 1988. *Bird Finding in New England*. David R. Godine, Boston, MA.

Virginia:

Beck, R., and D. Peake (eds.) 1985. *Virginia Birding Site Guide*. Virginia Society of Ornithology, Richmond.

Duda, M. 1994. *Virginia Wildlife Viewing Guide*. Falcon Press, Helena, MT.

Kain, T. (ed.) 1987. *Virginia's Birdlife: Annotated Checklist*. Virginia Society of Ornithology, Richmond.

Simpson, M.B., Jr. 1992. *Birds of the Blue Ridge Mountains*. University of North Carolina Press, Chapel Hill.

Wilds, C. 1992. *Finding Birds in the National Capital Area*. Smithsonian Institution Press, Washington, DC.

Washington:

La Tourrette, J. 1993. *Washington Wildlife Viewing Guide*. Falcon Press, Helena, MT.

Lewis, M.G., and F.A. Sharpe. 1987. *Birding in the San Juan Islands*. Mountaineers, Seattle, WA.

Wahl, T.R., and D.R. Paulson. 1991. *Guide to Birdfinding in Washington*. T.R. Wahl, Bellingham, WA.

West Virginia:

Hall, G.A. 1983. *West Virginia Birds*. Carnegie Museum of Natural History, Pittsburgh, PA.

Wisconsin:

Judd, M. 1994. *Wisconsin Wildlife Viewing Guide*. Falcon Press, Helena, MT.

Robbins, S.D., Jr. 1991. *Wisconsin Birdlife, Population and Distribution, Past and Present*. University of Wisconsin Press, Madison.

Temple, S.A., and J.R. Cary. 1987. *Wisconsin's Birds: Seasonal and Geographic Guide*. University of Wisconsin Press, Madison.

Tessen, D.D. 1989. *Wisconsin's Favorite Bird Haunts*. Wisconsin Society for Ornithology, De Pere.

Wyoming:

Dorn, J.L., and R.D. Dorn. 1990. *Wyoming Birds*. Mountain West, Cheyenne, WY.

Johnsgard, P.A. 1986. *Birds of the Rocky Mountains*. Colorado Associated University Press, Boulder.

Scott, O.K. 1993. *A Birder's Guide to Wyoming*. American Birding Association, Colorado Springs, CO.

Canada:

Finlay, J.C. (ed.) 1984. *A Bird Finding Guide to Canada*. Hurtig, Edmonton, AB.

Godfrey, W.E. 1986. *Birds of Canada*. National Museums of Canada, Ottawa, ON.

Alberta:

Butler, J. 1990. *Alberta Wildlife Viewing Guide*. Lone Pine, Edmonton, AB.

Calgary Field Naturalists' Society. 1991. *Alberta Birds 1971–1980, Vol I, Non-Passerines*. Calgary Field Naturalists' Society, Calgary, AB.

Calgary Field Naturalists' Society. 1993. *Alberta Birds 1971–1980, Vol II, Passerines*. Calgary Field Naturalists' Society, Calgary, AB.

Federation of Alberta Naturalists. 1992. *Atlas of Breeding Birds of Alberta*. Federation of Alberta Naturalists, Edmonton.

Johnsgard, P.A. 1986. *Birds of the Rocky Mountains*. Colorado Associated University Press, Boulder.

MacDonald, J.F. (ed.) 1993. *A Birdfinding Guide to the Calgary Region*. Calgary Field Naturalists' Society, Calgary, AB.

British Columbia:

Campbell, R.W., N.K. Dawe, I. McTaggart-Cowan, J.M. Cooper, G.W. Kaiser, and M.C.E. McNall. 1990. *The Birds of British Columbia, Vols. 1 and 2, The Nonpasserines*. Royal British Columbia Museum, Victoria.

Johnsgard, P.A. 1986. *Birds of the Rocky Mountains*. Colorado Associated University Press, Boulder.

Taylor, K. 1993. *A Birder's Guide to British Columbia*. Taylor, Victoria, BC.

Wareham, B. 1991. *British Columbia Wildlife Viewing Guide*. Lone Pine, Edmonton, AB.

Manitoba:

Chartier, B. 1994. *A Birder's Guide to Churchill*. American Birding Association, Colorado Springs, CO.

Cleveland, N.J., S. Edie, G.D, Grieef, G.E. Holland, R.F. Koes, J.W. Maynard, W.P. Neily, P. Taylor, and R. Tkachuk. 1988. *Birder's Guide to Southeastern Manitoba*, 2nd ed. Manitoba Naturalists Society, Winnipeg.

Cuthbert, C. et al. 1990. *Birder's Guide to Southwestern Manitoba*. Birder's Guide to Southwestern Manitoba, Brandon.

New Brunswick:

Burrows, R. 1992. *Birding in Atlantic Canada: Acadia*. Jesperson Press, St. John's, NF.

Erskine, A.J. 1992. *Atlas of Breeding Birds of the Maritime Provinces*. Nimbus, Halifax, NS.

Newfoundland:

Burrows, R. 1989. *Birding in Atlantic Canada: Newfoundland*. Jesperson Press, St. John's, NF.

Erskine, A.J. 1992. *Atlas of Breeding Birds of the Maritime Provinces*. Nimbus, Halifax, NS.

Nova Scotia:

Burrows, R. 1988. *Birding in Atlantic Canada: Nova Scotia*. Jesperson Press, St. John's, NF.

Cohrs, J.S. (ed.) 1991. *Birding Nova Scotia*. Nova Scotia Bird Society, Halifax.

Erskine, A.J. 1992. *Atlas of Breeding Birds of the Maritime Provinces*. Nimbus, Halifax, NS.

Tufts, R.W. 1986. *Birds of Nova Scotia*, 3rd ed. Nova Scotia Museum, Halifax.

Ontario:

Cadman, M.D., P.F.J. Eagles, and F.M. Helleiner. 1987. *Atlas of the Breeding Birds of Ontario*. University of Waterloo Press, Waterloo, ON.

Goodwin, C.E. 1994. *A Bird-finding Guide to Ontario*. University of Toronto Press, Toronto, ON.

James, R.D., P.L. McLaren, and J.C. Barlow. 1991. Annotated checklist of the birds of Ontario. *Life Sciences Miscellaneous Publications*, Royal Ontario Museum, Toronto.

Prince Edward Island:

Burrows, R. 1992. *Birding in Atlantic Canada: Acadia*. Jesperson Press, St. John's, NF.

Erskine, A.J. 1992. *Atlas of Breeding Birds of the Maritime Provinces*. Nimbus, Halifax, NS.

Quebec:

Bannon, P. 1991. *Birdfinding in the Montreal Area*. Centre de conservation de la faune ailee, Montreal, PQ.

Girard, S. *Birdwatching Itinerary of the Gaspé Peninsula*. Club des ornithologues de la Gaspésie, Pabos Mills, PQ.

Todd, W.E. Clyde. 1980. *Birds of the Labrador Peninsula*. University of Toronto Press, Toronto, ON.

Saskatchewan:

Adams, C., C. Escott, B. Luterbach, and R. Kreba. 1988. *A Guide to Bird-finding in the Regina Area*. Saskatchewan Natural History Society, Regina.

APPENDIX C

Cited references and suggested readings

Cited references

American Ornithologists' Union. 1983. *Check-list of North American Birds*, 6th ed. American Ornithologists' Union, Washington, D.C.

American Ornithologists' Union. 1989. Thirty-seventh supplement to the American Ornithologists' Union *Check-list of North American Birds*. *Auk* 106(3): 532–538.

American Ornithologists' Union. 1991. Thirty-eighth supplement to the American Ornithologists' Union *Check-list of North American Birds*. *Auk* 108(3): 675–682.

American Ornithologists' Union. 1993. Thirty-ninth supplement to the American Ornithologists' Union *Check-list of North American Birds*. *Auk* 110(3): 750–754.

Askins, R.A. 1993. Population trends in grassland, shrubland, and forest birds in Eastern North America. *Current Ornithology* 11: 1–34.

Bent, A.C. 1939. Life histories of North American woodpeckers. *United States National Museum Bulletin* 174.

Bent, A.C. 1946. Life histories of North American jays, crows, and titmice. *United States National Museum Bulletin* 191.

Bent, A.C. 1949. Life histories of North American thrushes, kinglets, and their allies. *United States National Museum Bulletin* 196.

Bent, A.C. 1953. Life histories of North American wood warblers. *United States National Museum Bulletin* 203.

Bent, A.C. 1958. Life histories of North American blackbirds, orioles, tanagers, and allies. *United States National Museum Bulletin* 211.

Bent, A.C. 1968. Life histories of North American cardinals, grosbeaks, buntings, towhees, finches, sparrows, and allies. *United States National Museum Bulletin* 237, Part 2.

British Birds. 1993. The 'British Birds' List of English Names of Western Palearctic Birds. *British Birds* 86(1): Supplement.

Butcher, G.S., M.R. Fuller, L.S. McAllister, and P.H. Geissler. 1990. An evaluation of the Christmas Bird Count for monitoring population trends of selected species. *Wildlife Society Bulletin* 18: 129–134.

Carson, R. 1962. *Silent Spring*. Houghton Mifflin, Boston.

Cadman, M.D., P.F.J. Eagles, and F.M. Helleiner. 1987. *Atlas of the Breeding Birds of Ontario*. University of Waterloo Press, Waterloo, Ontario.

Campbell, R.W., N.K. Dawe, I. McTaggart-Cowan, J.M. Cooper, G.W. Kaiser, and M.C.E. McNall. 1990. *The Birds of British Columbia, Vol. II: nonpasserines, diurnal birds of prey through woodpeckers*. Royal British Columbia Museum, Victoria, British Columbia.

Chandler, R.J. 1989. *The Facts on File Field Guide to North Atlantic Shorebirds*. Facts on File, New York.

Cressie, N. 1989. Geostatistics. *The American Statistician* 43: 197–202.

Cressie, N. 1990. The origins of kriging. *Mathematical Geology* 22(3): 239–252.

Cyr, A. and J. Larivee. 1993. A checklist approach for monitoring neotropical migrant birds: twenty year trends in birds of Quebec using EPOQ. Pp. 229–236 in D.M. Finch and P.W. Stangel (eds.), *Status and Management of Neotropical Migrating Birds*. USDA Forest Service General Technical Report RM-229.

DeSante, D., and P. Pyle. 1986. *Distributional Checklist of North American Birds*. Artemesia Press, Lee Vining, CA.

Droege, S. and J.R. Sauer. 1990. *North American Breeding Bird Survey Annual Summary 1989*. U.S. Fish and Wildlife Service Biological Report 90(8).

Ehrlich, P.R., D.S. Dobkin, and D. Wheye. 1988. *The Birder's Handbook: a field guide to the natural history of North American birds*. Simon & Schuster, New York.

Faanes, C.A. and D. Bystrak. 1981. The role of observer bias in the North American Breeding Bird Survey. *Studies in Avian Biology* 6: 353–359.

Finch D.M. and P.W. Stangel (eds.). 1993. *Status and Management of Neotropical Migratory Birds*. USDA Forest Service General Technical Report RM-229.

Godfrey, W.E. 1986. *The Birds of Canada*, rev. ed. National Museum of Natural Sciences, Ottawa, Ontario.

Hagan, J.M. and D.W. Johnston (eds.). 1992. *Ecology and Conservation of Neotropical Migrant Landbirds*. Smithsonian Institution Press, Washington DC.

Hayman, P., J. Marchant, and T. Prater. 1986. *Shorebirds: an identification guide to the waders of the world*. Houghton Mifflin, Boston.

Holt, H.R. 1989. *A Birder's Guide to Florida*. L&P Press, Denver, CO.

Holt, H.R. 1992. *A Birder's Guide to the Rio Grande Valley of Texas*. American Birding Association, Colorado Springs, CO.

Isaaks, E.H., and R.M. Srivastava. 1989. *An Introduction to Applied Geostatistics*. Oxford University Press, Oxford.

Janssen, R.B. 1987. *Birds in Minnesota*. University of Minnesota Press, Minneapolis.

Johnsgard, P.A. 1979. *Birds of the Great Plains: breeding species and their distribution*. University of Nebraska Press, Lincoln.

Johnsgard, P.A. 1986. *Birds of the Rocky Mountains: with particular reference to National Parks in the Northern Rocky Mountain Region*. Colorado Associated University Press, Boulder.

Johnsgard, P.A. 1988. *North American Owls*. Smithsonian Institution Press, Washington, D.C.

Kessel, B. 1989. *Birds of the Seward Peninsula, Alaska: Their biogeography, seasonality, and natural history*. University of Alaska Press, Fairbanks.

Kricher, J.C. 1993. *A Field Guide to the Ecology of Western Forests*. Houghton Mifflin, Boston.

Martin, R.P., and G.D. Lester. 1990. Atlas and census of wading bird and seabird nesting colonies in Louisiana 1990. *Special Publication No. 3*, Louisiana Department of Wildlife and Fisheries and the Louisiana Natural Heritage Program, Baton Rouge, LA.

Monson, G., and A.R. Phillips. 1981. *Annotated Checklist of the Birds of Arizona*, 2nd rev. ed. University of Arizona Press, Tucson, AZ.

National Geographic Society. 1983. *Field Guide to the Birds of North America*. National Geographic Society, Washington, D.C.

Ouellet, H. 1993. Bicknell's Thrush: Taxonomic status and distribution. *Wilson Bulletin* 105(4): 545–572.

Palmer, R.S. (ed.). 1962. *Handbook of North American Birds, Vol. 1: Loons through flamingos*. Yale University Press, New Haven, CT.

Palmer, R.S. (ed.). 1976. *Handbook of North American Birds, Vol. 2: Waterfowl, part 1*. Yale University Press, New Haven, CT.

Palmer, R.S. (ed.). 1988a. *Handbook of North American Birds, Vol. 4: Diurnal raptors, part 1*. Yale University Press, New Haven, CT.

Palmer, R.S. (ed.). 1988b. *Handbook of North American Birds, Vol. 5: Diurnal Raptors, part 2*. Yale University Press, New Haven, CT.

Peterson, R.T., and V.M. Peterson. 1990. *A Field Guide to Western Birds*, 3rd rev. ed. Houghton Mifflin, Boston.

Peterson, R.T., and V.M. Peterson. 1980. *A Field Guide to the Birds*, 4th rev. ed. Houghton Mifflin, Boston.

Pyle, P., N. Nur, and D.F. DeSante. 1994. Trends in nocturnal migrant landbird populations at Southeast Farallon Island, California, 1968–1992. *Studies in Avian Biology* 15: 58–74.

Rappole, J.H., and G.W. Blacklock. 1994. *Birds of Texas: a field guide*. Texas A&M University Press, College Station, Texas.

Robbins, C.S. 1981. Effect of time of day on bird activity. *Studies in Avian Biology* 6: 275–286.

Robbins, C.S., B. Bruun, and H.S. Zim. 1983. *Birds of North America*. Golden Press, New York.

Robbins, C.S., J.R. Sauer, R.S. Greenberg, and S. Droege. 1989. Population declines in North American birds that migrate to the Neotropics. *Proceedings of the National Academy of Sciences* 86: 7658–7662.

Sauer, J.R. and S. Droege (eds.). 1990a. *Survey Designs and Statistical Methods for the Estimation of Avian Population Trends*. U.S. Fish and Wildlife Service Biological Report 90(1).

Sauer, J.R. and S. Droege. 1990b. Recent population trends of the Eastern Bluebird. *Wilson Bulletin* 102: 239–252.

Sauer, J.R., D.D. Dolton, and S. Droege. 1994. Mourning Dove population trend estimates from Call-Count and North American Bird surveys. *Journal of Wildlife Management* 58(3): 506–515.

Stangel, P.(ed.) 1993. Partners in Flight Annual Report, 1992. *Partners in Flight* 3(1).

Stephens, D.A., and S.H. Sturts. 1991. Idaho bird distribution. *Special Publication No. 11*, Idaho Museum of Natural History, Pocatello, ID.

Temple, S.A. and J.A. Wiens. 1989. Bird populations and environmental changes: can birds be bioindicators? *American Birds* 43: 260–270.

Temple, S.A. and J.R. Cary. 1990. Using checklist records to reveal trends in bird populations. Pp. 98–104 *in* J.R. Sauer, and S. Droege. *Survey Designs and Statistical Methods for the Estimation of Avian Population Trends*. U.S. Fish and Wildlife Service Biological Report 90(1).

Toops, C., and W.E. Dilley. 1986. *Birds of South Florida: An interpretive guide*. Conway Printing Company, Conway, AR.

Unitt, P. 1984. *The Birds of San Diego County*. San Diego Society of Natural History, San Diego, CA.

Suggested readings

Chapter 1

Barker, R.J. and J.R. Sauer. 1992. Modelling population change from time series data. Pp. 182–196 *in* D.R. McCullough and R.H. Barrett (eds.), *Wildlife 2001: Populations*. Elsevier Science Publishers, New York.

Brown, J.H. and B.A. Maurer. 1987. Evolution of species assemblages: effects of energetic constraints and species dynamics on the diversification of the North American avifauna. *American Naturalist* 130: 1–17.

Bystrak, D. 1979. The Breeding Bird Survey. *Sialia* 1: 74–79.

Bystrak, D. 1981. The North American Breeding Bird Survey. *Studies in Avian Biology* 6: 34–42.

Flather, C.H., S.J. Brady, and D.B. Inkley. 1992. Regional habitat appraisals of wildlife communities: a landscape-level evaluation of a resource planning model using avian distribution data. *Landscape Ecology* 7: 137–147.

Maurer, B.A. and S.G. Heywood. 1993. Geographic range fragmentation and abundance in neotropical migratory birds. *Conservation Biology* 7: 501–509.

Peterjohn, B.G. and J.R. Sauer. 1993. North American Breeding Bird Survey Annual Summary, 1990-1991. *Bird Populations* 1: 52–67.

Robbins, C.S., D. Bystrak, and P.H. Geissler. 1986. *The Breeding Bird Survey: Its first fifteen years, 1965–1979*. U.S. Fish and Wildlife Service, Resource Publication 157.

Robbins, C.S., S. Droege, and J.R. Sauer. 1989. Monitoring bird populations with Breeding Bird Survey and atlas data. *Annales Zoologici Fennici* 26: 297–304.

Chapter 2

Cressie, N.A.C. 1991. *Statistics for Spatial Data*. John Wiley and Sons, Inc., New York.

Golden Software. 1994. *SURFER® for Windows Users Guide*. Golden Software, Inc., Golden, CO.

Root, T. 1988a. *Atlas of Wintering North American Birds*. Chicago University Press, Chicago.

Root, T. 1988b. Environmental factors associated with avian distributional boundaries. *Journal of Biogeography* 15: 489–505.

Root, T. 1988c. Energetic constraints on avian distributions and abundances. *Ecology* 69: 330–339.

Chapter 5

Droege, S. and J.R. Sauer. 1989. *North American Breeding Bird Survey Annual Summary 1988*. U.S. Fish and Wildlife Service Biological Report 89(13).

Ehrlich, P.R., D.S. Dobkin, and D. Wheye. 1992. *Birds in Jeopardy: the imperiled and extinct birds of the United States and Canada, including Hawaii and Puerto Rico*. Stanford University Press, Stanford, CA.

Goriup, P.D. (ed.). 1988. *Ecology and Conservation of Grassland Birds*. ICBP Technical Publication 7.

Jehl, J.R., Jr., and N.K. Johnson (eds.). 1994. *A Century of Avifaunal Change in Western North America*. Studies in Avian Biology No. 15, Cooper Ornithological Society.

Knopf, F.L. 1994. Avian assemblages on altered grasslands. *Studies in Avian Biology* 15: 247–257.

Terborgh, J. 1990. *Where Have All the Birds Gone?* Princeton University Press, Princeton, NJ.

APPENDIX D

Birding ethics

American Birding Association Code of Ethics
(Reprinted with permission.)

We, the Membership of the American Birding Association, believe that all birders have an obligation at all times to protect wildlife, the natural environment, and the rights of others. We therefore pledge ourselves to provide leadership in meeting this obligation by adhering to the following general guidelines of good birding behavior.

I. Birders must always act in ways that do not endanger the welfare of birds or other wildlife.
In keeping with this principle, we will
- Observe and photograph birds without knowingly disturbing them in any way.
- Avoid chasing or repeatedly flushing birds.
- We will only sparingly use recordings and similar methods of attracting birds and not use these methods in heavily birded areas.
- Keep an appropriate distance from nests and nesting colonies so as to not disturb the birds or expose them to danger.
- Refrain from handling birds or eggs unless engaged in recognized research activities.

II. Birders must always act in ways that do not harm the natural environment.
In keeping with this principle, we will
- Stay on existing roads, trails, and pathways whenever possible to avoid trampling or otherwise disturbing fragile habitat.
- Leave all habitat as it was found.

III. Birders must always respect the rights of others.
In keeping with this principle, we will
- Respect the privacy and property of others by observing 'No Trespassing' signs and by asking permission to enter private or posted lands.
- Observe all laws and the rules and regulations that govern public use of birding areas.
- Practice common courtesy in our contacts with others. For example, limit requests for information, and make them at reasonable hours of the day.
- Always behave in a manner that will enhance the image of the birding community in the eyes of the public.

IV. Birders in groups should assume special responsibilities
As group members, we will
- Take special care to alleviate the problems and disturbances that are multiplied when more people are present.
- Act in consideration of the group's interest, as well as our own.
- Support by our actions the responsibility of the group leader(s) for the conduct of the group.

As group leaders, we will
- Assume responsibility for the conduct of the group.
- Learn and inform the group of any special rules, regulations, or conduct applicable to the area, or habitat being visited.
- Limit groups to a size that does not threaten the environment or the peace and tranquility of others.
- Teach others birding ethics by our words and example.

The goals of the American Birding Association (ABA), a not-for-profit organization, are to promote recreational birding, contribute to the development of bird identification and population studies, and to help foster public appreciation of birds and their role in the environment. Recognizing that this depends on a diverse and viable avifauna, the ABA strongly supports efforts to protect wild birds and their habitats. For more information on the American Birding Association, write or call:

American Birding Association
P.O. Box 6599
Colorado Springs, CO 80934
(800) 850-2473

Index

Index Note: *bold type refers to maps*

Accipiter cooperii, 265
   A. gentilis, 266
Actitis macularia, **71,** 273
Aechmorphorus clarkii, 258
   A. occidentalis, **20,** 257
Aeronautes saxatalis, **98,** 281
Agelaius phoeniceus, **232,** 312
   A. tricolor, **233,** 313
Aimophila aestivalis, **215,** 308
   A. botterii, **215,** 308
   A. cassinii, **216,** 308
   A. ruficeps, **216,** 308
Aix sponsa, **34,** 261
Ajaia ajaja, **30,** 260
Alectoris chukar, **57,** 268
Ammodramus bairdii, **222,** 310
   A. caudacuctus, **224,** 310
   A. henslowii, 310
   A. leconteii, **223,** 310
   A. maritimus, **224,** 310
   A. savannarum, **223,** 310
Amphispiza belli, **221,** 309
   A. bilineata, **220,** 309
Anas acuta, **37,** 262
   A. americana, **39,** 262
   A. clypeata, **38,** 262
   A. crecca, **35,** 261
   A. cyanoptera, **38,** 262
   A. discors, **37,** 262
   A. fulvigula, **36,** 262
   A. platyrhynchos, **36,** 262
   A. rubirpes, **35,** 261
   A. strepera, **39,** 262
Anhinga anhinga, **23,** 258
Ani
   Groove-billed, **91,** 279
   Smooth-billed, **91,** 279
Anthus rubescens, 298
   A. spragueii, **171,** 298
Aphelocoma coerulescens, **138,** 290
   A. coerulescens coerulescens, **138,** 290
   A. ultramarina, **139,** 291
Aquila chrysaetos, **53,** 267
Aramus guarauna, **67,** 271
   A. colubris, **100,** 281
Ardea herodias, **24,** 259
Arremonops rufivirgatus, **212,** 307
Asio flammeus, 280
Auklet, Rhinoceros, 277
Auriparus flaviceps, **149,** 293
Avocet, American, **70,** 272
Aythya affinis, **41,** 263
   A. americana, **40,** 263
   A. collaris, **41,** 263
   A. marila, 263
   A. valisineria, **40,** 262

Bartramia longicauda, **72,** 273
Bittern
   American, **24,** 259
   Least, 259
Blackbird
   Brewer's, **235,** 313
   Red-winged, **232,** 312
   Rusty, 313
   Tricolored, **233,** 313
   Yellow-headed, **234,** 313
Bluebird
   Eastern, **160,** 296
   Mountain, **161,** 296
   Western, **160,** 296
Bobolink, **232,** 312
Bobwhite, Northern, **62,** 269
Bombycilla cedrorum, **171,** 298
   B. garrulus, 298
Bonasa umbellus, **59,** 268
Botaurus lentiginosus, **24,** 259
Brachyramphus marmoratus, 277
Branta canadensis, **34,** 261
Bubo virginianus, **92,** 279
Bubulcus ibis, **27,** 259
Bucephala albeola, 264
   B. clangula, **42,** 264
   B. islandica, **43,** 264
Bufflehead, 264
Bunting
   Indigo, **210,** 307
   Lark, **221,** 309
   Lazuli, **209,** 307
   Painted, **211,** 307
   Snow, 312
   Varied, **210,** 307
Bushtit, **149,** 293
Buteo albicaudatus, **52,** 266
   B. albonotatus, 266
   B. brachyurus, 266
   B. jamaicensis, **52,** 267
   B. lagopus, 267
   B. lineatus, **50,** 266
   B. nitidus, **50,** 266
   B. platypterus, 266, **510**
   B. regalis, **53,** 267
   B. swainsoni, **51,** 266
Butorides virescens, **28,** 260

Calamospiza melanocorys, **221,** 309
Calcarius lapponicus, 312
   C. mccownii, **230,** 312
   C. ornatus, **231,** 312
   C. pictus, 312
Calidris alpina, 273
   C. minutilla, 273
   C. ptilocnemis, 273
Callipepla californica, **64,** 270

Callipepla californica, contd.
   C. gambelii, **63**, 269
   C. squamata, **63**, 269
Calypte anna, **101**, 282
   C. costae, **101**, 282
Camptostoma imberbe, **115**, 285
Campylorhynchus brunneicapillus, **152**, 294
Canvasback, **40**, 262
Caprimulgus carolinensis, **96**, 280
   C. vociferus, **96**, 281
Caracara, Crested, **54**, 267
Caracara plancus, **54**, 267
Cardellina rubrifrons, **202**, 305
Cardinal, Northern, **207**, 306
Cardinalis cardinalis, **207**, 306
   C. sinuatus, **207**, 306
Carduelis flammea, 315
   C. lawrencei, **245**, 316
   C. pinus, **244**, 316
   C. psaltria, **244**, 316
   C. tristis, **245**, 316
Carpodacus cassinii, **242**, 315
   C. mexicanus, **243**, 315, **321**
   C. perpureus, **242**, 315
Casmerodius albus, **25**, 259
Catbird, Gray, **166**, 297
Cathartes aura, **45**, 265
Catharus fuscescens, **162**, 296
   C. guttatus, **163**, 296
   C. minimus, 296
   C. minimus bicknelli, **162**, 296
   C. ustulatus, **163**, 296
Catherpes mexicanus, **153**, 294
Catoptrophorus semipalmatus, **71**, 272
Centrocercus urophasianus, **59**, 269
Cepphus columba, 277
Cerorhinca monocerata, 277
Certhia americana, **152**, 294
Ceryle alcyon, **104**, 282
Chachalaca, Plain, **56**, 268
Chaetura pelagica, **97**, 281
   C. vauxi, **98**, 281
Chamaea fasciata, **165**, 297
Charadrius alexandrinus, 271
   C. montanus, **68**, 271
   C. semipalmatus, 271
   C. vociferus, **68**, 271
   C. wilsonia, 271
Chat, Yellow-breasted, **203**, 305
Chickadee
   Black-capped, **144**, 292
   Boreal, **146**, 292
   Carolina, **144**, 292
   Chestnut-backed, **146**, 292
   Mexican, **145**, 292
   Mountain, **145**, 292
Chlidonias niger, **83**, 277
Chloroceryle americana, 282
Chondestes grammacus, **220**, 309
Chordeiles acutipennis, **94**, 280
Chordeilis minor, **94**, 280
Chuck-will's-widow, **96**, 280
Chukar, **57**, 268
Cinclus mexicanus, **157**, 295
Circus cyaneus, **49**, 265

Cistothorus palustris, **156**, 295
   C. platensis, **156**, 295
Clangula hyemalis, 263
Coccothraustes vespertinus, **246**, 316
Coccyzus americanus, **89**, 279
   C. erythropthalmus, **89**, 279
   C. minor, **90**, 279
Colaptes auratus, **112**, 285
   C. auratus auratus, **113**, 285
   C. auratus cafer, **113**, 285
   C. auratus chrysoides, **114**, 285
Colinus virginianus, **62**, 269
Columba fasciata, **85**, 278
   C. leucocephala, **84**, 278
   C. livia, **84**, 278
Columbina inca, **87**, 278
   C. passerina, **87**, 278
Contopus borealis, **115**, 285
   C. pertinax, **116**, 285
   C. sordidulus, **116**, 286
   C. virens, **117**, 286
Coot, American, **66**, 271
Coragyps atratus, **45**, 264
Cormorant
   Brandt's, 258
   Double-crested, **22**, 258
   Neotropic, **22**, 258
   Pelagic, 258
Corvus brachyrhynchos, **141**, 291
   C. caurinus, **142**, ***291***
   C. corax, **143**, 292
   C. cryptoleucus, **143**, 291
   C. ossifragus, **142**, 291
Cowbird
   Bronzed, **237**, 314
   Brown-headed, **237**, 314
Crane, Sandhill, **67**, 271
Creeper, Brown, **152**, 294
Crossbill
   Red, **243**, 315
   White-winged, 315
Crotophaga ani, **91**, 279
   C. sulcirostris, **91**, 279
Crow
   American, **141**, 291
   Fish, **142**, 291
   Northwestern, **142**, 291
Cuckoo
   Black-billed, **89**, 279
   Mangrove, **90**, 279
   Yellow-billed, **89**, 279
Curlew, Long-billed, **72**, 273
Cyanocitta cristata, **137**, 290
   C. stelleri, **136**, 290
   C. yncas, **137**, 290
Cyngus buccinator, **33**, 261
   C. columbianus, 261
   C. olor, **33**, 261
Cynanthus latirostris, **99**, 281
Cypseloides niger, **97**, 281
Cyrtonyx montezumae, **62**, 269

Dendragapus canadensis, 268
   D. obscurus, **58**, 268

Dendrocygna autumnalis, **32,** 261
    D. bicolor, **32,** 261
Dendroica caerulescens, **186,** 301
    D. castanea, **193,** 303
    D. cerulea, **194,** 303
    D. coronata, **186,** 302
    D. coronata auduboni, **187,** 302
    D. coronata coronata, **187,** 302
    D. discolor, **192,** 303
    D. dominica, **190,** 302
    D. fusca, **190,** 302
    D. graciae, **191,** 303
    D. magnolia, **185,** 301
    D. nigrescens, **188,** 302
    D. occidentalis, **189,** 302
    D. palmarun, **192,** 303
    D. pensylvanica, **184,** 301
    D. petechia, **184,** 301
    D. pinus, **191,** 303
    D. striata, **193,** 303
    D. tigrina, **185,** 301
    D. townsendi, **188,** 302
    D. virens, **189,** 302
Dickcissel, **211,** 307
Dipper, American, **157,** 295
Dolichonyx oryzivorus, **232,** 312
Dove
    Inca, **87,** 278
    Mourning, **86,** 278
    Rock, **84,** 278
    Spotted, **85,** 278
    White-tipped, **88,** 278
    White-winged, **86,** 278
Dowitcher, Short-billed, 274
Dryocopus pileatus, **114,** 285
Duck
    American Black, **35,** 261
    Harlequin, 263
    Mottled, **36,** 262
    Ring-necked, **41,** 263
    Ruddy, **44,** 264
    Wood, **34,** 261
    see also Whistling-duck
Dumetella carolinensis, **166,** 297
Dunlin, 273

Eagle
    Bald, **48,** 265
    Golden, **53,** 267
Egret
    Cattle, **27,** 259
    Great, **25,** 259
    Reddish, **27,** 259
    Snowy, **25,** 259
Egretta caerulea, **26,** 259
    E. rufuscens, **27,** 259
    E. thula, **25,** 259
    E. tricolor, **26,** 259
Eider, Common, **42,** 263
Elanoides forficatus, **46,** 265
Elanoides leucurus, **47,** 265
Empidonax alnorum, **118,** 286
    E. difficilis, **121,** 287
    E. flaviventris, **117,** 286

E. hammondii, **120,** 286
E. minimus, **119,** 286
E. oberholseri, **120,** 286
E. occidentalis, **122,** 287
E. traillii, **119,** 286
E. virescens, **118,** 286
Empidonax wrightii, **121,** 287
Eremophila alpestris, **131,** 289
Eudocimus albus, **29,** 260
Euphagus carolinus, 313
    E. cyanocephalus, **235,** 313

Falco columbarius, **55,** 267
    F. mexicanus, **56,** 267
    F. peregrinus, **55,** 267
    F. sparverius, **54,** 267
Falcon
    Peregrine, **55,** 267
    Prairie, **56,** 267
Finch
    Cassin's, **242,** 315
    Gray-crowned Rosy, 315
    House, **243,** 315, **321**
    Purple, **242,** 315
Flicker
    Gilded, **114,** 285
    Northern, **112,** 285
    Red-shafted, **113,** 285
    Yellow-shafted, **113,** 285
Flycatcher
    species richness, **250**
    Acadian, **118,** 286
    Alder, **118,** 286
    Ash-throated, **125,** 287
    Brown-crested, **126,** 288
    Cordilleran, **122,** 287
    Dusky, **120,** 286
    Dusky-capped, **124,** 287
    Gray, **121,** 287
    Great Crested, **125,** 288
    Hammond's, **120,** 286
    Least, **119,** 286
    Olive-sided, **115,** 285
    Pacific-slope, **121,** 287
    Scissor-tailed, **130,** 289
    Sulphur-bellied, **127,** 288
    Vermilion, **124,** 287
    Willow, **119,** 286
    Yellow-bellied, **117,** 286
Fregata magnificens, **23,** 258
Frigatebird, Magnificent, **23,** 258
Fulica americana, **66,** 271

Gadwall, **39,** 262
Gallinago gallinago, **73,** 274
Gallinula chloropus, 270
Gallinule, Purple, **66,** 270
Gavia immer, **18,** 257
    G. pacifica, 257
    G. stellata, 257
Geococcyx californianus, **90,** 279
Geothlypis trichas, 305
Glaucidium gnoma, 279

Gnatcatcher
  Black-tailed, **159**, 295
  Blue-gray, **158**, 295
  California, **159**, 295
Godwit
  Hudsonian, 273
  Marbled, **73**, 273
Golden-plover, American, 271
Goldeneye
  Barrow's, **43**, 264
  Common, **42**, 264
Goldfinch
  American, **245**, 316
  Lawrence's, **245**, 316
  Lesser, **244**, 316
Goose, Canada, **34**, 261
Goshawk, Northern, 266
Grackle
  Boat-tailed, **236**, 313
  Common, **236**, 313
  Great-tailed, **235**, 313
Grebe
  Black-necked, **20**, 257
  Clark's, 258
  Eared, **20**, 257
  Horned, **19**, 257
  Pied-billed, **19**, 257
  Red-necked, 257
  Slovonian, **19**, 257
  Western, **20**, 257
Grosbeak
  Black-headed, **208**, 306
  Blue, **209**, 307
  Evening, **246**, 316
  Pine, 315
  Rose-breasted, **208**, 306
Ground-dove, Common, **87**, 278
Grouse
  Blue, **58**, 268
  Ruffed, **59**, 268
  Sage, **59**, 269
  Sharp-tailed, **61**, 269
  Spruce, 268
Grus canadensis, **67**, 271
Guillemot, Pigeon, 277
Guiraca caerulea, **209**, 307
Gull
  Bonaparte's, 275
  California, **77**, 275
  Franklin's, 274
  Glaucous, 275
  Glacous-winged, **78**, 275
  Great Black-backed, **79**, 275
  Heermann's, **76**, 275
  Herring, **77**, 275
  Laughing, 274
  Mew, 275
  Ring-billed, **76**, 275
  Western, **78**, 275
Gymnorhinus cyanocephalus, **139**, 291

Haematopus bachmani, **69**, 272
  H. palliatus, **69**, 272
Haliaeetus leucocephalus, **48**, 265

Harrier, Northern, **49**, 265
Hawk
  Broad-winged, **51**, 266
  Cooper's, 265
  Ferruginous, **53**, 267
  Gray, **50**, 266
  Harris', **49**, 266
  Red-shouldered, **50**, 266
  Red-tailed, **52**, 267
  Rough-legged, 267
  Short-tailed, 266
  Swainson's, **51**, 266
  White-tailed, **52**, 266
  Zone-tailed, 266
Helmitheros vermivorus, **196**, 304
Heron
  species richness, **249**
  Great Blue, **24**, 259
  Green, **28**, 260
  Little Blue, **26**, 259
  Tricolored, **26**, 259
  see also Night-heron
Himantopus mexicanus, **70**, 272
Hirundo fulva, **135**, 290
  H. pyrrhonota, **134**, 290
  H. rustica, **135**, 290
Histrionicus histrionicus, 263
Hummingbird
  Allen's, **103**, 282
  Anna's, **101**, 282
  Black-chinned, **100**, 281
  Blue-throated, **99**, 281
  Broad-billed, **99**, 281
  Broad-tailed, **102**, 282
  Calliope, **102**, 282
  Costa's, **101**, 282
  Ruby-throated, **100**, 281
  Rufous, **103**, 282
Hyloocichla mustelina, **164**, 297

Ibis
  Glossy, **29**, 260
  White, **29**, 260
  White-faced, **30**, 260
Icteria cirens, **203**, 305
  I. cucullatus, **238**, 314
  I. galbula, **240**, 314
  I. galbula bullockii, **241**, 314
  I. galbula galbula, **240**, 314
  I. graduacauda, **239**, 314
  I. gularis, **239**, 314
  I. mississippiensis, **48**, 265
  I. parisorum, **241**, 315
  I. spurius, **238**, 314
Ixobrychus exilis, 259
Ixoreus naevius, **165**, 297

Jaeger
  Long-tailed, 274
  Parasitic, 274
Jay
  Blue, **137**, 290
  Florida, **138**, 290

Index 359

Gray, **136,** 290
Gray-breasted, **139,** 291
Green, **137,** 290
Pinyon, **139,** 291
Scrub, **138,** 290
Steller's, **136,** 290
Junco
   Dark-eyed, **228,** 311
   Gray-headed, **230,** 312
   Oregon, **229,** 311
   Slate-colored, **228,** 311
   White-winged, **229,** 312
   Yellow-eyed, **230,** 312
Junco hyemalis, **228,** 311
   J. hyemalis aikeni, **229,** 312
   J. hyemalis caniceps, **230,** 312
   J. hyemalis hyemalis, **228,** 311
   J. hyemalis oreganus, **229,** 311
   J. phaeonotus, **230,** 312

Kestrel, American, **54,** 267
Killdeer, **68, 271**
Kingbird
   Cassin's, **128,** 288
   Couch's, **127,** 288
   Eastern, **129,** 288
   Gray, **130,** 289
   Thick-billed, **128,** 288
   Western, **129,** 288
Kingfisher
   Belted, **104,** 282
   Green, 282
Kinglet
   Golden-crowned, **157,** 295
   Rugby-crowned, **158,** 295
Kiskadee, Great, **126,** 288
Kite
   American Swallow-tailed, **46,** 265
   Mississippi, **48,** 265
   Snail, **47,** 265
   White-tailed, **47,** 265
Kittiwake, Black-legged, 276

Lagopus lagopus, 268
   L. mutus, 268
Lampornis clemenciae, **99,** 281
Lanius ludovicianus, **172,** 299
Lark, Horned, **131,** 289
Larus argentatus, **77,** 275
   L. atricilla, 274
Larus argenteus
   L. californicus, **77,** 275
   L. canus, 275
   L. delawarensis, **76,** 275
   L. glaucescens, **78,** 275
   L. heermanni, **76,** 275
   L. hyperboreus, 275
   L. marinus, **79,** 276
   L. occidentalis, **78,** 275
   L. philadelphia, 275
   L. pipixcan, 274
Leptotila verreauxi, **88,** 278
Leucosticte tephrocotis, 315

Limnodromus griseus, 274
Limnothlypis swainsonii, **196,** 304
Limosa fedoa, **73,** 273
   L. haemastica, 273
Limpkin, **67,** 271
Longspur
   Chestnut-collared, **231,** 312
   Lapland, 312
   McCown's, **231,** 312
   Smith's, 312
Loon
   Common, **18,** 257
   Pacific, 257
   Red-throated, 257
Lophodytes cucullatus, 264
Loxia curvirostra, **243,** 315
   L. leucoptera, 315

Magpie
   Black-billed, **140,** 291
   Yellow-billed, **141,** 291
Mallard, **36,** 262
Martin, Purple, **132,** 289
Meadowlark
   Eastern, **233,** 313
   Western, **234,** 313
Melanerpes aurifrons, **106,** 283
   M. carolinus, **107,** 283
   M. erythrocephalus, **105,** 283
   M. formicivorus, **105,** 283
   M. lewis, 283
   M. uropygialis, **106,** 283
Melanitta fusca, 264
   M. nigra, 263
   M. perspicillata, 263
Meleagris gallopavo, **61,** 269
Melospiza georgiana, **226,** 311
   M. lincolnii, **226,** 311
   M. melodia, **225,** 310
Merganser
   Common, **43,** 264
   Hooded, 264
   Red-breasted, **44,** 264
Mergus merganser, **43,** 264
   M. serrator, **44,** 264
Merlin, **55,** 267
Mimus polyglottos, **166,** 297
Mniotilta varia, **194,** 303
Mockingbird, Northern, **166,** 297
Molothrus aeneus, **237,** 314
   M. ater, **237,** 314
Moorhen, Common, 270
Murre, Common, 277
Murrelet, Marbled, 277
Myadestes townsendi, **161,** 296
Mycteria americana, **31,** 260
Myiarchus cinerascens, **125,** 287
   M. crinitus, **125,** 288
   M. tuberculifer, **124,** 287
   M. tyrannulus, **126,** 288
Myioborus pictus, **203,** 305
Myiodynastes luteiventris, **127,** 288

Night-heron
  Black-crowned, 260
  Yellow-crowned, **28,** 260
Nighthawk
  Common, **94,** 280
  Lesser, **94,** 280
Nucifraga columbiana, **140,** 291
Numenius americanus, **72,** 273
  N. phaeopus, 273
Nutcracker, Clark's, **140,** 291
Nuthatch
  Brown-headed, **151,** 293
  Pgymy, **151,** 293
  Red-breasted, **150,** 293
  White-breasted, **150,** 293
Nyctanassa violacea, **28,** 260
Nycticorax nycticorax, 260
Nyctidromus albicollis, **95,** 280

Oldsquaw, 263
Oporornis agilis, **199,** 304
  O. formosus, **198,** 304
  O. philadelphia, **199,** 304
  O. tolmiei, 305
Oreortyx pictus, **64,** 270
Oreoscoptes montanus, **167,** 297
Oriole
  Altamira, **239,** 314
  Audubon's, **239,** 314
  Baltimore, **240,** 314
  Bullock's, **241,** 314
  Hooded, **238,** 314
  Northern, **240,** 314
  Orchard, **238,** 314
  Scott's, **241,** 315
Ortalis vetula, **56,** 268
Osprey, **46,** 265
Ovenbird, **197,** 304
Overall species richness, **248**
Owl
  Barn, 279
  Barred, **93,** 280
  Burrowing, **92,** 280
  Great Horned, **92,** 279
  Short-eared, 280
  Spotted, 280
Oxyura jamaicensis, **44,** 264
Oystercatcher
  American, **69,** 272
  Black, **69,** 272

Pandion haliaetus, **46,** 265
Parabuteo unicinctus, **49,** 266
Partridge, Gray, **57,** 268
Parula, Northern, **183,** 301
Parula americana, **183,** 301
Parus atricapillus, **144,** 292
  P. bicolor, 293
  P. bicolor atricristatus, 293
  P. carolinensis, **144,** 292
  P. gambeli, **145,** 292
  P. gambeli, **145,** 292
  P. hudsonicus, **147,** 292

  P. inornatus, **146,** 292
  P. rufescens, **146,** 292
  P. sclateri, **145,** 292
  P. wollweberi, **147,** 292
Passer domesticus, **247,** 316
  P. montanus, **247,** 316
Passerculus sandwichensis, **222,** 310
Passerella iliaca, **225,** 310
Passerina amoena, **209,** 307
  P. ciris, **211,** 307
  P. cyanea, **210,** 307
  P. versicolor, **210,** 307
Pauraque, **95,** 280
Pelecanus erythrorhynchos, **21,** 258
  P. occidentalis, **21,** 258
Pelican
  American White, **21,** 258
  Brown, **21,** 258
Perdix perdix, **57,** 268
Perisoreus canadensis, **136,** 290
Peucedramus taeniatus, **204,** 305
Pewee, Greater, **116,** 285
Phainopepla, **172,** 299
Phainopepla nitens, **172,** 299
Phalacrocorax auritus, **22,** 258
  P. brasilianus, **22,** 258
  P. pelagicus, 258
  P. penicillatus, 258
Phalaenoptilus nuttallii, **95,** 280
Phalarope
  Red-necked, 274
  Wilson's, **74,** 274
Phalaropus lobatus, 274
  P. tricolor, **74,** 274
Phasianus colchicus, **58,** 268
Pheasant, Ring-necked, **58,** 268
Pheucticus ludovicianus, **208,** 306
  P. melancephalus, **208,** 306
Phoebe
  Black, **122,** 287
  Eastern, **123,** 287
  Say's, **123,** 287
Phylloscopus borealis, 295
Pica nuttalli, **141,** 291
  P. pica, **140,** 291
Picoides albolarvatus, **112,** 284
  P. arcticus, 285
  P. borealis, 284
  P. nuttallii, **110,** 284
  P. pubescens, **110,** 284
  P. scalaris, **109,** 284
  P. stricklandi, **111,** 284
  P. tridactylus, 284
  P. villosus, **111,** 284
Pigeon
  Band-tailed, **85,** 278
  White-crowned, **84,** 278
Pinocola enucleator, 315
Pintail, Northern, **37,** 262
Pipilo aberti, **214,** 308
  P. chlorurus, **212,** 307
  P. crissalis, **213,** 308
  P. erythrophthalmus, **213,** 307
  P. fuscus, **214,** 308
Pipit

American, 298
Sprague's, **171,** 298
Piranga flava, **205,** 306
  P. ludoviciana, **206,** 306
  P. olivacea, **206,** 306
  P. rubra, **205,** 306
Pitangus sulphuratus, **126,** 288
Plectrophenax nivalis, 312
Plegadis chihi, **30,** 260
  P. falchinellus, **29,** 260
Plover
  Mountain, **68,** 271
  Semipalmated, 271
  Snowy, 271
  Wilson's, 271
Pluvialis dominica, 271
Podiceps auritus, **19,** 257
  P. grisegena, 257
  P. nigricollis, **20,** 257
Podilymbus podiceps, **19,** 257
Polioptila caerulea, **158,** 295
  P. californica, **159,** 295
  P. melanura, **159,** 295
Pooecetes gramineus, **219,** 309
Poorwill, Common, **95,** 280
Porphyrula martinica, **66,** 270
Porzana carolina, **65,** 270
Prairie-chicken
  Greater, **60,** 269
  Lesser, **60,** 269
Progne subis, **132,** 289
Protonotaria citrea, **195,** 304
Psaltriparus minimus, **149,** 293
Ptarmigan
  Rock, 268
  Willow, 268
Pgymy-owl, Northern, 279
Pyrocephalus rubinus, **124,** 287
Pyrrhuloxia, **207,** 306

Quail
  California, **64,** 270
  Gambel's, **63,** 269
  Montezuma, **62,** 269
  Montain, **64,** 270
  Scaled, **63,** 269
Quiscalus major, **236,** 313
  Q. mexicanus, **235,** 313
  Q. quiscula, **236,** 313

Rail
  Clapper, **65,** 270
  King, 270
  Virginia, 270
  Yellow, 270
Rallus elegans, 270
  R. limicola, 270
  R. longirostris, **65,** 270
Raven
  Chihuahuan, **143,** 291
  Common, **143,** 292
Recurvirostra americana, **70,** 272
Redhead, **40,** 263

Redpoll, common, 315
Redstart
  American, **195,** 303
  Painted, **203,** 305
Regulus calendula, **158,** 295
Regulus satrapa, **157,** 295
Riparia riparia, **134,** 289
Rissa tridactyla, 276
Roadrunner, Greater, **90,** 279
Robin, American, **164,** 297
Rostrhamus sociabilis, **47,** 265
Rynchops niger, **83,** 277

Salpinctes obsoletus, **153,** 294
Sandpiper
  Least, 273
  Rock, 273
  Solitary, 272
  Spotted, **71,** 273
  Upland, **72,** 273
Sapsucker
  Red-breasted, **108,** 283
  Red-naped, **108,** 283
  Williamson's, **109,** 284
  Yellow-bellied, **107,** 283
Sayornis nigricans, **122,** 287
  S. phoebe, **123,** 287
  S. saya, **123,** 287
Scaup
  Greater, 263
  Lesser, **41,** 263
Scolopax minor, 274
Scoter
  Black, 263
  Common, 263
  Surf, 263
  Velvet, 264
  White-winged, 264
Seiurus aurocapillus, **197,** 304
  S. motacilla, **198,** 304
  S. noveboracensis, **197,** 304
Selasphorus platycercus, **102,** 282
  S. rufus, **103,** 282
  S. sasin, **103,** 282
Setophaga ruticilla, **195,** 303
Shoveler, Northern, **38,** 262
Shrike, Loggerhead, **172,** 299
Sialia currucoides, **161,** 296
  S. mexicana, **160,** 296
  S. sialis, **160,** 296
Siskin, Pine, **244,** 316
Sitta canadensis, **150,** 293
  S. carolinensis, **150,** 293
  S. pusilla, **151,** 293
  S. pygmaea, **151,** 293
Skimmer, Black, **83,** 277
Skua *See* Jaeger
Snipe, Common, **73,** 274
Solitaire, Townsend's, **161,** 296
Somateria mollissima, **42,** 263
Sora, **65,** 270
Sparrow
  species richess, **251**
  American Tree, 308

Sparrow *contd.*
  Bachman's, **215,** 308
  Baird's, **222,** 310
  Black-chinned, **219,** 309
  Black-throated, **220,** 309
  Botteri's, **215,** 308
  Brewer's, **218,** 309
  Cassin's, **216,** 308
  Chipping, **217,** 308
  Clay-colored, **217,** 309
  Eurasian Tree, **247,** 316
  Field, **218,** 309
  Fox, **225,** 310
  Golden-crowned, 311
  Grasshopper, **223,** 310
  Harris', 311
  Henslow's, 310
  House, **247,** 316
  Lark, **220,** 309
  Le Conte's, **223,** 310
  Lincoln's, **226,** 311
  Olive, **212,** 307
  Rufous-crowned, **216,** 308
  Sage, **221,** 309
  Savannah, **222,** 310
  Seaside, **224,** 310
  Sharp-tailed, **224,** 310
  Song, **225,** 310
  Swamp, **226,** 311
  Vesper, **219,** 309
  White-crowned, **227,** 311
  White-throated, **227,** 311
Speotyto cunicularia, **92,** 280
Sphyrapicus nuchalis, **108,** 283
  S. ruber, **108,** 283
  S. thyroideus, **109,** 284
  S. varius, **107,** 283
Spiza americana, **211,** 307
Spizella arborea, 308
  S. atrogularis, **219,** 309
  S. breweri, **218,** 309
  S. pallida, **217,** 309
  S. passerina, **217,** 308
  S. pusilla, **218,** 309
Spoonbill, Roseate, **30,** 260
Starling, European, **173,** 299
Stelgidopteryx serripennis, **133,** 289
Stullula calliope, **102,** 282
Stercorarius longicaudus, 274
  S. parasiticus, 274
Sterna aleutica, 277
Sterna alutica
  S. antillarum, **82,** 277
  S. caspia, **80,** 276
  S. forsteri, **82,** 276
  S. hirundo, **81,** 276
  S. maxima, **81,** 276
  S. nilotica, **80,** 276
  S. paradisaea, 276
  S. sandvicensis, 276
Silt, Black-necked, **70,** 272
Stork, Wood, **31,** 260
Streptopelia chinensis, **85,** 278
Strix occidentalis, 280
  S. varia, **93,** 280

Sturnella magna, **233,** 313
  S. neglecta, **234,** 313
Sturnus vulgaris, **173,** 299
Swallow
  Bank, **134,** 289
  Barn, **135,** 290
  Cave, **135,** 290
  Cliff, **134,** 290
  Northern Rough-winged, **133,** 289
  Tree, **132,** 289
  Violet-green, **133,** 289
Swan
  Mute, **33,** 261
  Trumpeter, **33,** 261
  Tundra, 261
Swift
  Black, **97,** 281
  Chimney, **97,** 281
  Vaux's, **98,** 281
  White-throated, **98,** 281

Tachycineta bicolor, **132,** 289
  T. thalassina, **133,** 289
Tanager
  Hepatic, **205,** 306
  Scarlet, **206,** 306
  Summer, **205,** 306
  Western, **206,** 306
Teal
  Blue-winged, **37,** 262
  Cinnamon, **38,** 262
  Green-winged, **35,** 261
Tern
  Aleutian, 277
  Arctic, 276
  Black, **83,** 277
  Caspian, **80,** 276
  Common, **81,** 276
  Forster's, **82,** 276
  Gull-billed, **80,** 276
  Least, **82,** 277
  Royal, **81,** 276
  Sandwich, 276
Thrasher
  Bendire's, **168,** 298
  Brown, **167,** 297
  California, **169,** 298
  Crissal, **170,** 298
  Curve-billed, **169,** 298
  Le Conte's, **170,** 298
  Long-billed, **168,** 297
  Sage, **167,** 297
Thrush
  species richness, **250**
  Bicknell's, **162,** 296
  Gray-cheeked, 296
  Hermit, **163,** 296
  Swainson's, **163,** 296
  Varied, **165,** 297
  Wood, **164,** 297
Thryomanes bewickii, **154,** 294
Thryothorus ludovicianus, **154,** 294
Titmouse
  Black-crested, 293

Bridled, **147,** 292
Plain, **147,** 292
Tufted, 293
Towhee
  Abert's, **214,** 308
  California, **213,** 308
  Canyon, **214,** 308
  Green-tailed, **212,** 307
  Rufous-sided, **213,** 307
Toxostoma bendirei, **168,** 298
  T. crissale, **170,** 298
  T. curvirostre, **169,** 298
  T. lecontei, **170,** 298
  T. longirostre, **168,** 297
  T. redivivum, **169,** 298
  T. rufum, **167,** 297
Tringa flavipes, 272
  T. melanoleuca, 272
  T. solitaria, 272
Troglodytes aedon, **155,** 294
  T. troglodytes, **155,** 294
Trogon, Elegant, **104,** 282
Trogon elegans, **104,** 282
Turdus migratorius, **164,** 297
Turkey, Wild, **61,** 269
Tympanuchus cupido, **60,** 269
  T. pallidicinctus, **60,** 269
  T. phasianellus, **61,** 269
Tyrannulet, Northern Beardless, **115,** 285
Tyrannus bendirei
  T. crassirostris, **128,** 288
  T. dominicensis, **130,** 289
  T. forficatus, **130,** 289
  T. tyrannus, **129,** 288
  T. verticalis, **129,** 288
  T. vociferans, **128,** 288
Tyrannus couchii, **127,** 288
Tyto alba, 279

Uria aalge, 277

Veery, **162,** 296
Verdin, **149,** 293
Vermivora celata, **181,** 300
  V. chrysoptera, **180,** 300
  V. luciae, **183,** 301
  V. peregrina, **181,** 300
  V. pinus, **180,** 300
  V. ruficapilla, **182,** 301
  V. virginiae, **182,** 301
Vireo
  Bell's, **174,** 299
  Black-capped, **175,** 299
  Black-whiskered, **179,** 300
  Gray, **175,** 299
  Hutton's, **177,** 300
  Philadelphia, **178,** 300
  Red-eyed, **178,** 300
  Solitary, **176,** 299
  Warbling, **177,** 300
  White-eyed, **174,** 299
  Yellow-throated, **176,** 299
Vireo altiloquus, **179,** 300
  V. atricapillus, **175,** 299
  V. bellii, **175,** 299
  V. flavifrons, **176,** 299
  V. gilvus, **177,** 300
  V. griseus, **174,** 299
  V. huttoni, **177,** 300
  V. olivaceus, **178,** 300
  V. philadelphicus, **178,** 300
  V. solitarius, **176,** 299
  V. vicinior, **175,** 299
Vulture
  Black, **45,** 264
  Turkey, **45,** 275

Warbler
  species richness, **251**
  Arctic, 295
  Audubon's, **187,** 302
  Bay-breasted, **193,** 303
  Black-and-white, **194,** 303
  Black-throated Blue, **186,** 301
  Black-throated Gray, **188,** 302
  Black-throated Green, **189,** 302
  Blackburnian, **190,** 302
  Blackpoll, **193,** 303
  Blue-winged, **180,** 300
  Canada, **202,** 305
  Cape May, **185,** 301
  Cerulean, **194,** 303
  Chestnut-sided, **184,** 301
  Connecticut, **199,** 304
  Golden-winged, **180,** 300
  Grace's, **191,** 303
  Hermit, **189,** 302
  Hooded, **201,** 305
  Kentucky, **198,** 304
  Lucy's, **183,** 301
  MacGillivray's, 305
  Magnolia, **185,** 301
  Mourning, **199,** 304
  Myrtle, **187,** 302
  Nashville, **182,** 301
  Olive, **204,** 305
  Orange-crowned, **181,** 300
  Palm, **192,** 303
  Pine, **191,** 303
  Prairie, **192,** 303
  Prothonotary, **195,** 304
  Red-faced, **202,** 305
  Swainson's, **196,** 304
  Tennessee, **181,** 300
  Townsend's, **188,** 302
  Virginia's, **182,** 301
  Wilson's, **201,** 305
  Worm-eating, **196,** 304
  Yellow, **184,** 301
  Yellow-rumped, **186,** 302
  Yellow-throated, **190,** 302
Waterfowl, species richness, **249**
Waterthrush
  Louisiana, **198,** 304
  Northern, **197,** 304

Waxwing
    Bohemian, 298
    Cedar, **171,** 298
Whimbrel, 273
Whip-poor-will, **96,** 281
Whistling-ducks
    Black-bellied, **32,** 261
    Fulvous, **32,** 261
Wigeon, American, **39,** 262
Willet, **71,** 272
Wilsonia canadensis, **202,** 305
    W. citrina, **201,** 305
    W. pusilla, **201,** 305
Wood-pewee
    Eastern, **117,** 286
    Western, **116,** 286
Woodcock, American, 274
Woodpecker
    Acorn, **105,** 283
    Black-backed, 285
    Downy, **110,** 284
    Gila, **106,** 283
    Golden-fronted, **106,** 283
    Hairy, **111,** 284
    Ladder-backed, **109,** 284
    Lewis', 283
    Nuttall's, **110,** 284
    Pileated, **114,** 285
    Red-bellied, **107,** 283
    Red-cockaded, 284
    Red-headed, **105,** 283
    Strickland's, **111,** 284
    Three-toed, 284
    White-headed, **112,** 284
Wren
    Bewick's, **154,** 294
    Cactus, **152,** 294
    Canyon, **153,** 294
    Carolina, **154,** 294
    House, **155,** 294
    Marsh, **156,** 295
    Rock, **153,** 294
    Sedge, **156,** 295
    Winter, **155,** 294
Wrentit, **165,** 297

Xanthocephalus xanthocephalus, **234,** 313

Yellowlegs
    Greater, 272
    Lesser, 272
Yellowthroat, Common, 305